thomson com

changing the way the world learns[sm]

To get extra value from this book for no additional cost, go to:

http://www.thomson.com/wadsworth.html

thomson.com is the World Wide Web site for Wadsworth/ITP and is your direct source to dozens of on-line resources. *thomson.com* helps you find out about supplements, experiment with demonstration software, search for a job, and send e-mail to many of our authors. You can even preview new publications and exciting new technologies.

thomson.com: *It's where you'll find us in the future.*

The Abortion Controversy

25 Years After *Roe v. Wade*

A Reader

SECOND EDITION

LOUIS P. POJMAN
UNITED STATES MILITARY ACADEMY
WEST POINT

FRANCIS J. BECKWITH
TRINITY INTERNATIONAL UNIVERSITY

WADSWORTH PUBLISHING COMPANY
I(T)P® An International Thomson Publishing Company

Belmont, CA • Albany, NY • Bonn • Boston • Cincinnati • Detroit • Johannesburg • London • Madrid
Melbourne • Mexico City • New York • Paris • Singapore • Tokyo • Toronto • Washington

Publisher: Peter Adams
Editorial Assistant: Kelly Bush
Assistant Editor: Kerri Abdinoor
Marketing Manager: David Garrison
Project Editor: John Walker
Print Buyer: Stacey Weinberger
Permissions Editor: Robert Kauser
Production: Robin Gold/Forbes Mill Press
Copy Editor: Robin Gold
Cover Designer: Lisa Langhoff
Compositor: Forbes Mill Press
Printer: Transcontinental Printing

For more information, contact Wadsworth Publishing Company, 10 Davis Drive,
Belmont, CA 94002, or electronically at http://www.thomson.com/wadsworth.html

International Thomson Publishing Europe
Berkshire House 168-173
High Holborn
London, WC1V 7AA, England

International Thomson Editores
Campos Eliseos 385, Piso 7
Col. Polanco
11560 México D.F. México

Thomas Nelson Australia
102 Dodds Street
South Melbourne 3205
Victoria, Australia

International Thomson Publishing Asia
221 Henderson Road
#05-10 Henderson Building
Singapore 0315

Nelson Canada
1120 Birchmount Road
Scarborough, Ontario
Canada M1K 5G4

International Thomson Publishing Japan
Hirakawacho Kyowa Building, 3F
2-2-1 Hirakawacho
Chiyoda-ku, Tokyo 102, Japan

International Thomson Publishing GmbH
Königswinterer Strasse 418
53227 Bonn, Germany

International Thomson Publishing Southern Africa
Building 18, Constantia Park
240 Old Pretoria Road
Halfway House, 1685 South Africa

Library of Congress Cataloging-in-Publication Data

The abortion controversy : 25 years after Roe v. Wade : a reader /
    [compiled by] Louis P. Pojman, Francis J. Beckwith. — [Rev. ed.]
        p.   cm.
    Includes bibliographical references.
    ISBN 0-534-55764-3
    1. Abortion.   2. Abortion—Moral and ethical aspects.   I. Pojman,
Louis P.   II. Beckwith, Francis.
HQ767.A175   1998
363.46'0973—dc21   98-10664

This book is printed on acid-free recycled paper.

Contents

Preface

Abortion is the most heated issue in contemporary North America—an issue that divides society and threatens to tear it asunder. On almost any given day one reads or hears of a prolife or prochoice demonstration, a controversy over a particular abortion case, or some other incident related to abortion. Many of us have experienced the breaking of friendships, social ostracism, and public violence over this issue. Our conviction is that the issues surrounding the abortion debate are difficult and that philosophical reflection can throw light on these issues.

We have put together an anthology, presenting arguments on all major sides of the dispute (in a dialectic, or pro-con, format) and including the most important articles on the subject. We have divided the work into eight major areas and have included introductions to each part of the work and to each reading. The book contains 29 readings (including important excerpts of the two major Supreme Court decisions and an assessment by Justice Ruth Bader Ginsburg), four of which have been commissioned for this work. In addition we provide study questions at the end of each reading and bibliographies at the end of each section.

We, Francis Beckwith and Louis Pojman, the editors, have both written on abortion and hold opposite positions on it. We have debated the topic in public, and we are still friends! We respect each other's position and arguments. It should be helpful to the reader to know that all sides of the dispute are represented in this text.

We have benefited from the support and constructive criticisms of the editor of the series in which the first edition of this book appeared, Robert Ginsberg; the publishers of the edition, Art & Nancy Bartlett; and Peter Adams, the Wadsworth editor who encouraged us to do a revised edition. This second edition, though containing the classic readings on abortion, includes recent works by David Boonin-Vail, Keith Pavlischek, Naomi Wolf, Ronald Dworkin, and Francis Beckwith. This edition also has a new section, "Abortion, Faith, and State Neutrality," which deals with the question of whether it violates state neutrality on religion for the government to take a position on the moral question of abortion.

As with the first edition, we dedicate this work to our wives, Trudy and Frankie, to whom we owe an immense debt of gratitude.

Francis J. Beckwith
Trinity Graduate School
Trinity International University
(Deerfield, Illinois)
California Campus
Anaheim, California

Louis P. Pojman
Department of English
  and Philosophy
United States Military Academy
West Point, New York

Introduction
to the Book

January 22, 1998, marked the 25th anniversary of *Roe v. Wade,* the U.S. Supreme Court decision that asserted that the right to abortion is supported by the U.S. Constitution. Although abortion is the most controversial moral and social issue in contemporary America—its mention often eliciting emotional outbursts by well-meaning yet zealous partisans—it is not an issue over which many people give much serious philosophical reflection. Just when one thinks that passions have subsided, a new controversy or event comes to the forefront.

In 1996 and again in 1997, President Bill Clinton vetoed the U.S. Congress' prohibition of what anti–abortion activists call "partial-birth abortion." Also known as D & X (for dilation and extraction) abortion, this procedure is performed in some second-trimester and third-trimester abortions. Using ultrasound, the doctor grips the fetus's legs with forceps. The fetus is then pulled out through the birth canal and delivered with the exception of its head. While the head is in the womb, the doctor penetrates the fetus's skull with scissors, opens the scissors to enlarge the hole, and then inserts a catheter. The fetus's brain is vacuumed out, resulting in the skull's collapse. The doctor then completes the womb's evacuation by removing a dead fetus.

Although a vast majority of the members of Congress as well as the American people (included in this number are many who are prochoice) supported the ban, many prochoice interest groups did not. Their reason: Any limitation on abortion rights—even if it means forbidding what nearly everyone finds morally abhorrent—is to concede some ground to the opposition, which might begin the slippery slope toward making all abortions illegal.

Some prochoice Congressmen, including Senate minority leader Tom Daschal, proposed an alternative bill, which prolife activists refused to consider. In this bill, D & X abortions would be banned, though the bill makes an exception for cases in which the pregnant woman's life or health is in danger. According to prolife activists and some members of Congress, this "loophole," as they call it, would be tantamount to having no ban at all, because physicians who perform D & X abortions will go on performing them as they had before by simply defining health or life in the broadest possible way. Even though prolifers could have countered Daschal's compromise bill by proposing one in which health and life are more narrowly defined, they did not. Their reason: Any concession—even if it means allowing abortions in cases that *most prolifers* find morally permissible—is to give up some ground to the opposition, which might be perceived by the general public as well as the media as a political defeat.

In March 1993, Dr. David Gunn, a Pensacola, Florida physician was murdered in front of the women's health clinic at which he practiced. In our violent society, such an incident, though tragic, is not unusual. But this incident was different, very different from an ordinary criminal homicide. The physician was an abortionist; the assailant, a prolife activist. The first was dedicated to helping women by terminating the lives of their unborn fetuses. The latter was so dedicated to saving the lives of unborn human fetuses that he saw nothing inconsistent or immoral with killing a physician who performs abortions.

At a 1989 Operation Rescue abortion clinic-blocking in Las Vegas, Nevada, an incident went unreported by the media and unprevented by the police present at the scene. The physician who owned the clinic gave prochoice demonstrators receptacles of urine which they subsequently poured on the rescuers while jeering at them; the rescuers took the abuse without retaliation as they continued to pray and sing hymns.

In July 1993, Louis Pojman, co-editor of this text, mailed a large portion of this manuscript together with other material from his home in Oxford, Mississippi, to Berkeley, California, where he was to spend his sabbatical year. Pojman had written a list of the contents on the outside of the box, including the words, "ABORTION PROJECT." When the package arrived in Berkeley in early August, Pojman joked with the post man that it appeared lighter in weight than it was when he sent it several days earlier. Upon opening the box, Pojman noticed that the abortion manuscript was missing and had been replaced by a large mail-order catalog. Evidently someone who works for the post office, a zealous abortion partisan no doubt, violated federal law and opened the package and stole the manuscript.

Although Dr. Gunn's murder was the first of its kind in the 25-year history of America's abortion controversy, and no doubt an isolated incident, a small number of people who oppose abortion engage in civil disobedience by blocking the doors to abortion clinics, and others have actually planted and set off bombs in clinics (but not yet during business hours when people are present in the buildings). And, as we saw in the story of the Las Vegas clinic, the prochoice movement has its extremists as well, though they, like their prolife counterparts, make up a tiny percentage of their movement. They have engaged in such activities as vandalism, desecration of prolife churches, and verbal harassment. The fact that a postal worker would risk termination and possible time in prison is further evidence of how far people will go to ensure political victory (for whichever side of the abortion debate they are supporting). The tone of the abortion debate is getting ugly and will never be resolved by the extremist tactics advocated by partisans on either side.

On May 1, 1993, the editors of this book, Francis J. Beckwith and Louis P. Pojman debated each other on the issue of abortion on the campus of Taylor University (Upland, Indiana). Pojman defended the prochoice position, arguing that the fetus, although a human being, is not a person. Beckwith argued for the prolife position, defending the claim that the fetus during all of pregnancy is a human person. Each participant presented his case in a philosophically respectable manner, replying to the other's arguments and concluding in a spirit of collegiality and mutual respect. Nobody was shot; nobody was assaulted. There was passionate debate, but it was wrapped in civility.

Our debate, although not containing enough vitriolic sound-bites to make the CBS evening news, is the sort of activity that is needed in the United States so that as a nation we can come to grips with the philosophical and legal issues that are central to the debate over abortion. Of course, there is no assurance that we will arrive at a compromise or an answer to this important moral and legal problem. But we have to move beyond the irrationality, stereotyping, and political posturing that tends to predominate the abortion debate as it is depicted in the popular media.[1] It is our hope that this book will contribute to raising the level of debate by providing the reader with the best arguments by those on all sides of the debate. Because each editor takes a different position on the abortion issue, we believe that this text is arguably the most balanced book of its kind.

BAD REASONING IN THE POPULAR
DEBATE OVER ABORTION

The arguments for abortion rights are put forth in the political arena with greater vigor and rhetorical hostility than ever before. However, many of these arguments, presented by those on both sides of the abortion debate, are riddled with fallacious reasoning.

Consider the following prolife examples.[2] In response to the prochoice argument that abortion is justified because there are too many unwanted children, the prolife advocate will often cite statistics that there are a great number of childless couples seeking children for adoption.[3] There are several problems with this prolife response. First, why should this point even matter? If there were no such couples, would abortion *ipso facto* become morally correct? If the unborn have an inherent right to life, a principle that is the foundation of the prolife position, why should the absence or presence of a couple who wants a child make a difference? Second, a sophisticated prochoice advocate would remain unconvinced, because according to his position a woman has a right to an abortion but has no obligation to make sure other people can adopt children. Why should the abortion rights advocate accept prolife assumptions? And third, it follows from these two points that the prolife advocate's appeal to adoption puts him or her in the odd position of appearing to support the prochoice assumption that only if the unborn are wanted do they have value. This is a fatal concession for the prolife cause.

Another popular prolife argument goes something like this: Because the unborn entity is a human being from the moment of conception, and because it is morally wrong in almost all circumstances to kill human beings, therefore, abortion in almost all circumstances is morally wrong. Although the prolifer is certainly correct that the unborn entity is a human being in the genetic sense from the moment of conception,[4] it is not clear from the biological facts alone, without philosophical reflection, that the fetus is a human *person* and possesses the rights that go with such a status. (The human being/human person distinction is discussed by the contributors in Part V.) Also, some prochoice advocates, such as Judith Jarvis Thomson, have argued that even if the fetus is a human person from conception or sometime very early in pregnancy, abortion is still morally justified. She argues that the unborn's presence in the pregnant woman's body entails a conflict of rights if the pregnant woman does not want to be pregnant. Therefore, the unborn, regardless of whether it is a fully human person with a right to life, cannot use the body of another against her will. Hence, a pregnant woman's removal of an unborn entity from her body, even though it will probably result in its death, is no more immoral than an ordinary person's refusal to donate his kidney to another in need of one, even though this refusal will probably result in the death of the prospective recipient. Thomson's argument and those similar to it will be the focus of Part IV.

Of course, popular arguments put forth by prochoice advocates fare no better. One argument goes like this: If abortion is made illegal, then women will once again be harmed by unsafe and illegal abortions performed by back-alley butchers. But there is a serious problem with this argument. If we are to accept the contention of the author of the majority opinion in *Roe v. Wade,* Justice Harry Blackmun, that if the fetus is a person then abortion is homicide and cannot be a Constitutional right,[5] the illegal-abortion argument turns out to be question-begging. That is to say, the argument assumes without reason the very thing, if false, that would invalidate the prochoicer's case, namely, that the unborn human being is not fully a person. In other words, only by assuming that the unborn are not fully human does the argument work. For if the unborn are fully human, this prochoice argument is tantamount to saying that because people die or are harmed while killing other people (that is, unborn people), the state should make it safe for them to do so. Hence, only by assuming that the unborn are not fully human does this prochoice argument work. Therefore, it begs the question. Even Mary Anne Warren, a prochoice advocate, clearly recognizes that her position on abortion cannot rest on this argument if it is not first demonstrated that the unborn entity is not fully human. She writes, "the fact that restricting access to abortion has tragic side effects does not, in itself, show that the restrictions are unjustified, since murder is wrong regardless the consequences of prohibiting it."[6]

This same criticism can be applied to other popular prochoice arguments, such as those which appeal to the difficulty of childrearing, the upsetting of one's career, or the poverty of the mother. In none of the cases do we think that the execution of the child is justified *after* it born. Therefore, if we are to take Justice Blackmun seriously (as most abortion-rights advocates do), it is the status of the unborn, not the other issues, that must be addressed.

Another argument that is very popular and used to defend abortion rights in the first two trimesters of pregnancy is the argument from fetal viability. Viability is the time at which the unborn can live outside its mother's womb. Some abortion-rights advocates have argued that because the unborn in the first two trimesters cannot survive independent of its mother, it is not a complete, independent human life, and hence not a human person. In arguing for increased state interest in fetal life after viability, Blackmun makes use of the viability argument in his dissenting opinion in *Webster v. Reproductive Health Services* (1989):

> The viability line reflects the biological facts and truths of fetal development; it marks the threshold moment prior to which a fetus cannot survive separate from the woman and cannot reasonably and objectively be regarded as a subject of rights or interests distinct from, or paramount to, those of the pregnant woman. At the same time, the viability standard takes account of the undeniable fact that as the fetus evolves into its postnatal form, and as it loses its dependence on the uterine environment, the State's interest in the fetus' potential human life, and in fostering a regard for human life in general, becomes compelling.[7]

Although many people use this argument to defend fetal personhood after viability rather than merely a state's interest in potential human life as Blackmun argues,[8] it nevertheless is a circular argument. Blackmun is claiming that the state has an interest in protecting fetal life only when that life can live outside the womb. But why is this correct? Because, we are told, prior to being able to live outside the womb, the fetus has no interests or rights. But this is clearly a case of circular reasoning, for Blackmun is assuming (that the fetus has no interests or rights prior to viability) what he is trying to prove (that the fetus has no interests or rights prior to viability). This argument is no more compelling than the one given by the zealous UNLV basketball fan who argues that the Rebels are the best team because no team is better (which, of course, is the same as being the best team).[9]

Certainly, we can find a number of other examples of poor reasoning by partisans in the popular abortion debate, but these should suffice to show that the debate in the public square must be brought to a higher level.

COMMON GROUND BETWEEN PROLIFERS
AND PROCHOICERS

Some people do not realize that the two main positions in the abortion debate have a great deal more in common than meets the eye. In fact, the differences between the two positions lie not in their values but in certain factual disputes and the application of these common values.

First, each side believes that all human persons possess certain inalienable rights regardless of whether their governments protect these rights. That is why both sides appeal to what each believes is a fundamental right. The prolife advocate appeals to "life," whereas the prochoice advocate appeals to "liberty" or "choice."

Second, each side believes that its position best exemplifies its opponent's fundamental value. The prochoice advocate does not deny that "life" is a value, but argues that his or her position's appeal to human liberty is a necessary ingredient by which an individual can pursue the fullest and most complete life possible. Furthermore, more sophisticated prochoice advocates argue that the unborn are not human persons. And for this reason, the unborn do not have a right to life if their life hinders the liberty of a being who is a person (that is, the pregnant woman). Others, such as Thomson, argue that even if the unborn entity is a human person, it has no right to use the body of another against that person's will, because such a usage of another's body demands of that person great risk and sacrifice, one that goes beyond any ordinary moral obligation. Hence, because a pregnant woman is not morally obligated to put herself at great risk and to make a significant sacrifice for another, she is morally justified in removing her unborn offspring even if such a removal results in its death.

On the other hand, the prolife advocate does not eschew "liberty," but believes that all human liberty is limited by another human person's right to life. For example, one has a right to freely pursue any goal one believes is consistent with one's happiness, such as attending a Boston Celtics basketball game. However, one has no right to freely pursue this goal at the expense of another's life or liberty, such as running over pedestrians with one's car so that one can get to the game on time. And of course, the prolife advocate argues that the unborn are persons with full right to life. And because the act of abortion typically results in the death of the unborn, abortion, unless the mother's life is in danger (since it is a prima facie greater good that one person should live rather than two die, which would be the result of such a pregnancy were it to continue) is not morally justified.

We believe, then, that the main dispute in the abortion debate does not involve differing values, but disagreement about both the application of these values and the truth of certain facts. The prochoice advocate does not deny that human persons have a right to life. He or she just believes that this right to life is not extended to the unborn because they are not human persons or their existence demands that another (the pregnant woman) is asked to make significant nonobligatory sacrifices. The prolife advocate does not deny that human persons have the liberty to make choices that they believe are in their best interests, and believes that this liberty does not entail the right to choose abortion, because such choice conflicts with the life, liberty, and interests of another human person (the unborn entity).

Because there is a common ground between two moral positions that are often depicted as absolutely polarized, we can coherently reason and argue about the issue of abortion. And because there is a common ground of values, the question about which position is correct rests on which one is best established by the facts and is consistent with our common values.

OVERVIEW OF THE TEXT

This book is divided into eight parts, each dealing with a different aspect of the abortion debate. Part I, "Breaking through the Stereotypes," consists of an essay authored by husband and wife Daniel Callahan and Sidney Callahan. Daniel, who takes a moderate prochoice position on abortion and Sidney, who opposes all abortion except to save the life of the pregnant woman, show in their essay how many people on the two main sides of the abortion debate tend to stereotype their opponents and ignore the many values and beliefs they hold in common. Part II, "The Major Supreme Court Decisions," consists of abridged versions of the two most important U.S. Supreme Court decisions on abortion: *Roe v. Wade* (1973) and *Planned Parenthood v. Casey* (1992). Evaluation of the Supreme Court's reasoning in *Roe v. Wade* is the focus of Part III, "Evaluations of *Roe v. Wade*." This part includes an essay by U.S. Supreme Court Justice Ruth Bader Ginsburg.

Parts IV, V, and VI consist of the arguments for and against abortion rights that are predominant on the contemporary philosophical scene. Part IV, "Arguments from a Woman's Right to Her Body," includes Judith Jarvis Thomson's classic treatment, as well as a supporting piece by David Boonin-Vail and critiques by Francis J. Beckwith and Keith Pavlischek. Pavlischek's essay was revised especially for this text.

Part V, "Personhood Arguments on Abortion," deals with what most philosophers consider the most important question in the abortion debate: When does human personhood begin in the development of an unborn human entity. This section includes the highly influential essays of John T. Noonan, Michael Tooley, Philip E. Devine, L. W. Sumner, and Norman Gillespie, as well as recent essays by Stephen D. Schwarz and Louis P. Pojman, the last of which was written for this volume.

Part VI, "Beyond the Personhood Argument," addresses the moral question without appealing to arguments regarding the beginning of personhood. Included in this section are articles by Jane English, Harry Gensler, and Don Marquis, all of which have made a substantial contribution to the abortion debate. We have also included Peter McInerney's critique of Marquis's article and two essays commissioned for this anthology: Gerald Paske's critique of Marquis's argument and a reply by Don Marquis to his critics.

Part VII, "Feminist Arguments on Abortion," deals with the question of whether abortion rights are inexorably tied to feminism. That is, can one be prolife and a feminist at the same time, or does moral opposition to abortion on the basis of fetal personhood disqualify one as a feminist? The contributors in this section are Sally Markowitz, Naomi Wolf, Celia Wolf-Devine, and Caroline Whitbeck.

Part VIII, "Abortion, Faith, and State Neutrality," deals with the question of whether state neutrality on religion is violated if government takes a position on the moral question of abortion. Francis J. Beckwith and Ronald Dworkin take different positions on this question.

Not only do we hope that this text will make a contribution in helping us all to better understand those with whom we disagree on this important issue, but we also hope that this text will be used by teachers of ethics, law, and medicine who desire for their students to think profoundly, insightfully, and critically about what is probably the most important moral issue of our time.

NOTES

1. This is not to imply that there are not intelligent and concerned people in the public arena on either side of the abortion debate. In fact, we have both met such people. However, it is our observation that these people are those who rarely make the media appearances on programs that most Americans watch (for example, television talk shows).

2. Some prolifers fully acknowledge that some popular prolife arguments, such as those discussed in this introduction, are not very good and in some cases need to be buttressed with more sophisticated philosophical arguments. See, for example, Francis J. Beckwith, *Politically Correct Death: Answering the Arguments for Abortion Rights*. Grand Rapids, Mich.: Baker Book House, 1993, 14–15, 45–46, 91–135.

3. See, for example Dr. and Mrs. J. C. Willke, *Abortion: Questions and Answers,* revised edition. Cincinnati: Hayes, 1988, 305–313.

4. See Andre F. Hellegers, "Fetal Development," in *Biomedical Ethics,* eds. Thomas A. Mappes and Jane S. Zembaty. New York: McGraw-Hill, 1981, 405–409.

5. Blackmun writes, "If the suggestion of personhood [of the unborn] is established, the appellant's case, of course, collapses, for the fetus' right to life is then guaranteed specifically by the [Fourteenth Amendment]." (Justice Harry Blackmun, "Excerpts from Opinion in *Roe v. Wade*" in *The Problem of Abortion,* 2nd ed., ed. Joel Feinberg. Belmont, Calif.: Wadsworth, 1984, 195.

6. Mary Anne Warren, "On the Moral and Legal Status of Abortion," in *The Problem of Abortion,* 103.

7. Justice Blackmun in *Webster v. Reproductive Health Services* (1989) as found in *The United States Law Week* 57, no. 50 (July 27, 1989): 5040.

8. Some have argued that the *Roe* Court's broadly applicable provision that abortion could not be restricted after viability if it is done to preserve the life or health of the pregnant woman (that is, "health" is so broadly defined as to include psychological, emotional, and familial health: see the Court's definition of health in *Doe v. Bolton* (410 U.S. 179, 192 [1973]) makes Blackmun's viability criterion practically

irrelevant. It seems, however, that the Court in *Webster v. Reproductive Health Services* (1989) and *Planned Parenthood v. Casey* (1992) allows states to more strictly interpret the *Roe* health provision to prohibit nearly all post-viability abortions except when the woman's life can be saved only by performing an abortion. For a discussion of the legal scholarship on this issue, see Beckwith, *Politically Correct Death,* 31–37, and John Hart Ely, "The Wages of Crying Wolf: A Comment on *Roe v. Wade,*" *Yale Law Journal* 82 (1973).

9. Other flaws in the viability argument have been pointed out elsewhere. See, for example, Beckwith, *Politically Correct Death,* 99–101; Stephen D. Schwarz, *The Moral Question of Abortion,* Chicago: Loyola University Press, 1990, 44–47; and Andrew Varga, *The Main Issues in Bioethics,* 2nd ed., New York: Paulist, 1984, 62–63.

FOR FURTHER READING

Baird, Robert M., and Stuart E. Rosenbaum, eds. *The Ethics of Abortion: Pro-Life vs. Pro-Choice.* Revised edition. Buffalo, N.Y.: Prometheus, 1993.

Beckwith, Francis J. *Politically Correct Death: Answering the Arguments for Abortion.* Grand Rapids, Mich.: Baker Book House, 1993.

Callahan, Daniel. *Abortion: Law, Choice, and Morality.* New York: Macmillan, 1970.

Dworkin, Ronald. *Life's Dominion: An Argument About Abortion, Euthanasia and Individual Freedom.* New York: Alfred A. Knopf, 1993.

Dwyer, Susan, and Joel Feinberg, eds. *The Problem of Abortion.* Third edition. Belmont, Calif.: Wadsworth, 1996.

Garfield, Jay L., and Patricia Hennessy, eds. *Abortion: Moral and Legal Perspectives.* Amherst: University of Massachusetts Press, 1984.

Hilgers, Thomas, Dennis J. Horan, and David Mall, eds. *New Perspectives on Human Abortion.* Frederick, Md.: University Publications of America, 1981.

Lee, Patrick. *Abortion and Unborn Human Life.* Washington, DC: The Catholic University of America Press, 1996.

McConogh, Eileen, *Breaking the Abortion Deadlock: From Choice to Consent.* New York: Oxford University Press, 1996.

Muldoon, Maureen, ed. *The Abortion Debate in the United States and Canada: A Source Book.* New York: Garland Publishing, 1991.

Noonan, John T., ed. *The Morality of Abortion.* Cambridge, Mass.: Harvard University Press, 1970.

Schwartz, Lewis M., ed. *Arguing About Abortion.* Belmont, Calif.: Wadsworth, 1993.

Schwarz, Stephen D. *The Moral Question of Abortion.* Chicago: Loyola University Press, 1990.

Tribe, Laurence. *Abortion: The Clash of Absolutes.* New York: Norton, 1990.

Breaking through the Stereotypes

INTRODUCTION

Stereotypes dominate our thinking, whether we realize it or not. The late North Carolina State men's basketball coach, Jim Valvano, used to tell a story that illustrates this point. Coach Valvano went to the airport to pick up a new recruit whom the team's assistant coaches were raving about. They said he was a great ballhandler, shooter, leaper, and rebounder, with a good dose of quickness. The coach arrived at the gate waiting for the new recruit to exit from the plane. He waited for several minutes and saw no one who in his mind could possibly resemble the player he expected to see. A skinny man, about 5 feet 6 inches tall, who looked lost, approached Coach Valvano asking him if he was from North Carolina State University. The coach replied, "yes." The young man said, "Hi, my name is Spudd Webb, I'm your new recruit." Valvano was shocked. He expected to greet a muscular young man with an athletic build who was at least a couple of inches over six feet. Despite the fact that Spudd was not the stereotypical college basketball player, he had a stellar career at North Carolina State and played professional ball in the National Basketball Association (NBA).

Although generalizations can be helpful in making some judgments, stereotyping entire groups of people tends to cloud our ability to make thoughtful evaluations of the arguments presented by these people. We sometimes ignore the arguments because we have already labeled the people. This is especially true in the controversy over abortion. According to the conventional wisdom," the stereotypical prolife advocate is a right-wing fundamentalist Christian or Roman Catholic male who wants to oppress women in the name of supporting "traditional values." Although this might be true in some cases, this stereotype does not capture the diversity of the prolife movement. Some prolifers are leftists, feminists, liberal Protestants, liberal Catholics, women, libertarians, atheists, agnostics, Jews, Muslims, and so forth. In fact, there are some "right-wingers" who would *not* consider themselves prolife.[1] Prolife proponents include such individuals as Nat Hentoff (liberal Jewish atheist), former Pennsylvania governor Robert Casey (liberal Democrat), Doris Gordon (libertarian atheist), Stanley Hauerwas (liberal Protestant theologian), and Sidney Callahan (feminist psychologist).

The stereotype of the prochoice advocate fares no better. She is portrayed as a radical feminist (probably lesbian) who is a religious liberal, atheist, or agnostic. In addition, the stereotypical abortion-rights supporter has had several abortions herself, despises traditional family life, and is sexually promiscuous. Although there are certainly prochoice partisans who fit this description, there is great diversity among those who support abortion rights. Included in their ranks are Roman Catholics, Jews, Evangelicals, conservatives, men, and believe it or not, anti-feminists.[2] In fact, some defenders of abortion rights despise abortion and recoil at the sexual promiscuity that they believe is undermining the traditional family. They simply believe that making abortion illegal is not good public policy. Prochoice proponents include such individuals as former Massachusetts Governor William Weld (conservative Republican), Robert Wennberg (Evangelical philosopher), Nicholas Davidson (anti-feminist), former New York Governor Mario Cuomo (Roman Catholic), and Virginia Ramey Mollenkott (Evangelical feminist).

Although many of us would not admit it, stereotyping has prevented us from really listening to other people's arguments. We resist the message because we don't like the messenger. One wonders how many people are sympathetic to or verbally espouse the prochoice position simply because prolifers are often linked to the religious right (and such individuals as Jerry Falwell or Pat Robertson), which many people perceive as radically opposed to individual liberties. On the other hand, one wonders how many people resist the prochoice message because in the minds of many it is associated with the National Organization for Women (NOW), ACT-UP (the radical gay rights group), and far left political movements, which many people perceive as radically anti-family. It is time we started critically evaluating the message rather than ignoring the message by focusing only on the messenger.

This section contains one article. Written by Daniel Callahan (a moderate prochoice bioethicist) and his wife Sidney Callahan (a prolife psychologist), the piece is an insightful and critical analysis of stereotyping in the abortion debate and the common values held by many on both sides.

NOTES

1. For example, take the position of the late conservative Evangelical theologian. Walter Martin. See Walter R. Martin. *Abortion: Is It Always Murder ?* Santa Ana, Ca.: Vision House, 1977.

2. See the defense of abortion rights in the following antifeminist work: Nicholas Davidson, *The Failure of Feminism.* Buffalo, N.Y.: Prometheus, 1988, 123–131.

1

Breaking through the Stereotypes

DANIEL CALLAHAN AND SIDNEY CALLAHAN

Daniel Callahan is Director of the Hastings Center, a nonpartisan bioethics think tank outside of New York City. Sidney Callahan is Professor of Psychology, Mercy College. Daniel and Sidney are husband and wife. Daniel is a moderate prochoice advocate. Sidney supports the prolife position.

The following article is a brief account of a study conducted by the Callahans. This study investigated the beliefs and views of people who oppose abortion rights as well as those who support those rights. Among the many things discovered by this study is that prolifers and prochoicers, in general, are difficult to label as either totally conservative or totally liberal in their value systems. In fact, according to the Callahans, prolifers and prochoicers hold a number of values in common, which perhaps can serve as a basis for dialogue.

Apart from some of the nastier reasons people impute to each other, just why is it that there are such profound differences about abortion? For at least twenty years now we have asked that question of each other, just as we have asked how our own differences and those of others might be reconciled. Ever since the topic of abortion became of interest to us, in the 1960s, we have disagreed. Well over half of our thirty years of marriage have been marked (though rarely marred) by an ongoing argument. For all of that period, one of

Reprinted from *Commonweal* (October 5, 1984), by permission.

us (Daniel) has taken a prochoice position and the other (Sidney) a prolife position (to use, somewhat reluctantly, the common labels).

At one time, while Daniel was writing a book on the subject, we talked about it every day for four years. Thereafter, Sidney wrote a number of articles on abortion, some of which would be copied and distributed by prolife protesters at Daniel's lectures. Whether observers made the connection between the two Callahans was not always clear, but we experienced the conflict first-hand. Over the years, every argument, every statistic, every historical example cited in the literature has been discussed between us. As Eliza Doolittle of *My Fair Lady* says about "words": "There's not a one I haven't heard."

Yet we continue to disagree. How can that be? Our desire to better understand our own differences and those of others led us not long ago to organize a small research project at The Hastings Center, supported by a grant from the Ford Foundation. As a social psychologist, Sidney had earlier investigated the differing views and personal characteristics people have about the making and keeping of promises. She found that the moral stance one takes on that common moral problem reflects deep and pervasive premises about the self and the world. In Daniel's work on biomedical ethics, he has similarly observed that people bring to specific moral issues their broad outlooks toward themselves and the world; but those outlooks are often not immediately apparent on the surface of their conventional arguments and moral stances.

Why not, we thought, look at the problem by considering the different ways in which abortion opponents understand themselves and the world? How do they bring that wider and deeper understanding to bear on this difficult, divisive issue? Many people, we reluctantly suspect, are not greatly interested in understanding in some sympathetic way why abortion is so divisive an issue. To recall Karl Marx's expression, they want to change the world, not understand it. In the larger political arena, it is victory that counts. But given the depth and apparent intractability of abortion differences, we think that in the long run most persons in the society will have to find a way to live with differences.

Our project, therefore, sought to see if we could provide some better insight into how individuals weigh and order their values when dealing with abortion. Though they came up from time to time, we did not directly deal with the most common issues in the abortion debate—when does life begin? What should the law be? and so on—but instead with the way in which abortion as a problem is situated within the terrain of a person's general, more encompassing values. We hoped that, if we could not entirely escape the common forms of sociological or psychological reductionism, we might at least bring to them some greater complexity and penetration. We sought only understanding, not a compromise solution, a consensus position, or a political recommendation.

A few other decisions gave the project its final shape. With the exception of Daniel, all the other participants would be women. They would be equally drawn from the prochoice and the prolife side. And they would focus their discussion on four broad themes: feminism, the family, childbearing and childrearing, and the political and cultural nature of our society. Those topics, we believe, provide for many in our society the background framework of values that often shape abortion attitudes.

Finally, although we wanted a group that was evenly divided on the moral and political issues, we also wanted one that could effectively talk and work together. Thus there was no pretense that the group would be representative of all the ethnic, religious, political, and cultural groups active in the abortion debate. But it was to be representative of one important, if sometimes overlooked, group—those women who, though they differ, are willing to talk with those on the other side, willing to make the effort to empathize with those who hold opposing views, and willing to see if they can find some shared ground to keep their dialogue alive. The results of our discussion were sufficient to persuade us that a more complex, nuanced, and fruitful argument is possible. That argument is more fully laid out in the book we edited as an outcome of the project *Abortion: Understanding Differences* (Plenum Press, 1984).

The general debate has seen an effort, on all sides, to make abortion fit into some overall coherent scheme of values, one that combines personal convictions and consistency with more broadly held social values. Abortion poses a supreme test in trying to achieve that coherence. It stands at the juncture of a number of value systems, all of which continually joust with each other for dominance, but none of which by itself can do full justice to all the values that, with varying degrees of insistence and historical rootedness, clamor for attention and respect. Here we will try to present a composite picture of the positions presented at our meetings. Not all the participants might have perceived the discussion the way we did, but we think the following account would gain general support.

The values that sustain and give theoretical legitimacy to both the prolife and prochoice movements are commonplace and command widespread respect. Neither has invented unusual moral principles nor idiosyncratic values. Consider first the prolife position. It is committed to respect for an individual's right to life, even if that right is uncertain or in doubt in borderline cases (or even if there is doubt about whether it is "life"); the need to protect the weak and powerless, at the least to preserve them from the harm that can be done by the more powerful and at the most to provide them with an opportunity to develop their full potential; the legitimacy of writing moral convictions and principles into law, particularly when that seems necessary to protect the rights of others (as in the civil rights movement); the value, not of fatalism but of accepting accidents and mischance as a part of life, and a denial of violent solutions as a way out of such vicissitudes; an obligation on the part of the community, whether through mediating institutions or the state, to provide support for those whose troubles (for example, an unwanted pregnancy) might lead them to forced, destructive choices; and, finally, the conviction that moral values and ideals toward nascent life should be upheld even at the cost of individual difficulties and travail.

The values that were identified as integral to the prolife position are a mixture of those ordinarily labeled "liberal" and "conservative. The prolife movement cannot, in its essence, be reduced to a simple conservative nostalgia or backlash, however much that might characterize some of its activist leaders and many of its mainline features. In the formulations of some, the prolife movement can just as well go in a recognizably liberal direction. What probably most distinguishes it in that rendering from the more garden varieties of liberalism is its willingness to live with—and accept—externally imposed tragedy as a part of life. That has not been a traditional part of secular liberalism, which has always been far more inclined toward instrumental rationality than the version that has surfaced in the prolife movement. The liberal community itself, however, has engaged in some sharp criticism of the part of its tradition that has stressed "rationalization" (a rational socially engineered solution to personal and political problems) and "emancipation" (freedom from the restraint of society and rejection of moral traditions). Hence, not only can the prolife movement make a strong claim to upholding many traditional liberal values, it can also (in some important formulations) lay claim to reflecting some recent developments intrinsic to liberalism's self-definition.

The prochoice movement can lay an equally strong claim to an important piece of the American and Western tradition. By stressing freedom of choice, it gives centrality to the sovereignty of the individual conscience, especially in cases of moral doubt. It also recognizes a closely related principle: that those who must personally bear the burden of their moral choices ought to have the right to make those choices. By its emphasis on the unique burden of women in pregnancy and childrearing, it has fostered the enfranchisement of women in controlling their own destinies. In its polity, the prochoice movement is at one with that recently emergent tradition that would free procreational choices from the control of the state and, more generally, give the benefit of uncertainty in matters of conscience to the individual rather than to the government. Its recognition of the injustice inherent in the known pattern of illegal abortion—that of *de facto* discrimination in favor of the affluent and the powerful—makes an important contribution to a more just society. Through its concern for choice and control in procreation, the prochoice movement has focused attention on parental responsibility, helping to remove childbearing from the realm of biological chance and sexual inevitability. By sundering a once necessary relationship between sexual activity and procreation, it helps provide an adaptation to a world that no longer needs, nor can afford, unlimited childbearing.

Just as the prolife movement can be said to have its conservative and liberal wings, the same is true of the prochoice movement. In its libertarian formulation, it is heavily weighted toward the maximization of individual choice and the privatization of moral judgment. The basic concern is not so much with the social and economic conditions under which choices are made, or with the ethical criteria by which they ought to be made, but solely with preserving the right to make a choice. But that is not the only prochoice formulation. In a different rendering—what might be called liberal communitarianism—the prochoice movement recognizes that a socially forced choice in favor of abortion is not a fully free choice; that a lack of communal, economic, and social support often coerces an abortion that would not be necessary in a more just society; that private moral choices are subject to moral judgments and standards; and that what ought to be an inherently difficult tragic choice can easily be trivialized and routinized—tacitly sanctioned and advanced by a society that promotes narcissism, prefers technological fixes to structural change, and is all too happy to see abortion put to the service of reducing welfare burdens.

There are, we think, two different abortion debates now taking place, one of them tense, open and familiar, the other more relaxed, less public, and surprising in some of its features. At one level, there is a fairly primitive, monochromatic struggle that takes place between the most public and vociferous activists on both sides. Kristin Luker's research on those groups (presented in our project before its appearance in book form in *Abortion and the Politics of Motherhood)* has vividly laid out the background values and assumptions that animate their convictions. There is a prolife movement dedicated to the preservation of the nuclear family, the centrality of childbearing in the life of women, and a religious rather than a secular view of life. As a mirror image of that movement, there is a prochoice ideology dedicated to female emancipation from the body and a repressive nuclear family, a subordination of childbearing to other personal goals, a celebration of rational control of self in place of the acceptance of fate, and a secular rather than a religious view of life.

At that level, the debate admits no accommodation. It is a living out, in bold relief, of the struggle between modernity and traditionalism that has been waged since at least the age of The Enlightenment. For both the prochoice modernizers and the prolife traditionalists, abortion serves as a perfect symbol for such pervasive issues as the roles and rights of the sexes, the family, the relationship between law and morality, the nature and malleability of social reality, and the place of reason and choice in human life. But by choosing to cast the issues in those fundamental terms, and by making abortion carry the weight of a Manichean-life struggle between the good (evil) past and the good (evil) present, each side has doomed itself to an utter inability to talk with the other side, the likelihood that neither side can wholly triumph in the future, and the disheartening prospect of never-ending, never-decided civil strife for everyone else.

For all those reasons, it is the debate at the other level that bears attention, cultivation, and development. Our own project discussions manifested some traits significantly different from those sketched above. Four features of that discussion are worth noting.

The first, already alluded to, is that participants from each side combined both liberal and conservative, modernizing and traditionalist, ingredients in their respective positions. Each side is uncomfortable with the more stark options and tight combinations of values pursued at the extremes of the debate. They thus felt free—and indeed, in many ways, compelled—to appropriate and adapt from both poles to fashion a different kind of synthesis. Both, strikingly, borrow from the various civil-rights struggles of the recent past. The prolife groups point out that a fundamental aim of the civil rights efforts was to protect and give voice to those without power—to give them an equal moral standing in the community. For them, the task is to extend to the fetus the rights won by women and racial minority groups; fetal rights are not inherently hostile to women's rights. The prochoice groups, sensitive to the deprivations of women who are given no options in their reproductive lives, want to provide women with a choice about something central to their lives. Yet, though they differ about the meaning of the various civil-rights struggles, those battles serve as a common reference point for both. Most critically, neither side finds the understanding and interpretation of the other outlandish or implausible.

Second, both sides tended to share a distrust of that form of libertarianism that would wholly sunder the individual from the community, setting up the private self as an isolated agent bound by no moral standards other than those perceived or devised by the agent. In this, they not only share some of the conservative and neoconservative critiques of liberalism, but share as well a similar questioning that has become part of the liberal tradition itself, whether from Marxist or other sources. They are, however, hardly less distrustful of that form of traditionalism that believes the past must be preserved in all of its purity. They want to be able to use the past selectively, preserving what remains valuable, rejecting what has been either harmful or wholly overtaken by time, and in general seeing the past as a resource requiring constant adjustment and adaptation for life in the present.

Third, they are uncomfortable with the labels *prolife* and *prochoice*. Those terms, they are well aware, were devised for polemical and political purposes, not for carefully nuanced distinctions. *Prolife* is misleading because it begs the question of what actually serves human life and welfare; *prochoice* is not less misleading because it begs the question of whether freedom of choice ought to be made an ultimate moral value regardless of the nature of the choice to be exercised. Put another way, prolife begs the question of moral means. The labels are also disliked because of a suggestion that one must be wholly one or the other. But the more complex reality is that many in the prolife group will not condemn out of hand all women who have abortions; and many in the prochoice group are repelled by the banal moral arguments used to justify many abortions. Neither group, in short, is happy when *prolife* or *prochoice* seems to require a *reductio ad absurdum,* or inflexible, insensitive moral rules, to be pursued regardless of consequence.

Fourth, both sides are concerned about the conditions that lead or drive women to abortions, and about the social, economic, and cultural contexts of abortion decisions. They rejected, on the one hand, that rendering of the prolife position that construes all choices in favor of abortion as merely personal convenience or crass expediency; and, on the other, that version of the prochoice position that is interested only in the easy availability of abortion, regardless of cause or motivation. They are willing to pursue together an understanding of ways to limit a forced choice of abortion because of poverty or the oppression of women, or lack of social support for childbearing; and they are no less willing to pursue together those social reforms that would be more supportive of troubled pregnancies.

Why, then, sharing so much in their beliefs about how the abortion problem should be understood, and sharing some mutual criticisms of the assumptions and premises of those who fight at what we have called the first level, do they still differ? In part, they can differ because of the relative weight they give to various considerations; ever so faintly tilting one way or another can be decisive when the political and legal choices are so narrow. But in the end it came down, we think, to what is perhaps one of the most profound and subtle value differences of all. That is the matter of one's general hopes and beliefs about the world, human nature, and reality. Put simply, for many who are prochoice, abortion is a necessary evil, one that must be tolerated and supported until such time as better sex education, more effective contraception, and a more just social order make possible fewer troubled pregnancies. And even then, there will still be some justifiable reasons for abortion; it will never disappear. For the prolife group, it is a ban on abortion that must be the necessary evil, one that must be advanced as a long-term step in devising a social order that is more supportive of women and childbearing, more dedicated to an eradication of violence as a solution to personal or social threats.

Both sides, then, are prepared to agree that abortion is undesirable, a crude solution to problems that would better be solved by other means. The crucial difference, however, is that those on the prochoice side believe that the world as it is must be acknowledged, and not just as it might or ought to be. Here and now, in our present social reality, there are women who need or desire abortions. Future solutions to the general problem of abortion, at some unspecified date, will do them no good. They have to live with the reality they encounter. They cannot be asked to bear personally the burden of helping to create a better future, which, even if possible, is not within their individual power to bring about. By contrast, the prolife group believes that a better future cannot be achieved unless we begin now to live the ideals that we want to achieve, unless we are prepared to make present sacrifices toward future goals, and unless aggression toward the fetus is denied, however high the individual cost of denying it. The acceptance of reality as it is implicitly legitimates the *status* quo, undercuts efforts to bring about social change and sanctions violence as an acceptable method of coping with problems.

Differences of that kind run deeply, pitting fundamentally discrepant attitudes and predispositions against each other. The dichotomies are expressed in our ordinary language when "idealists" are contrasted with "realists," or when the "hard-nosed" are pitted against the "starry-eyed." The liberal prolife group, it sometimes seems, favors the equivalent of unilateral disarmament on abortion and is willing to bear the hazards of a stance that will put many women at risk of disaster. They are willing to make a moral bet that the violence inherent in abortion will, in the long run, be repudiated. The public, they think, will eventually respond to the principled witness of those who reject it. The prochoice group, for its part, is hesitant to indulge hopes of that kind. They are unwilling to ask women to give up a viable solution to their present problems in the name of a yet-to-be future, one that might never come.

Perhaps the most striking outcome of our project was the way it broke many stereotypes. Too often it is assumed that a commitment to feminism entails a prochoice position, but that is only one version of feminism, not necessarily its essence. Too often it is assumed that a commitment to the family as an enduring value entails a prohibition of abortion, but that does not follow either. Too often it is assumed that a prochoice stand entails treating children as disposable goods, of value only if wanted. But that is too often a parody of the genuine affirmation of the value of children that can be a central part of a prochoice position. Too often it is assumed that a society that values the rights of individuals must deny the value of community and thus any social restrictions on abortion choices, but in some renderings a denial of abortion can be a way of affirming rights.

There is no suggestion here that the differences are any less sharp than ever, or to deny that even slight differences can have a significant social impact. We only suggest that the relationship of abortion to such deeper values as feminism, the family, childrearing, and the political culture are open to more flexible, interesting possibilities than has been apparent in much of the public debate. If our own domestic wrangles have not led to a general shift in position for either of us, it has nonetheless been valuable. Neither of us has remained unchanged by the other.

STUDY QUESTIONS

1. What are some of the values the Callahans believe prolifers and prochoicers hold in common? In light of this, why do the Callahans believe that each group comes to different conclusions?

2. What do you think the Callahans would say to the claims of *New York Times* columnist Anthony Lewis that the 1993 murder in Pensacola of an abortionist by a prolife extremist showed that almost all prolifers are "religious fanatics" who want to impose "God's word on the rest of us"?

3. Some prolife authors, such as George Grant (in his book, *Grand Illusions),* have documented the apparently racist comments and ideas by Planned Parenthood founder Margaret Sanger, as well as some of her contemporary allies. How do you think the Callahans would respond to this prolife tactic?

FOR FURTHER READING

Brody, Baruch. *Abortion and the Sanctity of Human Life: A Philosophical View*. Cambridge, Mass.: MIT Press, 1975. A defense of a conservative perspective on abortion by a Jewish philosopher.

Callahan, Daniel and Sidney Callahan. *Abortion: Understanding Differences*. New York: Plenum, 1984.

Gordon, Doris. "Abortion and Rights: Applying Libertarian Principles Correctly." *Studies in Prolife Feminism* 1.2 (Spring 1995). Gordon, an atheist Libertarian, defends the prolife view in this essay.

Mollenkott, Virginia Ramey. "Reproductive Choice: Basic to Justice for Women." *Christian Scholar's Review* 17 (March 1988).

Nathanson, Bernard (with Richard Ostling). *Aborting America*. New York: Doubleday, 1979. Nathanson, a co-founder of the National Association to Repeal Abortion Laws (N.A.R.A.L., now known as the National Abortion Rights Action League) and an obstetrician and gynecologist who once owned one of the largest abortion clinics in New York City, defends a strong anti-abortion position from a purely humanistic and non-religious perspective. Nathanson was an agnostic the time of the publication of his book.

Olasky, Marvin. "The Village's Prolife Voice." *Christianity Today*. (June 24, 1991). An interview with *Village Voice* writer Nat Hentoff who is a prolife advocate, atheist, and an attorney who has worked with the American Civil Liberties Union (ACLU).

Religious Coalition for Abortion Rights. *Words of Choice*. Washington, DC: Religious Coalition for Abortion Rights, 1991.

Sider, Ron. *Completely Pro-Life: Building a Consistent Stance*. Downers Grover, Ill.: Inter-Varsity, 1987. A prolife perspective by a theologian on the political left.

Sound Advice for All Prolife Activists and Candidates Who Wish to Include Concern for Women's Rights in Their Prolife Advocacy: Feminists for Life Debate Handbook. Kansas City, Mo.: Feminists for Life of America.

Wennberg, Robert. *Life in the Balance: Exploring the Abortion Controversy*. Grand Rapids, Mich.: Eerdmans, 1985. Although Evangelical Christians are assumed to be all prolife, Wennberg, an Evangelical who teaches at Westmont College (Santa Barbara, California), takes a moderate prochoice position on abortion.

PART II

The Major Supreme Court Decisions

INTRODUCTION

This section contains abridged versions of two major abortion decisions of the United States Supreme Court: *Roe v. Wade* (1973) and *Planned Parenthood v. Casey* (1992). The reader should pay close attention to the Court's reasoning process in each decision, paying particular attention to the factual claims and legal and historical precedent to which the Court appeals for support. These factors will be the focus of the articles in Part III.

Apart from the Court's reasoning process, the conclusions in each one of these decisions are fascinating and, unfortunately, not usually the subject of detailed presentation in the national media (especially television). Arguing that the right to abortion is as constitutionally fundamental as freedom of religion or speech, Justice Harry Blackmun, who wrote the majority opinion in *Roe,* divided pregnancy into three trimesters. He ruled that aside from normal procedural guidelines (for example, an abortion must be safely performed by a licensed physician), a state has no right to restrict abortion in the first six months of pregnancy. In the last trimester (after fetal viability, the time at which the fetus can live outside the womb even with technological assistance) the state has a right, although not an obligation, to restrict abortions to only those cases in which the mother's life or health is jeopardized, because, according to Blackmun, the state may have a legitimate interest in prenatal life. But this health exception for third trimester abortions, some scholars have argued, is so broad in principle that *Roe* turns out to be a much more permissive decision than most realize. In *Roe*'s companion decision, *Doe v. Bolton* (1973), the court ruled that "health" must be taken in its broadest possible medical context, and it must be defined "in light of all factors—physical, emotional, psychological, familial, and the woman's age—relevant to the well-being of the patient. All these factors relate to health."[1] This is one of the reasons why the U.S. Senate Judiciary Committee in 1983, after much critical evaluation of *Roe,* concluded that "no significant legal barriers of any kind whatsoever exist today in the United States for a woman to obtain an abortion for any reason during any stage of her pregnancy."[2]

In an important decision that set the stage for the 1992 Casey decision, *Webster v. Reproductive Health Services* (1989), the Court, in a 5 to 4 vote reversed a lower-court decision and upheld a Missouri statute that contains several provisions, one of which forbids physicians to perform abortions after the fetus is twenty weeks old (except, of course, when the woman's life is in imminent peril). The statute requires physicians to have their pregnant patients who are seeking an abortion to undergo a test to determine the gestational age of the fetus if the physician believes that the pregnant woman might be twenty weeks pregnant. *Webster* modified *Roe* in at least two significant ways. First, it rejected the trimester breakdown of pregnancy that is found in *Roe.* Chief Justice William Rehnquist, who wrote the majority opinion, argued that the trimester breakdown is not found in the Constitution and that the Court sees no reason why a state's interest in protecting the fetus should arrive at the point of viability. Second, the *Webster* Court ruled as constitutional the portion of the Missouri statute that forbade the use of government funds and employees in performing and counseling for a nontherapeutic abortion. Although the Court chipped away at *Roe*'s foundation, it did not overturn it.

In *Planned Parenthood v. Casey* (1992), the Supreme Court was asked to consider the constitutionality of five provisions of the Pennsylvania Abortion Control Act of 1982. This act requires that (1) "a woman seeking an abortion give her informed consent prior to the procedure, and specifies that she be provided with certain information at least 24 hours before the abortion is performed." (2) The act "mandates the informed consent of one parent for a minor to obtain an abortion, but provides a judicial bypass procedure." (3) It also "commands that, unless certain exceptions apply, a married woman seeking an abortion must sign a statement indicating that she has notified her husband." (4) However, the act defines and allows for "a 'medical emergency' that will excuse compliance with forgoing requirements." (5) The act also imposes "certain reporting requirements on facilities providing abortion services."[3]

The Court upheld as constitutional four of the five provisions, rejecting the third one based on what it calls the "undue burden" standard. This is a significant departure from *Roe*. *Roe* affirms abortion as a fundamental constitutional right and thus makes any possible restrictions subject to strict scrutiny (that is, possible restrictions must be essential to meeting a compelling public need to be valid, for example, laws that forbid yelling fire in a crowded theater pass strict scrutiny when subject to the fundamental right of freedom of expression). However, the *Casey* Court, by subscribing to the undue burden standard, does not support the right to abortion as fundamental. Consequently, the states can enact abortion restrictions that might not be able to withstand strict scrutiny but nevertheless do not place on the woman an undue burden. Admitting that the undue burden standard "has no basis in constitutional law," Justices O'Connor, Kennedy, and Souter suggest that when courts apply this standard when evaluating abortion regulations, "judges will have to make the subjective, unguided determination whether the regulations place 'substantial obstacles' in the path of a woman seeking an abortion, undoubtedly engendering a variety of conflicting views."[4]

One passage from *Casey* has received a lot of attention in the literature, because it seems to constitutionally ground the right to abortion in "the right to personal autonomy" rather than "the right to privacy." The passage reads as follows:

> Our law affords constitutional protection to personal decisions relating to marriage, procreation, family relationships, child rearing, and education…These matters, involving the most intimate and personal choices a person may make in a lifetime, choices central to personal dignity and autonomy, are central to the liberty protected by the Fourteenth Amendment. At the heart of liberty is the right to define one's own concept of existence, of meaning, of the universe, and of the mystery of human life. Beliefs about these matters could not define the attributes of personhood were they formed under compulsion by the State.[5]

It is no wonder that some commentators have called this the "mystery passage,"[6] though lower courts have found it to be no mystery at all, and have interpreted the passage to mean that personal autonomy trumps nearly every state interest in one's personal decision making. For example, in a 1994 U.S. District Court case in which the court ruled that a prohibition against physician-assisted suicide is unconstitutional, *Compassion in Dying v. Washington,* Judge Barbara Rothstein employed the logic of *Casey*:

> Like the abortion decision, the decision of a terminally ill person to end his or her life "involves the most intimate and personal choices a person can make in a lifetime," and constitutes a "choice central to personal dignity and autonomy."[7]

The U.S. Supreme Court seems for the time being to have rejected this interpretation of *Casey* when on June 26, 1997, it overturned both Judge Rothstein's ruling as well as an opinion delivered by a federal appeals court that upheld her ruling. Nevertheless, it is an interpretation that finds acceptance among some of the more influential social and legal philosophers. For instance, consider the comments of Ronald Dworkin:

> Our Constitution takes no sides in these ancient disputes about life's meaning. But it does protect people's right to die as well as live, so far as

possible in the light of their own intensely personal convictions about "the mystery of human life." It insists that these values are too central to personality, too much at the core of liberty, to allow a majority to decide what everyone must believe.[8]

Even though the Court since *Webster* has rejected *Roe*'s trimester framework, its requirement that restrictions be subject to "strict scrutiny," and that a woman has a fundamental right to abortion, it nevertheless concluded in *Casey* that *Roe* as a precedent must be respected, based apparently on the right to personal autonomy. Maybe this is why Chief Justice Rehnquist, in his dissent in *Casey*, made the comment: *"Roe* continues to exist, but only in the way a storefront on a western movie set exists: a mere facade to give the illusion of reality."[9]

NOTES

1. *Doe v. Bolton* 410 U.S. 179, 192 (1973).

2. Report, Committee on the Judiciary, U.S. Senate, on Senate Resolution 3, 98th Congress, 98–149, 7 June 1983, 6. Among the scores of works which address this legal issue are the following: John Hart Ely, "The Wages of Crying Wolf: A Comment on *Roe v. Wade*," *Yale Law Journal* 82 (1973): 921; Lynn Wardle and Mary Anne Q. Wood, *A Lawyer Looks at Abortion*, Provo, Utah: Brigham Young University Press, 1982, 12; Stephen M. Krason, *Abortion: Politics, Morality, and the Constitution*, Lanham, Md.: University Press of America, 1984, 103–104; Francis J. Beckwith, *Politically Correct Death: Answering the Arguments for Abortion Rights*, Grand Rapids, Mich.: Baker Book House, 1993, Chapter 2; Jacqueline Nolan Haley, "Haunting Shadows from the Rubble of *Roe*'s Right to Privacy," *Suffolk University Law Review* 9 (1974): 152–153; Roger Wertheimer, "Understanding Blackmun's Argument: The Reasoning of *Roe v. Wade*," in *Abortion: Moral and Legal Perspectives*, eds. Jay L. Garfield and Patricia Hennessy, Amherst: University of Massachusetts Press, 1984, 120–121; and Mary Anne Glendon, *Abortion and Divorce in Western Law*, Cambridge, Mass.: Harvard University Press, 1987, 22–24.

3. *Planned Parenthood v. Casey*, nos. 91–744 and 91–902 (1992): I (Syllabus).

4. Ibid., VIII.

5. *Planned Parenthood v. Casey*, 112 Sup. Ct. 2791, 2807 (1992). Although this is the same decision as cited in notes 3 and 4, this present citation comes from a different text of Casey.

6. See Gerard V. Bradley, "Shall We Ratify the New Constitution?: The Judicial Manifesto in *Casey* and *Lee*," in *Benchmarks: Great Constitutional Controversies in the Supreme Court*, ed. Terry Eastland. Washington, DC: Ethics and Public Policy Center/Grand Rapids, Mich.: Eerdmans, 1995, 117–140.

7. As quoted in Timothy Egan, "Federal Judge Says Ban on Suicide Aid is Unconstitutional," *New York Times* (May 5, 1994), A24.

8. Ronald Dworkin, "When Is It Right to Die?," *New York Times* (May 17 1994), A19.

9. *Planned Parenthood v. Casey* (note 3 citation), 12 (Rehnquist J., dissenting).

2

Roe v. Wade (1973)

U.S. SUPREME COURT

Jane Roe (a pseudonym for Norma McCorvey), a resident of Texas, claimed to have become pregnant as a result of a gang rape (which was found later to be a false charge). According to Texas law (essentially unchanged since 1856), a woman can have an abortion only if it is performed to save her life. Because Roe's pregnancy was not life-threatening, she sued the state of Texas. In 1970, the unmarried Roe filed a class action suit in federal court in Dallas. The federal court ruled that the Texas law was unconstitutionally vague and overbroad and infringed on a person's right to reproductive freedom. The state of Texas appealed to the Supreme Court of the United States. After the case was argued twice before the Court, on January 22, 1973, the Court in Roe v. Wade *agreed with the federal district court and ruled that the Texas law was unconstitutional and that not only must all the states including Texas permit abortions in cases of rape but also in all cases in accordance with the pregnant woman's own choice.*

The following are excerpts from two opinions in Roe. *The first, by Justice Harry Blackmun, is the Court's majority opinion. The second by Justice William Rehnquist (who is currently the Court's Chief Justice), is a dissenting opinion.*

MR. JUSTICE BLACKMUN delivered the opinion of the Court…

The principal thrust of appellant's attack on the Texas statutes is that they improperly invade a right, said to be possessed by the pregnant woman, to choose to terminate her pregnancy. Appellant would discover this right in the concept of personal "liberty" embodied in the Fourteenth Amendment's Due

Process Clause; or in personal, marital, familial, and sexual privacy said to be protected by the Bill of Rights or its penumbras, see *Griswold v. Connecticut,* 381 U.S. 479 (1965); *Eisenstadt v. Baird* 405 U.S. 438 (1972); *id.,* at 460 (WHITE, J., concurring in result); or among those rights reserved to the people by the Ninth Amendment, *Griswold v. Connecticut,* 381 U.S., at 486 (Goldberg, J., concurring). Before addressing this claim, we feel it desirable briefly to survey, in several aspects, the history of abortion, for such insight as that history may afford us, and then to examine the state purposes and interests behind the criminal abortion laws.

It perhaps is not generally appreciated that the restrictive criminal abortion laws in effect in a majority of States today are of relatively recent vintage. Those laws, generally proscribing abortion or its attempt at any time during pregnancy except when necessary to preserve the pregnant woman's life, are not of ancient or even of common-law origin. Instead, they derive from statutory changes effected, for the most part, in the latter half of the 19th century.

Ancient attitudes. These are not capable of precise determination. We are told that at the time of the Persian Empire, abortifacients were known and that criminal abortions were severely punished. We are also told, however, that abortion was practiced in Greek times as well as in the Roman Era, and that "it was resorted to without scruple." The Ephesian, Soranos, often described as the greatest of the ancient gynecologists, appears to have been generally opposed to Rome's prevailing free abortion practices. He found it necessary to think first of the life of the mother, and he resorted to abortion when, upon this standard, he felt the procedure advisable. Greek and Roman law afforded little protection to the unborn. If abortion was prosecuted in some places, it seems to have been based on a concept of a violation of the father's right to his offspring. Ancient religion did not bar abortion.

The Hippocratic Oath. What then of the famous Oath that has stood so long as the ethical guide of the medical profession and that bears the name of the great Greek (460(?)–377(?) B.C.), who has been described as the Father of Medicine, the "wisest and the greatest practitioner of his art," and the "most important and most complete medical personality of antiquity," who dominated the medical schools of his time, and who typified the sum of the medical knowledge of the past? The Oath varies somewhat according to the particular translation, but in any translation the content is clear: "I will give no deadly medicine to anyone if asked, nor suggest any such counsel; and in like manner I will not give to a woman a pessary to produce abortion," or "I will neither give a deadly drug to anybody if asked for it, nor will I make a suggestion to this effect. Similarly, I will not give to a woman an abortive remedy."

Although the Oath is not mentioned in any of the principal briefs in this case or in *Doe v. Bolton, post,* p. 179, it represents the apex of the development of strict ethical concepts in medicine, and its influence endures to this day.

Why did not the authority of Hippocrates dissuade abortion practice in his time and that of Rome? The late Dr. Edelstein provides us with a theory: The Oath was not uncontested even in Hippocrates day; only the Pythagorean school of philosophers frowned upon the related act of suicide. Most Greek thinkers, on the other hand, commended abortion, at least prior to viability. See Plato, Republic, V, 461; Aristotle, Politics, VII, 1335b 25. For the Pythagoreans, however, it was a matter of dogma. For them the embryo was animate from the moment of conception, and abortion meant destruction of living being. The abortion clause of the Oath, therefore, "echoes Pythagorean doctrines," and "[i]n no other stratum of Greek opinion were such views held or proposed in the same spirit of uncompromising austerity."

Dr. Edelstein then concludes that the Oath originated in a group representing only a small segment of Greek opinion and that it certainly was not accepted by all ancient physicians. He points out that medical writings down to Galen (A.D. 130–200) "give evidence of the violation of almost every one of its injunctions.' But with the end of antiquity a decided change took place. Resistance against suicide and against abortion became common. The Oath came to be popular. The emerging teachings of Christianity were in agreement with the Pythagorean ethic. The Oath "became the nucleus of all medical ethics" and "was applauded as the embodiment of truth." Thus, suggests Dr. Edelstein, it is "a Pythagorean manifesto and not the expression of an absolute standard of medical conduct."

This, it seems to us, is a satisfactory and acceptable explanation of the Hippocratic Oath's apparent rigidity. It enables us to understand, in historical context, a long-accepted and revered statement of medical ethics.

The common law. It is undisputed that at common law, abortion performed *before* "quickening"—the first recognizable movement of the fetus *in utero*, appearing usually from the 16th to the 18th week of pregnancy—was not an indictable offense. The absence of a common-law crime for pre-quickening abortion appears to have developed from a confluence of earlier philosophical, theological, and civil and canon law concepts of when life begins. These disciplines variously approached the question in terms of the point at which the embryo or fetus became "formed" or recognizably human, or in terms of when a "person" came into being, that is, infused with a "soul" or "animated." A loose consensus evolved in early English law that these events occurred at some point between conception and live birth. This was "mediate animation." Although Christian theology and the canon law came to fix the point of animation at 40 days for a male and 80 days for a female, a view that persisted until the 19th century, there was otherwise little agreement about the precise time of formation or animation. There was agreement, however, that prior to this point the fetus was to be regarded as part of the mother, and its destruction, therefore, was not homicide. Due to continued uncertainty about the precise time when animation occurred, or to the lack of any empirical basis for the 40–80-day view, and perhaps to Aquinas' definition of movement as one of the two first principles of life, Bracton focused upon quickening as the critical point. The significance of quickening was echoed by later common-law scholars and found its way into the received common law in this country.

Whether abortion of a *quick* fetus was a felony at common law, even a lesser crime, is still disputed. Bracton, writing early in the 13th century, thought it homicide. But the later and predominant view, following the great common-law scholars, has been that it was, at most, a lesser offense. In a frequently cited passage, Coke took the position that abortion of a woman "quick with childe" is "a great misprision, and no murder." Blackstone followed, saying that while abortion after quickening had once been considered manslaughter (though not murder), "modern law" took a less severe view. A recent review of the common-law precedents argues, however, that those precedents contradict Coke and that even post-quickening abortion was never established as a common-law crime. This is of some importance because while most American courts ruled, in holding or dictum, that abortion of an unquickened fetus was not criminal under their received common law, others followed Coke in stating that abortion of a quick fetus was a "misprision," a term they translated to mean "misdemeanor." That their reliance on Coke on this aspect of the law was uncritical and, apparently in all the reported cases, dictum (due probably to the paucity of common-law prosecutions for post-quickening abortion), makes it now appear doubtful that abortion was ever firmly established as a common-law crime even with respect to the destruction of a quick fetus....

The American law. In this country, the law in effect in all but a few States until mid-19th century was the pre-existing English common law. Connecticut, the first State to enact abortion legislation, adopted in 1821 that part of Lord Ellenborough's Act that related to a woman "quick with child." The death penalty was not imposed. Abortion before quickening was made a crime in that State only in 1860. In 1828, New York enacted legislation that, in two respects, was to serve as a model for early anti-abortion statutes. First, while barring destruction of an unquickened fetus as well as a quick fetus, it made the former only a misdemeanor, but the latter second-degree manslaughter. Second, it incorporated a concept of therapeutic abortion by providing that an abortion was excused if it "shall have been necessary to preserve the life of such mother, or shall have been advised by two physicians to be necessary for such purpose." By 1840, when Texas had received the common law, only eight American States had statutes dealing with abortion. It was not until after the War Between the States that legislation began generally to replace the common law. Most of these initial statutes dealt severely with abortion after quickening but were lenient with it before quickening. Most punished attempts equally with completed abortions. While many statutes included the exception for an abortion thought by one or more physicians to be necessary to save the mother's life, that provision soon disappeared and the typical law required that the procedure actually be necessary for that purpose.

Gradually, in the middle and late 19th century the quickening distinction disappeared from the statutory law of most States and the degree of the offense and the penalties were increased. By the end of the 1950s, a large majority of the jurisdictions banned abortion, however and whenever performed, unless done to save or preserve the life of the mother. The exceptions, Alabama and the District of Columbia, permitted abortion to preserve the mother's health. Three States permitted abortions that were not "unlawfully" performed or that were not "without lawful justification," leaving interpretation of those standards to the courts. In the past several years, however, a trend toward liberalization of abortion statutes has resulted in adoption, by about one-third of the States, of less stringent laws, most of them patterned after the ALI Model Penal Code, § 230.3.

It is thus apparent that at common law, at the time of the adoption of our Constitution, and throughout the major portion of the 19th century, abortion was viewed with less disfavor than under most American statutes currently in effect. Phrasing it another way, a woman enjoyed substantially broader right to terminate a pregnancy than she does most in States today. At least with respect to the early stage of pregnancy and very possibly without such a limitation, the opportunity to make this choice was present in this country well into the 19th century. Even later, the law continued for some time to treat less punitively an abortion procured in early pregnancy.

The position of the American Medical Association. The anti-abortion mood prevalent in this country in the late 19th century was shared by medical profession. Indeed, the attitude of the profession may have played a significant role in the enactment of stringent criminal abortion legislation during that period.

An AMA Committee on Criminal Abortion was appointed in May 1857. It presented its report, 12 Trans. of the Am. Med. Assn. 73–78 (1859), to the Twelfth Annual Meeting. That report observed that the Committee had been appointed to investigate criminal abortion "with a view to its general suppression." It deplored abortion and its frequency, and it listed three causes of "this general demoralization":

> "The first of these causes is a wide-spread popular ignorance of the true character of the crime—a belief, even among mothers themselves, that the foetus is not alive till after the period of quickening.
>
> "The second of the agents alluded to is the fact that the profession themselves are frequently supposed careless of foetal life....
>
> "The third reason of the frightful extent of this crime is found in the grave defects of our laws, both common and statute, as regards the independent and actual existence of the child before birth, as a living being. These errors, which are sufficient in most instances to prevent conviction, are based, and only based, upon mistaken and exploded medical dogmas. With strange inconsistency, the law fully acknowledges the foetus in utero and its inherent rights, for civil purposes; while personally and as criminally affected, it fails to recognize it, and to its life as yet denies all protection." *Id.,* at 75-76.

The Committee then offered, and the Association adopted, resolutions protesting "against such unwarrantable destruction of human life," calling upon state legislatures to revise their abortion laws, and requesting the cooperation of state medical societies "in pressing the subject." *Id.,* at 28, 78.

In 1871 a long and vivid report was submitted by the Committee on Criminal Abortion. It ended with the observation, "We had to deal with human life. In a matter of less importance we could entertain no compromise. An honest judge on the bench would call things by their proper names. We could do no less." 22 Trans. of the Am. Med. Assn. 258 (1871). It proffered resolutions, adopted by the Association, *id.,* at 38–39, recommending, among other things, that it "be unlawful and unprofessional for any physician to induce abortion or premature labor, without the concurrent opinion of at least one respectable consulting physician, and then always with a view to the safety of the child—if that be possible," and calling "the attention of the clergy of all denominations to the perverted views of morality entertained by a large class of females—aye, and men also, on this important question."

Except for periodic condemnation of the criminal abortionist, no further formal AMA action took place until 1967. In that year, the Committee on Human Reproduction urged the adoption of a stated policy of opposition to induced abortion, except when there is "documented medical evidence" of a threat to the health or life of the mother, or that the child "may be born with incapacitating physical deformity or mental deficiency," or that a pregnancy resulting from legally established statutory or forcible rape or incest may constitute a threat to the mental or physical health of the patient," two other physicians "chosen because of their recognized professional competence have examined the patient and have concurred in writing," and the procedure "is performed in a hospital accredited by the Joint Commission on Accreditation of Hospitals." The providing of medical information by physicians to state legislatures in their consideration of legislation regarding therapeutic abortion was "to be considered consistent with the principles of ethics of the American Medical Association." This recommendation was adopted by the House of Delegates. Proceedings of the AMA House of Delegates 40–51 (June 1967).

In 1970, after the introduction of a variety of proposed resolutions, and of a report from its Board of Trustees, a reference committee noted "polarization of the medical professional on this controversial issue"; division among those who had testified; a difference of opinion among AMA councils and committees; "the remarkable shift in testimony" in six months, felt to be influenced "by the rapid changes in state laws and by the judicial decisions which tend to make abortion more freely available," and a feeling "that this trend will continue." On June 25, 1970, the House of Delegates adopted preambles and most of the resolutions proposed by the reference committee. The preambles emphasized "the best interests of the patient," "sound clinical judgment," and "informed patient consent," in contrast to "mere acquiescence to the patient's demand." The resolutions asserted that abortion is a medical procedure that should be performed by a licensed physician in an accredited hospital only after consultation with two other physicians and in conformity with state law, and that no party to the procedure should be required to violate personally held moral principles. Proceedings of the AMA House of Delegates 220 (June 1970). The AMA Judicial Council rendered a complementary opinion.

The position of the American Public Health Association. In October 1970, the Executive Board of the APHA adopted Standards for Abortion Services. These were five in number:

"a. Rapid and simple abortion referral must be readily available through state and local public health departments medical societies, or other nonprofit organizations.

"b. An important function of counseling should be to simplify and expedite the provision of abortion services; it should not delay the obtaining of these services.

"c. Psychiatric consultation should not be mandatory. As in the case of other specialized medical services, psychiatric consultation should be sought for definite indications and not on a routine basis.

"d. A wide range of individuals from appropriately trained, sympathetic volunteers to highly skilled physicians may qualify as abortion counselors.

"e. Contraception and/or sterilization should be discussed with each abortion patient." Recommended Standards for Abortion Services, 61 Am. J. Pub. Health 396 (1971).

Among factors pertinent to life and health risks associated with abortion were three that "are recognized as important":

"a. the skill of the physician,

"b. the environment in which the abortion is performed and above all

"c. the duration of pregnancy, as determined by uterine size and confirmed by menstrual history." *Id.*, at 397.

It was said that "a well-equipped hospital" offers more protection "to cope with unforeseen difficulties than an office or clinic without such resources… The factor of gestational age is of overriding importance." Thus, it was recommended that abortions in the second trimester and early abortions in the presence of existing medical complications be performed in hospitals as inpatient procedures. For pregnancies in the first trimester, abortion in the hospital with or without overnight stay "is probably the safest practice." An abortion in an extramural facility, however, is an acceptable alternative "provided arrangements exist in advance to admit patients promptly if unforeseen complications develop." Standards for an abortion facility were listed. It was said that at present abortions should be performed by physicians or osteopaths who are licensed to practice and who have "adequate training."…

Three reasons have been advanced to explain historically the enactment of criminal abortion laws in the 19th century and to justify their continued existence.

It has been argued occasionally that these laws were the product a Victorian social concern to discourage illicit sexual conduct. Texas, however, does not advance this justification in the present case, and it appears that no court or commentator has taken the argument seriously. The appellants and *amici* contend, moreover, that this is not a proper state purpose at all and suggest that, if it were, the Texas statutes are overbroad in protecting it since the law fails to distinguish between married and unwed mothers.

A second reason is concerned with abortion as a medical procedure. When most criminal abortion laws were first enacted, the procedure was a hazardous one for the woman. This was particularly true prior to the development of antisepsis. Antiseptic techniques, of course were based on discoveries by Lister, Pasteur, and others first announced in 1867, but were not generally accepted and employed until about the turn of the century. Abortion mortality was high. Even after 1900, and perhaps until as late as the development of antibiotics in the 1940's, standard modern techniques such as dilation and curettage were not nearly so safe as they are today. Thus, it has been argued that a State's real concern in enacting a criminal abortion law was to protect the pregnant woman, that is, to restrain her from submitting to a procedure that placed her life in serious jeopardy.

Modern medical techniques have altered this situation. Appellants and various *amici* refer to medical data indicating that abortion in early pregnancy, that is, prior to the end of the first trimester, although not without its risk, is now relatively safe. Mortality rates for women undergoing early abortions, where the procedure is legal, appear to be as low as or lower than the rates for normal childbirth. Consequently, any interest of the State in protecting the women from an inherently hazardous procedure, except when it would be equally dangerous for her to forgo it, has largely disappeared. Of course, important state interests in the areas of health and medical standards do remain. The State has a legitimate interest in seeing to it that abortion, like any other medical procedure, is performed under circumstances that insure maximum safety for the patient. This interest obviously extends at least to the performing physician and his staff, to the facilities involved, to the availability of aftercare, and to adequate provision for any complication or emergency that might arise. The prevalence of high mortality rates at illegal "abortion mills" strengthens, rather than weakens, the State's interest in regulating the conditions under which abortions are performed. Moreover, the risk to the woman increases as her pregnancy continues. Thus the State retains a definite interest in protecting the woman's own health and safety when an abortion is proposed at a late stage of pregnancy.

The third reason is the State's interest—some phrase it in terms of duty—in protecting prenatal life. Some of the argument for this justification rests on the theory that a new human life is present from the moment of conception. The State's interest and general obligation to protect life then extends, it is argued, to prenatal life. Only when the life of the pregnant mother herself is at stake, balanced against the life she carries within her, should the interest of the embryo or fetus not prevail. Logically, of course, a legitimate state interest in this area need not stand or fall on acceptance of the belief that life begins at conception or at some other point prior to live birth. In assessing the State's interest, recognition may be given to the less rigid claim that as long as at least *potential* life is involved, the State may assert interests beyond the protection of the pregnant woman alone.

Parties challenging state abortion laws have sharply disputed in some courts the contention that a purpose of these laws, when enacted, was to protect prenatal life. Pointing to the absence of legislative history to support the contention, they claim that most state laws were designed solely to protect the woman. Because medical advances have lessened this concern, at least with respect to abortion in early pregnancy, they argue that with respect to such abortions the laws can no longer be justified by any state interest. There is some scholarly support for this view of original purpose. The few state courts called upon to interpret their laws in the late 19th and early 20th centuries did focus on the State's interest in protecting the woman's health rather than in preserving the embryo and fetus. Proponents of this view point out that in many States, including Texas, by statute or judicial interpretation, the pregnant woman herself could not be prosecuted for self-abortion or for cooperating in an abortion performed upon her by another. They claim that adoption of the "quickening" distinction through received common law and state statutes tacitly recognizes the greater health hazards inherent in late abortion and impliedly repudiates the theory that life begins at conception.

It is with these interests, and the weight to be attached to them, that this case is concerned.

The Constitution does not explicitly mention any right of privacy. In a line of decisions, however, going back perhaps as far as *Union Pacific R. Co. v. Botsford,* 141 U.S. 250, 251 (1891), the Court has recognized that a right of personal privacy, or a guarantee of certain areas or zones of privacy does exist under the Constitution. In carrying contexts, the Court or individual Justices have, indeed, found at least the roots of that right in the First Amendment, in the Fourth and Fifth Amendments, in the penumbras of the Bill of Rights, in the Ninth Amendment, or in the concept of liberty guaranteed by the first section of the Fourteenth Amendment. These decisions make it clear that only personal rights that can be deemed "fundamental" or "implicit in the concept of ordered liberty," are included in this guarantee of personal privacy. They also make it clear that the right has some extension to activities relating to marriage, procreation, contraception, family relationships, and child rearing and education.

This right of privacy, whether it be founded in the Fourteenth Amendment's concept of personal liberty and restrictions upon state action, as we feel it is, or, as the District Court determined, in the Ninth Amendment's reservation of rights to the people, is broad enough to encompass a woman's decision whether or not to terminate her pregnancy. The detriment that the State would impose upon the pregnant woman by denying this choice altogether is apparent. Specific and direct harm medically diagnosable even in early pregnancy may be involved. Maternity, or additional offspring, may force upon the woman a distressful life and future. Psychological harm may be imminent. Mental and physical health may be taxed by child care. There is also the distress, for all concerned, associated with the unwanted child, and there is the problem of bringing a child into a family already unable, psychologically and otherwise, to care for it. In other cases, as in this one, the additional difficulties and continuing stigma of unwed motherhood may be involved. All these are factors the woman and her responsible physician necessarily will consider in consultation.

On the basis of elements such as these, appellant and some *amici* argue that the woman's right is absolute and that she is entitled to terminate her pregnancy at whatever time, in whatever way, and for whatever reason she alone chooses. With this we do not agree. Appellant's arguments that Texas either has no valid interest at all in regulating the abortion decision, or no interest strong enough to support any limitation upon the woman's sole determination, are unpersuasive. The Court's decisions recognizing a right of privacy also acknowledge that some state regulation in areas protected by that right is appropriate. As noted above, a State may properly assert important interests in safeguarding health, in maintaining medical standards, and in protecting potential life. At some point in pregnancy, these respective interests become sufficiently compelling to sustain regulation of the factors that govern the abortion decision. The privacy right involved, therefore, cannot be said to be absolute. In fact, it is not clear to us that the claim asserted by some *amici* that one has an unlimited right to do with one's body as one pleases bears a close relationship to the right of privacy previously articulated in the Court's decisions. The Court has refused to recognize an unlimited right of this kind in the past.

We, therefore, conclude that the right of personal privacy includes the abortion decision, but that this right is not unqualified and must be considered against important state interests in regulation.

We note that those federal and state courts that have recently considered abortion law challenges have reached the same conclusion.

Although the results are divided, most of these courts have agreed that the right of privacy, however based, is broad enough to cover the abortion decision, that the right, nonetheless, is not absolute and is subject to some limitations; and that at some point the state interests as to protection of health, medical standards, and prenatal life, become dominant. We agree with this approach.

Where certain "fundamental rights" are involved, the Court has held that regulation limiting these rights may be justified only by a "compelling state interest," and that legislative enactments must be narrowly drawn to express only the legitimate state interests at stake.

In the recent abortion cases, cited above, courts have recognized these principles. Those striking down state laws have generally scrutinized the State's interests in protecting health and potential life, and have concluded that neither interest justified broad limitations on the reasons for which a physician and his pregnant patient might decide that she should have an abortion in the early stages of pregnancy. Courts sustaining state laws have held that the State's determinations to protect health or prenatal life are dominant and constitutionally justifiable.

The District Court held that the appellee failed to meet his burden demonstrating that the Texas statute's infringement upon Roe's rights was necessary to support a compelling state interest, and that, although the appellee presented "several compelling justifications for state presence in the area of abortions," the statutes outstripped these justifications and swept "far beyond any areas of compelling state interest." Appellant and appellee both contest that holding. Appellant, as has been indicated, claims an absolute right that bars any state imposition of criminal penalties in the area. Appellee argues that the State's determination to recognize and protect prenatal life from and after conception constitutes a compelling state interest. As noted above, we do not agree fully with either formulation.

A. The appellee and certain *amici* argue that the fetus is a "person" within the language and meaning of the Fourteenth Amendment. In support of this, they outline at length and in detail the well-known facts of fetal development. If this suggestion of personhood is established, the appellant's case, of course, collapses, for the fetus' right to life would then be guaranteed specifically by the Amendment. The appellant conceded as much on reargument. On the other hand, the appellee conceded on reargument that no case could be cited that holds that a fetus is a person within the meaning of the Fourteenth Amendment.

The Constitution does not define "person" in so many words. Section 1 of the Fourteenth Amendment contains three references to "person." In nearly all these instances, the use of the word is such that it has application only postnatally. None indicates, with any assurance, that it has any possible pre-natal application.

All this, together with our observation, *supra,* that throughout the major portion of the 19th century prevailing legal abortion practices were far freer than they are today, persuades us that the word "person," as used in the Fourteenth Amendment, does not include the unborn. This is in accord with the results reached in those few cases where the issue has been squarely presented. Indeed, our decision in *United States v. Vuitch,* 402 U.S. 62 (1971), inferentially is to the same effect, for we there would not have indulged in statutory interpretation favorable to abortion in specified circumstances if the necessary consequence was the termination of life entitled to Fourteenth Amendment protection.

This conclusion, however, does not of itself fully answer the contentions raised by Texas, and we pass on to other considerations.

B. The pregnant woman cannot be isolated in her privacy. She carried an embryo and, later, a fetus, if one accepts the medical definitions of the developing young in the human uterus. See Dorland's Illustrated Medical Dictionary 478–479, 547 (24th ed. 1965). The situation therefore is inherently different from martial intimacy, or bedroom possession of obscene material, or marriage, or procreation, or education, with which *Eisenstadt* and *Griswold,*

Stanley, Loving, Skinner, and *Pierce* and *Meyer* were respectively concerned. As we have intimated above, it is reasonable and appropriate for a State to decide that at some point in time another interest, that of health of the mother or that of potential human life, becomes significantly involved. The woman's privacy is no longer sole and any right of privacy she possesses must be measured accordingly.

Texas urges that, apart from the Fourteenth Amendment, life begins at conception and is present throughout pregnancy, and that, therefore, the State has a compelling interest in protecting that life from and after conception. We need not resolve the difficult question of when life begins. When those trained in the respective disciplines of medicine, philosophy, and theology are unable to arrive at any consensus, the judiciary, at this point in the development of man's knowledge, is not in a position to speculate as to the answer.

It should be sufficient to note briefly the wide divergence of thinking on this most sensitive and difficult question. There has always been strong support for the view that life does not begin until live birth. This was the belief of the Stoics. It appears to be the predominant, though not the unanimous, attitude of the Jewish faith. It may be taken to represent also the position of a large segment of the Protestant community, insofar as that can be ascertained; organized groups that have taken a formal position on the abortion issue have generally regarded abortion as a matter for the conscience of the individual and her family. As we have noted, the common law found greater significance in quickening. Physicians and their scientific colleagues have regarded that event with less interest and have tended to focus either upon conception, upon live birth, or upon the interim point at which the fetus becomes "viable," that is, potentially able to live outside the mother's womb, albeit with artificial aid. Viability is usually placed at about seven months (28 weeks) but may occur earlier, even at 24 weeks. The Aristotelian theory of "mediate animation," that held sway throughout the Middle Ages and the Renaissance in Europe, continued to be official Roman Catholic dogma until the 19th century, despite opposition to this "ensoulment" theory from those in the Church who would recognize the existence of life from the moment of conception. The latter is now, of course, the official belief of the Catholic Church. As one brief *amicus* discloses, this is a view strongly held by many non–Catholics as well, and by many physicians. Substantial problems for precise definition of this view are posed, however, by new embryological data that purport to indicate that conception is a "process" over time, rather than an event, and by new medical techniques such as menstrual extraction, the "morning-after" pill, implantation of embryos, artificial insemination, and even artificial wombs.

In areas other than criminal abortion, the law has been reluctant to endorse any theory that life, as we recognize it, begins before live birth or to accord legal rights to the unborn except in narrowly defined situations and except when the rights are contingent upon live birth. For example, the traditional rule of tort law denied recovery for prenatal injuries even though the child was born alive. That rule has been changed in almost every jurisdiction. In most States, recovery is said to be permitted only if the fetus was viable, or at least quick, when the injuries were sustained, though few courts have squarely so held. In a recent development, generally opposed by the commentators, some States permit the parents of a stillborn child to maintain an action for wrongful death because of prenatal injuries. Such an action, however, would appear to be one to vindicate the parents' interest and is thus consistent with the view that the fetus, at most, represents only the potentiality of life. Similarly, unborn children have been recognized as acquiring rights or interests by way of inheritance or other devolution of property, and have been represented by guardians *ad litem*. Perfection of the interests involved, again, has generally been contingent upon live birth. In short, the unborn have never been recognized in the law as persons in the whole sense.

In view of all this, we do not agree that, by adopting one theory of life, Texas may override the rights of the pregnant woman that are at stake. We repeat, however, that the State does have an important and legitimate interest in preserving and protecting the health of the pregnant woman, whether she be a resident of the State or a nonresident who seeks medical consultation and treatment there, and that it has still *another* important and legitimate interest in protecting the potentiality of human life. These interests are separate and distinct. Each grows in substantiality as the woman approaches term and, at a point during pregnancy, each becomes "compelling."

With respect to the State's important and legitimate interest in the health of the mother, the "compelling" point, in the light of present medical knowledge, is at approximately the end of the first trimester. This is so because of the now-established medical fact, referred to above, that until the end of the first trimester mortality in abortion may be less than mortality in normal childbirth. It follows that, from and after this point, a State may regulate the abortion procedure to the extent that the regulation reasonably relates to the preservation and protection of maternal health. Examples of permissible state regulation in this area are requirements as to the qualifications of the person who is to perform the abortion; as to the licensure of that person; as to the facility in which the procedure is to be performed, that is, whether it must be a hospital or may be a clinic or some other place of less-than-hospital status; as to the licensing of the facility; and the like.

This means, on the other hand, that, for the period of pregnancy prior to this "compelling" point, the attending physician, in consultation with his patient, is free to determine, without regulation by the State, that, in his medical judgment, the patient's pregnancy should be terminated. If that decision is reached, the judgment may be effectuated by an abortion free of interference by the State.

With respect to the State's important and legitimate interest in potential life, the "compelling" point is at viability. This is so because the fetus then presumably has the capability of meaningful life outside the mother's womb. State regulation protective of fetal life after viability thus has both logical and biological justifications. If the State is interested in protecting fetal life after viability, it may go so far as to proscribe abortion during that period, except when it is necessary to preserve the life or health of the mother.

To summarize and to repeat:

1. A state criminal abortion statute of the current Texas type, that excepts from criminality only a *lifesaving* procedure on behalf of the mother, without regard to pregnancy stage and without recognition of the other interests involved, is violative of the Due Process Clause of the Fourteenth Amendment.

(a) For the stage prior to approximately the end of the first trimester, the abortion decision and its effectuation must be left to the medical judgment of the pregnant woman s attending physician.

(b) For the stage subsequent to approximately the end of the first trimester, the State, in promoting its interest in the health of the mother, may, if it chooses, regulate the abortion procedure in ways that are reasonably related to maternal health.

(c) For the stage subsequent to viability, the State in promoting its interest in the potentiality of human life may, if it chooses, regulate, and even proscribe, abortion except where it is necessary, in appropriate medical judgment, for the preservation of the life or health of the mother.

2. The State may define the term "physician" as it has been employed in the preceding paragraphs of this Part XI of this opinion, to mean only a physician currently licensed by the State, and may proscribe any abortion by a person who is not a physician as so defined.

In *Doe v. Bolton, post*, p. 179, procedural requirements contained in one of the modern abortion statutes are considered. That opinion and this one, of course, are to be read together.

This holding, we feel, is consistent with the relative weights of the respective interests involved, with the lessons and examples of medical and legal history, with the lenity of the common law, and with the demands of the profound problems of the present day. The decision leaves the State free to place increasing restrictions on abortion as the period of pregnancy lengthens, so long as those restrictions are tailored to the recognized state interests. The decision vindicates the right of the physician to administer medical treatment according to his professional judgment up to the points where important state interests provide compelling justifications for intervention. Up to those points, the abortion decision in all its aspects is inherently, and primarily, a medical decision, and basic responsibility for it must rest with the physician. If an individual practitioner abuses the privilege of exercising proper medical judgment, the usual remedies, judicial and intra-professional, are available.

Mr. Justice Rehnquist, dissenting.

The Court's opinion brings to the decision of this troubling question both extensive historical fact and a wealth of legal scholarship. While the opinion thus commands my respect, I find myself nonetheless in fundamental disagreement with those parts of it that invalidate the Texas statute in question, and therefore dissent.

The Court's opinion decides that a State may impose virtually no restriction on the performance of abortions during the first trimester of pregnancy. Our previous decisions indicate that a necessary predicate for such an opinion is a plaintiff who was in her first trimester of pregnancy at some time during the pendency of her lawsuit. While a party may vindicate his own constitutional rights, he may not seek vindication for the rights of others. The Court's statement of facts in this case makes clear, however that the record in no way indicates the presence of such a plaintiff. We know only that plaintiff Roe at the time of filing her complaint was a pregnant woman; for aught that appears in this record, she may have been in her *last* trimester of pregnancy as of the date the complaint was filed.

Nothing in the Court's opinion indicates that Texas might not constitutionally apply its proscription of abortion as written to a woman in that stage of pregnancy. Nonetheless, the Court uses her complaint against the Texas statute as a fulcrum for deciding that States may impose virtually no restrictions on medical abortions performed during the *first* trimester of pregnancy. In deciding such a hypothetical lawsuit, the Court departs from the longstanding admonition that it should never "formulate a rule of constitutional law broader than is required by the precise facts to which it is to be applied." *Liverpool, New York & Philadelphia S.S. Co. v. Commissioners of Emigration,* 113 U.S. 33, 39 (1885).

Even if there were a plaintiff in this case capable of litigating the issue which the Court decides, I would reach a conclusion opposite to that reached by the Court. I have difficulty in concluding, as the Court does, that the right of "privacy" is involved in this case. Texas, by the statute here challenged, bars the performance of a medical abortion by a licensed physician on a plaintiff such as Roe. A transaction resulting in an operation such as this is not "private" in the ordinary usage of that word. Nor is the "privacy" that the Court finds here even a distant relative of the freedom from searches and seizures protected by the Fourth Amendment to the Constitution, which the Court has referred to as embodying a right to privacy. *Katz v. United States,* 389 U.S. 347 (1967).

If the Court means by the term "privacy" no more than that the claim of a person to be free from unwanted state regulation of consensual transactions may be a form of "liberty" protected by the Fourteenth Amendment, there is no doubt that similar claims have been upheld in our earlier decisions on the basis of that liberty. I agree with the state-meat of Mr. Justice Stewart in his concurring opinion that the "liberty," against deprivation of which without due process the Fourteenth Amendment protects, embraces more than the rights found in the Bill of Rights. But that liberty is not guaranteed absolutely against deprivation, only against deprivation without due process of law. The test traditionally applied in the area of social and economic legislation is whether or not a law such as that challenged has a rational relation to a valid state objective. The Due Process Clause of the Fourteenth Amendment undoubtedly does place a limit, albeit a broad one, on legislative power to enact laws such as this. If the Texas statute were to prohibit an abortion even where the mother's life is in jeopardy. I have little doubt that such a statute would lack a rational relation to a valid state objective under the test stated in *Williamson, supra.* But the Court's sweeping invalidation of any restrictions on abortion during the first trimester is impossible to justify under that standard, and the conscious weighing of competing factors that the Court's opinion apparently substitutes for the established test is far more appropriate to a legislative judgment than to a judicial one.

The Court eschews the history of the Fourteenth Amendment in its reliance on the "compelling state interest" test. But the Court adds a new wrinkle to this test by transposing it from the legal considerations associated with the Equal Protection Clause of the Fourteenth Amendment to this case arising under the Due Process Clause of the Fourteenth Amendment. Unless I misapprehend the consequences of this transplanting of the "compelling state interest test," the Court's opinion will accomplish the seemingly impossible feat of leaving this area of the law more confused than it found it.

While the Court's opinion quotes from the dissent of Mr. Justice Holmes in *Lochner v. New York*, 198 U.S. 45, 74 (1905), the result it reaches is more closely attuned to the majority opinion of Mr. Justice Peckham in that case. As in *Lochner* and similar cases applying substantive due process standards to economic and social welfare legislation, the adoption of the compelling state interest standard will inevitably require this Court to examine the legislative policies and pass on the wisdom of these policies in the very process of deciding whether a particular state interest put forward may or may not be "compelling." The decision here to break pregnancy into three distinct terms and to outline the permissible restrictions the State may impose in each one, for example, partakes more of judicial legislation than it does of a determination of the intent of the drafters of the Fourteenth Amendment.

The fact that a majority of the States reflecting, after all, the majority sentiment in those States, have had restrictions on abortions for at least a century is a strong indication, it seems to me, that the asserted right to an abortion is not "so rooted in the traditions and conscience of our people as to be ranked as fundamental," *Snyder v. Massachusetts,* 291 U.S. 97, 105 (1934). Even today, when society's views on abortion are changing the very existence of the debate is evidence that the "right" to an abortion is not so universally accepted as the appellant would have us believe.

To reach its result, the Court necessarily has had to find within the scope of the Fourteenth Amendment a right that was apparently completely unknown to the drafters of the Amendment. As early as 1821, the first state law dealing directly with abortion was enacted by the Connecticut Legislature. Conn. Stat., Tit. 22 § § 14, 16. By the time of the adoption of the Fourteenth Amendment in 1868, there were at least 36 laws enacted by state or territorial legislatures limiting abortion. While many States have amended or updated their laws, 21 of the laws on the books in 1868 remain in effect today. Indeed, the Texas statute struck down today was, as the majority notes, first enacted in 1857 and "has remained substantially unchanged to the present time."

There apparently was no question concerning the validity of this provision or of any of the other state statutes when the Fourteenth Amendment was adopted. The only conclusion possible from this history is that the drafters did not intend to have the Fourteenth Amendment withdraw from the States the power to legislate with respect to this matter.

STUDY QUESTIONS

1. In *Roe,* on what basis did the Court reason that the right to abortion is a fundamental right? How did the Court's appeal to the history of abortion in Western law, especially American law, influence its decision?

2. Briefly summarize Justice Rehnquist's dissent. Do you think he adequately addresses Justice Blackmun's case? Why or why not?

3. What is the Court's view of fetal personhood? Do you agree with its view? Why or why not?

3

Planned Parenthood v. Casey (1992)

U.S. SUPREME COURT

In Planned Parenthood v. Casey *(1992) the United States Supreme Court was asked to consider the constitutionality of five provisions of the Pennsylvania Abortion Control Act of 1982: (1) a woman seeking an abortion must give her informed consent before the procedure and be provided with certain information at least 24 hours before the abortion is performed; (2) the informed consent of one parent must be obtained for a minor to undergo an abortion, but a judicial bypass procedure is provided; (3) a married woman seeking an abortion must sign a statement indicating that she has notified her husband, unless certain exceptions apply (for example, she is being abused by her husband); (4) a "medical emergency" will excuse compliance with the statute's requirements; and (5) abortion-providing facilities must abide by certain reporting requirements. The Court upheld as constitutional four of the five provisions, rejecting the third one based on what it calls the "undue burden standard" (that is, does the provision constitute an undue burden for the woman seeking the abortion). Casey is significant because, although it upheld* Roe *as a legal precedent, it rejected* Roe's *trimester breakdown and its insistence that abortion is a fundamental constitutional right.*

The following are excerpts from opinions in Casey. *The first, by Justices O'Connor, Souter, and Kennedy, represents the Court's opinion. The second is Justice Antonin Scalia's dissent.*

JUSTICE O'CONNOR, JUSTICE KENNEDY, and JUSTICE SOUTER announced judgment of the Court and delivered the opinion of the Court with respect to Parts I, II, III, V-A, V-C, and VI, an opinion with respect to Part

V-E, in which JUSTICE STEVENS joins, and an opinion with respect to Parts IV, V-B, and V-D.

I

Liberty finds no refuge in a jurisprudence of doubt. Yet 19 years after our holding that the Constitution protects a woman's right to terminate her pregnancy in its early stages, *Roe v. Wade,* 410 U.S. 113 (1973), the definition of liberty is still questioned. Joining the respondents as *amicus curiae,* the United States, as it has done in five other cases in the last decade, again asks us to overrule *Roe.* See Brief for Respondents 104–117; Brief for United States as *Amicus Curiae* 8.

At issue in these cases are five provisions of the Pennsylvania Abortion Control Act of 1982 as amended in 1988 and 1989. 18 Pa. Cons. Stat. § § 3203–3220 (1990). Relevant portions of the Act are set forth in the appendix. *Infra,* at 60. The Act requires that a woman seeking an abortion give her informed consent prior to the abortion procedure, and specifies that she be provided with certain information at least 24 hours before the abortion is performed. § 3205. For a minor to obtain an abortion, the Act requires the informed consent of one of her parents, but provides for a judicial bypass option if the minor does not wish to or cannot obtain a parent's consent. § 3206. Another provision of the Act requires that, unless certain exceptions apply, a married woman seeking an abortion must sign a statement indicating that she has notified her husband of her intended abortion. § 3209. The Act exempts compliance with these three requirements in the event of a "medical emergency," which is defined in § 3203 of the Act. See § § 3203, 3205(a), 3206(a), 3209(c). In addition to the above provisions regulating the performance of abortions, the Act imposes certain reporting requirements on facilities that provide abortion services. §§3207(b), 3214(a), 3214(f)

Before any of these provisions took effect, the petitioners, who are five abortion clinics and one physician representing himself as well as a class of physicians who provide abortion services, brought this suit seeking declaratory and injunctive relief. Each provision was challenged as unconstitutional on its face. The District Court entered a preliminary injunction against the enforcement of the regulations, and, after a 3-day bench trial, held all the provisions at issue here unconstitutional, entering a permanent injunction against Pennsylvania's enforcement of them. 744 F. Supp. 1323 (ED Pa. 1990). The Court of Appeals for the Third Circuit affirmed in part and reversed in part, upholding all of the regulations except for the husband notification requirement. 947 F. 2d 682 (1991). We granted certiorari. 502 U.S. __ (1992).

The Court of Appeals found it necessary to follow an elaborate course of reasoning even to identify the first premise to use to determine whether the statute enacted by Pennsylvania meets constitutional standards. See 947 F. 2d, at 687–698. And at oral argument in this Court, the attorney for the parties challenging the statute took the position that none of the enactments can be upheld without overruling *Roe v. Wade* Tr. of Oral Arg. 5–6. We disagree with that analysis; but we acknowledge that our decisions after *Roe* cast doubt upon the meaning and reach of its holding. Further, the CHIEF JUSTICE admits that he would overrule the central holding of *Roe* and adopt the rational relationship test as the sole criterion of constitutionality. See *post,* at __. State and federal courts as well as legislatures throughout the Union must have guidance as they seek to address this subject in conformance with the Constitution. Given these premises, we find it imperative to review once more the principles that define the rights of the woman and the legitimate authority of the State respecting the termination of pregnancies by abortion procedures.

After considering the fundamental constitutional questions resolved by *Roe,* principles of institutional integrity, and the rule of *stare decisis,* we are led to conclude this: The essential holding of *Roe v. Wade* should be retained and once again reaffirmed.

It must be stated at the outset and with clarity that *Roe's* essential holding, the holding we affirm, has three parts. First is a recognition of the right of the woman to choose to have an abortion before viability and to obtain it without undue interference from the State. Before viability, the State's interests are not strong enough to support a prohibition of abortion or the imposition of a substantial obstacle to the woman's effective right to elect the procedure. Second is a confirmation of the State's power to restrict abortions after fetal viability, if the law contains exceptions for pregnancies which endanger a woman's life or health. And third is the principle that the State has legitimate interests from the outset of the pregnancy in protecting the health of the woman and the life of the fetus that may become a child. These principles do not contradict one another; and we adhere to each.

II

Constitutional protection of the woman's decision to terminate her pregnancy derives from the Due Process Clause of the Fourteenth Amendment. It declares that no State shall "deprive any person of life, liberty, or property, without due process of law." The controlling word in the case before us is "liberty." Although a literal reading of the Clause might suggest that it governs only the procedures by which a State may deprive persons of liberty, for at least 105 years, at least since *Mugler v. Kansas,* 123 U.S. 623, 660–661 (1887), the Clause has been understood to contain a substantive component as well, one "barring certain government actions regardless of the fairness of the procedures used to implement them." *Daniels v. Williams,* 474 U.S. 327, 331 (1986). As Justice Brandeis (joined by Justice Holmes) observed, "[d]espite arguments to the contrary which had seemed to me persuasive, it is settled that the due process clause of the Fourteenth Amendment applies to matters of substantive law as well as to matters of procedure. Thus all fundamental rights comprised within the term liberty are protected by the Federal Constitution from invasion by the States." *Whitney v. California,* 274 U.S. 357, 373 (1927) (Brandeis, J., con-curring). "[T]he guaranties of due process, though having their roots in Magna Carta's *'per legem terrae'* and considered as procedural safeguards 'against executive usurpation and tyranny,' have in this country 'become bulwarks also against arbitrary legislation.'" *Poe v. Ullman,* 367 U.S. 497, 541 (1961).

The most familiar of the substantive liberties protected by the Fourteenth Amendment are those recognized by the Bill of Rights. We have held that the Due Process Clause of the Fourteenth Amendment incorporates most of the Bill of Rights against the States. See, *e.g., Duncan v. Louisiana,* 391 U.S. 145, 147–148 (1968). It is tempting, as a means of curbing the discretion of federal judges, to suppose that liberty encompasses no more than those rights already guaranteed to the individual against federal interference by the express provisions of the first eight amendments to the Constitution. See *Adamson v. California,* 332 U.S. 46, 68–92 (1947) (Black, J., dissenting). But of course this Court has never accepted that view.

It is also tempting, for the same reason, to suppose that the Due Process Clause protects only those practices, defined at the most specific level, that were protected against government interference by other rules of law when the Fourteenth Amendment was ratified. But such a view would be inconsistent with our law. It is a promise of the Constitution that there is a realm of personal liberty which the government may not enter. We have vindicated this principle before. Marriage is mentioned nowhere in the Bill of Rights and interracial marriage was illegal in most States in the 19th century, but the Court was no doubt correct in finding it to be an aspect of liberty protected against state interference by substantive component of the Due Process Clause in *Loving v. Virginia,* 388 U.S. 1, 12 (1967) (relying, in an opinion for eight Justices, on the Due Process Clause).…

Neither the Bill of Rights nor the specific practices of States at the time of the adoption of the Fourteenth Amendment marks the outer limits of the substantive sphere of liberty which the Fourteenth Amendment protects. See U.S. Const., Amend. 9. As the second Justice Harlan recognized:

> "[T]he full scope of the liberty guaranteed by the Due Process Clause cannot be found in or limited by the precise terms of the specific guarantees elsewhere provided in the Constitution. This 'liberty' is not a series of isolated points pricked out in terms of the taking of property; the freedom of speech, press, and religion; the right to keep and bear arms; the freedom from unreasonable searches and seizures; and so on. It is a rational continuum which, broadly speaking, includes a freedom from all substantial arbitrary impositions and purposeless restraints,…and which also recognizes, what a reasonable and sensitive judgment must, that certain interests require particularly careful scrutiny of the state needs asserted to justify their abridgment." *Poe v. Ullman, supra,* at 543 (Harlan, J., dissenting from dismissal on jurisdictional grounds).

Justice Harlan wrote these words in addressing an issue the full Court did not reach in *Poe v. Ullman,* but the Court adopted his position four Terms later in *Griswold v. Connecticut, supra.* In *Griswold,* we held that the Constitution does not permit a State to forbid a married couple to use contraceptives. That same freedom was later guaranteed, under the Equal Protection Clause, for unmarried couples.

Constitutional protection was extended to the sale and distribution of contraceptives in *Carey v. Population Services International, supra.* It is settled now, as it was when the Court heard arguments in *Roe v. Wade* that the Constitution places limits on a State's right to interfere with a person's most basic decisions about family and parenthood....

The inescapable fact is that adjudication of substantive due process claims may call upon the Court in interpreting the Constitution to exercise that same capacity which by tradition courts always have exercised: reasoned judgment. Its boundaries are not susceptible of expression as a simple rule. That does not mean we are free to invalidate state policy choices with which we disagree; yet neither does it permit us to shrink from the duties of our office. As Justice Harlan observed:

> "Due process has not been reduced to any formula; its content cannot be determined by reference to any code. The best that can be said is that through the course of this Court's decisions it has represented the balance which our Nation, built upon postulates of respect for the liberty of the individual, has struck between that liberty and the demands of organized society. If the supplying of content to this Constitutional concept has of necessity been a rational process, it certainly has not been one where judges have felt free to roam where unguided speculation might take them. The balance of which I speak is the balance struck by this country; having regard to what history teaches are the traditions from which it developed as well as the traditions from which it broke. That tradition is a living thing. A decision of this Court which radically departs from it could not long survive, while a decision which builds on what has survived is likely to be sound. No formula could serve as a substitute, in this area, for judgment and restraint." *Poe v. Ullman,* 367 U.S., at 542 (Harlan, J., dissenting from dismissal on jurisdictional grounds).

Men and women of good conscience can disagree, and we suppose some always shall disagree, about the profound moral and spiritual implications of terminating a pregnancy, even in its earliest stage. Some of us as individuals find abortion offensive to our most basic principles of morality, but that cannot control our decision. Our obligation is to define the liberty of all, not to mandate our own moral code. The underlying constitutional issue is whether the State can resolve these philosophic questions in such a definitive way that a woman lacks all choice in the matter, except perhaps in those rare circumstances in which the pregnancy is itself a danger to her own life or health, or is the result of rape or incest.

It is conventional constitutional doctrine that when reasonable people disagree the government can adopt one position or the other. That theorem, however, assumes a state of affairs in which the choice does not intrude upon a protected liberty. Thus, while some people might disagree about whether or not the flag should be saluted, or disagree about the proposition that it may not be defiled, we have ruled that a State may not compel or enforce one view or the other.

Our law affords constitutional protection to personal decisions relating to marriage, procreation, contraception, family relationships, child rearing, and education. Our cases recognize "the right of the *individual,* married or single, to be free from unwarranted governmental intrusion into matters so fundamentally affecting a person as the decision whether to bear or beget a child." *Eisenstadt v. Baird, supra,* at 453. Our precedents "have respected the private realm of family life which the state cannot enter." *Prince v. Massachusetts,* 321 U.S. 158, 166 (1944). These matters involving the most intimate and personal choices a person may make in a lifetime, choices central to personal dignity and autonomy, are central to the liberty protected by the Fourteenth Amendment. At the heart of liberty is the right to define one's own concept of existence, of meaning of the universe, and of the mystery of human life. Beliefs about these matters could not define the attributes of personhood were they formed under compulsion of the State.

These considerations begin our analysis of the woman's interest in terminating her pregnancy but cannot end it, for this reason: though the abortion decision may originate within the zone of conscience and belief, it is more than a philosophic exercise. Abortion is a unique act. It is an act fraught with consequences for others: for the woman who must live with the implications of her decision; for the persons who perform and assist in the procedure; for the spouse, family, and society which must confront the knowledge that these procedures exist, procedures some deem nothing short of an act of violence against innocent human life; and, depending on one's beliefs, for the life or potential life that is aborted. Though abortion is conduct, it does not follow that the State is entitled to proscribe it in all instances. That is because the liberty of the woman is at stake in a sense unique to the human condition and so unique to the law. The mother who carries a child to full term is subject to anxieties, to physical constraints, to pain that only she must bear. That these sacrifices have from the beginning of the human race been endured by woman with pride that ennobles her in the eyes of others and gives to the infant a bond of love cannot alone be grounds for the State to insist she make the sacrifice. Her suffering is too intimate and personal for the State to insist, without more, upon its own vision of the woman's role, however dominant that vision has been in the course of our history and our culture. The destiny of the woman must be shaped to a large extent on her own conception of her spiritual imperatives and her place in society.

It should be recognized, moreover, that in some critical respects the abortion decision is of the same character as the decision to use contraception, to which *Griswold v. Connecticut, Eisenstadt v. Baird* and *Carey v. Population Services International* afford constitutional protection. We have no doubt as to the correctness of those decisions. They support the reasoning in *Roe* relating to the woman's liberty because they involve personal decisions concerning not only the meaning of procreation but also human responsibility and respect for it. As with abortion, reasonable people will have differences of opinion about these matters. One view is based on such reverence for the wonder of creation that any pregnancy ought to be welcomed and carried to full term no matter how difficult it will be to provide for the child and ensure its well-being. Another is that the inability to provide for the nurture and care of the infant is a cruelty to the child and an anguish to the parent. These are intimate views with infinite variations, and their deep, personal character underlay our decisions in *Griswold, Eisenstadt,* and *Carey.* The same concerns are present when the woman confronts the reality that, perhaps despite her attempts to avoid it, she has become pregnant.

It was this dimension of personal liberty that *Roe* sought to protect, and its holding invoked the reasoning and the tradition of the precedents we have discussed, granting protection to substantive liberties of the person. *Roe* was, of course, an extension of those cases and, as the decision itself indicated, the separate States could act in some degree to further their own legitimate interests in protecting pre-natal life. The extent to which the legislatures of the States might act to outweigh the interests of the woman in choosing to terminate her pregnancy was a subject of debate both in *Roe* itself and in decisions following it.

While we appreciate the weight of the arguments made on behalf of the State in the case before us, arguments which in their ultimate formulation conclude that *Roe* should be overruled, the reservations any of us may have in reaffirming the central holding of *Roe* are outweighed by the explication of individual liberty we have given combined with the force of *stare decisis.* We turn now to that doctrine.

III

A

The obligation to follow precedent begins with necessity, and a contrary necessity marks its outer limit. With Cardozo, we recognize that no judicial system could do society's work if it eyed each issue afresh in every cases that raised it. See B. Cardozo, The Nature of the Judicial Process 149 (1921). Indeed, the very concept of the rule of law underlying our own Constitution requires such continuity over time that a respect for precedent is, by definition, indispensable. See Powell, Stare Decisis and Judicial Restraint, 1991 Journal of Supreme Court History 13, 16. At the other extreme, a different necessity would make itself felt if a prior judicial ruling should come to be seen so clearly as error that its enforcement was for that very reason doomed.

Even when the decision to overrule a prior case is not, as in the rare, latter instance, virtually foreordained, it is common wisdom that the rule of *stare decisis* is not an "inexorable command," and certainly it is not such in every constitutional case....Rather, when this Court reexamines a prior holding, its judgment is customarily informed by a series of prudential and pragmatic considerations designed to test the consistency of overruling a prior decision with the ideal of the rule of law, and to gauge the respective costs of reaffirming and overruling a prior case. Thus, for example, we may ask whether the rule has proved to be intolerable simply in defying practical workability, *Swift & Co. v. Wickham,* 382 U.S. 111, 116 (1965); whether the rule is subject to a kind of reliance that would lend a special hardship to the consequences of overruling and add inequity to the cost of repudiation, e.g., *United States v. Title Ins. & Trust Co.,* 265 U.S. 472, 486 (1924); whether related principles of law have so far developed as to have left the old rule no more than a remnant of abandoned doctrine, see *Patterson v. McLean Credit Union,* 491 U.S. 164, 173–174 (1989); or whether facts have so changed or come to be seen so differently, as to have robbed the old rule of significant application or justification.

So in this case we may inquire whether *Roe's* central rule has been found unworkable; whether the rule's limitation on state power could be removed without serious inequity to those who have relied upon it or significant damage to the stability of the society governed by the rule in question; whether the law's growth in the intervening years has left *Roe's* central rule a doctrinal anachronism discounted by society; and whether *Roe's* premises of fact have so far changed in the ensuing two decades a to render its central holding somehow irrelevant or unjustifiable in dealing with the issue it addressed.

1

Although *Roe* has engendered opposition, it has in no sense proven "unworkable," representing as it does a simple limitation beyond which a state law is unenforceable. While *Roe* has, of course, required judicial assessment of state laws affecting the exercise of the choice guaranteed against government infringement, and although the need for such review will remain as a consequence of today's decision, the required determinations fall within judicial competence.

2

The inquiry into reliance counts the cost of a rule's repudiation as it would fall on those who have relied reasonably on the rule's continued application. Since the classic case for weighing reliance heavily in favor of following the earlier rule occurs in the commercial context, see *Payne v. Tennessee, supra,* at __ (slip op., at __, where advance planning of great precision is most obviously a necessity, it is no cause for surprise that some would find no reliance worthy of consideration in support of *Roe.*

While neither respondents nor their *amici* in so many words deny that the abortion right invites some reliance prior to its actual exercise, one can readily imagine an argument stressing the dissimilarity of this case to one involving property or contract. Abortion is customarily chosen as an unplanned response to the consequence of unplanned activity or to the failure of conventional birth control, and except on the assumption that no intercourse would have occurred but for *Roe's* holding, such behavior may appear to justify no reliance claim. Even if reliance could be claimed on that unrealistic assumption, the argument might run, any reliance interest would be *de minimis.* This argument would be premised on the hypothesis that reproductive planning could take virtually immediate account of any sudden restoration of state authority to ban abortions.

To eliminate the issue of reliance that easily, however, one would need to limit cognizable reliance to specific instances of sexual activity. But to do this would be simply to refuse to face the fact that for two decades of economic and social developments, people have organized intimate relationships and made choices that define their views of themselves and their places in society, in reliance on the availability of abortion in the event that contraception should fail. The ability of women to participate equally in the economic and social life of the Nation has been facilitated by their ability to control their reproductive lives. See, *e.g.,* R. Petchesky, Abortion and Woman's Choice 109, 133, no. 7 (rev. ed. 1990). The Constitution serves human values, and while the effect of reliance on *Roe* cannot be exactly measured, neither can the certain cost of overruling *Roe* for people who have ordered their thinking and living around that case be dismissed.

3

No evolution of legal principle has left *Roe's* doctrinal footings weaker than they were in 1973. No development of constitutional law since the case was decided has implicitly or explicitly left *Roe* behind as a mere survivor of obsolete constitutional thinking.

It will be recognized, of course, that *Roe* stands at an intersection of two lines of decisions, but in whichever doctrinal category one reads the case, the result for present purposes will be the same. The *Roe* Court itself placed its holding in the succession of cases most prominently exemplified by *Griswold v. Connecticut,* 381 U.S. 479 (1965), see *Roe,* 410 U.S., at 152–153. When it is so seen, *Roe* is clearly in no jeopardy, since subsequent constitutional developments have neither disturbed, nor do they threaten to diminish, the scope of recognized protection accorded to the liberty relating to intimate relationships, the family, and decisions about whether or not to beget or bear a child....

Roe, however, may be seen not only as an exemplar of *Griswold* liberty but as a rule (whether or not mistaken) of personal autonomy bodily integrity, with doctrinal affinity to cases recognizing limits on governmental power to mandate medical treatment or to bar its rejection. If so, our cases since *Roe* accord with *Roe's* view that a State's interest in protection of life falls short of justifying any plenary override of individual liberty claims....

Finally, one could classify *Roe* as *sui generis.* If the case is so viewed, then there clearly has been no erosion of its central determination. The original holding resting on the concurrence of seven Members of the Court in 1973 was expressly affirmed by a majority of six in 1983,...

More recently, in *Webster v. Reproductive Health Services,* 492 U.S. 490 (1989), although two of the present authors questioned the trimester framework in a way consistent with our judgment today, see *id.,* at 518 (REHNQUIST C. J., joined by WHITE, and KENNEDY, JJ.); *id.,* at 529 (O'CONNOR, J., concurring in part and concurring in judgment), a majority of the Court either decided to reaffirm or declined to address the constitutional validity of the central holding of *Roe.* See *Webster,* 492 U.S., at 521 (REHNQUIST, C. J., joined by WHITE and KENNEDY, JJ.); *id.,* at 525–526 (O'CONNOR, J., concurring in part and concurring in judgment); *id.* at 537, 553 (BLACKMUN, J. joined by BRENNAN and MARSHALL, JJ., concurring in part and dissenting in part); *id.,* at 561–563 (STEVENS, J., concurring part and dissenting in part).

Nor will courts building upon *Roe* be likely to hand down erroneous decisions as a consequence. Even on the assumption that the central holding of *Roe* was in error, that error would go only to the strength of the state interest in fetal protection, not to the recognition afforded by the Constitution to the woman's liberty. The latter aspect of the decision fits comfortably within the framework of the Court's prior decisions including *Skinner v. Oklahoma ex rel. Williamson,* 316 U.S. 535 (1942), *Griswold, supra, Loving v. Virginia,* 388 U.S. 1 (1967), and *Eisenstadt v. Baird,* 405 U.S. 438 (1972), the holdings of which are "not a series of isolated points," but mark a "rational continuum." *Poe v. Ullman,* 367 U.S., at 453 (1961) (Harlan, J., dissenting). As we described in *Carey v. Population Services International, supra,* the liberty which encompasses those decisions

> "includes 'the interest in independence in making certain kinds of important decisions.' While the outer limits of this aspect of [protected liberty] have not been marked by the Court, it is clear that among the decisions that an individual may make without unjustified government interference are personal decisions relating to marriage, procreation, contraception, family relation-ships, and child rearing and education.'" *Id.,* at 68–685 (citations omitted).

The soundness of this prong of the *Roe* analysis is apparent from consideration of the alternative. If indeed the woman's interest in deciding whether to bear and beget a child had not been recognized as in *Roe,* the State might as readily restrict a woman's right to choose to carry a pregnancy to term as to terminate it, to further asserted state interests in population control, or eugenics, for example. Yet *Roe* has been sensibly relied upon to counter any such suggestions....In any event, because *Roe's* scope is confined by the fact of its concern with postconception potential life, a concern otherwise likely to be implicated only by some forms of contraception protected independently under *Griswold* and later cases, any error in *Roe* is unlikely to have serious ramifications in future cases.

4

We have seen how time has overtaken some of *Roe's* factual assumptions: advances in maternal health care allow for abortions safe to the mother later in pregnancy than was true in 1973, and advances in neonatal care have advanced viability to a point somewhat earlier....But these facts go only to the scheme of time limits on the realization of competing interests, and the divergences from the factual premises of 1973 have no bearing on the validity of *Roe's* central holding, that viability marks the earliest point at which the State's interest in fetal life is constitutionally adequate to justify a legislative ban on nontherapeutic abortions. The soundness or unsoundness of that constitutional judgment in no sense turns on whether viability occurs at approximately 28 weeks, as was usual at the time of *Roe,* at 23 to 24 weeks, as it sometimes does today, or at some moment even slightly earlier in pregnancy, as it may if fetal respiratory capacity can somehow be enhanced in the future. Whenever it may occur, the attainment of viability may continue to serve as the critical fact, just as it has done since *Roe* was decided; which is to say that no change in *Roe's* factual underpinning has left its central holding obsolete, and none supports an argument for overruling it.

5

The sum of the precedential inquiry to this point shows *Roe's* underpinnings unweakened in any way affecting its central holding. While it has engendered disapproval, it has not been unworkable. An entire generation has come of age free to assume *Roe's* concept of liberty in defining the capacity of women to act in society, and to make reproductive decisions; no erosion of principle going to liberty or personal autonomy has left *Roe's* central holding a doctrinal remnant; *Roe* portends no developments at odds with other precedent for the analysis of personal liberty: and no changes of fact have rendered viability more or less appropriate as the point at which the balance of interests tips. Within the bounds of normal *stare decisis* analysis, then, and subject to the considerations on which it customarily turns, the stronger argument is for affirming *Roe's* central holding, with whatever degree of personal reluctance any of us may have, not for overruling it.

B

In a less significant case, *stare decisis* analysis could, and would, stop at the point we have reached. But the sustained and widespread debate *Roe* has provoked calls for some comparison between that case and others of comparable dimension that have responded to national controversies and taken on the impress of the controversies addressed. Only two such decisional lines from the past century present themselves for examination, and in each instance the result reached by the Court accorded with the principles we apply today.

The first example is that line of cases identified with *Lochner v. York,* 198 U.S. 45 (1905), which imposed substantive limitations on legislation limiting economic autonomy in favor of health and welfare regulation, adopting, in Justice Holmes' view, the theory of *laissez-faire. Id.,* at 75 (Holmes, J. dissenting). The *Lochner* decisions were exemplified by *Adkins v. Children's Hospital of D. C.,* 261 U.S. 525 (1923), in which this Court held it to be an infringement of constitutionally protected liberty of contract to require the employers of adult women to satisfy minimum wage standards. Fourteen years later, *West Coast Hotel Co. v. Parrish,* 300 U.S. 379 (1937), signalled the demise of *Lochner* by overruling *Adkins.* In the meantime, the Depression had come and, with it, the lesson that seemed unmistakable to most people by 1937, that the interpretation of contractual freedom protected in *Adkins* rested on fundamentally false factual assumptions about the capacity of a relatively unregulated market to satisfy minimal levels of human welfare. See *West Coast Hotel Co., supra,* at 399. As Justice Jackson wrote of the constitutional crisis of 1937 shortly before he came on the bench, "The older world of *laissez faire* was recognized everywhere outside the Court to be dead." R. Jackson, The Struggle for Judicial Supremacy 85 (1941). The facts upon which the earlier case had premised a constitutional resolution of social controversy had proved to be untrue, and history's demonstration of their untruth not only justified but required the new choice of constitutional principle that *West Coast Hotel* announced. Of course, it was true that the Court lost something by its misperception, or its lack of prescience, and the Court-packing crisis only magnified the loss; but the clear demonstration that the facts of economic life were different from those previously assumed warranted the repudiation of the old law.

The second comparison that 20th century history invites is with the cases employing the separate–but–equal rule for applying the Fourteenth Amendment's equal protection guarantee. They began with *Plessy v. Ferguson,* 163 U.S. 537 (1896), holding that legislatively mandated racial segregation in public transportation works no denial of equal protection, rejecting the argument that racial separation enforced by the legal machinery of American society treats the black race as inferior. The *Plessy* Court considered "the underlying fallacy of the plaintiff's argument to consist in the assumption that the enforced separation of the two races stamps the colored race with a badge of inferiority. If this be so, it is not by reason of anything found in the act, but solely because the colored race chooses to put that construction upon it." *Id.,* at 551. Whether, as a matter of historical fact, the Justices in the *Plessy* majority believed this or not, see *id.,* at 557, 562 (Harlan, J., dissenting), this understanding of the implication of segregation was the stated justification for the Court's opinion. But this understanding of the facts and the rule it was stated to justify were repudiated in *Brown v. Board of Education,* 347 U.S. 483 (1954). As one commentator observed, the question before the Court in *Brown* was "whether discrimination inheres in that segregation which is imposed by law in the twentieth century in certain specific states in the American Union. And that question has meaning and can find an answer only on the ground of history and of common knowledge about the facts of life in the times and places aforesaid." Black, The Lawfulness of the Segregation Decisions, 69 Yale L. J. 421, 427 (1960).

The Court in *Brown* addressed these facts of life by observing that whatever may have been the understanding in *Plessy's* time of the power of segregation to stigmatize those who were segregated with a "badge of inferiority," it was clear by 1954 that legally sanctioned segregation had just such an effect, to the point that racially separate public educational facilities were deemed inherently unequal. 374 U.S., at 494–495. Society's understanding of the facts upon which a constitutional ruling was sought in 1954 was thus fundamentally different from the basis claimed for the decision in 1896. While we think

Plessy was wrong the day it was decided, see *Plessy, supra,* at 552–564 (Harlan, J., dissenting), we must also recognize that the *Plessy* Court's explanation for its decision was so clearly at odds with the facts apparent to the Court in 1954 that the decision to reexamine *Plessy* was on this ground alone not only justified but required.

West Coast Hotel and *Brown* each rested on facts, or an understanding of facts, changed from those which furnished the claimed justifications for the earlier constitutional resolutions. Each case was comprehensible as the Court's response to facts that the country could understand, or had come to understand already, but which the Court of an earlier day, as its own declarations disclosed, had not been able to perceive. As the decisions were thus comprehensible they were also defensible, not merely as the victories of one doctrinal school over another by dint of numbers (victories though they were), but as applications of constitutional principle to facts as they had not been seen by the Court before. In constitutional adjudication as elsewhere in life, changed circumstances may impose new obligations, and the thoughtful part of the Nation could accept each decision to overrule a prior case as a response to the Court's constitutional duty.

Because the case before us presents no such occasion it could be seen as no such response. Because neither the factual underpinnings of *Roe's* central holding nor our understanding of it has changed (and because no other indication of weakened precedent has been shown) the Court could not pretend to be reexamining the prior law with any justification beyond a present doctrinal disposition to come out differently from the Court of 1973. To overrule prior law for no other reason than that would run counter to the view repeated in our cases, that a decision to overrule should rest on some special reason over and above the belief that a prior case was wrongly decided....

C

The examination of the conditions justifying the repudiation of *Adkins* by *West Coast Hotel* and *Plessy* by *Brown* is enough to suggest the terrible price that would have been paid if the Court had not overruled as it did. In the present case, however, as our analysis to this point makes clear, the terrible price would be paid for overruling. Our analysis would not be complete, however, without explaining why overruling *Roe's* central holding would not only reach an unjustifiable result under principles of *stare decisis,* but would seriously weaken the Court's capacity to exercise the judicial power and to function as the Supreme Court of a Nation dedicated to the rule of law. To understand why this would be so it is necessary to understand the source of this Court's authority, the conditions necessary for its preservation, and its relationship to the country's understanding of itself as a constitutional Republic.

The root of American governmental power is revealed most clearly in the instance of the power conferred by the Constitution upon the Judiciary of the United States and specifically upon this Court. As Americans of each succeeding generation are rightly told, the Court cannot buy support for its decisions by spending money and, except to a minor degree, it cannot inde-pendently coerce obedience to its decrees. The Court's power lies, rather, in its legitimacy; a product of substance and perception that shows itself in the people's acceptance of the Judiciary as fit to determine what the Nation's law means and to declare what it demands.

The underlying substance of this legitimacy is of course the warrant for the Court's decisions in the Constitution and the lesser sources of legal princi-ple on which the Court draws. That substance is expressed in the Court's opinions, and our contemporary understanding is such that a decision with-out principled justification would be no judicial act at all. But even when jus-tification is furnished by apposite legal principle, something more is required. Because not every conscientious claim of principled justification will be ac-cepted as such, the justification claimed must be beyond dispute. The Court must take care to speak and act in ways that allow people to accept its deci-sions on the terms the Court claims for them, as grounded truly in principle, not as compromises with social and political pressures having, as such, no bear-ing on the principled choices that the Court is obliged to make. Thus, the Court's legitimacy depends on making legally principled decisions under cir-cumstances in which their principled character is sufficiently plausible to be accepted by the Nation.

The need for principled action to be perceived as such is implicated to some degree whenever this, or any other appellate court, overrules a prior case. This is not to say, of course, that this Court cannot give a perfectly satis-factory explanation in most cases. People understand that some of the Consti-tution's language is hard to fathom and that the Court's Justices are sometimes able to perceive significant facts or to understand principles of law that eluded their predecessors and that justify departures from existing decisions. However upsetting it may be to those most directly affected when one judicially derived rule replaces another, the country can accept some correction of error with-out necessarily questioning the legitimacy of the Court.

In two circumstances, however, the Court would almost certainly fail to receive the benefit of the doubt in overruling prior cases. There is, first, a point beyond which frequent overruling would overtax the country's belief in the Court's good faith. Despite the variety of reasons that may inform and justify a decision to overrule, we cannot forget that such a decision is usually perceived (and perceived correctly) as, at the least, a statement that a prior de-cision was wrong. There is a limit to the amount of error that can plausibly be imputed to prior courts. If that limit should be exceeded, disturbance of prior rulings would be taken as evidence that justifiable reexamination of principle had given way to drives for particular results in the short term. The legitimacy of the Court would fade with the frequency of its vacillation.

That first circumstance can be described as hypothetical; the second is to the point here and now. Where, in the performance of its judicial duties, the Court decides a case in such a way as to resolve the sort of intensely divisive controversy reflected in *Roe* and those rare, comparable cases, its decision has a dimension that the resolution of the normal case does not carry. It is the dimension present whenever the Court's interpretation of the Constitution calls the contending sides of a national controversy to end their national division by accepting a common mandate rooted in the Constitution.

The Court is not asked to do this very often, having thus addressed the Nation only twice in our lifetime, in the decisions of *Brown* and *Roe*. But when the Court does act in this way, its decision requires an equally rare precedential force to counter the inevitable efforts to overturn it and to thwart its implementation. Some of those efforts may be mere unprincipled emotional reactions; others may proceed from principles worthy of profound respect. But whatever the premises of opposition may be, only the most convincing justification under accepted standards of precedent could suffice to demonstrate that a later decision overruling the first was anything but a surrender to political pressure, and an unjustified repudiation of the principle on which the Court staked its authority in the first instance. So to overrule under fire in the absence of the most compelling reason to reexamine a watershed decision would subvert the Court's legitimacy beyond any serious question....

The country's loss of confidence in the judiciary would be underscored by an equally certain and equally reasonable condemnation for another failing in overruling unnecessarily and under pressure. Some cost will be paid by anyone who approves or implements a constitutional decision where it is unpopular, or who refuses to work to undermine the decision or to force its reversal. The price may be criticism or ostracism, or it may be violence. An extra price will be paid by those who themselves disapprove of the decision's results when viewed outside of constitutional terms, but who nevertheless struggle to accept it, because they respect the rule of law. To all those who will be so tested by following, the Court implicitly undertakes to remain steadfast, lest in the end a price be paid for nothing. The promise of constancy, once given, binds its maker for as long as the power to stand by the decision survives and the understanding of the issue has not changed so fundamentally as to render the commitment obsolete. From the obligation of this promise this Court cannot and should not assume any exemption when duty requires it to decide a case in conformance with the Constitution. A willing breach of it would be nothing less than a breach of faith, and no Court that broke its faith with the people could sensibly expect credit for principle in the decision by which it did that.

It is true that diminished legitimacy may be restored, but only slowly. Unlike the political branches, a Court thus weakened could not seek to regain its position with a new mandate from the voters, and even if the Court could somehow go to the polls, the loss of its principled character could not be retrieved by the casting of so many votes. Like the character of an individual, the legitimacy of the Court must be earned over time. So, indeed, must be the character of a Nation of people who aspire to live according to the rule of law. Their belief in themselves as such a people is not readily separable from their understanding of the Court invested with the authority to decide their constitutional cases and speak before all others for their constitutional ideals. If the Court's legitimacy should be undermined, then, so would the country be in its very ability to see itself through its constitutional ideals. The Court's concern with legitimacy is not for the sake of the Court but for the sake of the Nation to which it is responsible.

The Court's duty in the present case is clear. In 1973, it confronted the already-divisive issue of governmental power to limit personal choice to undergo abortion, for which it provided a new resolution based on the due process guaranteed by the Fourteenth Amendment. Whether or not a new social consensus is developing on that issue, its divisiveness is no less today than in 1973, and pressure to overrule the decision, like pressure to retain it, has grown only more intense. A decision to overrule *Roe's* essential holding under the existing circumstances would address error, if error there was, at the cost of both profound and unnecessary damage to the Court's legitimacy; and to the Nation's commitment to the rule of law. It is therefore imperative to adhere to the essence of *Roe's* original decision, and we do so today.

IV

From what we have said so far it follows that it is a constitutional liberty of the woman to have some freedom to terminate her pregnancy. We conclude that the basic decision in *Roe* was based on a constitutional analysis which we cannot now repudiate. The woman's liberty is not so unlimited, however, that from the outset the State cannot show its concern for the life of the unborn, and at a later point in fetal development the State's interest in life has sufficient force so that the right of the woman to terminate the pregnancy can be restricted.

That brings us, of course, to the point where much criticism has been directed at *Roe,* a criticism that always inheres when the Court draws a specific rule from what in the Constitution is but a general standard. We conclude, however, that the urgent claims of the woman to retain the ultimate control over her destiny and her body, claims implicit in the meaning of liberty, require us to perform that function. Liberty must not be extinguished for want of a line that is clear. And it falls to us to give some real substance to the woman's liberty to determine whether to carry her pregnancy to full term.

We conclude the line should be drawn at viability, so that before that time the woman has a right to choose to terminate her pregnancy. We adhere to this principle for two reasons. First, as we have said, is the doctrine of *stare decisis*. Any judicial act of line-drawing may seem somewhat arbitrary, but *Roe* was a reasoned statement, elaborated with great care. We have twice reaffirmed it in the face of great opposition....Although we must overrule those parts of *Thornburgh* and *Akron I* which, in our view, are inconsistent with *Roe's* statement that the State has a legitimate interest in promoting the life or potential life of the unborn, see *infra,* at ___, the central premise of those cases represents an unbroken commitment by this Court to the essential holding of *Roe*. It is that premise which we reaffirm today.

The second reason is that the concept of viability, as we noted in *Roe,* is the time at which there is a realistic possibility of maintaining and nourishing a life outside the womb, so that the independent existence of the second life can in reason and all fairness be the object of state protection that now overrides the rights of the woman. See *Roe v. Wade,* 410 U.S., at 163. Consistent with other constitutional norms, legislatures may draw lines which appear arbitrary without the necessity of offering a justification. But courts may not. We must justify the lines we draw. And there is no line other than viability which is more workable. To be sure, as we have said, there may be some medical developments that affect the precise point of viability, see *supra,* at ___ but this is an imprecision within tolerable limits given that the medical community and all those who must apply its discoveries will continue to explore the matter. The viability line also has, as a practical matter, an element of fairness. In some broad sense it might be said that a woman who fails to act before viability has consented to the State's intervention on behalf of the developing child.

The woman's right to terminate her pregnancy before viability is the most central principle of *Roe v. Wade.* It is a rule of law and a component of liberty we cannot renounce.

On the other side of the equation is the interest of the State in the protection of potential life. The *Roe* Court recognized the State's "important and legitimate interest in protecting the potentiality of human life." *Roe, supra,* at 162. The weight to be given this state interest, not the strength of the woman's interest, was the difficult question faced in *Roe.* We do not need to say whether each of us, had we been Members of the Court when the valuation of the State interest came before it as an original matter, would have concluded, as the *Roe* Court did, that its weight is insufficient to justify a ban on abortions prior to viability even when it is subject to certain exceptions. The matter is not before us in the first instance, and coming as it does after nearly 20 years of litigation in *Roe's* wake we are satisfied that the immediate question is not the soundness of *Roe's* resolution of the issue, but the precedential force that must be accorded to its holding. And we have concluded that the essential holding of *Roe* should be reaffirmed.

Yet it must be remembered that *Roe v. Wade* speaks with clarity in establishing not only the woman's liberty but also the State's "important and legitimate interest in potential life." *Roe, supra,* at 163. That portion of the decision in *Roe* has been given too little acknowledgment and implementation by the Court in its subsequent cases. Those cases decided that any regulation touching upon the abortion decision must survive strict scrutiny, to be sustained only if drawn in narrow terms to further a compelling state interest....Not all of the cases decided under that formulation can be reconciled with the holding in *Roe* itself that the State has legitimate interests in the health of the woman and in protecting the potential life within her. In resolving this tension, we choose to rely upon *Roe,* as against the later cases.

Roe established a trimester framework to govern abortion regulations. Under this elaborate but rigid construct, almost no regulation at all is permitted during the first trimester of pregnancy; regulations designed to protect the woman's health, but not to further the State's interest in potential life, are permitted during the second trimester; and during the third trimester, when the fetus is viable, prohibitions are permitted provided the life or health of the mother is not at stake. *Roe v. Wade, supra,* at 163–166. Most of our cases since *Roe* have involved the application of rules derived from the trimester framework....

The trimester framework no doubt was erected to ensure that the woman's right to choose not become so subordinate to the State's interest in promoting fetal life that her choice exists in theory but not in fact. We do not agree, however, that the trimester approach is necessary to accomplish this objective. A framework of this rigidity was unnecessary and in its later interpretation sometimes contradicted the State's permissible exercise of its powers.

Though the woman has a right to choose to terminate or continue her pregnancy before viability, it does not at all follow that the State is prohibited from taking steps to ensure that this choice is thoughtful and informed. Even in the earliest stages of pregnancy, the State may enact rules and regulations designed to encourage her to know that there are philosophic and social arguments of great weight that can be brought to bear in favor of continuing the pregnancy to full term and that there are procedures and institutions to allow adoption of unwanted children as well as a certain degree of state assistance if the mother chooses to raise the child herself. "'[T]he Constitution does not forbid a State or city, pursuant to democratic processes, from expressing a preference for normal childbirth.'" *Webster v. Reproductive Health Services,* 492 U.S., at 511 (opinion of the Court) (quoting *Poelker v. Doe,* 432 U.S. 519, 521 (1977). It follows that States are free to enact laws to provide a reasonable framework for a woman to make a decision that has such profound and lasting meaning. This, too, we find consistent with *Roe's* central premises, and indeed the inevitable consequence of our holding that the State has an interest in protecting the life of the unborn.

We reject the trimester framework, which we do not consider to be part of the essential holding of *Roe.* See *Webster v. Reproductive Health Services, supra,* at 518 (opinion of REHNQUIST, C. J.); *id.,* at 529 (O'CONNOR, J., concurring in part and concurring in judgment) (describing the trimester framework as "problematic"). Measures aimed at ensuring that a woman's choice contemplates the consequences for the fetus do not necessarily interfere with the right recognized in *Roe,* although those measures have been found to be inconsistent with the rigid trimester framework announced in that case. A logical reading of the central holding in *Roe* itself, and a necessary reconciliation of the liberty of the woman and the interest of the State in promoting prenatal life, require, in our view, that we abandon the trimester framework as a rigid prohibition on all previability regulation aimed at the protection of fetal life. The trimester framework suffers from these basic flaws: in its formulation it misconceives the nature of the pregnant woman's interest; and in practice it undervalues the State's interest in potential life, as recognized in *Roe.*

As our jurisprudence relating to all liberties save perhaps abortion has recognized, not every law which makes a right more difficult to exercise is *ipso facto,* an infringement of that right. An example clarifies the point. We have held that not every ballot access limitation amounts to an infringement of the right to vote. Rather, the States are granted substantial flexibility in establishing the framework within which voters choose the candidates for whom they wish to vote. *Anderson v. Celebrezze,* 460 U.S. 780, 788 (1983); *Norman v. Reed,* 502 U.S. ___ (1992).

The abortion right is similar. Numerous forms of state regulation might have the incidental effect of increasing the cost or decreasing the availability of medical care, whether for abortion or any other medical procedure. The fact that a law which serves a valid purpose, one not designed to strike at the right itself, has the incidental effect of making it more difficult or more expensive to procure an abortion cannot be enough to invalidate it. Only where state regulation imposes an undue burden on a woman's ability to make this decision does the power of the State reach into the heart of the liberty protected by the Due Process Clause....

For the most part, the Court's early abortion cases adhered to this view. In *Maher v. Roe,* 432 U.S. 464, 473–474 (1977), the Court explained: "*Roe* did not declare an unqualified 'constitutional right to an abortion,' as the District Court seemed to think. Rather, the right protects the woman from unduly burdensome interference with her freedom to decide whether to terminate her pregnancy."...

These considerations of the nature of the abortion right illustrate that it is an overstatement to describe it as a right to decide whether to have an abortion "without interference from the State," *Planned Parenthood of Central Mo. v. Danforth* 428 U.S. 52, 61 (1976). All abortion regulations interfere to some degree with a woman's ability to decide whether to terminate her pregnancy. It is, as a consequence, not surprising that despite the protestations contained in the original *Roe* opinion to the effect that the Court was not recognizing an absolute right, 410 U.S., at 154–155, the Court's experience applying the trimester framework has led to the striking down of some abortion regulations which in no real sense deprived women of the ultimate decision. Those decisions went too far because the right recognized by *Roe* is a right "to be free from unwarranted governmental intrusion into matters so fundamentally affecting a person as the decision whether to bear or beget a child." *Eisenstadt v. Baird,* 405 U.S., at 453. Not all governmental intrusion is of necessity unwarranted; and that brings us to the other basic flaw in the trimester framework: even in *Roe's* terms, in practice it undervalues the State's interest in the potential life within the woman.

Roe v. Wade was express in its recognition of the State's "important and legitimate interest[s] in preserving and protecting the health of the pregnant woman [and) in protecting the potentiality of human life." U.S., at 162. The trimester framework, however, does not fulfill *Roe's* own promise that the State has an interest in protecting fetal life or potential life. *Roe* began the contradiction by using the trimester framework to forbid any regulation of abortion designed to advance that interest before viability. *Id.,* at 163. Before viability, *Roe* and subsequent cases treat all governmental attempts to influence a woman's decision on behalf of the potential life within her as unwarranted.

This treatment is, in our judgment, incompatible with the recognition that there is a substantial state interest in potential life throughout pregnancy. Cf. *Webster,* 492 U.S., at 519 (opinion of REHNQUIST, C. J.); *Akron I, supra,* at 461 (O'CONNOR, J., dissenting).

The very notion that the State has a substantial interest in potential life leads to the conclusion that not all regulations must be deemed unwarranted. Not all burdens on the right to decide whether to terminate a pregnancy will be undue. In our view, the undue burden standard is the appropriate means of reconciling the State's interest with the woman's constitutionally protected liberty.

The concept of an undue burden has been utilized by the Court as well as individual members of the Court, including two of us, in ways that could be considered inconsistent....Because we set forth a standard of general application to which we intend to adhere, it is important to clarify what is meant by an undue burden.

A finding of an undue burden is a shorthand for the conclusion that a state regulation has the purpose or effect of placing a substantial obstacle in the path of a woman seeking an abortion of a nonviable fetus. A statute with this purpose is invalid because the means chosen by the State to further the interest in potential life must be calculated to inform the woman's free choice, not hinder it. And a statute which, while furthering the interest in potential life or some other valid state interest, has the effect of placing a substantial obstacle in the path of a woman's choice cannot be considered a permissible means of serving its legitimate ends. To the extent that the opinions of the Court or of individual Justices use the undue burden standard in a manner that is inconsistent with this analysis, we set out what in our view should be the controlling standard. Cf. *McCleskey v. Zant,* 499 U.S. __ , __ (1991) (slip op. at 20) (attempting to "define the doctrine of abuse of the writ with more precision" after acknowledging tension among earlier cases). In our considered judgment, an undue burden is an unconstitutional burden. See *Akron II, supra,* at ____ (opinion of KENNEDY, J.) Understood another way, we answer the question, left open in previous opinions discussing the undue burden formulation, whether a law designed to further the State's interest in fetal life which imposes an undue burden on the woman's decision before fetal viability could be constitutional. See, *e.g., Akron I, supra,* at 462–463 (O'CONNOR, J., dissenting). The answer is no.

Some guiding principles should emerge. What is at stake is the women's right to make the ultimate decision, not a right to be insulated from all others in doing so. Regulations which do no more than create a structural mechanism by which the State, or the parent or guardian of a minor, may express profound respect for the life of the unborn are permitted, if they are not a substantial obstacle to the woman's exercise of the right to choose. See *infra,* at __-__ (addressing Pennsylvania's parental consent requirement). Unless it has that effect on her right of choice, a state measure designed to persuade her to choose childbirth over abortion will be upheld if reasonably related to that goal. Regulations designed to foster the health of a woman seeking an abortion are valid if they do not constitute an undue burden.

Even when jurists reason from shared premises, some disagreement is inevitable....That is to be expected in the application of any legal standard which must accommodate life's complexity. We do not expect it to be otherwise with respect to the undue burden standard. We give this summary:

(a) to protect the central right recognized by *Roe v. Wade* while at the same time accommodating the State's profound interest in potential life, we will employ the undue burden analysis as explained in this opinion. An undue burden exists, and therefore a provision of law is invalid, if its purpose or effect is to place a substantial obstacle in the path of a woman seeking an abortion before the fetus attains viability.

(b) We reject the rigid trimester framework of *Roe v. Wade.* To promote the State's profound interest in potential life, throughout pregnancy the State may take measures to ensure that the woman's choice is informed, and measures designed to advance this interest will not be invalidated as long as their purpose is to persuade the woman to choose childbirth over abortion. These measures must not be an undue burden on the right.

(c) As with any medical procedure, the State may enact regulations to further the health or safety of a woman seeking an abortion. Unnecessary health regulations that have the purpose or effect of presenting a substantial obstacle to a woman seeking an abortion impose an undue burden on the right.

(d) Our adoption of the undue burden analysis does not disturb the central holding of *Roe v. Wade,* and we reaffirm that holding. Regardless of whether exceptions are made for particular circumstances, a State may not prohibit any woman from making the ultimate decision to terminate her pregnancy before viability.

(e) We also reaffirm *Roe's* holding that "subsequent to viability, the State in promoting its interest in the potentiality of human life may, if it chooses, regulate, and even proscribe, abortion except where it is necessary, in appropriate medical judgment, for the preservation of the life or health of the mother." *Roe v. Wade,* 410 U.S., at 164–165....

JUSTICE SCALIA, with whom THE CHIEF JUSTICE, JUSTICE WHITE, and JUSTICE THOMAS join, concurring in the judgment in part and dissenting in part.

My views on this matter are unchanged from those I set forth in my separate opinions in *Webster v. Reproductive Health Services,* 492 U.S. 490, 532 (1989) (SCALIA, J., concurring in part and concurring in judgment), and *Ohio v. Akron Center for Reproductive Health,* 497 U.S. 502, 520 (1990) *(Akron II)* (SCALIA, J., concurring). The States may, if they wish, permit abortion-on-demand, but the Constitution does not *require* them to do so. The permissibility of abortion, and the limitations upon it, are to be resolved like most important questions in our democracy: by citizens trying to persuade one another and then voting. As the Court acknowledges, "where reasonable people disagree the government can adopt one position or the other."...The Court is correct in adding the qualification that this "assumes a state of affairs in which the choice does not intrude upon a protected liberty,"...—but the crucial part of that qualification is the penultimate word. A State's choice between two positions on which reasonable people can disagree is constitutional even when (as is often the case) it intrudes upon a "liberty" in the absolute sense. Laws against bigamy, for example—which entire societies of reasonable people disagree with—intrude upon men and women's liberty to marry and live with one another. But bigamy happens not to be a liberty specially "protected" by the Constitution.

That is, quite simply, the issue in this case: not whether the power of a woman to abort her unborn child is a "liberty" in the absolute sense; or even whether it is a liberty of great importance to many women. Of course it is both. The issue is whether it is a liberty protected by the Constitution of the United States. I am sure it is not. I reach that conclusion not because of anything so exalted as my views concerning the "concept of existence, of meaning, of the universe, and of the mystery of human life."...Rather, I reach it for the same reason I reach the conclusion that bigamy is not constitutionally protected—because of two simple facts: (1) the Constitution says absolutely nothing about it, and (2) the longstanding traditions of American society have permitted it to be legally proscribed. *Akron II supra,* at 520 (SCALIA, J., concurring).

The Court destroys the proposition, evidently meant to represent my position, that liberty" includes "only those practices, defined at the most specific level, that were protected against government interference by other rules of law when the Fourteenth Amendment was ratified,"...(citing *Michael H. v. Gerald D.,* 491 U.S. 110, 127, n. 6 (1989) (opinion of SCALIA, J.). That is not, however, what *Michael H.* says; it merely observes that, in defining "liberty," we may not disregard a specific, "relevant tradition protecting, or denying protection to, the asserted right," 491 U.S., at 127, n. 6. But the Court does not wish to be fettered by any such limitations on its preferences. The Court's statement that it is "tempting" to acknowledge the authoritativeness of tradition in order to "cur[b] the discretion of federal judges,"...is of course rhetoric rather than reality; no government official is "tempted" to place restraints upon his own freedom of action, which is why Lord Acton did not say "Power tends to purify." The Court's temptation is in the quite opposite and more natural direction—towards systematically eliminating checks upon its own power; and it succumbs.

Beyond that brief summary of the essence of my position, I will not swell the United States Reports with repetition of what I have said before; and applying the rational basis test, I would uphold the Pennsylvania statute in its entirety. I must, however, respond to a few of the more outrageous arguments in today's opinion, which it is beyond human nature to leave unanswered. I shall discuss each of them under a quotation from the Court's opinion to which they pertain.

"The inescapable fact is that adjudication of substantive due process claims may call upon the Court in interpreting the Constitution to exercise that same capacity which by tradition courts always have exercised: reasoned judgment."...

Assuming that the question before us is to be resolved at such a level of philosophical abstraction, in such isolation from the traditions of American society, as by simply applying "reasoned judgment," I do not see how that could possibly have produced the answer the Court arrived at in *Roe v. Wade,* 410 U. S. 113 (1973). Today's opinion describes the methodology of *Roe,* quite accurately, as weighing against the woman's interest the State's important and legitimate interest in protecting the potentiality of human life." ... (quoting *Roe, supra,* at 162). But "reasoned judgment" does not begin by begging the question, as *Roe* and subsequent cases unquestionably did by assuming that what the State is protecting is the mere "potentiality of human life." ...The whole argument of abortion opponents is that what the Court calls the fetus and what others call the unborn child *is a human life.* Thus, whatever answer *Roe* came up with after conducting its "balancing" is bound to be wrong, unless it is correct that the human fetus is in some critical sense merely potentially human. There is of course no way to determine that as a legal matter; it is in fact a value judgment. Some societies have considered newborn children not yet human, or the incompetent elderly no longer so.

The authors of the joint opinion, of course, do not squarely contend that *Roe v. Wade* was a *correct* application of "reasoned judgment"; merely that it must be followed, because of *stare decisis....*But in their exhaustive discussion of all the factors that go into the determination of when *stare decisis* should be observed and when disregarded, they never mention "how wrong was the decision on its face?" Surely, if "[t]he Court's power lies...in its legitimacy, a product of substance and perception,"...the "substance" part of the equation demands that plain error be acknowledged and eliminated. *Roe* was plainly wrong—even on the Court's methodology of "reasoned judgment," and even more so (of course) if the proper criteria of text and tradition are applied.

The emptiness of the "reasoned judgment" that produced *Roe* is displayed in plain view by the fact that, after more than 19 years of effort by some of the brightest (and most determined) legal minds in the country, after more than 10 cases upholding abortion rights in this Court, and after dozens upon dozens of *amicus* briefs submitted in this and other cases, the best the Court can do to explain how it is that the word "liberty" *must* be thought to include the right to destroy human fetuses is to rattle off a collection of adjectives that simply decorate a value judgment and conceal a political choice. The right to abort, we are told, inheres in "liberty" because it is among "a person's most basic decisions,"...; it involves a "most intimate and personal choic[e],"...; it is "central to personal dignity and autonomy,"...; it "originate[s] within the zone of conscience and belief," *ibid.;* it is "too intimate and personal" for state interference,...; it reflects "intimate views" of a "deep, personal character,"...at all involves "intimate relationships," and notions of "personal autonomy and bodily integrity,"…; and it concerns a particularly 'important decisio[n].'"…But it is obvious to anyone applying "reasoned judgment" that the same adjectives can be applied to many forms of conduct that this Court (including one of the Justices in today's majority, see *Bowers v. Hardwick* 478 U.S. 186 (1986)) has held are *not* entitled to constitutional protection—because, like abortion, they are forms of conduct that have long been criminalized in American society. Those adjectives might be applied, for example, to homosexual sodomy, polygamy, adult incest, and suicide, all of which are equally "intimate" and "deep[ly] personal" decisions involving "personal autonomy and bodily integrity," and all of which can constitutionally be proscribed because it is our unquestionable constitutional tradition that they are proscribable. It is not reasoned judgment that supports the Court's decision; only personal predilection. Justice Curtis's warning is as timely today as it was 135 years ago:

> "[W]hen a strict interpretation of the Constitution, according to the fixed rules which govern the interpretation of laws, is abandoned, and the theoretical opinions of individuals are allowed to control its meaning, we have no longer a Constitution; we are under the government of individual men, who for the time being have power to declare what the Constitution is, according to their own views of what it ought to mean." *Dred Scott v. Sandford,* 19 How. 393, 621 (1857) (CURTIS, J., dissenting).

"Liberty finds no refuge in a jurisprudence of doubt."…

One might have feared to encounter this august and sonorous phrase in an opinion defending the real *Roe v. Wade,* rather than the revised version fabricated today by the authors of the joint opinion. The shortcomings of *Roe* did not include lack of clarity: Virtually all regulation of abortion before the third trimester was invalid. But to come across this phrase in the joint opinion—which calls upon federal district judges to apply an "undue burden" standard as doubtful in application as it is unprincipled in origin—is really more than one should have to bear.

The joint opinion frankly concedes that the amorphous concept of "undue burden" has been inconsistently applied by the Members of this Court in the few brief years since that "test" was first explicitly propounded by JUSTICE O'CONNOR in her dissent in *Akron I, supra.*…Because the three Justices now wish to "set forth a standard of general application," the joint opinion announces that "it is important to clarify what is meant by an undue burden." …I certainly agree with that, but I do not agree that the joint opinion succeeds in the announced endeavor. To the contrary, its efforts at clarification make clear only that the standard is inherently manipulable and will prove hopelessly unworkable in practice.

The joint opinion explains that a state regulation imposes an undue burden" if it "has the purpose or effect of placing a substantial obstacle in the path of a woman seeking an abortion of a nonviable fetus."…An obstacle is "substantial," we are told, if it is "calculated[,] [not] to inform the woman's free choice, [but to] hinder it."…This latter statement cannot possibly mean what it says. *Any* regulation of abortion that is intended to advance what the joint opinion concedes is the State's "substantial" interest in protecting unborn life will be "calculated [to] hinder" a decision to have an abortion. It thus seems more accurate to say that the joint opinion would uphold abortion regulations only if they do not *unduly* hinder the woman's decision. That, of course, brings us right back to square one: Defining an "undue burden" as an "undue hindrance" (or a "substantial obstacle") hardly "clarifies" the test. Consciously or not, the joint opinion's verbal shell game will conceal raw judicial policy choices concerning what is "appropriate" abortion legislation.

The ultimately standardless nature of the "undue burden" inquiry is a reflection of the underlying fact that the concept has no principled or coherent legal basis. As THE CHIEF JUSTICE points out, *Roe's* strict-scrutiny standard "at least had a recognized basis in constitutional law at the time *Roe* was decided." …while "[t]he same cannot be said for the 'undue burden' standard, which is created largely out of whole cloth by the authors of the joint opinion."… The joint opinion is flatly wrong in asserting that "our jurisprudence relating to all liberties save perhaps abortion has recognized" the permissibility of laws that do not impose an "undue burden." … It argues that the abortion right is similar to other rights in that a law "not designed to strike at the right itself, [but which] has the incidental effect of making it more difficult or more expensive to [exercise the right,]" is not invalid.…I agree, indeed I have forcefully urged, that a law of general applicability which places only an incidental burden on a fundamental right does not infringe that right, see *R. A. V v. St. Paul,* 505 U.S. ___ , ___ (1992) (slip op. at 11); *Employment Division, Dept. of Human Resources of Ore. v. Smith,* 494 U.S. 872, 878–882 (1990), but that principle does not establish the quite different (and quite dangerous) proposition that a law which *directly* regulates a fundamental right will not be found to violate the Constitution unless it imposes an "undue burden." It is that, of course, which is at issue here: Pennsylvania has *consciously and directly* regulated conduct that our cases have held is constitutionally protected. The appropriate analogy, therefore, is that of a state law requiring purchasers of religious books to endure a 24-hour waiting period, or to pay a nominal additional tax of 1¢. The joint opinion cannot possibly be correct in suggesting that we would uphold such legislation on the ground that it does not impose a "substantial obstacle" to the exercise of First Amendment rights. The "undue burden" standard is not at all the generally applicable principle the joint opinion pretends it to be; rather, it is a unique concept created specially for this case, to preserve some judicial foothold in this ill-gotten territory. In claiming otherwise, the three Justices show their willingness to place all constitutional rights at risk in an effort to preserve what they deem the "central holding in *Roe.*"…

The rootless nature of the "undue burden" standard, a phrase plucked out of context from our earlier abortion decisions…is further reflected in the fact that the joint opinion finds it necessary expressly to repudiate the more narrow formulations used in JUSTICE O'CONNOR's earlier opinions.…Those opinions stated that a statute imposes an "undue burden" if it imposes *absolute obstacles or severe* limitations on the abortion decision," *Akron I,* 462 U.S., at 464.... Those strong adjectives are conspicuously missing from the joint opinion, whose authors have for some unexplained reason now determined that a burden is "undue" if it merely imposes a "substantial" obstacle to abortion decisions....JUSTICE O'CONNOR has also abandoned (again without explanation) the view she expressed in *Planned Parenthood Assn. of Kansas City, Mo., Inc. v. Ashcroft,* 462 U.S. 476 (1983) (dissenting opinion), that a medical regulation which imposes an "undue burden" could nevertheless be upheld if it "reasonably relate[s] to the preservation and protection of maternal health," *id.,* at 505 (citation and internal quotation marks omitted). In today's version, even health measures will be upheld only *"if they do not constitute an undue burden"*...(emphasis added). Gone too is JUSTICE O'CONNOR's statement that "the State possesses *compelling* interests in the protection of potential human life...throughout pregnancy," *Akron I, supra,* at 461 (emphasis added); see also *Ashcroft, supra,* at 505 (O'CONNOR, J., concurring in judgment in part and dissenting in part); instead, the state's interest in unborn human life is stealthily downgraded to a merely "substantial" or "profound" interest....(That had to be done, of course, since designating the interest as "compelling" throughout pregnancy would have been, shall we say, a "substantial obstacle" to the joint opinion's determined effort to reaffirm what it views as the "central holding" of *Roe.*)...And "viability" is no longer the "arbitrary" dividing line previously decried by JUSTICE O'CONNOR in *Akron I, id.,* at 461; the Court now announces that "the attainment of viability may continue to serve as the critical fact."...It is difficult to maintain the illusion that we are interpreting a Constitution rather than inventing one, when we amend its provisions so breezily.

Because the portion of the joint opinion adopting and describing the undue-burden test provides no more useful guidance than the empty phrases discussed above, one must turn to the 23 pages applying that standard to the present facts for further guidance. In evaluating Pennsylvania's abortion law, the joint opinion relies extensively on the factual findings of the District Court, and repeatedly qualifies its conclusions by noting that they are contingent upon the record developed in this case. Thus, the joint opinion would uphold the 24-hour waiting period contained in the Pennsylvania statute's informed consent provision, 18 Pa. Cons. Stat. §3205 (1990), because "the record evidence shows that in the vast majority of cases, a 24-hour delay does not create any appreciable health risk."...The three Justices therefore conclude that "on the record before...we are not convinced that the 24-hour waiting period constitutes an undue burden."...The requirement that a doctor provide the information pertinent to informed consent would also be upheld because "there is no evidence on this record that [this requirement] would amount in practical terms to a substantial obstacle to a woman seeking an abortion."...Similarly, the joint opinion would uphold the reporting requirements of the Act, § § 3207, 3214, because "there is no...showing on the record before us" that these requirements constitute a "substantial obstacle" to abortion decisions....But at the same time the opinion pointedly observes that these reporting requirements may increase the costs of abortions and that "at some point [that fact] could become a substantial obstacle."...Most significantly, the joint opinion's conclusion that the spousal notice requirement of the Act, see §3209, imposes an "undue burden" is based in large measure on the District Court's "detailed findings of fact," which the joint opinion sets out at great length....

I do not, of course, have any objection to the notion that, in applying legal principles, one should rely only upon the facts that are contained in the record or that are properly subject to judicial notice. But what is remarkable about the joint opinion's fact-intensive analysis is that it does not result in any measurable clarification of the "undue burden" standard. Rather, the approach of the joint opinion is, for the most part, simply to highlight certain facts in the record that apparently strike the three Justices as particularly significant in establishing (or refuting) the existence of an undue burden; after describing these facts, the opinion then simply announces that the provision either does or does not impose a "substantial obstacle" or an "undue burden."...We do not know whether the same conclusions could have been reached on a different record, or in what respects the record would have had to differ before an opposite conclusion would have been appropriate. The inherently standardless nature of this inquiry invites the district judge to give effect to his personal preferences about abortion. By finding and relying upon the right facts, he can invalidate, it would seem, almost any abortion restriction that. strikes him as "undue"—subject, of course, to the possibility of being reversed by a Circuit Court or Supreme Court that is as unconstrained in reviewing his decision as he was in making it.

To the extent I can discern *any* meaningful content in the "undue burden" standard as applied in the joint opinion, it appears to be that a State may not regulate abortion in such a way as to reduce significantly its incidence. The joint opinion repeatedly emphasizes that an important factor in the "undue burden" analysis is whether the regulation "prevent[s] a significant number of women from obtaining an abortion."...; whether a "significant number of women...are likely to be deterred from procuring an abortion."...; and whether the regulation often "deters" women from seeking abortions....We are not told, however, what forms of "deterrence" are impermissible or what degree of success in deterrence is too much to be tolerated. If, for example, a State required a woman to read a pamphlet describing, with illustrations, the facts of fetal development before she could obtain an abortion, the effect of such legislation might be to "deter" a "significant number of women" from procuring abortions, thereby seemingly allowing a district judge to invalidate it as an undue burden. Thus, despite flowery rhetoric about the State's "substantial" and "profound" interest in "potential human life," and criticism of *Roe* for undervaluing that interest, the joint opinion permits the State to pursue that interest only so long as it is not too successful. As JUSTICE BLACKMUN recognizes (with evident hope)..., the "undue burden" standard may ultimately require the invalidation of each provision upheld today if it can be shown, on a better record, that the State is too effectively "express [ing] a preference for childbirth over abortion."...Reason finds no refuge in this jurisprudence of confusion.

> **"While we appreciate the weight of the arguments...that *Roe* should be overruled, the reservations any of us may have in reaffirming the central holding of *Roe* are outweighed by the explication of individual liberty we have given combined with the force of *stare decisis*."...**

The Court's reliance upon *stare decisis* can best be described as contrived. It insists upon the necessity of adhering not to all of *Roe,* but only to what it calls the "central holding." It seems to me that *stare decisis* ought to be applied even to the doctrine of *stare decisis,* and I confess never to have heard of this new, keep-what-you-want-and-throw-away-the-rest version. I wonder whether, as applied to *Marbury v. Madison,* 1 Cranch 137 (1803), for example, the new version of *stare decisis* would be satisfied if we allowed courts to review the constitutionality of only those statutes that (like the one in *Marbury)* pertain to the jurisdiction of the courts.

I am certainly not in a good position to dispute that the Court *has saved* the "central holding" of *Roe,* since to do that effectively I would have to know what the Court has saved, which in turn would require me to understand (as I do not) what the "undue burden" test means. I must confess, however, that I have always thought, and I think a lot of other people have always thought, that the arbitrary trimester framework, which the Court today discards, was quite as central to *Roe* as the arbitrary viability test, which the Court today retains. It seems particularly ungrateful to carve the trimester framework out of the core of *Roe,* since its very rigidity (in sharp contrast to the utter indeterminability of the "undue burden" test) is probably the only reason the Court is able to say, in urging *stare decisis,* that *Roe* "has in no sense proven 'unworkabl,'"...I suppose the Court is entitled to call a "central holding" whatever it wants to call a "central holding"—which is, come to think of it, perhaps one of the difficulties with this modified version of *stare decisis.* I thought I might note, however, that the following portions of *Roe* have not been saved:

- Under *Roe,* requiring that a woman seeking an abortion be provided truthful information about abortion before giving informed written consent is unconstitutional, if the information is designed to influence her choice, *Thornburgh,* 476 U.S., at 759–765; *Akron I,* 462 U.S., at 442–445. Under the joint opinion's "undue burden" regime (as applied today, at least) such a requirement is constitutional....

- Under *Roe,* requiring that information be provided by a doctor, rather than by nonphysician counselors, is unconstitutional, *Akron I, supra,* at 446–449. Under the "undue burden" regime (as applied today, at least) it is not....

- Under *Roe,* requiring a 24-hour waiting period between the time the woman gives her informed consent and the time of the abortion is unconstitutional, *Akron I, supra,* at 449–451. Under the "undue burden" regime (as applied today, at least) it is not....

- Under *Roe,* requiring detailed reports that include demographic data about each woman who seeks an abortion and various information about each abortion is unconstitutional, *Thornburgh, supra,* at 465–768. Under the "undue burden" regime (as applied today, at least) it generally is not....

> **"Where, in the performance of its judicial duties, the Court decides a case in such a way as to resolve the sort of intensely divisive controversy reflected in *Roe...,* its decision has a dimension that the resolution of the normal case does not carry. It is the dimension present whenever the Court's interpretation of the Constitution calls the contending sides of a national controversy to end their national division by accepting a common mandate rooted in the Constitution."...**

The Court's description of the place of *Roe* in the social history of the United States is unrecognizable. Not only did *Roe* not, as the Court suggests, *resolve* the deeply divisive issue of abortion; it did more than anything else to nourish it, by elevating it to the national level where it is infinitely more difficult to resolve. National politics were not plagued by abortion protests, national abortion lobbying, or abortion marches on Congress, before *Roe v. Wade* was decided. Profound disagreement existed among our citizens over the issue—as it does over other issues, such as the death penalty—but that disagreement was being worked out at the state level. As with many other issues, the division of sentiment within each State was not as closely balanced as it was among the population of the Nation as a whole, meaning not only that more people would be satisfied with the results of state-by-state resolution, but also that those results would be more stable. Pre-*Roe,* moreover, political compromise was possible.

Roe's mandate for abortion-on-demand destroyed the compromises of the past, rendered compromise impossible for the future, and required the entire issue to be resolved uniformly, at the national level. At the same time, *Roe* created a vast new class of abortion consumers and abortion proponents by eliminating the moral opprobrium that had attached to the act. ("If the Constitution *guarantees* abortion, how can it be bad?"—not an accurate line of thought, but a natural one.) Many favor all of those developments, and it is not for me to say that they are wrong. But to portray *Roe* as the statesmanlike "settlement" of a divisive issue, a jurisprudential Peace of Westphalia that is worth preserving, is nothing less than Orwellian. *Roe* fanned into life an issue that has inflamed our national politics in general, and has obscured with its smoke the selection of Justices to this Court in particular, ever since. And by keeping us in the abortion-umpiring business, it is the perpetuation of that disruption, rather than of any *pax Roeana,* that the Court's new majority decrees.

> **"[T]o overrule under fire... would subvert the Court's legitimacy...**
>
> **"To all those who will be...tested by following, the Court implicitly undertakes to remain steadfast...The promise of constancy, once given, binds its maker for as long as the power to stand by the decision survives and...the commitment [is not] obsolete...**
>
> **"[The American people's] belief in themselves as...a people [who aspire to live according to the rule of law] is not readily separable from their understanding of the Court invested with the authority to decide their constitutional cases and speak before all others for their constitutional ideals. If the Court's legitimacy should be undermined, then, so would the country be in its very ability to see itself through its constitutional ideals."...**

The Imperial Judiciary lives. It is instructive to compare this Nietzschean vision of us unelected, life-tenured judges—leading a Volk who will be "tested by following," and whose very "belief in themselves" is mystically bound up in their "understanding" of a Court that "speak[s] before all others for their constitutional ideals"—with the somewhat more modest role envisioned for these lawyers by the Founders.

> "The judiciary...has...no direction either of the strength or of the wealth of the society, and can take no active resolution whatever. It may truly be said to have neither FORCE nor WILL but merely judgment..." The Federalist No. 78, pp. 393–394 (G. Wills ed. 1982).

Or, again to compare this ecstasy of a Supreme Court in which there is, especially on controversial matters, no shadow of change or hint of alteration ("There is a limit to the amount of error that can plausibly be imputed to prior courts"...), with the more democratic views of a more humble man:

> "[T]he candid citizen must confess that if the policy of the Government upon vital questions affecting the whole people is to be irrevocably fixed by decisions of the Supreme Court,...the people will have ceased to be their own rulers, having to that extent practically resigned their Government into the hands of that eminent tribunal." A. Lincoln, First Inaugural Address (Mar. 4, 1861),...

It is particularly difficult, in the circumstances of the present decision, to sit still for the Court's lengthy lecture upon the virtues of "constancy"..., of "remain[ing] steadfast"..., and adhering to "principle."...Among the five Justices who purportedly adhere to *Roe,* at most three agree upon the principle that constitutes adherence (the joint opinion's "undue burden" standard)—and that principle is inconsistent with *Roe,* see 410 U.S., at 154–156. To make matters worse, two of the three, in order thus to remain steadfast, had to abandon previously stated positions.…It is beyond me how the Court expects these accommodations to be accepted "as grounded truly in principle, not as compromises with social and political pressures having, as such, no bearing on the principled choices that the Court is obliged to make."…The only principle the Court "adheres" to, it seems to me, is the principle that the Court must be seen as standing by *Roe.* That is not a principle of law (which is what I thought the Court was talking about), but a principle of *Realpolitik*—and a wrong one at that.

I cannot agree with, indeed I am appalled by, the Court's suggestion that the decision whether to stand by an erroneous constitutional decision must be strongly influenced—*against* overruling, no less—by the substantial and continuing public opposition the decision has generated. The Court's judgment that any other course would "subvert the Court's legitimacy" must be another consequence of reading the error-filled history book that described the deeply divided country brought together by *Roe.* In my history book, the Court was covered with dishonor and deprived of legitimacy by *Dred Scott v. Sandford,* 19 How. 393 (1857), an erroneous (and widely opposed) opinion that it did not abandon, rather than by *West Coast Hotel Co. v. Parrish,* 300 U.S. 379 (1937), which produced the famous "switch in time" from the Court's erroneous (and widely opposed) constitutional opposition to the social measures of the New Deal. (Both *Dred Scott* and one line of the cases resisting the New Deal rested upon the concept of "substantive due process" that the Court praises and employs today. Indeed, *Dred Scott* was "very possibly the first application of substantive due process in the Supreme Court, the original precedent for *Lochner v. New York* and *Roe v. Wade.*" D. Currie, The Constitution in the Supreme Court 271 (1985) (footnotes omitted).)

But whether it would "subvert the Court's legitimacy" or not, the notion that we would decide a case differently from the way we otherwise would have in order to show that we can stand firm against public disapproval is frightening. It is a bad enough idea, even in the head of someone like me, who believes that the text of the Constitution, and our traditions, say what they say and there is no fiddling with them. But when it is in the mind of a Court that believes the Constitution has an evolving meaning.…; that the Ninth Amendment's reference to "othe[r]" rights is not a disclaimer, but a charter for action.…; and that the function of this Court is to "speak before all others for [the people's] constitutional ideals" unrestrained by meaningful text or tradition—then the notion that the Court must adhere to a decision for as long as the decision faces "great opposition" and the Court is "under fire" acquires a character of almost czarist arrogance. We are offended by these marchers who descend upon us, every year on the anniversary of *Roe,* to protest our saying that the Constitution requires what our society has never thought the Constitution requires. These people who refuse to be "tested by following" must be taught a lesson. We have no Cossacks, but at least we can stubbornly refuse to abandon an erroneous opinion that we might otherwise change—to show how little they intimidate us.

Of course, as THE CHIEF JUSTICE points out, we have been subjected to what the Court calls "political pressure" by *both* sides of this issue....Maybe today's decision *not* to overrule *Roe* will be seen as buckling to pressure from *that* direction. Instead of engaging in the hopeless task of predicting public perception—a job not for lawyers but for political campaign managers—the Justices should do what is *legally* right by asking two questions: (1) Was *Roe* correctly decided? (2) Has *Roe* succeeded in producing a settled body of law? If the answer to both questions is no, *Roe* should undoubtedly be overruled.

In truth, I am as distressed as the Court is—and expressed my distress several years ago, see *Webster,* 492 U.S., at 535—about the "political pressure" directed to the Court: the marches, the mail, the protests aimed at inducing us to change our opinions. How upsetting it is, that so many of our citizens (good people, not lawless ones, on both sides of this abortion issue, and on various sides of other issues as well) think that we Justices should properly take into account their views, as though we were engaged not in ascertaining an objective law but in determining some kind of social consensus. The Court would profit, I think, from giving less attention to the *fact* of this distressing phenomenon, and more attention to the *cause* of it. That cause permeates today's opinion: a new mode of constitutional adjudication that relies not upon text and traditional practice to determine the law, but upon what the Court calls "reasoned judgment,"...which turns out to be nothing but philosophical predilection and moral intuition. All manner of "liberties," the Court tells us, inhere in the Constitution and are enforceable by this Court—not just those mentioned in the text or established in the traditions of our society....Why even the Ninth Amendment—which says only that "[t]he enumeration in the Constitution of certain rights shall not be construed to deny or disparage others retained by the people"—is, despite our contrary understanding for almost 200 years, a literally boundless source of additional, unnamed, unhinted-at "rights," definable and enforceable by us, through "reasoned judgment."...

What makes all this relevant to the bothersome application of "political pressure" against the Court are the twin facts that the American people love democracy and the American people are not fools. As long as the Court thought (and the people thought) that we Justices were doing essentially lawyers' work up here—reading text and discerning our society's traditional understanding of that text—the public pretty much left us alone. Texts and traditions are facts to study, not convictions to demonstrate about. But if in reality our process of constitutional adjudication consists primarily of making *value judgments;* if we can ignore a long and clear tradition clarifying an ambiguous text, as we did, for example, five days ago in declaring unconstitutional invocations and benedictions at public-high-school graduation ceremonies, *Lee v. Weisman,* 505 U.S. ___ (1992); if, as I say, our pronouncement of constitutional law rests primarily on value judgments, then a free and intelligent people's attitude towards us can be expected to be *(ought to be)* quite different. The people know that their value judgments are quite as good as those taught in any law school—maybe better. If, indeed, the "liberties" protected by the Constitution are, as the Court says, undefined and unbounded, then the people *should* demonstrate, to protest that we do not implement *their* values instead of *ours.* Not only that, but confirmation hearings for new Justices *should* deteriorate into question-and-answer sessions in which Senators go through a list of their constituents' most favored and most disfavored alleged constitutional rights, and seek the nominee's commitment to support or oppose them. Value judgments, after all, should be voted on, not dictated; and if our Constitution has somehow accidentally committed them to the Supreme Court, at least we can have a sort of plebiscite each time a new nominee to that body is put forward.

STUDY QUESTIONS

1. Justices O'Connor, Kennedy, and Souter in *Casey* argue that *Roe* must be preserved as a precedent. On what bases do they draw this conclusion?

2. According to the Court, a law that attempts to limit a fundamental right must be able to withstand *strict scrutiny,* whereas a law which attempts to limit a liberty must not pose an *undue burden.* How does the Court distinguish the strict scrutiny standard from the undue burden standard? How does this distinction apply to *Casey*'s effect on *Roe?*

3. What is the basis of Justice Scalia's scathing dissent? Do you think his arguments are plausible? Why or why not?

FOR FURTHER READING

Beckwith, Francis J. *Politically Correct Death: Answering the Arguments for Abortion Rights.* Grand Rapids, Mich.: Baker Book House, 1993. Chapter 2.

Butler, J. Douglas, and David F. Walbert, eds. *Abortion, Medicine, and the Law.* New York: Facts on File Publications, 1986.

Drucker, Dan. *Abortion Decisions of the Supreme Court, 1973 through 1989: A Comprehensive Review with Historical Commentary.* Jefferson, N.C.: McFarland and Company, 1990.

Glendon, Mary Anne. *Abortion and Divorce in Western Law.* Cambridge, Mass.: Harvard University Press, 1987.

Krason, Stephen M. *Abortion: Politics, Morality, and the Constitution.* Lanham, Md.: University Press of America, 1984, 77–90.

Mohr, James. *Abortion in America: The Origins and Evolution of National Policy, 1800–1900.* New York: Oxford University Press, 1978.

Olasky, Marvin. *Abortion Rites: A Social History of Abortion in America.* Wheaton, Ill.: Crossway, 1992.

Tribe, Laurence. *Abortion: The Clash of Absolutes.* New York: Norton, 1990. Chapter 2.

Wardle, Lynn D., and Mary Anne Q. Wood. *A Lawyer Looks at Abortion.* Provo, UT: Brigham Young University Press, 1982.

Wertheimer, Roger. "Understanding Blackmun's Argument: The Reasoning of *Roe v. Wade.*" In *Abortion: Moral and Legal Perspectives,* edited by Jay L. Garfield and Patricia Hennessy. Amherst: University of Massachusetts Press, 1984.

PART III

Evaluations of
Roe v. Wade

INTRODUCTION

In a debate during the 1992 presidential primaries, candidates from the Democratic Party (among them then-future President Bill Clinton) were asked whether each supported the U.S Supreme Court decision *Roe v. Wade* (1993), the decision that ruled that state anti-abortion laws were unconstitutional because they violated a woman's right to privacy. Every one of the candidates answered the question with a resounding "yes," usually adding the comment, "I believe in a woman's right to choose." What is interesting about this reply is that it seems to be assuming that if one believes in abortion-rights as a public policy one automatically supports *Roe v. Wade* as a legal decision. But this is a mistake. *Roe* is a very controversial decision with scores of critics, both prolife and prochoice.

This section contains three essays that criticize *Roe* from different perspectives. The first essay, by Dennis Horan and Thomas Balch ("*Roe v. Wade:* No Basis in Law, Logic, or History") attacks the factual and logical bases for *Roe,* arguing that the Court's reasoning is unsound and that the history and law appealed to by the Court is factually incorrect. Horan and Balch are prolife legal scholars. The second essay ("*Roe v. Wade:* A Study in Male Ideology") is by feminist legal scholar Catharine MacKinnon, who critiques *Roe* from a radical feminist perspective arguing that far from liberating women, *Roe's* constitutional basis (that is, the right to privacy) is a product of male ideology and thus merely reinforces male oppression of women by control over their sexuality.

U.S. Supreme Court Justice Ruth Bader Ginsburg is the author of the third essay ("Some Thoughts on Autonomy and Equality in Relation to *Roe v. Wade*"). Originally published in the *North Carolina Law Review* in 1985, this essay criticizes the Court for trying to justify abortion rights by the right to privacy. Ginsburg argues that the Court should have argued that since women are uniquely burdened by pregnancy, they deserve equal protection under the law, that is, a right to abortion.

4

Roe v. Wade: No Basis in Law, Logic, or History

DENNIS J. HORAN AND THOMAS J. BALCH

Dennis J. Horan, who passed away in 1988, was Chairman, Americans United for Life Legal Defense Fund. He also served as a Lecturer in Law at the University of Chicago Law School. Thomas J. Balch is Staff Counsel, National Center for the Medically Dependent and Disabled and former Staff Counsel, Americans United for Life Legal Defense Fund.

In this essay Horan and Balch argue that the legal and historical precedent appealed to by Justice Blackmun in Roe v. Wade *does not stand up to critical scrutiny. That is, the Court's interpretation of common-law, nineteenth-century abortion law, and the intent of the drafters of the Constitution is seriously flawed and, when correctly interpreted, works against the conclusion arrived at in* Roe. *In addition, Horan and Balch argue that Blackmun's reasoning process in* Roe *(that is, his logic) is flawed as well.*

I. *ROE* AND ITS CRITICS

In the history of American constitutional jurisprudence, few Supreme Court decisions have come to be recognized as so faulty, and with such damaging social consequences that history has branded them not only as controversial or erroneous but also as watersheds of ignominy.

Reprinted from *Abortion and the Law: Reversing* Roe v. Wade *Through the Courts*, eds. Dennis J. Horan, Edward R. Grant, and Paige C. Cunningham (Washington, DC: Georgetown University Press, 1987). Reprinted by permission. Endnotes edited.

Dred Scott v. Sandford ruled that blacks were not citizens, *Plessy v. Ferguson* upheld racial segregation, and *Lochner v. New York* said that legislatures could not enact maximum hour laws to protect workers from the superior bargaining power of employers. *Roe v. Wade* is in this unenviable tradition. It is difficult to find a contemporary decision whose reasoning is more universally questioned by the community of legal scholars. It is attacked by thinkers who, like John Hart Ely, support legal abortion as a matter of legislative policy and criticized by those who support its result as a matter of constitutional law.

After surveying the decision, editors of the *Michigan Law Review,* introducing a Symposium on the Law and Politics of Abortion, wrote that "the consensus among legal academics seems to be that, whatever one thinks of the holding, the opinion is unsatisfying."[1] Richard Morgan notes,

> Rarely does the Supreme Court invite critical outrage as it did in *Roe* by offering so little explanation for a decision that requires so much. The stark inadequacy of the Court's attempt to justify its conclusions...suggests to some scholars that the Court, finding no justification at all in the Constitution, unabashedly usurped the legislative function...Even some who approve of *Roe's* form of judicial review concede that the opinion itself is inscrutable.[2]

Joseph Dellapenna has asserted that the opinion is so poorly written that even its defenders begin by apologizing for the difficulties in following the reasoning of the Court.[3] Heymann and Barzelay, although they defend *Roe's* consistency with "principles that are justified in both reason and precedent," regret that "these principles were never adequately articulated by the opinion of the Court." "This failure," they write, "leaves the impression that the abortion decisions rest in part on unexplained precedents, in part on an extremely tenuous relation to provisions of the Bill of Rights, and in part on a raw exercise of judicial fiat."[4]

The Court's articulation of its position is so embarrassing that the invariable approach of legal scholars writing in support of *Roe's* holdings is to "rewrite" the opinion, suggesting some constitutional rationale not proffered by the Court that attempts to justify its conclusions. Archibald Cox speaks for many: "The failure to confront the issue in principled terms leaves the opinion to read like a set of hospital rules and regulations, whose validity is good enough this week but will be destroyed with new statistics upon the medical risks of child-birth and abortion or new advances in providing for the separate existence of a foetus."[5]

Virtually every aspect of the historical, sociological, medical, and legal arguments Justice Harry Blackmun used to support the *Roe* holdings has been subjected to intense scholarly criticism. The unprecedented extremity of the Court's opinion is well known. After Justice Blackmun announced the Court's opinion on January 22, 1973, not a single abortion statute in any state of the Union still stood. Even the law of New York, the "abortion capital of the country," which allowed abortion on demand through the twenty-fourth week of pregnancy, was too protective of the unborn for the majority of the United

States Supreme Court. For under *Roe,* it is constitutionally impossible for any state to prohibit abortions at any time during pregnancy.

The Court held:

(a) For the stage prior to approximately the end of the first trimester, the abortion decision and its effectuation must he left to the medical judgment of the pregnant woman's attending physician.

(b) For the stage subsequent to approximately the end of the first trimester, the State, in promoting its interest in the health of the mother, may, if it chooses, regulate the abortion procedure in ways that are reasonably related to maternal health.

(c) For the stage subsequent to viability, the State in promoting its interest in the potentiality of human life may, if it chooses, regulate, and even proscribe, abortion except where it is necessary, in appropriate medical judgment for the preservation of the life *or health* of the mother.

On the same day that the Court decided *Roe,* it also decided the companion case *Doe v. Bolton.* The Court emphasized, in *Roe,* "That opinion and this one, of course, are to be read together." In *Doe,* the Court, making reference to its earlier decision in *United States v. Vuitch,* construed the meaning of "mother's life or health."

That…has been construed to bear upon psychological as well as physical well-being…[T]he medical judgment may be exercised in the light of all factors—physical, emotional, psychological, familial, and the woman's age—relevant to the well-being of the patient. All these factors may relate to health. This allows the attending physician the room he needs to make his best medical judgment. And it is room that operates for the benefit, not the disadvantage, of the pregnant woman.[6]

In *Roe,* the Court expanded on the factors the physician might consider:

Maternity, or additional offspring, may force upon the woman a distressful life and future. Psychological harm may be imminent. Mental and physical health may be taxed by child care. There is also the distress, for all concerned, associated with the unwanted child, and there is the problem of bringing a child into a family already unable, psychologically and otherwise, to care for it. In other cases…the additional difficulties and continuing stigma of unwed motherhood may be involved. All these are factors the woman and her responsible physician necessarily will consider in consultation.

Thus it is clear that, under the Supreme Court's abortion decisions no state may constitutionally prohibit abortion at any time during pregnancy. After the end of the first trimester (first three months), it may make some regulations to protect *maternal* health, but not to impede abortion. After viability, the state may "proscribe" abortion only when the woman considering abortion can find no physician willing to say that her mental health would, for example, be "taxed by child care" or suffer "distress…associated with the unwanted child."

In effect, "[t]he statutes of most states must be unconstitutional *even as applied to the final trimester…*[E]ven after viability the mother's life *or health* (which presumably is to be defined very broadly indeed, so as to include what many might regard as the mother's convenience…) must, as a matter of constitutional law, take precedence over… the fetus's *life…*"[7]

The lower courts have followed this analysis. In *American College of Obstetricians and Gynecologists v. Thornburgh,* a federal court of appeals was quite explicit:

[A] physician may perform an abortion even after viability when necessary "to preserve maternal life or health." It is clear from the Supreme Court cases that "health" is to be broadly defined. As the Court stated in *Doe v. Bolton,* the factors relating to health include those that are: "physical, emotional, psychological, familial, [as well as] the woman's age." 410 U.S. at 192.

…[I]t is apparent that the Pennsylvania legislature was hostile to this definition. Section 3210(b) [of the state's abortion law] contains the statement, "The potential psychological or emotional impact on the mother of the unborn child's survival shall not be deemed a medical risk to the mother." Had the legislature imposed this qualification on the language "maternal… health."… we would have no hesitation in declaring that provision unconstitutional.

Similarly, in *Schulte v. Douglas,* a federal district court declared unconstitutional a Nebraska statute that attempted to prohibit abortion after viability unless it was necessary to protect the woman from imminent peril substantially endangering her life or health. This, Judge Warren Urbom held, prevents postviability abortions "even when in the physician's judgment a different course should be undertaken to preserve the mother…from a *non-imminent* peril that endangers her life or health *less than substantially*….This the state has no authority to do."

In effect, as long as a woman can find a physician willing to perform the abortion, she has a constitutional right to obtain an abortion at *any* time during pregnancy. When the Court asserts that such an extreme position is required by the Constitution, one expects an especially compelling rationale. Few have found *Roe* convincing.

II. HISTORICAL CRITIQUES OF *ROE*

After Justice Blackmun recited the case history and disposed of the procedural questions of justiciability, standing, and abstention, he did not launch directly into analysis of the substantive issues at stake. Instead, he began with a lengthy discussion of the history of legal and societal attitudes toward abortion. Why? Justice Blackmun maintained that, until the mid-nineteenth century, abortion was generally and freely available and not forbidden by the law and should be recognized as an aspect of the liberty the framers of the Fourteenth

Amendment intended to protect. Thus, a historical discussion must be seen as a predicate for the Court's holding that the right of privacy incorporated by the Fourteenth Amendment into the U.S. Constitution should be deemed to encompass abortion as a time-treasured right.

Before considering Justice Blackmun's version of the history of abortion, it is worth putting that history in perspective. Today, virtually all who oppose abortion do so because abortion kills unborn human life. Therefore, in examining the history of abortion it is natural to focus our understanding on the attitudes of previous historical eras toward the child in the womb. To what extent, and at what point in gestation, did each epoch recognize the child as a human person? Did they, on that ground, condemn abortion as a form of homicide?

Regarding these important questions, scholarly research reveals that recognition of the unborn as "persons in the whole sense" was largely determined by the biological and medical knowledge of each historical era. The ovum and the actual nature of fertilization were discovered in the nineteenth century. Prior to this, scientists and contemporaneous jurists supposed that human life commenced at "formation," "animation," or "quickening." Abortion was seen as unquestionably homicidal only after the gestational point at which, in light of the science of the time, human life was finally understood to be present.

Justice Blackmun's conclusion that in prior eras abortion in early pregnancy was not seen as homicidal is irrelevant. Indeed, an approach coinciding with historical continuity; *pace* Blackmun, would be to protect the unborn from the time of fertilization because that is when modern science teaches us that the life of an individual human organism comes into being.

Another aspect important to an historical analysis of abortion is that there was widespread disapproval and prohibition of abortion during early pregnancy before, in the view of the science of the time, human life had been infused. The motives for this repudiation of early abortion may not be the same as those that would appeal to today's society as justifying legal interdiction.

Our ancestors' biologically incorrect notions of when human life begins led Blackmun to assert that, historically, "abortion was viewed with less disfavor than under most American statutes currently in effect" (in January, 1973) and "[p]hrasing it another way, a woman enjoyed a substantially broader right to terminate a pregnancy than she does…today." Examination of the condemnation of abortion, apart from views on the beginning of human life, proves this conclusion incorrect.

A. Ancient and Medieval Attitudes

Blackmun's recounting of the history of abortion began with ancient attitudes and the Hippocratic oath. Relying exclusively for both areas on the dated work of historian Ludwig Edelstein, he concluded that the ancient Greeks and Romans had resorted to abortion with great frequency and that it had met with widespread approbation. Conversely, Martin Arbagi demonstrates that temple inscriptions and other ancient writings disclose considerable opposition to abortion in the Greco-Roman world. Opposition spread and intensified from earlier to later ancient time—a tendency that manifested itself long before Christianity had any influence.[8]

Apart from remarking that the Persian Empire banned abortion, Justice Blackmun's survey of the ancient world was limited to Greece and Rome. Yet, it is significant that abortion was condemned in the twelfth century B.C. by Assyrians, Hittites, early Hindus, Buddhists of India, and Indian law. There is some evidence that the ancient Egyptians took a similar attitude. Most of this information was available in the epical work of Eugene Quay, which Blackmun cited but failed to incorporate into his opinion.[9]

Justice Blackmun recognized that the oath of Hippocrates, composed in ancient Greece, forbade the practice of abortion. Apparently, in view of the longstanding honor paid to the Hippocratic oath, Blackmun felt the need to diminish its importance. In fact, he brought this question up *sua sponte,* because, "Although the Oath is not mentioned in any of the principal briefs in this case or in [the companion case of] *Doe v. Bolton...,* it represents the apex of the development of strict ethical concepts in medicine, and its influence endures to this day." Citing Edelstein, Blackmun argued that the oath, rather than establishing significant pre-Christian opposition to abortion, was merely the manifesto of an idiosyncratic and unrepresentative sect of Pythagoreans.

Harold Brown makes a further point:

> The unspoken implication of the Court's argument seems to be that the Hippocratic Oath need not be taken seriously as an expression of medical ethics because, at the outset, it was the view of a minority...and later, when it came to enjoy majority acceptance, this only took place because the majority by that time had embraced Christianity. Edelstein's conclusion is somewhat different...In all countries, in all epochs, in which monotheism, in its purely religious or its more secularized form, was the accepted creed, the Hippocratic Oath was applauded as the embodiment of truth. Not only the Jews and the Christians, but the Arabs, the medieval doctors, men of the Renaissance, scholars of the enlightenment and scientists of the nineteenth century embraced the ideals of the oath.[10]

In short, the Court's discussion of the oath amounts to a *non sequitur:* Even were its scholarship and conclusions about the oath's origins unassailable, the Court did not diminish the significance of the Hippocratic oath as a longstanding and near-universal condemnation of abortion by the organized medical profession.

Despite the fact that studies and commentaries on that period were available to the Court, Justice Blackmun left a historical gap of more than a thousand years when he leaped directly from ancient attitudes and the Hippocratic oath to Anglo-American common law; John Noonan, in 1970, wrote about the rejection of abortion as *An Almost Absolute Value in History.* During that period, the ethics and law of Western civilization were dominated by the Judeo-Christian perspective; in fact, every adequate survey of historical attitudes toward abortion has to come to terms with the longstanding opposition to abortion by Jews and Christians. True, there was both ignorance and debate, appropriate to the science of the time, about "ensoulment" and what was viewed as the coming of full humanity to the fetus. But opposition to abortion, with minor exceptions, was constant.

The Septuagint, the Greek version of the Hebrew Bible used by third century B.C. Jews of the Diaspora, contained a version of Exodus which decreed capital punishment for one who aborted a formed fetus. The Didache (first century A.D.), known as the "Teaching of the Twelve Apostles," proclaimed to the early Christian Church, "You shall not slay the child by abortions. You shall not kill what is generated." Other early Christian writings such as the Epistle of Barnabas and the Apocalypse of Peter contained similar prohibitions. In the West, the Fathers of the Church, from second century Clement of Alexandria through Tertullian and Jerome to Augustine, condemned abortion. In the East, St. John Chrysostom and St. Basil of Cappadocia preached against all abortion. These early teachings were concretized in the prohibitions of penitentials and of canons enacted by synods and councils which, in turn, found their way into the law of the state, such as the Frankish kingdom of Charlemagne. These were followed by canon law. A decretal of Gregory IX grouped the penalty for abortion with that for means of sterilization. Of both it was said, "[l]et it be held as homicide."

This treatment of abortion and contraception as crimes demanding severe punishment was coupled with a general attitude that abortion was not "true" homicide until the fetus was "ensouled"—something held to occur at formation or quickening. That distinction, taken from Aristotle, was introduced by theologians in the fifth century and was dominant until the seventeenth century. John Connery describes Aristotle's essentially biological theory of "delayed animation":

> To Aristotle…life at conception came from a vegetative soul. After conception, this would eventually be replaced by an animal soul, and the latter finally by a human soul. The difficult question was when this human soul was infused, or as it is sometimes put, when the fetus became a human being. Aristotle held that this occurred when the fetus was formed, 40 days after conception for the male fetus and 90 days for the female. Aristotle also used the criterion of movement. If the aborted fetus showed signs of movement, it was considered human. But since this coincided with the time of formation, the time estimate was the same…It was easy to argue for delayed animation when one thought that semen gradually turned into blood and then into flesh and bone and eventually into a human fetus."[11]

Through the Middle Ages, civil law on the continent of Europe was based on the Roman law. Connery notes that from the end of the second century through the thirteenth century, that law applied the same punishment to abortion throughout pregnancy. In the thirteenth century, the Italian jurist Accursio first interpreted the law to impose a higher punishment for abortion after formation: Such abortion was classified as homicide and incurred capital punishment. This late application to the civil law of the Aristotelian view that had long dominated church penitential discipline did not eliminate or lessen the penalty for preformation abortion; it only heightened it for postformation abortion.

B. The Common Law on Abortion

Ignoring this civil law background, which was important for its relation to the beginnings of the English common law, the Supreme Court paid considerable attention to the content of English common law. From the thirteenth through the sixteenth centuries, the common law courts coexisted with the ecclesiastical courts in England—much as state courts coexist with federal courts today. Just as state and federal courts have independent jurisdiction over some matters and concurrent jurisdiction over others, so it was with the medieval, royal, and church courts. The ecclesiastical courts dealt with many secular matters such as wills, slander, and informal contracts.[12] As Dellapenna's research discloses, "at least prior to 1600, royal courts did not concern themselves about abortion, but…royally-sustained ecclesiastical courts did."[13]

Justice Blackmun's view of the common law focused almost exclusively on the royal courts. He followed the position of Cyril Means, legal counsel to the National Association for the Repeal of Abortion Laws, and concluded that it is "doubtful that abortion was ever firmly established as a common-law crime even with respect to the destruction of a quick fetus." Means's and Blackmun's position has been resoundingly refuted in articles by Dellapenna, Robert Byrn, and Robert Destro. Essentially, Means's position rests on his attribution of deceit and distortion to Chief Justice Sir Edward Coke. He was the great sixteenth and seventeenth century jurist who successfully led the fight to capture, for the common law courts, most of the jurisdiction exercised up to then by the ecclesiastical courts. In the process, Coke was a leader in systematizing, expanding, and recording the common law. In his famous *Institutes,* he declared that, while not "murder," abortion of a woman "quick with childe" was a "great misprision."

Means, based on his interpretation of two fourteenth-century cases he called *The Twinslayer's Case* and *The Abortionist's Case,* and two sixteenth-century commentaries, Sir William Stanford's *Les Plees del Coron* and William Lamborde's *Eirenorcha, Or of the Office of the Justice of the Peace,* concluded that Coke was mistaken. Means asserted that these sources established that abortion was never a crime at common law. He brushed aside the earlier evidence of the thirteenth-century commentators Bracton and Fleta, who described abortion of a formed and animated fetus as homicide. He scornfully accused Coke of distorting the law to fit the view of abortion he had taken as attorney general in a case argued in 1601; and he dismissed Blackstone, whose name was synonymous with "law" for eighteenth and nineteenth century American lawyers, as an uncritical follower of Coke. Blackstone's work, well known by the framers of the Constitution and the architects of the Fourteenth Amendment, called it a "great misprision" "[t]o kill a child in its mother's womb."

The intricacies of legal history and the explication of the scanty texts of these decisions and commentaries are complex. Means's interpretation of *The Twinslayer's Case* and *The Abortionist's Case* rested on the assumption that the dismissals of charges brought against abortionists in those cases were because abortion was not a crime at common law. Instead, as Byrn, Dellapenna, and Destro have demonstrated, the dismissals were clearly based on problems of proof. Robert Destro argued from the text of the cases and included a key paragraph in *The Twinslayer's Case* ignored by Means. He concluded, and the documents affirm, that as a matter of substantive law, postquickening abortion was a common law crime. The same can be said of Stanford's commentary.

The primitive nature of biological knowledge and abortion technology made it next to impossible to prove that the child was alive before the supposed abortion *and* that the abortion was the cause of death. It was compounded by rigidly technical procedural requirements and led to the conclusion by the sixteenth-century commentary that abortion was not punished as a crime.

In the 1601 *Sims Case,* a solution to some of these difficulties in proof was offered: when a child was born alive, but showed the marks of an abortion, and subsequently died, murder could be proved. This position was adopted by Coke and carried through to Blackstone. There is a plethora of cases since Coke holding postquickening abortion a common law crime—cases ignored by Means or dismissed by him as being based on Coke's "distortion." Yet, as Destro asks, "[e]ven assuming that Coke's view was completely at variance with the earliest common law precedents…one question remains to be answered: Why did Coke's view persevere and gain acceptance by virtually every court which considered the matter?"[14] Suppose someone were to contend today that racial segregation was "never" unconstitutional because *Brown v. Board of Education* was inconsistent with *Plessy v. Ferguson* and other precedents, and that the many subsequent desegregation cases in the Supreme Court and other federal courts were based on an uncritical acceptance of *Brown.* Justifiably, the argument would be laughed out of court.

Coke's views became so firmly established from the seventeenth through the nineteenth century that it takes a remarkably selective vision to deny that abortion of a quickened fetus was a common law crime at the time of the adoption of the Constitution or the Fourteenth Amendment. In the words of Robert Byrn, "For the Supreme Court in *Roe v. Wade* to cite the 'lenity' of the common law as a basis for holding that unborn children do not possess a fundamental right to live and to the law's protection at any time up to birth, is a perversion of Bracton, Coke, Hawkins and Blackstone. The whole history of the common law cries out against the jurisprudence of *Wade.*"[15]

C. Nineteenth Century Statutory Reform

After evaluation of the common law, Justice Blackmun described the nineteenth-century English and American statutory enactments on abortion. Then, after charting the changing positions of the American Medical Association, the

American Public Health Association, and the American Bar Association on abortion, he analyzed reasons behind the nineteenth-century enactment of statutes against abortion throughout pregnancy.

Following Cyril Means's thesis, Blackmun maintained that the nineteenth century's statutory prohibitions of abortion, even back to the moment of conception, were enacted not to aid prenatal life but to protect maternal health against the danger of unsafe operations. Blackmun made several key factual errors and completely failed to mention the important scientific developments that prompted the statutory changes. As Victor Rosenblum has noted,

> Only in the second quarter of the nineteenth century did biological research advance to the extent of understanding the actual mechanism of development. The nineteenth century saw a gradual but profoundly influential revolution in the scientific understanding of the beginning of individual mammalian life. Although sperm had been discovered in 1677, the mammalian egg was not identified until 1827. The cell was first recognized as the structural unit of organisms in 1839, and the egg and sperm were recognized as cells in the next two decades. These developments were brought to the attention of the American state legislatures and public by those professionals most familiar with their unfolding import—physicians. It was the new research finding which persuaded doctors that the old "quickening" distinction embodied in the common and some statutory law was unscientific and indefensible.[16]

Beginning about 1857, the American Medical Association (AMA) led a "physicians' crusade" to enact laws protecting the unborn from the time of conception. These vigorous physicians rested their argument primarily on the living nature of the fetus in early pregnancy, and it was their efforts that passed the laws. As Dellapenna noted, twenty-six of thirty-six states had prohibited abortion by the end of the Civil War as had six of the ten territories. "The assertion by Justice Blackmun that such legislation did not become widespread until after the 'War Between the States' is simply wrong."[17] Justice Blackmun ignored this clear history—an extraordinary omission in light of his quotation, in *Roe,* of statements from the principal resolutions of the AMA during "the 'physicians' crusade."

Blackmun gave three reasons for the notion that the laws were enacted to protect maternal health rather than the child. All have been rebutted. First, citing only one New Jersey decision, he said, "The few state courts called upon to interpret their laws in the late nineteenth and early twentieth century did focus on the state's interests in protecting the woman's health rather than in preserving the embryo and fetus." To the contrary, John Gorby has demonstrated that there are eleven state court decisions explicitly affirming that protection of the unborn was a purpose of their nineteenth-century abortion statutes, and nine others that imply the same position. Robert Destro and Gorby have both independently demonstrated that the isolated New Jersey citation misstates the purpose even of that jurisdiction's law.[18]

Second, Blackmun argued, "In many States…by statute or judicial interpretation, the pregnant woman herself could not be prosecuted for self-abortion or for cooperating in an abortion performed upon her by another." John Gorby replies,

> The explanation for this legal phenomenon is that there are special circumstances surrounding the commitment of an act, circumstances which the lawmaker may properly and reasonably consider in formulating means to protect state interests and values…in the abortion situation, the assumed stresses on the woman burdened by an unwanted pregnancy. These factors may justify and explain different treatment of the woman or even the physician in the abortion context, just as they justify or explain different treatment of the child of tender years or even of one who kills another under severe provocation.[19]

Finally, Blackmun contended, "Adoption of the 'quickening' distinction through received common law and state statutes tacitly recognizes the greater health hazard inherent in late abortion and impliedly repudiates the theory that life begins at conception." Robert Sauer demolishes this notion:

> Although a number of the initial state laws contained a distinction based on quickening which gave lower value to early foetal life, the large majority of state laws never made this distinction, and most of these laws referred to a woman as "being with child" or some similar phrase which attributed a human status to the foetus. Furthermore, many of the states which initially had this distinction written into their law later dropped it and also referred to a woman at any period of her pregnancy as "being with child."[20]

Common law was not the only means available or used to prevent abortion. In the ecclesiastical courts and in church law, the notion, based on the inaccurate biology of the time, that the fetus became a human being only at formation or quickening did not prevent the authorities from condemning abortion during all stages of gestation. Although problems of proof prevented the common law from punishing abortion of an unquickened fetus, they allowed society to use other endeavors to prevent abortion throughout pregnancy.

Professor Dellapenna has made a valuable contribution to accurately understanding the history of abortion by pointing out the varying technical methods used to attempt abortion at different periods in history. Historically, these methods involved the use of drugs, potions (often either ineffectual or fatally poisonous), beatings, or other risky efforts to induce trauma that would trigger abortion. After 1750, methods involving the insertion of objects into the uterus were introduced; and surgery, initially highly dangerous, was used sometime later.

Today, we naturally think of abortive surgical procedures being performed by physicians. Yet into the nineteenth century, midwives attended women during childbirth and pregnancy and performed most abortions. Following the institution of similar systems in continental Europe in the fifteenth century, England developed a system of regulating and licensing midwives in the early sixteenth century. These regulations required midwives' oaths swearing that they would not give advice or medicines to women enabling them to abort. No distinction was made on the basis of the stage of pregnancy. A similar practice was instituted in colonial America: Records exist of a New York City ordinance requiring midwives to take such an oath as early as 1716. Possibly the nineteenth century "physicians' crusade" extended the protection of statutory law back to conception because midwives had lost their prominence as abortion providers.

Evidence is overwhelming that the Court's abortion history is fatally flawed. Contrary to Justice Blackmun's assertion that "restrictive criminal abortion laws...are of relatively recent vintage...not of ancient or even of common-law origin," abortion was condemned even in ancient times and the consensus of Western civilization was opposed to abortion throughout the duration of pregnancy. True, the precise penalties varied, depending on what science held to be the point at which human life began. As the result of nineteenth-century biological discoveries the existence of human life from the time of conception became clear. Members of the American medical community were aware of new evidence and the increasing frequency of abortion resulting from technological developments in abortion methodology. They successfully led a reform movement that extended the full protection of the criminal law to the time of fertilization. These statutory amendments were neither anomalous nor explained by motivations other than fetal protection; they were the logical outgrowth of the interaction of "an almost absolute value in history" and the teachings of evolving science.

History provides no excuse for Justice Blackmun's conclusion that "at common law, at the time of the adoption of our Constitution, and throughout the major portion of the nineteenth century...a woman enjoyed a substantially broader right to terminate a pregnancy" than in most states immediately before *Roe v. Wade*. That "right" was *never* present in America until 1973. That erroneous conclusion is of paramount importance, since it is from its misguided version of abortion history that the Court implicitly draws what meager support it can for the notion that abortion is time-treasured and incorporated into the Fourteenth Amendment.

III. ABORTION AS A CONSTITUTIONAL RIGHT

Immediately after his historical survey, Justice Blackmun turned to the essence of what he found to be the abortion right. "The Fourteenth Amendment's concept of personal liberty," the Court ruled, "is broad enough to encompass a woman's decision whether or not to terminate her pregnancy." This textually unsupported assertion has been subjected to an avalanche of criticism—

some of it from the most respected legal minds in the country. Indeed, this portion of the opinion has stimulated more negative jurisprudential evaluation than any other section and the critique comes from various parts of the ideological spectrum.

Listing cases recognizing some form of a "right of privacy," Justice Blackmun acknowledged that "[t]hese decisions make it clear that only personal rights that can be deemed 'fundamental' or 'implicit in the concept of ordered liberty'...are included in this guarantee of personal privacy." What makes abortion "implicit" in the very nature of "ordered liberty"? Justice Blackmun wrote that the right of privacy has been deemed to encompass marriage, procreation, contraception, family relationships, and child rearing and education. Without abortion a woman may suffer direct harm, distressful life, or psychological harm. Mental and physical health may be taxed by child care, also the distress associated with the unwanted child and the additional difficulties and continuing stigma of unwed mothers.

This is the entirety of Blackmun's argument. Norman Vieira, one of many critics, said in response:

> No elaborate discussion is required to expose the glaring non sequitur in the Court's argument. Plainly the fact that *some* family matters are constitutionally protected does not demonstrate that abortion is constitutionally protected. Nor does the added fact that abortion laws disadvantage pregnant women establish their invalidity. Legal restrictions are placed on family autonomy in fields ranging from divorce to euthanasia despite the heavy costs thereby exacted from the individuals concerned.[21]

In 1973 John Ely made an early and telling attack on *Roe's* postulation of this right. Referring to the Court's delineation of the difficulties of undesired pregnancy, he wrote,

> All of this is true and ought to be taken very seriously. But it has nothing to do with privacy in the Bill of Rights sense or any other the Constitution suggests...What is unusual about *Roe* is that the liberty involved is accorded...a protection more stringent, I think it is fair to say, than that the present Court accords the freedom of the press explicitly guaranteed by the First Amendment. What is frightening about *Roe* is that this superprotected right is not inferrable from the language of the Constitution, the framers' thinking respecting the specific problem in issue, any general value derivable from the provisions they included, or the nation's governmental structure. Nor is it explainable in terms of the unusual political impotence of the group judicially protected vis-à-vis the interest that legislatively prevailed over it. And that, I believe...is a charge that can responsibly be leveled at no other decision of the past twenty years.[22]

Remember that Ely has written that, were he a legislator, he would vote for a bill legalizing abortion nearly to the extent allowed by the Supreme Court.

Vieira and Ely are not alone. Archibald Cox wrote, "The Court failed to establish the legitimacy of the decision by not articulating a principle of sufficient abstractness to lift the ruling above the level of a political judgment.[23] Judge Richard Posner warns that "*Wade* raise[s]…the question whether we have a written Constitution, with the limitations thereby implied on the creation of new constitutional rights, or whether the Constitution is no more than a grant of discretion to the Supreme Court to mold public policy in accordance with the Justices' own personal and shifting preferences."[24]

At least two commentators have noted the incoherence of the striking contrast between the Court's treatment of privacy with regard to abortion, which the justices clearly like, and with regard to sexually explicit material, which they just as clearly do not. Indeed, the very notion that abortion should be subsumed under a right of "privacy" is strange. As Joseph O'Meara objects, "[T]here is nothing private about an abortion." It occurs not at home, like sex or the reading of obscenity, but in a public clinic.[25]

IV. ABORTION AND HUMAN PERSONHOOD

Having read into the Constitution a right that was not in the text, Justice Blackmun then proceeded to read out of the Constitution the application of a right basic to that text. Recognizing that if the Fourteenth Amendment's protection of the right to life is extended to the unborn the case for abortion collapses, he developed the argument for his conclusion that "the word 'person'…does not include the unborn." As John Hart Ely has noted, after employing the most imaginative possible construction of the Fourteenth Amendment to find a right of abortion, the Court resorted to the most literalistic possible form of strict construction to avoid finding the unborn to be persons.[26]

Professors Byrn, Destro, and Gorby have independently provided comprehensive, point-by-point rebuttals of the Court's objections to unborn personhood. The opinion argued that the word "person," as used in clauses elsewhere in the Constitution, has application only postnatally. Ely wrote that the Court "might have added that most of them were plainly drafted with *adults* in mind, but I suppose that wouldn't have helped."[27] As John Gorby has pointed out:

> [T]hese other clauses…do not provide an answer to the question of the scope of constitutional personhood. In the clauses mentioned by the Court, the concept of "person" was broad and undefined and the function of the specific constitutional clause was to limit the broader class of persons for a particular purpose. For example, for a person to be…a representative, a senator or the President, he must be twenty-five, thirty, and thirty-five years of age respectively…The fact that a 24-year-old is not qualified for these offices suggests only that there are "persons" who are not qualified for the House, Senate or the Presidency…; it does not suggest when the 24-year-old became a "person," or that he became a person at birth."[28]

For example, the Court says, "[w]e are not aware that in the taking of any census a fetus has ever been counted." As one commentator put it:

The Court seems to be saying that, because a word is narrowly defined in the context of a practical application (census taking) due to the impracticability or susceptibility to large error of including fetuses within the meaning of the term, that it should also be narrowly defined, to the exclusion of an entire class of potential "persons," when determining what persons are deserving of constitutional protection of the right to life.[29]

The Court fails to recognize that the Apportionment Clause merely provides for a decennial census "in such manner as [Congress] shall by law direct." "Although Congress has never done so, it would be neither irrational nor unconstitutional for it to direct that account also be taken of the unborn whenever the census-taker is made aware of their existence," writes Destro. "The fact that Congress has never done so is irrelevant." He and Byrn observe that corporations are not counted in the census, yet they are Fourteenth Amendment persons.[30]

Blackmun objects that, under the challenged Texas law, the existence of an exception to save the life of the mother is inconsistent with regard to the unborn as persons entitled to equal protection with their mothers. But the doctrines of self-defense and legal necessity allow persons acting out of self-protection to kill another human being, releasing themselves from the liability for killing a born person. "Balance of interest tests are commonplace," Epstein points out. "That process of balancing can take place even if the unborn child is treated as a person under the Due Process Clause…We might as well conclude that self-defense should never be treated as a justification for the deliberate killing of another person under the law of either crime or tort. No one could believe that the constitutional right to life extends that far."[31]

Blackmun raises what the Court regards as "two other inconsistencies between Fourteenth Amendment status [of the unborn as a person] and the typical abortion statute." The first is that the woman who submits to an abortion is not liable for punishment for the abortion. But this says nothing about the personhood of the unborn child; it represents a societal judgment about the degree of culpability of the mother. The law provides very different penalties for the secretive, hardened assassin who kills for cash, the angered spouse who kills during a family quarrel, the driver who causes the death of another by accident, or the individual whom duress or disturbance has made incapable either of avoiding the killing or of appreciating the significance of the act. The punishment ranges from death to probation to nothing at all, but this represents no judgment by the legislature or the judiciary that any of the victims were other than persons equal before the law.

In the context of abortion, society may reasonably conclude that most women who seek it are in a situation of immense stress and pressure, and that few of them are aware of the full humanity of the child within the womb. Society may reasonably choose to regard the woman as a second victim rather than a perpetrator and instead punish the professional who performs abortions for money. Since anyone who performs an abortion is culpable, this does not diminish protection for the unborn child. Indeed, as a practical matter, it may increase that protection for it allows a prosecutor to employ the woman's testimony against the abortionist.

The second "inconsistency" is explained by the response to the first. Justice Blackmun objected that the penalty for abortion is less than that for murder. "If the fetus is a person, may the penalties be different?" As Byrn responds,

> The law recognizes "degrees of evil" and states may treat offenders accordingly. Killing an unborn child may, in legislative judgment, involve less personal malice than killing a child after birth even though the result is the same—just as, for instance, a legislature may choose to categorize, as something less than murder, intentional killing under the influence of extreme emotional disturbance or intentionally aiding and abetting a suicide. Such legislative recognitions of degrees of malice in killing have nothing to do with the fourteenth amendment personhood of the victims.[32]

The Court opined that together with its observation that "throughout the major portion of the nineteenth century prevailing legal practices were far freer than they are today," these four arguments led to the conclusion that the unborn are not Fourteenth Amendment persons. The Court's historical flaws have been amply documented and, as shown, the four arguments that constitute its "strict constructionist" approach to the Fourteenth Amendment's use of "person" fail on their own grounds.

How *should* the Court have construed the term "person" in the Fourteenth Amendment? It could have referred to the test for personhood it had previously enunciated in *Levy v. Louisiana:* Persons are those who "are humans, live, and have their being." It could have looked at the legislative history of the Fourteenth Amendment and to the words of its sponsor, John Bingham. Under the Amendment, he said during the congressional debates, "[a] State has not the right to deny equal protection to every human being." In reaction to the exclusion of blacks from constitutional protection, the post-Civil War Congress sought to establish once and for all that every biological human being within the national jurisdiction could be entitled to the equal protection of the laws, without allowing any other discriminating criteria. A number of law review articles have carefully argued this point. Unfortunately, all of this argument and evidence was totally ignored by the Supreme Court.

V. THE BEGINNING OF HUMAN LIFE

Justice Blackmun acknowledged that even if the unborn lack Fourteenth Amendment protection, a legislature might still assert a compelling interest in prenatal life. In response he argued that no consensus exists on the temporal origin of human life. His effort "to note…the wide divergence of thinking" on "when life begins" is sprinkled with factual errors: incorrect citation of a medical textbook concerning the range of gestational ages associated with viability, a mistaken statement of "Roman Catholic dogma," a rendering of the decision of certain influential medical advocates of abortifacients who wanted to redefine "conception" to mean "implantation" as "new embryological data that purport to indicate that conception is a 'process' over time," and thus posing "substantial problems" for the view that life begins at conception.

Its larger failure lies in a basic misunderstanding of the nature of the debate. Two pages purporting to summarize the views of the Stoics, various religions, and physicians, together with a cursory summary of the treatment of the unborn in various areas of the law, constitute the evidence mustered in support of what are probably the two best known sentences in *Roe:*

> We need not resolve the difficult question of when life begins. When those trained in the respective disciplines of medicine, philosophy, and theology are unable to arrive at any consensus, the judiciary, at this point in the development of man's knowledge, is not in a position to speculate as to the answer.

The Court's conclusion, together with the jumbled "divergence of thinking" it cites on the matter, confuse two distinct questions. One is the strictly scientific question of when a human being comes into existence. The other is the ethical, sociological, and legal question of what value to place on that existence: whether all human beings ought to be regarded as equal in their entitlement to rights or whether those rights should be accorded only to human beings who possess certain qualities such as certain levels of self-consciousness, societal interaction, or the like. The first question was a subject of legitimate dispute before the scientific discoveries of the nineteenth century—which explains some of the "diversity" Justice Blackmun recounts. The second question is admittedly being disputed today, and that accounts for the bulk of the "diversity."

The first question is now settled, however. There is an unequivocal consensus among informed scientists that fertilization constitutes the coming into existence of an individual human organism.[33] And the second question, although far from settled in contemporary America, ought as a legal matter to be regarded as settled by the value judgment incorporated in the Fourteenth Amendment that all biological human beings are to be accorded equal protection of law. As Dr. Harrison has warned, "[t]o substitute consensus for soundness as the criterion by which to decide the worth of an argument is to admit a principle of irrationality into the decision-making process. That the issue being decided is as far-reaching in its consequences as is the abortion problem only compounds the damage."[34]

Even taking the Court at its word about the unsettled and unsettleable nature of the controversy, a number of commentators have found the implications of its reasoning extraordinary and its derived holdings inconsistent. One commentator writes,

> What the Court does seem to have said is that the question of when life begins is an extremely unsettled and controversial issue, and for that reason alone, any legislative purpose that is based on a purported resolution of the issue is irrational...This is an extremely strict requirement that

affords the judiciary a powerful weapon to use against legislation that it finds offensive in some manner, for few issues that reach the Supreme Court are demonstrably noncontroversial.[35]

Taking note of Blackmun's ultimate conclusion, that no legislature may "by adopting one theory of life…override the rights of the pregnant woman that are at stake," Richard Epstein protests "this formulation of the issue begged the important question; because it assumes that we know that the woman's rights must prevail even before the required balance takes place. We could as well claim that the Court, by adopting another theory of life, has decided to override the rights of the unborn child which the law of Texas tries to protect… [I]t is simple fiat and power that gives his position its legal effect."[36]

Indeed, Blackmun's laconic assumption that the lack of consensus means not that the matter must be left to the legislatures, but that abortion must be permitted has been subject to as much criticism as the initial holding that the right of privacy includes abortion. Commentator after commentator has noted that his balancing as presented by the Court is quite arbitrary, and has no warrant in the Constitution. "[T]he Court's decision lacks legitimacy," writes Erwin Chemerinsky, who is sympathetic to its result, "because it seems to be an arbitrary, unjustified set of choices."[37] "The quintessence of a balancing test," Elliott Silverstein points out, "is the formulation of the rights and interests on both sides. If one side is ignored or slighted, the judicial process becomes a mere exercise in sophistry…If the Court really means, when it says it need not decide when life begins, that it need not recognize the State's valid interest in instilling respect for life, then *Roe* is, indeed, a dangerous precedent."[38]

VI. THE TRIMESTER APPROACH: JUDICIAL LEGISLATION

The final portion of the decision, with its line drawing by convenient trimesters, and its weighting of state interests by medical statistics, has been almost universally recognized as legislation pure and simple. "Neither historian, layman, nor lawyer," says Archibald Cox, "will be persuaded that all the details prescribed in *Roe v. Wade* are part of either natural law or the Constitution."[39]

The decision is an excellent example of the problems with the judiciary as legislature. As Ely says, the opinion draws "lines with an apparent precision one generally associates with a commission's regulations. A commissioner can readily redraw regulations on the basis of a better understanding of the facts or purely for administrative convenience. However, what the Court writes is graven in constitutional stone and can only be altered by constitutional amendment or Court reversal. The Court's lines in *Roe,* where they are not arbitrary, are grounded in questionable or changeable data."[40]

Why did the Court conclude that the state could regulate on behalf of maternal health only after the second trimester? Apparently because it was persuaded that abortion is safer than childbirth during the first trimester. Yet, Hilgers and O'Hare have shown that the mortality statistics relied on by the Court give an inaccurate measure of the comparative safety of abortion and childbirth.[41] The Court's exclusive reliance on mortality figures quite ignored the question of morbidity, and there is abundant evidence of physical and psychological problems short of death associated with abortion. Even were they correct, the assumptions provide no basis for concluding that there is no state interest in health regulations during the first trimester. "The Court gave no reason why it should make a difference whether it is safer to undergo an abortion or carry the pregnancy to full term," writes one commentator. "[T]hough it may be safer for a particular patient to undergo open heart surgery than to forego the operation and do nothing, the state still has an interest in ensuring that if the patient chooses to have the operation, it is performed as safely as possible."[42] Thus, as Arnold Loewy says, "[t]he fact that abortion [during the first trimester] is safer than childbirth is irrelevant unless the Court is also holding that such regulation in regard to childbirth would be unconstitutional."[43] John Hart Ely's comment is written in tones of astonishment: "[e]ven a sure sense that abortion during the first trimester is safer than childbirth would serve only to blunt a state's claim that it is, for reasons relating to maternal health, entitled to *proscribe* abortion; it would not support the inference the Court draws, that *regulations designed to make the abortion procedure safer* during the first trimester are impermissible."[44]

The only plausible basis for the Court's ruling that the first trimester remain free of health regulation is what Robert Destro calls, "the Court's concern that state health regulations might turn into 'roadblocks' barring access to legalized abortion."[45] Because medical practices and skills change over time, a practical effect of the Court's analysis is to render this aspect of the constitutional test of abortion statutes subject to a variable technological standard. An abortion statute that is constitutional today may be unconstitutional tomorrow as a result of changes in medical techniques.

The Court went on to choose viability as the point in pregnancy after which states could actually prohibit abortion, unless a physician then judged it necessary for the life or health of the mother. As we have seen, this distinction is illusory; with "health" as broadly defined as the Court requires, there is no practical difference between it and abortion on demand. However, the Court clearly sought to give the impression that viability does make a difference, and commentators have persistently observed that Justice Blackmun did not, or could not, say *why.* The opinion says that "the fetus then presumably has the capability of meaningful life outside the mother's womb" and therefore drawing a line at viability "thus has both logical and biological justifications." The ruling made no attempt to detail what "meaningful life" is, why the capability for it is significant, or what the "logical and biological justifications" might be. If the capacity for independent life was to be the criterion, that capacity certainly does not occur at viability. Any newborn infant is totally dependent on others for food, shelter, and care. Certainly, when the Court recognized that "artificial means might be used to make a newborn "viable," it contemplated incubators and other extraordinary medical support systems on which the child would be utterly dependent.

The changeability of the capacity of medical science is even more pronounced in the case of viability than in that of abortion and childbirth safety. Remarkable progress has been made in recent decades in pushing back the time of viability. This means that a child of the same intrinsic development is subject to disposal or protection depending solely on when he or she is conceived. Such an arbitrary dependency on things wholly extrinsic to the individual in determining whether the individual has value and is worthy of protection is wholly indefensible.

VII. CONCLUSION

The Court's majority opinion in *Roe v. Wade* is riddled with factual errors and logical incongruities. Its analysis is as poor as its results are tragic. The thoroughness and breadth of the criticisms directed at *Roe* fully justify the conclusion of Justice Sandra Day O'Connor that "*Roe*...is clearly on a collision course with itself...[It has] no justification in law or logic."

STUDY QUESTIONS

1. Briefly review Horan and Balch's historical critique of *Roe v. Wade*. Do you think such a critique is important in evaluating the legal acceptability of *Roe*?

2. Justice Blackmun argued that the right to abortion is based constitutionally on the right to privacy. How do Horan and Balch respond to this contention? Do you think they succeed in their response? Why or why not?

3. What is Horan and Balch's assessment of the Court's conclusion about the value of fetal life? Do you agree or disagree with their assessment? Why or why not?

4. Horan and Balch criticize the Court for engaging in legislation in its trimester breakdown of pregnancy. Briefly present their argument against the Court. Do you think it succeeds? Why or why not?

NOTES

1. *Editor's Preface, Symposium on the Law and Politics of Abortion* 77 Michigan Law Review, unpaginated preceding 1569 (1979).

2. Morgan, *Roe v. Wade and the Lesson of the Pre-Roe Case Law,* 77 Michigan Law Review 1724, 1724 (1979) (footnotes omitted).

3. Dellapenna, The History of Abortion: Technology, Morality, and the Law, 40 University of Pittsburgh Law Review 359, 361 n. 11 (1979).

4. Heyman and Barzelay, *The Forest and the Trees: Roe v. Wade and its Critics,* 53, Boston University Law Review 384 (1973).

5. Cox, *The Role of the Supreme Court in American Government.* New York: Oxford University Press, 113–114 (1976). *See also* Epstein, *Substantive Due Process by Any Other Name,* 1973 Sup. Ct. Rev. 159, 184.

6. *Doe v. Bolton,* 410 U.S. 179, 191–192 (1973).

7. Ely, *The Wages of Crying Wolf: A Comment on Roe v. Wade,* 82 Yale Law Journal 921 n.19 (1973) (emphasis in original).

8. See S. Krason & Hollberg, *The Law and History of Abortion: The Supreme Court Refuted* (1984); and Special Project, *Survey of Abortion Law,* 1980 Ariz. St. L. J. 67, 77.

9. Quay, *Justifiable Abortion—Medical and Legal Foundations* (Pt. 2) 49 Georgetown Law Journal 395 (1961) cited in *Roe v. Wade,* 410 U.S. H3, 130 n.9 (1973).

10. See also Brown, *What the Supreme Court Didn't Know: Ancient and Early Christian Views on Abortion,* 1 Human Life Rev. 5, 13 (1975).

11. Quotation is from text delivered at American United for Life conference Chicago, March 31, 1984.

12. Dellapenna, *supra* note 12, at 367 and n. 46 (1974).

13. *Id.* at 368.

14. Destro, *Abortion and the Constitution. The Need for a Life-Protective Amendment,* 63 California Law Review 1273 (1975).

15. Byrn, *An American Tragedy: The Supreme Court on Abortion* 41 Fordham Law Review 827 (1973).

16. *The Human Life Bill Hearings on S. 158 Before the Subcomm. on Separation of Powers of the Senate Comm. on the judiciary,* 97th Cong., 1st Sess. 474 (statement of Victor Rosenblum, Professor of Law, Northwestern University).

17. Dellapenna, *supra* note 3, at 389.

18. Gorby, *The "Right" to an Abortion, the Scope of Fourteenth Amendment "Personhood" and the Supreme Court's Birth Requirement,* 1979 Southern Illinois Law Review 1, 16–17 n. 84; Destro, *supra* note 14, at 1273–1275.

19. Gorby, *supra* note 18, at 20.

20. Sauer, *Attitudes to Abortion in America, 1800–1973,* 28 Population Studies 58 (1974).

21. Vieira, *Roe and Doe: Substantive Due Process and the Right of Abortion,* 25 Hastings Law Journal 867, 873 (1974).

22. Ely, *supra* note 7, at 932, 935–936 (footnotes omitted).

23. Cox, *supra* note 5, at 113.

24. Posner, *The Uncertain Protection of Privacy by the Supreme Court,* 1979 Supreme Court Review 173, 199 (footnotes omitted).

25. O'Meara, *Abortion: The Court Decides a Non-Case,* 1974 Supreme Court Review 337, 340.

26. Ely, *supra* note 7, at 926.

27. *Id.,* at 925–926.

28. Gorby, *supra* note 18, at 11–12.

29. Comment, Roe v. Wade—*The Abortion Decision—An Analysis and Its Implications,* 10 San Diego Law Review 844, 855 (1973).

30. *See Santa Clara County v. Southern Pacific Railroad Co.,* 118 U.S. 394, 396 (1886); Destro, *supra* note 14, at 1284; Byrn, *supra* note 15, at 852–853.

31. Epstein, *Substantive Due Process by Any Other Name,* 1973 Supreme Court Review 159.

32. Byrn, *supra* note 15, at 855.

33. The evidence for the existence of individual human life from the time of fertilization has been set forth in cogent detail in the 1981 report of the Senate Judiciary Committee's Subcommittee on Separation of Powers on the Human Life Bill. Subcomm. on Separation of Powers, Senate Comm. on the Judiciary, The Human Life Bill—S. 158, 97th Cong., 1st Sess. 7–13 (1981).

34. Harrison, *The Supreme Court and Abortion Reform Means to an End,* 19 New York Law Forum 691(1974).

35. Comment, Roe v. Wade—*Abortion Decision-An Analysis and Its Implications, supra* note 29, at 850–851.

36. Epstein, *supra* note 31, at 182.

37. Chemerinsky, *Rationalizing the Abortion Debate: Legal Rhetoric and the Abortion Controversy,* 31 Buffalo Law Review 142 (1982).

38. Silverstein, *From Comstockery Through Population Control: Inevitability of Balancing*

6 North Carolina Central law Journal 39–40 (1974).

39. Cox, *supra* note 5, at 114.

40. Ely, *supra* note 7, at 921 n. 19 (emphasis in original).

41. Hilgers & O'Hare, *Abortion Related Maternal Mortality: An In-Depth Analysis,* in New Perspectives on Human Abortion. Hilgers, Horan, and Mall, eds. Washington D.C.: University Publications of America, 1981 69–91.

42. Comment, *Technological Advances and Roe v. Wade: The Need to Rethink Abortion Law,* 29 U.C.L.A. Law Review 1194, 1199 n. 41 (1982).

43. Loewy, *Abortive Reasons and Obscene Standards: A Comment on the Abortion and Obscenity Cases,* 52 North Carolina Law Review 233, n. 58 (1973).

44. Ely, *supra* note 7, at 942 n. 117 (emphasis in original).

45. Destro, *supra* note 14, at 1294.

5

Roe v. Wade: A Study in Male Ideology

CATHARINE MACKINNON

Catharine MacKinnon is Professor of Law at the University of Michigan Law School in Ann Arbor, Michigan.

In this essay, Professor MacKinnon, a prochoice advocate, argues that Roe, *because it was based on the constitutional right to privacy, assumed a view of female sexuality held by both the liberal proponents and the conservative opponents of abortion rights: Women control their sexual behavior. By keeping the sex act behind the veil of "privacy," MacKinnon believes that* Roe *reinforces male control of female sexuality because women do not in truth freely choose to engage in sexual intercourse. Now that the possibility of childbirth is eliminated because of legalized abortion, MacKinnon argues, "the availability of abortion thus removes the one remaining legitimized reason that women have had for refusing sex besides the headache." As long as women are "forced" by male ideology to engage in sexual intercourse (even though women may think they have freely engaged in it), basing the right to abortion on the right to privacy, as the Court did in* Roe, *does not truly liberate women. According to MacKinnon, the right to privacy does not protect women from marital rape, battery, or exploitation.*

Reprinted from Catharine A. MacKinnon, *Feminism Unmodified: Discourses on Life and Law.* (Cambridge: Harvard University Press, 1987). Reprinted by permission.

In a society where women entered sexual intercourse willingly, where adequate contraception was a genuine social priority, there would be no abortion issue…Abortion is violence…It is the offspring, and will continue to be the accuser of a more pervasive and prevalent violence, the violence of rapism. Adrienne Rich, *Of Woman Born* (1976)

Roe v. Wade[1] guaranteed the right to choose abortion, subject to some countervailing considerations, by conceiving it as a private choice, included in the constitutional right to privacy. In this critique of that decision, I first situate abortion and the abortion right in the experience of women. The argument is that abortion is inextricable from sexuality, assuming that the feminist analysis of sexuality is our analysis of gender in-equality. I then criticize the doctrinal choice to pursue the abortion right under the law of privacy. The argument is that privacy doctrine reaffirms and reinforces what the feminist critique of sexuality criticizes: the public/private split. The political and ideological meaning of privacy as a legal doctrine is connected with the concrete consequences of the public/private split for the lives of women. This analysis makes *Harris v. McRae*,[2] in which public funding for abortions was held not to be required, appear consistent with the larger meaning of *Roe*.

I will neglect two important explorations, which I bracket now. The first is this: What are babies to men? On one level, men respond to women's rights to abort as if confronting the possibility of their own potential nonexistence—at *women's* hands, no less. On another level, men's issues of potency, of continuity as a compensation for mortality, of the thrust to embody themselves or their own image in the world, underlie their relation to babies (as well as to most else). To overlook these meanings of abortion to men as men is to overlook political and strategic as well as fundamental theoretical issues and to misassess where much of the opposition to abortion is coming from. The second issue I bracket is one that, unlike the first, has been discussed extensively in the abortion debate: the moral rightness of abortion itself. My stance is that the abortion choice must be legally available and must be *women's*, but not because the fetus is not a form of life. In the usual argument, the abortion decision is made contingent on whether the fetus is a form of life. I cannot follow that. Why should women not make life or death decisions? This returns us to the first bracketed issue.

The issues I will explore have largely not been discussed in the terms I will use. Instead, I think, women's embattled need to survive in a world hostile to our survival has precluded our exploring these issues as I am about to. That is, the perspective from which we have addressed abortion has been shaped and constrained by the very situation that the abortion issue puts us in and requires us to address. We have not been able to risk thinking about these issues on our own terms because the terms have not been ours. The attempt to grasp women's situation on our own terms, from our own point of view, defines the feminist impulse. If doing that is risky, our situation also makes it risky not to. So, first feminism, then law.

Most women who seek abortions became pregnant while having sexual intercourse with men. Most did not mean or wish to conceive. In contrast to this fact of women's experience, which converges sexuality with reproduction with gender, the abortion debate has centered on separating control over sexuality from control over reproduction, and on separating both from gender and the life options of the sexes. Liberals have supported the availability of the abortion choice as if the woman just happened on the fetus. The political right, imagining that the intercourse preceding conception is usually voluntary, urges abstinence, as if sex were up to women, while defending male authority, specifically including a wife's duty to submit to sex. Continuing with this logic, many opponents of state funding of abortions, such as supporters of some versions of the Hyde Amendment, would permit funding of abortions when pregnancy results from rape or incest.[3] They make *exceptions* for those special occasions during which they presume women did *not* control sex. From all this I deduce that abortion's proponents and opponents share a tacit assumption that women significantly do control sex.

Feminist investigations suggest otherwise. Sexual intercourse, still the most common cause of pregnancy, cannot simply be presumed co-equally determined. Feminism has found that women feel compelled to preserve the appearance—which, acted upon, becomes the reality—of male direction of sexual expression, as if male initiative itself were what we want, as if it were that which turns us on. Men enforce this. It is much of what men want in a woman. It is what pornography eroticizes and prostitutes provide. Rape—that is, intercourse with force that is recognized as force—is adjudicated not according to the power or force that the man wields, but according to indices of intimacy between the parties. The more intimate you are with your accused rapist, the less likely a court is to find that what happened to you was rape. Often indices of intimacy include intercourse itself. If "no" can be taken as "yes," how free can "yes" be?

Under these conditions, women often do not use birth control because of its social meaning, a meaning we did not create. Using contraception means acknowledging and planning the possibility of intercourse, accepting one's sexual availability, and appearing nonspontaneous. It means appearing available to male incursions. A good user of contraception can be presumed sexually available and, among other consequences, raped with relative impunity. (If you think this isn't true, you should consider rape cases in which the fact that a woman had a diaphragm in is taken as an indication that what happened to her was intercourse, not rape. "Why did you have your diaphragm in?") From studies of abortion clinics, women who repeatedly seek abortions (and now I'm looking at the repeat offenders high on the list of the right's villains, their best case for opposing abortion as female irresponsibility), when asked why, say something like, "The sex just happened." Like every night for two and a half years.[4] I wonder if a woman can be presumed to control access to her sexuality if she feels unable to interrupt intercourse to insert a diaphragm; or worse, cannot even want to, aware that she risks a pregnancy she knows she does not want. Do you think she would stop the man for any other reason, such as, for instance, the real taboo—lack of desire? If she would not, how is sex, hence its consequences, meaningfully voluntary for women? Norms of sexual rhythm and romance that are felt interrupted by women's needs are constructed against women's interests. Sex doesn't look a whole lot like freedom when it appears normatively less costly for women to risk an undesired, often painful, traumatic, dangerous, sometimes illegal, and potentially life-threatening procedure than to protect themselves in advance. Yet abortion policy has never been explicitly approached in the context of how women get pregnant, that is, as a consequence of intercourse under conditions of gender inequality: that is, as an issue of forced sex.

Now, law. In 1973 *Roe v. Wade* found that a statute that made criminal all abortions except those to save the life of the mother violated the constitutional right to privacy.[5] The privacy right had been previously created as a constitutional principle in a case that decriminalized the prescription and use of contraceptives.[6] Note that courts use the privacy rubric to connect contraception with abortion through privacy in the same way that I just did through sexuality. In *Roe* that right to privacy was found "broad enough to encompass a woman's decision whether or not to terminate her pregnancy." In 1977 three justices observed, "In the abortion context, we have held that the right to privacy shields the woman from undue state intrusion in and external scrutiny of her very personal choice."[7]

In 1981 the Supreme Court in *Harris v. McRae* decided that this right to privacy did not mean that federal Medicaid programs had to fund medically necessary abortions. Privacy, the Court had said, was guaranteed for "a woman's *decision* whether or not to terminate her pregnancy." The Court then permitted the government to support one decision and not another: to fund continuing conceptions and not to fund discontinuing them. Asserting that decisional privacy was nevertheless constitutionally intact, the Court stated that "although the government may not place obstacles in the path of a woman's exercise of her freedom of choice, it need not remove those not of its own creation."[8] It is apparently a very short step from that which the government has a duty *not* to intervene in to that which it has *no* duty to intervene in.

The idea of privacy, if regarded as the outer edge of the limitations on government, embodies, I think, a tension between the preclusion of public exposure or governmental intrusion, on the one hand, and autonomy in the sense of protecting personal self-action on the other. This is a tension, not just two facets of one whole right. In the liberal state this tension is resolved by demarking the threshold of the state at its permissible extent of penetration into a domain that is considered free by definition: the private sphere. It is by this move that the state secures to individuals what has been termed "an inviolable personality" by ensuring what has been called "autonomy or control over the intimacies of personal identity."[9] The state does this by centering its self-restraint on body and home, especially bedroom. By staying out of marriage and the family, prominently meaning sexuality—that is to say, heterosexuality—from contraception through pornography to the abortion decision, the law of privacy proposes to guarantee individual bodily integrity, personal exercise of moral intelligence, and freedom of intimacy.[10] But if one asks whether *women's* rights to these values have been guaranteed, it appears that the law of privacy works to translate traditional social values into the rhetoric of individual rights as a means of subordinating those rights to specific social imperatives.[11] In feminist terms, I am arguing that the logic of *Roe* consummated in *Harris* translates the ideology of the private sphere into the individual woman's legal right to privacy as a means of subordinating women's collective needs to the imperatives of male supremacy.

This is my retrospective on *Roe v. Wade*. Reproduction is sexual, men control sexuality, and the state supports the interest of men as a group. *Roe* does not contradict this. So why was abortion legalized? Why were women even imagined to have such a right as privacy? It is not an accusation of bad faith to answer that the interests of men as a social group converged with the definition of justice embodied in law in what I call the male point of view. The way the male point of view constructs a social event or legal need will be the way that social event or legal need is framed by state policy. For example, to the extent that possession is the point of sex, illegal rape will be sex with a woman who is not yours unless the act makes her yours. If part of the kick of pornography involves eroticizing the putatively prohibited, illegal pornography—obscenity—will be prohibited enough to keep pornography desirable without ever making it truly illegitimate or unavailable. If, from the male standpoint, male is the implicit definition of human, maleness will be the implicit standard by which sex equality is measured in discrimination law. In parallel terms, abortion's availability frames, and is framed by, the conditions men work out among themselves to grant legitimacy to women to control the reproductive consequences of intercourse.

Since Freud, the social problem posed by sexuality has been perceived as the problem of the innate desire for sexual pleasure being repressed by the constraints of civilization. In this context, the inequality of the sexes arises as an issue only in women's repressive socialization to passivity and coolness (so-called frigidity), in women's so-called desexualization, and in the disparate consequences of biology, that is, pregnancy. Who defines what is sexual, what sexuality therefore is, to whom what stimuli are erotic and why, and who defines the conditions under which sexuality is expressed—these issues are not even available to be considered. "Civilization's" answer to these questions fuses women's reproductivity with our attributed sexuality in its definition of what a woman is. We are defined as women by the uses to which men put us. In this context it becomes clear why the struggle for reproductive freedom has never included a woman's right to refuse sex. In this notion of sexual liberation, the equality issue has been framed as a struggle for women to have sex with men on the same terms as men: "without consequences." In this sense the abortion right has been sought as freedom from the reproductive consequences of sexual expression, with sexuality defined as centered on heterosexual genital intercourse. It is as if biological organisms, rather than social relations, reproduced the species. But if your concern is not how more people can get more sex, but who defines sexuality—pleasure and violation both—then the abortion right is situated within a very different problematic: the social and political problematic of the inequality of the sexes. As Susan Sontag said, "Sex itself is not liberating for women. Neither is more sex....The question is, what sexuality shall women be liberated to enjoy?"[12] To address this requires reformulating the problem of sexuality from the repression of drives by civilization to the oppression of women by men.

Arguments for abortion under the rubric of feminism have rested on the right to control one's own body—gender neutral. I think that argument has been appealing for the same reasons it is inadequate: socially, women's bodies have not been ours; we have not controlled their meanings and destinies. Feminists tried to assert that control without risking pursuit of the idea that something more might be at stake than our bodies, something closer to a net of relations in which we are (at present unescapably) gendered.[13] Some feminists have noticed that our right to decide has become merged with the right of an overwhelmingly male profession's right not to have its professional judgment second-guessed by the government.[14] But most abortion advocates argue in rigidly and rigorously gender-neutral terms.

Thus, for instance, Judith Jarvis Thomson's argument that an abducted woman had no obligation to be a celebrated violinist's life support system meant that women have no obligation to support a fetus.[15] The parallel seems misframed. No woman who needs an abortion—no woman, period—is valued, no potential a woman's life might hold is cherished, like a gender-neutral famous violinist's unencumbered possibilities. The problems of gender are thus underlined here rather than solved, or even addressed. Too, the underlying recognition in the parallel of the origin of the problem in rape—the origin in force, in abduction, that gives the hypothetical much of its moral weight—would confine abortions to instances in which force is recognized as force, like rape or incest. The applicability of this to the normal case of abortion is neither embraced nor disavowed, although the parallel was meant to apply to the normal case, as is abortion policy, usually. This parable is constructed precisely to begin the debate after sex occurred, yet even it requires discussion of intercourse in relation to rape in relation to conception, in order to make sense. Because this issue has been studiously avoided in the abortion context, the unequal basis on which woman's personhood is being constructed is obscured.

In the context of a sexual critique of gender inequality, abortion promises to women sex with men on the same reproductive terms as men have sex with women. So long as women do not control access to our sexuality, abortion facilitates women's heterosexual availability. In other words, under conditions of gender inequality sexual liberation in this sense does not free women; it frees male sexual aggression. The availability of abortion removes the one remaining legitimized reason that women have had for refusing sex besides the headache. As Andrea Dworkin put it, analyzing male ideology on abortion, "Getting laid was at stake."[16] The Playboy Foundation has supported abortion rights from day one; it continues to, even with shrinking disposable funds, on a level of priority comparable to that of its opposition to censorship.

Privacy doctrine is an ideal vehicle for this process. The liberal ideal of the private—and privacy as an ideal has been formulated in liberal terms-holds that, so long as the public does not interfere, autonomous individuals interact freely and equally. Conceptually, this private is hermetic. It *means* that which is inaccessible to, unaccountable to, unconstructed by anything beyond itself. By definition, it is not part of or conditioned by anything systematic or outside of it. It is personal, intimate, autonomous, particular, individual, the original source and final outpost of the self, gender neutral. It is, in short, defined by everything that feminism reveals women have never been allowed to be or to have, and everything that women have been equated with and defined in terms of *men's* ability to have. To complain in public of inequality within it contradicts the liberal definition of the private. In this view, no act of the state contributes to—hence should properly participate in—shaping the internal alignments of the private or distributing its internal forces. Its inviolability by the state, framed as an individual right, presupposes that the private is not already an arm of the state. In this scheme, intimacy is implicitly thought to guarantee symmetry of power. Injuries arise in violating the private sphere, not within and by and because of it.

In private, consent tends to be presumed. It is true that a showing of coercion voids this presumption. But the problem is getting anything private to be perceived as coercive. Why one would allow force in private—the "why doesn't she leave" question asked of battered women—is a question given its urgency by the social meaning of the private as a sphere of choice. But for women the measure of the intimacy has been the measure of the oppression. This is why feminism has had to explode the private. This is why feminism has seen the personal as the political. The private is the public for those for whom the personal is the political. In this sense, there is no private, either normatively or empirically. Feminism confronts the fact that women have no privacy to lose or to guarantee. We are not inviolable. Our sexuality is not only violable, it is—hence, we are—seen *in* and *as* our violation. To confront the fact that we have no privacy is to confront the intimate degradation of women as the public order.

In this light, a right to privacy looks like an injury got up as a gift. Freedom from public intervention coexists uneasily with any right that requires social preconditions to be meaningfully delivered. For example, if inequality is socially pervasive and enforced, equality will require intervention, not abdication, to be meaningful. But the right to privacy is not thought to require social change. It is not even thought to require any social preconditions, other than nonintervention by the public. The point of this for the abortion cases is not that indigency—which was the specific barrier to effective choice in *Harris*—is well within the public power to remedy, nor that the state is exempt in issues of the distribution of wealth. The point is rather that *Roe v. Wade* presumes that government nonintervention into the private sphere promotes a woman's freedom of choice. When the alternative is jail, there is much to be said for this argument. But the *Harris* result sustains the ultimate meaning of privacy in *Roe:* Women are guaranteed by the public no more than what we can get in private—that is, what we can extract through our intimate associations with men. Women with privileges get rights.

So women got abortion as a private privilege, not as a public right. We got control over reproduction that is controlled by "a man or The Man," an individual man or the doctors or the government. Abortion was not decriminalized; it was legalized. In *Roe* the government set the stage for the conditions under which women gain access to this right. Virtually every ounce of control that women won out of this legalization has gone directly into the hands of men—husbands, doctors, or fathers—or is now in the process of attempts to reclaim it through regulation.[17] This, surely, must be what is meant by reform.

It is not inconsistent, then, that framed as a privacy right, a woman's decision to abort would have no claim on public support and would genuinely not be seen as burdened by that deprivation. Privacy conceived as a right against public intervention and disclosure is the opposite of the relief that *Harris* sought for welfare women. State intervention would have provided a choice women did *not* have in private. The women in *Harris,* women whose sexual refusal has counted for particularly little, needed something to make their privacy effective.[18] The logic of the Court's response resembles the logic by which women are supposed to consent to sex. Preclude the alternatives, then call the sole remaining option "her choice." The point is that the alternatives are precluded *prior to* the reach of the chosen legal doctrine. They are precluded by conditions of sex, race, and class—the very conditions the privacy frame not only leaves tacit but exists to *guarantee.*

When the law of privacy restricts intrusions into intimacy, it bars change in control over that intimacy. The existing distribution of power and resources within the private sphere will be precisely what the law of privacy exists to protect. It is probably not coincidence that the very things feminism regards as central to the subjection of women—the very place, the body; the very relations, heterosexual; the very activities, intercourse and reproduction; and the very feelings, intimate—form the core of what is covered by privacy doctrine. From this perspective, the legal concept of privacy can and has shielded the place of battery, marital rape, and women's exploited labor; has preserved the central institutions whereby women are *deprived* of identity, autonomy, control and self-definition; and has protected the primary activity through which male supremacy is expressed and enforced. Just as pornography is legally protected as individual freedom of expression—without questioning whose freedom and whose expression and at whose expense—abstract privacy protects abstract autonomy, without inquiring into whose freedom of action is being sanctioned at whose expense.

To fail to recognize the meaning of the private in the ideology and reality of women's subordination by seeking protection behind a right *to* that privacy is to cut women off from collective verification and state support in the same act. I think this has a lot to do with why we can't organize women on the abortion issue. When women are segregated in private, separated from each other, one at a time, a right to that privacy isolates us at once from each other and from public recourse. This right to privacy is a right of men "to be let alone"[19] to oppress women one at a time. It embodies and reflects the private sphere's existing definition of womanhood. This is an instance of liberalism called feminism, liberalism applied to women as if we *are* persons, gender neutral. It reinforces the division between public and private that is *not* gender neutral. It is at once an ideological division that lies about women's shared experience and that mystifies the unity among the spheres of women's violation. It is a very material division that keeps the private beyond public redress and depoliticizes women's subjection within it. It keeps some men out of the bedrooms of other men.

STUDY QUESTIONS

1. Why does Professor MacKinnon believe that *Roe v. Wade*'s reliance on the right to privacy helps to reinforce traditional sexist notions of the relationship between men and women? Do you agree with her? Why or why not?

2. Why does Professor MacKinnon believe that the right to privacy does not protect women from marital rape, battery, or exploitation? Do you agree with her? Why or why not?

3. MacKinnon writes: "In this notion of sexual liberation, the equality issue has been framed as a struggle for women to have sex with men on the same terms as men: without consequences." Why does MacKinnon believe this notion of sexual liberation applies to the issue of abortion rights for women? And why does MacKinnon believe that this notion is inevitably harmful and oppressive to women? What are your thoughts on this matter?

NOTES

1. See my article, Feminism, Marxism, Method and the State," *Signs* 8 (1983): 635–658.

2. This is not to suggest that the decision should have gone the other way, or to propose individual hearings to determine coercion prior to allowing abortions. Nor is it to criticize Justice Blackmun, author of the majority opinion in *Roe,* who probably saw legalizing abortion as a way to help women out of a desperate situation, which it has done.

3. As of 1973, ten states that made abortion a crime had exceptions for rape and incest; at least three had exceptions for rape only. Many of these exceptions were based on Model Penal Code Section 230.3 (Proposed Official Draft 1962), quoted in *Doe v. Bolton,* 410 U.S. 179, 205–207, App. B (1973), permitting abortion, *inter alia,* in cases of rape, incest, or other felonious intercourse. References to states with incest and rape exceptions can be found in *Roe v. Wade,* 410 U.S. 113 n. 37 (1973). Some versions of the Hyde Amendment, which prohibits use of public money to fund abortions, have contained exceptions for cases of rape or incest. All require immediate reporting of the incident.

4. Kristin Luker, *Taking Chance's: Abortion and the Decision Not to Contracept.* Berkeley and Los Angeles: University of California Press, 1976.

5. *Roe v. Wade,* 410 U.S. 113 (1973).

6. *Griswold v. Connecticut,* 381 U.S. 479 (1965).

7. *Eisenstadt v. Baird,* 405 U.S. 438 (1972).

8. *Harris v. McRae,* 448 U.S. 297 (1980).

9. T. Gerety, "Redefining Privacy," *Harvard Civil Rights Civil Liberties Law Review* 12 (1977): 233–296, at 236.

10. Kenneth I. Karst, "The Freedom of Intimate Association," *Yale Law Journal* 89 (1980): 624; "Developments—The Family," *Harvard Law Review* 93 (1980): 1157–1383; *Doe v. Commonwealth Atty,*

403 F. Supp. 1199 (E.D. Va. 1975), *aff'd* without opinion, 425 U.S. 901 (1976) but cf. *People v. Onofre,* 51 N.Y. 2d 476 (1980), *cert. denied* 451 U.S. 987 (1981).

11. Tom Grey, "Eros, Civilization and the Burger Court," *Law and Contemporary Problems* 43 (1980): 83.

12. Susan Sontag, "The Third World of Women," *Partisan Review* 40 (1973): 188.

13. See Adrienne Rich, *Of Woman Born: Motherhood as Experience and Institution.* New York: Bantam Books, 1977, Chapter 3, "The Kingdom of the Fathers," especially pages 47, 48: "The child that I carry for nine months can be defined *neither* as me or as not-me" (emphasis in the original).

14. Kristin Booth Glen, "Abortion in the Courts: A Lay Women's Historical Guide to the New Disaster Area," *Feminist Studies* 4 (1978): 1.

15. Judith Jarvis Thomson, "A Defense of Abortion," *Philosophy and Public Affairs* 1 (1971): 47–66. Republished in this volume as Chapter 7.

16. Andrea Dworkin, *Right Wing Women.* New York: Perigee, 1983. You must read this book. See also Friedrich Engels arguing on removing private housekeeping into social industry, *Origin of the Family, Private Property and the State.* New York: International Publishers, 1942.

17. *H. L. v. Matheson,* 450 U.S. 398 (1981); *Poe v. Gerstein; Bellotti v. Baird,* 443 U.S. 622 (1979); but cf. *Planned Parenthood of Central Missouri v. Danforth,* 428 U.S. 52 (1976).

18. See Dworkin, *Right Wing Women,* 98–99.

19. S. Warren and L. Brandeis, "The Right to Privacy;" *Harvard Law Review* 4 (1890) 190, 205, but note that the right of privacy under some *state* constitutions has been held to *include* funding for abortions: *Committee to Defend Reproductive Rights v. Meyers,* 29 Cal. 3d 252 (1981); *Moe v. Society of Admin. and Finance,* 417 N.E. 2d 387 (Mass. 1981).

6

Some Thoughts on Autonomy and Equality in Relation to *Roe v. Wade*

RUTH BADER GINSBURG

Ruth Bader Ginsburg is an Associate Justice of the United States Supreme Court and is the second woman to be appointed to the Court. (The first was Sandra Day O'Connor, an appointee of President Ronald W. Reagan.) Ginsburg was appointed by President Bill Clinton in June 1993.

In this article, Justice Ginsburg criticizes the Court for basing Roe v. Wade *on the right to privacy rather than on the equal protection clause of the Constitution. She argues that since women are unique in their ability to be burdened by pregnancy, giving men a distinct advantage in social and political advancement, women should have the right to abortion based on the constitutional principle that all people deserve equal protection under the law. Thus, by permitting women to undergo abortions on the basis of the equal protection clause, the Court would have made a clear stand for gender equity on firm constitutional grounds rather than basing its decision on the controversial and constitutionally vague right to privacy.*

These remarks contrast two related areas of constitutional adjudication: gender-based classification and reproductive autonomy. In both areas, the Burger Court, in contrast to the Warren Court, has been uncommonly active. The two areas are intimately related in this practical sense: the law's response to questions subsumed under these headings bears pervasively on the situation

Reprinted from *University of North Carolina Law Review* (1985). Reprinted by permission. Footnotes edited.

of women in society. Inevitably, the shape of the law on gender-based classification and reproductive autonomy indicates and influences the opportunity women will have to participate as men's full partners in the nation's social, political, and economic life.

Doctrine in the two areas, however, has evolved in discrete compartments. The High Court has analyzed classification by gender under an equal protection/sex discrimination rubric; it has treated reproductive autonomy under a substantive due process/personal autonomy headline not expressly linked to discrimination against women. The Court's gender classification decisions overturning state and federal legislation, in the main, have not provoked large controversy; the Court's initial 1973 abortion decision, *Roe v. Wade,* on the other hand, became and remains a storm center. *Roe v. Wade* sparked public opposition and academic criticism, in part, I believe, because the Court ventured too far in the change it ordered and presented an incomplete justification for its action. I will attempt to explain these twin perspectives on *Roe* later in this essay.

Preliminarily, I will relate why an invitation to speak at Chapel Hill on any topic relating to constitutional law led me to think about gender-based classification coupled with *Roe* and its aftermath. In 1971, just before the Supreme Court's turning-point gender-classification decision in *Reed v. Reed,* and over a year before *Roe v. Wade,* I visited a neighboring institution to participate in a conference on women and the law. I spoke then of the utility of litigation attacking official line-drawing by sex. My comments focused on the chance in the 1970s that courts, through constitutional adjudication, would aid in evening out the rights, responsibilities, and opportunities of women and men. I did not mention the abortion cases then on the dockets of several lower courts—I was not at that time or any other time thereafter personally engaged in reproductive-autonomy litigation. Nonetheless, the most heated questions I received concerned abortion.

The questions were pressed by black men. The suggestion, not thinly veiled, was that legislative reform and litigation regarding abortion might have less to do with individual autonomy or discrimination against women than with restricting population growth among oppressed minorities. The strong word "genocide" was uttered more than once. It is a notable irony that, as constitutional law in this domain has unfolded, women who are not poor have achieved access to abortion with relative ease; for poor women, however, a group in which minorities are disproportionately represented, access to abortion is not markedly different from what it was in pre-*Roe* days.

I will summarize first the Supreme Court's performance in cases challenging explicit gender-based classification—a development that has encountered no significant backlash—and then turn to the far more turbulent reproductive autonomy area.

The Warren Court uncabined the equal protection guarantee in diverse settings, but line-drawing by sex was a quarter in which no change occurred in the 1950s and 1960s. From the 1860s until 1971, the record remained unbroken: The Supreme Court rejected virtually every effort to overturn sex-based classification by law. Without offense to the Constitution, for example, women could be kept off juries and could be barred from occupations ranging from lawyer to bartender.

In the 1970s overt sex-based classification fell prey to the Burger Court's intervention. Men could not be preferred to women for estate administration purposes, the Court declared in the pivotal *Reed v. Reed* decision. Married women in the military could not be denied fringe benefit—family housing and health care allowances—accorded married men in military service, the High Court held in *Frontiero v. Richardson*. Social security benefits, welfare assistance, and workers' compensation secured by a male's employment must be secured, to the same extent, by a female's employment, the Supreme Court ruled in a progression of cases: *Weinberger v. Wiesenfeld, Califano v. Goldfarb, Califano v. Westcott,* and *Wengler v. Druggists Mutual Insurance Co.* Girls are entitled to the same parental support as boys, the Supreme Court stated in *Stanton v. Stanton.* Evidencing its neutrality, the Court declared in *Craig v. Boren* that boys must be permitted to buy 3.2 percent beer at the same age as girls and, in *Orr v. Orr,* that alimony could not be retained as a one-way street: A state could compel able men to make payments to women in need only if it also held women of means accountable for payments to men unable to fend for themselves. Louisiana's rule, derived from Napoleon's Civil Code, designating husband head and master of the household, was held in *Kirchberg v. Feenstra* to be offensive to the evolving sex equality principle.

However sensible—and noncontroversial—these results, the decisions had a spectacular aspect. The race cases that trooped before the Warren Court could be viewed as moving the federal judiciary onto the course set by the Reconstruction Congress a century earlier in the post–Civil War amendments. No similar foundation, set deliberately by actors in the political arena, can account for the Burger Court sex discrimination decisions. Perhaps for that reason, the Court has proceeded cautiously. It has taken no giant step. In its most recent decision, *Mississippi University for Women v. Hogan,* the High Court recognized the right of men to a nursing school education at an institution maintained by the state for women only. But it earlier had declined to condemn a state property tax advantage reserved for widows, a state statutory rape law penalizing males but not females, and draft registration limited to males. It has formally reserved judgment on the question whether, absent ratification of an equal rights amendment, sex, like race, should rank as a suspect classification.

The Court's gender-based classification precedent impelled acknowledgment of a middle-tier equal protection standard of review, a level of judicial scrutiny demanding more than minimal rationality but less than a near-perfect fit between legislative ends and means. This movement away from the empty-cupboard interpretation of the equal protection principle in relation to sex equality claims largely trailed and mirrored changing patterns in society—most conspicuously, the emergence of the two-career family. The Court's decisions provoked no outraged opposition in legislative chambers. On the contrary, in a key area in which the Court rejected claims of impermissible sex-based classification, Congress indicated a different view, one more sensitive to discrimination against women.

That area, significantly in view of the Court's approach to reproductive choice, was pregnancy. In 1974 the Court decided an issue pressed by pregnant school teachers forced to terminate their employment, or take unpaid maternity leave, months before the anticipated birth date. Policies singling out pregnant women for disadvantageous treatment discriminated invidiously on the basis of sex, the teachers argued. The Court bypassed that argument; instead, the Court rested its decision holding mandatory maternity leaves unconstitutional on due process/conclusive presumption reasoning. Some weeks later, the Court held that a state-operated disability income protection plan could exclude normal pregnancy without offense to the equal protection principle. In a statutory setting as well, under Title VII, the Court later ruled, as it earlier had held in a constitutional context, that women unable to work due to pregnancy or childbirth could be excluded from disability coverage. The classifications in these disability cases, according to the Court, were not gender-based on their face, and were not shown to have any sex-discriminatory effect. All "non-pregnant persons," women along with men, the Court pointed out, were treated alike.

With respect to Title VII, Congress prospectively overruled the Court in 1978. It amended the statute to state explicitly that classification on the basis of sex includes classification on the basis of pregnancy. That congressional definition is not controlling in constitutional adjudication, but it might stimulate the Court one day to revise its position that regulation governing "pregnant persons" is not sex-based.

Roe v. Wade, in contrast to decisions involving explicit male/female classification, has occasioned searing criticism of the Court, over a decade of demonstrations, a stream of vituperative mail addressed to Justice Blackmun (the author of the opinion), annual proposals for overruling *Roe* by constitutional amendment, and a variety of measures in Congress and state legislatures to contain or curtail the decision. In 1973, when *Roe* issued, abortion law was in a state of change across the nation. There was a distinct trend in the states, noted by the Court, "toward liberalization of abortion statutes." Several states had adopted the American Law Institute's Model Penal Code approach setting out grounds on which abortion could be justified at any stage of pregnancy; most significantly, the Code included as a permissible ground preservation of the woman's physical or mental health. Four states—New York, Washington, Alaska, and Hawaii—permitted physicians to perform first-trimester abortions with virtually no restrictions. This movement in legislative arenas bore some resemblance to the law revision activity that eventually swept through the states establishing no-fault divorce as the national pattern.

The Texas law at issue in *Roe* made it a crime to "procure an abortion" except "by medical advice for the purpose of saving the life of the mother." It was the most extreme prohibition extant. The Court had in close view two pathmarking opinions on reproductive autonomy: first, a 1965 precedent, *Griswold v. Connecticut,* holding inconsistent with personal privacy, somehow sheltered by due process, a state ban on the use of contraceptives even by married couples; second, a 1972 decision, *Eisenstadt v. Baird,* extending *Griswold* to strike down a state prohibition on sales of contraceptives except to married persons by prescription. The Court had already decided *Reed v. Reed,* recognizing the arbitrariness in the 1970s of a once traditional gender-based classification, but it did not further pursue that avenue in *Roe.*

The decision in *Roe* appeared to be a stunning victory for the plaintiffs. The Court declared that a woman, guided by the medical judgment of her physician, had a "fundamental" right to abort a pregnancy, a right the Court anchored to a concept of personal autonomy derived from the due process guarantee. The Court then proceeded to define with precision that state regulation of abortion henceforth permissible. The rulings in *Roe,* and in a companion case decided the same day, *Doe v. Bolton,* were stunning in this sense: they called into question the criminal abortion statutes of every state, even those with the least restrictive provisions.

Roe announced a trimester approach Professor Archibald Cox has described as "read[ing] like a set of hospital rules and regulations."[1] During the first trimester, "the abortion decision and its effectuation must be left to the medical judgment of the pregnant woman's attending physician"[2]; in the next, roughly three-month stage, the state may, if it chooses, require other measures protective of the woman's health.[3] During the final months, "the stage subsequent to viability," the state also may concern itself with an emerging interest, the "potentiality of human life"; at that stage, the state "may, if it chooses, regulate, and even proscribe, abortion except where it is necessary, in appropriate medical judgment, for the preservation of the life or health of the mother."[4]

Justice O'Connor, ten years after *Roe,* described the trimester approach as "on a collision course with itself."[5] Advances in medical technology would continue to move *forward* to the point at which regulation could be justified as protective of a woman's health, and to move *backward* the point of viability, when the state could proscribe abortions unnecessary to preserve the patient's life or health. The approach, she thought, impelled legislatures to remain *au courant* with changing medical practices and called upon courts to examine legislative judgments, not as jurists applying "neutral principles," but as "science review boards."[6]

I earlier observed that, in my judgment, *Roe* ventured too far in the change it ordered. The sweep and detail of the opinion stimulated the mobilization of a right-to-life movement and an attendant reaction in Congress and state legislatures. In place of the trend "toward liberalization of abortion statutes" noted in *Roe,* legislatures adopted measures aimed at minimizing the impact of the 1973 rulings, including notification and consent requirements, prescriptions for the protection of fetal life, and bans on public expenditures for poor women's abortions.

Professor Paul Freund explained where he thought the Court went astray in *Roe,* and I agree with his statement. The Court properly invalidated the Texas proscription, he indicated, because "[a] law that absolutely made criminal all kinds and forms of abortion could not stand up; it is not a reasonable accommodation of interests."[7] If *Roe* had left off at that point and not adopted what Professor Freund called a "medical approach,"[8] physicians might have been less pleased with the decision, but the legislative trend might have continued in the direction in which it was headed in the early 1970s. "[S]ome of the bitter debate on the issue might have been averted," Professor Freund believed; "[t]he animus against the Court might at least have been diverted to the legislative halls."[9] Overall, he thought that the *Roe* distinctions turning on trimesters and viability of the fetus illustrated a troublesome tendency of the modern Supreme Court under Chief Justices Burger and Warren "to specify by a kind of legislative code the one alternative pattern that will satisfy the Constitution."[10]

I commented at the outset that I believe the Court presented an incomplete justification for its action. Academic criticism of *Roe,* charging the Court with reading its own values into the due process clause, might have been less pointed had the Court placed the woman alone, rather than the woman tied to her physician, at the center of its attention. Professor Karst's commentary is indicative of the perspective not developed in the High Court's opinion; he solidly linked abortion prohibitions with discrimination against women.[11] The issue in *Roe,* he wrote, deeply touched and concerned "women's position in society in relation to men."[12]

It is not a sufficient answer to charge it all to women's anatomy—a natural, not man-made, phenomenon. Society, not anatomy, "places a greater stigma on unmarried women who become pregnant than on the men who father their children."[13] Society expects, but nature does not command, that "women take the major responsibility...for child care"[14] and that they will stay with their children, bearing nurture and support burdens alone, when fathers deny paternity or otherwise refuse to provide care or financial support for unwanted offspring.

I do not pretend that, if the Court had added a distinct sex discrimination theme to its medically oriented opinion, the storm *Roe* generated would have been less furious. I appreciate the intense divisions of opinion on the moral question and recognize that abortion today cannot fairly be described as nothing more than birth control delayed. The conflict, however, is not simply one between a fetus' interests and a woman's interests, narrowly conceived, nor is the overriding issue state versus private control of a woman's body for a span of nine months. Also in the balance is a woman's autonomous charge of her full life's course—as Professor Karst put it, her ability to stand in relation to man, society, and the state as an independent, self-sustaining, equal citizen.

On several occasions since *Roe* the Court has confronted legislative responses to the decision. With the notable exception of the public funding cases, the Court typically has applied *Roe* to overturn or limit efforts to impede access to abortion. I will not survey in the brief compass of this essay the Court's series of opinions addressing regulation of the abortion decision-making process; specifications regarding personnel, facilities, and medical procedures; and parental notification and consent requirements in the case of minors.[15] Instead, I will simply highlight the Court's statement last year reaffirming *Roe's* "basic principle that a woman has a fundamental right to make the highly personal choice whether or not to terminate her pregnancy." In *City of Akron v. Akron Center for Reproductive Health, Inc.,* the Court acknowledged arguments it continues to hear that *Roe* "erred in interpreting the Constitution." Nonetheless, the Court declared it would adhere to *Roe* because *"stare decisis,* while perhaps never entirely persuasive on a constitutional question, is a doctrine that demands respect in a society governed by the rule of law."

I turn, finally, to the plight of the woman who lacks resources to finance privately implementation of her personal choice to terminate her pregnancy. The hostile reaction to *Roe* has trained largely on her.

Some observers speculated that the seven-two judgment in *Roe* was motivated at least in part by pragmatic considerations—population control concerns, the specter of coat hanger abortions, and concerns about unwanted children born to impoverished women. I recalled earlier the view that the demand for open access to abortions had as its real purpose suppressing minorities. In a set of 1977 decisions, however, the Court upheld state denial of medical expense reimbursement or hospital facilities for abortions sought by indigent women. Moreover, in a 1980 decision, *Harris v. McRae,* the Court found no constitutional infirmity in the Hyde Amendment, which excluded even medically necessary abortions from Medicaid coverage. After these decisions, the Court was accused of sensitivity only to the Justices' own social milieu—"of creating a middle-class right to abortion."

The argument for constitutionally mandated public assistance to effectuate the poor woman's choice ran along these lines. Accepting that our Constitution's Bill of Rights places restraints, not affirmative obligations, on government, counsel for the impoverished women stressed that childbirth was publicly subsidized. As long as the government paid for childbirth, the argument proceeded, public funding could not be denied for abortion, often a safer and always a far less expensive course, short and long run. By paying for childbirth but not abortion, the complainants maintained, government increased spending and intruded on or steered a choice *Roe* had ranked as a woman's "fundamental" right.

The Court responded that, like other individual rights secured by the Constitution, the right to abortion is indeed a negative right. Government could not intervene by blocking a woman's utilization of her own resources to effectuate her decision. It could not "'impose its will by force of law.'" But *Roe* did not demand government neutrality, the Court reasoned; it left room for substantive government control to this extent: Action "deemed in the public interest"—in this instance, protection of the potential life of the fetus—could be promoted by encouraging childbirth in preference to abortion.

Financial need alone, under the Court's jurisprudence, does not identify a class of persons whose complaints of disadvantageous treatment attract close scrutiny. Generally, constitutional claims to government benefits on behalf of the poor have prevailed only when tied to another bark—a right to travel interstate, discrimination because of out-of-wedlock birth, or gender-based discrimination. If the Court had acknowledged a woman's equality aspect, not simply a patient–physician autonomy constitutional dimension to the abortion issue, a majority perhaps might have seen the public assistance cases as instances in which, borrowing a phrase from Justice Stevens, the sovereign had violated its "duty to govern impartially."

I have tried to discuss some features of constitutional adjudication concerning sex equality, in relation to the autonomy and equal-regard values involved in cases on abortion. I have done so tentatively and with trepidation. *Roe v. Wade* is a decision I approached gingerly in prior comment; until now I have limited my remarks to a brief description of what others have said. While I claim no original contribution, I have endeavored here to state my own reflections and concerns.

Roe, I believe, would have been more acceptable as a judicial decision if it had not gone beyond a ruling on the extreme statute before the Court. The political process was moving in the early 1970s, not swiftly enough for advocates of quick, complete change, but majoritarian institutions were listening and acting. Heavy-handed judicial intervention was difficult to justify and appears to have provoked, not resolved, conflict.

The public funding of abortion decisions appear incongruous following so soon after the intrepid 1973 rulings. The Court did not adequately explain why the "fundamental" choice principle and trimester approach embraced in *Roe* did not bar the sovereign, at least at the previability stage of pregnancy, from taking sides.

Overall, the Court's *Roe* position is weakened, I believe, by the opinion's concentration on a medically approved autonomy idea, to the exclusion of a constitutionally based sex-equality perspective. I understand the view that for political reasons the reproductive autonomy controversy should be isolated from the general debate on equal rights, responsibilities, and opportunities for women and men. I expect, however, that organized and determined opposing efforts to inform and persuade the public on the abortion issue will continue through the 1980s. In that process there will be opportunities for elaborating in public forums the equal-regard conception of women's claims to reproductive choice uncoerced and unsteered by government.

STUDY QUESTIONS

1. Justice Ginsburg argues that the legal reasoning on which *Roe v. Wade* is based might have precipitated, rather than discouraged, anti-abortion measures. How does she support this contention? Do you agree with her? Why or why not?

2. Why does Justice Ginsburg believe that it would have been better for the cause for abortion rights had *Roe* been based on the equal protection clause rather than the right to privacy? Do you agree with her? Why or why not?

3. Would it matter to Justice Ginsburg's appeal to the equal protection clause if it is conclusively proven to everyone's satisfaction that the fetus is a human person? If not, how do you believe she would respond to a critic who argues that Justice Ginsburg is saying that it is morally permissible for women to achieve equality with men by killing other persons (fetuses)?

NOTES

1. A. Cox, *The Role of the Supreme Court in American Government* 113 (1976).

2. *Roe v. Wade,* 410 U.S. at 164.

3. *Id.*

4. *Id.* at 164–165.

5. *City of Akron v. Akron Center for Reproductive Health, Inc.,* 103 S. Ct. 2481, 2507.

6. *Id.*

7. Freund, *Storms over the Supreme Court,* 69 A.B.A. J. 1474, 1480 (1983).

8. *Id.*

9. *Id.*

10. *Id.*

11. Karst, "Forward: Equal Citizenship under the Fourteenth Amendment," 91 *Harvard Law Review,* 58 (1977).

12. *Id.*

13. *Id.* at 57.

14. *Id.*

15. *City of Akron v. Akron Center for Reproductive Health.*

FOR FURTHER READING

Bork, Robert. *The Tempting of America: The Political Seduction of the Law.* New York: Simon & Schuster, 1989. Bork makes critical comments about *Roe* throughout his book, but especially on pages 111–126.

Bradley, Gerard V. "Shall We Ratify the New Constitution?: The Judicial Manifesto in *Casey* and *Lee.*" In *Benchmarks: Great Constitutional Controversies in the Supreme Court,* ed. Terry Eastland. Grand Rapids, Mich.: Eerdmans, 1995.

Brody, Baruch. *Abortion and the Sanctity of Human Life: A Philosophical View.* Cambridge, Mass.: M.I.T. Press, 1975. Chapter 9.

Ely, John Hart. "The Wages of Crying Wolf: A Comment on *Roe v. Wade.*" *Yale Law Journal* 82 (1973).

Glendon, Mary Anne. *Abortion and Divorce in Western Law.* Cambridge, Mass.: Harvard University Press, 1987.

Horan, Dennis J., Edward R. Grant, and Paige C. Cunningham, eds. *Abortion and the Law: Reversing* Roe v. Wade *Through the Courts.* Washington, DC: Georgetown University Press, 1987.

Krason, Stephen. *Abortion: Morality, the Law, and the Constitution.* Lanham, Md.: University Press of America, 1984, 90–333.

Noonan, John T., Jr., "Raw Judicial Power." In *The Zero People,* ed. Jeff Lane Hensley. Ann Arbor, Mich.: Servant, 1983.

Tribe, Laurence. *Abortion: The Clash of Absolutes.* New York: W.W. Norton, 1990. Chapters 2, 3, and 5.

Witherspoon, James S. "Reexamining *Roe:* Nineteenth-Century Abortion Statutes and the Fourteenth Amendment. *St. Mary's Law Journal* 17 (1985).

PART IV

Arguments from a Woman's Right to Her Body

INTRODUCTION

The emphasis in the philosophical debate over abortion has been the status of the fetus. That is to say, most of the works written on this topic have reasoned as follows:

1. The fetus is a person if and only if abortion in almost every case is unjustified homicide.
2. The fetus is (or is not) a person, therefore,
3. Abortion is (or is not) in almost every case unjustified homicide.

Supreme Court Justice Harry Blackmun, who wrote the majority opinion in *Roe v. Wade* (1973), seems to reason this way as well: "If the suggestion of personhood [of the unborn] is established, the appellant's case, of course, collapses, for the fetus' right to life is then guaranteed specifically by the [Fourteenth Amendment]."[1]

On the other hand, the popular debate over abortion, as portrayed on radio and television talk shows, appears to emphasize the bodily rights of the pregnant woman. In 1971, Professor Judith Jarvis Thomson provided this popular portrayal with a highly sophisticated philosophical argument. She questioned the truth of the first premise in the previous argument: if and only if the fetus is a person, abortion in almost every case is unjustified homicide. In the article reprinted in this volume ("A Defense of Abortion"), which by 1986 was "the most widely reprinted essay in all of contemporary philosophy,"[2] Thomson

115

argues that even if the fetus is a person with a right to life, this does not mean that a woman must be forced to use her bodily organs to sustain its life. Just as one does not have a right to use another's kidney if one's kidney has failed, the unborn entity, although having a basic right to life, does not have a right to life so strong that it outweighs the pregnant woman's right to personal bodily autonomy.

It should be noted that Thomson's argument was not used in the two landmark Supreme Court decisions that have supported abortion rights, such as *Roe v. Wade* and *Doe v. Bolton* (1973). However, in his book, *Abortion: The Clash of Absolutes* (1990), Laurence Tribe argues that "perhaps the Supreme Court's opinion in *Roe,* by gratuitously insisting that the fetus cannot be deemed a 'person,' needlessly insulted and alienated those for whom the view that the fetus is a person represents a fundamental article of faith or bedrock personal commitment." He suggests that the "Court could instead have said: Even if the fetus is a person, our Constitution forbids compelling a woman to carry it for nine months and become a mother."[3]

Responding to Thomson's argument, as well as two other arguments, is Francis J. Beckwith (Chapter 8), who maintains that Thomson's case is flawed in at least nine ways. He argues, among other things, that Thomson fails to take into consideration fundamental moral intuitions that ground family life and our obligations toward children who, because they are naturally weak and helpless, have a prima facie right to their parents' protection. In response to Beckwith's reasoning as well as other authors who have proposed similar critiques of Thomson's argument, David Boonin-Vail (Chapter 9) defends Thomson's case against what he calls the Responsibility Objection. Boonin-Vail critiques this objection and concludes that Thomson's argument withstands the attacks of its critics. This section concludes with an essay by Keith Pavlischek, who argues that the logic of Thomson's case proves too much, for it supports a perspective that most defenders of abortion-rights detest, paternal irresponsibility after birth (that is, "Dead-beat Dads"). In concluding remarks written exclusively for this volume, Pavlischek ends his essay with a reply to Boonin-Vail's analysis of his argument.

NOTES

1. Justice Harry Blackmun, "Excerpts from Opinion in *Roe v. Wade,*" in *The Problem of Abortion,* 2nd ed., ed, Joel Feinberg, Belmont, Calif.: Wadsworth, 1984, 195.

2. According to her editor, William Parent, Judith Jarvis Thomson, *Rights, Restitution, and Risk,* Cambridge, Mass.: Harvard University Press, 1986, vii.

3. Laurence Tribe, *Abortion: The Clash of Absolutes,* New York: Norton, 1990, 135.

7

A Defense of Abortion

JUDITH JARVIS THOMSON

Judith Jarvis Thomson is Professor of Philosophy at Massachusetts Institute of Technology. In the following article Thomson argues that a woman has a right to an abortion even if the fetus is a human person.

Using a series of examples including the imagined case of a famous violinist who needs your kidney for nine months, she argues that just as you have a right to unplug yourself from the violinist, the pregnant woman has a right to an abortion. Although she rejects the idea that the fetus has a right to life which overrides the mother's right to her own body, Thomson distinguishes cases where it would be a good thing for a woman to refrain from having an abortion.

Most opposition to abortion relies on the premise that the foetus is a human being, a person, from the moment of conception. The premise is argued for, but, as I think, not well. Take, for example, the most common argument. We are asked to notice that the development of a human being from conception through birth into childhood is continuous; then it is said that to draw a line, to choose a point in this development and say 'before this point the thing is not a person, after this point it is a person' is to make an arbitrary choice, a choice for which in the nature of things no good reason can be given. It is concluded that the foetus is, or anyway that we had better say it is, as a person from the moment of conception. But this conclusion does not

Reprinted from *Philosophy and Public Affairs*, vol. 1, no. 1 (1911). Reprinted by permission.

follow. Similar things might be said about the development of an acorn into an oak tree, and it does not follow that acorns are oak trees, or that we had better say they are. Arguments of this form are sometimes called 'slippery slope arguments'—the phrase is perhaps self-explanatory—and it is dismaying that opponents of abortion rely on them so heavily and uncritically.

I am inclined to agree, however, that the prospects for 'drawing a line' in the development of the foetus look dim. I am inclined to think also that we shall probably have to agree that the foetus has already become a human person well before birth. Indeed, it comes as a surprise when one first learns how early in its life it begins to acquire human characteristics. By the tenth week for example, it already has a face, arms and legs, fingers and toes; it has internal organs, and brain activity is detectable. On the other hand, I think that the premise is false, that the foetus is not a person from the moment of conception. A newly fertilized ovum, a newly implanted clump of cells, is no more a person than an acorn is an oak tree. But I shall not discuss any of this. For it seems to me to be of great interest to ask what happens if, for the sake of argument, we allow the premise. How, precisely, are we supposed to get from there to the conclusion that abortion is morally impermissible? Opponents of abortion commonly spend most of their time establishing that the foetus is a person and hardly any time explaining the step from there to the impermissibility of abortion. Perhaps they think the step too simple and obvious to require much comment. Or perhaps instead they are simply being economical in argument. Many of those who defend abortion rely on the premise that the foetus is not a person, but only a bit of tissue that will become a person at birth, and why pay out more arguments than you have to? Whatever the explanation, I suggest that the step they take is neither easy nor obvious, it calls for closer examination than it is commonly given, and that when we do give it this closer examination, we shall feel inclined to reject it.

I propose, then, that we grant that the foetus is a person from the moment of conception. How does the argument go from here? Something like this, I take it. Every person has a right to life. So the foetus has a right to life. No doubt the mother has a right to decide what shall happen in and to her body; everyone would grant that. But surely a person's right to life is stronger and more stringent than the mother's right to decide what happens in and to her body, and so outweighs it. So the foetus may not be killed; an abortion may not be performed.

It sounds plausible. But now let me ask you to imagine this. You wake up in the morning and find yourself back to back in bed with an unconscious violinist. A famous unconscious violinist. He has been found to have a fatal kidney ailment, and the Society of Music Lovers has canvassed all the available medical records and found that you alone have the right blood type to help. They have therefore kidnapped you, and last night the violinist's circulatory system was plugged into yours, so that your kidneys can be used to extract poisons from his blood as well as your own. The director of the hospital now tells you, "Look, we're sorry the Society of Music Lovers did this to you—we would never have permitted it if we had known. But still, they did it, and the violinist now is plugged into you. To unplug you would be to kill him. But never mind, it's only for nine months. By then he will have recovered from his ailment and can safely be unplugged from you." Is it morally incumbent on you to accede to this situation? No doubt it would be very nice of you if you did, a great kindness. But do you *have* to accede to it? What if it were not nine months, but nine years? Or longer still? What if the director of the hospital says, "Tough luck, I agree, but you've now got to stay in bed, with the violinist plugged into you, for the rest of your life. Because remember this. All persons have a right to life, and violinists are persons. Granted you have a right to decide what happens in and to your body, but a person's right to life outweighs your right to decide what happens in and to your body. So you cannot ever be unplugged from him." I imagine you would regard this as outrageous, which suggests that something really is wrong with that plausible-sounding argument I mentioned a moment ago.

In this case, of course, you were kidnapped; you didn't volunteer for the operation that plugged the violinist into your kidneys. Can those who oppose abortion on the ground I mentioned make an exception for a pregnancy due to rape? Certainly. They can say that persons have a right to life only if they didn't come into existence because of rape; or they can say that all persons have a right to life, but that some have less of a right to life than others, in particular, that those who came into existence because of rape have less. But these statements have a rather unpleasant sound. Surely the question of whether you have a right to life at all, or how much of it you have, shouldn't turn on the question of whether or not you are the product of a rape. And in fact the people who oppose abortion on the ground I mentioned do not make this distinction, and hence do not make an exception in case of rape.

Nor do they make an exception for a case in which the mother has to spend the nine months of her pregnancy in bed. They would agree that would be a great pity, and hard on the mother, but all the same, all persons have a right to life, the foetus is a person, and so on. I suspect, in fact, that they would not make an exception for a case in which, miraculously enough, the pregnancy went on for nine years, or even the rest of the mother's life.

Some won't even make an exception for a case in which continuation of the pregnancy is likely to shorten the mother's life; they regard abortion as impermissible even to save the mother's life. Such cases are nowadays very rare, and many opponents of abortion do not accept this extreme view. All the same, it is a good place to begin: A number of points of interest come out in respect to it.

1. Let us call the view that abortion is impermissible even to save the mother's life "the extreme view." I want to suggest first that it does not issue from the argument I mentioned earlier without the addition of some fairly powerful premises. Suppose a woman has become pregnant, and now learns that she has a cardiac condition such that she will die if she carries the baby to term. What may be done for her? The foetus, being a person, has a right to life, but as the mother is a person, too, so has she a right to life. Presumably they have an equal right to life. How is it supposed to come out that an

abortion may not be performed? If mother and child have an equal right to life, shouldn't we perhaps flip a coin? Or should we add to the mother's right to life her right to decide what happens in and to her body, which everybody seems to be ready to grant—the sum of her rights now outweighing the foetus's right to life?

The most familiar argument here is the following. We are told that performing the abortion would be directly killing[1] the child, whereas doing nothing would not be killing the mother, but only letting her die. Moreover, in killing the child, one would be killing an innocent person, for the child has committed no crime, and is not aiming at his mother's death. And then there are a variety of ways in which this might be continued. (1) But as directly killing an innocent person is always and absolutely impermissible, an abortion may not be performed. Or, (2) as directly killing an innocent person is murder, and murder is always and absolutely impermissible, an abortion may not be performed.[2] Or, (3) as one's duty to refrain from directly killing an innocent person is more stringent than one's duty to keep a person from dying, an abortion may not be performed. Or, (4) if one's only options are directly killing an innocent person or letting a person die, one must prefer letting the person die, and thus an abortion may not be performed.[3]

Some people seem to have thought that these are not further premises that must be added if the conclusion is to be reached, but that they follow from the very fact that an innocent person has a right to life.[4] But this seems to me to be a mistake, and perhaps the simplest way to show this is to bring out that while we must certainly grant that innocent persons have a right to life, the theses in (1) to (4) are all false. Take (2), for example. If directly killing an innocent person is murder, and thus is impermissible, then the mother's directly killing the innocent person inside her is murder, and thus is impermissible. But it cannot seriously be thought to be murder if the mother performs an abortion on herself to save her life. It cannot seriously be said that she *must* refrain, that she must sit passively by and wait for her death. Let us look again at the case of you and the violinist. There you are, in bed with the violinist, and the director of the hospital says to you, "It's all most distressing, and I deeply sympathize, but you see this is putting an additional strain on your kidneys, and you'll be dead within the month. But you *have* to stay where you are all the same. Because unplugging you would be directly killing an innocent violinist, and that's murder, and that's impermissible." If anything in the world is true, it is that you do not commit murder, you do not do what is impermissible, if you reach around to your back and unplug yourself from that violinist to save your life.

The main focus of attention in writings on abortion has been on what a third party may or may not do in answer to a request from a woman for an abortion. This is in a way understandable. Things being as they are, there isn't much a woman can safely do to abort herself. So the question asked is what a third party may do, and what the mother may do, if it is mentioned at all, is deduced, almost as an afterthought, from what it is concluded that third parties may do. But it seems to me that to treat the matter in this way is to refuse to grant to the mother that very status of person that is so firmly insisted on for the foetus. For we cannot simply read what a person may do from what a third party may do. Suppose you find yourself trapped in a tiny house with a growing child. I mean a very tiny house, and a rapidly growing child—you are already up against the wall of the house and in a few minutes you'll be crushed to death. The child on the other hand won't be crushed to death; if nothing is done to stop him from growing he'll be hurt, but in the end he'll simply burst open the house and walk out a free man. Now I could well understand it if a bystander were to say, "There's nothing we can do for you. We cannot choose between your life and his, we cannot be the ones to decide who is to live, we cannot intervene." But it cannot be concluded that you too can do nothing, that you cannot attack it to save your life. However innocent the child may be, you do not have to wait passively while it crushes you to death. Perhaps a pregnant woman is vaguely felt to have the status of house, to which we don't allow the right of self-defense. But if the woman houses the child, it should be remembered that she is a person who houses it.

I should perhaps stop to say explicitly that I am not claiming that people have a right to do anything whatever to save their lives. I think, rather, that there are drastic limits to the right of self-defense. If someone threatens you with death unless you torture someone else to death, I think you have not the right, even to save your life, to do so. But the case under consideration here is very different. In our case there are only two people involved, one whose life is threatened, and one who threatens it. Both are innocent: the one who is threatened is not threatened because of any fault, the one who threatens does not threaten because of any fault. For this reason we may feel that we bystanders cannot intervene. But the person threatened can.

In sum, a woman surely can defend her life against the threat to it posed by the unborn child, even if doing so involves its death. And this shows not merely that the theses in (1) to (4) are false; it shows also that the extreme view of abortion is false, and so we need not canvass any other possible ways of arriving at it from the argument I mentioned at the outset.

2. The extreme view could of course be weakened to say that while abortion is permissible to save the mother's life, it may not be performed by a third party but only by the mother herself. But this cannot be right either. For what we have to keep in mind is that the mother and the unborn child are not like two tenants in a small house which has, by an unfortunate mistake, been rented to both: the mother *owns* the house. The fact that she does adds to the offensiveness of deducing that the mother can do nothing from the supposition that third parties can do nothing. But it does more than this: It casts a bright light on the supposition that third parties can do nothing. Certainly it lets us see that a third party who says "I cannot choose between you" is fooling himself if he thinks this is impartiality. If Jones has found and fastened on a certain coat, which he needs to keep him from freezing, but which Smith also needs to keep him from freezing, then it is not impartiality that says "I cannot choose between you" when Smith owns the coat. Women have said again and again "This body is *my* body!" and they have reason to feel angry, reason to feel that

it has been like shouting into the wind. Smith, after all, is hardly likely to bless us if we say to him, "Of course it's your coat, anybody would grant that it is. But no one may choose between you and Jones who is to have it."

We should really ask what it is that says "no one may choose" in the face of the fact that the body that houses the child is the mother's body. It may be simply a failure to appreciate this fact. But it may be something more interesting, namely the sense that one has a right to refuse to lay hands on people, even where it would be just and fair to do so, even where justice seems to require that somebody do so. Thus justice might call for somebody to get Smith's coat back from Jones, and yet you have a right to refuse to be the one to lay hands on Jones, a right to refuse to do physical violence to him. This, I think, must be granted. But then what should be said is not "no one may choose," but only "*I* cannot choose," and indeed not even this, but "*I* will not *act*," leaving it open that somebody else can or should, and in particular that anyone in a position of authority, with the job of securing people's rights, both can and should. So this is no difficulty. I have not been arguing that any given third party must accede to the mother's request that he perform an abortion to save her life, but only that he may.

I suppose that in some views of human life the mother's body is only on loan to her, the loan not being one which gives her any prior claim to it. One who held this view might well think it impartiality to say "I cannot choose." But I shall simply ignore this possibility. My own view is that if a human being has any just, prior claim to anything at all, he has a just, prior claim to his own body. And perhaps this needn't be argued for here anyway, since, as I mentioned, the arguments against abortion we are looking at do grant that the woman has a right to decide what happens in and to her body.

But although they do grant it, I have tried to show that they do not take seriously what is done in granting it. I suggest the same thing will reappear even more clearly when we turn away from cases in which the mother's life is at stake, and attend, as I propose we now do, to the vastly more common cases in which a woman wants an abortion for some less weighty reason than preserving her own life.

3. Where the mother's life is not at stake, the argument I mentioned at the outset seems to have a much stronger pull. "Everyone has a right to life, so the unborn person has a right to life." And isn't the child's right to life weightier than anything other than the mother's own right to life, which she might put forward as ground for an abortion?

This argument treats the right to life as if it were unproblematic. It is not, and this seems to me to be precisely the source of the mistake,

For we should now, at long last, ask what it comes to, to have a right to life. In some views having a right to life includes having a right to be given at least the bare minimum one needs for continued life. But suppose that what in fact *is* the bare minimum a man needs for continued life is something he has no right at all to be given? If I am sick unto death, and the only thing that will save my life is the touch of Henry Fonda's cool hand on my fevered brow, then all the same, I have no right to be given the touch of Henry Fonda's cool hand on my fevered brow. It would be frightfully nice of him to fly in from the West Coast to provide it. It would be less nice, though no doubt well meant, if my friends flew out to the West Coast and carried Henry Fonda back with them. But I have no right at all against anybody that he should do this for me. Or again, to return to the story I told earlier, the fact that for continued life that violinist needs the continued use of your kidneys does not establish that he has a right to be given the continued use of your kidneys. He certainly has no right against you that *you* should give him continued use of your kidneys. For nobody has any right to use your kidneys unless you give him such a right, and nobody has the right against you that you shall give him this right—if you do allow him to go on using your kidneys, this is a kindness on your part, and not something he can claim from you as his due. Nor has he any right against anybody else that *they* should give him continued use of your kidneys. Certainly he had no right against the Society of Music Lovers that they should plug him into you in the first place. And if you now start to unplug yourself, having learned that you will otherwise have to spend nine years in bed with him, there is nobody in the world who must try to prevent you, in order to see to it that he is given something he has a right to be given.

Some people are rather stricter about the right to life. In their view, it does not include the right to be given anything, but amounts to, and only to, the right not to be killed by anybody. But here a related difficulty arises. If everybody is to refrain from killing that violinist, then everybody must refrain from doing a great many different sorts of things. Everybody must refrain from slitting his throat, everybody must refrain from shooting him—and everybody must refrain from unplugging you from him. But does he have a right against everybody that they shall refrain from unplugging you from him? To refrain from doing this is to allow him to continue to use your kidneys. It could be argued that he has a right against us that *we* should allow him to continue to use your kidneys. That is, while he had no right against us that we should give him the use of your kidneys, it might be argued that he anyway has a right against us that we shall not now intervene and deprive him of the use of your kidneys. I shall come back to third-party interventions later. But certainly the violinist has no right against you that *you* shall allow him to continue to use your kidneys. As I said, if you do allow him to use them, it is a kindness on your part, and not something you owe him.

The difficulty I point to here is not peculiar to the right to life. It reappears in connection with all the other natural rights; and it is something which an adequate account of rights must deal with. For present purposes it is enough just to draw attention to it. But I would stress that I am not arguing that people do not have a right to life—quite to the contrary, it seems to me that the primary control we must place on the acceptability of an account of rights is that it should turn out in that account to be a truth that all persons have a right to life. I am arguing only that having a right to life does not guarantee having either a right to be given the use of or a right to be allowed continued use of another person's body—even if one needs it for life itself. So the right to life will not serve the opponents of abortion in the very simple and clear way in which they seem to have thought it would.

4. There is another way to bring out the difficulty. In the most ordinary sort of case, to deprive someone of what he has a right to is to treat him unjustly. Suppose a boy and his small brother are jointly given a box of chocolates for Christmas. If the older boy takes the box and refuses to give his brother any of the chocolates, he is unjust to him, for the brother has been given a right to half of them. But suppose that, having learned that otherwise it means nine years in bed with that violinist, you unplug yourself from him. You surely are not being unjust to him, for you gave him no right to use your kidneys, and no one else can have given him any such right. But we have to notice that in unplugging yourself, you are killing him; and violinists, like everybody else, have a right to life, and thus in the view we were considering just now, the right not to be killed. So here you do what he supposedly has a right you shall not do, but you do not act unjustly to him in doing it.

The emendation which may be made at this point is this: the right to life consists not in the right not to be killed, but rather in the right not to be killed unjustly. This runs a risk of circularity, but never mind: it would enable us to square the fact that the violinist has a right to life with the fact that you do not act unjustly toward him in unplugging yourself, thereby killing him. For if you do not kill him unjustly, you do not violate his right to life, and so it is no wonder you do him no injustice.

But if this emendation is accepted, the gap in the argument against abortion stares us plainly in the face: it is by no means enough to show that the foetus is a person, and to remind us that all persons have a right to life—we need to be shown also that killing the foetus violates its right to life, that is, that abortion is unjust killing. And is it?

I suppose we may take it as a datum that in a case of pregnancy due to rape the mother has not given the unborn person a right to the use of her body for food and shelter. Indeed, in what pregnancy could it be supposed that the mother has given the unborn person such a right? It is not as if there were unborn persons drifting about the world, to whom a woman who wants a child says "I invite you in."

But it might be argued that there are other ways one can have acquired a right to the use of another person's body than by having been invited to use it by that person. Suppose a woman voluntarily indulges in intercourse, knowing of the chance it will issue in pregnancy, and then she does become pregnant; is she not in part responsible for the presence, in fact the very existence, of the unborn person inside her? No doubt she did not invite it in. But doesn't her partial responsibility for its being there itself give it a right to the use of her body? If so, then her aborting it would be more like the boy's taking away the chocolates, and less like your unplugging yourself from the violinist—doing so would be depriving it of what it does have a right to, and thus would be doing it an injustice.

And then, too, it might be asked whether or not she can kill it even to save her own life: If she voluntarily called it into existence, how can she now kill it, even in self-defense?

The first thing to be said about this is that it is something new. Opponents of abortion have been so concerned to make out the independence of the foetus, in order to establish that it has a right to life, just as its mother does, that they have tended to overlook the possible support they might gain from making out that the foetus is *dependent* on the mother, in order to establish that she has a special kind of responsibility for it, a responsibility that gives it rights against her which are not possessed by any independent person—such as an ailing violinist who is a stranger to her.

On the other hand, this argument would give the unborn person a right to its mother's body only if her pregnancy resulted from a voluntary act, undertaken in full knowledge of the chance a pregnancy might result from it. It would leave out entirely the unborn person whose existence is due to rape. Pending the availability of some further argument, then we would be left with the conclusion that unborn persons whose existence is due to rape have no right to the use of their mothers' bodies, and thus that aborting them is not depriving them of anything they have a right to and hence is not unjust killing.

And we should also notice that it is not at all plain that this argument really does go even as far as it purports to. For there are cases and cases, and the details make a difference. If the room is stuffy, and I therefore open a window to air it, and a burglar climbs in, it would be absurd to say, "Ah, now he can stay, she's given him a right to the use of her house—for she is partially responsible for his presence there, having voluntarily done what enabled him to get in, in full knowledge that there are such things as burglars, and that burglars burgle." It would be still more absurd to say this if I had had bars installed outside my windows, precisely to prevent burglars from getting in, and a burglar got in only because of a defect in the bars. It remains equally absurd if we imagine it is not a burglar who climbs in, but an innocent person who blunders or falls in. Again, suppose it were like this: people-seeds drift about in the air like pollen, and if you open your windows, one may drift in and take root in your carpets or upholstery. You don't want children, so you fix up your windows with fine mesh screens, the very best you can buy. As can happen, however, and on very, very rare occasions does happen, one of the screens is defective; and a seed drifts in and takes root. Does the person-plant who now develops have a right to the use of your house? Surely not—despite the fact that you voluntarily opened your windows, you knowingly kept carpets and upholstered furniture, and you knew that screens were sometimes defective. Someone may argue that you are responsible for its rooting, that it does have a right to your house, because after all you *could* have lived out your life with bare floors and furniture, or with sealed windows and doors. But this won't do—for by the same token anyone can avoid a pregnancy due to rape by having a hysterectomy, or anyway by never leaving home without a (reliable!) army.

It seems to me that the argument we are looking at can establish at most that there are *some* cases in which the unborn person has a right to the use of its mother's body, and therefore *some* cases in which abortion is unjust killing. There is room for much discussion and argument as to precisely which, if any. But I think we should side-step this issue and leave it open, for at any rate the argument certainly does not establish that all abortion is unjust killing.

5. There is room for yet another argument here, however. We surely must all grant that there may be cases in which it would be morally indecent to detach a person from your body at the cost of his life. Suppose you learn that what the violinist needs is not nine years of your life but only one hour: All you need do to save his life is to spend one hour in that bed with him. Suppose also that letting him use your kidneys for that one hour would not affect your health in the slightest. Admittedly you were kidnapped. Admittedly you did not give anyone permission to plug him into you. Nevertheless it seems to me plain you *ought* to allow him to use your kidneys for that hour—it would be indecent to refuse.

Again, suppose pregnancy lasted only an hour and constituted no threat to life or health. And suppose that a woman becomes pregnant as a result of rape. Admittedly she did not voluntarily do anything to bring about the existence of a child. Admittedly she did nothing at all which would give the unborn person a right to the use of her body. All the same it might well be said, as in the newly emended violinist story, that she *ought* to allow it to remain for that hour—that it would be indecent of her to refuse.

Now some people are inclined to use the term "right" in such a way that it follows from the fact that you ought to allow a person to use your body for the hour he needs, that he has a right to use your body for the hour he needs, even though he has not been given that right by any person or act. They may say that it follows also that if you refuse, you act unjustly toward him. This use of the term is perhaps so common that it cannot be called wrong; nevertheless it seems to me to be an unfortunate loosening of what we would do better to keep a tight rein on. Suppose that box of chocolates I mentioned earlier had not been given to both boys jointly, but was given only to the older boy. There he sits, stolidly eating his way through the box, his small brother watching enviously. Here we are likely to say "You ought not to be so mean. You ought to give your brother some of those chocolates." My own view is that it just does not follow from the truth of this that the brother has any right to any of the chocolates. If the boy refuses to give his brother any, he is greedy, stingy, callous—but not unjust. I suppose that the people I have in mind will say it does follow that the brother has a right to some of the chocolates, and thus that the boy does act unjustly if he refuses to give his brother any. But the effect of saying this is to obscure what we should keep distinct, namely the difference between the boy's refusal in this case and the boy's refusal in the earlier case, in which the box was given to both boys jointly, and in which the small brother thus had what was from any point of view clear title to half.

A further objection to so using the term "right" that from the fact that *A* ought to do a thing for *B*, it follows that *B* has a right against *A* that *A* do it for him, is that it is going to make the question of whether or not a man has a right to a thing turn on how easy it is to provide him with it, and this seems not merely unfortunate, but morally unacceptable. Take the case of Henry Fonda again. I said earlier that I had no right to the touch of his cool hand on my fevered brow, even though I needed it to save my life. I said it would be frightfully nice of him to fly in from the West Coast to provide me with it, but that I had no right against him that he should do so. But suppose he isn't on the West Coast. Suppose he has only to walk across the room, place a hand briefly on my brow—and lo, my life is saved. Then surely he ought to do it, it would be indecent to refuse. Is it to be said "Ah, well, it follows that in this case she has a right to the touch of his hand on her brow, and so it would be an injustice in him to refuse?" So that I have a right to it when it is easy for him to provide it, though no right when it's hard? It's rather a shocking idea that anyone's rights should fade away and disappear as it gets harder and harder to accord them to him.

So my own view is that even though you ought to let the violinist use your kidneys for the one hour he needs, we should not conclude that he has a right to do so—we should say that if you refuse, you are, like the boy who owns all the chocolates and will give none away, self-centered and callous, indecent in fact, but not unjust. And similarly, that even supposing a case in which a woman pregnant due to rape ought to allow the unborn person to use her body for the hour he needs, we should not conclude that he has a right to do so; we should conclude that she is self-centered, callous, indecent, but not unjust, if she refuses. The complaints are no less grave; they are just different. However, there is no need to insist on this point. If anyone does wish to deduce "he has a right" from "you ought to," then all the same he must surely grant that there are cases in which it is not morally required of you that you allow that violinist to use your kidneys, and in which he does not have a right to use them, and in which you do not do him an injustice if you refuse. And so also for mother and unborn child. Except in such cases as the unborn person has a right to demand it—and we were leaving open the possibility that there may be such case—nobody is morally *required* to make large sacrifices, of health, of all other interests and concerns, of all other duties and commitments for nine years, or even for nine months, in order to keep another person alive.

6. We have in fact to distinguish between two kinds of Samaritan: the Good Samaritan and what we might call the Minimally Decent Samaritan. The story of the Good Samaritan, you will remember, goes like this:

> A certain man went down from Jerusalem to Jericho, and fell among thieves, which stripped him of his raiment, and wounded him, and departed, leaving him half dead.
>
> And by chance there came down a certain priest that way; and when he saw him, he passed by on the other side.
>
> And likewise a Levite, when he was at the place, came and looked on him, and passed by on the other side.

But a certain Samaritan, as he journeyed, came where he was; and when he saw him he had compassion on him.

And went to him, and bound up his wounds, pouring in oil and wine, and set him on his own beast, and brought him to an inn, and took care of him.

And on the morrow, when he departed, he took out two pence, and gave them to the host, and said unto him, 'Take care of him; and whatsoever thou spendest more, when I come again, I will repay thee.' (Luke 10: 30-35)

The Good Samaritan went out of his way, at some cost to himself, to help one in need of it. We are not told what the options were, that is, whether or not the priest and the Levite could have helped by doing less than the Good Samaritan did, but assuming they could have, then the fact they did nothing at all shows they were not even Minimally Decent Samaritans, not because they were not Samaritans, but because they were not even minimally decent.

These things are a matter of degree, of course, but there is a difference, and it comes out perhaps most clearly in the story of Kitty Genovese who, as you will remember, was murdered while thirty-eight people watched or listened and did nothing at all to help her. A Good Samaritan would have rushed out to give direct assistance against the murderer. Or perhaps we had better allow that it would have been a Splendid Samaritan who did this, on the ground that it would have involved a risk of death for himself. But the thirty-eight not only did not do this, they did not even trouble to pick up a phone to call the police. Minimally Decent Samaritanism would call for doing at least that, and their not having done it was monstrous.

After telling the story of the Good Samaritan, Jesus said, 'Go, and do thou likewise.' Perhaps he meant that we are morally required to act as the Good Samaritan did. Perhaps he was urging people to do more than is morally required of them. At all events it seems plain that it was not morally required of any of the thirty-eight that he rush out to give direct assistance at the risk of his own life, and that it is not morally required of anyone that he give long stretches of his life—nine years or nine months—to sustaining the life of a person who has no special right (we were leaving open the possibility of this) to demand it.

Indeed, with one rather striking class of exceptions, no one in any country in the world is *legally* required to do anywhere near as much as this for anyone else. The class of exceptions is obvious. My main concern here is not the state of the law in respect to abortion, but it is worth drawing attention to the fact that in no state in this country is any man compelled by law to be even a Minimally Decent Samaritan to any person; there is no law under which charges could be brought against the thirty-eight who stood by while Kitty Genovese died. By contrast, in most states in this country women are compelled by law to be not merely Minimally Decent Samaritans, but Good Samaritans to unborn persons inside them. This doesn't by itself settle anything one way or the other because it may well be argued that there should be laws in this country—as there are in many European countries—compelling at least Minimally Decent Samaritanism. But it does show that there is a gross injustice in the existing state of the law. And it shows also that the groups currently working against liberalization of abortion laws, in fact working toward having it declared unconstitutional for a state to permit abortion, had better start working for the adoption of Good Samaritan laws generally, or earn the charge that they are acting in bad faith.

I should think, myself, that Minimally Decent Samaritan laws would be one thing, Good Samaritan laws quite another, and in fact highly improper. But we are not here concerned with the law. What we should ask is not whether anybody should be compelled by law to be a Good Samaritan, but whether we must accede to a situation in which somebody is being compelled—by nature, perhaps—to be a Good Samaritan. We have, in other words, to look now at third-party interventions. I have been arguing that no person is morally required to make large sacrifices to sustain the life of another who has no right to demand them, and this even where the sacrifices do not include life itself; we are not morally required to be Good Samaritans or anyway Very Good Samaritans to one another. But what if a man cannot extricate himself from such a situation? What if he appeals to us to extricate him? It seems to me plain that there are cases in which we can, cases in which a Good Samaritan would extricate him. There you are, you were kidnapped, and nine years in bed with that violinist lie ahead of you. You have your own life to lead. You are sorry but you simply cannot see giving up so much of your life to the sustaining of his. You cannot extricate yourself, and ask us to do so. I should have thought that—in light of his having no right to the use of your body—it was obvious that we do not have to accede to your being forced to give up so much. We can do what you ask. There is no injustice to the violinist in our doing so.

7. Following the lead of the opponents of abortion, I have throughout been speaking of the foetus merely as a person, and what I have been asking is whether or not the argument we began with, which proceeds only from the foetus's being a person, really does establish its conclusion. I have argued that it does not.

But of course there are arguments and arguments, and it may be said that I have simply fastened on the wrong one. It may be said that what is important is not merely the fact that the foetus is a person, but that it is a person for whom the woman has a special kind of responsibility issuing from the fact that she is its mother. And it might be argued that all my analogies are therefore irrelevant—for you do not have that special kind of responsibility for that violinist, Henry Fonda does not have that special kind of responsibility for me. And our attention might be drawn to the fact that men and women both *are* compelled by law to provide support for their children.

I have in effect dealt (briefly) with this argument in section 4 above; but a (still briefer) recapitulation now may be in order. Surely we do not have any such "special responsibility" for a person unless we have assumed it, explicitly or implicitly. If a set of parents do not try to prevent pregnancy, do not obtain an abortion, and then at the time of birth of the child do not put it out for adoption, but rather take it home with them, then they have assumed responsibility for it, they have given it rights, and they cannot *now* withdraw support from it at the cost of its life because they now find it difficult to go on providing for it. But if they have taken all reasonable precautions against having a child, they do not simply by virtue of their biological relationship to the child who comes into existence have a special responsibility for it. They may wish to assume responsibility for it, or they may not wish to. And I am suggesting that if assuming responsibility for it would require large sacrifices, then they may refuse. A Good Samaritan would not refuse—or anyway, a Splendid Samaritan, if the sacrifices that had to be made were enormous. But then so would a Good Samaritan assume responsibility for that violinist; so would Henry Fonda, if he is a Good Samaritan, fly in from the West Coast and assume responsibility for me.

8. My argument will be found unsatisfactory on two counts by many of those who want to regard abortion as morally permissible. First, while I do argue that abortion is not impermissible, I do not argue that it is always permissible. There may well be cases in which carrying the child to term requires only Minimally Decent Samaritanism of the mother, and this is a standard we must not fall below. I am inclined to think it a merit of my account precisely that it does *not* give a general yes or a general no. It allows for and supports our sense that, for example, a sick and desperately frightened fourteen-year-old schoolgirl, pregnant due to rape, may *of course* choose abortion, and that any law that rules this out is an insane law. And it also allows for and supports our sense that in other cases resort to abortion is even positively indecent. It would be indecent in the woman to request an abortion, and indecent in a doctor to perform it, if she is in her seventh month, and wants the abortion just to avoid the nuisance of postponing a trip abroad. The very fact that the arguments I have been drawing attention to treat all cases of abortion, or even all cases of abortion in which the mother's life is not at stake, as morally on a par ought to have made them suspect at the outset.

Secondly, while I am arguing for the permissibility of abortion in some cases, I am not arguing for the right to secure the death of the unborn child. It is easy to confuse these two things in that up to a certain point in the life of the foetus it is not able to survive outside the mother's body; hence removing it from her body guarantees its death. But they are importantly different. I have argued that you are not morally required to spend nine months in bed, sustaining the life of that violinist, but to say this is by no means to say that if, when you unplug yourself, there is a miracle and he survives, you then have a right to turn round and slit his throat. You may detach yourself even if this costs him his life; you have no right to be guaranteed his death, by some other means, if unplugging yourself does not kill him. There are some people who will feel dissatisfied by this feature of my argument. A woman may be utterly devastated by the thought of a child, a bit of herself, put out for adoption and never seen or heard of again. She may therefore want not merely that the child be detached from her, but more, that it die. Some opponents of abortion are inclined to regard this as beneath contempt—thereby showing insensitivity to what is surely a powerful source of despair. All the same, I agree that the desire for the child's death is not one which anybody may gratify, should it turn out to be possible to detach the child alive.

At this place, however, it should be remembered that we have only been pretending throughout that the foetus is a human being from the moment of conception. A very early abortion is surely not the killing of a person, and so is not dealt with by anything I have said here.

STUDY QUESTIONS

1. What is Thomson's argument for the permissibility of abortion? How effective is the analogy comparing abortion to detaching oneself from the world-famous violinist?

2. Under what conditions, if any, does the violinist have a right to use your kidney? If he only needs it for five minutes, does he have a right to your kidney? Should you allow him to use it? Explain.

3. Thomson's argument seems relevant to cases of rape, where the woman did not voluntarily have sex. Does it apply to cases where the woman voluntarily had sex?

NOTES

1. The term "direct" in the arguments I refer to is a technical one. Roughly, what is meant by 'direct killing' is either killing as an end in itself. or killing as a means to some end, for example, the end of saving someone else's life. See note 4, following, for a example of its use.

2. Cf. *Encyclical Letter of Pope Pius XI on Christian Marriage, St.* Paul Editions (Boston, n.d.), 32: "however much we may pity the mother whose health and even life is gravely imperiled in the performance of the duty allotted to her by nature, nevertheless what could ever be a sufficient reason for excusing in any way the direct murder of the innocent? This is precisely what we are dealing with here." John T. Noonan, Jr. ("An Almost Absolute Value in History," in *The Morality of Abortion,* ed. John T. Noonan, Jr., Cambridge, Mass.: Harvard, 1970, 43). Reads this as follows: "What cause can ever avail to excuse in any way the direct killing of the innocent? For it is a question of that."

3. The thesis in (4) is in an interesting way weaker than those in (1), (2), and (3): they rule out abortion even in cases in which both mother *and* child will die if the abortion is not performed. By contrast, one who held the view expressed in (4) could consistently say that one needn't prefer letting two persons die to killing one.

4. Cf. the following passage from Pius XII, *Address to the Italian Catholic Society of Midwives.* "The baby in the maternal breast has the right to life immediately from God.— Hence there is no man, no human authority, no science, no medical, eugenic, social, economic or moral 'indication' which can establish or grant a valid juridical ground for a direct deliberate disposition of an innocent human life, that is a disposition which looks to its destruction either as an end or as a means to another end perhaps in itself not illicit.—The baby, still not born, is a man in the same degree and for the same reason as the mother" (quoted in Noonan, *The Morality of Abortion,* 45).

8

Arguments from Bodily Rights: A Critical Analysis

FRANCIS J. BECKWITH

Francis J. Beckwith is Associate Professor of Philosophy, Culture, and Law and W. Howard Hoffman scholar at Trinity Graduate School and Trinity Law School, Trinity International University (Deerfield, Illinois), California campus.

In the following essay Beckwith contends that Thomson's argument (Chapter 7) is flawed for many reasons: (1) it assumes that moral obligations must be voluntary, (2) it denies special obligations to family members, (3) it denies prima facie rights of the unborn, (4) it ignores the distinction between killing and withholding treatment, (5) it does not take into consideration legal precedent, and (6) it seems inconsistent with radical feminism (a view espoused by many of the argument's proponents) in at least three ways: (i) its use of the burden of pregnancy, (ii) its appeal to libertarian principles, and (iii) its macho view of bodily control. However, before his critique of Thomson's argument, Beckwith critically evaluates two popular arguments for abortion rights that appeal to personal bodily autonomy: (1) argument from a woman's right over her own body, and (2) argument from abortion being safer than childbirth. According to Beckwith, the first argument fails because it begs the question as to the unborn's personhood, and the second fails because it is based on dubious statistics as well as a faulty comparison between the risks of childbirth and abortion.

Reprinted from Francis J. Beckwith, *Politically Correct Death: Answering the Arguments for Abortion Rights* (Grand Rapids, Mich.: Baker Book House, 1993), Chapter 7. Some notes and portions of the original text have been either revised or deleted for this anthology. Reprinted by permission.

Some abortion-rights advocates do not see the status of the unborn as the decisive factor in whether or not abortion is morally justified. They argue that the unborn's presence in the pregnant woman's body entails a conflict of rights if the pregnant woman does not want to be pregnant. Therefore, the unborn, regardless of whether it is fully human and has a full right to life, cannot use the body of another against her will. Hence, a pregnant woman's removal of an unborn entity from her body, even though it will probably result in that entity's death, is no more immoral than an ordinary person's refusal to donate his kidney to another in need of one, even though this refusal will probably result in the death of the prospective recipient. In this essay we will discuss such arguments from rights.

The most famous and influential argument from rights is the one presented by philosopher Judith Jarvis Thomson. However, before analyzing that argument, I want to respond to two popular arguments that are much less sophisticated than Thomson's. These arguments, unlike Thomson's, do not assume for the sake of argument that the unborn is fully human. but ignore altogether the question of the unborn's humanness.

ARGUMENT FROM A WOMAN'S RIGHT OVER HER OWN BODY

This argument asserts that because a woman has a right to control her own body, she therefore has a right to undergo an abortion for any reason she deems fit. Although it is not obvious that either the law or sound ethical reasoning supports such a strong view of personal autonomy (for example, laws against prostitution and suicide), this abortion-rights argument still fails logically even if we assume that such a strong view of personal autonomy is correct.

First, the unborn entity within the pregnant woman's body is not a part of her body, although many people, (even very intelligent ones) seem unaware of this fact. Consider the comments of philosopher Mortimer Adler, who claims that before viability the life the unborn "has is as a part of the mother's body, in the same sense that an individual's arm or leg is a part of a living organism. An individual's decision to have an arm or leg amputated falls within the sphere of privacy—the freedom to do as one pleases in all matters that do not injure others or the public welfare."[1] Even someone as knowledgeable on the abortion issue as Laurence Tribe of the Harvard Law School writes that "although the fetus at some point develops an independent identity and even an independent consciousness, it begins as a living part of the woman's body."[2] Both Adler and Tribe are completely mistaken. For one thing, the conceptus is a genetically distinct entity with its own individual gender, blood type, bone structure, and genetic code. Although the unborn entity is attached to her mother, she is not part of her mother. To say that the unborn entity is part of her mother is to claim that the mother possesses four legs, two heads, two noses, and with the case of a male fetus, a penis and two testicles. Moreover,

Bernard Nathanson points out "that the modern science of immunology has shown that the unborn child is not a part of a woman's body in the sense that her kidney or heart is."[3] This, of course, contradicts the claims of Adler and Tribe. Nathanson goes on to outline the scientific basis for this claim:

> Immunologic studies have demonstrated beyond cavil that when a pregnancy implants itself into the wall of the uterus at the eighth day following conception the defense mechanisms of the body, principally the white blood cells, sense that this creature now settling down for a lengthy stay is an intruder, an alien, and must be expelled. Therefore, an intense immunological attack is mounted on the pregnancy by the white blood cell elements, and through an ingenious and extraordinarily efficient defense system the unborn child succeeds in repelling the attack. In 10 percent or so of cases the defensive system fails and pregnancy is lost as a spontaneous abortion or miscarriage. Think how fundamental a lesson there is for us here: Even on the most minute microscopic scale the body has trained itself, or somehow in some inchoate way *knows,* how to recognize *self* from *non-self.*[4]

Furthermore, because scientists have been able to achieve conception in a petri dish (the "test-tube" baby), and this conceptus if it has white parents can be transferred to the body of a black woman and be born white, we know conclusively that the unborn is not part of the pregnant woman's body. Certainly a woman has a right to control her own body, but the unborn entity is not part of her body. Hence, abortion is not justified because no one's right to personal autonomy is so strong that it permits the arbitrary execution of others.

Second, this abortion–rights argument is guilty of special pleading. The concept of a personal right over one's own body presupposes the existence of a person who possesses such a right. Such a right also presupposes that this right to personal autonomy should not interfere with another person's identical right. This is why smoking is being prohibited in more and more public places. Many studies have shown conclusively that a smoker's habit affects not only his own lungs, but also the lungs of others who choose not to smoke. The smoker's "secondary smoke" can cause the nonsmoker to be ill and quite possibly acquire lung cancer if he is exposed to such smoke over a long period of time. Because the nonsmoker has a personal right over his own body, and he chooses not to fill it with nicotine, the smoker's personal right to smoke and fill his own body with nicotine is limited by the nonsmoker's personal right to remain healthy. This is because in the process of smoking the smoker passes on harmful secondary smoke to the unwilling nonsmoker.

Suppose a smoker, in arguing against a prohibition of smoking in public places, continually appeals to his "personal right" to control his own body. And suppose he dismisses out of hand any counterargument that appeals to the possible existence of other persons (nonsmokers) whose rights his actions may obstruct. This sort of argumentation would be a case of *special pleading,* a fallacy that occurs when someone selects pieces of evidence that confirm his position (in this case, the smoker's legitimate right to personal autonomy) and ignores counterexamples that conflict with it (in this case, the nonsmoker's legitimate right to personal autonomy). Therefore, for the abortion issue, when the abortion-rights advocate appeals to a woman's right to control her own body while ignoring the possibility that this control might entail the death of another, he is guilty of selecting principles that support his position (every person has a prima facie right to personal autonomy) while ignoring principles that conflict with it (every person has a prima facie obligation not to harm another). Thus the abortion-rights advocate is guilty of special pleading.

Of course, if the unborn entity is not fully human, this abortion-rights argument is successful. But this means that one begs the question when one argues for abortion rights from a woman's right to control her own body if one does not first show that the unborn entity is not fully human. Baruch Brody adds to this observation that although "it is surely true that one way in which women have been oppressed is by their being denied authority over their own bodies…, it seems to be that, as the struggle is carried on for meaningful amelioration of such oppression, it ought not to be carried so far that it violates the steady responsibilities all people have to one another." To cite a number of examples, "parents may not desert their children, one class may not oppress another, one race or nation may not exploit another. For parents, powerful groups in society, races, or nations in ascendancy, there are penalties for refraining from these wrong actions, but those penalties can in no way be taken as the justification for such wrong actions. Similarly, if the fetus is a human being, the penalty of carrying it cannot, I believe, be used as justification for destroying it."[5]

ARGUMENT FROM ABORTION BEING SAFER THAN CHILDBIRTH

This argument attempts to show that the pregnant woman has no moral obligation to carry her unborn offspring to term, regardless of whether or not it is fully human. The abortion-rights advocate argues that childbirth is an act that is not morally obligatory by the pregnant woman because an abortion is statistically safer than childbirth. The statistic often quoted to support this argument is one found in the most recent edition of the *American Medical Association Encyclopedia of Medicine:* "Mortality is less than one per 100,000 when abortion is performed before the 13th week, rising to three per 100,000 after the 13th week. (For comparison, maternal mortality for full-term pregnancy is nine per l00,000.)"[6] This argument can be outlined in the following way.

1. Among moral acts one is not morally obligated to perform are those that can endanger one's life (for example, the man who dove into the Potomac in the middle of winter to save the survivors of a plane crash).
2. Childbirth is more life-threatening than having an abortion.
3. Therefore, childbirth is an act one is not morally obligated to perform.
4. Therefore, abortion is justified.

The problem with this argument lies in the inference from 2 to 3. First, assuming that childbirth is on the average more life-threatening than abortion, it does not follow that abortion is justified in every case. The fact that one act, A, is more life-threatening *on the average* than another act, B, does not mean that one is not justified or obligated to perform A in *specific* situations where there is no prima facie reason to believe that A would result in death or severe physical impairment. To use an uncontroversial example, it is probably on the average less life-threatening to stay at home than to leave home and buy groceries (for example, one can be killed in a car crash, purchase and take tainted Tylenol, or be murdered by a mugger), yet it seems foolish, not to mention counterintuitive, to always act in every instance on the basis of that average. This is a form of the informal *fallacy of division,* which occurs when someone erroneously argues that what is true of a whole (the average) must also be true of its parts (every individual situation). One would commit this fallacy if one argued that because Beverly Hills is wealthier than Barstow, every individual person who lives in Beverly Hills is wealthier than every individual person who lives in Barstow.

Second, we can also imagine a situation in which someone is obligated to perform a particular moral action although there is statistically more risk in performing it than abstaining from it. That is to say, we can challenge the inference from 2 to 3 by pointing out that just because an act, X, is "more dangerous" relative to another act, Y, does not mean that a person is not morally obligated to perform X. For example, it would be statistically more dangerous for me (a swimmer) to dive into a swimming pool to save my wife (a nonswimmer) from drowning than it would be for me to abstain from acting. Yet this does not mean that I am not morally obligated to save my wife's life. Sometimes my moral obligation is such that it outweighs the relatively insignificant chance of danger I avoid by not acting. We could then argue that although childbirth might be "more dangerous" than abortion, the special moral obligation one has to one's offspring far outweighs the relatively insignificant danger one avoids by not acting on that moral obligation (on the statistical insignificance between abortion and childbirth [see later]).

Of course, if a specific act, X, is significantly dangerous (that is, there is a good chance that you will die or be severely harmed if you act)—such as the act performed by that man who dove into the freezing Potomac River to save the survivors of an airplane crash—then it would seem that an individual would not be obligated to perform X. However, if you had chosen to perform X, you would be performing an act of exceptional morality (what ethicists call a *supererogatory act*), although if you had refrained from X, you would not be considered a bad or an evil person. In light of these observations, the abortion-rights argument in question can be strengthened if changed in the following way:

1. Among moral acts you are not morally obligated to perform are those that can endanger your life.

2. A particular instance of childbirth, X, is more life-threatening to the pregnant woman than having an abortion.

3. Therefore, X is an act you are not morally obligated to perform.

4. Therefore, not-X via abortion is justified.

Although avoiding the pitfalls of the first argument, this one does not support the abortion-rights position. It is consistent with the prolife assertion that abortion is justified if it is employed to save the life of the mother. Therefore, whether or not abortion is statistically safer than childbirth is irrelevant to whether or not abortion is justified in particular cases where sound medical diagnosis indicates that childbirth will pose virtually no threat to the mother's life.

Two other observations can be made about the argument from abortion being safer than childbirth. First, the AMA statistics are misused and do not really establish the abortion-rights position. The statistics claim that the mortality rate for a woman in childbirth is 9 per 100,000 while mortality is less than 1 per 100,000 when abortion is performed before the thirteenth week, increasing to 3 per 100,000 after the thirteenth week. This is why abortion-rights advocates often claim that a first trimester abortion is nine times safer than childbirth. Although this assertion is technically true if you assume that the statistics are accurate, it is statistically insignificant. This becomes apparent when we convert the odds into percentages. If the mortality of childbirth is 9 per 100,000, then a woman has a 99.991 percent chance of surviving. If the mortality of a first-trimester abortion is 1 per 100,000, then a woman has a 99.999 percent chance of surviving. But the statistical difference between 99.991 percent and 99.999 percent (00.008 percent) is moot, especially if one considers the complex nature of both childbirth and abortion, as there are so many variables that can account for the small difference in the mortality rates.

Second, we can challenge the claim that abortion is safer than childbirth. David C. Reardon points out that claims that abortion is safer than childbirth are based on dubious statistical studies, simply because "accurate statistics are scarce because the reporting of complications is almost entirely at the option of abortion providers. In other words, abortionists are in the privileged position of being able to hide any information which might damage their reputation or trade." And because "federal court rulings have sheltered the practice of abortion in a 'zone of privacy,'" therefore "any laws which attempt to require that deaths and complications resulting from abortion are recorded, much less reported, are unconstitutional." This means that the "only information available on abortion complications is the result of data which is voluntarily reported."[7] From these and other factors,[8] Reardon concludes that

> Complication records from outpatient clinics are virtually inaccessible, or non-existent, even though these clinics provide the vast majority of all abortions. Even in Britain where reporting requirements are much better than in the United States, medical experts believe that less than 10 percent of abortion complications are actually reported to government health agencies.[9]

Reardon's study indicates that it might be more true to say that abortion is more dangerous than childbirth. His work deals with the physical risks as well as the psychological impact of abortion on women, in addition to the impact of abortion on later children. He concludes that the harm caused by abortion to the woman and her children is grossly understated by abortion-rights advocates.[10]

It should be noted that many scholars have disputed the claim of abortion-rights advocates that early abortions are safer than childbirth. These critics argue that the data used to draw this conclusion have been misinterpreted or are problematic. Consider the following example of how such a misinterpretation can occur. In a highly sophisticated study on the topic of abortion-related maternal mortality, Thomas W. Hilgers, M.D., a professor of obstetrics and gynecology at Creighton University, writes,

> Maternal mortality rates are generally expressed as the number of maternal deaths which occur—during the entire course of pregnancy and during the first three to six months following completion of the pregnancy—per 100,000 *live births*. The maternal mortality related to abortion, on the other hand, is expressed according to the type of procedure or the gestational age of the pregnancy per 100,000 *abortions*. In the latter case, the denominator is, in essence, the *number of cases* in which a particular procedure is carried out. With maternal mortality rates, this is not so. When the denominator is live births, a number of cases of pregnancy are automatically excluded from the denominator, while their associated maternal deaths are included in the numerator. This automatically strains the traditional comparison between the maternal mortality in natural pregnancy and that in abortion. Such comparisons lack statistical accuracy.[11]

Taking into consideration this and other statistical problems, Hilgers draws among many conclusions the following: "In comparing the relative risk of natural pregnancy versus that of legal abortion, *natural, pregnancy was found to be safer in both the first and second 20 weeks of pregnancy.*"[12]

Considering that the supposed fact that childbirth is not as safe as abortion played a substantial role in the U.S Supreme Court opinions that made abortion legal, *Roe v. Wade* (410 U.S. 113 [1973]) and *Doe v. Bolton* (410 U.S. 179 [1973]), exposing the logical and factual flaws of this claim helps to undermine the foundation of the Court's opinions.

ARGUMENT FROM UNPLUGGING
THE VIOLINIST

Judith Jarvis Thomson presents a philosophically sophisticated version of the argument from a woman's right to control her body.[13] Thomson argues that even if the unborn entity is a person with a right to life, this does not mean that a woman must be forced to use her bodily organs to sustain its life. Just as one does not have a right to use another's kidney if one's kidney has failed, the unborn entity, although having a basic right to life, does not have a right to life so strong that it outweighs the pregnant woman's right to personal bodily autonomy.

Presentation of the Argument

This argument is called "the argument from unplugging the violinist" because of a story Thomson uses to illustrate her position:

> You wake up in the morning and find yourself back to back in bed with an unconscious violinist. A famous unconscious violinist. He has been found to have a fatal kidney ailment, and the Society of Music Lovers has canvassed all the available medical records and found that you alone have the right blood type to help. They have therefore kidnapped you, and last night the violinist's circulatory system was plugged into yours, so that your kidneys can be used to extract poisons from his blood as well as your own. The director of the hospital now tells you, "Look, we're sorry the Society of Music Lovers did this to you—we would never have permitted it if we had known. But still, they did it, and the violinist now is plugged into you. To unplug you would be to kill him. But never mind, it's only for nine months. By then he will have recovered from his ailment and can safely be unplugged from you." Is it morally incumbent on you to accede to this situation? No doubt it would be very nice of you if you did, a great kindness. But do you *have* to accede to it? What if it were not nine months, but nine years? Or still longer? What if the director of the hospital says, "Tough luck, I agree, but you've now got to stay in bed, with the violinist plugged into you for the rest of your life. Because remember this. All persons have a right to life, and violinists are persons. Granted you have a right to decide what happens in and to your body, but a person's right to life outweighs your right to decide what happens in and to your body. So you cannot ever be unplugged from him." I imagine that you would regard this as outrageous.[14]

Thomson concludes that she is "only arguing that having a right to life does not guarantee having either a right to be given the use of or a right to be allowed continued use of another person's body—even if one needs it for life itself."[15] Thomson anticipates several objections to her argument, and in the process of responding to them further clarifies it. It is not important, however, that we go over these clarifications now, for some are not germane to the prolife position I am defending in this essay,[16] and the remaining will be dealt with in the following critique. In any event, It should not be ignored by the prolife advocate that Thomson's argument makes some important observations which have gone virtually unnoticed by the prolife movement. In defending the relevance of her story, Thomson points out that it is "of great interest to ask what happens if, for the sake of argument, we allow the premise [that the unborn are fully human or persons]. How, precisely, are we supposed to get from there to the conclusion that abortion is morally impermissible?" Thomson's argument poses a special difficulty because she believes that since pregnancy constitutes an infringement on the pregnant woman's personal rights by the unborn entity, the ordinary abortion, although it results in the death of an innocent human person, is not prima facie wrong.

A Critique of Thomson's Argument

There are at least nine problems with Thomson's argument. These problems can be put into three categories: ethical, legal, and ideological.

Ethical Problems with Thomson's Argument

1. *Thomson assumes volunteerism.* By using the story as a paradigm for all relationships, thus implying that moral obligations must be voluntarily accepted to have moral force, Thomson mistakenly infers that all true moral obligations to one's offspring are voluntary. But consider the following story. Suppose a couple has a sexual encounter that is fully protected by several forms of birth control short of surgical abortion (condom, the Pill, IUD), but nevertheless results in conception. Instead of getting an abortion, the mother of the conceptus decides to bring it to term, although the father is unaware of this decision. After the birth of the child, the mother pleads with the father for child support. Because he refuses, she takes legal action. Although he took every precaution to avoid fatherhood, thus showing that he did not wish to accept such a status, according to nearly all child-support laws in the United States, he would still be obligated to pay support *precisely because* of his relationship to this child.[17] As Michael Levin points out, "All child-support laws make the parental body an indirect resource for the child. If the father is a construction worker, the state will intervene unless some of his calories he expends lifting equipment go to providing food for his children."[18]

But this obligatory relationship is not based strictly on biology, for this would make sperm donors morally responsible for children conceived by their seed. Rather, the father's responsibility for his offspring stems from the fact that he engaged in an act, sexual intercourse, that he fully realized could result in the creation of another human being, although he took every precaution to avoid such a result. This is not an unusual way to frame moral obligations, for we hold drunk people whose driving results in manslaughter responsible for their actions, even if they did not intend to kill someone prior to becoming intoxicated. Such special obligations, although not directly undertaken voluntarily, are necessary in any civilized culture to preserve the rights of the vulnerable, the weak, and the young, who can offer very little in exchange for the rights bestowed on them by the strong, the powerful, and the postuterine in Thomson's moral universe of the social contract. Thus, Thomson is wrong, in addition to ignoring the *natural* relationship between sexual intercourse and human reproduction,[19] when she claims that if a couple has "taken all reasonable precautions against having a child, they do not by virtue of their biological relationship to the child who comes into existence have a special responsibility for it." "Surely we do not have any such 'special responsibility' for a person unless we have assumed it, explicitly or implicitly."[20] Hence, instead of providing reasons for rejecting any special responsibilities for one's offspring, Thomson simply dismisses the concept altogether.

2. *Thomson's argument is fatal to family morality.* It follows from the first criticism that Thomson's volunteerism is fatal to family morality, which has as

one of its central beliefs that an individual has special and filial obligations to his offspring and family that he does not have to other persons. Although Thomson might not consider such a fatality as being all that terrible because she might accept the feminist dogma that the traditional family is "oppressive" to women, a great number of ordinary men and women, who have found joy, happiness, and love in family life, find Thomson's voluneerism to be counter-intuitive. Christina Sommers has come to a similar conclusion:

> For it [the volunteerist thesis] means that there is no such thing as filial duty per se, no such thing as the special duty of mother to child, and generally no such thing as morality of special family or kinship relations. All of which is contrary to what people think. For most people think that we do owe special debts to our parents even though we have not volun-tarily assumed our obligations to them. Most people think that what we owe to our children does not have its origin in any voluntary undertak-ing, explicit or implicit, that we have made to them. And "preanalyti-cally," many people believe that we owe special consideration to our siblings even at times when we may not *feel* very friendly to them…The idea that to be committed to an individual is to have made a voluntarily implicit or explicit commitment to that individual is generally fatal to family morality. For it looks upon the network of felt obligation and ex-pectation that binds family members as a sociological phenomenon that is without presumptive moral force. The social critics who hold this view of family obligation usually are aware that promoting it in public policy must further the disintegration of the traditional family as an institution. But whether they deplore the disintegration or welcome it, they are bound in principle to abet it.[21]

3. A case can be made that the unborn does have a prima facie right to her mother's body. Assuming that there is such a thing as a special filial obligation, a princi-ple that does not have to be voluntarily accepted to have moral force, it is not obvious that the unborn entity in ordinary circumstances (that is, with the ex-ception of when the mother's life is in significant danger) does not have a nat-ural prima facie claim to her mother's body. There are several reasons to suppose that the unborn entity does have such a natural claim.

a. Unlike Thomson's violinist, who is artificially attached to another per-son to save his life and is therefore not naturally dependent on any particular human being, the unborn entity is a human being who by her very nature is dependent on her mother, for this is how human beings are at this stage of their development.

b. This period of a human being's natural development occurs in the womb. This is the journey that we all must take and is a necessary condition for any human being's postuterine existence. And this fact alone brings out the most glaring difference between the violinist and the unborn: The womb is the unborn's natural environment whereas being artificially hooked up to a stranger is not the natural environment for the violinist. It would seem, then, that the unborn has a prima facie natural claim on her mother's body.

c. This same entity, when she becomes a newborn, has a natural claim on her parents to care for her, regardless of whether her parents wanted her (see the story of the irresponsible father). This is why we prosecute child abusers, people who throw their babies in trash cans, and parents who abandon their children. Although it should not be ignored that pregnancy and childbirth entail certain emotional, physical, and financial sacrifices by the pregnant woman, these sacrifices are also endemic of parenthood in general (which ordinarily lasts much longer than nine months) and do not seem to justify the execution of troublesome infants and younger children whose existence entails a natural claim to certain financial and bodily goods that are under the ownership of their parents. If the unborn entity is fully human, as Thomson is willing to grant, why should the unborn's natural prima facie claim to her parents' goods differ before birth? Of course, a court will not force a parent to donate a kidney to her dying offspring, but this sort of dependence on the parent's body is highly unusual and is not part of the ordinary obligations associated with the natural process of human development, just as in the case of the violinist's artificial dependency on the reluctant music lover.

As Stephen D. Schwarz points out: "So, the very thing that makes it plausible to say that the person in bed with the violinist has no duty to sustain him; namely, that he is a stranger unnaturally hooked up to him, is precisely what is absent in the case of the mother and her child." That is to say, the mother "does have an obligation to take care of her child, to sustain her, to protect her, and especially, to let her live in the only place where she can now be protected, nourished, and allowed to grow, namely the womb."[22]

If Thomson responds to this argument by saying that birth is the threshold at which parents become fully responsible, then she has begged the question, for her argument was supposed to show us why there is no parental responsibility before birth. That is to say, Thomson cannot appeal to birth as the decisive moment at which parents become responsible to prove that birth is the time at which parents become responsible.

It is evident that Thomson's violinist illustration undermines the deep natural bond between mother and child by making it seem no different from that between two strangers artificially hooked up to each other so that one can "steal" the service of the other's kidneys. Never has something so human, so natural, so beautiful, and so wonderfully demanding of our human creativity and love been reduced to such a brutal caricature.

I am not saying that the unborn entity has an absolute natural claim to her mother's body, but simply that she has a prima facie natural claim. For one can easily imagine a situation in which this natural claim is outweighed by other important prima facie values, such as when a pregnancy significantly endangers the mother's life. Since the continuation of such a pregnancy would most likely entail the death of both mother and child, and since it is better that one human should live rather than two die, terminating such a pregnancy via abortion is morally justified.

Someone may respond to the three criticisms by agreeing that Thomson's illustration may not apply in cases of ordinary sexual intercourse, but only in cases in which pregnancy results from rape or incest, although it should be noted that Thomson herself does not press this argument. She writes, "Surely the question of whether you have a right to life at all, or how much of it you have, shouldn't turn on the question of whether or not you are the product of rape."[23]

But those who do press the rape argument may choose to argue in the following way: Just as the sperm donor is not responsible for how his sperm is used or what results from its use (for example, it might be stolen, or an unmarried woman might purchase it, inseminate herself, and give birth to a child), the raped woman, who did not voluntarily engage in intercourse cannot be held responsible for the unborn human who is living inside her.

But there is a problem with this analogy: The sperm donor's relinquishing of responsibility does not result in the death of a human person. The following story should help illustrate the differences and similarities between these two cases.

Suppose that the sperm donated by the sperm donor was stolen by an unscrupulous physician and inseminated into a woman. Although he is not morally responsible for the child that results from such an insemination, the donor is nevertheless forced by an unjust court to pay a large monthly sum for child support, a sum so large that it may drive him into serious debt, maybe even bankruptcy. This would be similar to the woman who became pregnant as a result of rape. She was unjustly violated and is supporting a human being against her will at an emotional and financial cost. Is it morally right for the sperm donor to kill the child he is supporting to allegedly right the wrong that has been committed against him? Not at all, because such an act would be murder. Now if we assume, as does Thomson, that the raped woman is carrying a being who is fully human (or "a person"), her killing of the unborn entity by abortion, except if the pregnancy has a strong possibility of endangering her life, would be as unjust as the sperm donor killing the child he is unjustly forced to support. As the victimized man can rightly refuse to pay the child support, the raped woman can rightly refuse to bring up her child after the pregnancy has come to term. She can choose to put the child up for adoption. But in both cases, the killing of child is not morally justified. Although neither the sperm donor nor the rape victim might have the same special obligation to their biological offspring as does the couple who voluntarily engaged in intercourse with no direct intention to produce a child, it seems that the more general obligation not to directly kill another human person does apply.

4. *Thomson ignores the fact that abortion is indeed killing and not merely the withholding of treatment.* Thomson makes an excellent point: Namely, there are times when withholding or withdrawing medical treatment is morally justified. For instance, I am not morally obligated to donate my kidney to Fred, my next-door neighbor, simply because he needs a kidney to live. In other words, I am not obligated to risk my life so that Fred can live a few years longer. Fred should not expect that of me. If, however, I donate one of my kidneys to Fred, I will have acted above and beyond the call of duty because I

will have performed a supererogatory moral act. But this case is not analogous to pregnancy and abortion.

Levin argues that there is an essential difference between abortion and the unplugging of the violinist. In the case of the violinist (as well as my relationship to Fred's welfare), "the person who withdraws [or withholds] his assistance is not completely responsible for the dependency on him of the person who is about to die, while the mother *is* completely responsible for the dependency of her fetus on her. When one is completely responsible for dependence, refusal to continue to aid is indeed killing." For example, "if a woman brings a newborn home from the hospital, puts it in its crib and refuses to feed it until it has starved to death, it would be absurd to say that she simply refused to assist it and had done nothing for which she should be criminally liable."[24] In other words, just as the withholding of food kills the child after birth, in the case of abortion, the abortion kills the child. In neither case is there any ailment from which the child suffers and for which highly invasive medical treatment, with the cooperation of another's bodily organs, is necessary to cure this ailment and save the child's life.

Or consider the following case, which can be applied to the case of pregnancy resulting from rape or incest. Suppose a person returns home after work to find a baby at his doorstep. Suppose that no one else is able to take care of the child, but this person has only to take care of the child for nine months (after that time a couple will adopt the child). Imagine that this person, because of the child's presence, will have some bouts with morning sickness, water retention, and other minor ailments. If we assume with Thomson that the unborn child is as much a person as you or I, would "withholding treatment" from this child and its subsequent death be justified on the basis that the homeowner was only "withholding treatment" of a child he did not ask for to benefit himself? Is any person, born or unborn, obligated to sacrifice his life because his death would benefit another person? Consequently, there is no doubt that such "withholding" of treatment (and it seems totally false to call ordinary shelter and sustenance "treatment") is indeed murder.

But is it even accurate to refer to abortion as the "withholding of support or treatment"? Professors Schwarz and R. K. Tacelli make the important point that although "a woman who has an abortion is indeed 'withholding support' from her unborn child…abortion is far more than that. It is the active killing of a human person—by burning him, by crushing him, by dismembering him."[25] Euphemistically calling abortion the "withholding of support or treatment" makes about as much sense as calling suffocating someone with a pillow the withdrawing of oxygen.

In summary, I agree with Professor Brody when he concludes, "Thomson has not established the truth of her claim about abortion, primarily because she has not sufficiently attended to the distinction between our duty to save X's life and our duty not to take it." But "once one attends to that distinction, it would seem that the mother, in order to regain control over her body, has no right to abort the fetus from the point at which it becomes a human being."[26]

Legal Problems with Thomson's Argument

There are at least two legal problems with Thomson's argument: One has to do with tort law, and the other has to do with parental responsibility and child-welfare law.

1. *Thomson's argument ignores tort law.* Judge John T. Noonan of the U.S. Ninth Circuit Court of Appeals points out that "while Thomson focuses on this fantasy [the violinist story], she ignores a real case from which American tort law has generalized."[27]

> On a January night in Minnesota, a cattle buyer, Orlando Depue, asked a family of farmers, the Flateaus, with whom he had dined, if he could remain overnight at their house. The Flateaus refused and, although Depue was sick and had fainted, put him out of the house into the cold night. Imposing liability on the Flateaus for Depue's loss of his frostbitten fingers, the court said: "In the case at bar defendants were under no contract obligation to minister to plaintiff in his distress; but humanity demanded they do so, if they understood and appreciated his condition...The law as well as humanity required that he not be exposed in his helpless condition to the merciless elements." Depue was a guest for supper although not a guest after supper. The American Law Institute, generalizing, has said that it makes no difference whether the person is a guest or a trespasser. He has the privilege of staying. His host has the duty not to injure him or put him into an environment where he becomes nonviable. The obligation arises when one "understands and appreciates" the condition of the other.

Noonan concludes that "although the analogy is not exact, the case is much closer to the mother's situation than the case imagined by Thomson, and the emotional response of the Minnesota judges seems to be a truer reflection of what humanity requires."

2. *Thomson's argument ignores family law.* Thomson's argument is inconsistent with the body of well-established family law, which presupposes parental responsibility of a child's welfare. And, of course, assuming as Thomson does that the unborn are fully human, this body of law would also apply to parents' responsibility for their unborn children. According to legal scholars Dennis J. Horan and Burke J. Balch, "All 50 states, the District of Columbia, American Samoa, Guam, and the U.S. Virgin Islands have child abuse and neglect statutes which provide for the protection of a child who does not receive needed medical care." They further state that "a review of cases makes it clear that these statutes are properly applied to secure emergency medical treatment and sustenance (food or water, whether given orally or through intravenous or nasogastric tube) for children when parents, with or without the acquiescence of physicians, refuse to provide it."[28] Evidently, "pulling the plug" on a perfectly healthy unborn entity, assuming that it is a human person, would clearly violate these statutes.

For example, in a case in New York, the court ruled that the parents' actions constituted neglect when they failed to provide medical care to a child with leukemia: "The parent…may not deprive a child of life-saving treatment, however well-intentioned. Even when the parents' decision to decline necessary treatment is based on constitutional grounds such as religious beliefs, it must yield to the State's interests, as parens patriae, in protecting the health and welfare of the child."[29] The fact of the matter is that the "courts have uniformly held that a parent has the legal responsibility of furnishing his dependent child with adequate food and medical care."[30]

It is evident then that child-protection laws reflect our deepest moral intuitions about parental responsibility and the utter helplessness of infants and small children. And without these moral scruples—which are undoubtedly undermined by "brave new notions" of a socially contracted "voluntaristic" family (Thomson's view)—the protection of children and the natural bonds and filial obligations that are an integral part of ordinary family life will become a thing of the past. This seems too high a price for bodily autonomy.

Ideological Problems with the Use of Thomson's Argument

There are at least three ideological problems in the use of Thomson's argument by others. The latter two problems are usually found in the books, speeches, articles, or papers of those in the feminist or abortion-rights movements who sometimes uncritically use Thomson's argument or ones similar to it. In fact, Thomson might agree with most or all of the following critique.

1. *Inconsistent use of the burden of pregnancy.* Thomson has to paint pregnancy in the most horrific of terms to make her argument seem plausible. Dr. Bernard Nathanson, an obstetrician/gynecologist and former abortion provider, objects "strenuously to Thomson's portrayal of pregnancy as a nine-month involuntary imprisonment in bed. This casts an unfair and wrong-headed prejudice against the consideration of the state of pregnancy and skews the argument." Nathanson points out that "pregnancy is not a 'sickness.' Few pregnant women are bedridden and many, emotionally and physically, have never felt better. For these it is a stimulating experience, even for mothers who originally did not 'want' to be pregnant." Unlike the person who is plugged into Thomson's violinist, "alpha [the unborn entity] does not hurt the mother by being 'plugged in'…except in the case of well-defined medical indications." And "in those few cases where pregnancy is a medical penalty, it is a penalty lasting nine months."[31]

Compare and contrast Thomson's portrayal of pregnancy with the fact that researchers have recently discovered that many people believe that a pregnant woman cannot work as effectively as a nonpregnant woman who is employed to do the same job in the same work place. This has upset a number of feminists, and rightfully so. They argue that a pregnant woman is not incapacitated or ill, but can work just as effectively as a nonpregnant woman.[32] But why then do feminists who use Thomson's argument argue, when it comes to abortion, that pregnancy is similar to being bedridden and hooked up to a violinist for nine months? When it comes to equality in the workplace (with which I agree with the feminists), there is no problem. But in the case of morally justifying abortion rights, pregnancy is painted in the most horrific of terms. Although not logically fatal to the abortion-rights position, this sort of double-mindedness is not conducive to good moral reasoning.

2. *The libertarian principles underlying Thomson's case are inconsistent with the state-mandated agenda of radical feminism.* If Thomson's illustration works at all, it works contrary to the statist principles of radical feminism (of course, a libertarian feminist need not be fazed by this objection). Levin points out that "while appeal to an absolute right to the disposition of one's body coheres well with other strongly libertarian positions (laissez-faire in the marketplace, parental autonomy in education of their children, freedom of private association), this appeal is most commonly made by feminists who are antilibertarian on just about every other issue." For example, "feminists who advocate state-mandated quotas, state-mandated comparable worth pay scales, the censorship of 'sexist' textbooks in the public schools, laws against 'sexually harassing speech' and legal limitations on private association excluding homosexuals, will go on to advocate abortion on the basis of an absolute libertarianism at odds with every one of those policies."[33] Although this criticism is ad hominem, as was the previous one, it underscores the important political fact that many abortion-rights advocates are more than willing to hold and earnestly defend contrary principles for the sake of legally mandating their ideological agenda.

This sort of inconsistency is evident in abortion-rights activity throughout the United States. In the state of Nevada, those who supported an abortion-rights referendum in November of 1990 told the voting public that they wanted to "get the government off of our backs and out of the bedrooms." But when the state legislature met in January these same abortion-rights supporters, under the auspices of the Nevada Women's Lobby, proposed legislation that asked for the taxpayers of the state to fund school-based sex clinics (which will refer teenage girls to abortion services and are euphemistically called health clinics) and assorted other programs. Forgetting that many of us keep our wallets in our back pockets and place them in the evening on our dressers in our bedrooms, the members of the Nevada Women's Lobby did not hesitate to do in January what they vehemently opposed in November: to get the government on our backs and *in* our bedrooms. The libertarians of November became the social engineers of March.

3. *Thomson's argument implies a macho view of bodily control, a view inconsistent with true feminism.* Some have pointed out that Thomson's argument or the reasoning behind it is actually quite antifeminist.[34] In response to a similar argument from a woman's right to control her own body, one feminist publication asks, "What kind of control are we talking about? A control that allows for violence against another human being is a macho, oppressive kind of control. Women rightly object when others try to have that kind of control over them, and the movement for women's rights asserts the moral right of women to be free from the control of others." After all, "abortion involves violence against a small, weak and dependent child. It is macho control, the very kind the feminist movement most eloquently opposes in other contexts."[35]

Celia Wolf-Devine observes that "abortion has something…in common with the behavior ecofeminists and pacifist feminists take to be characteristically masculine; it shows a willingness to use violence in order to take control. The fetus is destroyed by being pulled apart by suction, cut in pieces, or poisoned." Wolf-Devine goes on to point out that "in terms of social thought… it is the masculine models which are most frequently employed in thinking about abortion. If masculine thought is naturally hierarchical and oriented toward power and control, then the interests of the fetus (who has no power) would naturally be suppressed in favor of the interests of the mother. But to the extent that feminist social thought is egalitarian, the question must be raised of why the mother's interests should prevail over the child's…Feminist thought about abortion has…been deeply pervaded by the individualism which they so ardently criticize."[36]

STUDY QUESTIONS

1. How does Beckwith argue against Thomson's position on abortion? Do you think he is successful? Why or why not?

2. Beckwith does not believe that Thomson's argument even applies to the case of the woman pregnant due to rape. Do you think that Beckwith is correct in his assessment? Do you think his analogies are successful when arguing for this position?

3. Why, according to Beckwith, does Thomson's argument seem inconsistent with radical feminism at three different points? Do you think he is correct? Why or why not?

NOTES

1. Mortimer J. Adler, *Haves Without Have-Nots: Essays for the 21st Century on Democracy and Socialism.* New York: Macmillan, 1991, 210.

2. Laurence H. Tribe, *Abortion: The Clash of Absolutes.* New York: Norton, 1990, 102.

3. Bernard N. Nathanson, M.D., *The Abortion Papers: Inside the Abortion Mentality.* New York: Frederick Fell, 1983, 150.

4. Ibid., 150–151.

5. Baruch Brody, *Abortion and the Sanctity of Human Life: A Philosophical View.* Cambridge, Mass.: M.I.T. Press, 1975, 30.

6. *American Medical Association Encyclopedia of Medicine,* ed. Charles B. Clayman, M.D. New York: Random House, 1989, 58.

7. David C. Reardon, *Aborted Women: Silent No More.* Westchester, Ill.: Crossway, 1987, 90. Reardon cites a *Chicago Sun Times* piece ("The Abortion Profiteers," 12 November 1978), in which writers Pamela Zekman and Pamela Warrick "reveal how undercover investigators in abortion clinics found that clinic employees routinely checked 'no complications' before the abortion was even performed." (Reardon, *Aborted Women,* 343).

8. Some other reasons for underreporting could be the following: Few outpatient clinics provide follow-up examinations; long-term complications may develop (for example, sterility, incompetent uterus) that cannot be detected without prolonged surveillance; of the women who require emergency treatment after an outpatient abortion, more than 60 percent go to a local hospital rather than returning to the abortion clinic; some women who are receiving treatment for such long-term complications as infertility can either hide their abortion or not know that it is relevant. (Ibid., 91).

9. Ibid.

10. See ibid., 89–160, 219–231.

11. Thomas W. Hilgers, M.D. and Dennis O'Hare, "Abortion Related Maternal Mortality: An In-Depth Analysis," in *New Perspectives on Human Abortion,* ed. Thomas W. Hilgers, M.D., Dennis J. Horan, and David Mall. Frederick, Md.: University Publications of America, 1981, 69–70. See also Robert Marshall and Charles Donovan, *Blessed Are the Barren: The Social Policy of Planned Parenthood.* San Francisco: Ignatius, 1991, 187–210.

12. Hilgers and O'Hare, "Mortality," 90.

13. Judith Jarvis Thomson, "A Defense of Abortion," in *The Problems of Abortion,* 2nd ed., ed. Joel Feinberg. Belmont, Calif.: Wadsworth, 1984, 173–187. This article was originally published in *Philosophy and Public Affairs* 1 (1971): 47–66.

14. Thomson, "Defense of Abortion," 174–175.

15. Ibid., 180.

16. For example, in clarifying her own view, Thomson criticizes the absolutist position on abortion that it is morally impermissible to have an abortion even if the life of the mother is in significant danger. Needless to say, I agree with Thomson that this view is seriously flawed and have spelled out my reasons for this in the introduction, Chapters 1 and 6 of *Politically Correct Death: Answering the Argument for Abortion Rights.* Grand Rapids, Mich.: Baker Books House, 1993.

17. See *In the Best Interest of the Child: A Guide to State Child Support and Paternity Laws,* ed. Carolyn Royce Kastner and Lawrence R. Young, Child Support Enforcement Beneficial Laws Project. National Conference of State Legislatures, 1981, n.p.

18. Michael Levin, review of *Life in the Balance* by Robert Wennberg, *Constitutional Commentary* 3 (Summer 1986): 511.

19. The lengths to which Thomson will go to deny the natural relationship between sex, reproduction, and filial obligations is evident in her use of the following

analogy: "If the room is stuffy, and I therefore open a window to air it, and a burglar climbs in, it would be absurd to say. 'Ah, now he can stay, she's given him a right to use her house—for she is partially responsible for his presence there, having voluntarily done what enabled him to get in, in full knowledge that there are such things as burglars, and that burglars burgle'" (Thomson, "Defense of Abortion," 182). Because there is no natural dependency between burglar and homeowner, as there is between child and parent, Thomson's analogy is way off the mark. Burglars don't belong in other people's homes; whereas preborn children belong in no other place except their mother's wombs.

20. Thomson, "Defense of Abortion," 186.

21. Sommers, "Philosophers Against the Family," 774–775.

22. Stephen D. Schwarz, *The Moral Question of Abortion*. Chicago: Loyola University Press, 1990, 118.

23. Thomson, "Defense of Abortion," 175.

24. Michael Levin, *Feminism and Freedom*. New Brunswick, N.J.: Transaction, 1987, 288–289.

25. Stephen D. Schwarz and R. K. Tacelli, "Abortion and Some Philosophers: A Critical Examination," *Public Affairs Quarterly* 3 (April 1989): 85.

26. Brody, *Abortion*, 30.

27. John T. Noonan, "How to Argue About Abortion," in *Morality in Practice,* 2nd ed., ed. James P. Sterba. Belmont, Calif.: Wadsworth, 1988, 150. This article is from Noonan's "Responding to Persons: Methods of Moral Argument in Debate over Abortion," *Theology Digest* (1973): 291–307.

28. Dennis J. Horan and Burke J. Balch, *Infant Doe and Baby Jane Doe: Medical Treatment of the Handicapped Newborn,* Studies in Law & Medicine Series. Chicago: Americans United for Life, 1985, 2.

29. *In re Storar,* 53 N.Y. 2d 363, 380–381, 420 N.E. 2d 64, 73, 438 N.Y.S. 2d 266, 275 (1981), as quoted in ibid., 2–3.

30. Horan and Balch, *Infant Doe,* 3–4.

31. Bernard Nathanson, M.D., *Aborting America.* New York: Doubleday, 1979, 220.

32. Michelle Healy "At Work: Maternity Bias," *USA Today* (30 July 1990): 1A. Conducted by researcher Hal Gruental of State University of New York, Albany, this survey found that 41 percent of those interviewed (133 women and 122 men at eight businesses in the Northeast) "said they think pregnancy hurts a woman's job performance."

33. Levin, review of *Life in the Balance,* 507–508.

34. Although not dealing exclusively with Thomson's argument, Celia Wolf-Devine's article is quite helpful: "Abortion and the 'Feminine Voice,'" *Public Affairs Quarterly* 3 (July 1989): 181–197. See also Doris Gordon, "Abortion and Thomson's Violinist," a paper published by Libertarians for Life, 1991 (13424 Hathaway Drive, Wheaton, Md. 20906; 301-460-4141); Janet Smith, "Abortion as a Feminist Concern," in *The Zero People,* ed. Jeffe Lane Hensley, Ann Arbor, Mich.: Servant, 1983, 77–95; and John T. Wilcox, "Nature as Demonic in Thomson's Defense of Abortion," *The New Scholasticism* 63 (Autumn 1989): 463–484.

35. n.a., *Sound Advice for all Prolife Activists and Candidates Who Wish to Include a Concern for Women's Rights in Their Prolife Advocacy: Feminists for Life Debate Handbook.* Kansas City, Mo.: Feminists for Life of America, n.d., 15–16.

36. Wolf-Devine, "Abortion," 86, 87.

9

A Defense of "A Defense of Abortion"

On the Responsibility Objection to Thomson's Argument[*]

DAVID BOONIN-VAIL[**]

David Boonin-Vail is Assistant Professor of Philosophy at Tulane University in New Orleans, Louisiana. In this essay, Boonin-Vail critically evaluates two versions of what he calls the Responsibility Objection to Thomson's defense of abortion rights (see Chapter 7): (1) the tacit consent version, and (2) the negligence version. Those who defend the tacit consent version agree with Thomson that the fetus does not have a right to use the woman's body without her consent. However, they argue that there is good reason to believe that the woman (except in rape cases) has given her tacit consent. Those who defend the negligence version maintain that the pregnant woman who gets an abortion is like a driver who is partially responsible for an automobile accident that strikes an innocent pedestrian, but then the driver leaves the scene, and by not lending her assistance (for example, calling 911) puts the victim in harm's way. Boonin-Vail provides several reasons why both versions of the Responsibility Objection fail. He concludes that because of its failure, the Responsibility Objection provides no reason to reject Thomson's argument.

---

*Published by permission from David Boonin-Vail, "A Defense of 'A Defense of Abortion': On the Responsibility Objection to Thomson's Argument," *Ethics* 107.2 (January 1997).

** I would like to thank the Senate Committee on Research at Tulane University for a grant which provided financial support for work on this paper during the summer of 1995. I would also like to thank Leonard Boonin, Luc Bovens, Alisa Carse, Jon Mandle, Ruth Sample, Bonnie Steinbock, Jim Stone, Alec Walen, Sara Worley, and an audience at Tulane University for helpful comments on various earlier versions of the paper, the anonymous referees and associate editors of *Ethics* for their useful criticisms of a later version, and Marcia Baron for her careful and encouraging editorial guidance throughout as the paper gradually moved from initial submission to its final form.

Since Thomson's argument turns crucially on the analogy between a woman's being pregnant and your being plugged into the famous violinist,[1] her critics are left with essentially three lines of response: They can attempt to identify a morally relevant disanalogy between the two cases, they can embrace the conclusion that it would be impermissible for you to unplug yourself from the violinist, or they can reject the authority of such arguments from analogy. I will assume for the purposes of this paper that you accept the legitimacy of arguing from cases of the sort that Thomson exploits and that you agree that it would be morally permissible for you to unplug yourself from the violinist. The question, then, is whether there is a morally relevant disanalogy between the two cases. Numerous objections of this sort have been proposed in the literature, but I want here to focus on one such objection in particular, and surely the most common: the claim that even if Thomson's analogy is successful in every other respect, her argument can establish only that abortion is permissible in cases involving rape.[2] Your being plugged into the violinist against your will is like a woman's being impregnated against her will, it is conceded, but it is not like a woman's becoming pregnant as a result of consensual intercourse. As with the case of you and the violinist, the rape victim cannot be held responsible for the well-being of the fetus because she did not choose to be raped, but the woman who is not raped can and should be held responsible for the well-being of the fetus because she engaged in intercourse voluntarily. Call this the Responsibility Objection.

The Responsibility Objection can be developed in two importantly distinct ways, although the distinction is often overlooked in cursory rebuttals to Thomson that take the force of the objection to be virtually self-evident. On one version, the claim is that because the woman's pregnancy is the result of a voluntary action, she should be understood as having tacitly waived her right to expel the fetus or (what amounts to the same thing) as having tacitly granted the fetus a right to stay. This version, which I will call the Tacit Consent Version, agrees with Thomson that the fetus cannot have a right to the use of the woman's body unless the woman consents to give it such a right, but claims that (in nonrape cases) there is good reason to conclude that the woman has in fact so consented. The alternative version of the Responsibility Objection denies that consent, even tacit consent, is necessary in order for the voluntariness of the woman's intercourse to deprive the woman of her right to refuse to aid the fetus. On this version, which I will call the Negligence Version, the woman is like a person who is partly responsible for an accident that leaves an innocent bystander in need of her assistance (the bystander will die, for example, unless he receives a series of physically demanding blood transfusions from her over the next nine months).[3] One need not argue that by running the risk of causing such an accident, the woman has tacitly consented to give such bystanders the use of her body in order to believe that she has nonetheless acquired a duty to save them that she would not have acquired if, say, someone else had been (partly) responsible for the accident. On either version, Thomson's argument fails to apply to cases in which the woman is (partly) responsible for the fact that she is pregnant.[4]

The claim that when a woman is partially responsible for her pregnancy, the fetus has acquired the right to the use of her body seems to many people to be a devastating objection to Thomson's argument, and, although Thomson anticipates the objection, she does not provide a satisfactory reply. She responds by suggesting that a woman who becomes pregnant because of contraceptive failure cannot reasonably be thought of as being responsible for the pregnancy,[5] but this reply is unsatisfactory for at least two reasons. First, and perhaps most obviously, even if one concedes to Thomson the case of contraceptive failure, the response itself seems to concede that a woman who fails to use contraception in the first place can be held responsible for her unwanted pregnancy and can thus be understood as having given the fetus a right to the use of her body. A significant number of unwanted pregnancies arise in cases where contraception is not used, and the result would then be that, so far as Thomson's argument is concerned, it is impermissible for these women to have abortions.

Second, and more important, it can plausibly be argued that, since contraceptive devices are known to be imperfect, a woman who has intercourse using one is responsible for the results since she knowingly and voluntarily runs the risk of becoming pregnant. Hunters, after all, can still acquire a duty to provide blood to an innocent bystander they have accidentally shot, even if they took every reasonable precaution to avoid this result short of not going hunting in the first place. So if Thomson cannot defend abortion in the case where contraception is not used, then she may well be unable to defend it even in the case where it is used, and if that is so, then her defense of abortion will really be only a defense of abortion in cases of rape. And since only a very small fraction of abortions involve pregnancies arising from rape, and since a significant portion of those who generally oppose abortion are willing to make an exception in such cases anyhow, it will turn out that, if the Responsibility Objection is not defeated, Thomson's argument will prove a greater contribution to critics of abortion than to its defenders. In this sense, the Responsibility Objection is the most important of all the many objections that have been aimed at her argument. I will argue in what follows, however, that neither version of the Responsibility Objection should be accepted and that if Thomson's argument succeeds in cases involving rape, then it succeeds in nonrape cases as well.

THE TACIT CONSENT VERSION

I will begin with the Tacit Consent Version, which seems to be the more common version of the Responsibility Objection and which, indeed, is often pressed even by those of Thomson's readers who are generally sympathetic with her conclusions. As one such writer has put it, "The fetus *does* have a right to use the pregnant woman's body [in nonrape cases] because she is (partly) responsible for its existence. By engaging in intercourse, knowing that this may result in the creation of a person inside her body, she implicitly gives the resulting person a right to remain."[6] The Tacit Consent Version turns on two claims: (1) that because the woman's act of intercourse is voluntary, she should be understood as having tacitly consented to something with respect to the state of affairs in which there is now a fetus developing inside of her body, and (2) that what she should be understood as having tacitly consented to with respect to this state of affairs is, in particular, the fetus's right to have the state of affairs continue for as long as this is necessary for it to remain alive. Both claims should be rejected.

Let me begin with claim 1, the claim that the fact of the woman's act of intercourse is voluntary counts as evidence of her having tacitly consented to something with respect to the resulting state of affairs, There is surely something plausible sounding about this, since if the notion of tacit consent is to make sense at all it must arise from voluntary rather than involuntary actions, but I want to suggest that it rests on a confusion between a person's (a) voluntarily bringing about a state of affairs S and (b) voluntarily doing an action A foreseeing that this may lead to a state of affairs S. My claim is that only *a* is a plausible candidate for grounding tacit consent in the relation between an agent and a state of affairs she is (or is partly) responsible for having brought about, and that any attempt to apply tacit consent to nonrape cases of pregnancy must appeal to *b*.[7] If this is right, then we have no grounds for concluding that the woman who has intercourse without contraception has tacitly consented to anything with respect to the state of affairs in which a fetus is now developing inside her body.

To see this, let us first consider what one would have to believe in order to affirm the claim that when a woman has voluntary intercourse without contraception and becomes pregnant as a result, she has tacitly consented to give the fetus a right to stay. In general terms, we could begin by saying that P has done a voluntary act A that caused the state of affairs S to exist, where S is the state of affairs in which Q is now infringing on P's right to X.[8] We want to know what conditions would be sufficient to make it be the case that P has tacitly consented to give Q the right to continue doing this. We could say that it is sufficient that A be voluntary and that A cause S. But this would imply that P consented to S even if P had no knowledge that A could lead to S. And this would amount to saying that if a woman has intercourse without contraception and does not understand that intercourse can lead to conception, then she has tacitly consented to carry the fetus to term. Since this is plainly unacceptable, we must at least add the requirement that A cause S in a manner that is foreseeable to P.

Let us assume that these three criteria—voluntariness, causality, and foreseeability—are necessary in order to avoid unacceptable implications.[9] It seems correct that all three are satisfied in the case where a woman's pregnancy arises from voluntary intercourse: her action was voluntary, was the proximate cause of the pregnancy that now infringes on her right to control her body, and was the cause of this state of affairs in a manner that was foreseeable to her (assuming that she understood that intercourse can lead to pregnancy). But all of this will show that a woman who engages in intercourse without contraception has tacitly consented to something with respect to the resulting state of affairs only if these conditions are not merely necessary, but sufficient. And the claim that these conditions are sufficient for having consented is implausible. Now, of course, one could argue against the claim that these conditions are sufficient for consent by arguing that no conditions short of explicit consent are sufficient. But since I want to identify a feature of this position that should be unacceptable even to those who embrace the general notion of tacit consent, I want to assume that tacit consent in and of itself is a perfectly reasonable doctrine and to argue by means of an example that puts this assumption in a favorable light. So let us focus on a relatively uncontroversial instance of tacit consent: If you voluntarily leave some money on the table in a restaurant as you are leaving after your meal is over, then you have tacitly waived your right to it and have consented to allow the waiter to have it. You have made no explicit announcement that you intend to relinquish control of the money, of course, and have said nothing explicit that would indicate that you wish the money to go to the waiter rather than the chef or the busboy or the owner, but it nonetheless seems reasonable to maintain that your action amounts to a tacit declaration of just this sort. And surely it is the voluntariness of your act that makes this assessment reasonable, since if you had instead left the money on the table because you had been forced to do so by a knife-wielding assailant, we would not be inclined to say that you had tacitly consented to anything about it.

But now consider the cases of Bill and Ted, each of whom has recently voluntarily exited a restaurant having voluntarily placed some money on the table at which he was dining alone. In Bill's case, the state of affairs in which he is no longer in the restaurant and some of his money is on the table is a state of affairs he voluntarily brought about: after he finished eating, he stood up, took some money out of his wallet, placed it on the table, and walked out the door. In Ted's case, the state of affairs is not one which he voluntarily brought about, but rather one which foreseeably arose from a voluntary action of his. As Ted sat down to eat, he discovered that the crumpled wad of dollar bills in his pants pocket made him uncomfortable, so he put them down on the table while he was eating, intending to put them back in his pocket when it was time to leave. A friend who was leaving the restaurant when Ted sat down saw this and warned Ted not to put the money there on the grounds that he might forget about it, but Ted foolishly refused, and when the friend urged that he at least tie a piece of string around his finger to remind himself to put the money back in his pocket before leaving, Ted declined, saying that he didn't like the way having a piece of string tied around his finger "made him feel" while he was trying to enjoy a meal. Unfortunately, Ted was so lost in the rapture of his meal that he did indeed forget to put the money back in his pocket, and about ten minutes after he left the restaurant, he suddenly realized his mistake and headed back to clear things up.

Now clearly Ted has no one to blame but himself. It isn't as if someone else forcibly removed the money from his pocket and put it on the table. Still, it is surely unacceptable to say that by putting the money on the table when he sat down Ted tacitly agreed to let the waiter keep it if as a foreseeable consequence of this act the money was still on the table when he left. Yet if the three conditions identified as necessary conditions for consent are also taken to be sufficient, there can be no way to account for the distinction between the cases of Bill and Ted. In Ted's case, just as in Bill's, all three criteria for waiving one's rights are satisfied: Ted's putting his money on the table without tying a piece of string on his finger was voluntary, was the proximate cause of his leaving the money in the restaurant, which in turn was a foreseeable (even if unintended) consequence of his act. These three criteria cannot distinguish between the cases of Bill and Ted precisely because they overlook the distinction between *a* and *b* noted earlier. The cases are different because Bill voluntarily brings about the state of affairs in which he has left the restaurant with his money still on the table, while Ted does not. Ted voluntarily puts the money on the table foreseeing that this may result in the state of affairs in which he has left it in the restaurant. And the lesson of this is that even if deliberately creating a state of affairs counts as consenting to the burdens it imposes on you (as in the case of Bill), it does not follow that being partly responsible for that state of affairs counts as such consent (as in the case of Ted).

This analysis has the following implications for the application of tacit consent theory to cases of voluntary intercourse.[10] A woman who is merely (partly) responsible for her unwanted pregnancy has not voluntarily brought about the state of affairs in which the fetus is making demands on her body. She has voluntarily brought about the state of affairs in which a man is having sexual intercourse with her, foreseeing that this might bring about the further state of affairs. In this respect, she is like Ted rather than Bill. And since Ted's relation to the unwanted state of affairs he has produced is not sufficient to warrant the claim that he has consented to it, the same is true of her. We cannot justifiably insist that she has tacitly consented to waive the right to the control of her body. Suppose that once she discovers that she is pregnant she endeavors to have the pregnancy terminated. There she is like Ted when he returns to the restaurant to retrieve his money after he discovers that he has (foreseeably, but not deliberately) left it on the table. It seems clear that in Ted's case we must take this to mean that he has not agreed to waive his right to control over the money. Similarly, we must take this to mean that she did not give and has not given the fetus a right to the use of her body. The mere fact that her pregnancy resulted from voluntary intercourse for which she is responsible, then, cannot be reasonably understood as evidence that she has consented to anything with respect to the fetus.[11]

Let me make one further point about the distinction between voluntarily creating a particular state of affairs and voluntarily acting with the foresight that a particular state of affairs may result: Its importance is revealed by seeing what happens when it is ignored, and it is ignored in an analogy often offered by proponents of the Responsibility Objection. Langer, for example, motivates his defense of the objection with the following example:

Imagine a person who freely chooses to join the Society of Music lovers, knowing that there was a 1 in 100 chance of being plugged into the violinist if she joins the society. She certainly does not desire to be plugged into the violinist, but at the same time she desires to join the society and feels the one in one hundred odds are an acceptable risk. She goes ahead and joins, and much to her chagrin, her name is selected as the person to be plugged into the violinist. Is it unreasonable to say that she has waived her right to control over her own body? I think not.[12]

On this account, the woman who risks an unwanted pregnancy by voluntarily engaging in intercourse is like the woman who risks being plugged into the violinist by voluntarily joining the Society of Music lovers. And since the second woman clearly waives the right to control of her hotly, so does the first.

The problem with the analogy is this. Langer says that the second woman "freely chooses to *join*" the society, and this sounds as if it means that her voluntary action just is the action of agreeing to abide by the society's rules. And since the society's rules include entering every member in a lottery to decide who will be plugged into the violinist, it follows that her act is the act of agreeing to be entered into the lottery, from which it of course follows that if her name is called she must be understood as having waived her right to control her body. This is because her voluntary action just *is* the act of entering the lottery, rather than an action with the foreseeable consequence that others will treat her as if she had. In order for the two cases to be parallel, then, we must assume that the first woman has similarly agreed to enter her name in a comparable pregnancy lottery by virtue of her having engaged in voluntary intercourse. But we cannot assume that she has so agreed because whether she has is precisely the question we are attempting to answer.[13]

The problem with the analogy becomes more apparent, I think, if we set it straight by simply having the second woman freely choose to do some action foreseeing that it may lead to the society's taking her and plugging her into the violinist as the woman foresees that her voluntary intercourse without contraception may lead to pregnancy. So suppose instead that you are this woman, and that the society was known to have hired kidnappers who were lurking in the park at night. Your friends warned you: Don't go into the park alone at night because there are kidnappers from the Society of Music Lovers lurking there, and if you do go, then for God's sake carry some Mace. But you nonetheless voluntarily engaged in walking through the park, knowing that this might result in being kidnapped, and you didn't bring Mace with you just because you don't like the way that carrying protection "makes you feel" when you are trying to enjoy a stroll (after all, you told yourself, people take unprotected walks through the park all the time without becoming kidnapped).[14] Being harsh, your friends might later say that you got what you deserved, but they could not truthfully say that you got what you had tacitly consented to. And so it is again with the woman whose unwanted pregnancy arises from voluntary intercourse without contraception. She may be partly responsible for it, but, as with the forgetful customer who is partly responsible for his money being on the table after he has left the restaurant, this partial responsibility cannot reasonably be taken as evidence of consent.[15]

My argument against claim 1 of the Tacit Consent Version has to this point focused on the distinction between deliberately bringing about a particular state of affairs and deliberately doing an action foreseeing that a particular state of affairs may arise as a result. But before turning to claim 2 of the argument, I want to note a further difficulty with claim 1 that remains even if we picture the woman as deliberately becoming pregnant rather than merely being partly responsible for her pregnancy. So return for a moment to the case of Bill, who deliberately left some of his money on the restaurant table after his meal and proceeded to walk out the door. Why are we so confident that this counts as evidence that he has consented to transfer his right to control the money to the waiter, rather than to the owner, or the busboy, or the customers at the next table? Or why isn't it simply a waiver of his right to the money with the result that whoever sees it first is entitled to take it? Presumably, this is because there is a well-established convention that constitutes the background against which the act is performed. If the act of leaving money on the table took place in a culture where there was no convention about tipping, then it would be unreasonable to take the act as consenting to transfer the right to the money to the waiter, And this suggests that there is at least one further necessary condition for an act to count as evidence of consent: It must take place in a culture where there is a convention by which it is so understood. Indeed, this is presumably true of explicit consent as well, insofar as a handshake, for example, will only be evidence of consent if it takes place in a context where it is so understood, But this creates a further problem with the attempt to use tacit consent theory as grounds for raising an objection to Thomson. It is unclear, to say the least, that in our culture there is such a convention, and it is certainly clear that in other cultures there is no such convention. Consider a woman in China who already has as many children as she is permitted by her culture to have.[16] It just seems patently false to insist that if she engages in voluntary intercourse without using contraception then she is tacitly consenting to allow the fetus to stay. If anything, she will be understood as having tacitly agreed *not* to allow the fetus to stay, though I do not mean to press this suggestion. The point is simply that a person's act cannot be taken as tacitly consenting to anything unless it takes place in a context where it is generally understood as constituting such consent.[17]

I have been concerned to this point to argue against claim 1 of the Tacit Consent Version, the claim that, because the woman's act of intercourse is voluntary, she should be understood as having tacitly consented to something with respect to the state of affairs in which there is now a fetus making demands on her body. If my argument has been successful, then the woman who has intercourse without contraception is not like you if you voluntarily plug yourself into the violinist, but is rather like you if you voluntarily engage in some pleasurable activity with the foresight that this might end up causing you to become plugged into the violinist, And in that case, if my suggestion has been accepted, you have not agreed to give the violinist the right to your body. But let us now suppose that I have been mistaken about this. let us suppose that the woman is just like you if you freely walk into the violinist's room, sit down next to him, and plug yourself in. I will take it that this implies that you have consented to being plugged in. But what follows from this?

I think that there is at least one thing that does follow: Suppose that the procedure involved in unplugging you from the violinist is itself somewhat painful and costly. If you were involuntarily plugged into the violinist, then whoever forced you to be plugged in should have to bear the costs of and compensate you for the suffering involved in the unplugging. But if you freely plugged yourself in, then you should have to bear these costs on your own. So we might say that freely plugging yourself into the violinist constitutes consent to bear the costs of unplugging yourself. But does it constitute consent to more, and, in particular, consent to remain plugged in for the nine-month period that the violinist requires? This too seems implausible. Suppose that because of your unique compatibility, the violinist will die unless you undergo a series of nine painful bone marrow extractions over the next nine months, and, with a clear understanding of the nature of the procedure and its potential risks, you freely volunteer to begin the treatment. After the second round of extraction, however, you find that the burden is considerably more than you are willing to bear on his behalf. Do we really believe that it would now be impermissible for you to discontinue providing aid to the violinist merely because you began the procedure voluntarily? This would seem implausible. It would be to say that the violinist's right to life does not entitle him to seven more extractions of bone marrow from you if the first two were done involuntarily, but that it does entitle him to seven more extractions if the first two were done voluntarily.[18] And if I am right about this, then even if we picture the woman's unwanted pregnancy as evidence of consent (and I have already argued that this is unwarranted), it should not be understood as consent to keep the fetus in her care for as long as is necessary for the fetus to survive.[19] I conclude that both claims of the Tacit Consent Version should be rejected, and that the objection thus fails to undermine Thomson's analogy for typical nonrape cases such as those in which a woman voluntarily has intercourse without contraception. If Thomson's analogy is successful in rape cases, then the Tacit Consent Version fails to show that it is not also successful in nonrape cases as well.

THE NEGLIGENCE VERSION

Let us now consider what I am calling the Negligence Version of the Responsibility Objection. This version of the objection dispenses with the claim that the woman has tacitly consented to assist the fetus and instead argues that she is like someone who is partly responsible for an accident that has caused an innocent bystander to be in need of her assistance. Tooley, for example, argues that Thomson's position is undermined by considering a case in which you engage in a pleasurable activity knowing that it may have the unfortunate side effect of destroying someone's food supply. You did not intend to cause the loss of food, let us assume, but it nonetheless resulted from your voluntary actions, and in a manner that was foreseeable in the sense that you knew your actions risked causing a loss of this sort. Surely most of us will agree that you do owe it to the bystander or victim to save his life even at some considerable cost to yourself, even though you need not be understood as having consented to do so by virtue of your having undertaken the risky action voluntarily. But if this is so, then the woman whose pregnancy is the accidental but foreseeable result of her voluntary actions owes the fetus the use of her hotly even if she did not tacitly consent to this.[20]

Let me begin by noting one reason to be suspicious of analogies with cases of negligence in general. Beckwith, for example, argues that the claim that voluntarily engaging in intercourse with the foresight that this might result in pregnancy imposes a duty to care for the offspring "is not an unusual way to frame moral obligations, for we hold drunk people whose driving results in manslaughter responsible for their actions, even if they did not *intend* to kill someone prior to becoming intoxicated."[21] But in the case of drunk or negligent driving, we already agree that people have a right not to be run over by cars and then determine that a person who risks running over someone with a car can be held culpable if that person has an accident which results in the violation of this right.[22] In the case of an unintended pregnancy, on the other hand, the question of whether or not the fetus has a right not to be aborted is precisely the question at issue. So it is difficult to see how an argument from an analogy with negligence can avoid begging the question.

But there is an even more fundamental problem with this version of the Responsibility Objection. The problem can be most clearly identified by asking precisely why we are so confident that the one who stands in need of your assistance has the right to it in the sorts of cases that Tooley, Beckwith, and Carrier employ. Presumably, as a first approximation, we would say something like this: It is because if you *hadn't* done the voluntary action that foreseeably led him to be in need of your assistance, he wouldn't be in need of your assistance in the first place. And this seems reasonable enough. But now consider that there are two distinct ways in which this counterfactual claim can be true: (1) if you had not done the action, he would not now exist (and so would not now exist in a state of dependency on you); and (2) if you had not done the action, he would now exist, but not in a state of dependency on you. Assuming that your voluntarily doing the action makes you responsible for the resulting state of affairs, we can recast this distinction as one between two different senses in which you might be responsible for the state of affairs in which P now stands in need of your assistance in order to survive:

1. You are responsible for the fact that P exists.
2. You are responsible for the fact that, given that P exists, P stands in need of your assistance.

The first thing to note is simply that these two senses are distinct. As Silverstein has pointed out, one could be responsible for P's predicament in either, neither, or both senses, generating four distinct possibilities that can easily be conflated.[23] In Thomson's (kidnapping) version of the story, you are not responsible for the violinist in either sense 1 or sense 2. The proponent of the Negligence Version of the Responsibility Objection agrees that you are permitted to unplug yourself in this case and concedes that, unless there is another morally relevant asymmetry, this case is relevantly similar to that of a woman whose pregnancy results from rape. He then argues that in cases of voluntary intercourse, the woman is responsible for the fetus, so that while Thomson's example is relevantly similar to rape cases, it is not relevantly similar to nonrape cases. But in cases such as Beckwith's, Carrier's, and Tooley's, in which you cause an accident as a result of some voluntary action of yours, you are responsible for the bystander in sense 2 and not sense 1, while even in nonrape cases, the woman is responsible for the fetus only in sense 1 and not in sense 2. She is responsible for the existence of the fetus, that is, since her voluntary actions foreseeably caused the fetus to exist, but she is not responsible for the fact that, given the existence of the fetus, the fetus stands in need of assistance from her. In the cases of Beckwith, Carrier, and Tooley, there were numerous alternative courses of action available to you that would have resulted in the bystander's still existing and not in a state of dependency on you, but in the case of the pregnant woman, there was no course of action available to her that would have resulted in the fetus's existing without needing assistance from her. So this condition of the fetus, given that it exists, is not something that she is responsible for. Because of this distinction, we cannot yet say that the rape case is unlike the nonrape case in a morally relevant way. We can say only that the rape case is like the nonrape case in terms of responsibility in sense 2 and is unlike the nonrape case in terms of responsibility in sense 1. And this means that the Negligence Version of the Responsibility Objection can he sustained only if we agree that the difference in terms of responsibility in sense 1 alone is itself morally relevant.[24] This assumption stands in need of defense but is typically not even noted, let alone defended, but those who press the Negligence Version of the Responsibility Objection. The question, then, is what we should say about cases in which you are responsible for another in sense 1 but not in sense 2.

It is perhaps not immediately apparent how to go about answering this question. One wants to consider cases in which you do some action such that, had you not done it, this dependent person would not now exist, and given that you have done it, this person is now dependent on you. And it may seem that there really are no such cases other than those in which the act is simply the act of conceiving the person. If that is so, then we cannot usefully illuminate the case of voluntary intercourse by appealing to other cases and may simply have to conclude that we have a case here that cannot be resolved either way by appealing to more general principles. But this pessimism is premature. For there is another kind of action which is such that had you not done the action the person would not now exist: not the act of *creating* his life, but the act of *extending* it. Suitably constructed, such cases offer a means of testing the relative significance of the different senses of responsibility involved in the objection. And when they are consulted, the Negligence Version is undermined.

Consider first the following story[25]:

> **Imperfect Drug:** You are the violinist's doctor. Seven years ago, you discovered that the violinist had contracted a rare disease that was on the verge of killing him. The only way to save his life that was available to you was to give him a drug that cures the disease but has one unfortunate side effect: Five to ten years after ingestion, it often causes the kidney ailment Thomson has described. Knowing that you alone would have the appropriate blood type to save the violinist were his kidneys to fail, you prescribed the drug and cured the disease. The violinist has now been struck by the kidney ailment. If you do not allow him the use of your kidneys for nine months, he will die.

In this story, you are responsible for the violinist in the first sense. He currently exists only because, in giving him the drug, you voluntarily acted in a way which foreseeably caused him to exist at this time. But you are not responsible for the violinist in the second sense. Given that he (still) exists, you are not responsible for his need of your kidneys because there was no course of action available to you seven years ago that would have caused it both to be the case that the violinist would now be alive and to be the case that he was not in need of the use of your kidneys.[26] This is what makes Imperfect Drug importantly different from what I will call

> **Malpractice:** Same as Imperfect Drug, except that you could have given the violinist a perfect drug which would have cured him with no side effects. But out of indifference or laziness, you chose to give him the imperfect drug.

In the case of Malpractice, you are responsible for the violinist in both senses. I suspect that most people will think that you do owe the violinist the use of your kidneys in Malpractice but that you do not in the case of Imperfect Drug. We might put the reason for this in a few ways. We might say that in Malpractice there is a clear sense in which you harmed him by giving him the drug you gave him, while in Imperfect Drug there is no sense in which you harmed him. Or we might put it like this: suppose that, in the first case, you had told the violinist that you could either give him the imperfect drug or no drug at all, and that if you gave him the imperfect drug you would refuse to lend him the use of your kidneys should he later develop the kidney ailment. Presumably, the violinist would have chosen to take the drug rather than the alternative. But suppose that, in the second case, you had told him that you could either give him the imperfect drug or the perfect drug or no drug at all, and that if you gave him the imperfect drug and he later developed the kidney ailment you would refuse to lend him the use of your kidneys.

Presumably, for consistency, the violinist would have chosen to take the perfect drug. So we can say that you do not incur a further duty to assist the violinist when you make the choice that leaves him best off, or is the one he would have selected, but that you do incur such a duty when you fail to do so. And either way, if this is our response, then we must conclude that if you are responsible for another in sense 1, this only imposes an obligation on you if you are also responsible in sense 2. And if this is so, then the Negligence Version of the Responsibility Objection fails: Pregnancies that arise from voluntary intercourse are relevantly similar to Imperfect Drug rather than to Malpractice.[27] And so, again, if Thomson's argument succeeds in rape cases, it succeeds in nonrape cases as well.[28]

A few objections that might be raised against this argument merit notice. The argument rests on the claim that if you are responsible for someone in sense 1 but not in sense 2, then you incur no duty to assist that person at some cost to yourself. But this claim can be challenged in two ways. The first arises from the possibility that by being responsible for a person only in sense 1, you could still harm him or do other than he would have chosen to have you do, and thus still have a duty to provide the needed assistance. Consider, for example, the case of

> **Really Imperfect Drug:** Same as Imperfect Drug except that the situation arose a few weeks ago, and the only way to save his life that was available to you was to give him a drug which in every case causes continuous excruciating pain for a few weeks which then ceases with the onset of kidney failure. Knowing that the drug would certainly cause both the pain and the kidney failure, and knowing that you alone would have the appropriate blood type to save the violinist once his kidneys failed and to enable him to then go on and live a healthy, happy, independent life, you gave him the drug that cured the disease and caused the pain to begin. The violinist has now been struck by the kidney ailment.

Let us assume, what some might deny, that the violinist is better off dying right away of the rare disease than taking the drug, if he is only going to endure a few weeks of agony and then die of the kidney failure anyhow. Let us also assume that he is better off still if he takes the drug and endures the pain and is then saved from the kidney failure and enjoys the rest of his life. In that case, while you are not responsible for the fact that, given that the violinist exists, he needs the use of your kidneys, it is nonetheless true that if you refrain from assisting him now, he will have been made worse off by your having given him the drug than he would have been had you let him die at that time (or that he would have chosen no drug at all over drug with no subsequent kidney assistance). And this makes it plausible to suppose that you now have a duty to save him from the kidney failure, even at some substantial cost to yourself. If we accept this analysis, then we must modify our original claim to read: if you are responsible for a person in sense 1 but not in sense 2, then you incur no duty to assist that person at some cost to yourself *unless his or her existence without your assistance is itself a harm.*[29]

This modification of the argument will affect its ability to undermine the Negligence Version of the Responsibility Objection, however, only if we believe that a fetus is made worse off by being conceived and then aborted than it would have been if it had never been conceived in the first place. I cannot pretend to offer a conclusive rebuttal to this claim here, so it will have to suffice simply to note that the claim is controversial at best, unintelligible at worst (since the fetus would not "have been" anything had it not been conceived), and that proponents of the Negligence Version have thus far failed to make a convincing case for it or even to recognize that such a case is required by their position. But it may be worth noting, in addition, that the sorts of arguments typically offered in defense of the claim in other contexts are unsatisfactory.

Michael Davis offers one argument for the claim that the fetus is made worse off by being made to live a short time and then being killed than if it would have been if it had never existed at all by appealing to the following example:

> To be killed is bad, so bad that merely being brought into existence for a time is not necessarily enough to make up for it. We would not, I take it, allow a scientist to kill a ten-year-old child just because the scientist had ten years ago "constructed" the child out of a dollar's worth of chemicals, had reared it for ten years in such a way as to make it impossible for the child's care to be given to anyone else for another eight years, and now found the care of the child a far greater burden than he had expected.[30]

But this example simply does not support the conclusion. For suppose we agree that we would not allow such a scientist to kill his or her child. Davis simply assumes that this must be so because the killing is so bad *for the child* that the high quality of the child's (short) life does not make up for it. Only on this assumption would our saying that the scientist does something impermissible commit us to the claim that one is made worse off by being made to live a short time and then being killed than if one had never existed. But this assumption is unwarranted. It seems much more likely that our response to Davis's example (assuming that we share his response) reveals instead that we believe that some acts are impermissible even though they leave no one worse off than they would otherwise have been. Suppose, for example, that a woman knows that if she conceives a child now it will live a just barely worthwhile life and die at fifteen but that if she waits a month she will conceive a child who will live an extremely happy life to a ripe old age. We might well criticize her if she has the first child rather than the second, but that is no evidence that we think that *this* child is made worse off than if he had never lived. It is instead evidence that we think (if we do criticize her) that there are wrongs that harm no one. Similarly, if we share Davis's response to the scientist example, this is not because we think the child would have been better off never having been conceived.

A second defense of the claim that a fetus is made worse off by being conceived and then aborted than it would have been had it never been conceived arises from the following thought: death, especially premature death, is a great harm to the one who suffers it, while the provision of a very short amount of life, especially life of the sort one enjoys during the first few months after conception, is a relatively small benefit to the one who receives it. So one who is conceived and then aborted is granted a relatively small benefit and then a relatively great harm, which seems to add up, on the whole, to a worse state than that of one who is not conceived in the first place and who thus receives no benefit and no harm.

This argument is unacceptable for two reasons. In the first place, as Nagel has pointed out, "if death is an evil at all, it cannot be because of its positive features, but only because of what it deprives us of."[31] But if to say that death is a great harm to the fetus is to say that death deprives the fetus of great goods it would enjoy if it were to go on living, this provides no support for the claim that the fetus would have been better off still if it had enjoyed no such goods in the first place.[32] In addition, the argument would seem equally to imply that a six-year-old child who leads a happy life and then dies in her sleep would have been better off never having been conceived. After all, the totality of goods she has so far enjoyed, and if the harm of death consists in the greatness of the good it deprives one of, then this would mean that the harms in her life greatly outweighed the benefits. But as tragic as her death is, the conclusion that she would have been better off never having been conceived is plainly absurd. Of course, it is open to the proponent of the Negligence Version to attempt to articulate and defend a conception of the nature of death on which it turns out both that the fetus is worse off being conceived and then aborted than not being conceived and that this is not so of the six-year-old who dies in her sleep,[33] but in the absence of such a defense, the attempt to defend the objection to Thomson's argument by appealing to cases such as Really Imperfect Drug is unsuccessful.

A second response to the argument I have developed to this point would be to insist that if you are responsible for a person in sense 1 but not in sense 2, then you can still incur a duty to assist that person at some cost to yourself even if his or her existence without your assistance is *not* itself a harm. And Langer offers what seems to be a plausible example to support this claim: his relationship with his one-year-old son: "I am responsible for his existence, but I am not responsible for the condition in which he finds himself....He is in a condition which requires constant physical attention, long-term financial aid, and significant psychological nurture...I have caused his existence, but I certainly have not caused him to be in this terrible, needy condition. Do I not have an obligation to care for his needs?"[34] This is plainly a case in which someone is responsible for another in sense 1 but not in sense 2 (since there was no option available to Langer on which his son would both exist and not be in this needy condition), yet it is not (or at least need not be) the case that Langer's son would be harmed by being born and living for only a year as opposed to never being conceived in the first place. If it is necessary that Langer be guilty of harming his son by conceiving him in order for him now to have an obligation to care for him, then, since Langer has not harmed his son by conceiving him, he has no obligation to care for him. But Langer takes it that we all think he does have such an obligation since "the laws and moral intuitions of our society strongly oppose child abandonment."[35] And if that is so, then you can be responsible for assisting someone even if you are only responsible for them in sense 1 and not in sense 2, and even if you have not harmed them relative to their never having been conceived. And that is the sense in which a pregnant woman is responsible for the fetus she conceives as a result of voluntary intercourse.

Let us assume that we agree that you have a duty to care for your one-year-old son in such circumstances.[36] It does not follow from this that you always have a duty to assist those for whom you are responsible in sense 1 and not sense 2. It follows only that you can *sometimes* have such a duty. This would indeed force a further revision in our claim. Now we cannot even say that harming another is necessary in order for you to have a duty to assist them in those cases where you are responsible for someone only in sense 1. Even this revision, however, strong as it is, does not suffice to rescue the Negligence Version of the Responsibility Objection from the problem I have identified. The objection, remember, claims that nonrape cases are relevantly different from rape cases *because* they differ in terms of being responsible in sense 1; the objection is only forceful, then, if being responsible in sense 1 is, in and of itself, enough to make the difference between owing support and not owing support. It must, that is, be a sufficient condition for owing support. But the fact (assuming that it is fact) that you can *sometimes* have a duty to care for someone you are responsible for only in sense 1 does not show that being responsible in sense 1 is in and of itself sufficient to generate that duty. The argument presented earlier still shows that being responsible in sense 1 is not sufficient to generate this duty since it does not generate this duty in the case of Imperfect Drug. If this is a duty you only sometimes have when you are responsible in sense 1 but not in sense 2, then it is sufficient only in conjunction with (and perhaps only because of) other considerations. And the burden would then be on the proponent of the objection to show that these other considerations obtain in the case of pregnancy, and not just in the case of the father of the one-year-old. Otherwise, the claim that you have a duty to care for your one-year-old son for whom you are responsible in sense 1 but not sense 2 is perfectly compatible with the claim that being responsible in sense 1 is not sufficient to make the nonraped woman have a duty to assist the fetus she is carrying if the rape victim does not have such a duty.

And, indeed, there is good reason to doubt that such a case could be made. For, in an ironic way, what seems plausible about the Tacit Consent Version seems to come back to haunt the Negligence Version. After all, a plausible case can be made for saying that a mother (to switch back to the woman's perspective and keep the analogy tighter) who brings a baby to term and takes it home with her has tacitly agreed to care for it. Nothing that was said in criticism of the Tacit Consent Version of the Responsibility Objection would count against this claim, since voluntarily bringing a baby home is voluntarily bringing about the state of affairs in which the baby is under one's care, while voluntarily having intercourse is only acting in a way that foreseeably can lead to the state of affairs in which there is a developing fetus in the womb. But if this is so, then we can account for Langer's duty to his son without conceding that responsibility in sense 1 is in itself sufficient to generate a duty to care. We can say that the mother (and father) of the one-year-old owe care to their child either because (*a*) such a duty follows from tacit consent alone which is reasonably inferred from bringing the child home after it is born but not merely from engaging in voluntary intercourse (in which case the fact that Langer is responsible for his son in sense 1 is entirely superfluous to accounting for his duty to care for him), or (*b*) such a duty follows from such consent only when it is conjoined with being responsible for the child in sense 1 (in which case the fact that he is responsible for his son in sense 1 is necessary but not sufficient). The first of the two accounts seems far more plausible, since account *b* is difficult to square with the assumption that the duty adoptive parents have to the children they adopt is the same as the duty biological parents have to their offspring.[37] But choosing between the two is not necessary: On either of these accounts, the morally relevant distinction that explains why the parent of a one-year-old son has a duty to care for him while the victim of rape does not have a duty to care for her fetus would fail to distinguish the woman whose pregnancy arises from rape from the woman whose pregnancy arises from voluntary intercourse.[38]

A final objection to my rebuttal of the Negligence Version which merits attention is this[39]: In attempting to make the case for the claim that being responsible for another in sense 1 alone is not sufficient to distinguish rape cases from nonrape cases, I have followed the sort of example exploited by Silverstein, in which the doctor who is responsible for the fact that her patient is still alive does not owe him additional assistance unless she is also responsible for the fact that the patient is dependent on her given that he is still alive. This is the claim, in short, that cases of voluntary intercourse that result in pregnancy are morally like Imperfect Drug rather than Malpractice. But it is open to someone to agree that voluntary intercourse is like Imperfect Drug in this particular respect, but to insist that there is a much more important sense in which they differ and that undermines the analogy. In particular, one could argue as follows: In Imperfect Drug, the doctor is responsible for the patient's existence because she did an act, namely, the act of giving the patient the drug, that was done in response to the patient's needs. But in voluntary intercourse, the woman is responsible for the fetus's existence not because she was acting in response to its needs (after all, the fetus didn't exist at that point) but merely because she selfishly wanted to engage in a pleasurable activity.[40] And one could claim that the doctor is free of further responsibility not by virtue of the fact that she is only responsible in sense 1, but in virtue of the *way in which* she is only responsible in sense 1. Because she was acting in the patient's interest, she has done all she is obligated to do for him, but because the woman who engages in voluntary intercourse was not acting in the fetus's interest, she has not yet done all she is obligated to do for the fetus. Indeed, she hasn't yet done anything for the fetus. Thus, one could agree that the doctor owes aid in Malpractice but not in Imperfect Drug, and also agree that the woman who engages in voluntary intercourse is responsible in sense 1 but not sense 2, but still conclude that she owes aid to the fetus by virtue of her voluntary behavior while the doctor in Imperfect Drug does not.

Let us assume that this difference in the agent's motivation undermines the analogy between pregnancies that arise from voluntary intercourse and the case of Imperfect Drug.[41] I believe that the point of the analogy can be sustained by turning to a new analogy that parallels voluntary pregnancy more closely than does Imperfect Drug. Indeed, this is a useful revision on its own, even if one does not think it a necessary one, because it reveals how easily even defenders of Thomson such as Silverstein can be led to impute a greater degree of responsibility to the pregnant woman than the circumstances warrant. In particular, the altruistic doctor deliberately causes the patient to live longer by her considerate act of giving him the drug. But the pleasure-seeking woman does not deliberately cause the fetus to come into existence so that she can experience pleasure, she deliberately engages in intercourse so that she can experience pleasure with the recognition that a fetus may come into existence as a result. Silverstein's case against the Negligence Version, then, by overlooking the distinction that undermines the Tacit Consent Version, rests on an example that compares the pregnant woman to one who is responsible in sense 1 in a more direct way than she really is. And if we reconstruct Silverstein's point with this distinction in mind, we can produce an analogy that avoids the potentially problematic discrepancy in motives. So instead, consider,

> **Pleasure-Seeking Doctor:** You are a doctor who wishes to engage in a very pleasurable activity. The activity is such that if you engage in it, there is a good chance that it will cause some gas to be released, which will result in adding extra years to the life of some violinist in the world, who will then contract the familiar kidney ailment from which only you will be able to save him by the familiar means described earlier. There are certain devices that you can use during the activity that reduce the chances of gas emission but do not eliminate them entirely, but you do not like the way the use of such devises "makes you feel" when you engage in the pleasurable activity. So you engage in the activity, and without such devices. As a result, there is a violinist who has some extra time added to his life and then gets the ailment, He now stands in need of the use of your kidneys.

In this case, you are responsible for the violinist in sense 1, but not in sense 2. You are in this respect like the woman whose pregnancy is the result of voluntary intercourse. And in this case, unlike Imperfect Drug, you are responsible for the violinist's existence at this point, not because you were admirably responding to his needs, but because his present existence was (foreseeably but not intentionally) caused by an act you engaged in just because it would be pleasurable. The new example, then, eliminates the possibly relevant difference in motivations noted above. But now ask: Do you believe that you are obligated to provide the violinist with the use of your hotly? This seems to me most implausible. Why should the fact that you have already added some years to his life mean that you have to add more, just because your motive in performing the action that foreseeably added some years to his life was purely selfish? And if this is so, then my objection to the Negligence Version can be sustained even if one rejects the sort of example with which Silverstein attempts to press his.

I conclude, therefore, that there are good reasons to reject both versions of the Responsibility Objection and no good reasons to accept either. If Thomson's argument is successful in rape cases, then it is successful in nonrape cases as well. Whether or not Thomson's argument is successful in rape cases in the first place, of course, is another question. I am inclined to believe that it is, but that will have to be the topic of another paper.[42]

STUDY QUESTIONS

1. Define and present both versions (tacit consent and negligence) of the Responsibility Objection to Thomson's argument.

2. Present and explain Professor Boonin-Vail's critique of the tacit consent version of the Responsibility Objection. Do you think he succeeds in his case? Why or why not? Explain and defend your answer.

3. Present and explain Professor Boonin-Vail's critique of the negligence version of the Responsibility Objection. Do you think he succeeds in his case? Why or why not? Explain and defend your answer.

NOTES

1. Judith Jarvis Thomson, "A Defense of Abortion," *Philosophy and Public Affairs* 1 (1971): 47–66, reprinted in *Arguing about Abortion,* ed. Lewis M. Schwartz (Belmont, Calif.: Wadsworth, 1993), 113–127. All references to Thomson are to the pagination in the Schwartz edition.

2. The objection is ubiquitous in the literature. In addition to the proponents of the objection cited here, see also, for example, Robert N. Wennberg, *Life in the Balance: Exploring the Abortion Controversy,* Grand Rapids, Mich.: Eerdmans, 1985, 160–162; John T. Wilcox. "Nature as Demonic in Thomson's Defense of Abortion," in *The Ethics of Abortion: Pro-Life vs. Pro-Choice,* rev. ed., ed. Robert M. Baird and Stuart E. Rosenbaum, Buffalo, N.Y.: Prometheus, 1993, 212–225; Mary Anne

Warren, "On the Moral and Legal Status of Abortion" in Schwartz, ed., 232; Paul D. Feinberg, "The Morality of Abortion." in *Thou Shalt Not Kill: The Christian Case against Abortion.* ed. Richard L. Ganz, New Rochelle, N.Y.: Arlington House, 1978, 143; Judith A. Boss, *The Birth Lottery: Prenatal Diagnosis and Selective Abortion,* Chicago: Loyola University Press, 1993, 102; Alan Donagan, *The Theory of Morality,* Chicago: University of Chicago Press, 1977, 169–170.

3. The example of the particular burden involved comes from L. S. Carrier, "Abortion and the Right to Life," *Social Theory and Practice* 3 (1975): 398–399, though very similar examples can he found in a number of other writers who press this objection.

4. The Responsibility Objection is also at times given an indirect defense by appealing to the claim that if the objection is rejected, then there is no way to account for the presumed legitimacy of those laws that require men to pay child support to defray the costs of raising children conceived as a result of their having engaged in intercourse voluntarily. As one such critic has put it, "If such a minimal life-sustaining sacrifice [that is, sustaining a pregnancy through to term] cannot be required of the mother before birth, how could even minimal child support be required of the father after birth?" (Keith J. Pavlischek, "Abortion Logic and Paternal Responsibility: One More look at Judith Thomson's 'A Defense of Abortion,'" *Public Affairs Quarterly* 7 [1993]: 348). This strategy merits a more detailed examination than I can give it here, but it should suffice for my present purposes to note that the nature of the burdens involved in the two cases is fundamentally different. The woman is required to suffer a distinctly intimate and physical burden while the man is required only to hand over some money. Of course, it might be pointed out that in order for the man to raise the necessary money he may also have to suffer a significant degree of physical pain and discomfort. As another such critic has pointed out, "If the father is a construction worker, the state will intervene unless some of the calories he expends lifting equipment go to providing food for his children" (Michael Levin, quoted in Francis J. Beckwith, "Arguments from the Bodily Rights: A Critical Analysis," in *The Abortion Controversy,* ed. Louis P. Pojman and Francis J. Beckwith, Boston: Jones & Bartlett, 1994, 164). But surely it does not follow from the fact that one can choose to earn one's money doing painful physical labor and then be required to make a financial sacrifice for a given cause that one can also be required to do a comparable amount of painful physical labor on behalf of that cause. If the state determined that it would be in the public interest to build a new highway, for example, it would hardly follow from the claim that it would be morally permissible for the state to take some of the construction worker's income to help

pay for the highway that it would also be morally permissible for the State to force the construction worker to help to build the highway. As a result of this difference in the nature of the burdens involved, an opponent of the Responsibility Objection to Thomson's argument need not be an opponent of child-support laws.

5. She is not completely explicit about this, but this is plainly the point of her examples of bars or screens failing to prevent unwanted burglars or people-seeds from getting in through a window (Thomson, 121).

6. Bonnie Steinbock, *Life before Birth: The Moral and Legal Status of Embryos and Fetuses.* Oxford: Oxford University Press, 1992, 78.

7. For two possible exceptions to this claim, see n. 10 following.

8. This formulation might seem to beg the question, since if we conclude that the voluntariness of P's doing A counts as evidence of P's having consented to S, then it won't be the case that S involves Q's infringing on some right of P's. Strictly speaking, then, we should say that S is the state of affairs in which Q is doing something that infringes on P's right to X unless P does or has done something to grant Q the right to do this.

9. These requirements are typically acknowledged and defended by those who defend the Tactic Consent Version of the objection. See, for example, Richard Linger, "Abortion and the Right to Privacy," *Journal of Social Philosophy,* 23 (1992): 23–51.

10. It might objected that very little, if anything, about cases of voluntary intercourse follows from my analysis of the sufficient conditions for consent on the grounds that the analysis itself arises from a relatively trivial example. Relatively little is at stake in the question of who has the right to the use of (what was at least initially) Ted's money, but a great deal is at stake in the question of who has the right to the use of the pregnant woman's body. So one might well think that even if Ted has the right to take the money back from the waiter, it does not follow that the woman has the right to take the use of her

body back from the fetus, and that attending to the example of tipping can thus do little to illuminate the moral problem of abortion. I certainly agree that the woman's right to abort the fetus does not follow from Ted's right to reclaim his money. There may be any number of important differences between the two cases. But viewing this as a problem for my analysis misconstrues the purpose of the example. I am not arguing that the woman has a right to abort the fetus because she has not consented to refrain from doing so. Rather, I am responding to an argument that claims that she lacks the right to abort the fetus because she has consented to refrain from doing so. That argument turns on the claim that the voluntariness of the action which produced the state of affairs justifies the attribution of consent, not on the claim that she is obligated to sustain the fetus because its very life is at stake. And the example of Bill and Ted demonstrates that this claim about consent is untenable. It may be worth noting, however, that the importance of the distinction between a and b that I have been arguing for would be revealed even if we focused on less straightforward and more controversial examples of consent. Suppose one believed, for example, that if you take off your coat and put it in the arms of a homeless person who needs the coat in order to survive the winter, then you have tacitly consented to let him keep the coat for as long as he needs it. It might be thought that in some respects this is more representative of what is at stake in cases of abortion. Still, this would not support the conclusion that if you take your coat off on a windy day because you want to experience the pleasure of a chilling breeze against your bare skin, then you must let the homeless person keep it if, as a foreseeable (but unintended and undesired) consequence of your action, the coat is blown into his arms. Again, there may be good reason to believe that you would be obligated to let the homeless person keep the coat at that point, but the reason cannot plausibly be grounded in the claim that you have consented to let him keep it, and that is the claim I am concerned to address in this Section. 1

have avoided appealing to such cases (you let someone into your house because it is cold outside, and so on) in developing my argument for the importance of the distinction between a and b because it is less clear that people will agree that you have consented to let the person keep the coat (or stay in your house) for as long as he needs to even in the case where you deliberately hand it to him (or let him in; perhaps you only mean to let him use the coat until you are ready to go home or to remain in your home until you are ready to go to bed), and I want to work from a case that puts the tacit consent claim itself in the most favorable possible light.

11. Two exceptions might be urged here. One is the case of a woman who freely chooses to have an embryo implanted in her. This does seem to be a case in which she voluntarily brings about the state of affairs in which there is a fetus making demands on her body, rather than one in which she merely foresees that her action may lead to this state of affairs. It thus seems plausible to think of it as a genuine case in which, if one believes in tacit consent, one will have good grounds for thinking that consent has been given. The other is what might be called the case of intentional conception, one in which the woman deliberately refrained from using contraception because she wanted to become pregnant. She does seem to do more than merely foresee that the subsequent state of affairs may arise, and so it can again seem plausible to suppose that in this case she has consented to it. Each sort of exception seems plausible, but each raises difficulties. In the case of the embryo implant, we would need to be careful about specifying the content of the rights waiver that was consented to; as Sara Worley has pointed out to me, it may seem implausible to suppose that a woman who consents to have multiple embryos implanted in her as a part of infertility treatment should be understood as waiving the right later to remove one in order to improve the prospects of survival for the others. And as Marcia Baron has noted, such a woman might also be understood as tacitly agreeing only to bear at least one child by virtue of such a procedure without having agreed to bear all of them. In

the case of the intentional conception, on the other hand, there is a sense in which it does not seem right to say that, strictly speaking, the woman intentionally becomes pregnant. She does what she hopes will lead to pregnancy, but there are many factors beyond her control which may lead one to conclude that the pregnancy should not be understood as a state of affairs that she voluntarily creates. I will leave the question about how to treat both cases open and thus accept the possibility that my argument against the Tacit Consent Version does not apply in either or both of these cases. Since abortions arising from such cases are relatively rare, however, this is at most a very small concession.

12. Langer, 42. Although he does not note this, the same example is used to make the same point by Warren, 232–233.

13. It might be argued that in a society that legally prohibits abortion except in cases of rape a woman who engages in voluntary intercourse enters precisely such a lottery. Even if we think that such a woman has tacitly consented to carry the fetus to term, however, this would only be because she has tacitly agreed to obey a law, not because she has granted a right to the fetus. And Thomson's argument is addressed to the proponent of the claim that abortion is impermissible because it violates the fetus's right to life.

14. In constructing the analogy in this way. I do not mean to suggest that when a couple has intercourse without contraception this is always the result of a deliberate policy devised exclusively to increase their level of physical pleasure. The story might be modified to say that you thought you had Mace with you but at the last minute could not find it, or that you usually carry Mace but forgot this one time, or that you are deterred from purchasing Mace because you are made to feel shameful when you go to the store to buy it, or that your religious leaders have told you that it is immoral, and so on. I will stick with my version because I want to show that even in what amounts to a kind of "worse case" scenario for Thomson's argument. the woman's voluntary action does not give the fetus any more

right to the use of her body than it would have in cases involving rape.

15. It might be thought that the concession here that it would be fair to say that you had gotten what you deserve plays into the hands of Thomson's critics. After all, wouldn't it then follow that the pregnant woman has also gotten what she deserves? But all that can plausibly be meant here is that it is fair to make you bear the costs of extricating yourself from the situation, since it is not as if someone else had forced you into the park. And the concession that in those cases in which the woman is (partly) responsible for her pregnancy, she should also be (partly) responsible for bearing whatever physical, economic, and psychological costs an abortion may involve seems perfectly reasonable and surely consistent with Thomson's position.

16. I am aware that the following example simplifies in some respects the present policy of the Chinese government; if any of the simplifications affect the argument, we can simply treat this as a fictional version of China.

17. In addition, it is worth noting that not every act is a suitable candidate for counting as evidence of consent to something. If the act is such that refraining from performing it is itself a substantial burden to the agent, then viewing the act as consenting to S amounts to coercing the agent into consenting to S, and expressions of consent that are coerced are generally recognized to be nonbinding. And as Smith points out, a strong case can be made for saying that refraining from voluntary intercourse is a substantial enough burden to undermine the suitability of voluntary intercourse as a sign of consenting to anything (Holly M. Smith, "Intercourse and Moral Responsibility for the Fetus," in *Abortion and the Status of the Fetus,* ed. William B. Bondeson et al., Dordrecht: Reidel, 1983, 237–238).

18. Similarly, Kamm points out that voluntarily bringing someone into your house does not constitute a tacit agreement to let him stay. She also notes that accepting the view that voluntarily beginning to aid makes discontinuing aid impermissible would deter many people

from offering aid in the first place, since once they started voluntarily it would become impermissible for them to discontinue, and they might be genuinely uncertain about whether they would be willing to provide all of the aid needed but willing to try as long as they would be free to stop if they so desired (Frances Myrna Kamm. *Creation and Abortion* Oxford: Oxford University Press, 1992, 23, 108).

19. There may, of course, be other important differences between the bone marrow case and the pregnancy case. The cost in terms of suffering may be different, and refraining from giving more bone marrow might seem to he a case of letting die while refraining from continuing the pregnancy might he a case of killing. One might, then, consistently believe that you don't have to keep giving bone marrow while you do have to keep supporting a fetus. My point here is simply that this will have to be for reasons other than the fact that the support was begun voluntarily, so that the mere fact of voluntary initiation of support does not imply a duty to continue it. But the Tacit Consent Version depends on its being the case that the fact of voluntary initiation itself does imply such a duty.

20. Michael Tooley, *Abortion and Infanticide* (Oxford: Clarendon, 1983), 45. The same objection is made by means of similar examples by, for example, Carrier, 398–399; Francis Beckwith, "Personal Bodily Rights, Abortion, and Unplugging the Violinist," *International Philosophical Quarterly,* 32 (1992): 111–112, and "Arguments from Bodily Rights," 164.

21. Beckwith, "Personal Bodily Rights, Abortion, and Unplugging the Violinist," 111–112, and "Arguments from Bodily Rights," 164 (Beckwith makes this claim in the contest of defending the father's responsibility to care for the offspring, but it is presumably meant to apply equally to the case of the mother).

22. Even this claim is by no means unproblematic, as the literature on moral luck demonstrates.

23. Harry S. Silverstein. "On a Woman's 'Responsibility' for the fetus," *Social Theory and Practice* 13 (1987): 106.

24. Note that my claim is not that it would be improper to use the term "negligent" to describe the behavior of a woman who has intercourse without using birth control (although something like "irresponsible" might be more apt). My claim is simply that, whatever we call her action, it lacks the feature of characteristically negligent acts such as those cited by Tooley, Beckwith, and others that plausibly justifies attributing a right to assistance to the one who stands in need of assistance as a foreseeable result of the action.

25. This is a condensed and slightly modified version of an example given by Silverstein, "On a Woman's 'Responsibility' for the Fetus," 106–107.

26. In his response to an objection raised by Langer. Silverstein is more clear that this is the central point of his argument. See Richard Langer, "Silverstein and the 'Responsibility Objection,'" *Social Theory and Practice* 19 (1993): 348–349; Harry S. Silverstein, "Reply to Langer," *Social Theory and Practice* 19 (1993): 361 ff.

27. Of course, one might maintain that even in Malpractice, the doctor does not owe the violinist the use of his kidneys (and one could hold this even while believing that the violinist was nonetheless entitled to something as compensation or punitive damages). And it would then follow that Thomson's argument would be secure even if it turned out that the pregnancy case was more like Malpractice than like Imperfect Drug. Since this assessment seems controversial at best, and since I claim that Thomson's argument can be defended without it, I will not rely on it here though I do not mean to be insisting that it is mistaken.

28. One might well be inclined to object at this point that the woman is responsible for helping the fetus precisely *because* there was no way for her to make it the case that the fetus exists without making it the case that the fetus exists in a state of dependence on her, while there was a way for her to avoid making it the case that the fetus exists in the first place: she could simply have abstained from having intercourse. But this would seem equally to imply that you are responsible for aiding the violinist in Imperfect Drug. There was

no way for you to make it the case that the violinist (still) exists without making it the case that he exists in a state of dependence on you, but there was a way for you to avoid making it be the case that he still exists in the first place: You could simply have abstained from giving him the drug.

29. Silverstein himself accepts this emendation, and it also runs parallel to the notion of a "baseline" employed by Kamm, who argues that you are (or may be) obligated only to ensure that the violinist not be made worse off than he would have been had you not been hooked up to him in the first place. See Silverstein, On a Woman's 'Responsibility' for the Fetus," 111; Kamm, for example, 26–43, 89–90.

30. Michael Davis, "Foetuses, Famous Violinists, and the Right to Continued Aid," *Philosophical Quarterly* 33 (1983): 277.

31. Thomas Nagel, "Death" in his *Mortal Questions*. Cambridge: Cambridge University Press, 1979, 1.

32. This response is pressed persuasively by Kamm, who also argues that the claim is importantly at odds with our attitudes toward women who are prone to miscarriage: We do not think it wrong for them to try to have children even if it takes several attempts, but surely we would think it wrong if we thought this meant making several fetuses worse off than they would have been had they never been conceived. See Kamm, 84–87.

33. One might appeal in part to the idea that being unjustly killed is worse than simply dying in one's sleep, but this claim too is a bit difficult to make sense of and would in any event clearly beg the question at issue, which is whether or not the killing of the fetus is unjust.

34. Langer, "Silverstein and the 'Responsibility Objection,'" 351–352.

35. Ibid., 352.

36. It is worth noting that even this part of Langer's argument is subject to doubt. After all, it does not follow from the claim that "child abandonment" is immoral that a parent has a duty to provide for his child's needs. That would follow only if one also believed that a parent had a duty not to put this child up for adoption, but most people (especially, perhaps, opponents of abortion) believe that it is perfectly permissible for a parent to have someone else incur the costs of raising his child. So one might simply reply to Langer's question by saying no, he does not have an obligation to care for his son's needs. If he no longer wishes to be a parent, it is permissible for him to put his son up for adoption.

37. Even if the "adoption" is really a kidnapping, as in the case where a woman steals a baby from the hospital and takes it home to raise as her own, we will still presumably believe that her duty to care for the infant is as strong as the duty of any parent to care for her child, and this would again favor account *a* over account *b*.

38. None of what is said in this paragraph. of course, implies or presupposes that a woman who declines to bring her newborn home has no duty to care for it at all. Suppose she gives birth in an abandoned field. One might hold the view that there are no positive duties to assist others, in which case one will hold that if she does not wish to raise the child herself she is morally free to walk away and leave the infant to die. But one need not hold this view. One could believe that there are positive duties to assist others at least in cases where the burden is relatively small and the benefit relatively great, and so hold that the woman would at least be obligated to incur the cost of carrying the child to town and providing for it until it could be taken to a hospital. But then she will have this obligation equally even if she comes across a newborn that someone else has abandoned in the field, so this will again fail to support the view that Thomson's argument is undermined by the difference between the voluntariness of intercourse in nonrape cases and the involuntariness of kidnapping in the violinist case. And in addition, it will be unlikely to follow that a woman would be obligated to sustain her pregnancy since the burdens of pregnancy are not so trivial. Of course, one might endorse the existence of a positive duty to assist another who will otherwise die even where the burden to you in doing so is quite substantial, provided that (a) the

benefit to the other still significantly outweighs the burden to you and (b) you are
the only one who can save the individual.
This would justify a duty to continue the
pregnancy even granting that the burden is
substantially greater than what we are
typically required to undergo for the benefit of others. But then it will seem equally
to follow that you are obligated to remain
plugged into the violinist in Thomson's
story, since the benefit to the violinist
significantly outweighs the burden to you
and you are the only one who can save
him. So even this view of positive rights
will fail to undermine Thomson's analogy.

39. I am grateful to Alec Walen for bringing this objection to my attention.

40. One might well complain here that
the importance of a sexual relationship to
living a well-lived life is trivialized by
picturing the woman as merely pursuing
physical pleasure. The assumption that
such pleasure is all that can be involved is
surely too narrow, but I want to assume
for the sake of the argument that this

really is all the woman (and her partner)
are seeking, and to question what follows
from this.

41. It is by no means obvious that this
assumption should be accepted. We might
well think that this simply reveals a difference in the moral merit of their characters
but not a difference in the obligations that
arise from their actions.

42. Or two. See my "Death Comes for
the Violinist," *Social Theory and* Practice
23.3 (Fall 1997), which responds to the
objection that Thomson's analogy is undermined either by the importance of the
distinction between killing and letting die
or by the importance of the distinction
between intending death and foreseeing it,
and "A Further Defense of 'A Defense of
Abortion'" (unpublished), which responds
to a number of additional objections,
including those that accept Thomson's
analogy but hold either that unplugging
yourself from the violinist is not permissible or that arguments from such analogies
are unsound.

10

Abortion Logic and Paternal Responsibilities

One More Look at Judith Thomson's Argument and a Critique of David Boonin-Vail's Defense of It*

KEITH PAVLISCHEK

Keith Pavlischek is Director of Crossroads (Wynnewood, Pennsylvania), a program of Evangelicals for Social Action and the Center for Public Justice. He is the executive editor of the Crossroads Monograph Series on Faith and Public Policy.

In this critical analysis of Professor Thomson's argument (see Chapter 7), Dr. Pavlischek puts forth an argument similar to one employed only briefly in Beckwith's critique of Thomson (see Chapter 8). Pavlischek argues that the logic of Thomson's case—that parents have no "special responsibility" toward their children—proves too much, for it supports a perspective that most defenders of abortion-rights detest, paternal irresponsibility after birth (that is, "Dead-beat Dads"). In concluding remarks written exclusively for this volume, Pavlischek ends his essay with a reply to Boonin-Vail's analysis of his argument (Chapter 9).

INTRODUCTION

The central and most important claim of the prolife movement is that a fetus is a human being from the moment of conception, that abortion involves the taking of innocent human life, and that because the fundamental and overriding function of any legal system is to protect innocent human life it should be

---

*This essay is a revised version of an article originally published in *Public Affairs Quarterly* 7 (October 1993). This revised version was commissioned for this volume.

proscribed by law. A corollary to this central claim is that an intimate connection exists between the way a culture (including its legal system) understands and treats the unborn and the way it understands and acts toward other vulnerable members of society.[1] Often dismissed as falling prey to the slippery slope fallacy. the claim of the corollary is that if as a culture we are cavalier about the preservation and protection of those who are most vulnerable, the unborn, we will also tend to have a similarly cavalier attitude with respect to other physically and mentally vulnerable citizens.[2] Our attitudes toward the unborn will inevitably come to be manifested not only in the way we treat deformed and handicapped infants or the "unproductive" elderly, but also in the way we treat children generally. The claim is that children, being the weakest and most vulnerable members of society, are likely to suffer the most at the hands of the strong and most powerful. One should therefore expect a marked rise in incidents of child neglect, abandonment and abuse in an abortionist culture.

All this is, of course, terribly oversimplified. But even if the corollary could be explicated more precisely, it would be remarkably difficult to demonstrate. Empirically, establishing a causal nexus between the increase in the number of abortions since *Roe v. Wade* and an increase in incidents of child neglect, abandonment and abuse is next to impossible. A wide variety of other societal causes from a lack of adequate education to (depending on who you ask) too little or too much social welfare spending can plausibly be said to contribute to this or any other social problem, as contemporary debates over the nature and cause of poverty make abundantly clear. And conceptually, there does not seem to be a strictly logical connection between abortion logic and the neglect and abandonment of children. If the prochoice advocate makes a strong conceptual distinction between a child after birth or, if less radical, the stage at which the fetus becomes "viable" and that of a fetus prior to either of these stages of human development, he can, it would seem, morally distinguish the way he advocates treating the unborn and the way he would want children treated.

Notwithstanding these types of objections, prolife advocates persist in claiming that there is in some sense a significant connection between a culture's thinking and behavior toward fetal life and that of other vulnerable members of society.[3] In this essay I want to examine the conceptual connection in one relevant area, that of child abandonment and neglect, and leave aside broader issues such as euthanasia, the treatment of deformed and handicapped infants, and more explicit child abuse. I intend to focus the issue more narrowly on the relation between abortion and *paternal* abandonment of children. I will argue that while indeed many cases of paternal abandonment and neglect can be consistently condemned by both prolife advocates and defenders of abortion on demand. there nevertheless remain a significant number of cases that cannot be consistently condemned by prochoice advocates. Given certain moderate prochoice assumptions. I argue that in many cases there should be no legal requirement that men financially support their children and that a father should legally be able to opt out of all parental responsibilities.

The aim of my argument is a modest one—to force a dilemma on defenders of permissive abortion laws: either surrender the defense of abortion on demand and allow the passage of laws restricting abortion, or surrender the advocacy of paternal responsibility for children of mothers who choose to forego an abortion.

I propose to examine the question of paternal responsibilities within the context of Judith Jarvis Thomson's renowned essay, "A Defense of Abortion."[4] This well-anthologized article is useful not only because it proved to be so influential in the debate over legalized abortion and has become a bit of a classic in the literature on the subject, but also because Thomson believes she is advocating a relatively moderate prochoice position. Thomson acknowledges that her position will be found unsatisfactory "by many of those who want to regard abortion as morally permissible (65). But in her view removing a non-viable fetus from the mother's body and thereby letting it die is significantly different from removing a viable fetus from the mother's body and then killing it. Some prochoice advocates object to this as a limitation of choice. But for Thomson, although the former may be permissible, the latter is not.[5] The "right to an abortion" is not, for her, extensionally equivalent to a "right to a dead fetus." Her position thus uncouples, at least at first glance, the connection between the fetus (nonviable or viable) living in the mother's womb on the one hand and the infant (or viable fetus) outside the mother's womb on the other. So, if what I have to say about paternal responsibility is sound relative to Thomson's position, then it is also sound for those more radial prochoice positions that are less inclined to make that distinction.[6]

The overall thrust of my argument will be to show that if, given the logic of the moderate prochoice position, the most reasonable course to follow would be to surrender the defense of paternal support laws for those children whose fathers would rather have had their children aborted, it will lend some credence not only to the prolife insistence on the corollary that an intimate connection exists between the way we collectively relate to the unborn and the way we relate to our children after birth—but also to the claim made by some prolife feminists that the abortion mentality simply reaffirms the worst historical failings, neglect and chauvinism of males.[7]

I

Thomson's strategy is to begin by conceding, for the sake of argument, that the fetus is a person from the moment of conception.[8] Then, relying on a series of analogies or thought experiments, she aims to demonstrate that even if the fetus is granted full personhood status, a woman has the right to obtain an abortion even though it would in some cases be "indecent" to exercise her right.

The first of her analogies and perhaps the most well-known and influential invites us to consider the question of abortion in the event of a pregnancy resulting from rape. It is her story of the violinist (see Chapter 7)...

The purpose of Thomson's analogy is to defeat the central prolife argument, which I stated less formally at the beginning of this essay:

1. The fetus is a person from the moment of conception.

2. Every person has a right to life.

3. A mother has the right to decide what will happen in and to her body.

4. However, a person's right to life is stronger and more stringent than the mother's right to decide what happens in and to her body.

5. Therefore, the fetus may not be killed and an abortion may not be performed.

Her strategy is to concede (1), attack (4) and (hereby foist a dilemma on the opponent of abortion: If the prolife advocate says once innocent life exists we should not directly take it, she would be obligated to being plugged into the violinist as long as it takes. If, on the other hand, she concedes that this case is significantly different because she did not *consent* to it, then she is forced to admit that the argument against abortion collapses, at least in certain situations. And, of course, once (4) is shown to be implausible in the case of rape, then it will be easier for her to advance to the next stage of her argument and show it to be implausible in other cases in which full consent is absent, particularly in those pregnancies resulting from contraceptive failure.

Now, however much Thomson's "violin player" analogy may have helped us see why "abortion in cases of rape is a very special and different matter,"[9] it doesn't really raise any special problems as far as paternal child support is concerned. In this situation, the question of paternal support would arise only in the event that the mother chose to carry the child to term and the father was in a position in which he could be compelled by law to support her and the child. The significant question that would arise relative to the issue of child support would simply involve the *extent* to which the father is morally and legally obligated to support the child, not the more specific question, with which we are concerned, of *whether* the law ought to require of the father some sort of child support in the first place.

No doubt a situation such as this certainly might cause us to ponder a set of interesting questions: How much beyond the basic needs of the child must the father contribute? Should the father be forced by law to contribute financially everything above what is needed for the child's basic needs? What might be the larger culture's obligations to the child should the father be unable to support her at all? A discussion of these questions might prove illuminating in matters of child support generally. But reasons for requiring paternal support in the first place must be given, not assumed.

In any case, the issue of whether or not the father of a child brought into the world as a result of rape could be completely relieved of financial responsibility, if it was within his financial means to provide it, is not likely to be controversial. I mention Thomson's first analogy mainly because it serves to introduce a picture of how we are to understand the parent-fetus/person relation that will be more relevant when we look at her second analogy. Here Thomson asks us to imagine that

People-seeds drift about in the air like pollen, and if you open your windows, one may drift in and take root in your carpets or upholstery. You
don't want children, so you fix up your widows with fine mesh screens,
the very best you can buy. As can happen, however, and on very very rare
occasions does happen, one of the screens is defective, and a seed drifts in
and takes root. Does the personplant who now develops have a right to
the use of your house? Surely not…(59)

By this analogy Thomson intends to broaden her defense of abortion to
those cases in which the mother willingly and knowingly risked pregnancy.
The point of her example is meant to show that pregnancy resulting from contraceptive failure confers no "special responsibility" on the parents for the child.

Surely, we do not have any such "special responsibility" for a person unless we have assumed it, explicitly or implicitly. If a set of parents do not
try to prevent pregnancy, do not obtain an abortion, but rather take it
home with them, then they have assumed responsibility for it, they have
given it rights, and they cannot *now* withdraw support from it at the cost
of its life because they now find it difficult to go on providing for it. But
if they have taken all reasonable precautions against having a child, they
do not by virtue of their biological relationship to the child who comes
into existence have a special responsibility for it. They may wish to assume responsibility for it, or they may not wish to. And I am suggesting
that if assuming responsibility for it would require large sacrifices, then
they may refuse. (65)

Now, to gain a clearer perspective on the implications of Thomson's argument for *paternal* responsibility in cases of contraceptive failure, we must first
uncouple Thomson's "set of parents,"[10] for we should not simply assume that
"they" will agree on the action to be taken after conception. Assuming that
they agreed to engage in sexual intercourse and to take reasonable contraceptive
measures, we are then confronted with four possibilities and four outcomes:

1. The mother does not confer human significance on or assume "special
   responsibility" for the fetus-person, nor does the father.

   Outcome = UNPROBLEMATIC ABORTION

2. The mother does not confer human significance on or assume "special
   responsibility" for the fetus-person, the father does.

   Outcome = PROBLEMATIC ABORTION (with no paternal notification obligation?)

3. The mother does confer human significance on or assume "special
   responsibility" for the fetus-person, the father does also.

   Outcome = UNPROBLEMATIC BIRTH

4. The mother does confer human significance on or assume "special
   responsibility' for the fetus-person, the father does not.

   Outcome = PROBLEMATIC BIRTH (with no paternal support obligation?)

Situations (1) and (3) are explicitly addressed in the cited passage and are unproblematic since the parents agree on the action to be taken. The entire point of Thomson's essay is to show that in the case of (1) an abortion should at the very least be legally permissible. That an abortion would also result in situation (2) is implied by her analogies. Her argument clearly suggests that the will of the mother must trump the will of the father when abortion is being considered and there is disagreement. If we prefer to speak in terms of the first analogy we can say that she is the one who is "plugged-in" to the violinist. Or, if we prefer the second analogy, it is her "house" in which the fetus-person has set up residence. And since one cannot infer a special responsibility from these simple facts one would have to assume that the mere fact that a man is the biological father would carry no moral weight either. Here one finds the theoretical grounding for the general prochoice opposition to paternal notification laws, not to mention the outright hostility to paternal consent.[11] Given this, the question to be addressed is whether this is consistent with a paternal support requirement in situation (4).

Situations (3) and (4) both result in the birth of the child. While there is parental agreement in situation (3) the birth occurs primarily because the mother has willed that it be so. The will of the father, as far as birth *per se* is concerned, is an entirely secondary matter. Although the birth itself is rather unproblematic, the fact that both the father and mother agree to have the child does make it relevant to the issue of child support. Since the father agrees to "take it home with them," he has at least tacitly assumed responsibility for the child and has thus incurred an obligation for child support equal to that of the mother. The "taking home" signifies the assumption of that responsibility. For the father to support the child at this point would then become an obligation of justice, a point that both prochoice and prolife advocates can presumably agree on without much difficulty.

Thus far, then, the conceptual distinction between abortion and child abandonment and neglect can plausibly be maintained by prochoice advocates, which means that the stronger and broader connection posited by the corollary has yet to be established. However, the issue of paternal responsibility becomes more problematic in the case of (4), when the mother wants to bear the child but the father wants her to have an abortion. *Thomson does not address this in her article. But where would her argument take her if she had?*

II

The obvious problem for the defender of abortion on demand who would also advocate some sort of "get-tough legislation" on "dead-beat Dads" (to employ the contemporary political jargon) is to justify holding the father morally or legally responsible for an act that flows solely from an act of the mother's will, namely her choice to give birth to a child. How, given Thomson's reasoning on the question of abortion, can a father be forced to make serious sacrifices and assume "special responsibility" for a child to whom *he* does not will to confer any special status? More precisely, how can he, as an autonomous rational agent, be bound by law to a child that achieves legal personhood status solely by an act of *the mother's* will? It certainly would seem strange to suggest that the mother could be relieved of potential parental burdens and responsibilities in *all* situations but the father could not under *any* circumstances. To some this may even appear sexist.

To see how conceptually difficult it will be legally or morally to bind the father to such an obligation, we must first recognize how and why, according to Thomson, the *mother* can relieve herself of any "special responsibility" prior to birth and then ask under what conditions the father could also.

Thomson's argument leans heavily on the distinction between what a person can demand as a right and what is required by minimal moral decency. What she means by "minimal moral decency" is illustrated by another analogy intended to call our attention to the difference between what she calls a Minimally Decent Samaritan and a Good (or Splendid) Samaritan. She asks us to suppose that she is sick unto death and the only thing that will save her is a touch of Henry Fonda's cool hand on her brow.

> It would be frightfully nice of him to fly in from the West Coast to provide it. It would be less nice, though no doubt well meant, if my friends flew out to the West Coast and carried Henry Fonda back with them. But I have no right at all against anybody that he should do this for me. (55)

Fonda, according to Thomson, would certainly be a Good or Splendid Samaritan if he made the sacrifice by flying all the way from the West Coast, but he has no obligation to do it, and she would have no right to demand it. But what if, she asks, Henry Fonda is not on the West Coast but in the hospital room next door? Well, in that case, while it may be the minimally moral thing for him to do, she still has no right to it and he has no obligation to provide it. Hence it would be wrong to compel him by law to provide it (61). And, of course, if the law could not compel him, it surely cannot compel a mother to sacrifice nine months of her life and a lot more after birth in support of the fetus-person. That would require her to be not only a Minimally Decent Samaritan but a Good or Splendid Samaritan.

Thomson further illustrates the significance of the distinction between minimal moral decency and the obligations of justice with a variation on the "dying violinist" analogy. She asks us to suppose that what the violinist needs is not nine months of your life but only one hour. Spending that one hour will not affect your life in the slightest and yet you can save his life. Even though you were kidnapped and did not give anyone permission to plug him into you, Thomson argues that one *ought* to do so (here is another reason her position is considered "moderate") for it would be morally indecent to refuse.

> Even supposing a case in which a woman pregnant due to rape ought to allow the unborn person to use her body for the hour he needs, we should not conclude that he has a right to do so; we should conclude that she is self-centered, callous, indecent, but not unjust if she refuses. (61)

Again, the point to be made by this strong distinction between minimal moral decency and the requirements of justice is to demonstrate that while abortion *may* be an affront to the former, it can rarely if ever be said to violate the latter.[12]

But if such a minimal life-sustaining sacrifice cannot be required of the mother *before* birth, how could even minimal child support be required of the father *after* birth? If the sacrifice of the pregnant woman can at best be a requirement (if that) of "decency" and not an obligation of justice, should not the same thing be said of the father? The "requirement" that the father meet the basic needs of his child, if he can do so, certainly seems to be no more than a requirement of minimal decency rather than an obligation of justice. And this, of course, would seem to imply that while we might have to say it is not "nice" for a father to fail to provide support for his child, it would not be unjust if he failed to do so, which would in turn imply that it would be wrong to have a law requiring him to do so. Would this not be imposing someone else's (minimally decent) morality on him?

Now the most obvious response to this line of reasoning is simply to assert that there is a significant distinction of great moral weight between the unborn fetus and a child who has already been born. Given Thomson's working assumption that the fetus is a person just as much as the infant, one might question just why the brute fact of birth should carry significantly more moral weight. But let's suppose for the sake of argument that the birth of a child *does* confer greater moral significance. This forces on us several crucial questions: Given Thomson's argument, what is the minimal extent to which the father should be held responsible by law for the fetus-person, if he declares, prior to birth, that he does not want the child? More precisely, what actions may the father take prior to birth that may plausibly be taken to relieve himself of the responsibilities and burdens of child support should he find himself in a situation in which the mother attempts to trump his will by having the child?

One option would be for him simply to offer to provide half the cost of procuring an abortion, including, if he were sufficiently generous, the cost of travel to and from the abortion clinic. His argument might be that even though it is her "house," he bears at least 50 percent of the responsibility for the entrance of the people-seed and therefore should pay half the cost of extermination. This would, I suppose, render his action minimally decent.

Of course, a minimally decent person could do a bit more by factoring into his financial calculations a number of other relevant considerations. He could offer to pay more than simply half of the cost to procure an abortion, but less than the full amount, arguing perhaps that the emotional effects on the woman should be compensated for financially in some way. If he is indeed a Minimally Decent Samaritan, he will most likely recognize that this is the least he could do, given that she does not want to have an abortion at all, and may therefore offer to compensate her for a certain amount of emotional stress. He could also offer to pay the entire cost of procuring an abortion, which would seem to exceed his "fair share." But that would imply that he would be approaching the status of a "Good Samaritan," if not a "Splendid Samaritan," and this, according to Thomson, cannot be prescribed by law.[13] Of course, all these calculations would matter only if the woman finally concedes to having the abortion even though she is predisposed not to.

But what if she doesn't have the abortion? Would a *mere good faith offer* of any of the above suffice to relieve the father of further moral and legal obligations? It would certainly seem so. He has, after all, taken all the responsible actions one might expect of a minimally decent person to relieve the mother of the considerably heavier personal and financial burdens of raising a child. Again, if he is a "Good Samaritan," he may go beyond the call of duty and calculate the "costs" to the mother of providing a "house" for the child during the nine months of pregnancy and render that much financial assistance. A "Splendid Samaritan" might even offer to provide something for the child after birth. But one is hard-pressed to see how, given Thomson's argument, it would be *unjust* if he failed to do so. If the mother could absolve herself of responsibility by securing an abortion, then the father should be able to absolve himself of responsibility by providing his fair share of the means for her to obtain one.

A good faith financial offer to pay a fair share would appear to legally be the *most* one could require, but even that would depend on one's willingness to legislate minimally decent Samaritan laws more generally.[14] But the *most* reasonable conclusion when the mother wants the child and the father doesn't, given Thomson's perspective, would be to say simply that *the father should bear no legal responsibility for the fetus-person either before or after birth.* We can reasonably say of him what Thomson says of the woman attached to the violinist for only an hour: He ought to do something, to do nothing would be morally indecent, but there is a significant difference between the demands of moral decency and the demands of justice. We may consider him indecent if he refuses to provide anything at all for the child. He is, after all, the biological father. But if no "special kind of responsibility" issues from the fact that the woman is the mother of a fetus-person, even when that fetus-person is living in her "house," it is difficult if not impossible to see how the father/fetus-person relationship could create legal obligations greater than that of the mother. And it is easy enough to imagine a man, who is a Minimally Decent Samaritan, saying something like this to a woman who chose to have the child and wants financial support from the father:

> I'm personally opposed to those fathers who refuse to support their children, but I refuse to impose my own (minimally decent) morality on the rest of society. It's not that I'm for child neglect, I'm just prochoice. After all, when you invited him and those pesky people-seeds into your house, you knew the risk. It was small, you took all the precautions, but, well, accidents happen. Because it's your house and not his, you bear the complete responsibility for what happens there and for what comes out of there, not him. It would be nice if he were a Minimally Decent Samaritan. It would even be nicer if he were a Good Samaritan and he offered to help you and your child out. You may have at one time thought he was at least a Minimally Decent Samaritan. But he isn't. That's unfortunate, but you can't force him to be one by passing and enforcing child support laws.

I suspect that few would explicitly say this sort of thing. But, given the increase in paternal neglect and its associated problems, such as neglected child-support payments,[15] one might suppose that the view is not uncommon. One can fairly safely assume that the reason so many young males support permissive abortion laws is not primarily an overwhelming concern with equality for women. In any case, this sort of view does seem entirely consistent with a "moderate" prochoice position, and seems to follow quite reasonably and naturally from it. So, at least partially, the corollary holds. All that is required of a father legitimately to abandon his child is a good faith declaration of non-responsibility prior to birth.

III

It would seem then, that the prolife feminist claim that the abortion mentality simply reaffirms past male failings and neglect has some plausibility. But what about the broader claim expressed in the corollary? It might be argued that the assertion of a broader connection between abortion logic and the way a culture treats other vulnerable members of society has not at all been established. In fact, in three of the four possible outcomes after conception it would seem that the prochoice advocate can keep his view of the fetus and his view of other vulnerable members of society entirely separate. Even if the prochoice advocate is willing to concede that he has a problem in this one instance, he might simple concede such situations arise so infrequently that the fear expressed in the corollary is unwarranted.

But the prolife concern is not, I think, so easily dismissed. The problem arises not simply with the logic of the prochoice position in the narrow sense, but with the metaphors, images, and perspectives it invites us to employ. The claim of the corollary requires a broader perspective and a broader question: Can the metaphors, imagery, and perspectives of even the "moderate" prochoice position evoke the sort of caring, nurturing, and sharing attitudes required for a culture to have positive regard for the vulnerable? That Thomson has serious problems in this regard has been demonstrated quite conclusively in Gilbert Meilaender's illuminating critique of Thomson in his essay "The Fetus as Parasite and Mushroom."[16]

Meilaender calls our attention to the way in which the "violin player" and "people-seed" analogies subtly distort the whole issue of abortion. For the remainder of the essay, I want to follow the lead of Meilaender and suggest that by encouraging a radically individualistic logic and rhetoric, Thomson's argument also subtly serves to undermine the resources of culture to care for the vulnerable in a more general sense. And, of course, if this is so, the corollary has greater credence.

Meilaender argues that despite her claim to take the humanity of the fetus seriously, Thomson's violin-player analogy invites us to picture the fetus not as a genuine person, but rather as some sort of a parasite (51). And, of course, in a purely biological sense, it is. During pregnancy the fetus does live off the mother and the dependence is entirely one-way. The fetus contributes nothing to the mother and yet draws from her nutrients, immunological defenses, hormonal secretions, blood, digestive functions, and makes use of her circulatory and waste-disposal systems for a full nine months.[17] That's what renders Thomson's analogy initially plausible. But Meilaender thinks that there are alternative ways of interpreting this biological phenomenon and suggests that we should not be so quick to acquiesce in this particular imagery. Although it is clear that we *can* picture the fetus in the mother's womb as simply one more example of parasitism, it is equally clear that we need not do so. "Nature provides us with countless examples of dependence. But nature's book must be read" (54).

Perhaps we should instead, he suggests, see in the conception and growth of the fetus in the mother's womb, "a striking act of creativity," and a witness to "the self-spending that such creativity requires" (51–52). That for nine months the child lives within the mother provides for Meilaender a "paradigm of human dependence," and even "vicariousness."

> We may see there a sign of what is truly human: an inescapable witness to the self-spending that human life requires and to the bonds of vicarious dependence that encompasses the lives of us all. We may see there a sign—indeed, more than that, an embodiment—of the fact that we *do* live off others who never invited us to do so or granted us any rights thereto. And we may even find there an invitation to recognize that we cannot, without forfeiting our humanity, turn from the giving which is the other side of that receiving (52).

For Meilaender the mother-fetus relation symbolizes our communal dependence on one another. However, for Thomson, the fact that the fetus lives off the mother is at best mere biology—a brute biological fact. And because brute facts are mute facts, the relation between child and mother can tell us nothing of human significance.

Meilaender's alternative picture not only forces us to ask whether we should so readily acquiesce in Thomson's picture of the fetus as a parasite, but more important, I think, should invite us to question whether a culture can easily alter its imagery of human existence simply because a birth has taken place. Birth too, if we are to adopt Thomson's understanding, would seem to be just one more brute biological fact. Can we realistically expect the simple brute fact of human birth to induce a fundamental shift in perspective and a change in attitude toward the child? I suppose it can, but it need not.

Indeed, if the mother-child relationship is all mere biology before birth it certainly cannot be more than that for the father before birth. And since, in the situation with which we are concerned, the father does not will to bring his daughter home, she can quite easily be seen by him as nothing more than that after birth either. After all, his biological relationship with the child is one step removed from that of the mother. To a father who takes seriously Thomson's view of the matter, it would seem that the birth of a child cannot signify anything other than mere biology.[18] When all is said and done, it is only through a raw act of will signified by "taking it home" that the fetus-person becomes more than a mere parasite. And if the father does not will that it be so, it is quite difficult to see how we could fault him for continuing to view the child as parasitic, as a mere burden on *his* existence. When we begin with the picture of the fetus in the womb offered by Thomson, it is not unfair to ask whether we can expect a father to come to see vicariousness not simply as a burden, but rather, in Meilaender's pregnant phrase, as "an essential part of creative human love" (52). Indeed, Thomson seems to take quite literally, at least on this question, Hobbes' belief that there exists "no obligation on any man, which ariseth not from some act of his own" *(Leviathan,* 21). That would include, it seems, so-called "paternal obligations."

But again, the issue extends further than mere *paternal* responsibility because of the radically individualist nature of Thomson's perspective. This becomes even clearer with Meilaender's criticism of her "people-seed" analogy. He labels this "the fetus as mushroom" because it recalls the sort of imagery found, significantly enough, in Thomas Hobbes' *De Cive.* He calls our attention to the passage where Hobbes suggest that we "consider men as if but even now sprung out of the earth, and suddenly, like mushroom, come to full maturity, without all kind of engagement to each other"[19] (57). For Meilaender, to picture the fetus in this way is to

> deny human, personal significance to a biological relationship that marks each of us.... We can think of Creatures like the mushrooms her analogy suggests. But we cannot think of them in the terms her argument purports to grant: as human beings. For she has abstracted them from one of the relation-ships that importantly characterize our humanity (58).

Taken together, Meilaender suggests, Thomson's analogies subtly distort the discussion to the point where we must seriously question whether she really discusses the issue of abortion in the terms she says she will grant. We cannot, he insists, heed her analogies of fetus as parasite and mushroom *and* her prior affirmation that she will grant from the outset that the fetus is a human being (56). Thus, despite Thomson's working assumption, genuine human significance is, in true Hobbsean fashion, not something given to us as a gift to be received, but rather bestowed by human beings as an act of will, specifically when the parent recognizes or acknowledges the child and thereby takes responsibility for it. In short, the analogies employed by Thomson reflect "an excessively individualistic notion of human personhood, a notion oblivious to the bonds that tie us to one another" (48).

That, when all is said and done, is why this picture dovetails so neatly not only with paternal abandonment, irresponsibility, and (not to put too fine a point on it) child abuse, but also with the neglect of deformed and handicapped infants, the unproductive elderly and the weak and dispossessed. By calling our attention to the essentially Hobbsean pedigree of her position, Meilaender urges us to consider what the implications might be for those fetus-persons and others unable rationally to negotiate a social contract.[20] The result, at least in part, is clear. We know that the fetus-person has all the rights of parasites and mushrooms. And a child only seems to have rights because they have been conferred, not by nature or nature's God, but by the parents, through an act of will. And what happens when that will weakens after birth under the strains of caring for infants and toddlers? Perhaps that is when the broader connection between the way we think and behave toward fetal life and other vulnerable members of society—the claim advanced in the corollary—first becomes culturally manifest.

CONCLUSION

Now, I suspect there will be those who will not think that there is something unjust or even odd about a state of affairs in which the father can abandon his child for a relatively small cost, or indeed at no cost at all. Nothing in this essay is likely to be persuasive to someone unwilling to call into question the fundamental presuppositions, images, and metaphors that lead to such a position. However, many who advocate permissive abortion laws and who identify themselves as "prochoice," are not likely to be happy with a situation in which the woman is for all intents and purposes forced to become the sole provider for her child(ren). Many are likely to think that there is something unjust in all this. Of course, accounting for why it is unjust is another matter. And reconciling it with certain central prochoice assumptions is another.

A large part of the problem for many who are sympathetic toward the prochoice position is that much of the rhetoric trades heavily on a welcomed increase in the autonomy and independence gained by a woman faced with an "unplanned" or "unwanted" pregnancy. That's why those who defend permissive abortion laws have considerable difficulty coming to grips with situations in which the option of abortion does not enhance the autonomy of the woman, but rather seriously compromises it by placing on her almost insurmountable financial and emotional burdens that in turn put her at a significant social and economic disadvantage *vis à vis* the father and other men.

If, indeed, we are confronted with a situation in which the father can completely opt out of child support and thereby force a woman either to have an abortion or to bear the costs of raising a child, and this seems to follow quite logically from Thomson's defense of the "moderate" prochoice position, perhaps we should ask whether we should acquiesce in these assumptions in the first place. Perhaps we should and just be willing to live with the implications. But perhaps we should not. Maybe this unhappy state of affairs stems from a seriously distorted picture of what we, as human beings—fetuses, babies, fathers and mothers, handicapped and deformed infants, and the unproductive elderly—are all about.

Perhaps we should instead *begin* our reflections with what for most will be the intuitive notion that men *do* have a simple obligation arising from the demands of justice to support the children they have fathered. Suppose we then work back from there. Perhaps we should ask this: With what presuppositions, understandings of the human condition, perspectives, images, and so on, should we begin if we want to conclude with a public policy that will encourage fathers to care, support, and nurture a child, one that would, in short, insist that when discussing the specific question of paternal responsibilities we are dealing not with a mere nicety of moral decency but indeed with an obligation of justice from which one cannot so easily opt out? Where do we begin our reflections such that the result would be a civil society that will, through the encouragement of law and the threat of its sanctions, insist that a father live up to his parental obligations?

I have briefly tried to suggest that Thomson and Meilaender offer two distinct visions with which to begin. And their alternative visions, I would think, are likely to usher into belief systems or moral paradigms that are, for all practical purposes, incommensurate. It is here, indeed, that we have a class of absolutes[21] and perhaps what might be called a fundamental *religious* conflict.[22] For this reasons, I doubt one could *prove* that we should picture the fetus, parental responsibility, and the human condition in the way Meilaender suggests rather than the way Thomson and the prochoice movement suggests. I confess that I, along with Meilaender, don't find it illuminating to picture the fetus or the human community in the ways suggested by Thomson's analogies. However, the wider culture, including the legal system, can. And since paternal neglect and abandonment seems to be such a problem, one can say with some confidence that it has to some extent adopted Thomson's way of looking at things. But if a culture does come to prefer her perspective, we should perhaps insist that it have the courage of its convictions and let these "fathers" off the legal hook, accepting them perhaps as the price to be paid for accepting a "moderate" prochoice position. But then again we might hold fathers responsible from the moment of conception. What that might imply for the question of abortion is, I think, obvious.[23]

POSTSCRIPT: A REPLY TO BOONIN-VAIL

David Boonin-Vail accurately summarizes my argument as an indirect defense of the responsibility objection to abortion (see Chapter 9). My approach is to ask what the implications might be for paternal responsibilities if what Judith Jarvis Thomson believes about the source of maternal responsibilities is true. As Boonin-Vail observes, I think the prochoice position in general and Thomson's position in particular cannot account for the legitimacy of laws requiring men to pay child support for children conceived through voluntary intercourse. My response to Boonin-Vail follows the same approach. His article leads me to ask what the implications are for paternal responsibilities if what he understands about human sexuality is true.

Essentially Boonin-Vail argues that voluntary sexual intercourse simply does not signal any intrinsic commitment or obligation on the part of either the father or the mother for a child created from that act. Neither party tacitly consents to such an obligation merely by engaging in sexual intercourse. The generation of life is thus completely severed from the responsibility for the life created from the act. I think this is a consistent way of viewing the matter if one believes what Boonin-Vail believes about consent and more generally the nature of moral obligation. There are, of course, other ways to think about such things but that would carry us far afield into competing conceptions of metaphysics and the nature of morality. I am here concerned to ask what this way of thinking implies concerning paternal responsibility and to determine whether philosophers such as Thomson and Boonin-Vail can live with the unhappy implications of their metaphysical convictions. If not, then we have good warrant for looking elsewhere to account for our moral intuitions about paternal responsibilities.

I suspect that Boonin-Vail is at least mildly concerned about the possible implications his defense of abortion might have for paternal responsibilities. As I said in the original version of my article, I find it "strange to suggest that the mother could be relieved of potential parental burdens and responsibilities in all situations but the father could not under any circumstances." Boonin-Vail seems to think this strange too, but his argument suggests no reason for him to think it strange at all. I simply cannot see how he could consistently morally condemn or legally punish fathers who in certain rather common circumstances completely abandon their children to the care of their mothers.

His initial comment that "the nature of the burdens involved in the two cases [maternal responsibilities and paternal responsibilities] is fundamentally different," is not at all promising. Boonin-Vail implies that merely because the mother's burden is "distinctly intimate and physical" it is a greater or more profound burden than, say, requiring a father to support his daughter with monthly child support payments for 18 years or so. But one would hardly be thought irrational to think that forced appropriation of the father's time and labor over almost two decades counts for less than the physical burdens of pregnancy for a mere nine months.

Boonin-Vail's analogy to *general* taxation for the public purpose of building a highway is not very promising either. The obvious difference is that all citizens are taxed to support a highway, but paternal support laws are by definition selective—The financial burden is targeted on the biological father of the child. It is specifically *his* burden to bear, not the general public's, as in the case of the highway. The analogy would be well taken if and only if Boonin-Vail were prepared to argue that the responsibilities for paternal child abandonment should be shifted from the biological father to the broader society. That would make it more akin to taxation for highways, but that would not be a paternal support requirement but rather a public or governmental support requirement more akin to welfare.

More fundamentally, given Boonin-Vail's belief that moral obligation arises solely from "consent," I am entirely perplexed why he might think that the "distinctly intimate and personal" burden on the mother is at all be relevant to the question of paternal responsibilities in the first place. From the perspective of the father, that is nothing more than an interesting biological fact. One could fairly ask just what gives Boonin-Vail (and perhaps an electoral majority of those who think like him) the right to appropriate someone else's time and labor for the support of a child, which, if his consent were respected, would have been safely and legally exterminated. Why should a brute act of will on the part of the mother trump the father's will? Surely, given his stress on the necessity of consent, the imposition of such a coercive burden on the father against his will must count as a profound injustice. Which is not to imply, of course, that Boonin-Vail should favor paternal abandonment. It is merely that he should be "prochoice" in the matter. Paternal abandonment, one might expect him to argue, should be safe, legal, and rare—though not publicly funded.

In sum, one would expect Boonin-Vail to argue that differences in (potential) burdens to be borne are simply irrelevant to the more fundamental similarity between the father's and the mother's purported responsibility to a child. And that the more fundamental similarity has to do with the source of the moral obligation, which accrue to them solely through consent. (Tacit consent would work if you can find an act that would signal it or would stand in for the paper it's not written on.) If the absence of consent allows one to opt out of all maternal responsibility to one's offspring (and that, after all, is the central point of his article), it must also allow one to opt out of all paternal responsibility. Whatever the burdens on the mother might be, they simply can carry no moral weight for the father.

This implies conversely that once you locate the source of maternal responsibility, you will likely begin to locate the source of paternal responsibility. Boonin-Vail concedes that a father may indeed have rather extensive obligations to his one-year-old son. But, of course, the source of that obligation resides solely in the tacit consent of the parent(s) signified by the conventionally recognized act of "taking the infant home." This raises interesting questions about how we are to think of horrible cases in which women give birth at home then discard their babies in the trash.[24] Nevertheless, having emphatically rejected the idea that responsibility comes with the act of sexual reproduction itself, that is, with the state of being the *parent* of the child conceived, the tacit consent signalled by "taking the child home" is as good a way to morally ground a parent's obligations as any.

But if that is where one locates the source of maternal obligation, one might expect that this, or something quite like it, would also be the source of paternal obligation. However, if the father—convinced perhaps by Boonin-Vail's argument that his sexual activity carries with it no obligations to a child who might be conceived—abandoned both the mother and child during her pregnancy, or encouraged her to have an abortion, or offered to pay for her abortion, or simply declared he didn't want the responsibilities of fatherhood, why should he concede that the mother's act of "taking the child home," constitutes tacit consent on *his* part. At best, it constitute tacit consent only on her part. He should be entirely off the hook.

Now, I think this conclusion follows quite obviously from Boonin-Vail's understanding of human sexuality. I believe that conclusion is a poor way to think about such things, but one can hardly deny that this perspective is widely extant in our culture and will seem quite plausible to many readers, especially college-age males. I do confess to a certain perplexity at why women might think this way, since for obvious physical reasons it allows men to walk away from any responsibilities quite easily. Men can walk away simply because their burden is considerably less "intimate and physical."

That, of course, is not a good enough reason for a philosopher to abandon the metaphysical and anthropological convictions that, if widely held, might lead to such a state of affairs. We could perhaps, just be living in an absurd universe, where we should not expect the kind of connection between sexuality and parenthood that many religious believers find there. And, it could very well be that our culture should be liberated from such Puritanical judgments against certain types of male sexual behavior once labeled "irresponsible." Perhaps we should be liberated from moral judgments against fathers who abandon the children they conceive, just as we have been liberated against Puritanical moral judgments against mothers who abort the children they have conceived.

But perhaps our philosophical squeamishness and moral embarrassment over the paternal neglect and sexual irresponsibility implicit in abortion logic should tell us something. Perhaps our unease points to a deeper truth in older traditions of moral reflection—traditions that make much less of "consent" between autonomous contractors, traditions that tend to think there is a "telos" to human sexuality, and traditions that think that the mother-child relationship is a sign of something deeper and more meaningful. Perhaps it will lead us to think more seriously about the link between the widespread acceptance of abortion and the "culture of death."[25] Perhaps it even suggests an enlarged understanding of "consent" in which philosophers might also consider the will of Another, who may grieve over little ones who are so easily dispatched because the consenting parties are bigger and stronger, and because the victim's consent is never sought. Perhaps.[26]

STUDY QUESTIONS

1. What is the thrust of Pavlischek's argument and how does he support it? Do you think he succeeds in doing so? Why or why not? Explain your answer.

2. Pavlischek states, "I doubt that one could *prove* that we should picture the fetus, parental responsibility, and the human condition in the way Meilaender suggests rather than the way Thomson and the prochoice movement suggests." What does Pavlischek mean by this? Explain your answer.

3. How does Pavlischek respond to Boonin-Vail's critique of the Responsibility Objection to Thomson's argument? Present and explain Pavlischek's argument. What do you think Pavlischek means by a "telos" to human sexuality? Do you think he succeeds in refuting Boonin-Vail's case? Why or why not?

NOTES

1. I call this a "corollary" because the opponent of abortion need not accept its truth to maintain her opposition to abortion.

2. For an argument that attempts to extend this reasoning to future generations and distant peoples, see James Sterba, "Abortion, Distant Peoples and Future Generations" in *The Demands of Justice*. Notre Dame, University of Notre Dame Press, 1980, 126–150. Sterba's article provided the initial impetus toward my attempt to apply abortion logic generally, and Thomson's article specifically, to the issue of paternal responsibilities.

3. One example of a statement expressing the corollary can be found in the *Statement on Abortion* (1985) by the U.S. Catholic Conference in which a committee chaired by Cardinal Joseph Bernardin displayed part of his "seamless garment" or "consistent ethic of life." The committee urged consistency not only in regard to abortion but also in the areas of war, poverty, and euthanasia. After asserting that the church "has always seen that the child's helplessness, both before and after birth, far from diminishing his or her right to life, increases our moral obligation to respect and to protect that right," the committee then adds:

> The church also realizes that a society which tolerates the direct destruction of innocent life, as in the current practice of abortion, is in danger of losing its respect for life in all other contexts. It likewise knows that protecting unborn life will ultimately benefit all human life, not only the unborn. (17)

An earlier expression of the corollary can be found in the *Statement on Abortion* (1977) by the Evangelical Free Church of America:

> We hold that the eclectic morality upheld by the courts relative to abortion forebodes ill, not only for the defenseless, but also for the aged and the infirm, and represents an over-all trend which, if persisted in, will have repugnant consequences in the lives and

consciences of every individual in our nation and in our national heritage and destiny.

These statements can be found in *Abortion: Official Church Statements from Religions Bodies and Ecumenical Organizations,* J. Gordon Melton, editor. Detroit: Gale Research Inc., 1989, 17 and 50.

4. *Philosophy and Public Affairs,* vol. I, no. I. References to Thomson's article will be parenthetically inserted into the text.

5. Thus, Thomson insists that "while I am arguing for the permissibility of abortion in some cases, I am not arguing for the right to secure the death of the unborn child. It is easy to confuse these two things in that up to a certain point in the life of the fetus it is not able to survive outside the mother's body; hence removing it from her body guarantees its death. But they are importantly different....There are some people who will feel dissatisfied by this feature of my argument. A woman may be utterly devastated by the thought of a child, a bit of herself, put out for adoption and never seen or heard of again. She may therefore want not merely that the child be detached from her, but more, that it die. Some opponents of abortion are inclined to regard this as beneath contempt—thereby showing insensitivity to what is surely a powerful source of despair. All the same, I agree that the desire for the child's death is not one which anybody may gratify, should it turn out to be possible to detach the child live" (66).

6. For an early feminist article criticizing Thomson as being too moderate, see Mary Anne Warren's "On the Moral and Legal Status of Abortion." This article originally appeared in *Monist,* vol. 57, No. 1, and can be found along with Thomson's article in *Women and Values: Readings in Recent Feminist Philosophy,* ed. by Marilyn Pearsall. Belmont, Calif.: Wadsworth, 1986, 279–291.

Warren argues for both the legality and morality of aborting even a seven- or eight-month fetus. While conceding that the mature fetus is *somewhat* more person-like than a younger fetus since it can feel and respond to pain and even may have a rudimentary form of consciousness, she nevertheless insists that

> It seems safe to say that it is not fully conscious, in the way that an infant of a few months is, and that it cannot reason, or communicate messages of indefinitely many sorts, does not engage in self-motivated activity, and has no self-awareness. Thus in the relevant respects, a fetus, even a fully developed one, is considerably less personlike than is the average mature mammal, indeed the average fish. And I think that a rational person must conclude that if the right to life of a fetus is to be based upon its resemblance to a person, then it cannot be said to have any more right to life than, let us say, a newborn guppy (which also seems capable of feeling pain), and that a right of that magnitude could never override a woman's right to obtain an abortion, at any stage of her pregnancy. (288)

7. For a succinct statement of the Feminist Prolife position, see Sidney Callahan's "Abortion and the Sexual Agenda" in *Commonweal* 113 (April 25, 1986), 232–238. Permissive abortion law, according to Callahan, simply "confirms the sexual and social status quo" (238). Callahan argues that in Western culture at least since the nineteenth century "most women have espoused a version of sexual function in which sex acts are embedded within deep emotional bonds and secure long-term commitments. Within these committed 'pair bonds' males assume parental obligations." She observes that "many of the most influential women in the nineteenth-century women's movement preached and lived this sexual ethic, often by the side of exemplary feminist men." However, it coexisted in competition with a "more male-oriented model of erotic or amative sexuality," which "endorses sexual permissiveness without long-term commitment of reproductive focus" and "emphasizes pleasure, play, passion, individual self-expression, and romantic games of courtship and conquest." While this erotic model has often worked for men and for certain cultural elites, "for the average woman, it is quite destructive."

Women can only play the erotic game successfully when like the *"Cosmopolitan* woman," they are young, physically attractive, economically powerful, and fulfilled enough in a career to be willing to sacrifice family life. Abortion is also required. As our society increasingly endorses this male-oriented, permissive view of sexuality, it is all too ready to give women abortion on demand. Abortion helps a woman's body to be more like a man's. (236–237)

Incidentally, I should also mention that my argument will lend some plausibility to a prochoice feminist position such as that of Catharine MacKinnon. See for instance, her essay "More Than Simply a Magazine: Playboy's Money" in *Feminism Unmodified: Discourses on Life and Law.* Cambridge: Harvard University Press, 1987, where she argues that it is not at all surprising that *Playboy* magazine has supported and funded abortion rights from the very beginning:

> Abortion offers women the liberal feminist dream of being real women— that is, available to be freely fucked— while still being able to live out a socially male biography—*not having to be responsible for children*. This is the "equality" it offers us. I hope this makes clear why liberal so-called feminists and the pornographers wind up on the same side of things. (144–145, emphasis mine.)

In another essay, "Not a Moral Issue," MacKinnon defends Andrea Dworkin's view that "the liberal defense of pornography as sexual liberation…is a defense not only of force and sexual terrorism, but of the subordination of women" (149). A key question is whether her support of legislation restricting pornography is consistent with her refusal to do so with abortion. For MacKinnon's view of abortion more generally see her essay "Privacy v. Equality: Beyond *Roe v. Wade,"* 103–116 in the same volume.

8. Although I am calling Thomson's position "moderate," Gilbert Meilaender has rightly called my attention to the fact that in another sense Thomson's view is not at all moderate. Because she is willing to contemplate the killing of an acknowledged person, her view is, in fact, quite

radical relative to those who do *not* concede the personhood of the fetus. But this means that, in addition to my argument working against those who take a more radical stand on the question of whether the fetus may be legitimately killed when "unattached" to the mother, it will work as well against those who do not grant fetal personhood regardless of whether the fetus is attached or unattached.

9. Gilbert Meilaender, "The Fetus as Parasite and Mushroom" in *The Limits of Love*. University Park, Pa., and London: The Pennsylvania State University Press, 1987, 50. However, because she runs together pregnancy resulting from forcible intercourse with other cases, Meilaender is less sure that Thomson sees why abortion in cases of pregnancy resulting from rape is a different matter. "Thomson seems oblivious to what is surely more important than the fact that the mother did not 'invite' this fetus in—namely, the nature of the relationship in which the fetus was conceived, a relationship which strikes most of us as not only less than human but inhuman" (51).

10. It should not be assumed when I speak of the mother and father that they are married or that, given Thomson's assumptions, it should matter. I'm going to assume that a husband could opt out of support for a child for the same reasons as one not married to the mother. As we will see, this follows quite naturally from Thomson's individualistic assumptions.

11. See for instance the chapter "Men's Attempts to Veto Women's Abortion Decisions" (17–19) in the National Abortion Rights Action League booklet *Who Decides?: A Reproductive Rights Manual* (NARAL Foundation, January 1990). This chapter is particularly notable for its evident failure to distinguish between the concepts of "notification" and "consent." Predictably enough, NARAL rejects attempts by "anti-abortion activists" to promote paternal notification laws as cases involving "fathers rights."

> The term "father" in this context begs the question of who will decide if a woman may have an abortion. The men initiating these cases are not "fathers" but are seeking to become fathers

by forcing a woman to bear a child against her wishes. (19).

One can only conclude that a man only becomes a father at birth, a view apparently shared by Planned Parenthood and a majority of the Supreme Court judges. Of the Pennsylvania abortion restrictions challenged in *Planned Parenthood v. Casey,* the paternal notification requirement of the Pennsylvania statute was the only requirement not upheld.

12. The implications of this distinction for a less "moderate" prochoice advocate are summed up nicely by Mary Anne Warren:

> Whether or not it would be *indecent* (whatever that means) for a woman in her seventh month to obtain an abortion just to avoid having to postpone a trip to Europe, it would not, in itself, be *immoral,* and therefore it ought to be permitted. (288)

It is important to note that after the publication of her article in *The Monist* Warren received many letters pointing out that her argument justified infanticide as well as abortion. And she concedes the point in a "Postscript on Infanticide":

> Now, if I am right in holding that it is only people who have a full-fledged right to life, and who can be murdered, and if the criteria of personhood are as I described them, then it obviously follows that killing a newborn infant isn't murder. (289)

But she hastens to add that it does not follow from this that it is *permissible* (whatever that means), mainly because

> even if its parents do not want it and would not suffer from its destruction, there are other people who would like to have it, and would, in all probability, be deprived of a great deal of pleasure by its destruction. Thus, infanticide is wrong for reasons analogous to those which make it wrong to wantonly destroy natural resources, or great works of art....So long as there are people who want an infant preserved, and who are willing and able to provide the means of caring for it, under reasonably human conditions, it is *ceteris peribus,* wrong to destroy it. (289–290)

We're not told whether the "morality" involved with preserving an infant's life long enough to find adoptive parents requires Minimally Decent Samaritanism or Good or Splendid Samaritanism.

13. The effect of this argument is to transform the old male tendency to say something like "Get rid of it, honey, I'll pay for it," into a moral virtue.

14. Thomson seems rather ambivalent about this:

> I should think that Minimally Decent Samaritan laws would be one thing, Good Samaritan laws another, and in fact highly improper. What we should ask is not whether anybody should be compelled by law to be a Good Samaritan, but whether we must accede to a situation in which somebody is being compelled—by nature, perhaps—to be a Good Samaritan. (64)

I find quite incredible the way Thomson collapses the phenomenon of pregnancy into the notion of Good Samaritanism. Is it the "attachment" of the fetus that makes pregnancy Good Samaritan like," or is it the degree of sacrifice? If the latter, might this imply that parental care of infants, as tiresome a task if ever there was one, is analogously a Good Samaritan phenomenon? Would this mean that parents have no justice obligation to their children? Or am I simply pushing Thomson down a slippery slope?

15. Sec Lorraine A. Schmall, "Women and Children First, but Only If the Men Are Union Members: Hiring Halls and Delinquent Child Supporters" in the *Notre Dame Journal of Law, Ethics and Public Policy,* vol. 6 (1992), 449–552, particularly Section III, aptly titled, "Delinquent Fathers Are a Societal Problem of Enormous Proportion."

The problems cluster around two related failures. First, court-ordered levels of support for divorced mothers are frequently far below what is practically needed for them to support their children. Schmall cites evidence collected in interviews with California family law judges that "greater concern was more often shown for the husband who had to support the children than for the wife who

had to raise them. The California jurists stress the importance of maintaining *his* standard of living and *his* incentive to earn" (495). But even apart from the failure of courts to assess sufficient child support payments "fathers simply do not pay," reports Schmall, even when noncustodial fathers are able to make payments. The figures express the extent and magnitude of the problem:

> Six years ago [1986] 5,390,000 women were awarded child support, but only 3,243,000 actually received any payments. Additionally, the mean amount of child support payments received amounted to $1,510 annually. If the full amount due had been paid, the mean amount would have been $2,460. (493)

Moreover, testimony at recent Congressional hearings on legislation to strengthen child support collection identified "willful disregard of court orders, a pattern that people assumed was limited to lower income men, was now common among fathers of all social classes, because it was asserted judges failed to enforce the law" (494).

16. Meilaender, *op. cit.* Page numbers from this article will be inserted parenthetically in the text.

17. Although Meilaender finds the imagery of fetus as parasite only implicit in Thomson's article, it is explicit in Rosalind Pollack Petchesky's defense of abortion in *Abortion and Woman's Choice* (Longman, 1984). Petchesky simply asserts that "on the level of biology alone…the fetus is a parasite." And she concludes from this that "the concept of viability *whenever* it may occur, is meaningless." Though she later concedes that the phenomenon of pregnancy is also "characterized by mutual dependency in a social and moral sense," the bottom line is that "it is her [that is, the pregnant woman's] consciousness that is the condition of its [that is, the fetus's humanization…" 350–351.

18. Perhaps this is why, as Callahan observes, "Childbirth often appears in prochoice literature as a painful, traumatic, life-threatening experience." "Ironically," she adds, "some prochoice men and women think and talk of pregnancy and

child-birth with the same repugnance that ancient ascetics displayed toward orgasms and sexual intercourse." She suggests that "the similarity may not be accidental." Callahan, *op. cit.*, 237.

19. The citation can be found in Thomas Hobbes, *Man and Citizen,* ed. Bernard Gert (Garden City, New York: Double-day Anchor, 1972), vol. VIII, 1. Commenting on this passage, the feminist political theorist Christine Di Stiphano argues that because he denies any significance to the mother-child relationship there is no room for nurture within the family in Hobbes's slate of nature; "men are not born of, much less nurtured by, women, or anyone else for that matter." See her "Masculinity as Ideology in political Theory: Hobbesian Man Considered," *Women's Studies International Forum,* vol. 6 (1983) 638.

That Thomson's position in particular, and the feminist position on abortion more generally, is still put in terms of rights language is noteworthy given that so much of contemporary feminist political and moral philosophy has rejected the language of rights and liberal individualism as alienating. For many feminists, liberal individualism and the social contract theory advanced by those such as Hobbes is rooted in a metaphysics that falsely asserts that individuals are autonomous and separate from one another in a very strong sense. They thus generally wish to deny much of the force of liberal distinctions between the public and the private, the individual and community, and the self and the other. As Robert K. Fullwinder summarizes it, the general feminist defense of abortion in terms of individual rights

> is of no small consequence, since the feminist attack on liberal individualism implies a politics in which the community may legitimately regulate "personal" dimensions of life. Feminist proposals concerning pornography, marital rape, sexual harassment, wife-beating, and so on, are grounded in this politics. There is no reason in *principle* why other persons. or the community as a whole, shouldn't have some say in what happens in families, in other

intimate relationships, or even in the bodies of persons.

Fullwinder adds that the claim of autonomy and bodily integrity makes sense only if we presuppose a metaphysic similar to something like that of liberal individualism. After noting that many feminists tend to frame the abortion issue by relying on a language and metaphysic they otherwise deplore largely for "strategic reasons," he then suggests that nevertheless this attraction to rights-language reflects "unresolved tensions within feminist theory itself." See Robert K. Fullwinder "Feminism and Liberal Individualism," *Philosophy and Public Policy,* vol. 10 (1990), 8–9.

20. For an important feminist understanding of the way social contract theory fundamentally distorts the mother/child relation, see Virginia Held's "Non-Contractual Society: A Feminist View," in *Science, Morality, and Feminist Theory,* ed. Marsha Hanen and Kai Nielson. Calgary: University of Calgary Press, 1987, 111–137. Held argues that the conceptions of power exemplified in the tradition which runs from Hobbes and Locke to Hegel and Marx "are of little use for understanding the aspects of power involved in the [mother-child] relation" (132). She later notes, "Anyone in the social contract tradition who has noticed the relation of mothering person and child at all has supposed it to belong to some domain outside the realm of the 'free market' and outside the 'public' realm of politics and the law." She suggests, however, "mothering is at the heart of society." What does this imply for social theory?

> If the dynamic relation between mothering person and child is taken as the primary social relation, then it is the model of 'economic man' that can be seen to be deficient as a model for society and morality, and unsuitable for all but a special context. A domain such as law, if built on no more than contractual foundations, can then be recognized as one limited domain among others; law protects some moral rights when people are too immoral or weak to respect them without the force of law.

But it is hardly a majestic edifice that can serve as a model for morality. (137)

Or, we might add, for the question of abortion and paternal responsibility.

21. See Laurence Tribe's *Abortion: A Clash of Absolutes.* New York: Norton, 1990. I would simply add that the defense and opposition to child support laws also involves a "clash of absolutes."

22. Some might argue that since indeed what is at stake in the abortion controversy is a religious issue, then, given the First Amendment's prohibition of establishing religion and guaranteeing religious freedom, public law must simply default to abortion on demand. To hold otherwise would be, so the argument goes, to impose one's religion on the prochoice advocate. But this argument proves too much. For if abortion is a religious matter, then so is the issue of paternal support and neglect. Thus, laws requiring paternal support could also just as plausibly be said to be a "religious" imposition on a father who did not share the "religious" person's view of parental responsibility. In short, that knife cuts both ways.

23. An almost identical version of this article, minus the postscript, was presented on October 30, 1992, at the Midwestern Regional Meeting of the Society of Christian Philosophers at the University of St. Thomas, St. Paul, Minnesota. I want to thank Alissa Carse, Sidney Callahan, Jean Bethke Elshtain, Todd Flanders, Stanley Hauerwas, Gayne Nerney and Gilbert Meilaender for their comments on earlier drafts, but most of all, for their encouragement.

24. Or of those cases in which, say, they are dumped in the trash on prom night in a rush to get back on the dance floor. I refer, of course, to a story which, as I write, has been front page news. I should add, however, that on the day in which I am making final editorial revisions to this essay, the newspaper tells me that the coroners have determined that the young woman may have strangled the baby before discarding it in the trash. If so, then strictly speaking, this specific example may not be directly relevant here. It would be relevant, however, if Boonin-Vail could not make good his IOU regarding the distinction between killing and letting die. (See note 42 of Chapter 9.)

25. The reference is to the observation by the Polish philosopher and poet Karol Wojtyla. Wojtyla, better known as Pope John Paul II, traces the roots of the "culture of death" to a perverse idea of freedom, which is seen as disconnected from any reference to truth and objective good. It asserts itself in an individualistic way, without the constitutive link of relationships with others. Wojtyla associates this with a practical materialism, which gives priority to having over being, and to the satisfaction of personal pleasure over respect for those who are weak. This view ends by considering life worthwhile only to the extent that it is productive and enjoyable. These views are articulated in the encyclical *Evangelium Vitae (The Gospel of Life)* especially paragraphs 19–21.

26. I want to thank Bruce Ballard, Fred Clark, Bob Morrison, and Frank Beckwith for their helpful comments on an early draft of this postscript.

FOR FURTHER READING

Beckwith, Francis J. "From Personhood to Bodily Autonomy: The Shifting Legal Focus in the Abortion Debate." In *Bioethics and the Future of Medicine*, eds. John Kilner, Nigel M. de S. Cameron, and David Schiedermayer. Grand Rapids, Mich.: Eerdmans, 1995.

Boonin-Vail, David. "Death Comes for the Violinist." *Social Theory and Practice* 23.3 (Fall 1997).

Brody, Baruch. *Abortion and the Sanctity of Human Life: A Philosophical View*. Cambridge, Mass.: M.I.T. Press, 1975,26–33.

Gordon, Doris. "Abortion and Rights: Applying Libertarian Principles Correctly." *Studies in Prolife Feminism* 1.2 (Spring 1995).

Kamm, F.M. *Creation and Abortion: A Study in Moral and Legal Philosophy*. New York: Oxford University Press, 1992.

Keenan, James. "Reply To Beckwith: Abortion—Whose Agenda Is It Anyway?" *International Philosophical Quarterly* 32 (June 1992).

Levin, Michael. Review of *Life in the Balance* by Robert Wennberg. *Constitutional Commentary* 3 (Summer 1986).

McDonagh, Eileen. *Breaking the Abortion Deadlock: From Choice to Consent*. New York: Oxford University Press, 1996.

Tribe, Laurence. *Abortion: The Clash of Absolutes*. New York: W.W. Norton, 1990, 129–135.

Wilcox, John T. "Nature as Demonic in Thomson's Defense of Abortion." *The New Scholasticism* 3 (Autumn 1989).

PART V

Personhood Arguments on Abortion

INTRODUCTION

Why is abortion a moral issue? Take a fertilized egg, a zygote, a tiny sphere of cells. By itself it is hard to see what is so important about such an inconspicuous piece of matter. It is virtually indistinguishable from other clusters of cells, or zygotes of other animals. Now take an adult human being, a class of beings that we all intuitively feel to be worthy of high respect and having rights, including the right to life. To kill an innocent human being is an act of murder and universally condemned. Yet no obvious line of division separates that single-cell zygote from the adult it will become. Hence, the problem of abortion.

A set of arguments has grown up around these two features of (1) the apparent difference between the fetus and adult and (2) the continuity of development from the zygote to the adult. Conservatives—those who hold that a fetus has a right to life—emphasize that no cutoff point or clear demarcation exists between the fetus and the infant and the adult. In the first reading of Part V, John Noonan argues that because it is always wrong to kill innocent human beings and since fetuses are innocent human beings, it is wrong to kill fetuses. He makes an exception when the mother's life is in danger because something of comparable worth is at stake. Noonan argues that conception is the only non-arbitrary cutoff place between nonpersonhood and personhood.

Phillip Devine and Stephen Schwarz further develop the conservative position. Schwarz specifically argues against the liberal position that fetuses are not persons.

Liberals—those who hold that it is (almost) always morally permissible to have an abortion—emphasize that an enormous difference exists between the fetus and the child, let alone the adult. Michael Tooley argues against Noonan that fetuses are not persons, that is, beings with a serious right to life, because persons must have characteristics such as a concept of a continuing self or mental substance, which fetuses apparently lack. Louis Pojman defends the liberal argument against its critics, addressing the main objections, including the issue of whether the liberal position justifies infanticide.

Moderates—those who hold that it is sometimes morally permissible and sometimes not morally permissible to have an abortion—criticize both conservatives and liberals for accepting extreme and simplistic positions. The truth is in the middle, a complex balancing of considerations. Norman Gillespie argues against both the liberal and conservative positions. Conservatives are mistaken because they hold that just because we cannot find a definite cutoff point between conception and birth, the fetus must have the same right to life that an infant has. Liberals are mistaken because they hold that simply because a fetus lacks the moral properties that an adult has, it also lacks all rights to life. Fetuses may have rights even though we cannot say exactly when personhood begins.

In our final reading, L. W. Sumner further develops with great intricacy the moderate position. He argues that regarding early abortions (those done before the end of the first trimester), the liberal position is more plausible, but regarding late abortions (those done after the first trimester), the conservative position is more plausible.

11

Abortion Is Morally Wrong

JOHN T. NOONAN, JR.

John T. Noonan, Jr., a judge on the Ninth Circuit Court of Appeals, was for many years Professor of Law at the University of California, Berkeley. In this selection Noonan defends the conservative view that an entity becomes a person at conception and that abortion, except to save the mother's life, is morally wrong. He uses an argument from probabilities to show that his criterion of humanity is objectively based.

The most fundamental question involved in the long history of thought on abortion is this: How do you determine the humanity of a being? To phrase the question that way is to put in comprehensive humanistic terms what the theologians either dealt with as an explicitly theological question under the heading of "ensoulment" or dealt with implicitly in their treatment of abortion. The Christian position as it originated did not depend on a narrow theological or philosophical concept. It had no relation to theories of infant baptism. It appealed to no special theory of instantaneous ensoulment. It took the world's view on ensoulment as that view changed from Aristotle to Zacchia. There was, indeed, theological influence affecting the theory of ensoulment finally adopted, and, of course, ensoulment itself was a theological concept, so that the position was always explained in theological terms. But the theological notion of ensoulment could easily be translated into humanistic language by substituting "human" for "rational soul"; the problem of knowing when a man is a man is common to theology and humanism.

Reprinted by permission from *The Morality of Abortion: Legal and Historical Perspectives* (Cambridge, Mass.: Harvard University Press,). Copyright 1970 by the President and Fellows of Harvard College.

If one steps outside the specific categories used by the theologians, the answer they gave can be analyzed as a refusal to discriminate among human beings on the basis of their varying potentialities. Once conceived, the being was recognized as man because he had man's potential. The criterion for humanity, thus, was simple and all-embracing: If you are conceived by human parents, you are human.

The strength of this position may be tested by a review of some of the other distinctions offered in the contemporary controversy over legalizing abortion. Perhaps the most popular distinction is in terms of viability. Before an age of so many months, the fetus is not viable, that is, it cannot be removed from the mother's womb and live apart from her. To that extent, the life of the fetus is absolutely dependent on the life of the mother. This dependence is made the basis of denying recognition to its humanity.

There are difficulties with this distinction. One is that the perfection of artificial incubation may make the fetus viable at any time: It may be removed and artificially sustained. Experiments with animals already show that such a procedure is possible. This hypothetical extreme case relates to an actual difficulty: There is considerable elasticity to the idea of viability. Mere length of life is not an exact measure. The viability of the fetus depends on the extent of its anatomical and functional development. The weight and length of the fetus are better guides to the state of its development than age, but weight and length vary. Moreover, different racial groups have different ages at which their fetuses are viable. Some evidence, for example, suggests that Negro fetuses mature more quickly than white fetuses. If viability is the norm, the standard would vary with race and with many individual circumstances.

The most important objection to this approach is that dependence is not ended by viability. The fetus is still absolutely dependent on someone's care in order to continue existence; indeed a child of one or three or even five years of age is absolutely dependent on another's care for existence; uncared for, the older fetus or the younger child will die as surely as the early fetus detached from the mother. The unsubstantial lessening in dependence at viability does not seem to signify any special acquisition of humanity.

A second distinction has been attempted in terms of experience. A being who has had experience, has lived and suffered, who possesses memories, is more human than one who has not. Humanity depends on formation by experience. The fetus is thus "unformed" in the most basic human sense.

This distinction is not serviceable for the embryo which is already experiencing and reacting. The embryo is responsive to touch after eight weeks and at least at that point is experiencing. At an earlier stage, the zygote is certainly alive and responding to its environment. The distinction may also be challenged by the rare case where aphasia has erased adult memory: Has it erased humanity? More fundamentally, this distinction leaves even the older fetus or the younger child to be treated as an unformed inhuman thing. Finally, it is not clear why experience as such confers humanity. It could be argued that certain central experiences such as loving or learning are necessary to make a man human. But then human beings who have failed to love or to learn might be excluded from the class called man.

A third distinction is made by appeal to the sentiments of adults. If a fetus dies, the grief of the parents is not the grief they would have for a living child. The fetus is an unnamed "it" till birth and is not perceived as personality until at least the fourth month of existence when movements in the womb manifest a vigorous presence demanding joyful recognition by the parents.

Yet feeling is notoriously an unsure guide to the humanity of others. Many groups of humans have had difficulty in feeling that persons of an other tongue, color, religion, sex, are as human as they. Apart from reactions to alien groups, we mourn the loss of a ten-year-old boy more than the loss of his one-day-old brother or his 90-year-old grandfather. The difference felt and the grief expressed vary with the potentialities extinguished, or the experience wiped out; they do not seem to point to an substantial difference in the humanity of baby, boy, or grandfather.

Distinctions are also made in terms of sensation by the parents. The embryo is felt within the womb only after about the fourth month. The embryo is seen only at birth. What can be neither seen nor felt is different from what is tangible. If the fetus cannot be seen or touched at all, it cannot be perceived as man.

Yet experience shows that sight is even more untrustworthy than feeling in determining humanity. By sight, color became an appropriate index for saying who was a man, and the evil of racial discrimination was given foundation. Nor can touch provide the test; a being confined by sickness, "out of touch" with others, does not thereby seem to lose his humanity. To the extent that touch still has appeal as a criterion, it appears to be a survival of the old English idea of "quickening"—a possible mistranslation of the Latin *animatus* used in the canon law. To that extent, touch as a criterion seems to be dependent on the Aristotelian notion of ensoulment, and to fall when this notion is discarded.

Finally, a distinction is sought in social visibility. The fetus is not socially perceived as human. It cannot communicate with others. Thus, both subjectively and objectively, it is not a member of society. As moral rules are rules for the behavior of members of society to each other, they cannot be made for behavior toward what is not yet a member. Excluded from the society of men, the fetus is excluded from the humanity of men.

By force of the argument from the consequences, this distinction is to be rejected. It is more subtle than that founded on an appeal to physical sensation, but it is equally dangerous in its implications. If humanity depends on social recognition, individuals or whole groups may be dehumanized by being denied any status in their society. Such a fate is fictionally portrayed in *1984* and has actually been the lot of many men in many societies. In the Roman empire, for example, condemnation to slavery meant the practical denial of most human rights, in the Chinese Communist world, landlords have been classified as enemies of the people and so treated as nonpersons by the state. Humanity does not depend on social recognition, though often the failure of society to recognize the prisoner, the alien, the heterodox as human has led to the destruction of human beings. Anyone conceived by a man and a woman is human. Recognition of this condition by society follows a real event in the objective order, however imperfect and halting the recognition. Any attempt to limit humanity to exclude some group runs the risk of furnishing authority and precedent for excluding other groups in the name of the consciousness or perception of the controlling group in the society.

A philosopher may reject the appeal to the humanity of the fetus because he views "humanity" as a secular view of the soul and because he doubts the existence of anything real and objective that can be identified as humanity. One answer to such a philosopher is to ask how he reasons about moral questions without supposing that there is a sense in which he and the others of whom he speaks are human. Whatever group is taken as the society which determines who may be killed is thereby taken as human. A second answer is to ask if he does not believe that there is a right and wrong way of deciding moral questions. If there is such a difference, experience may be appealed to: to decide who is human on the basis of the sentiment of a given society has led to consequences which rational men would characterize as monstrous.

The rejection of the attempted distinctions based on viability and visibility, experience and feeling, may be buttressed by the following considerations: Moral judgments often rest on distinctions, but if the distinctions are not to appear arbitrary fiat, they should relate to some real difference in probabilities. There is a kind of continuity in all life, but the earlier stages of the elements of human life possess tiny probabilities of development. Consider for example, the spermatozoa in any normal ejaculate: There are about 200,000,000 in any single ejaculate, of which one has a chance of developing into a zygote. Consider the oocytes that may become ova: there are 100,000 to 1,000,000 oocytes in a female infant, of which a maximum of 390 are ovulated. But once spermatozoon and ovum meet and the conceptus is formed, such studies as have been made show that roughly in only 20 percent of the cases will spontaneous abortion occur. In other words, the chances are about 4 out of 5 that this new being will develop. At this stage in the life of the being there is a sharp shift in probabilities, an immense jump in potentialities. To make a distinction between the rights of spermatozoa and the rights of the fertilized ovum is to respond to an enormous shift in possibilities. For about twenty days after conception the egg may split to form twins or combine with another egg to form a chimera, but the probability of either event happening is very small.

It may be asked, What does a change in biological probabilities have to do with establishing humanity? The argument from probabilities is not aimed at establishing humanity but at establishing an objective discontinuity that may be taken into account in moral discourse. As life itself is a matter of probabilities, as most moral reasoning is an estimate of probabilities, so it seems in accord with the structure of reality and the nature of moral thought to found a moral judgment on the change in probabilities at conception. The appeal to probabilities is the most commonsensical of arguments, to a greater or smaller degree all of us base our actions on probabilities, and in morals, as in law, prudence and negligence are often measured by the account one has taken of the probabilities. If the chance is 200,000,000 to 1 that the movement in the bushes into which you shoot is a man's, I doubt if many persons would hold you careless in shooting; but if the chances are four out of five that the movement is a human being's, few would acquit you of blame. Would the argument be different if only one out of ten children conceived came to term? Of course this argument would be different. This argument is an appeal to probabilities that actually exist, not to any and all states of affairs that may be imagined.

The probabilities as they do exist do not show the humanity of the embryo in the sense of a demonstration in logic any more than the probabilities of the movement in the bush being a man demonstrate beyond all doubt that the being is a man. The appeal is a "buttressing" consideration, showing the plausibility of the standard adopted. The argument focuses on the decisional factor in any moral judgment and assumes that part of the business of a moralist is drawing lines. One evidence of the nonarbitrary character of the line drawn is the difference of probabilities on either side of it. If a spermatozoon is destroyed, one destroys a being that had a chance of far less than 1 in 200 million of developing into a reasoning being, possessed of the genetic code, a heart, and other organs, and capable of pain. If a fetus is destroyed, one destroys a being already possessed of the genetic code, organs, and sensitivity to pain, and one that had an 80 percent chance of developing further into a baby outside the womb who, in time, would reason.

The positive argument for conception as the decisive moment of humanization is that at conception the new being receives the genetic code. It is this genetic information that determines his characteristics, that is the biological carrier of the possibility of human wisdom, that makes him a self-evolving being. A being with a human genetic code is man.

This review of current controversy over the humanity of the fetus emphasizes what a fundamental question the theologians resolved in asserting the inviolability of the fetus. To regard the fetus as possessed of equal rights with other humans was not, however, to decide every case where abortion might be employed. It did decide the case where the argument was that the fetus should be aborted for its own good. To say a being was human was to say it had a destiny to decide for itself that could not be taken from it by another man's decision. But human beings with equal rights often come in conflict with each other, and some decision must be made as whose claims are to prevail. Cases of conflict involving the fetus are different only in two respects: the total inability of the fetus to speak for itself and the fact that the right of the fetus regularly at stake is the right to life itself.

The approach taken by the theologians to these conflicts was articulated in terms of "direct" and "indirect." Again, to look at what they were doing from outside their categories, they may be said to have been drawing lines or "balancing values." "Direct" and "indirect" are spatial metaphors; "line-drawing" is another. "To weigh" or "to balance" values is a metaphor of a more complicated mathematical sort hinting at the process which goes on in moral judgments. All the metaphors suggest that, in the moral judgments made, comparisons were necessary, that no value completely controlled. The principle of double effect was no doctrine fallen from heaven, but a method of analysis appropriate where two relative values were being compared. In Catholic moral theology, as it developed, life even of the innocent was not taken as an absolute. Judgments on acts affecting life issued from a process of weighing. In the weighing, the fetus was always given a value greater than zero, always a value separate and independent from its parents. This valuation was crucial and fundamental in all Christian thought on the subject and marked it off from any approach that considered that only the parents' interests needed to be considered.

Even with the fetus weighed as human, one interest could be weighed as equal or superior: that of the mother in her own life. The casuists between 1450 and 1895 were willing to weigh this interest as superior. Since 1895, that interest was given decisive weight only in the two special cases of the cancerous uterus and the ectopic pregnancy. In both of these cases the fetus itself had little chance of survival even if the abortion were not performed. As the balance was once struck in favor of the mother whenever her life was endangered, it could be so struck again. The balance reached between 1895 and 1930 attempted prudentially and pastorally to forestall a multitude of exceptions for interests less than life.

The perception of the humanity of the fetus and the weighing of fetal rights against other human rights constituted the work of the moral analysts. But what spirit animated their abstract judgments? For the Christian community, it was the injunction of Scripture to love your neighbor as yourself. The fetus as human was a neighbor; his life had parity with one's own. The commandment gave life to what otherwise would have been only rational calculation.

The commandment could be put in humanistic as well as theological terms: Do not injure your fellow man without reason. In these terms, once the humanity of the fetus is perceived, abortion is never right except in self-defense. When life must be taken to save life, reason alone cannot say that a mother must prefer a child's life to her own. With this exception, now of great rarity, abortion violates the rational humanist tenet of the equality of human lives.

For Christians the commandment to love had received a special imprint in that the exemplar proposed of love was the love of the Lord for his disciples. In the light given by this example, self-sacrifice carried to the point of death seemed in the extreme situations not without meaning. In the less extreme cases, preference for one's own interests to the life of another seemed to express cruelty or selfishness irreconcilable with the demands of love.

STUDY QUESTIONS

1. Where does Noonan draw the line between being human and nonhuman? Do you agree with him? Explain.

2. Has Noonan successfully argued that abortion is immoral? How would he argue against abortion in cases of rape?

3. Examine Noonan's argument from the relevance of probabilities in determining whether a fetus will become a fully formed human person. What are the implications of this suggestion? Is it sound?

12

In Defense of Abortion and Infanticide

MICHAEL TOOLEY

Michael Tooley, after teaching for many years at the Australian National University, is now Professor of Philosophy at the University of Colorado, Boulder. Here is Tooley's abstract of his article:

This essay deals with the question of the morality of abortion and infanticide. The fundamental ethical objection traditionally advanced against these practices rests on the contention that human fetuses and infants have a right to life. This claim will be the focus of attention here. The basic issue to be discussed, then, is what properties a thing must possess to have a right to life. My approach will be to set out and defend a basic moral principle specifying a condition an organism must satisfy if it is to have a right to life. It will be seen that this condition is not satisfied by human fetuses and infants, and thus that they do not have a right to life. So unless there are other objections to abortion and infanticide that are sound, one is forced to conclude that these practices are morally acceptable ones.[1] In contrast, it may turn out that our treatment of adult members of some other species is morally indefensible. For it is quite possible that some nonhuman animals do possess properties that endow them with a right to life.

ABORTION AND INFANTICIDE

What reason is there for raising the question of the morality of infanticide? One reason is that it seems very difficult to formulate a completely satisfactory pro–abortion position without coming to grips with the infanticide issue. For the problem that the liberal on abortion encounters here is that of specifying a cutoff point that is not arbitrary: At what stage in the development of a human being does it cease to be morally permissible to destroy it, and why?

It is important to be clear about the difficulty here. The problem is not, as some have thought, that since there is a continuous line of development from a zygote to a newborn baby, one cannot hold that it is seriously wrong to destroy a newborn baby without also holding that it is seriously wrong to destroy a zygote, or any intermediate stage in the development of a human being. The problem is rather that if one says that it is wrong to destroy a newborn baby but not a zygote or some intermediate stage, one should be prepared to point to a *morally relevant* difference between a new-born baby and the earlier stage in the development of a human being.

Precisely the same difficulty can, of course, be raised for a person who holds that infanticide is morally permissible, since one can ask what morally relevant difference there is between an adult human being and a newborn baby. What makes it morally permissible to destroy a baby, but wrong to kill an adult? So the challenge remains. But I shall argue that in the latter case there is an extremely plausible answer.

Reflecting on the morality of infanticide forces one to face up to this challenge. In the case of abortion a number of events—quickening or viability, for instance—might be taken as cutoff points, and it is easy to overlook the fact that none of these events involves any morally significant change in the developing human. In contrast, if one is going to defend infanticide, one has to get very clear about what it is that gives something a right to life.

One of the interesting ways in which the abortion issue differs from most other moral issues is that the plausible positions on abortion appear to be extreme ones. For if a human fetus has a right to life, one is inclined to say that, in general, one would be justified in killing it only to save the life of the mother, and perhaps not even in that case.[2] Such is the extreme anti-abortion position. On the other hand, if the fetus does not have a right to life, why should it be seriously wrong to destroy it? Why would one need to point to special circumstance—such as the presence of genetic disease, or a threat to the woman's health—in order to justify such action? The upshot is that there does not appear to be any room for a moderate position on abortion as one finds, for example, in the Model Penal Code recommendations.[3]

Aside from the light it may shed on the abortion question, the issue of infanticide is both interesting and important in its own right. The theoretical interest has been mentioned earlier: It forces one to face up to the question of what it is that gives something a right to life. The practical importance need not be labored. Most people would prefer to raise children who do not suffer from gross deformities or from severe physical, emotional, or intellectual handicaps. If it could be shown that there is no moral objection to infanticide, the happiness of society could be significantly and justifiably increased.

The suggestion that infanticide may be morally permissible is not an idea that many people are able to consider dispassionately. Even philosophers tend to react in a way that seems primarily visceral—offering no arguments and dismissing infanticide out of hand.

Some philosophers have argued, however, that such a reaction is not inappropriate, on the ground that, first, moral principles must, in the final analysis, be justified by reference to our moral feelings, or intuitions, and secondly, infanticide is one practice that is judged wrong by virtually everyone's moral intuition. I believe, however, that this line of thought is unsound, and I have argued elsewhere that even if one grants, at least for the sake of argument, that moral intuitions are the final court of appeal regarding the acceptability of moral principles, the question of the morality of infanticide is not one that can be settled by an appeal to our intuitions concerning it.[4] If infanticide is to be rejected, an argument is needed, and I believe that the considerations advanced in this essay show that it is unlikely that such an argument is forthcoming.

WHAT SORT OF BEING CAN POSSESS A RIGHT TO LIFE?

The issues of the morality of abortion and of infanticide seem to turn primarily upon the answers to the following four questions:

1. What properties, other than potentialities, give something a right to life?
2. Do the corresponding potentialities also endow something with a right to life?
3. If not, do they at least make it seriously wrong to destroy it?
4. At what point in its development does a member of the biologically defined species *Homo sapiens* first possess those nonpotential properties that give something a right to life?

The argument to be developed in the present section bears upon the answers to the first two questions.

How can one determine what properties endow a being with a right to life? An approach that I believe is very promising starts from the observation that there appear to be two radically different sorts of reasons why an entity may lack a certain right. Compare, for example, the following two claims:

1. A child does not have a right to smoke.
2. A newspaper does not have a right not to be torn up.

The first claim raises a substantive moral issue. People might well disagree about it, and support their conflicting views by appealing to different moral theories. The second dispute, in contrast, seems an unlikely candidate for moral dispute. It is natural to say that newspapers just are not the sort of thing that can have any rights at all, including a right not to be torn up. So there is no need to appeal to a substantive moral theory to resolve the question whether a newspaper has a right not to be torn up.

One way of characterizing this difference, albeit one that will not especially commend itself to philosophers of a Quinean bent, is to say that the second claim, unlike the first, is true in virtue of a certain *conceptual* connection, and that is why no moral theory is needed in order to see that it is true. The explanation, then, of why it is that a newspaper does not have a right not to be torn up, is that there exists some property P such that, first, newspapers lack property P, and, second, it is a conceptual truth that only things with property P can be possessors of rights.

What might property P be? A plausible answer, I believe, is set out and defended by Joel Feinberg in his paper, "The Rights of Animals and Unborn Generations."[5] It takes the form of what Feinberg refers to as the *interest principle*: "...the sorts of beings who *can* have rights are precisely those who have (or can have) interests."[6] And then, since "interests must be compounded somehow out of conations,"[7] it follows that things devoid of desires, such as newspapers, can have neither interests nor rights. Here, then, is one account of the difference in status between judgments such as (1) and (2) above.

Let us now consider the right to life. The interest principle tells us that an entity cannot have any rights at all, and, *a fortiori,* cannot have a right to life, unless it is capable of having interests. This in itself may be a conclusion of considerable importance. Consider, for example, a fertilized human egg cell. Someday it will come to have desires and interests. As a zygote, however, it does not have desires, nor even the *capacity* for having desires. What about interests? This depends upon the account one offers of the relationship between desires and interests. It seems to me that a zygote cannot be properly spoken of as a subject of interests. My reason is roughly this. What is in a thing's interest is a function of its present and future desires, both those it will actually have and those it could have. In the case of an entity that is not presently capable of any desires, its interests must be based entirely upon the satisfaction of future desires. Then, since satisfaction of future desires presupposes the continued existence of the entity in question, anything which has an interest that is based upon the satisfaction of future desires must also have an interest in its own continued existence. Therefore, something that is not presently capable of having any desires at all—like a zygote—cannot have any interests at all unless it has interest in its own continued existence. I shall argue shortly, however, that a zygote cannot have such an interest. From this it will follow that it cannot have any interests at all, and this conclusion, together with the interest principle, entails that not all members of the species *Homo sapiens* have a right to life.

The interest principle involves, then, a thesis concerning a necessary condition that something must satisfy if it is to have a right to life, and it is a thesis that has important moral implications. It implies, for example, that abortions, if performed sufficiently early, do not involve any violation of a right to life.

But on the other hand, the interest principle provides no help with the question of the moral status of human organisms once they have developed to the point where they do have desires, and thus are capable of having interests. The interest principle states that they *can* have rights. It does not state whether they *do* have rights—including, in particular, a right not to be destroyed.

It is possible, however, that the interest principle does not exhaust the connections between rights and interests. It formulates only a very general connection: A thing cannot have any rights at all unless it is capable of having at least some interest. May there not be more specific connections, between particular rights and particular sorts of interests? The following line of thought lends plausibility to this suggestion. Consider animals such as cats. Some philosophers are inclined to hold that animals such as cats do not have any rights at all. But let us assume, for the purpose of the present discussion, that cats do have some rights, such as a right not to be tortured, and consider the following claim:

3. A cat does not have a right to a university education.

How is this statement to be regarded? In particular, is it comparable in status to the claim that children do not have a right to smoke, or, instead, to the claim that newspapers do not have a right to be torn up? To the latter, surely. Just as a newspaper is not the sort of thing that can have any rights at all, including a right not to be destroyed, so one is inclined to say that a cat, though it may have some rights, such as a right not to be tortured, is not the sort of thing that can possibly have a right to a university education.

This intuitive judgment about the status of claims such as (3) is reinforced, moreover, if one turns to the question of the grounds of the interest principle. Consider, for example, the account offered by Feinberg, which he summarizes as follows:

> Now we can extract from our discussion of animal rights a crucial principle for tentative use in the resolution of the other riddles about the applicability of the concept of a right, namely, that the sorts of beings who *can* have rights are precisely those who have (or can have) interests. I have come to this tentative conclusion for two reasons: (1) because a right holder must be capable of being represented and it is impossible to represent a being that has no interests, and (2) because a right holder must be capable of being a beneficiary in his own person, and a being without interests is a being that is incapable of being harmed or benefited, having no good or "sake" of its own. Thus a being without interests has no "behalf" to act in, and no "sake" to act for.[8]

If this justification of the interest principle is sound, it can also be employed to support principles connecting particular rights with specific sorts of interests. Just as one cannot represent a being that has no interests at all, so one cannot, in demanding a university education for a cat, be representing the cat unless one is thereby representing some interest that the cat has, and that would be served by its receiving a university education. Similarly, one cannot be acting for the sake of a cat in arguing that it should receive a university education unless the cat has some interest that will thereby be furthered. The conclusion, therefore, is that if Feinberg's defense of the interest principle is sound, other, more specific principles must also be correct. These more specific principles can be summed up, albeit somewhat vaguely, by the following, *particular-interests principle.*

> It is a conceptual truth that an entity cannot have a particular right, R, unless it is at least capable of having some interest, I, which is furthered by its having right R.

Given this particular-interests principle, certain familiar facts, whose importance has not often been appreciated, become comprehensible. Compare an act of killing a normal adult human being with an act of torturing one for five minutes. Though both acts are seriously wrong, they are not equally so. Here, as in most cases, to violate an individual's right to life is more seriously wrong than to violate his right not to have pain inflicted upon him. Consider, however, the corresponding actions in the case of a newborn kitten. Most people feel that it is seriously wrong to torture a kitten for five minutes, but not to kill it painlessly. How is this difference in the moral ordering of the two types of acts, between the human case and the kitten case, to be explained? One answer is that while normal adult human beings have both a right to life and a right not to be tortured, a kitten has only the latter. But why should this be so? The particular-interest principle, however, suggests a possible explanation. Though kittens have some interests, including, in particular, an interest in not being tortured, which derives from their capacity to feel pain, they do not have an interest in their own continued existence and, hence, do not have a right not to be destroyed. This answer contains, of course, a large promissory element. One needs a defense of the view that kittens have no interest in continued existence. But the point here is simply that there is an important question about the rationale underlying the moral ordering of certain sorts of acts, and that the particular-interests principle points to a possible answer.

This fact lends further plausibility, I believe, to the particular-interests principle. What one would ultimately like to do, of course, is to set out an analysis of the concept of a right, show that the analysis is indeed satisfactory, and then show that the particular-interests principle is entailed by the analysis. Unfortunately, it will not be possible to pursue such an approach here, since formulating an acceptable analysis of the concept of a right is a far from trivial matter. What I should like to do, however, is to touch briefly upon the problem of providing such an analysis, and then to indicate the account that seems to me most satisfactory—an account which does entail the particular-interests principle.

It would be widely agreed, I believe, both that rights impose obligations and that the obligations they impose upon others are *conditional* upon certain factors. The difficulty arises when one attempts to specify what the obligations are conditional upon. There seems to be two main views in this area. According to the one, rights impose obligations that are conditional upon the interests of the possessor of the right. To say that Sandra has a right to something is thus to say, roughly, that if it is in Sandra's interest to have that thing, then others are under an obligation not to deprive her of it. According to the second view, rights impose obligations that are conditional upon the right's not having been waived. To say that Sandra has a right to something is to say, roughly, that if Sandra has not given others permission to take the thing, then they are under an obligation not to deprive her of it.

Both views encounter serious difficulties. On the one hand, in the case of minors, and nonhuman animals, it would seem that the obligations that rights impose must be taken as conditional upon the interests of those individuals, rather than upon whether they have given one permission to do certain things. On the other, in the case of individuals who are capable of making informed and rational decisions, if that person has not given one permission to take something that belongs to him, it would seem that one is, in general, still under an obligation not to deprive him of it, even if having that thing is no longer in his interest.

As a result, it seems that a more complex account is needed of the factors upon which the obligations imposed by rights are conditional. The account which I now prefer, and which I have defended elsewhere,[9] is this: "A has a right to X" means the same as:

> A is such that it can be in A's interest to have X, and either (1) A is not capable of making an informed and rational choice whether to grant others permission to deprive him of X, in which case, if it is in A's interest not to be deprived of X, then, by this fact alone, others are under a prima facie obligation not to deprive A of X, *or* (2) A is capable of making an informed and rational choice whether to grant others permission to deprive him of X, in which case the others are under a prima facie obligation not to deprive A of X if and only if A has not granted them permission to do so.

And if this account, or something rather similar is correct, then so is the particular-interests principle.

What I now want to do is simply apply the particular-interests principle to the case of the right to life. First, however, one needs to notice that the expression, "right to life," is not entirely happy, since it suggests that the right in question concerns the continued existence of a biological organism. That this is incorrect can be brought out by considering possible ways of violating an individual's right to life. Suppose, for example, that future technological developments make it possible to change completely the neural networks in a brain, and that the brain of some normal adult human being is thus completely reprogrammed so that the organism in question winds up with memories (or rather, apparent memories), beliefs, attitudes, and personality traits totally different from those associated with it before it was subjected to reprogramming. (The Pope is reprogrammed, say, on the model of Bertrand Russell.) In such a case, however beneficial the change might be, one would surely want to say that *someone* had been destroyed, that an adult human being's right to life had been violated, even though no biological organism had been killed. This shows that the expression, "right to life," is misleading, since what one is concerned about is not just the continued existence of a biological organism.

How, then, might the right in question be more accurately described? A natural suggestion is that the expression, "right to life," refers to the right of a subject of experiences and other mental states to continue to exist. It might be contended, however, that this interpretation begs the question against certain possible views. For someone might hold—and surely some people in fact do—that while continuing subjects of experiences and other mental states certainly have a right to life, so do some other organisms that are only potentially such continuing subjects, such as human fetuses. A right to life, on this view, is *either* the right of a subject of experiences to continue to exist *or* the right of something that is only potentially a continuing subject of experiences to become such an entity.

This view is, I believe, to be rejected, for at least two reasons. First, this view appears to be clearly incompatible with the interest principle. Second, this position entails that the destruction of potential persons is, in general, prima facie seriously wrong, and I shall argue, in the next section, that the latter view is incorrect.

Let us consider, then, the right of a subject of experiences and other mental states to continue to exist. The particular-interests principle implies that something cannot possibly have such a right unless its continued existence can be in its interest. We need to ask, then, what must be the case if the continued existence of something is to be in its interest.

It will help to focus our thinking, I believe, if we consider a crucial case, stressed by Derek Parfit. Imagine a human baby that has developed to the point of being sentient, and of having simple desires, but that is not yet capable of having any desire for continued existence. Suppose, further, that the baby will enjoy a happy life and will be glad that it was not destroyed. Can we or can we not say that it is in the baby's interest not to be destroyed?

To approach this case, let us consider a closely related one, namely, that of a human embryo that has not developed sufficiently far to have any desires, or even any states of consciousness at all, but that will develop into an individual who will enjoy a happy life, and who will be glad that his mother did not have an abortion. Can we or can we not say that it is the embryo's interest not to be destroyed?

Why might someone be tempted to say that it is in the embryo's interest that it not be destroyed? One line of thought which, I believe, tempts some people, is this. Let Mary be an individual who enjoys a happy life. Then, though some philosophers have expressed serious doubts about this, it might very well be said that it was certainly in Mary's interest that a certain embryo was not destroyed several years earlier. And this claim, together with the tendency to use expressions such as "Mary before she was born" to refer to the embryo in question, may lead one to think that it was in the embryo's interest not to be destroyed. But this way of thinking involves conceptual confusion. A subject of interests, in the relevant sense of "interest," must necessarily be a subject of conscious states, including experiences and desires. This means that in identifying Mary with the embryo, and attributing to it her interest in its earlier nondestruction, one is treating the embryo as if it were itself a subject of consciousness. But by hypothesis, the embryo being considered has not developed to the point where there is any subject of consciousness associated with it. It cannot, therefore, have any interests at all, and *a fortiori,* it cannot have any interest in its own continued existence.

Let us now return to the first case—that of a human baby that is sentient, and that has simple desires, but which is not yet capable of having more complex desires, such as a desire for its own continued existence. Given that it will develop into an individual who will lead a happy life and who will be glad that the baby was not destroyed, does one want to say that the baby's not being destroyed is in the baby's own interest?

Again, the following line of thought may seem initially tempting. If Mary is the resulting individual, then it was in Mary's interest that the baby not have been destroyed. But the baby just *is* Mary when she was young. So it must have been in the baby's interest that it not have been destroyed.

Indeed, this argument is considerably more tempting in the present case than in the former, since here there is something that is a subject of consciousness, and which it is natural to identify with Mary. I suggest, however, that when one reflects upon the case, it becomes clear that such an identification is justified only if certain further things are the case. Thus, on the one hand, suppose that Mary is able to remember quite clearly some of the experiences that the baby enjoyed. Given that sort of causal and psychological connection, it would seem perfectly reasonable to hold that Mary and the baby are one and the same subject of consciousness, and thus, that if it is in Mary's interest that the baby not have been destroyed, then this must also have been in the baby's interest. On the other hand, suppose that not only does Mary, at a much later time, not remember any of the baby's experiences, but the experiences in question are not psychologically linked, either via memory or in any other way, to mental states enjoyed by the human organism in question at *any* later time. Here it seems to me clearly incorrect to say that Mary and the baby are one and the same subject of consciousness, and therefore it cannot be correct to transfer, from Mary to the baby, Mary's interest in the baby's not having been destroyed.

Let us now return to the question of what must be the case if the continued existence of something is to be in its own interest. The picture that emerges from the two cases just discussed is this. In the first place, nothing at all can be in an entity's interest unless it has desires at some time or other. But more than this is required if the continued existence of the entity is to be in its own interest. One possibility, which will generally be sufficient, is that the individual have, at the time in question, a desire for its own continued existence. Yet it also seems clear that an individual's continued existence can be in its own interest even when such a desire is not present. What is needed, apparently, is that the continued existence of the individual will make possible the satisfaction of some desires existing at other times. But not just any desires existing at other times will do. Indeed, as is illustrated both by the case of the baby just discussed and by the deprogramming/reprogramming example, it is not even sufficient that they be desires associated with the same physical organism. It is crucial that they be desires that belong to one and the same subject of consciousness.

The critical question, then, concerns the conditions under which desires existing at different times can be correctly attributed to a single, continuing subject of consciousness. This question raises a number of difficult issues that cannot be considered here. Part of the rationale underlying the view I wish to advance will be clear, however, if one considers the role played by memory in the psychological unity of an individual over time. When I remember a past experience, what I know is not merely that there was a certain experience which someone or other had, but that there was an experience that belonged to the *same* individual as the present memory beliefs, and it seems clear that this feature of one's memories is, in general, a crucial part of what it is that makes one a continuing subject of experiences, rather than merely a series of psychologically isolated, momentary subjects of consciousness. This suggests something like the following principle:

> Desires existing at different times can belong to a single, continuing subject of consciousness only if that subject of consciousness possesses, at some time, the concept of a continuing self or mental substance.[10]

Given this principle, together with the particular-rights principle, one can set out the following argument in support of a claim concerning a necessary condition that an entity must satisfy if it is to have a right to life:

1. The concept of a right is such that an individual cannot have a right at time *t* to continued existence unless the individual is such that it can be in its interest at time *t* that it continue to exist.

2. The continued existence of a given subject of consciousness cannot be in that individual's interest at time *t* unless *either* that individual has a desire, at time *t*, to continue as a subject of consciousness, *or* that individual can have desires at other times.

3. An individual cannot have a desire to continue to exist as a subject of consciousness unless it possesses the concept of continuing self or mental substance.

4. An individual existing at one time cannot have desires at other times unless there is at least one time at which it possesses the concept of a continuing self or mental substance.

Therefore,

5. An individual cannot have a right to continued existence unless there is at least one time at which it possesses the concept of a continuing self or mental substance.

This conclusion is obviously significant. But precisely what implications does it have with respect to the morality of abortion and infanticide? The answer will depend upon what relationship there is between, on the one hand, the behavioral and neurophysiological development of a human being, and, on the other, the development of that individual's mind. Some people believe that there is no relationship at all. They believe that a human mind, with all its mature capacities, is present in a human from conception onward, and so is there before the brain has even begun to develop, and before the individual has begun to exhibit behavior expressive of higher mental functioning. Most philosophers, however, reject this view. They believe, on the one hand, that there is, in general, a rather close relation between an individual's behavioral capacities and its mental functioning, and, on the other, that there is a very intimate relationship between the mind and the brain. As regards the latter, some philosophers hold that the mind is in fact identical with the brain. Others maintain that the mind is distinct from the brain, but causally dependent upon it. In either case, the result is a view according to which the development of the mind and the brain are necessarily closely tied to one another.

If one does adopt the view that there is a close relation between the behavioral and neurophysiological development of a human being, and the development of its mind, then the previous conclusion has a very important, and possibly decisive implication with respect to the morality of abortion and infanticide. For when human development, both behavioral and neurophysiological, is closely examined, it is seen to be most unlikely that human fetuses, or even newborn babies, possess any concept of a continuing self.[11] And in the light of the above conclusion, this means that such individuals do not possess a right to life.

But is it reasonable to hold that there is a close relation between human behavioral and neurophysiological development, and the development of the human mind? Approached from a scientific perspective, I believe that there is excellent reason for doing so. Consider, for example, what is known about how, at later stages, human mental capacities proceed in step with brain development, or what is known about how damage to different parts of the brain can affect, in different ways, an individual's intellectual capacities.

Why, then, do some people reject the view that there is a close relationship between the development of the human mind, and the behavioral and neurophysiological development of human beings? There are, I think, two main reasons. First, some philosophers believe that the scientific evidence is irrelevant because they believe that it is possible to establish, by means of a purely metaphysical argument, that a human mind, with its mature capacities, is present in a human from conception onward. I have argued elsewhere that the argument in question is unsound.[12]

Second, and more commonly, some people appeal to the idea that it is a divinely revealed truth that human beings have minds from conception onward. There are a number of points to be made about such an appeal. First, the belief that a mind, or soul, is infused into a human body at conception by God is not an essential belief within many of the world's religions. Second, even with religious traditions, such as Roman Catholicism, where the belief is a very common one, it is by no means universally accepted. Thus, for example, the

well-known Catholic philosopher, Joseph Donceel, has argued very strongly
for the claim that the correct position on the question of ensoulment is that
the soul enters the body only when the human brain has undergone a sufficient process of development.[13] Third, there is the question of whether it is
reasonable to accept the religious outlook that is being appealed to in support
of the contention that humans have minds that are capable of higher intellectual activities from conception onward. This question raises very large issues
in philosophy of religion, which cannot be pursued here. But it should at least
be said that most contemporary philosophers who have reflected upon religious beliefs have come to the view that there is not sufficient reason even for
believing in the existence of God, let alone for accepting the much more detailed religious claims which are part of a religion such as Christianity. Finally,
suppose that one nonetheless decides to accept the contention that it is a divinely revealed truth that humans have, from conception onward, minds that
are capable of higher mental activities, and that one appeals to this purported
revelation in order to support the claim that all humans have a right to life.
One needs to notice that if one then goes on to argue, not merely that abortion is wrong, but that there should be a law against it, one will encounter a
very serious objection. For it is surely true that it is inappropriate, at least in a
pluralistic society, to appeal to specific religious beliefs of a nonmoral sort—
such as the belief that God infuses souls into human bodies at conception—in
support of legislation that will be binding upon everyone, including those
who either accept different religious beliefs, or none at all.

IS IT MORALLY WRONG TO DESTROY
POTENTIAL PERSONS?

In this section I shall consider the question of whether it can be seriously
wrong to destroy an entity, not because of the nonpotential properties it
presently possesses, but because of the properties it will later come to have, if
it is not interfered with. First, however, we need to be clear why this is such a
crucial question. We can do this by considering a line of thought that has led
some people to feel that the anti-abortionist position is more defensible than
that of the pro-abortionist. The argument in question rests upon the gradual
and continuous development of an organism as it changes from a zygote into
an adult human being. The anti-abortionist can point to this development,
and argue that it is morally arbitrary for a pro-abortionist to draw a line at
some point in this continuous process—such as at birth, or viability—and to
say that killing is permissible before, but not after, that particular point.

The pro-abortionist reply would be, I think, that the emphasis on the continuity of the process is misleading. What the anti-abortionist really doing is
simply challenging the pro-abortionist to specify what properties a thing must
have in order to have a right to life, and to show that the developing organism
does acquire those properties at the point in question. The pro-abortionist may

then be tempted to argue that the difficulty in meeting this challenge should not be taken as grounds for rejecting his position. For the anti–abortionist cannot meet this challenge either; he is equally unable to say what properties something must have if it is to have a right to life.

Although this rejoinder does not dispose of the anti-abortionist argument, it is not without bite. For defenders of the view that abortion is almost always wrong have failed to face up to the question of the *basic* moral principles on which their position rests, where a basic moral principle is one whose accept-ability does not rest upon the truth of any factual claim of a nonmoral sort.[14] They have been content to assert the wrongness of killing any organism, from a zygote on, if that organism is a member of the biologically defined species *Homo sapiens.* But they have overlooked the point that this cannot be an ac-ceptable *basic* moral principle, since difference in species is not in itself a morally relevant difference.[15]

The anti-abortionist can reply that it is possible to defend his position, but not a pro-abortionist position, *without* getting clear about the properties a thing must possess if it is to have a right to life. For one can appeal to the fol-lowing two claims: First, that there is a property, even if one is unable to spec-ify what it is, that (1) is possessed by normal adult humans, and (2) endows any being possessing it with a right to life. Second, that there are properties that satisfy (1) and (2), at least one those properties will be such that any or-ganism potentially possessing that property has a right to life even now, simply in virtue of that potentiality—where an organism possesses a property poten-tially if it will come to have it in the normal course of its development.

The second claim—which I shall refer to as the potentiality principle—is crucial to the anti-abortionist's defense of his position. Given that principle, the anti-abortionist can defend his position without grappling with the very difficult question of what nonpotential properties an entity must possess in order to have a right to life. It is enough to know that adult members of *Homo sapiens* do have such a right. For then one can employ the potentiality princi-ple to conclude that any organism that belongs to the species *Homo sapiens,* from a zygote on—with the possible exception of those that suffer from cer-tain gross neurophysiological abnormalities—must also have a right to life.

The pro-abortionist, in contrast, cannot mount a comparable argument. He cannot defend his position without offering at least a partial answer to the question of what properties a thing must possess in order to have a right to life.

The importance of the potentiality principle, however, goes beyond the fact that it provides support for an anti-abortion position. For it seems that if the potentiality principle is unsound, then there is no acceptable defense of an extreme conservative view on abortion.

The reason is this: Suppose that the claim that an organism's having certain potentialities is sufficient grounds for its having a right to life cannot be sus-tained. The claim that a fetus that is a member of *Homo sapiens* has a right to life can then be attacked as follows. The reason an adult member of *Homo sapi-ens* has a right to life, but an infant ape, say, does not, is that there are certain physiological properties that the former possesses and the latter does not. Now even if one is unsure exactly what the relevant psychological characteristics are, it seems clear that an organism in the early stages of development from a zygote into an adult member of *Homo sapiens* does not possess those properties. One need merely compare a human fetus with an ape fetus. In early stages of development, neither will have any mental life at all. (Does a zygote have a mental life? Does it have experiences? Or beliefs? Or desires?) In later stages of fetal development some mental events presumably occur, but these will be of a very rudimentary sort. The crucial point, however, is that given what we know through comparative studies of, on the one hand, brain development. and, on the other behavior after birth, it is surely reasonable to hold that there are no significant differences in the respective mental lives of a human fetus and an ape fetus. There are, of course, physiological differences, but these are not in themselves morally significant. *If* one held that potentialities were relevant to the ascription of a right to life, one could argue that the physiological differences, though not morally relevant in themselves, are morally relevant in virtue of their causal consequences: They will lead to later psychological differences that are morally relevant, and for this reason the physiological differences are themselves morally significant. But if the potentiality principle is not available, this line of argument cannot be used, and there will then be no differences between a human and an ape fetus that the anti-abortionist can use as grounds for ascribing a right to life to the former but not to the latter.

This argument assumes, of course, that the anti-abortionist cannot successfully argue that there are religious reasons for holding that, even when potentialities are set aside, there is a morally relevant difference between human fetuses and ape fetuses. In the previous section I indicated, however, why it is very unlikely that any religious line of argument can be satisfactory in the present context.

The conclusion seems to be then, that the anti-abortionist position is defensible only if the potentiality principle is sound. Let us now consider what can be said against that principle. One way of attacking it is by appealing to the conclusion advanced in the previous section, to the effect that an individual cannot have a right to continued existence unless there is at least one time at which it possesses the concept of continuing self or mental substance. This principle entails the denial of the potentiality principle. Or more precisely, it does so in conjunction with the presumably uncontroversial empirical claim that a fertilized human egg cell, which does possess the relevant potentialities, does not possess the concept of a continuing self or mental substance.

Alternatively, one could appeal to the more modest claim involved in the interest principle and use it to argue that since a fertilized human egg cell cannot have any interests at all, it cannot have any rights, and *a fortiori* cannot have a right to life. So potentialities alone cannot endow something with a right to life.

Given these lines of argument, is there any reason not to rest the case at this point? I want to suggest that there are at least two reasons why one needs to take a closer look at the potentiality principle. The first is that some people who are anti-abortionists may wish to reject not only the particular-interests principle, but also the more modest interest principle, and although I believe that this response to the above arguments is unsound, I think it is important to see whether there aren't other arguments that are untouched by this reply.

A second, and more important, reason why it is unwise to base one's case against the anti-abortionist entirely upon an appeal to principles such as the interest principle is this. The anti-abortionist can modify his position slightly and avoid the arguments in question. Specifically, he can abandon his claim that a human fetus has a right to life, but contend that it is nevertheless seriously wrong to kill it. Some philosophers would feel that such modification cannot possibly be acceptable, on the ground that no action can be seriously wrong unless it violates someone's right to something. It seems to me, however, that this latter view is in fact mistaken.[16] In any case, let us consider the position that results from this modification. An anti-abortionist who is willing to adopt this position can then appeal, not to the potentiality principle, but to the following, *modified potentiality principle:*

> If there are properties possessed by normal adult human beings that endow any organism possessing them with a right to life, then at least one of those properties is such that it is seriously wrong to kill any organism that potentially possesses that property, simply in virtue of that potentiality.

Since this modified potentiality principle is not concerned with the attribution of rights to organisms, it cannot be attacked by appealing to the interest principle, or to the particular-interests principle, or to some analysis of the concept of a right.

Let us now consider how the case against the anti-abortionist position can be strengthened. I shall advance three arguments that are objections to both the original and the modified potentiality principles. Since the original potentiality principle cannot be correct unless the modified one is, it will suffice to consider only the modified principle. The basic issue, then, is this: Is there any property J which satisfies the following three conditions:

1. There is a property, K, such that any individual possessing property K has a right to life, and there is a scientific law, L, to the effect that any organism possessing property J will, in the normal course of events, come to possess property K at some later time.

2. Given the relationship just described between property J and property K, it is seriously wrong to kill anything possessing property J.

3. If property J were not related to property K in the way indicated, the fact that an organism possessed property J would not make it seriously wrong to kill it.

In short, the question is whether there is a property, J, that makes it seriously wrong to kill something *only because* J stands in a certain causal relation to a second property, K, which is such that anything possessing that property *ipso facto* has a right to life.

My first objection turns upon the claim that if one accepts the modified potentiality principle, one ought also to accept the following, *generalized potentiality principle.*

If there are any properties possessed by normal adult human beings that endow any organism possessing them with a right to life, then at least one of those properties is such that it is seriously wrong to perform any action that will prevent some system, which otherwise would have developed the property, from doing so.

This generalized potentiality principle differs from the original and the modified potentiality principles in two respects. First, it applies to systems of objects and not merely to organisms. I think that this first generalization is one that ought to be accepted by anyone who accepts either the original or the modified principle. For why should it make any difference whether the potentiality resides in a single organism, or in a system of organisms that are so interrelated that they will in the normal course of affairs, due to the operation of natural laws, causally give rise to something that possesses the property in question? Surely it is only the potentiality for a certain outcome that matters and not whether there are one or more objects interacting and developing in a predetermined way to produce that outcome.

In thinking about this issue, it is important not to confuse *potentialities* with mere *possibilities.* The generalized potentiality principle does not deal with collection of objects that merely have the capacity to interact in certain ways. The objects must already be interrelated in such a way that in the absence of external interference, the laws governing their future interaction and development will bring it about that the system will develop the property in question.

The second difference is that the original and modified potentiality principles deal only with the *destruction* of organisms, while the generalized principle deals with any action that prevents an organism, or system, from developing the relevant property. I think that the anti-abortionist will certainly want to accept this generalization. For suppose that by exposing a human zygote to appropriate radiation one could transform it into a frog zygote. A woman could then undergo a two-step abortion: first the human zygote would be transformed into a frog zygote and then the frog zygote would be destroyed. Assuming that one doesn't view the destruction of a frog zygote as seriously wrong, one must either hold that it is seriously wrong to prevent a human zygote from developing its potentialities, or else conclude that the two-step abortion technique is morally permissible. The latter option would not appear to be viable, let alone a welcome one, for the anti-abortionist. For why should it be morally permissible to destroy a human organism in two steps, one of which limits its potentialities and the other of which destroys the resulting organism, but seriously wrong to collapse these two steps into one limiting its potentialities and destroying it by a single action? I think that the anti-abortionists would agree that there is no significant moral distinction here, and thus would accept the second generalization involved in the expanded potentiality principle.

Suppose, now, that artificial wombs have been perfected. A healthy, unfertilized human egg cell has been placed in one, along with a large number of spermatozoa. If the device is turned on, the spermatozoa will be carried, via a conveyor belt, to the unfertilized egg cell, where, we can assume, fertilization will take place. The device is such, moreover, that no outside assistance will be needed at any future stage, and nine months later a normal human baby will emerge from the artificial womb. Given these assumptions—all of which are certainly empirically possible—once such a device has been turned on, there will exist an active potentiality that will, if not interfered with, give rise to something that will become an adult human being, and so will have a right to life. But would it be seriously wrong to destroy that potentiality—as might be done, for example, by turning off the machine, or by cutting the conveyor belt, so that fertilization does not take place? Most people, I believe, would certainly not think that such actions were seriously wrong. If that view is correct, the generalized potentiality principle must be rejected as unsound.

In short, the first argument against the modified potentiality principle, and hence against the original potentiality principle, is as follows. It is reasonable to accept the modified principle only if it is also reasonable to accept the generalized potentiality principle because whether the potentialities reside in a single organism or in a system does not seem to be a morally significant difference. But to accept the generalized potentiality principle is to commit oneself to the view that interference with an artificial womb so as to prevent fertilization from taking place is just as seriously wrong as abortion, and for precisely the same reason. If, as seems plausible, this is not a acceptable view, then one cannot reasonably accept either the original or the modified potentiality principle.

Let us now turn to my second argument against the modified potentiality principle. This argument turns upon the following crucial claim:

> Let C be any type of causal process where there is some type of occurrence, E, such that processes of type C would possess no intrinsic moral significance were it not for the fact that they result in occurrences of type E.

Then,

> The characteristic of being an act of intervening in a process of type C that prevents the occurrence of a outcome of type E makes an action intrinsically wrong to precisely the same degree as does the characteristic of being an act of ensuring that a causal process of type C, which it was in one's power to initiate, does not get initiated.

This principle, which I shall refer to as the moral symmetry principle with respect to action, would be rejected by some philosophers. They would argue that there is an important distinction to be drawn between "what we owe people in the form of aid, and what we owe them in the way of noninterference,"[17] and that the latter, "negative duties," are duties that it is more serious to neglect than the former, "positive" ones. This view arises from an intuitive response to examples such as the following. Even if it is wrong not to send food to starving people in other parts of the world, it is more wrong still to kill someone. And isn't the conclusion, then, that one's obligation to refrain from killing someone is a more serious obligation than one's obligation to save lives?

I want to argue that this is not the correct conclusion. I think that it is tempting to draw this conclusion if one fails to consider the motivation likely to be associated with the respective actions. If someone performs an action he knows will kill someone else, this will usually be good reason for concluding that he wanted the death of the person in question. In contrast, failing to help someone may indicate only apathy, laziness, selfishness, or an amoral outlook: the fact that a person knowingly allows another to die is not normally grounds for concluding that he desired that person's death. Someone who knowingly kills another is thus more likely to be seriously defective from a moral point of view than someone who fails to save another's life.

If we are not to be led to false conclusions by our intuitions about certain cases, we must explicitly assume identical motivations in the two situations. Compare, for example, the following: (1) Jones sees that Smith will be killed by a bomb unless he warns him. Jones' reaction is, "How fortunate, this will save me the trouble of killing Smith myself." So Jones allows Smith to be killed by the bomb, even though he could have easily warned him. (2) Jones wants Smith dead, and therefore shoots him. Is one to say that there is a significant difference between the wrongness of Jones' behavior in these two cases? I suggest that it is not plausible to hold that there is a significant difference here.

If this is right, then it would appear to be a mistake to draw a distinction between positive and negative duties and to hold the latter impose stricter obligations than the former. The differences in our intuitions about situations that involve giving aid to others, and corresponding situations that involve not interfering with others, is to be explained by reference to probable differences in the motivations that are likely to be present in the two sorts of situations, and not by reference to a distinction between positive and negative duties. For once it is specified that the motivation is the same in the two situations, it seems clear that inaction is as wrong in the one case as action is in the other.

There is another point that may be relevant. Action involves effort, whereas inaction usually does not. It does not usually require any effort to refrain from killing someone, but saving someone's life may require a considerable effort. One needs to ask, then, how large a sacrifice a person is morally required to make to save the life of another. If the sacrifice is a very significant one, it may be that one is not morally obliged to save the life of another in that situation. Superficial reflection upon such cases might easily lead one to introduce the distinction between positive and negative duties, but again it seems clear that this would be a mistake. The point is not that one has a greater duty to refrain from killing others than to perform actions that will save them. It is rather that positive actions require effort, and this means that in deciding what to do a person has to take into account his own right to do what he wants with his life, and not only the other person's right to life. In order to avoid this confusion, then, one needs to confine oneself to consideration of situations in which the positive action requires no greater sacrifice than is involved in the inaction.

What I have been arguing, in brief, is this. It is probably true, for example, that most cases of killing are morally worse than most cases of merely letting die. This, however, is not an objection to the moral symmetry principle, since that principle does not imply that, all things considered, acts of killing are, in general, morally on a par with cases of allowing someone to die. What the moral symmetry principle implies is rather that, *other things being equal,* it is just as wrong to fail to save someone as it is to kill someone. If one wants to test this principle against one's moral intuitions, one has to be careful to select pairs of situations in which all other morally relevant factors—such as motivation, and risk to the agent—are equivalent. And I have suggested that when this is done, the moral symmetry principle is by no means counterintuitive.[18]

My argument against the modified potentiality principle can now be stated. Suppose at some future time a chemical were to be discovered which, when injected into the brain of a kitten, would cause the kitten to develop into a cat possessing a brain of the sort possessed by humans, and consequently into a cat having all the psychological capabilities characteristic of normal adult humans. Such cats would be able to think, to use language, and so on. Now it would surely be morally indefensible in such a situation to hold that it is seriously wrong to kill an adult member of the species *Homo sapiens* without also holding that it is wrong to kill any cat that has undergone such a process of development: There would be no morally significant differences.

Second, imagine that one has two kittens, one of which has been injected with a special chemical, but which has not yet developed those properties that in themselves endow something with a right to life, and the other of which has not been injected with the special chemical. It follows from the moral symmetry principle that the action of injecting the former with a "neutralizing" chemical that will interfere with the transformation process and prevent the kitten from developing those properties that in themselves would give it a right to life is prima facie no more seriously wrong than the action of intentionally refraining from injecting the second kitten with the special chemical.

It perhaps needs to be emphasized here that the moral symmetry principle does not imply that neither action is morally wrong. Perhaps both actions are wrong, even seriously so. The moral symmetry principle implies only that if they are wrong, they are so to precisely the same degree.

Third, compare a kitten that has been injected with the special chemical and then had it neutralized, with a kitten that has never been injected with the chemical. It is clear that it is no more seriously wrong to kill the former than to kill the latter. For although their bodies have undergone different processes in the past, there is no reason why the kittens need differ in any way with respect to either their present properties or their potentialities.

Fourth, again consider two kittens, one of which has been injected with the special chemical, but which has not yet developed those properties that in themselves would give it a right to life, and the other of which has not been injected with the chemical. It follows from the previous two steps in the argument that the combined action of injecting the first kitten with a neutralizing chemical and then killing it is no more seriously wrong than the combined action of intentionally refraining from injecting the second kitten with the special chemical and then killing it.

Fifth, one way of neutralizing the action of the special chemical is simply to kill the kitten. And since there is surely no reason to hold that it is more seriously wrong to neutralize the chemical and to kill the kitten in a single step than in two successive steps, it must be the case that it is no more seriously wrong to kill a kitten that has been injected with the special chemical, but which has not developed those properties that in themselves would give it a right to life, than it is to inject such a kitten with a neutralizing chemical and then to kill it.

Next, compare a member of *Homo sapiens* that has not developed far enough to have those properties that in themselves give something a right to life, but which later will come to have them, with a kitten that has been injected with the special chemical but which has not yet had the chance to develop the relevant properties. It is clear that it cannot be any more seriously wrong to kill the human than to kill the kitten. The potentialities are the same in both cases. The only difference is that in the case of a human fetus the potentialities have been present from the beginning of the organism's development, while in the case of the kitten they have been present only from the time it was injected with the special chemical. This difference in the time at which the potentialities were acquired is not a morally relevant one.

It follows from the previous three steps in the argument that it is no more seriously wrong to kill a human being that lacks properties that in themselves, and irrespective of their causal consequences, endow something with a right to life, but which will naturally develop those properties, than it would be to intentionally refrain from injecting a kitten with the special chemical, and to kill it. But if it is the case that normal adult humans do possess properties that in themselves give them a right to life, it follows in virtue of the modified potentiality principle that it is seriously wrong to kill any human organism that will naturally develop the properties in question. Thus, if the modified potentiality principle is sound, we are forced by this argument to conclude that if there were a chemical that would transform kittens into animals having the psychological capabilities possessed by adult humans, it would be seriously wrong to intentionally refrain from injecting kittens with the chemical and to kill them instead.

But is it clear that this final conclusion is unacceptable? I believe that it is. It turns out, however, that this issue is *much* more complex than most people take it to be.[19] Here, however, it will have to suffice to note that the vast majority of people would certainly view this conclusion as unacceptable. For although there are at present no special chemicals that will transform kittens in the required way, there are other biological organisms, namely unfertilized human egg cells, and special chemicals, namely human spermatozoa, that will transform those organisms in the required way. So if one were to hold that it was seriously wrong to intentionally refrain from injecting kittens with the special chemical and instead to kill them, one would also have to maintain that it was prima facie seriously wrong to refrain from injecting human egg cells with spermatozoa, and instead to kill them. So unless the anti-abortionist is prepared to hold that any woman, married or unmarried, does something seriously wrong every month that she intentionally refrains from getting pregnant, he cannot maintain that it would be seriously wrong to refrain from injecting the kitten with the special chemical, and instead to kill it.

In short, the previous argument shows that anyone who wants to defend the original or the modified potentiality principle must either argue against the moral symmetry principle, or hold that in a world in which kittens could be transformed into "rational animals," it would be seriously wrong to kill newborn kittens. But we have just seen that if one accepts the latter claim, one must also hold that it is seriously wrong to intentionally refrain from fertilizing a human egg cell and to kill it instead. Consequently, it seems very likely that any anti-abortionist rejoinder to the present argument will be directed against the moral symmetry principle. In the present essay I have not attempted to offer a thorough defense of that principle, although I have tried to show that what is perhaps the most important objection to it—the one that appeals to a distinction between positive and negative duties—rests upon a superficial analysis of our moral intuitions. Elsewhere, however, I have argued that a thorough examination of the moral symmetry principle sustains the conclusion that that principle is in fact correct.

There is one final point that needs to be made about the present argument, and that is that there are variations of it which do not involve the moral symmetry principle, but which also tell against the anti-abortionist position. These variations are suggested by the reflection that someone not quite convinced, for example, that failing to save is, in itself, just as seriously wrong as killing, may very well accept one of the following, more modest claims:

1. Failing to save someone is, in itself, almost as seriously wrong as killing.

2. Killing and failing to save are *comparable* in the technical sense of there being some number *n* such that failing to save *n* people is in itself, at least as seriously wrong as killing one person.

These claims can be generalized into principles similar to, but less controversial than, the moral symmetry principle. In the case of the second, we have the following, *moral comparability principle*.

Let C be any type of causal process where there is some type of occurrence, E, such that processes of type C would possess no intrinsic moral significance were it not for the fact that they result in occurrences of type E.

Then,

There is some number *n* such that the characteristic of being an act of ensuring that *n* causal processes of type C, which it was within one's power to initiate, do not get initiated, makes an action intrinsically wrong to at least the degree that the characteristic of being an act of intervening in a process of type C which prevents the occurrence of an event of type E does.

Given this moral comparability principle, one way of proceeding is simply to parallel the argument involving the moral symmetry principle. This will lead to the conclusion that there is some number n such that intentionally refraining from fertilizing n human egg cells is in itself at least as seriously wrong as destroying a human before it has acquired those nonpotential properties that would give it a right to life. Then, if it is granted that it is not seriously wrong to refrain from fertilizing n human egg cells, it follows that it is not in itself seriously wrong to destroy a human before it has acquired nonpotential properties that would give it a right to life.

Most people would readily grant the claim that it is not seriously wrong to intentionally refrain from fertilizing n human egg cells. It is worth noting, however, that there is a variant of the argument that avoids this assumption. Consider the moral status of destroying a human organism that has not yet acquired the nonpotential properties that would give it a right to life, and that, if allowed to survive, will lead an unhappy life. The moral comparability principle implies that there is some number n such that the destruction of such an entity is, in itself, no more seriously wrong than intentionally refraining from fertilizing n human egg cells that will result in n individuals who will lead unhappy lives. Since the latter is surely not even wrong, let alone seriously so, it follows that it is not seriously wrong to destroy a human organism that has not yet acquired those nonpotential properties that would give it a right to life, and that, if allowed to survive, will lead an unhappy life.

This variation of the comparability argument has led to a more modest conclusion. However, it is still a conclusion that tells against the view advanced by anti-abortionists, since they reject the claim that abortion is morally permissible in cases where the resulting individual will lead an unhappy life.

To sum up, what I have argued in the present section is this. The anti-abortionist position is defensible only if some version of the potentiality principle is sound. The original version of that principle is incompatible, however, both with the particular-interests principle and with the interest principle, and also with the account of the concept of a right offered above. The modified potentiality principle avoids these problems. There are, however, at least three other serious objections that tell against both the original potentiality principle and the modified one. It would seem, therefore, that there are excellent reasons for rejecting the potentiality principle, and with it, the anti-abortionist position.

SUMMARY AND CONCLUSIONS

In this paper I have advanced three main philosophical contentions:

1. An entity cannot have a right to life unless it is capable of having an interest in its own continued existence.

2. An entity is not capable of having an interest in its own continued existence unless it possesses, at some time, the concept of a continuing self, or subject of experiences and other mental states.

3. The fact that an entity will, if not destroyed, come to have properties that would give it a right to life does not in itself make it seriously wrong to destroy it.

If these philosophical contentions are correct, the crucial question is a factual one: At what point does a developing human being acquire the concept of a continuing self, and at what point is it capable of having an interest in its own continued existence? I have not examined this issue in detail here, but I have suggested that careful scientific studies of human development both behavioral and neurophysiological, strongly support the view that even newborn humans do not have the capacities in question. If this is right, then it would seem that infanticide during a time interval shortly after birth must be viewed as morally acceptable.

But where is the line to be drawn? And what is the precise cutoff point? If one maintained, as some philosophers do, that an individual can possess a concept only if it is capable of expressing that concept linguistically, then it would be a relatively simple matter to determine whether a given organism possessed the concept of a continuing subject of experiences and other mental states. It is far from clear, however, that this claim about the necessary connection between the possession of concepts and the having of linguistic capabilities is correct. I would argue, for example, that one wants to ascribe mental states of a conceptual sort—such as beliefs and desires—to animals that are incapable of learning a language, and that an individual cannot have beliefs and desires unless it possesses the concepts involved in those beliefs and desires. And if that view is right—if an organism can acquire concepts without thereby acquiring a way of expressing those concepts linguistically—then the question of whether an individual possesses the concept of a continuing self may be one that requires quite subtle experimental techniques to answer.

If this view of the matter is roughly correct, there are two worries that one is left with at the level of practical moral decisions, one of which may turn out to be deeply disturbing. The lesser worry is the question just raised: Where is the line to be drawn in the case of infanticide? This is not really a troubling question since there is no serious need to know the exact point at which a human infant acquires a right to life. For in the vast majority of cases in which infanticide is desirable due to serious defects from which the baby suffers, its desirability will be apparent at birth or within a very short time thereafter. Since it seems clear that an infant at this point in its development is not capable of possessing the concept of a continuing subject of experiences and other mental states, and so is incapable of having an interest in its own continued existence, infanticide will be morally permissible in the vast majority of cases in which it is, for one reason or another, desirable. The practical moral problem can thus be satisfactorily handled by choosing some short period of time, such as a week after birth, as the interval during which infanticide will be permitted.

The troubling issue that arises out of these reflections concerns whether adult animals belonging to species other than *Homo sapiens* may not also possess a right to life. For once one allows that an individual can possess concepts, and have beliefs and desires, without being able to express those concepts, or those beliefs and desires, linguistically, then it becomes very much an open question whether animals belonging to other species do not possess properties that give them a right to life. Indeed, I am strongly inclined to think that adult members of at least some nonhuman species do have a right to life. My reason is that, first, I believe that some nonhuman animals are capable of envisaging a future for themselves, and of having desires about future states of themselves. Second, that anything which exercises these capacities has an interest in its own continued existence. And third, that having an interest in one's own continued existence is not merely necessary, but also a sufficient condition, for having a right to life.

The suggestion that at least some nonhuman animals have a right to life is not unfamiliar, but is one that most of us are accustomed to dismissing very casually. The line of thought advanced here suggests that this attitude may very well turn out to be tragically mistaken. Once one reflects upon the question of the *basic* moral principles involved in the ascription of a right to life to organisms, one may find oneself driven to the conclusion that our everyday treatment of members of other species is morally indefensible and that we are in fact murdering innocent persons.

STUDY QUESTIONS

1. What are the four questions that Tooley considers in Section II of his essay and how does he address each question?

2. What, according to Tooley, is the morally relevant difference between a fetus and a normal adult person? What implications does this criterion have for infants?

3. What is the "interest principle"? Do you agree with Feinberg's analysis? Discuss possible criticisms. For example: Why can't a tree have an interest in having light and nutrition to grow properly? or What if I don't care about what really is in my interest?

4. Assess the overall strengths and weaknesses of Tooley's argument.

NOTES

1. My book, *Abortion and Infanticide* (Oxford University Press, 1983), contains a detailed examination of other important objections.

2. Judith Jarvis Thomson, in her article "A Defense of Abortion," *Philosophy & Public Affairs* 1, 1971, 47–66, argues very forcefully for the view that this conclusion is incorrect. For a critical discussion of her argument, see Chapter 3 of *Abortion and Infanticide.*

3. America Law Institute, *Model Penal Code* (Philadelphia, 1962), section 230.3.

4. *Abortion and Infanticide,* Chapter 10.

5. In *Philosophy and Environmental Crisis,* ed. William T. Blackstone Athens, Ga, 1974, 43–68.

6. Ibid., 51.

7. Ibid.,. 49–50

8. Ibid., 51.

9. *Abortion and Infanticide,* section 5.2.

10. For a fuller discussion, and defense of this principle, see ibid., section 5.3.

11. For a detailed survey of the scientific evidence concerning human development, see ibid., section 11.5.

12. Ibid., section 11.42.

13. For a brief discussion, see Joseph F. Donceel, "A Liberal Catholic's View," *Abortion in a Changing World,* 1, ed. R. E. Hal. New York, 1970. A more detailed philosophical discussion can be found in Donceel's "Immediate Animation and Delayed Hominization," *Theological Studies,* 31, 1970, 76–105.

14. Consider the belief that it is prima facie wrong to pull cats' tails. Here is a belief that is almost universally accepted, but very few people, if any, would regard it as a basic moral belief. For this belief rests upon a nonmoral belief, to the effect that pulling cats' tails causes them pain. If one came to believe that cats actually enjoy this, one would abandon the moral belief in question. So the belief, though widely and firmly accepted, is a derived moral belief, rather than a basic one.

15. For a much more extended discussion of this point, see, for example, Peter Singer's essay, "Animals and the Value of Life," *Matters of Life and Death,* ed. by Tom Regan (Philadelphia, 1980), or my own discussion in section 4.2 of *Abortion and Infanticide.*

16. *Abortion and Infanticide,* section 7.33.

17. Philippa Foot, "The Problem of Abortion and the Doctrine of the Double Effect," *The Oxford Review,* 5 (1967): 5–15. *See* the discussion of 11ff.

18. For a much more detailed defense of this view, see section 6.5 of *Abortion and Infanticide.*

19. A discussion of why this is so can be found in Chapter 7 of *Abortion and Infanticide.*

13

The Scope of the Prohibition Against Killing

PHILIP DEVINE

Philip Devine is Professor of Philosophy at Providence College in Providence, Rhode Island. Devine asks what kind of beings are protected by the rule against homicide. He examines three principles that specify the scope of the protection principle: (1) the species principle (any member of the human species is protected); (2) the present enjoyment principle (only those beings—human and nonhuman—who possess actual capacities, such as the ability to reason, are protected); and (3) the potentiality principle (any member of any species who has the potential for possessing the property designated in Principle 2. Devine, specifically mentioning Michael Tooley, rejects Principle 2 and ends up with a synthesis of Principles 1 and 3, which are adequate to provide a general anti-abortion thesis. Devine admits that grey areas exist, but in general and normally, abortion is immoral, for the fetus belongs to the human species and, in the normal course of things, will develop into a self-conscious, rational being.

What kinds of creatures, I shall be asking, constitute the class whose members the moral rule against homicide protects? What is the status of normal human fetuses and infants? of human defectives? of robots and androids? of dolphins and chimpanzees? Is it even prima facie wrong to kill such creatures, and if so, need the justifications for killing them be as compelling as those required to warrant killing a normal adult human? These questions are important not only for the ethics of homicide, but for ethics generally, since if a creature has no right not to be killed, it cannot have any other serious rights

Reprinted from *The Ethics of Homicide* (Ithaca, New York, Cornell University Press 1978) by permission. The editors removed footnotes as we edited the text.

in contexts where its interests and those of persons are in conflict. Such a conflict could always be resolved by killing the troublesome creature.

In what follows, I distinguish three principles of interpretation determining the limits of the moral rule against homicide and other moral rules protecting distinctively human rights. One of these, the *species principle,* will be founded on the kinship or solidarity that obtains among members of the same species. It seems best understood as a more precise version of the "Standard Belief" that Roger Wertheimer attributes to nearly everyone: that what warrants the ascription of human moral status to a creature is simply that creature's being human. (I say a more precise version, since Wertheimer believes that one can deny that a biologically human creature is a member of "the family of man," although why he thinks this is not completely clear.) The second, the *present enjoyment* (or *present possession) principle,* rests on the ability of human beings to assert their personhood by appeals or resistance. And the third, the *potentiality principle,* rests on the uniquely rich kinds of action and experience of which human beings are capable, and the uniquely severe loss suffered when the prospect of such life is frustrated, whether or not the organism whose existence has been ended or whose capacity for such life has been impaired has had some experience of it. The potentiality and present enjoyment principles seem best viewed as attempts to replace the Standard Belief with something thought more satisfactory. Our choice among these principles will determine our judgment of the moral status of fetuses, infants, and the moribund, and thus make a crucial difference to our judgments concerning abortion, infanticide, and euthanasia.

1. THE SPECIES PRINCIPLE

A first statement of the species principle as it applies to killing is as follows: Those creatures protected by the moral rule against homicide are the members of the human species, and only the members of the human species. This version of the principle protects all human organisms, whatever their degree of maturity or decay, including fetuses and embryos, but not robots or nonhuman animals, whatever the attainments of such beings might be.

The species principle does not mean, as Joseph Fletcher thinks, that "we would be human if we have opposable thumbs, are capable of face-to-face coitus and have a brain weighing 1,400 grams, whether a particular brain functions cerebrally or not." Obviously a creature might be morally and biologically human while lacking one of these traits—say a child born without hands (and thus without thumbs)—and it is easy to imagine a species that met the suggested criteria without being in any sense human. Membership in a biological species is a complex matter, but scientists are now well able to recognize biological humanity in the fine structure of an organism, without reference to such things as opposable thumbs. Jerome Lejeune puts the point nicely:

Let us take the example of trisomy 21 [a chromosome disorder], observed by amniocentesis. Looking at the chromosomes and detecting the extra 21, we say very safely "The child who will develop here will be a trisomic 21." But this phrase does not convey all the information. We have not seen only the extra 21; we have also seen all the 46 other chromosomes and concluded that they were human, because if they had been mouse or monkey chromosomes, we would have noticed.

In other words, even a human defective is a defective *human,* and this biological humanity is recognizable in the genetic structure of the organism even when the genetic structure itself is defective.

Some vagueness does afflict the species principle when it comes to deciding precisely when—at conception or shortly thereafter, when the unity and uniqueness of the nascent creature is secured—a human organism comes into existence, as well as how much breakdown is necessary before we say that a human organism has ceased to be. Ape-human hybrids and the like also pose a knotty problem. But none of these zones of vagueness render the principle unusable, nor do they provide any grounds for refusing to use the principle to condemn killing where the victim is unambiguously a human organism.

Finally, the species principle provides an adequate answer to the "acorn" argument, which has a surprising persistence in disputes about abortion. Whatever may be the case with dormant acorns, a germinating acorn is, while not an oak *tree,* still a member of the appropriate species of oak. If oaks had a serious right to life in their own right, so would oak saplings and germinating acorns. And the same reply can be made to those who would argue about abortion from the premise that a caterpillar is not a butterfly....

A more troubling charge is that of species chauvinism: the charge, that is, that the giving of a higher moral status to members of one's own species than to those of others is akin to regarding members of other races as subhuman. It would not be chauvinism in the strict sense to argue that between two intelligent species, members of one have no rights that members of the other are bound to respect, while each agent is morally required to respect the rights of members of his own species, in particular not to kill them unless he has a very compelling justification. It is, after all, considered worse (all other things being equal) to kill one's brother than a stranger, not because one's brother in himself is morally more worthy than the stranger, but because the relationship between brothers is itself morally significant. Nonetheless we would certainly want intelligent Martians to respect our rights, and might be prepared to respect theirs in return. And, if Martians were enough like human beings that the notion of human individuality could be extended to them, this respect for their rights would naturally take the form, *inter alia,* of regarding Martians as protected by our moral (and quite possibly our legal) rules against homicide.

But this line of thought can be accommodated by a modification of the species principle that does not alter its essential structure. According to this modification, what the moral rule against homicide protects is all members of intelligent species, including, but not limited to, the human. On this account determining whether a given creature is protected by the moral rule against homicide is a two-step process: first, identifying the species to which the creature belongs, and, second, deciding whether this species is in fact intelligent. For members of the human species, the human species continues to play a somewhat paradigmatic role, in setting the standard of intelligence that must be approached or exceeded for a species to be considered intelligent, and the same is true for members of other intelligent species. A human being will ask whether Martians as a species are intelligent enough by human standards to be regarded as persons, and an intelligent Martian will make the corresponding inquiry concerning human beings. In any case, all creatures protected by the original species principle are protected by the modified species principle as well.

Three problems of application arise for the modified species principle, of particular importance in assessing the claims that might be made on behalf of chimpanzees, whales, and dolphins. First, supposing one member of a species reaches the human level, what effect does this achievement have on the status of the other members of the species? Second, what kind of standards are to be employed in determining whether a given species is to be regarded as intelligent? Since we cannot, in answering these questions, rely on the considerations of lineage that settle nearly all questions of species membership, they will require very careful examination.

It seems that we want to regard an individual cat that has, through some chance or other, attained human intelligence as protected by the moral rule against homicide. To do so consistently with the species principle requires the adoption of one of two strategies: (1) the existence of such a cat renders the entire species *Felis domestica* an intelligent species, and all of its members protected by the moral rule against homicide (consider the plea such a cat might make on behalf of its less intelligent brethren) or (2) the intelligence of our super-cat might be considered as producing a different species, consisting of him alone, although he is still capable of breeding fertilely with other, less favored, cats. (He may wish to disassociate himself from other cats, and feel humiliated by his bodily likeness to subhuman creatures.) The first of these strategies would be plausible for the claims of dolphins and the like, all of which at least come somewhat close to human intelligence. The second would be more plausible for the claims of cats and dogs.

The second question is what traits are decisive for regarding a given individual as rendering his species intelligent. Self-consciousness (or consciousness of oneself as a subject of conscious states) might be suggested, as a necessary condition of the desire to live. Moral agency is another contender, since moral agents are presupposed by moral discourse as such. Finally, the use of language is the key to the rich kind of life enjoyed by human beings, so that it may be taken as what distinguishes the human from the subhuman. An attractive blend of these last two possibilities is participation in moral discourse: If we discover that Martians argue about the issues discussed in this book, we should be obliged to regard them for moral purposes as human.

The question of which traits are crucial is less important for the species than for other interpretations of the moral rule against homicide, since no attempt is made to draw lines within the human species. But even here it may be crucial—especially on some interpretations of what it is to speak a language—to the status of some nonhumans such as chimpanzees. What seems to be the case is that the distinction between human and nonhuman rests not on any one trait, but on an interlocking set of traits, that will wax and wane as a whole.

Finally, we need to ask (supposing that the relevant traits admit of degree) how much of them is required to make a species one of the human level. (If they do not, we will still have to adjudicate borderline cases.) It is worth noticing that our standards can be more demanding here than for either of the species principle's two rivals. In order to reach minimally tolerable results, the present enjoyment principle will have to demand very little of a creature before treating it as a person; the potentiality principle can ask for more, since what the creature will attain in due course, not what it attains now, is the standard. But the species principle can demand the production of saints, philosophers, musicians, scientists, or whatever else is thought to be the highest embodiment of human nature, since the bulk of the species can gain their morally privileged status through the achievements of their best members, so long as there is not a sharp break between the capacities of the best of a species and members of that species generally.

2. THE PRESENT ENJOYMENT PRINCIPLE

The appeal of the species principle, especially as modified and expanded to encompass intelligent nonhumans, to those who are prepared to be generous in their ascriptions of personhood is very great. To the extent, for instance, that we are prepared to regard even the most hopelessly retarded human being as a person, and the killing of such a one as murder, the species principle appears to provide the only plausible grounds for so doing. And even when its full effect is denied, the species principle still has important residues: Many who are prepared to defend both abortion and capital punishment balk at the execution of pregnant women, and some defenders of abortion also disapprove of experiments on live aborted "fetuses," as well as experiments on fetuses *in utero* when abortion is intended. And even if we were prepared to admit that the hopelessly retarded might be painlessly killed rather than cared for, still we would be most reluctant to countenance the use of such creatures for the kinds of experiments that are performed on animals, or their being killed for food. Finally, to the extent that we tend to think that there are organisms of the human species that may rightfully be treated as other than human—that may, for instance, be killed to relieve us of the burden of caring for and feeding them—we think in terms of human vegetables, not human brutes. The latter is quite as logical from the standpoint of a denial of the species principle.

Many, however, are not prepared to be so generous in extending the protection of the moral rule against homicide. Nor is this surprising, for the admission that a given creature is a person is morally very expensive and becomes more so as the lists of human rights grow longer. And caring for those who are persons on the species principle frequently places burdens on those who are persons on narrower principles, of which an unwanted pregnancy may be taken as emblematic. It is therefore well worth asking whether a narrower version of the rule against homicide is possible, one, that is, which is not merely an ad hoc modification of the rule designed to allow us to kill those whose existence we find particularly burdensome.

An obvious possibility is to drop the reference to the species and to require that a creature be in present possession of distinctively human traits before the killing of such a creature will be deemed homicide. Assuming that what we value human beings for is their capacities for rational and social life, perhaps we should place the kind of value that grounds the moral rule against homicide only on those that (now) have these capacities. Or again, we may be impressed by the various ways human beings (and not animals) insist on respect for their rights (including the right not to be killed) and feel that those who are incapable of making such appeals (or engaging in such resistance) do not deserve to be treated as persons. Let us call this principle the present enjoyment principle....

The most striking conflict between the present enjoyment principle and our intuitions—the implication of the principle that infants have no right to live—arises in the specific context of debates about abortion. Many such debates have been conducted within limits imposed by agreed-upon judgments concerning contraception and infanticide. Contraception, it has been agreed, is a morally legitimate way of avoiding undesired parenthood, and infanticide is not. The participants in the controversy have limited themselves to arguing that abortion (or a practice on the borderline between contraception and abortion) is more closely analogous to contraception than to infanticide, or more closely analogous to infanticide than to contraception. But some defenders of abortion have conceded—or even, like Tooley, insisted on and argued for—what has hitherto been the principal contention of opponents of abortion, that abortion and infanticide are essentially the same and maintained that there are no good grounds for regarding infanticide as a violation of anyone's right to live.

I shall be considering Tooley's views in some detail, since by his willingness to carry the case against fetal rights to its logical extreme, he manages to present the issues underlying the abortion debate with more than ordinary clarity. An examination of the arguments employed by those who have rested their defense of abortion on the fact that the fetus (and not the woman) is unable to envisage a future for itself, talk, enter into social relations, and so on, will show that their premises are brought to their logical conclusion in Tooley's articles.

I shall not here attempt a direct proof that Tooley is wrong, and that infants have a right to live, but shall limit myself to showing that Tooley's attempt to show that the infant cannot be correctly ascribed a right to live (that is, accorded the protection of the moral rule against homicide) does not succeed. How serious a limitation this is on a moral case against infanticide depends on one's view of the relationship between moral principles formulated by philosophers and socially established moral intuitions of a relatively concrete sort. In my view, the concrete intuitions embodied in our laws and customs, at least insofar as they are shared by the philosopher in his prereflective moments, are entitled to at least as much weight as the moral principles he finds plausible when they are stated in an abstract manner.

Hence, the feeling that exists against infanticide among persons of widely varying religious, political, and cultural attitudes will be taken as a datum for our inquiry. If it persistently resists attempts to accommodate it within our moral theories, we may be entitled to reject it. But if the arguments of this chapter are sound, we have no good reason to abandon our intuitions in this case.

The acceptability of an appeal to socially current intuitions may well be the chief issue between defenders of infanticide and me. But I think it can be shown that it is reasonable to appeal to such intuitions, and unreasonable to bar such appeals. That our moral intuitions are shaped by others—our parents, teachers, peers, and so on—before we are capable of thinking about morality for ourselves, I do not deny. But to regard this fact as in some way constituting an argument for the conclusion that the beliefs and attitudes so formed are as likely to be false as true is to deprive ourselves of any basis whatever for a moral theory. For there are indefinitely many moral theories, the doctrine that right conduct consists in maximizing pain and minimizing pleasure for instance, which are never seriously entertained by philosophers because they deviate so wildly from the moral intuitions shared by the philosopher and his community. And there are results, such as that it is our duty to kill as many people painlessly as we can, which suffice to invalidate even the most superficially attractive moral theory if they follow from this theory as a result. Moreover, to argue that a moral intuition is suspect because of its source in family or social life is to render one's moral conclusions irrelevant to that life, and thus to moral problems as human beings in fact experience them....

What I have done so far is to expound the species principle, and to state and give grounds for rejecting the present enjoyment principle. In particular, I have argued that there is no good reason to deny, as holders of the present enjoyment principle must, that infants have a right to live in principle no different from that enjoyed by adults. With this background, we are prepared to confront the question of abortion.

3. THE POTENTIALITY PRINCIPLE

I now turn to an exposition of and defense of the potentiality principle, an attempt to do justice to the competing claims of the potentiality and species principles, and an argument that at least the central cases of abortion are morally unacceptable.

I shall assume here that infants are protected by the moral rule against homicide. From this assumption it seems to follow immediately that fetuses, and other instances of human life from conception onward, are also so protected, so that, unless justified or mitigated, abortion is murder. For there seem to be only two possible grounds for asserting the humanity of the infant: (1) The infant is a member of the human species (species principle). (2) The infant will, in due course, think, talk, love, and have a sense of justice (potentiality principle). And both (1) and (2) are true of fetuses, embryos, and zygotes, as well as of infants. A zygote is alive (it grows) and presumably is an instance of the species *Homo sapiens* (of what other species might it be?), and it will, if nothing goes wrong, develop into the kind of creature that is universally conceded to be a person.

But a number of arguments still have to be answered before the humanity or personhood of the fetus can be asserted with confidence. All of them are reflected in, and lend plausibility to, Joel Feinberg's remark: "To assert that a single-cell zygote, or a tiny cluster of cells, as such, is a complete human being already possessed of all the rights of a developed person seems at least as counter-intuitive as the position into which some liberals [defenders of abortion] are forced, that newly born infants have no right to continue living." These arguments are (1) that if a fetus is a person because of its potential and its biological humanity, spermatozoa and ova must also be considered persons, which is absurd; (2) that personhood is something one acquires gradually, so that a fetus is only imperfectly a person; and (3) that there is an adequately defensible dividing point between the human and the nonhuman, the personal and the nonpersonal, that enables us to defend abortion (or "early" abortion) without being committed to the defense of infanticide.

1. Michael Tooley argues that if it is seriously wrong to kill infants or fetuses because they potentially possess human traits, it must also be seriously wrong to prevent systems of objects from developing into an organism possessing self-consciousness, so that artificial contraception will be just as wrong as infanticide. But only organisms can have a right to life, although something more like an organism than a mere concatenation of sperm and egg might have a right to something like life. And the same point can be reached if we speak not in terms of a right to life but of a moral rule against certain kinds of killing, for only an organism can be killed.

There is another, more complicated, argument against the contention that a spermatozoon and an ovum, not united, might be protected by the moral rule against homicide (or would be if infants and fetuses were). Since the moral rule against homicide is a rule that protects rights, it cannot obtain unless there is some specifiable individual whose rights would be violated were it breached. A sperm conjoined with an ovum in this way is not in any sense an individual; therefore it cannot have any rights. For this reason the prevention of such a combination's being fruitful cannot be a violation of the moral rule against homicide. An ejaculation contains many more spermatozoa than could possibly be united with ova, and it is difficult to see the sperm-plus-ovum combinations that do not prevail as somehow deprived of something on which they have a claim.

But it is hard to reject all rights-claims made on behalf of inchoate subjects. It is commonly held to be prima facie wrong to exterminate entire species of animals, and such a wrong could be committed without destroying any individual animal (for example, by rendering all members of the species sterile). It seems that many of us want to accord to the species as such a right to continue in existence as a species. (Compare the notion that genocide, the destruction of an entire race or ethnic group, is a crime over and above, and indeed apart from, the destruction of individual members of such a group.) How seriously we take talk of the rights of species depends on how seriously we take the interests of species. It will not do to refuse to admit the existence of such interests on the grounds that "a whole collection, as such, cannot have beliefs, expectations, wants, or desires," since such conditions are not necessary to the existence of interests. We can easily view the perpetuation of a species through its characteristic mode of reproduction as an act, not only of the individual organisms that engage in reproductive activity, but also of the species itself, acting through its members. It is thus possible to attribute an aim of preserving itself to the species as a whole and to see this aim as frustrated when a species becomes extinct.

If so, it seems also that human beings have at least a general duty to procreate, to the extent that it would be wrong to encompass, or to adopt maxims that entail, the dying-out of the human species. (What I have in mind are those who hold that truly virtuous or enlightened persons will abstain from sexual activity or reproduction, a view which has the result that the human species will be continued by fools or sinners, if by anyone.) Thus, it seems, unrealized human possibilities do have some sort of claim on us. Still, the distinction between an individual organism and an unrealized possibility of such an organism is surely great enough to block any attempt to bring such unrealized possibilities within the scope of the moral rule against homicide.

One can reply similarly to the contention that, since every cell in the body is a potential person (by cloning), and no very great moral weight attaches to the cells in the body, no very great moral weight attaches to potential persons. But even with cloning, an ordinary human cell is not only a merely potential person. it is also a merely potential organism. Belief that creatures that are potentially personal are persons is not the same as believing that anything from which such a creature might arise is also a person. One might, in view of the possibility of cloning, argue that a one-celled zygote is only a potential organism, essentially no different from an ovum or an ordinary cell, but the embryo and the fetus are clearly actual organisms, even if they are supposed to be merely potential persons. Hence, if to be potentially personal is to be a person, they are actual persons as well.

Spermatozoa and ova might be said to be living individuals in a sense. But it is clear that a spermatozoon cannot be considered a member of the human species or a being potentially possessing the traits we regard as distinctively human in the way a fetus or infant can. A developed human being issuing from a sperm alone is a possibility far outside the normal powers of the spermatozoon in the way a developed human being issuing from a fetus or infant is not outside the normal powers of those creatures.

The case of the ovum is more complicated, since parthenogenesis, reproduction from the ovum alone, takes place in at least some species. But, apart from considerations involving twinning and recombination (to be discussed below), fertilization still remains a relative bright line available for distinguishing prehuman organic matter from the developing human organism. Finally, we must remember that sperm and ovum are biologically parts of *other* human individuals (the parents).

2. Perhaps, however, it is a mistake to look for a bright line between prehuman organic matter and a developing human being or person. Perhaps personhood is a quality the developing human creature acquires gradually. This suggestion will always have a considerable appeal to the moderate-minded. For it avoids the harshness, or seeming harshness, of those who would require great suffering on the part of the woman carrying a fetus for the sake of that fetus's rights, while avoiding also the crudity of those who regard abortion as of no greater moral significance than cutting one's toenails, having a tooth pulled, or swatting a fly. Moreover, that abortion is morally less desirable the closer it is to birth—and not simply because a late abortion is more likely to harm the woman—is one of the few intuitions widely shared on all sides of the abortion controversy, and thus not to be despised. That abortion should become harder and harder to justify as pregnancy proceeds, without being ever as hard to justify as is the killing of a person, is a suggestion which ought therefore to be given the most serious attention.

The gradualist suggestion raises a problem of quite general scope. Not only as regards the distinction between prehuman organic matter and a human person, but also as regards that between human beings and brute animals, and that between a dying person and a corpse, our thought is pulled in two different directions. On the one hand, we find it natural to look for sharp, if not radical, breaks between different kinds of being, for evolutionary quanta so to speak. On the other hand, we are suspicious of sharp breaks and look for continuities at every point in nature. On a merely theoretical level, Kant's suggestion—that we regard the principle of continuity and the principle of speciation as regulative ideals or heuristic principles that, although contradictory if asserted together, are nonetheless useful in prompting the advance of knowledge; in other words, that we should look at both continuities and gaps—is most attractive. But it is of very little use to us here.

For what we are looking for is a way of making abortion decisions that offers some hope of rational agreement. And there seems to be no stable, nonarbitrary way of correlating stages of fetal development with justifying grounds. At the stage of development when the embryo most closely resembles a fish, the moderate on the abortion question will want to ascribe it stronger rights than he does fish, but weaker rights than he does full human beings. And the moderate, as I conceive him, regards an infant as a human person, though the difference between a human infant and an infant ape is not palpable. Turning to "indications," it is far from clear why incestuous conception, for instance, plays the kind of role it does in justifying abortion to many moderates.

There is a form of the moderate position that seems to escape this line of attack. Marvin Kohl defines and defends a "moderate feminist" view of abortion, according to which "a living potential human being has the prima facie right to life but…the actual right may be reasonably denied in cases of abortion on request." In other words, although the killing of a fetus requires justification, any reason that might prompt a woman to request an abortion is sufficient.

Kohl concedes that there is nothing in his view to prevent a woman from having an abortion for no reason at all, or more precisely, nothing in his view to permit Kohl to disapprove such abortions. But he sees no need for such a preventative. To suppose that a significant number of women will have frivolous abortions, thinks Kohl, is to be guilty of "the most deadly anti-women bias of all, namely: that unless women are carefully controlled they will kill their own progeny without reason because they are not fully rational creatures." In this way, Kohl combines a moderate assessment of the fetus with an avoidance of line-drawing. The issue of how much justification is required for killing a fetus is left to the good sense and discretion of the pregnant woman.

There are three answers to Kohl here: one qualitative, one quantitative, and one conceptual. The qualitative point is that while it is of course extremely unlikely that a woman will have an abortion for a lark, there is also evidence that women and couples (I do not know what Kohl considers a significant number) will sometimes request abortions for uncompelling reasons. There have been reports of women having abortions because the child turned out to be of the "wrong" sex and because a one-in-twenty chance of a cleft lip was diagnosed. Quantitatively, where permissive attitudes toward abortion prevail, the number of abortions has been known to exceed the number of live births. To defend such results one has to abandon all pretense of moderation about abortion and contend that the fetus has no right to live, even a prima facie one, against its mother. For—and this is the conceptual point— there is a connection between the concept of a right and the maxim that no one shall be judge in his own cause. I should remark in conclusion that I do not regard either women or men as fully rational beings. A writer on ethics who denies the irrational (even perverse) side of the human make-up, including his own, is doomed to irrelevance. In any case, questions of sexual bias, however important they may be in other contexts, are of very little relevance here. For the unborn, at least as much as women, may be victims of prejudice.

Moreover, if personhood or humanity admits of degrees before birth, then it would seem that it must admit of degrees after birth as well. And even if we can manage to block such inferences as that kings are more persons than peasants, Greeks more than barbarians, men more than women (or women more than men), or those with Ph.D.'s more than those with M.A.'s, according to this theory we should still expect that adults will be considered more fully human than children. But few hold and fewer still teach that a ten-year-old child can be killed on lighter grounds than an adult. Indeed the killing of small children is often considered worse than the killing of adults. (Although a parent who kills his child is likely to receive a less severe sentence than someone who kills an adult, this remnant of the *patria potestas* is the result of excuse or mitigation rather than of justification.)…

3. We are now prepared to address the question of the homicidal character of abortion head on. If we assume the personhood of the human infant when born, is there a point later than fertilization when the life of a human person may be said to begin?

a. One possible dividing point is that stage at which twinning, and the combination of two developing zygotes to form one organism, is no longer possible. If something that we could not help but regard as a person were to split, or merge with another person, in such a manner, we would be compelled, in order to ascertain what (if anything) was the continuation of our original person, to rely on such criteria as memory and character. Bodily continuity would not give an unambiguous result. But since a developing zygote has neither memory nor character, we are left without means of resolving questions of personal identity. The potentiality of acquiring memory or character may suffice to ground a claim of personhood, but only with an organism whose unity and uniqueness is firmly secured.

One can hardly leave the question in this state, however, since the question of dividing (and fusing) selves cuts very deep into the contested question of personal identity. Faced with the possibility of a dividing self, there are, I think, three different possible responses. One can employ such a possibility to undermine our idea of a person, of one being persisting throughout the human life span. Such a course would seem to overthrow a great deal of our moral universe, not least our ethics of homicide. A second strategy is the heroic course of regarding the self before a division as in fact two selves, so that each subsequent self will have the whole pre-split history as part of its past. The implausibility of this position need hardly be labored. The third possibility treats the question of who a given person is (in split cases) as relative to the temporal perspective from which the question is asked. Asked from before the split, the question leads us to pick out a Y-shaped "lifetime," including the pre-split self, and both subsequent branches. Asked from the perspective of afterwards, the question leads us to pick out one of the post-split selves, including the pre-split self as part of its history. The labored quality of this solution means that it can coexist with our concept of a person only when splits remain extraordinary (or a mere possibility): it is a precondition of the kind of language of selves that we have that selves normally neither split nor fuse. Hence there is a legitimate presumption against positions that require us to admit splitting or fusing selves, and hence also the capacity for fission and fusion enjoyed by the one-celled zygote is a legitimate moral difference between it and an infant or older embryo that warrants our regarding it as not a person. It hardly seems plausible to regard a distinction linked to our very concept of a person as arbitrary.

If this cut-off point is accepted, we are committed to the existence of bits of human biological material that are neither human organisms, nor parts of human organisms, but things that are becoming human organisms. But this of itself provides no warrant for extending the category of "human becoming" to embryos and fetuses generally. For the behavior of the zygote is quite clearly an anomaly, and any way we choose to deal with it is going to produce some degree of conceptual discomfort. At least where the context is an ethical one, the category of "human becoming" seems to be the least uncomfortable way of dealing with the problem. But being an embryo can still be part of the life cycle of members of the human species, as being a caterpillar is part of the life cycle of members of various species of butterfly. For the justification present in the zygotic case for introducing an anomalous concept is not present in the embryonic one.

b. None of the other proposed intra-uterine dividing points is in the end credible. The beginning of heart or brain activity gains its plausibility from the criteria of death, but the cessation of such activity is a criterion of death only because it is irreversible: When, as in the embryonic case, such activity will begin in due course, there is no reason to regard its absence as decisive on the personhood issue. Growth alone, combined with the possibility of future activity, seems sufficient to justify the finding that the distinctively human kind of life is present, unless we are able to find some other reason for denying the immature embryo the status of a person, or are prepared to revert to the present enjoyment principle and treat infants as well as fetuses as subpersonal.

Writing in defense of a brain-activity criterion, Baruch Brody asks,

> Imagine the following science-fiction case: Imagine that medical technology has reached the stage at which, when brain death occurs, the brain is removed, "liquefied," and "recast" into a new functioning brain. The new brain bears no relation to the old one (it has none of its memory traces and so on). If the new brain were put back into the old body, would the same human being exist or a new human being who made use of the body of the old one? I am inclined to suppose the latter. But consider the entity whose body has died. Is he not like the fetus? Both have the potential for developing into an entity with a functioning brain (we shall call this a weak potential) but neither now has the structure of a functioning brain.

The answer is that there is this crucial distinction between the two sorts of "weak potential." The weak potential of the fetus includes genetic information, with which the fetus will, in due course, generate a brain of its own. The weak potential of a brain-dead individual is merely the capacity to sustain a brain that can be imposed on it from the outside.

Of course, the absence of brain activity means that the unborn organism is not conscious, but once again this lack of consciousness, being merely temporary, has no decisive moral weight. Conversely, the responses to stimuli observed in very young embryos do not of themselves establish personhood—that must rest on the capacity for distinctively human development—whether or not these responses indicate consciousness in the usual sense. They do, however, like human form, provide a possible basis for sympathy....

c. Although birth is given considerable significance by our law and conventional morality (otherwise this section would not have to be written), it is still difficult to see how it can be treated as morally decisive. Considered as a shift from one sort of dependency to another, I believe it has little moral importance. The severance of the umbilical cord removes the child, not from the body of his mother, but from the placenta, an organ of his own for which he has no further use The social and administrative importance of birth is well accounted for in terms of practicality and discretion irrelevant to the abortion issue One example is the reckoning of United States citizenship from birth rather than conception; another is the practice of not counting fetuses in the census.

And the grounds given by H. Tristram Engelhardt for distinguishing between fetus and infant, "that the mother-fetus relationship is not an instance of a generally established social relation," whereas "the infant, in virtue of being able to assume the role "child," is socialized in terms of this particular role, and a personality is *imputed* to it," are in fact an argument for drawing the line some time, say twenty-four hours, after birth. It would be possible to postpone the imputation of personality (signalized by naming) for such a period in order to look for defects and decide whether to kill the infant or spare it. On the assumption, argued for in [Section I], that newborn infants are persons, Engelhardt's argument must therefore be rejected.

Finally, treating birth as the dividing point between the human and the nonhuman places a rationally indefensible premium on modes of abortion designed to kill the unborn infant within the womb, since once removed from the womb a fetus is born, and thus human by the suggested criterion, and is therefore entitled to be kept alive if prospects of success exist. Some might try to get around this by stipulating that whether a creature of the human species counts as an infant (with a right to life) or an abortus (which doesn't have one) depends on the intentions with which it is delivered. This kind of proposal seems quite arbitrary, however....

4. CLARIFYING THE POTENTIALITY PRINCIPLE

The case just made for regarding the fetus or embryo as a human person does not depend on identifying a person with a human organism. One could ascribe personhood to members of other intelligent species, and deny it to so-called human vegetables, while ascribing it to the (normal) fetus. The underlying premise of such an ascription is what has been called the potentiality principle.

Like the species principle, but unlike the present enjoyment principle, the potentiality principle accounts quite without difficulty for our ascription of humanity to infants and the unconscious and requires ascribing humanity to fetuses as well. According to this principle, there is a property, self-consciousness or the use of speech for instance, such that (i) it is possessed by adult humans, (ii) it endows any organism possessing it with a serious right to life, and (iii) it is such that any organism potentially possessing it has a serious right to life even now—where an organism possesses a property potentially if it will come to have that property under normal conditions for development. It is often convenient to speak of those who are regarded as persons under the potentiality principle, but not under the present enjoyment principle, as "potential persons." But this usage is misleading. For even a normal, awake adult can be thought of as a person for essentially the same reasons as an embryo: Both are capable of using speech and so on, although the embryo's capacity requires the more time and care before it is realized.

Notice that, whereas the potentiality principle in terms extends a right to live to all creatures potentially possessing self-consciousness or the use of speech, it could be narrowed to require that such organisms also possess certain additional properties $P_1 \ldots P_n$ (for example, exclusion of twinning, the presence of brain activity, or existence outside the uterus) to have a right to live. A defender of a narrowed version of the principle would, of course, have to show that the additional properties $P_1 \ldots P_n$ provided a morally relevant reason to ascribe rights to those having them and to deny rights to those not possessing them. I have had occasion to consider the merits of some suggestions along these lines above.

The basis of the potentiality principle is quite simple: What makes the difference between human beings and other life is the capacity human beings enjoy for a specially rich kind of life. The life already enjoyed by a human being cannot be taken away from him, only the prospect of such life in the future. But this prospect is possessed as much by an infant or fetus as by a full-grown adult. But it is not possessed by the irreversibly comatose, and thus they are morally speaking dead from the standpoint of the potentiality principle.

Tooley motivates his rejection of the potentiality principle by citing what he calls the Frankenstein example:

> Let us suppose that technology has advanced to the point, first, where it is possible to construct humans in the laboratory from inorganic compounds. Second, that it is possible to freeze animals, including humans, and then to thaw them out without damaging them. Third, that it is possible to program beliefs, desires, personality traits, and so on into an organism by bringing about certain brain states. Given these technological advances, suppose that we put together an adult human in the laboratory, carrying out the construction at a temperature at which the organism is frozen. We program in some happy set of beliefs, desires, and personality traits. If we now thaw out this organism we will have a conscious, adult human with beliefs, desires, and a distinct personality. But what if, as a result of all this work, we have developed ravenous appetites, and rather than thawing out the organism, we grind it up for hamburgers. Our action might be economically unwise and subject to culinary objections, but would it be open to moral criticism? In particular, would we be guilty of murdering an innocent person? I think most people would say the answer is no.

One reason those who consider such a case are likely to give for regarding such a creature (which I shall call a frozen android) as not a person is that it is artificially produced, not generated from human parents. But once it is granted that the artificial production of a creature need not make it a nonperson, it seems reasonable to consider the potential of the frozen android as making the proposed action one of murder. The more important point is that the eccentricity of the example, its distance from any problem I or my audience will ever confront, makes it difficult to sort out our moral and our nonmoral responses to it, and hence makes considered moral judgment on such cases nearly impossible. The best course is to decide them by analogy to, or by generalizations derived from, cases where our intuitions are surer. Thus if indeed the frozen android is a fair analogy to an infant, or if there is no plausible principle that distinguishes an infant from a frozen android or a frozen android from an infant, the rational course is to allow our intuitions concerning infants to control our result as to frozen androids even if this leads to a result that seems strange. The same is true of another example of Tooley's: the kitten injected in such a manner as to give it, upon maturity, the capacities of an adult human. My own judgment would be that the analogy holds and that frozen androids and injected kittens should both be accorded the right to live.

Tooley's chief criticism of the potentiality principle starts with what he calls "the moral symmetry principle with respect to action and inaction," which he phrases as follows:

> Let C be a causal process that normally leads to event E. Let A be an action that initiates process C, and let B be an action involving a minimal expenditure of energy that stops process C before outcome E occurs. Assume further that A and B do not have any further consequences, and that E is the only part or outcome of C which is morally significant in itself. Then there is no morally significant difference between intentionally performing action B and intentionally refraining from performing action A, assuming identical motivation in both cases.

Tooley argues that, if this principle is accepted, there is no essential moral difference between killing an infant and refraining from fertilizing a human egg, since in the one case the development of a self-conscious creature is prevented by action, and in the other case by inaction. So that if we accept the potentiality principle, we are forced to the conclusion that "any woman, married or unmarried, does something seriously wrong every month she intentionally avoids becoming pregnant," even when the means chosen for avoiding pregnancy is sexual abstinence.

I shall postpone my formal defense of the distinction between action and inaction until the next chapter. In this context, I shall limit myself to arguing intuitively that the moral symmetry principle is unacceptable, and give grounds for believing that the intuitive sense we all have that there is an important difference between not starting a life and stopping one once started is in fact sound. To reach the widest possible audience, I shall forgo arguing that, if the moral symmetry principle requires us to believe that there is no essential difference between infanticide and contraception, that of itself is sufficient to require us to reject the principle. That I forgo such an argument does not mean that I find it unacceptable. Certainly the intellectual costs of rejecting the principle are not great.

Consider the following method of interrogation, designed to get information out of those of great physical courage but sensitive conscience. The person interrogated is informed (correctly) that a child will be tortured until he talks: when he talks, the torture will be stopped. Now imagine this method being employed by an interrogator whose motive is simply patriotism against a captured soldier whose motive for not talking is also simply patriotism. Both say "I regret this child's suffering, but my country demands it." The causes of the war and the probable effects of victory for one side or the other are left unspecified and thus may be taken as irrelevant. One might think that the victory of those who are prepared to use blackmail of this sort would be a bad result, but supposing that the comrades of the person interrogated have used similar tactics does not alter the ethics of the situation. The motives and justifications of the two parties can thus be treated as the same. But to hold that the interrogator and the captured soldier are in any sense morally on a par is monstrous, or at any rate highly counterintuitive.

Some pragmatic considerations reinforcing our sense of difference between stopping life and not starting it follow. Obviously, not all ova can reach maturity if the human race is not going to be swamped. Avoiding the fertilization of most ova, whether by contraception or by some other means, is clearly preferable to destroying the product of conception at some later stage in its development (for example, in infancy). No one but a very imaginative philosopher is likely to see any connection between the former kind of action and the killing of adults (which nearly all agree is to be avoided), whereas the similarity between killing a baby and killing an adult is underlined by our murder laws among other things. Hence it is reasonable to ascribe to infants and fetuses a right to live while denying that ova have a right to be impregnated. Of course, to argue in this way is to concede that abortion has some good effects, in that it helps prevent overpopulation, but on any view of ethics I can think of, a wrong act—even a gravely wrong one—can have some good consequences.

One might also treat the coming-into-existence of specific human individuals by sexual reproduction as constituting the results of a kind of natural lottery. In the absence of a compulsion to attempt a task one cannot satisfactorily perform, or mindlessly to employ all technical devices available, it seems best, for instance, to leave the proportion of males to females in society to chance rather than controlling it technologically. Likewise the decision whether a given possible person should enter the population is best left, for the most part, to a combination of chance, personal decision motivated at most in part by a desire that a possible person should enter the population, and other elements alien to technocratic manipulation. But once a child has been conceived, the natural lottery has been completed, and it is time for talk about rights.

To these considerations may be added the considerations adduced in section 3, briefly, the importance of maintaining in our society a concern for the welfare of babies. Although such considerations do not themselves establish that immature human beings have a right to live in their own right, they do contribute to a cumulative argument having this conclusion. No such considerations are available tending to support the conclusion that ova have a right to be fertilized.

It may seem that pragmatic arguments such as I have offered are inconsistent with an insistence that an infant has a right to live not subject to consequentialist manipulation. But this is not so. I have been trying to show that our moral intuitions regarding infants possess a reasonable basis and thus to quiet skepticism concerning them. I do not wish to reduce these intuitions to their consequentialist ground or to deny that the right to live embodies a norm resistant, at least to a considerable extent, to consequentialist considerations. There are good consequences to be hoped for from protecting some interests from direct consequentialist overriding and bad consequences to be feared from failing to do so. In any case, even at the level of strictly consequentialist argumentation, the death of an infant seems a very different sort of result than some possible human being's not being conceived.

Finally, a word about the logic of the potentiality principle is in order. The potentiality principle relies heavily on the distinction between what happens in the ordinary course of events, as opposed to by miracle, freak accident, or extraordinary human intervention. Philosophers have sometimes expressed considerable difficulty with such distinctions, and if such difficulties were allowed to prevail, the potentiality principle would collapse, since anything that could be given self-consciousness or other distinctively human traits by some extraordinary manipulation would then be a person. But most of us can understand that a kitten's growing up into a rational being—even if it should happen without human intervention once in a million years—would not be part of the normal course of events, whereas the similar maturation of a human fetus or infant is. Although I have cited the case of a very rare occurrence, the distinction I have in mind is only in part statistical. Pregnancy for instance is a normal result of coitus, even though it results from coitus with relative infrequency. Hence also statistics on infant mortality and fetal loss are of little relevance to the question of what the normal development of a human infant or fetus is.

Nonetheless, the distinction between a potential person and something that might become a person under extraordinary conditions is dependent on the prevailing conditions of human experience and would change its complexion if these conditions were to be drastically altered. Joel Feinberg observes:

> If we lived in a world in which every biologically capable human female became pregnant once a year throughout her entire fertile period of life [without external intervention], then we would regard fertilization as something which happens to every ovum in "the natural course of events." Perhaps we would regard every unfertilized ovum, in such a world, as a potential person even possessed of rights corresponding to its future interests. It would perhaps make conceptual if not moral sense in such a world to regard deliberate nonfertilization as a kind of homicide.

What the ethics of such a world might be is a matter concerning which it is only possible to speculate. (The case for drawing the line at the beginning of recognizably human form rather than at "conception" would probably be much strengthened.) In any case, it should be possible to acknowledge that changes in human experiences, purposes, and techniques could produce changes in the application of concepts like "right" without regarding every new biomedical development as altering the parameters of moral discourse so fundamentally as to render all older ideas irrelevant. Hence we have good reasons to use the potentiality principle to ascribe personhood to immature human organisms, such as fetuses and infants, and not to spermatozoa and ova.

5. THE POTENTIALITY AND SPECIES PRINCIPLES

The potentiality and species principles both protect all normal human infants and unborn children, along with the reversibly unconscious and, of course, normal, awake adults. They differ importantly as to scope, however. According to the potentiality principle, a gravely retarded human (unable, let us say, ever to communicate with us at all as a person), and an irreversibly comatose human organism whose heart beats of its own accord are not persons, whereas they are members of the human species and as such are protected by the species principle. (The status of someone whose heart beats on only because it is artificially stimulated is unclear even on the species principle.) While generous impulses and an unwillingness to take the moral risk of acting on the narrower principle may predispose us to adopt the species principle, a surer foundation for choice is greatly to be desired.

In what follows, I shall offer a tentative synthesis of the two principles, which I hope will be at least to a minimum degree intuitively acceptable. I shall use the potentiality principle to specify the extension of the expression "person," while continuing to use "human being" as a morally significant expression. That is to say, I shall distinguish two classes of creatures, delimited by two versions of the moral rule against homicide: persons, that is, creatures having the capacity or potentiality of doing distinctively human things; and human beings, that is, members of the human species. (What is true of human beings could also be true of members of other intelligent species.) I shall suggest that a prima facie obligation to abstain from killing both kinds of creatures exists, but the obligation to abstain from killing persons is both primary and more stringent.

Respect for persons is morally fundamental. To deprive a person of his capacity to perform personal acts—to reduce a person to a thing, or displace him by one—is an act that can only be justified under the most stringent conditions. And killing is precisely such a reduction of the victim from personhood to thinghood or the annihilation of a person in favor of a thing. It is unclear whether the language of reduction, or the language of annihilation and replacement, is more appropriate here because of the suggestion that someone whose existence as a person has ceased may yet survive as a human being. For most purposes, reduction of a person to a thing may be taken as a portrayal of death which, while somewhat mythical because it supposes that a person is somehow identical with his corpse, is a good enough approximation that ethical conclusions can be drawn from it.

But the principle of respect for persons also extends, by what might be called the "overflow principle," to things closely associated with persons. Thus corpses ought not to be treated as ordinary garbage, and one might also argue that a modicum of reverence should be accorded the processes by which persons come to be. This line of thought explains the (otherwise quite bewildering) expression "the sanctity of life" (as opposed to the sanctity of the living individual), as well as the connection many have seen between questions of homicide and such questions as artificial insemination. Nothing more is claimed for the overflow principle here than that it helps explain a number of our intuitions, and helps suggest a way of bringing together the species and potentiality principles in a way that appears to do justice to the claims of each.

Human beings who are not persons (the expression "person" being used in the semitechnical sense explained above) are entitled to a degree of respect because of their close association with persons. First, all human beings are entitled to be presumed to be persons until it is absolutely clear that they have no capacity for personal activity. Second, even those human beings who clearly have no such capacity ought not to be killed except where the reasons for so doing are very strong and the resulting danger to the principle of respect for persons very small. Thus, for instance, even the most severely mentally retarded ought not to be killed, since to do so would endanger those (the majority of the retarded) who can, with effort, be brought to a human level of existence (roughly, can be taught to talk). On the other hand, one might perhaps allow the abortion to be performed on fetal indications, to avoid great suffering on the part of the parents, in cases of grave and irremediable mental defect (not, it deserves emphasis, on grounds of physical defect: an oddly shaped human being is no less a person for that reason). For fetuses are not very closely imaginatively linked with born persons. On these premises, disorders like Tay-Sachs disease, which by killing in early childhood prevent the development of significant human capacities, provide (given certainty of diagnosis) just enough justification for abortion on fetal indications. Down's syndrome (mongolism), on the other hand, does not. For some mongols at any rate manage to attain the capacity to speak to us as persons.

Again, an irreversibly comatose human being ought not to be hurried into the grave in order to advance the hospital schedule. But if his heart is needed to save the life of another, it might be taken from him for that end. (Notice, however, that all comas are, in the absence of very clear evidence, to be presumed reversible: one might, of course, terminate life-support systems on grounds of futility somewhat before the point of certainty, though the decision is a very grave one.) Where the body is kept going only by massive artificial aid, one might, indeed, conclude that what one has here is not even a human organism but a corpse with a beating heart.

To refuse to admit this concept—say, on the grounds that the death of a human organism just *means* "the system of those reciprocally dependent processes which assimilate oxygen, metabolize food, eliminate waste, and keep the organism in relative homeostasis are arrested in a way which the organism itself cannot reverse"—leads to paradoxical conclusions. These conclusions are that if the organism were to stop functioning in the way just mentioned and then be revived, we would have a case, not of saving life, but of reversing death. The most radical implications of advances in medical technology may be that one cannot define death simply by reference to an organic state, but must bring in the available medical resources as well.

The flat EEG, which has played a considerable role in recent discussion of "brain death," has a double relevance in this connection. As an indication of cessation of brain function, it is a possible criterion of organismic breakdown; it is also evidence of irreversible unconsciousness and thus of personal death. Conceivably, however, decisive evidence of irreversible unconsciousness could be obtained without flat EEG or other indices of the organism's breakdown. In that case the problems discussed in this section would become quite acute.

I appear to have somewhat compromised the rejection of graded person-hood that I insisted on in section 4. The tendency we have to require a sharply marked-off class of persons, outside of which creatures can have only very few and very weak rights but within which the greatest scrupulousness is required in respecting the rights of persons, perhaps cannot be maintained without qualification given the complexity of human situations. But a principle whose complex application is the result of the union of two identifiable, simpler principles is still preferable to a way of applying the concept "person" that invites opportunism, that is, ad hoc adjustment of rights in an arbitrary manner throughout the whole range of its application.

Implementation of the perspective just outlined does raise difficult problems, however. These problems do not arise in the case of abortion on fetal indications (extreme mental defect), since our institutions have for a long time distinguished, however shaky the ultimate justification for so doing, between abortion and the killing of the born. They arise in connection with the use as organ donors of those who have lost the capacity for human activity.

On the one hand, organ transplants do save lives, and it seems undesirable, at least if one can in good faith regard the donor as a cadaver, to carve out exceptions to the moral rule against homicide in order to justify them On the other, there are serious worries involved in blurring the questions "Is he alive?" and "Should he be let die (or killed)?" and with definitions of death that vary according to the definer's purposes. Some of these worries—for instance the possibility of "the protracting of the in-between state…and extracting from it all the profit we can"—might be laid to rest by stressing the principle of respect for human remains. But the central difficulty—the doubtful legitimacy of manipulating the time of death for transplant purposes—is still troublesome.

We might react to this difficulty by reverting to the species principle, with the result that the moral rule against homicide will protect not only all born human organisms, but also all human fetuses however defective they may be. We may feel that even the most gravely retarded human being—and even a human being who is unconscious and certain never to regain consciousness—is a person entitled in his own right not to be killed, though futile measures to prolong life would still not be required. (This is how we would feel, certainly, about someone lying on a railroad track, drugged to remain unconscious until the train ran him over, and quite possibly how we would feel about a premature infant with a beating heart whose biological death was imminent. It is when the cause of permanent unconsciousness is structural damage that our intuitions are unclear.)

We might justify our adoption of the species principle in the following way. No matter how unlikely it may be, it is never a fantastic supposition—never one requiring a miracle, freak accident, or technological intervention of a radical sort—that a human being should attain or regain consciousness at the personal level or become able to perform distinctively personal acts. On this interpretation, the species and potentiality principles merge fully.

Even so, it will still be possible for a human being or person to be succeeded by a mere animal in some sense continuous with him. A werewolf, who as a wolf has only the mental capacities of a wolf, should he become stuck in the wolf phase of his existence, would be a mere brute animal, although we might still treat the resulting wolf differently out of respect for what it had (in some sense) been.

The upshot of this discussion is that it is very difficult to choose decisively between the species and potentiality principles. And the choice between the principles is very important—philosophically, since it marks the crucial divide between those who believe that human beings have worth simply because they are human, and those who believe that they have worth because they are able to produce systems of philosophy, cities, works of art, and sophisticated manuals of sexual technique; and practically, since the choice and the calculation underlying it will crucially affect our attitude toward the severely mentally retarded (and perhaps others). On the other hand, there are important issues for which the results of accepting the two principles are the same. One of these is that the abortion of a normal fetus (and many defective ones too) can only be justified in ways which would justify the sacrifice of the life of a mature human being.

STUDY QUESTIONS

1. What are the three candidates for membership in the class of beings covered by the prohibition against homicide? How does Devine characterize each principle? Which are accepted and which are rejected?

2. What does Devine say about the proper cutoff point ("relative bright line") between a human being and a nonhuman being?

3. Explain the synthesis at which Devine finally arrives and show its bearing on the issue of abortion.

4. Do you find any problems with Devine's reasoning? Here is one point to consider: Is there a difference between being *potentially* something which is X and having the *capacity* for X? For example, a river has the potential for generating electricity but not the capacity for doing so until certain mechanisms (for example, gears and wheels) are arranged in the right relationship to the river. Can you see how this distinction could apply to the abortion issue? Does the fetus have merely the *potentiality* or also the *capacity* for those properties necessary for a right to life?

5. What is the significance of moral intuitions in Devine's theory? How seriously should we take our intuitions? To what issue does he apply this point? Do you agree with him?

14

Personhood Begins at Conception

STEPHEN SCHWARZ

Stephen Schwarz is Professor of Philosophy at the University of Rhode Island. Schwarz argues that prochoice advocates like Michael Tooley and Mary Anne Warren make a fundamental mistake in confusing the idea of being a person with functioning as a person. What matters is not whether something can function as a person (that is, can reason, has a concept of self, and so on) but whether it is a person. Employing a continuum argument (the life of a human person is a single continuum; the time in the womb is simply the first phase of this continuum), Schwarz argues that the being in the womb is an actual person, not a potential person. A single-celled zygote is not a potential person, but a nonfunctioning actual person, whose essence is the same as a functioning adult. Abortion and infanticide are simply abuses of power, unjust lethal discriminations against the powerless by the powerful.

A THEORY ABOUT HUMAN BEINGS
AND PERSONS

Let us now examine a theory that defends abortion on the grounds that the child in the womb, though undoubtedly a human being, is not a person, and that it is only the killing of persons that is intrinsically and seriously wrong. The theory consists of two major theses: First, that killing human beings is

Reprinted from Stephen Schwarz, *The Moral Question of Abortion* (Chicago: Loyola University Press, 1990) by permission. Endnotes have been removed.

not wrong; second, that the child (in the womb and for a time after birth) is human but not a person. I shall argue that both of these theses are mistaken.

This theory recognizes that abortion is the deliberate killing of an innocent human being, but it denies this is wrong because it denies that it is wrong to deliberately kill human beings. What *is* wrong is killing human beings who are persons. Now, of course, many human beings are persons, for example, normal adult human beings, and it is wrong to kill them because they are persons. But small infants, such as newborn babies or babies in the womb, though they are undoubtedly human, are not, according to this theory, persons. And so it is not intrinsically wrong to kill them. That is, it is not wrong in itself, though it may be wrong because of adverse consequences. A small child, therefore, has no right to life as a normal adult does, and if the child is unwanted, he may be killed.

Thus, the theory allows for abortion and infanticide alike. It rejects the typical pro-abortion lines, such as viability and birth. It agrees that there is no morally significant difference between "before" and "after." But instead of saying that killing a human being is *wrong* on both sides of such a line, it claims that it is *right* (or can be right) on both sides of the line.

Joseph Fletcher expresses this view when he remarks, "I would support the…position…that both abortion and infanticide can be justified if and when the good to be gained outweighs the evil—that neither abortion nor infanticide is as such immoral."

Michael Tooley has an essay entitled, "A Defense of Abortion and Infanticide." If the idea that killing babies is morally right is shocking to most people, Tooley replies in his essay that this is merely an emotional response, not a reasoned one. "The response, rather than appealing to carefully formulated moral principles, is primarily visceral," he says. And, "It is reasonable to suspect that one is dealing with a taboo rather than with a rational prohibition." His position is, "Since I do not believe human infants are persons, but only potential persons, and since I think that the destruction of potential persons is a morally neutral action, the correct conclusion seems to me to be that infanticide is in itself morally acceptable."

I want to show that the theories held by Fletcher, Tooley, and others are absolutely wrong. Infanticide and abortion are both morally wrong, as wrong as the deliberate killing of an older child or an adult, and thus our emotional response of shock and horror at killing babies is completely grounded in reason and moral principles. I want to show that a small child, after birth or still in the womb, *is* a person, as much a person as the rest of us; that the notion of person as used by these writers is a special one, a narrower concept, and not the one that is crucial for morality. I want to make clear why the attempts to show that a small child is not a person are mistaken, and that all human beings as such are persons.

THE ARGUMENT OF MARY ANNE WARREN

Mary Anne Warren examines "the traditional argument that since (1) it is wrong to kill innocent human beings, and (2) fetuses are innocent human beings, then (3) it is wrong to kill fetuses." This argument, she claims is "fallacious," because "the term 'human' has two distinct, but not often distinguished, senses." In premise one, human means person, or full-fledged member of the moral community, a being whom it is wrong to kill. In premise two, on the other hand, the term human refers merely to a member of the biological species human, as opposed, say, to a rabbit or an eagle. Warren's claim is that mere membership in a biological species is morally irrelevant and thus does not confer on the being in question a right to life.

"Yes, a fetus is biologically human (human in the genetic sense), but that does not make it the kind of being who has a right to life. It is only persons (those who are human in the moral sense) who have such a right. It is wrong to kill persons, and if a human being is not also a person he does not have a right to life, and it is, or often can be, morally right to destroy him." This, in essence, is Warren's argument.

Warren offers an analysis of what is a person, a full-fledged member of the moral community:

> I suggest that the traits which are most central to the concept of personhood, or humanity in the moral sense, are, very roughly, the following:
>
> 1. Consciousness (of objects and events external and/or internal to the being), and in particular the capacity to feel pain.
>
> 2. Reasoning (the *developed* capacity to solve new and relatively complex problems).
>
> 3. Self-motivated activity (activity which is relatively independent of either genetic or direct external control).
>
> 4. The capacity to communicate, by whatever means, messages of an indefinite variety of types; that is, not just with an indefinite number of possible contents, but on indefinitely many possible topics.
>
> 5. The presence of self-concepts, and self-awareness, either individual or racial, or both.

This, she acknowledges, is not a full analysis of the concept of a person. It is not a list of necessary and sufficient conditions for being a person. But, she says, this does not matter.

> All we need to claim, to demonstrate that a fetus is not a person, is that any being which satisfies *none* of (1)–(5) is certainly not a person. I consider this claim to be so obvious that I think anyone who denied it and claimed that a being which satisfied none of (1)–(5) was a person all the same, would thereby demonstrate that he had no notion at all of what a person is—perhaps because he had confused the concept of a person with that of genetic humanity.

We can now see Warren's argument for abortion in its entirety. A fetus is human in the genetic sense; that is morally irrelevant. A fetus is not human in the moral sense: He is not a person because he satisfies none of the criteria she has outlined. Not being a person, he has no right to life, and abortion is morally permissible. The same applies to the child after birth. "Killing a newborn infant isn't murder." Infanticide is wrong, according to Warren, only to the extent that the child is wanted, that there are couples who would like to adopt or keep him. "Thus, infanticide is wrong for reasons analogous to those which make it wrong to wantonly destroy natural resources, or great works of art."

But destroying natural resources or works of art is not always wrong, and certainly not wrong in the sense in which murder is wrong. Warren acknowledges this when she says, "It follows from my argument that when an unwanted or defective infant is born into a society which cannot afford and/or is not willing to care for it, then its destruction is permissible."

BEING A PERSON AND *FUNCTIONING* AS A PERSON

The failure of Warren's argument can be seen in light of the distinction between being a person and functioning as a person. Consider Warren's five characteristics of a person: consciousness, reasoning, self-motivated activity, the capacity to communicate, and the presence of self-concepts. Imagine a person in a deep, dreamless sleep. She is not conscious, she cannot reason, and so forth; she lacks all five of these traits. She is not functioning as a person; that is part of what being asleep means. But of course she is a person, she retains fully her status of being a person, and killing her while asleep is just as wrong as killing her while she is awake and functioning as a person.

Functioning as a person refers to all the activities proper to persons as persons, to thinking in the broadest sense. It includes reasoning, deciding, imagining, talking, experiencing love and beauty, remembering, intending, and much more. The term *function* does not refer here to bodily functions, but rather to those of the mind, though certain bodily functions, especially those of the brain, are necessary conditions for functioning as a person.

When Warren points out that a fetus satisfies none of the five traits she mentions, she shows only that a fetus does not function as a person, not that it lacks the being of a person, which is the crucial thing.

At this point several objections are likely to be raised: First, the sleeping person will soon wake up and function as a person, while the being in the womb will not.

In reply, neither the sleeping person nor the being in the womb now display the qualities of a functioning person. Both will display them. It is only a matter of time. Why should the one count as a real person because the time is short, while the other does not, simply because in her case the time is longer?

Second, the sleeping adult was already self-conscious, had already solved some problems. Therefore, she has a history of functioning as a person. The child in the womb has no such history. Thus Tooley argues that "an organism cannot have a serious right to life [be a person] unless it either now possesses, or did possess at some time in the past, the concept of a self... [what is required for functioning as a person]." The human being sound asleep counts as a person because she once functioned as a person; the child never did, so she does not count as a person.

True, there is a difference with respect to past functioning, but the difference is not morally relevant. The reason the child never functioned as a person is because her capacity to do so is not yet sufficiently developed. It cannot be, for she is near the beginning of her existence, in the first phase of her life.

Imagine a case of two children. One is born comatose, and he will remain so until the age of nine. The other is healthy at birth, but as soon as she achieves the concept of a continuing self for a brief time, she, too, lapses into a coma, from which she will not emerge until she is nine. Can anyone seriously hold that the second child is a person with a right to life, while the first child is not? In one case, self-awareness will come only after nine years have elapsed, in the other, it will return. In both cases, self-awareness will grow and develop. Picture the two unconscious children lying side by side. Almost nine years have passed. Would it not be absurd to say that only one of them is a person, that there is some essential, morally relevant, difference between them? Imagine someone about to kill both of them. Consistent with his theory, Tooley would have to say, "You may kill the first, for he is not a person. He is human only in the genetic sense, since he has no history of functioning as a person. You may not kill the second, since she does have such a history." If this distinction is absurd when applied to the two born human beings, is it any less absurd when applied to two human beings, one born (asleep in a bed), the other preborn (sleeping in the womb)?

In short, when it comes to functioning as a person, there is no moral difference between "did, but does not" (the sleeping adult) and "does not, but will" (the small child).

Third, a sleeping person has the capacity to function as a person and therefore counts as being a person, even though this capacity is not now actualized. In contrast, a child in the womb lacks this capacity, so he does not count as being a person.

This is the most fundamental objection, and probably underlies the preceding two objections. In considering it, compare the following beings:

A. A normal adult, sound asleep, not conscious.

B. An adult in a coma from which he will emerge in, say, six months and function normally as a person.

C. A normal newborn baby.

D. A normal baby soon to be born.

E. A normal "well-proportioned, small-scale baby" in the womb at seven weeks.

F. A normal embryo or zygote.

Case A, the normal adult sound asleep, is someone who has the being of a person, who is not now functioning as a person, and who clearly has the capacity to function as a person. I want to show now that all the other cases are essentially similar to this one. That is, if case A is a person—a full-fledged member of the moral community, a being with a right to life, whose value lies in his own being and dignity, and not merely in his significance for others (like natural resources and works of art), a being whose willful destruction is murder—each of the other cases is a person as well.

The objection claims that the being in the womb lacks the capacity to function as a person. True, it lacks what I shall call the *present immediate capacity* to function, where responses may be immediately elicited. Such a capacity means the capability of functioning, where such a capability varies enormously among people, and normally develops and grows (as a result of learning and other experiences).

The capability of functioning as a person is grounded in the *basic inherent capacity* to function. This is proper to the being of a person and it has a physical basis, typically the brain and nervous system. It is a capacity that grows and develops as the child grows and develops.

This basic inherent capacity may be fully accessible, as in a normal sleeping adult. It then exists in its present immediate form. It may also exist in other forms where it is latent, as in reversible coma. I shall call this the latent-1 capacity, where the basic inherent capacity is present but temporarily damaged or blocked. In a small child, the basic inherent capacity is there but insufficiently developed for the child to function in the manner of a normal adult. I shall call this the latent-2 capacity.

Let me turn to the actual refutation of this objection. I will begin with cases A through E (replies 1 and 2), then case F (3), then abnormal or handicapped human beings (4).

(1) The beings on our list, A through E, differ only with respect to their present immediate capacity to function. They are all essentially similar with respect to their basic inherent capacity, and through this, their being as persons.

Thus the adult in a coma, case B, is not essentially different from the sleeping person in case A. Person B is in a deep, deep sleep; person A in a comparatively superficial sleep. Person B cannot be awakened easily; person A can be. Person B is in a very long sleep; person A is in a short sleep, say 8 hours. Both have the basic inherent capacity: in A it is present immediate; in B it is latent-1. That is certainly not a morally relevant difference. If the status of persons is to be viewed in terms of capacity to function as a person, then surely a latent-1 capacity (temporarily blocked—person B) qualifies as much as a nonlatent capacity (present immediate—person A).

Consider now the newborn baby, case C. He too has the physical basis for functioning as a person (brain, nervous system, and so on). Only his overall development is insufficient for him to actually function on the level of the normal adult. He has a latent-2 capacity. Thus there is an essential similarity between cases B and C, the adult in a coma and the newborn baby. Neither has the present immediate capacity to function as a person. Both take longer than the sleeping adult (case A) to wake up from their slumber. But both have a latent capacity to function because they both have the basic inherent capacity to function. In the case of B, the impossibility of eliciting an immediate response is due to an abnormality, which brought on the coma. In the other, case C, this is due to the fact that the being is not yet far enough along in his process of development. In both cases the basic inherent capacity is there, it is merely latent.

Cases C and D, babies just after birth and just before birth, are clearly the same in terms of their capacity to function as persons. Birth is, among other things, the beginning of vast new opportunities to develop the basic inherent capacity to function by seeing, hearing, touching, and so on, a capacity that is equally present just before birth.

Case E, a baby at seven weeks, has "all the internal organs of the adult"; "after the eighth week no further primordia will form; and *everything* is already present that will be found in the full term baby." It is these "internal organs" and "primordia" that constitute the physical base for the basic inherent capacity to function as a person. They are substantially present in both the very young preborn child, at seven and eight weeks (case E), and the older preborn child (case D). Thus the cases D and E are essentially similar with respect to their basic inherent capacity and because of this, their being as persons.

In brief, cases A through E are essentially similar. Cases B through E are similar in themselves (each represents a latent capacity), and, taken together, in comparison with A (present immediate capacity). There is no essential difference among cases B through E. If a person whose lack of present immediate capacity to function is due to a disorder (as in case B) should be respected as a person, then surely a being whose lack of this capacity to function is due to insufficient development (cases C through E) should also be respected as a person. Both are beings with the potential to function as a person, and this they can only have if they have the basis for it, that is, the being of a person. Case B represents a latent-1 capacity, cases C through E, a latent-2 capacity; both are forms of the basic inherent capacity to function, proper to the nature of a person. If a latent-1 capacity (B) is a mark of a person, then surely a latent-2 capacity (C through E) is also a mark of a person. Both B and C through F represent beings who will have the capability to function as persons, who lack this capability now because of the condition of the working basis of this capability (brain, nervous system, and so forth). In one, that condition is one of disorder or blockage, in the other, the lack of development proper to the age of the being in question.

(2) The essential similarity among the beings A through E is also established if they are imagined as the same being: a being in the womb developing from seven weeks to birth (E to C), then lapsing into a coma (B), then recovering (A). Thus if there is a person at the end (A), there is also that same person at the beginning (E). It is the same person going through various stages, representing first a latent-2 capacity, then a latent-1 capacity, and finally a present immediate capacity.

I am now a being capable of functioning as a person (present immediate capacity). Many years ago I was a small newborn baby, and before that a smaller child in my mother's womb. My capabilities have changed, they have increased as my basic inherent capacity to function as a person has developed, but I remain always *the same person,* the same essential being, the being who has these growing capabilities. If I am essentially a person now, I was essentially a person then, when I was a baby. The fact that my capabilities to function as a person have changed and grown does not alter the absolute continuity of my essential being, that of a person. In fact, this variation in capabilities presupposes the continuity of my being as a person. It is *as a person* that I develop my capabilities to function as a person. It is because I am a person that I have these capabilities, to whatever degree.

And so the basic reality is being as a person. This is what entails your right to life, the wrongness of killing you, the necessity of respecting you as a person, and not just as a desired commodity like a natural resource. It is *being* a person that is crucial morally, not *functioning* as a person. The very existence and meaning of functioning as a person can have its basis only in the being of a person. It is because you have the being of a person that you can function as a person, although you might fail to function as a person and still retain your full being as a person.

(3) Let us turn now to case F, the zygote or embryo. There are three considerations that show the essential similarity between this case and cases A through E.

First: The continuum argument applies here as well. The adult now sleeping is the same being who was once an embryo and a zygote. There is a direct continuity between the zygote at F and the child at E, through to the adult at A. If the being at the later stages should be given the respect due to persons, then that same being should also be given this respect when he is at an earlier stage.

Second: It may be objected that the zygote lacks "a well-developed physical substratum of consciousness"—that it lacks the actual physical basis (brain, nervous system, etc.) for the basic inherent capacity to function as a person. This is incorrect. The zygote does not lack this physical basis; it is merely that it is now in a primitive, undeveloped form. The zygote has the essential structure of this basis; a structure that will unfold, grow, develop, mature, which takes time. As Blechschmidt states, "…the fertilized ovum (zygote) is already a form of man. Indeed, it is already active…All the organs of the developing organism are differentiation products of each unique [fertilized] human ovum." That is, the organs that form the physical basis for the more developed basic inherent capacity to function as a person (at various stages, E to A) are "differentiation products" of what is already present in the zygote. Thus the zygote has, in primitive form, the physical basis of his basic inherent capacity to function as a person. In the adult, this same basis exists in developed form.

The zygote actually has the basic inherent capacity to function as a person because he has the essential physical structure for this. This structure is merely undeveloped:

> The zygotic self cannot actually breathe, but he *actually has* the undeveloped capacity for breathing. Nor can this zygotic self actually think and love as an adult does, but he *actually has* the undeveloped capacity for thinking and loving. And the human zygote could not actually have such undeveloped capacities unless he actually IS the kind of being that *has*

such capacities. Just as it is obviously true that only a human being can have the *developed* capacities for thinking and loving, it should be obviously true that only a human being can have the *underdeveloped* capacities for thinking and loving.

Elsewhere, Robert Joyce remarks,

> A person is not an individual with a *developed* capacity for reasoning, willing, desiring, and relating to others. A person is an individual with a *natural* capacity for these activities and relationships, whether this natural capacity is ever developed or not—that is, whether he or she ever attains the functional capacity or not. Individuals of a rational, volitional, self-conscious *nature* may never attain or may lose the functional capacity for fulfilling this nature to any appreciable extent. But this inability to fulfill their nature does not negate or destroy the nature itself.

A being at the beginning of his development cannot be expected to possess what only that development can provide for him. He is already the being who will later function as a person, given time. The sleeping person is also a being who will later function as a person, only he will do it much sooner. What they each have now—a fully developed brain in one case, and a potential brain that will grow into a developed brain in the other case—is a basis for their capacity to function as persons. It is the same essential basis, one undeveloped, the other developed. It is merely a matter of degree; there is no difference in kind.

One must already *be* a human person in order to develop the human brain necessary for the present and immediate capacity to function as a person. As we noted earlier, *only a human being can develop a human brain, a human brain cannot develop before a human exists.* "Human being" means of course "human person," the same being in different phases of his existence.

Third: Imagine a person J solving new and relatively complex problems (item 2 on Mary Anne Warren's list).

1. Person J is *doing* this.
2. Person K *has the capacity* to do this (like the sleeping person A on the list).
3. Person L *has the capacity to learn* to do this (to learn what is necessary for having this capacity; for example, a child in school).
4. Person M *has the capacity to acquire,* by natural development, what is necessary for the capacity to learn to do this.

What is true of person M applies to a newborn baby (C), or a baby about to be born (D), or a much younger baby, at seven weeks (E). It applies equally to that same being at a still earlier stage of her development, as a zygote (F).

There is a continuity here. If being a person is approached from the point of view of capacity to function as a person, then clearly persons K, L, and M are essentially alike. Each is removed by one or more steps from the person J, who is actually functioning as a person. None of these steps is of moral or metaphysical significance. In reverse order from M to J, there is, respectively, a capacity to acquire, a capacity to learn, and a capacity to do what the next being represents. If doing is to count for being a person, then surely the capacity to do, the capacity to learn to do, and the capacity to acquire what is needed to learn to do must also count.

This chain argument shows not only the essential similarity between the zygote (F) and the child at later stages (C through E) but also the essential similarity among the beings A through F.

We are now in a better position to understand the real significance of past functioning as a person, which is present in the adult (asleep or in a coma), and absent from the child. It is a sign that the being in question is a person. Because a certain being has functioned in the past, he must be a person. But if he has not, or we do not know it, it does not follow that he is not a person. Other indications must also be examined. In the case of a small baby, born or preborn, including the zygote stage of a baby's existence, there are three such indications.

One, the *continuum of being,* the identity of the person. The baby is now the same being, the same "self" that the child will be later on. "I was once a newborn baby and before that, a baby inside my mother." Because it is a human being's essential nature to be a person, this being—as a zygote, as a seven-week-old baby, as a newborn—is always a person.

Two, the *continuum of essential structure* for the basic inherent capacity to function as a person. The baby as a zygote has the essential physical structure that represents this capacity. Both in the primitive form of development and in all later stages of development, there exists the same essential structure.

Three, the *continuum of capacities,* to acquire, learn, and do. The zygote has the capacity to acquire what is needed to learn to function as a person.

If a being is not now functioning as a person, is he a person? Two perspectives can be used in answering this question: present to past and present to future. An affirmative answer in either case suffices to indicate that the being in question is a person. Present to past: Yes, he is a person because he functioned as a person in the past. Present to future: Yes, he is a person because he will function as a person in the future, based on the three-fold continuum. The mistake of writers such as Tooley is to ignore the second of these.

(4) Let us turn, finally, to the case of abnormal, or handicapped, human beings. Does the analysis offered here—that the beings A through F are essentially similar with respect to their being as persons, and their basic inherent capacity to function as persons—apply equally to abnormal, or handicapped, human beings?

It certainly does. A handicapped person (physically, mentally, or both) has the same being of a person as the rest of us who are fortunate enough not to be so afflicted. He has, with this, the same dignity, the same rights as the rest of us. We must "do unto him" as we would want others to "do unto us" if we were afflicted with a handicap. Just as there is no morally relevant difference between a normal functioning person and a small child who cannot yet function as a person because of his lack of development, there is also no morally relevant difference between the normal functioning person and one incapable, or less capable, of doing so. Any one of us who now has the present immediate capacity to function as a person may lose it through a severe illness or accident. If that happened to you, you would still have the same status of being a person, the same dignity and rights of a person.

Even a very severely abnormal or handicapped human being has the basic inherent capacity to function as a person, which is a sign that he is a person. The abnormality represents a hindrance to the actual working of this capacity to its manifestation in actual functioning. It does not imply the absence of this capacity, as in a nonperson.

The normal adult and child were selected for this analysis because it is in them that the essence of functioning as a person, or its usual absence because of (normal) lack of development, can most easily be seen and understood. Once recognized there, it applies equally to all persons, regardless of the degree to which they are able to accomplish it.

To conclude this part of the main argument: Would Mary Anne Warren admit the adult sound asleep to the status of person? If not, she is saying it is acceptable to kill people in their sleep. Suppose she admits sleeping person A. She must then admit sleeping person B, the one in a longer, deeper sleep. The only differences are the length and nature of the sleep. In each case there is a being with a capacity to function as a person, who will, if not killed, wake up to exercise it. Clearly there is no morally relevant difference between them. This proves decisively that present immediate capacity to function as a person is not necessary to being a person. This is plainly true of the newborn baby C. Having then admitted B as a person, Warren is forced to admit C as well, for the two cases are essentially the same: no present immediate capacity to function as a person, the presence of a latent capacity, rooted in the basic inherent capacity.

With this, Warren's whole argument is destroyed. For she herself claims that, in terms of their intrinsic nature, their being (as persons or nonpersons), the newborn baby (C) and the preborn baby (D through F) are morally on a par. Neither (her argument shows) can now function as a person. Both, I have shown, have the basic inherent capacity to function as persons. In all of these cases, there is the same being, with the same essential structure of a person, differing only with respect to the degree of development of the capacity to function as a person.

Views like those of Warren and Tooley do not reach the crucial point: the fact that a human being functions as a person or has the present and immediate capacity to do so, is not the ground for his dignity, preciousness, and right to life; rather, that decisive ground is the fact of his *being* a person.

THE REALITY OF THE PERSON SEEN
THROUGH LOVE

Imagine a person you deeply love in a coma from which he will emerge in about thirty weeks, perfectly normal. Apply Warren's five criteria. He fails them all. He is not conscious, he cannot reason, he is incapable of self-motivated activity, he cannot communicate, he has no self-concepts or awareness of himself. This doesn't mean he is not a person; that he has no right to life of his own; that he could be killed if no one cared. He is just as real, just as precious, just as much a full person as if he were now capable of functioning as a person. It is just as important and necessary to respect him and care for him as if he were awake.

The child in the womb is in a comparable state, only his "sleep" is normal and is not preceded by a phase where he is able to function as a person. He is also unseen. But none of these makes a morally relevant difference. If one person in "deep sleep" (inability to function as a person) is to be respected and cared for, then the other person should be cared for and respected as well.

THE DISTINCTION APPLIED TO SOME
PRO-ABORTION VIEWS

Given our understanding of the distinction between being a person and functioning as a person, we can now come to a better understanding of some of the things put forward by defenders of abortion.

1. *Drawing Lines.* We examined ten suggested places to draw the line between what is supposed to be merely a *preparation* for a person and the actual person. Every line proved false. In each case the same fully real person is clearly present on both sides of it. No line marks any real difference with regard to *being* a person: The person is there before as well as after. But many of these lines do have a bearing on *functioning* as a person. Thus a baby after birth interacts with others in a way not possible before birth. A baby who has reached sentience has developed an important dimension of his capacity to function as a person. And the presence of a functioning brain marks a significant milestone in the child's development as a functioning person. If these lines seem to have any plausibility, it is because one has in mind functioning as a person. But the plausibility evaporates when one realizes that the crucial thing is not functioning as a person, but being a person.

2. *The Agnostic Position.* Realizing that these lines do not work, some people say that it is simply not known when a human person begins to exist. What should be said is, rather, that it is not known when *functioning* as a person begins, for there is indeed no single place on the continuum of human life at which this begins. It is a gradual development. But the *being* of the person is there all along. And the development is what it is because the being of the person is there all the way through: It is the person's development. Agnosticism regarding functioning as a person should not lead to agnosticism regarding being a person.

3. *The Gradualist Position.* False when applied to the *being* of a person, the gradualist position is absolutely valid when applied to *functioning* as a person. That is indeed a matter of degree. We gradually develop our basic inherent capacity to think and to communicate.

4. *The Notion of Potential Person.* False when applied to *being* a person, the notion of potential person has a validity when applied to *functioning* as a

person. If by "person" we mean "functioning person," for example, a normal adult making a complex decision or reading a book, then clearly a child in the womb, or just born, or even at age one, is only potentially such a person. A baby is a potential functioning person, but he is that only because he has the actual being of a person.

HUMAN IS NOT MERELY A BIOLOGICAL CATEGORY

The theory advanced by writers such as Fletcher, Tooley, and Warren holds that killing babies is permissible because they are not persons; whereas, in fact, they are nonfunctioning persons. A functioning person is one who either is now actually functioning as a person, or has the present immediate capacity to do so. What the theory holds is that only functioning persons (and those who were once such persons) are truly persons. It may, therefore, be called the *functioning-person theory.*

Advocates of the functioning-person theory hold that it is not in itself wrong to kill human beings; that this can only be wrong when the being in question is a "person," as defined by the theory (one who has the present immediate capacity to function as a person, or has had it in the past.) Such advocates hold that the single fact that a being is human does not constitute any reason for not deliberately killing it. Hence, they say, killing babies, born or preborn, is not in itself wrong. *If* it is ever wrong, it is so because these babies are wanted and would be missed by adults. The thesis, as Tooley puts it, is that "membership in a biological species is not morally significant *in itself.*" In the words of Singer, "Whether a being is or is not a member of our species is, in itself no more relevant to the wrongness of killing it than whether it is or is not a member of our race." Warren says that being human in the genetic sense does not give the being in question a right to life.

The thrust of this is to drive a wedge between two categories of beings—persons and human beings—and to hold that it is the former, not the latter, that is of moral significance. There are two fundamental and disastrous errors in this approach. The first concerns the category of persons and consists in equating this term with functioning persons (present or past), thereby excluding babies who have not yet developed the present immediate capacity to function as persons. The second error, closely related to the first, is to dismiss the category of human being as not (in itself) morally significant.

Proponents of the functioning-person theory are quite right in maintaining that there is a distinction between persons and human beings. They point out that there could be persons who are not human beings, for example, creatures on distant planets who can think, make decisions, feel gratitude, and so forth. They would certainly be persons without being human beings. In the Christian faith, angels are persons but not human beings. So, not all persons are necessarily human beings. But, I shall maintain, all human beings are persons (though not necessary functioning persons). Being human is not necessary to being a person (there could be others), but it is sufficient, for all human beings are persons.

The fundamental error here is the notion that human is a mere biological category, that it designates simply one of many zoological species. If this were so, if the difference between human and other species were like the difference between, say, cats and dogs, or tigers and bears, then of course it would be morally irrelevant. But human—though it may be viewed as a zoological species and compared to other species in the study of anatomy and physiology—is not simply a biological category. It is rather a mode of being a person.

Human designates, in its most significant meaning, a type of being whose nature it is to be a person. A person is a being who has the basic inherent capacity to function as a person, regardless of how developed this capacity is, or whether or not it is blocked, as in severe senility. We respect and value human beings, not because they are a certain biological species, but because they are persons, because it is the nature of human being to be a person. All human beings are persons, even if they can no longer function as persons (severe senility), or cannot yet function as persons (small babies), or cannot now function as persons (sound asleep or under anesthesia or in a coma).

The theory is correct when it says that it is persons who are of moral significance, and that persons need not be human persons (they may be Martians or angels). The error is to fail to recognize that humans are persons. Being human is a mode of existence of persons. So we should respect human beings—all human beings, regardless of race, degree of intelligence, degree of bodily health, degree of development as functioning persons—because they are persons.

"Do unto others as you would have them do unto you." Surely the class of others is not limited to functioning persons. It includes all human beings; perhaps others as well, but at least all human beings. "Do unto others" must include, very specifically, the lame, the retarded, the weak. It must include those no longer able to function as persons, as well as those not yet able to do so.

When we love another person, it is the *total human being* that we love, not just his or her rationality, or that which makes him or her capable of functioning as a person. We love their individual mode of being, expressed in many ways, such as gestures, facial features, tone of voice, expressions in the eyes, and so on. These are, of course, in one respect, bodily features. This does not render them merely biological in the sense dismissed by Singer, Tooley, and others. They are dimensions of the total human person.

The present immediate capacity to function as a person is not essential to this fundamental reality, the total human being. When a loved one is under anesthesia, he is still fully that person, that total human being. More than that, part of the beauty, the charm, the lovableness of a small child is that he is *only a child,* not yet matured, not yet (fully) capable of functioning as a person. The total human being in such a case does not even require the present capacity to function as a person.

Warren, Tooley, and Singer fall into the trap of seeing "human" as a mere biological category because of an earlier, and more fundamental, error: confusing person and functioning person (present or past), indeed, grouping the two together. For if it is assumed that "person" equals "functioning person," and if a small child is not a (fully) functioning person, it follows that the child is not a person. If the child is not a human *person*, "human" can then refer only to a biological species. Once one strips the child of his status as a person (on the grounds that he cannot now function as a person), what is there left except his being a member of a biological species? Separated from the notion of person, the notion of "human" is indeed only a biological species, and as such morally irrelevant.

The fallacy is, then, the separation of human and person, the failure to see that humans are precisely *human persons*. Humans are human persons, where "persons" includes nonfunctioning persons as well as functioning persons.

THE NOTION OF POTENTIAL PERSON

In arguing for his thesis that abortion is morally right, Tooley goes to great lengths to show that potential persons do not have a serious right to life. "There appears to be little hope of defending a conservative view [that is, that abortion is wrong] unless it can be shown that the destruction of potential persons is intrinsically wrong, and seriously so."

On the contrary, abortion is wrong because it destroys an actual person. The assumption that the being in the womb is merely a potential person is typical of the functioning-person theory. Thus Warren speaks of the "fetus" as a "potential person," and of "its potential for becoming a person." She denies that the latter "provides any basis whatever for the claims that it has any significant right to life."

What is potential about the child in the womb is not her *being* as a person, but rather her *functioning* as a person. That functioning is potential in the sense that she now has only a latent capacity to function, and not yet a present immediate capacity, because her basic inherent capacity has not yet had a chance to develop sufficiently.

The child in the womb is not, as the functioning-person theory maintains, a potential person, but rather a *potentially functioning actual person*. To be a potentially functioning person already ensures that the baby is a person, an actual, real, full person, for a potentially functioning person must necessarily be a person.

In the words of Joyce, "a one-celled person at conception is not a potential person, but an actual person with great potential for development and self-expression. That single-celled individual is just as actually a person as you and I."

I submit that there is no such thing as a potential person. The ovum and the sperm are preparations for a new person. Each of them is not that person in potential form because it is not that person at all. There is a radical break between sperm/ovum and the new person in the zygotic state. The transition from "potential x" to "actual x" always involves a continuity. Thus a medical student is recognized as a potential doctor because when the student *becomes* a doctor this will have happened within a continuity involving the same person. In contrast, as Joyce puts it, sperm and ovum…do not, even together, become a new human life, because they do not survive beyond conception.

"The sperm and the ovum," Joyce says, "are not potential [personal] life; rather they are potential *causes* of individual human life."

THE ACHIEVEMENT VIEW

The *functioning person theory* implies a certain elitism, something that may be called the *achievement view,* namely, that only human beings who have achieved a certain degree of development of the present immediate capacity to function as persons count as real persons. Thus Mary Anne Warren, Michael Tooley, and Peter Singer dismiss infants as nonpersons simply on the grounds that they have not yet achieved the status of functioning persons. But why hold that against them? That they have not achieved this status is perfectly normal, and could not be otherwise; for they have not yet reached that stage in their development over time when such capacity is normal. The achievement view is a clear example of discrimination: "You don't count as a real person, for you have not yet achieved the degree of development necessary for the present immediate capacity to function as a person."

The functioning-person theory is presented as if it were the product of careful, rational, philosophical analysis, a contribution to clear thinking. It gains this appearance largely from the element of truth it contains: that the concepts of "person" and "human being" are not identical, for there could be nonhuman persons. This hides its true nature, that it is in fact a form of elitism, leading to discrimination of the worst sort. For the theory implies that only some persons count: those who have achieved the status of functioning persons.

"At what point in its development does a fetus become a person?" (Or, when does it become human, meaning a person, since it is obviously human in the biological sense all along.) This whole question is misplaced. For there is a person, a human being, all along. It is only a matter of degree of development of the basic inherent capacity to function as a person. What we can now see, with new clarity, is that this question assumes the achievement view, indeed expresses it, and would collapse without it. Translated, the question reads, "How much must a human being achieve in the way of attaining the capability of functioning as a person to count as a person, that is, a being whose life we must respect?" The answer is clear: nothing. No achievement is necessary, and to demand it is elitism and discrimination. What is required is *being,* not achievement: being a person, having the nature of a person, regardless of how far along the achievement scale one has progressed.

It is wrong for a white to demand that real persons be white to count as persons. Blacks are equally persons, though they are "different." So too, it is wrong for a functioning person to demand that real persons be capable of functioning as persons. Small babies, incapable of this—or less capable—are equally persons, though they are "different." Being white is not a special achievement that blacks have failed to reach. Having the capability of functioning as a person, while it is an achievement, is equally irrelevant, morally. To demand it as a condition for membership in the class of persons is equally unjust and discriminatory.

It is wrong to discriminate against anyone who has not yet achieved the status of a functioning person. It is equally wrong to discriminate against anyone who is *no longer* capable of functioning because of severe senility. Likewise, it is wrong to discriminate against anyone who cannot now function, whether or not he ever could function in the past and whether or not he will be able to function in the future.

In the present context, in which we are analyzing a theory that raises—as a serious issue—the question of which human beings may be killed and which may not, it is not a matter of discrimination in merely a general sense, but something very specific, and particularly odious: It is a discrimination that takes advantage of a person's inability to function as a person and uses that against him or her as a pretext for killing that person. The effect of adopting the functioning-person theory would be to legitimize this taking advantage of a person's lack of ability. This is sheer "might over right," power and ability over frailty and (natural) disability. Those who have power and ability exercise it over those who do not—infants whom their theory can rule out as nonpersons. I submit that, quite generally, it is wrong for those who have the advantage of power and ability to take advantage of it over those who do not and to discriminate against them on the basis of this advantage. Let me express this in terms of the following moral principle:

It is always wrong for persons who have power and ability to take advantage of their status by discriminating against persons who are powerless, especially to kill them.

And, as a corollary: *It is always wrong to take advantage of anyone else's inability to function as a person by acts of discrimination that would deny that individual the full respect that is due to every person.*

This principle and its corollary apply not only to actions but also to rules and theories that would legitimatize such actions. Any theory that calls for or allows such discrimination is itself an immoral theory. (This is not a moral judgment on those who propose the theory, but strictly a judgment on the theory itself, in terms of its content and its logical consequences.) The functioning-person theory legitimizes the deliberate killing of small babies merely because they have not reached a sufficient level of development as predetermined by the theory. This is immoral.

STUDY QUESTIONS

1. According to Schwarz, what is the major failure in prochoice arguments like those of Mary Anne Warren and Michael Tooley? What does Schwarz say about this failure?

2. Consider Schwarz's counter example of the two neonates: One is born comatose and will remain so until the age of nine and the other is healthy at birth but as soon as she achieves the concept of a self, lapses into a coma until she is nine. Schwarz appeals to our intuitions to conclude that no essential difference exists between these two states, thus undermining the prochoice thesis that an actualized sense of selfhood is what gives one a right to life. Do you agree with Schwarz?

3. What is Schwarz's argument that fetuses and infants are actual persons, and not merely *potential* persons? How would a prochoice advocate respond to Schwarz's argument?

4. What is Schwarz's continuum argument (the one where cases A through F are compared)? Does it succeed in its objective?

5. According to Schwarz's position on personhood, would he be obligated to keep a permanently comatose person alive—through daily feeding and nursing care?

15

Abortion: A Defense of the Personhood Argument

LOUIS P. POJMAN

Louis P. Pojman is Professor of Philosophy at the United States Military Academy, West Point, New York. In this article, Pojman attempts to meet objections to the personhood argument for the permissibility of abortion. First, he argues that three of the four pro-abortion arguments on abortion fail, but that the personhood argument seems cogent. He then responds to criticisms, including that of Stephen Schwarz, against this argument. He shows why the liberal need not accept the permissibility of infanticide. Finally, he considers the moderate position as a possible alternative to the conservative-liberal controversy.

> Every unborn child must be regarded as a human person with all the rights of a human person, from the moment of conception. (Ethical and Religious Directive from Catholic Hospitals)

> [Abortion] during the first two or three months of gestation [is morally equivalent] to removal of a piece of tissue from the woman's body. (Thomas Szasz, "The Ethics of Abortion," *Humanist,* 1966)

No social issue divides our society as does the moral and legal status of the human fetus and the corresponding question of the moral permissibility of abortion. On the one hand, such organizations as the Roman Catholic Church and the Right-to-Life Movement, appalled by the 1.5 million abortions that

---

Although some of the material in this essay is based on material first set forth in Louis P. Pojman, *Life and Death: Grappling with the Moral Dilemmas of Our Time* (Boston: Jones and Bartlett, 1992), the essay itself was written for the first edition of this book.

take place in the United States each year, have exerted significant political pressure toward introducing a constitutional amendment that would grant full legal rights to fetuses. On the other hand, prochoice groups, such as the National Organization of Women (NOW), the National Abortion Rights Action League (NARAL), and feminist organizations have exerted enormous pressure on politicians to support pro-abortion legislation. The Republican and Democratic political platforms of the past three elections took diametrically opposite sides on this issue.

Opponents of abortion, like John Noonan and Stephen Schwarz, argue that because there is no non-arbitrary cutoff point between conception of the single-cell zygote and the full adult where we can say, "Here we do not have a human being and here we do," to draw the line anywhere but at conception is to justify infanticide, the killing of small children, the killing of teenagers, and the killing of the elderly.

In this essay I will examine the problem of abortion. But first I want to prove that no poor people exist in the world! I know you will agree that having a single penny does not make the difference between being wealthy or poor. Perhaps having a penny will make the difference in purchasing something, but that in itself does not constitute the difference between poverty and wealth. Then I hope you will agree that possessing a billion dollars constitutes being wealthy. Now take a penny away from our billionaire. Does the loss of one cent make him poor? Of course not. We have already agreed that the gain or loss of one penny does not make a difference with regard to whether someone is poor or wealthy. Now take another penny from him and another and another until he only is worth $1.25, the price of *The Sunday New York Times*. He is homeless and cannot even afford a half-gallon of milk, but by our argument, he is not poor, for all we did was subtract pennies from him one by one and such small increments cannot make a difference.

Of course, we could work the argument the other way around and prove that no one is rich—that everyone is poor. We will agree to the same crucial premise that a penny does not make a difference between wealth and poverty. We will agree that possessing only a penny makes no one rich. Then we will give a penny to our poor man, one by one, until he possesses a hundred billion pennies or a billion dollars.

Or consider this argument. No one is really bald, for taking a single hair from anyone with a complete head of hair cannot produce baldness, so we begin to take hairs from your head one by one until you have no hair at all on your head. At what point were you really bald? Surely, having merely one strand of hair is being bald, and adding a second makes no difference to the designation of being bald. So we can go from baldness to a full head of hair without ever finding a cutoff point where baldness ends and hairiness begins. Yet we are sure that there is a difference between baldness and having a full head of hair.

When does an accumulation of sand, soil, and rock become a mountain? A piece of sand, a speck of soil, and a tiny stone do not constitute a mountain, but if we keep adding sand, soil, and rocks long enough we will eventually end up with a structure as large as Mt. Everest!

You get the point. Concepts are not clear and do not fit easily onto reality, so that it may not make sense to speak of drawing a line between stages of development. These are examples of Slippery Slope Arguments, sometimes called "Edge of the Wedge Arguments." Such arguments have been used as the trump card of traditionalists opposed to social change. Give innovation an inch and it will take a mile. The first step to Auschwitz begins with a seemingly innocent concession to those who would promote social considerations over the sanctity of life.

The slippery slope arguments trade on the difficulty of applying concepts, which are vague, to reality, which is precise. That is, I have an absolutely precise number of hairs on my head, but the concept of baldness is imprecise. The fallacy of the slippery slope argument is to suppose that because there is no distinct cutoff point in reality where concepts change (rich to poor, and so forth), there is no real difference between state A and B. But there is. We know the difference between wealth and poverty even though we cannot define it in absolute monetary terms. We know the difference between a full head of hair and baldness even though we cannot say exactly where baldness begins. We know the difference between a hill and a mountain even though there is a grey area in between where we are not sure what to call it.

Now apply this point to the moral problem of abortion. Simply because we cannot discover a bright line separating a person from a nonperson does not rule out the existence of such a distinction. If we judge on the merits of the case that a relevant moral difference exists between fetal life and self-conscious human life, that difference can be as real as the difference between poverty and wealth or a mole hill and Mt. Whitney. Even though no perceptible difference might exist between any two successive stages, a real difference can appear between nonsuccessive stages.

THE LIBERAL POSITION

The liberal position asserts that it is always or almost always morally permissible for a woman to have an abortion. It allows abortion on demand. Four arguments for this position have been offered. They are as follows:

1. Subjectivism: Radical Relativism
2. Absolute Right to Privacy Argument (reproductive freedom)
3. The Quality of Life Argument (in cases of the probability of defective neonates)
4. The Personhood Argument

1. Subjectivism: Radical Relativism

Abortion is a private matter into which the law should not enter. No one should be forced to have children. H. Schur in his book, *Crimes without Victims,* calls abortion a victimless crime. Unfortunately, he supplies no argument for his view that fetuses are nonpersons. Schur assumes that morality is merely a matter of individual choice. Who are we to judge?

But subjectivism is a dubious doctrine. If fetuses are persons, then is not what we are doing tantamount to killing innocent people? Are not we all engaged in mass killings? And is not the killing of innocents to be condemned?

2. The Absolute Right to Privacy Argument

The National Organization of Women (NOW) and many radical feminists hold that because a woman has an absolute right to her own body on which a fetus is dependent, she may do whatever is necessary to detach the fetus from her, including putting it to death.

The first problem with this argument is that it is unclear whether we have any *absolute* rights at all. An absolute right always overrides all other considerations. It is doubtful whether we have many of these. The only ones I can think of are rights like the right not to be unnecessarily harmed or tortured. We have no reason to believe that our right to use our own body as we wish is an absolute right. Consider 500-pound Fat Fred who decides to sit down, but your money-packed wallet happens to be directly on the spot where he sits. You request him to move his body so that you can get your wallet, but he refuses, claiming that he has an absolute right to do with his body what he wills.

The doctrine of absolute rights to privacy or body use suffers from lack of intelligent support. Because our bodies are public and interact with other people's bodies and property, we need ways of adjudicating conflicts between them, but there is no such thing as an absolute right to do whatever we want with our bodies. The parent of dependent children does not have a right to remove his or her body to a different locale, abandoning the children. A citizen may be morally obligated to take his or her body to the army recruitment center when his or her nation is in danger and the draft board picks his or her number.

Although my right to do what I please with my body can include my right to deny its use to a creature who needs it (for example, the mayor of my town needs to attach himself to someone with a functioning liver), it does *not* give me a right to kill the mayor. I only have a right to disengage from him, not kill him. Because all current methods of abortion involve killing the fetus before disengagement, none of them can be justified by the libertarian argument.

The case is even more serious for the libertarian argument because the woman wanting an abortion has typically voluntarily put herself at risk for pregnancy. Suppose that President Clinton suddenly has a rare form of liver and double kidney failure, so that he needs to be plugged into a human being's kidneys and liver. The person will have to walk around with the President, sleep in his bed, and eat at his table for nine months. One hundred people with the right kinds of kidneys and livers are rounded up and invited to participate in a lottery. One person, the loser, will get plugged in to the president. Each of the one hundred people will win $1,000 for playing the game. You are one of the people invited to play. Would you play?

Most people asked, including myself, say that they would take the risk of playing the lottery. Once we agree to play we are obligated to accept the inconvenience if we lose. It would be absurd to back out, claiming an absolute right to privacy or bodily use.

The implications of the lottery game for abortion are obvious. Once people voluntarily engage in sex, they are engaged in the lottery game. Even if they use birth control devices, pregnancy might result. If the fetus is a person with a right to life, the woman cannot simply dismiss that right by invoking a superior right to privacy. She has suspended that right by engaging in an act that brought the new being into existence.

3. The Quality of life Argument

One strategy available to the liberal is to deny that life is of absolute value. Life may be a necessary condition for happiness and whatever makes life worth living, but not all life is worth living. The severely deformed, retarded, anencephalic[1] or hydrocephalic child might live a negative existence, in which case abortion might be warranted. Or suppose that a pregnant woman is informed that the fetus she is carrying has Tay-Sachs[2] disease or *spina bifida* and is told that if she aborts, in five months she will be able to conceive a normal child. If it is quality that counts, the woman not only may abort, but she has a positive duty to do so.

This argument can be extended to cover cases where the woman is incapable of providing an adequate upbringing for the child to be born, the case of the teenage pregnancy, the family with children which cannot afford another child. That the world is already overpopulated is another consideration arguing for abortion of unwanted children. No unwanted child should enter the world.

The Quality of Life Argument has merit—quality does count—but it has weaknesses that need to be examined. First, the argument against bringing unwanted children into the world can be offset by the availability of adoption. Many childless couples *want* these children. Nevertheless, not all children are likely to be adopted into loving homes, so that some abortions would still be permitted.

A more significant objection is that the Quality of Life Argument leaves the status of the fetus untouched. If the fetus is a person, then it makes no more sense to speak of aborting it because you do not think it will have an adequate quality of life than it does to kill a baby or ten-year old or ninety-year-old because you do not think he or she will have an adequate quality of life. Although quality counts, the critic contends, we do not have the right to "play God" in this way with people's lives. It is too dangerous.

The prochoice adherent has a response here—sometimes we must play God, for sometimes the prospects of suffering for all concerned are so dire and so likely that abortion, even if the fetus is a person, is permissible. In this sense, abortion is the lesser of evils, though still an evil.

This is essentially the moderate position as set forth by Daniel Callahan, L. W. Sumner, Baruch Brody, and Caroline Whitbeck.

4. The Personhood Argument

Our intuitions generally tell us that the fetus does not have the same moral status as the mother. Anti-abortionists often base their conclusions on our religious heritage, but even there the case is ambiguous. Although the notion of ensoulment argues for the personhood of the fetus, earlier Biblical ideas lend support for a distinction of status. For example, Exodus (21:22) says that if a man causes a woman to abort, he shall be punished, but if the woman's death follows, those responsible shall give "life for life, eye for eye, tooth for tooth."

Moreover, a tradition within the Roman Catholic Church, going at least as far back as Thomas Aquinas (1225–1274) and adopted at the Council of Vienna in 1312, called *hylomorphism,* holds that the human soul is to the body somewhat as the shape of a statue is to the actual statue. Thus, without a fully formed human shape, no human soul exists.[3]

Furthermore, serious difficulties arise in viewing the single-cell zygote or the conceptus as a person, given the phenomenon of twinning that can take place up to the third week of pregnancy. If the embryo splits into two (or three, four, or more) embryos, does one person (soul) become two (or more)? How can personhood, with its characteristic of complete unity, be divided?

But it is not enough for liberals to point out problems in the conservative position. The liberal must go to the heart of the matter and dismantle the conservative arguments for the fetus's right to life. The central one is offered by Noonan:

1. We ought never to kill innocent human beings.

2. Fetuses are innocent human beings.

3. Therefore we ought never to kill fetuses (that is, have abortions).

The liberal points out that the term *human being* is used ambiguously in the argument. Note that sometimes by *human being* we have a biological concept in mind, the species *Homo sapiens,* that at other times we have a psychological-moral concept in mind, someone with the characteristics of humans as we typically find them, characteristics such as rationality, freedom, and self-consciousness, which mark them off from other animals. In philosophy we sometimes refer the word *person* to this type of being. A person is someone who has an intrinsic right to life. If we apply this distinction to Noonan's argument, we see that it trades on this ambiguity.

In the first premise "human beings" refers to persons, while in the second it refers to *Homo sapiens.* The argument should read as follows:

1. We ought never to kill innocent *persons.*

2. Fetuses are innocent *Homo sapiens.*

3. Therefore we ought never to kill fetuses.

But this is an invalid argument, since it is not obvious that all *Homo sapiens* are persons.

The question is this: by virtue of what characteristics does someone have a right to life? The liberal will point out that it is a form of prejudice, similar to racism, sexism, nationalism, religionism, and ethnocentrism, to prefer one species to another simply because it is your species or to grant someone a right simply because he or she is a member of a biological group. Richard Ryder and Peter Singer in their works on animal rights call this prejudice *Speciesism.*

Speciesism violates the first principle of justice: Treat equals equally and unequals unequally. Suppose it turned out that one ethnic group or gender on average made better musicians than other groups. It would still be unjust automatically to allow all and only members of that group to enter music schools. Individuals have a right to be judged according to their ability, and so we would want to test individuals independently of ethnic group or gender to ascertain a candidate's capacity for musical performance.

What are the characteristics that give beings a right to life analogous to the characteristics that give candidates a right to enter music school? The liberal argues that certain properties that most adult humans have are the proper criteria for this distinction. These properties are intrinsically valuable traits that allow us to view ourselves as selves with plans and projects over time, properties like self-consciousness and rationality. Both conservatives and liberals agree that these qualities are intrinsically good. The liberal, however, tries, to draw out their implications: that our ability to make plans, to think rationally, and to have a self over time give us a special right to life. Although it is difficult to specify exactly what are the necessary and sufficient conditions for personhood, and liberals have described these conditions differently—some emphasizing desires and interests, others emphasizing agency or the ability to project into the future, others emphasizing the capacity for a notion of the self—they all point to a cluster of characteristics which distinguish children and adults from fetuses, infants, and most animals. And those characteristics enable us to interact and reciprocate on the social playing field of civilized existence.[4]

Joel Feinberg describes personhood this way:

> What makes me certain that my parents, siblings, and friends are people is that they give evidence of being conscious of the world and of themselves; they have inner emotional lives, just like me; they can understand things and reason about them, make plans, and act; they can communicate with me, argue, negotiate, express themselves, make agreements, honor commitments, and stand in relationships of mutual trust; they have tastes and values of their own; they can be frustrated or fulfilled, pleased or hurt.... In the commonsense way of thinking, persons are those beings who are conscious, have a concept and awareness of themselves, are capable of experiencing emotions, can reason and acquire understanding, can plan ahead, can act on their plans, and can feel pleasure and pain.[5]

A certain vagueness inheres in the specification of these qualities, and individuals possess them to different degrees—life is not neat and tidy—but we have an adequate idea of what they are. Practically, a typical test of whether someone is a person is the ability to reason about or emphatically communicate about interpersonal relations. Studies show that not only humans but gorillas, chimpanzees, and dogs have this ability.

I think that the phrase "rational self-consciousness" captures what we typically mean by this property. It distinguishes the average adult human from most of the animal kingdom. But not all humans have these qualities, whereas some animals may possess them. Severely retarded children, anencephalic babies, severely senile adults, and people in persistent vegetative states do not possess these properties, but dolphins, whales, chimpanzees, apes, and even some dogs and pigs may possess them. The following diagram represents the relationship between humans and animals with regard to personhood.

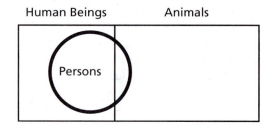

If rational self-consciousness marks the criterion for having a right to life, then fetuses do not have a right to life, since they are neither rational nor self-conscious.

THE CONSERVATIVE RESPONSE AND LIBERAL COUNTERRESPONSE

How do conservatives respond to this argument? First, they point out two counterintuitive implications of the liberal position, and then they point out something missing that changes the liberal's logic.

If the personhood argument were followed, we would be permitted to kill unconscious and severely retarded and senile humans—even normal people when they sleep, for none of these have the required characteristics for personhood. Second, the argument ignores the fact that the fetus is a *potential* person, and potentiality for self-consciousness should be seen as granting a being similar rights as an actual person. Finally, the argument would also sanction infanticide, something that most liberals are loath to allow.

Poignant as these objections are, the liberal has an adequate response to each of them. Regarding the killing of the retarded and senile, the liberal would point out that most of these people still have an adequate amount of self-consciousness and rationality and that it would be dangerous to put into practice a policy of doing away with all but the most obvious cases of irretrievable loss of selfhood. With regard to those who sleep or are unconscious, they still have the capacity for rational self-consciousness, so we may not kill them.

Potentiality is not enough, only actuality or capacity for self-consciousness is sufficient for granting someone a right to life. Let me illustrate this with an example from the 1992 presidential campaign. Suppose that during that campaign of the Democratic Party for the presidential nomination, Jerry Brown had suddenly appeared at the White House with his family and furniture. "I'm moving in here," he announces to an incredulous White House staff.

"You can't do. It's unlawful! President Bush rightly lives here," objects the staff member.

"You don't know what you're talking about. Don't you Republicans believe that a potential person has all the rights of an actual person? Well, on that same logic, a potential president has the same rights as an actual president. Since I am potentially the president, I'm taking advantage of my rights, so let me in."

Although the fetus may be a potential person, it is not yet an actual one; hence, it does not have the same rights as an actual person.

In this regard, Mary Anne Warren offers the following thought experiment:

> Suppose that our space explorer falls into the hands of an alien culture, whose scientists decide to create a few hundred thousand or more human beings, by breaking his body into its component cells, and using these to create fully developed human beings, with, of course, his genetic code. We may imagine that each of these newly created men will have all of the original man's abilities, skills, knowledge, and so on, and also have an individual self-concept, in short that each of them will be a bona fide (though hardly unique) person. Imagine that the whole project will take only seconds, and that its chances of success are extremely high, and that our explorer knows all of this, and also knows that these people will be treated fairly. I maintain that in such a situation he would have every right to escape if he could, and thus to deprive all of these potential people of their potential lives; for his right to life outweighs all of theirs together, in spite of the fact that they are all genetically human, all innocent, and all have a very high probability of becoming people very soon, if only he refrains from acting.[6]

Warren, in a later article, seems to have lost confidence in this argument, conceding that such bizarre situations are inadequate grounds for the refutation of the potentiality principle.[7] But the situation is not as bizarre as we might suppose.

Consider the implications of the thesis held by virtually all conservatives that the single-cell zygote has the same right to life as a fully conscious moral agent. If you believe that a single-cell zygote has a right to life, then you should refrain from washing, scratching, and brushing your teeth. Why? Because in doing so, you are killing thousands of single cells of *exactly the same nature* as the zygote. The only difference between other diploid cells in our body and the zygote is the location. The zygote fortuitously has gotten into the incubator, whereas the others have not. But that is an irrelevant distinction, having nothing to do with inherent rights or the quality of the cell itself. Given the prospects of cloning, any cell of your body could be developed into a fetus, a baby, and, finally, into an adult. If the zygote is sacred and possesses a right to life, the same goes for every other human cell in the world.

Some conservatives, like Stephen Schwarz, argue that the fetus is not a potential person but an actual person, an essential person, who simply is not functioning as an adult.[8]

Schwarz raises an important issue. If a sleeping person or temporarily comatose person is not to be killed because he or she has the potential for rational self-consciousness, should not the fetus be likewise protected since it too will eventually become rationally self-conscious? "Neither the sleeping person nor the being in the womb now display the qualities of a functioning person. Both will display them. It is only a matter of time. Why should the one count as a real person because the time is short, while the other does not, simply because in her case the time is longer?"

Rejecting the idea of potentiality altogether, Schwarz divides the relevant categories into varieties of capacities. Personhood is grounded in the *basic inherent capacity* to function as rational beings. But this basic capacity may not be presently operative, but only latent, as in a reversible coma, which Schwarz calls *latent-1 capacity,* or where it is insufficiently developed, as in a small child, which Schwarz calls *latent-2 capacity*. All of these capacities are sufficient for personhood. Schwarz argues that the single-cell zygote has the physical basis of the required capacities (that is, it has latent-2 capacity). "It is merely that it is now in a primitive, undeveloped form. The zygote has the essential structure of this basis; a structure that will unfold, grow, develop, mature, which takes time…The zygote actually has the basic inherent capacity to function as a person because he has the essential physical structure for this."[9] So the single-cell zygote is a full person.

But if every human zygote is a full person whose latent-2 capacity grants an inalienable right to life, every cell in our bodies must merit that same protection, since essentially it has the same structure as the cell in the pregnant woman's uterus. In fact, the ovum and the spermatozoon also have the essential genetic make-up, so that they would qualify as persons, and as such deserve full protection.

With regard to the matter of treating the fetus as a person with "latent-2 capacities" rather than as a potential person, Schwarz seems to be playing with words. "Latent-2 capacity" obscures the distinction between potentiality and actuality. The crucial distinction between a capacity and a potentiality goes like this. Consider a lump of clay. It does not have the capacity to hold water, but it has the potentiality for that capacity (Schwarz's latent-2 capacity). Suppose that I mold it into a cup. Now it has the capacity for holding water even though at present it is not holding any (what Schwarz calls a latent-1 capacity). The fetus only has the potentiality for self-consciousness, whereas the unconscious person has the capacity for it. The seemingly innocuous latent-1 and latent-2 capacities slur over the essential difference between having the potential for becoming a rational self-conscious person and actually being one who is not functioning as such. It makes all the difference in the world—as much difference as between a mere pack of clay and a clay cup with a lid on it so that it cannot presently take in liquid.

Although Schwarz is aware that liberals want to make something like this distinction, he thinks that on reflection our intuitions will lead us to a contrary judgment. Here is his thought experiment.

Consider the case of two children. "One is born comatose, and he will remain so until the age of nine. The other is healthy at birth, but as soon as she achieves the concept of a continuing self for a brief time, she, too, lapses into a coma, from which she will not emerge until she is nine." Then Schwarz asks, "Can anyone seriously hold that the second child is a person with a right to life, while the first child is not?"[10] My response is, "Yes, indeed, I can!"

My intuitions are exactly the opposite of Schwarz's, which makes me suspect that our intuitions are partly a function of the wider theories about human nature, personal identity, religion, and morality. Here is my assessment of Schwarz's counter example. First of all, children are not born with a sense of selfhood. They gradually achieve this property as they interact with their parents and older siblings. Piaget and other psychologists think that the child only attains such a sense in the second year of life. Schwarz's counter example presupposes that the sense of selfhood is a *fiat,* which reveals a deep misunderstanding of the psychological process of becoming self-aware.

Second, one must question the relevance of Schwarz's counter example. If the pro-abortionist believes that a sense of selfhood is the decisive property separating personhood from nonpersonhood, why should the fact that someone only enjoyed it for a short time be a reason for discounting it at all? Suppose Albert Einstein went into a nine-year comatose state immediately after arriving at his theory of relativity. He still possessed something valuable, which his fellow comatosee lacked. The question is not whether the girl in Schwarz's example possessed a sense of selfhood for a long time, but whether the sense of selfhood is a necessary and sufficient criterion for deontological personhood. The liberal argues that it is, and so he or she should not be moved by such counter examples.

Schwarz holds that an adult person is identical with his or her single-cell zygote. "My capabilities have changed; they have increased as my basic inherent capacity to function as a person has developed; but I remain always *the same person,* the same essential being…" But this identity of the adult with the zygote or blastocyst creates staggering difficulties. If I am exactly identical to my zygote, then I am exactly identical to whatever my zygote develops into. But early in the fetus's life, twinning sometimes occurs (not to speak of quintupling!). So, if I am an identical twin, I must be identical to my identical twin. So if my twin commits a murder, I may be executed for it, and if I marry Joan, my twin may properly sleep with her.

Unless one is willing to swallow such implications, this kind of conservative position on personal identity from the zygote to the adult is doomed to incoherence.

Infanticide

The most serious objection to the liberal position on abortion is that it leads to the permissibility of infanticide. Since there is no relevant difference between a fetus one day before birth and a baby one day after birth, if abortion of a fetus is permissible, so is the killing of a baby. What is the liberal's response to this charge?

The liberal's reply is a qualified, "Yes, but not necessarily." In a sense liberalism does lead to the permissibility of infanticide, but it need not. Let me explain.

The liberal can distinguish between a *natural right* (or deontological right) and a *social right* (or utilitarian right). A natural right is one that a person has simply by virtue of intrinsic qualities. A social right, on the other hand, is not intrinsic to the being, but bestowed by society. Society has the privilege and right of protecting things that it deems valuable or useful to its purposes. Just as it can grant a forest or endangered animal species a protective right, so it can give fetuses or infants such rights if it so chooses. The only necessary condition for granting something a social right is that we give a utilitarian reason for doing so. Since the entity at issue does not have sufficient intrinsic value to claim the right, there must be an instrumental reason for doing so.

We are more willing to extend a social right to infants than to fetuses because they are closer to personhood and because they are independent of the mother's body and can be adopted. If a state decided that good reasons existed to extend the social right to life to fetuses, it would be justified in doing so. But it does not have to, and if there were good utilitarian reasons for doing so, the state could remove the social right to life from infants. Because removing that right would most likely cause a social upheaval far beyond the present uproar over the legalization of abortion, this is unlikely to happen. Nonetheless, on the liberal argument, such a move could not be ruled out as morally unacceptable.

Let me succinctly set forth this argument in six steps so that you will be able to examine it carefully.

1. All and only actual persons have a deontological moral *right* to life (that is, potentiality or "latent-2 capacities" do not count).

2. Persons may be defined as beings who have the capacity for reason and self-conscious desire ("Reason Capacity").

3. Fetuses and infants do not have Reason Capacities and so do not have a deontological moral right to life.

4. However, there are social rights (utilitarian rights) that society may bestow on classes of beings for utilitarian reasons. This includes treating some potential persons as though they had full deontological rights.

5. There are good utilitarian reasons for treating infants (and perhaps fetuses in the latter stages of pregnancy) as "persons," giving them social rights.

6. Therefore, we ought to bestow a social right on infants and perhaps on viable fetuses. That is, once past a fixed time a woman loses her right to abort potential persons, except where they will be seriously defective or where the mother's life or health is endangered.

The distinction between a deontological right and a social or utilitarian right means that certain rights are largely beyond the authority of society to tamper with. The basic rights of persons are within this domain. However, optional rights, social rights, may be extended or withheld from beings not yet fully human but on the way to becoming so.

Good utilitarian reasons exist for forbidding infanticide, except perhaps where the handicap is so severe as to impede the prospects for a worthwhile life. Anencephalic, severely deformed, and incurably diseased neonates might well be killed at birth to prevent needless suffering. Infants, unlike fetuses, can be taken from the mother and adopted by others. They also have begun to play a social role in society. As Joel Feinberg argues

> It would be seriously wrong for a mother to kill her physically normal infant, [liberals] contend, even though such a killing would not violate anyone's right to life. The same reasons that make infanticide in the normal case wrong also justify its prohibition by the criminal law. The moral rule that condemns these killings and the legal rule that renders them punishable are both supported by "utilitarian reasons," that is, considerations of what is called "social utility," "the common good," "the public interest," and the like. Nature has apparently implanted in us an instinctive tenderness toward infants that has proven extremely useful to the species, not only because it leads us to protect our young from death, and thus keep our population up, but also because infants usually grow into adults, and in Benn's words, "if as infants *they* are not treated with some minimal degree of tenderness and consideration, they will suffer for it later, as persons." One might add that when they are adults, others will suffer for it, too, at their hands. Spontaneous warmth and sympathy toward babies then clearly has a great deal of social utility, and insofar as infanticide would tend to weaken that socially valuable response, it is, on utilitarian grounds, morally wrong.[11]

The core of the liberal position is the notion that we are not born persons but become such through adequate socialization. Becoming a person is not a biological given but an interactive *process.* Studies by Bruno Bettelheim and others of children suffering severe forms of infantile autism (a form of childhood schizophrenia) show that infants abandoned or severely neglected by parents (even intelligent, educated, middle-class parents) fail to learn to speak and take on animal characteristics: eat raw meat, drink by lapping, tear their clothes off and prefer to run around naked, howl, growl at humans, and often bite those who attend them. Reports of feral children are controversial, but abandoned infants who have been brought up by wolves take on wolf-like traits, not distinctively human ones. They lack language ability, lack a sense of self, and are unable to think abstractly.[12]

If a *Homo sapiens* is not born a person but becomes such through a complex process of socialization, personhood is a social achievement, and the liberal has grounds to permit abortion, and, in some instances, infanticide.

THE MODERATE POSITION

The moderate is caught in the middle of this controversy. He or she is dissatisfied with the arguments on both sides of the fence. Moderates object to the conservative prohibition of abortion because it is one-dimensional, seeing only the abstract right of the fetus and not the complications of life. The moderate contends against the conservative that the mother's psychological condition and the quality of life of the fetus must be taken into consideration in deciding on abortion. A victim of rape, a pregnant thirteen-year-old, or a poor woman with too many children is probably justified in getting an abortion.

But the moderate does not agree with the liberal on the issue of abortion on demand. Fetuses are potential persons in a way that other single cells in the body are not. They are already in process of developing into the kind of beings that will be socialized as self-conscious persons. The closer they come to birth, the more the presumption of life is in their favor.

Even though it is put forward by a conservative, John Noonan, the moderate is likely to accept the argument from probability.

> Consider, for example, the spermatozoa in any normal ejaculate. There are about 200,000,000 in any single ejaculate, of which one has a chance of developing into a zygote. Consider the oocytes that may become òva: There are 100,000 to 1,000,000 oocytes in a female infant, of which a maximum of 390 are ovulated. But once spermatozoa and ovum meet and the conceptus is formed, such studies as have been made show that roughly in only 20 percent of the cases will spontaneous abortion occur. In other words, the chances are about four out of five that this new being will develop. At this stage in the life of the being there is a sharp shift in probabilities, an immense jump in potentialities. To make a distinction between the rights of spermatozoa and the rights of the fertilized ovum is to respond to an enormous shift in possibilities. For about 20 days after conception the egg may split to form twins or combine with another egg to form a chimera, but the probability of either event happening is very small.[13]

Although Noonan is an anti-abortionist, this argument can be used by moderates because he is not arguing that biological probabilities establish essential humanity, but simply that it is commonsensical to suppose that the fetus will develop into a person. As Noonan continues, "If the chance is 200,000,000 to 1 that the movement in the bushes into which you shoot is a man's, I doubt if many persons would hold you careless in shooting; but if the chances are four out of five that the movement is a human being's, few would acquit you of blame."

The argument from probability does not give the fetus a clear right to life, but it shows that there is a presumption against aborting. That is, a difference still stands between a potential person and an actual person, but since there is a high probability that the fetus will become a person, we should only permit abortion for compelling reasons, where the mother's health or life is endangered or where the quality of life of the fetus will be seriously compromised.

Ultimately, the moderate position may be a practical social compromise between the liberal and conservative positions. Nevertheless, I do not think that it overcomes the logical point about potentiality. Regardless of probabilities, a potential president of the United States cannot simply on that basis move into the White House, and a potential person cannot claim a right to life. Unless the conservatives and moderates can show why the liberal arguments that I have defended in this essay are unsound, a fetus cannot be properly accorded a deontological right to life. Abortion, and in some instances, infanticide, are morally permissible.[15]

STUDY QUESTIONS

1. How does Louis Pojman see the slippery slope argument operating in the abortion dispute? Is he correct? Why or why not?

2. What are the four arguments set forth by liberals in defense of the permissibility of abortion, and what are their comparative strengths and weaknesses?

3. Explain the personhood argument. What is its view on potentiality? What is the difference between *potentiality* for something and having a *capacity* for something?

4. What is the difference between a deontological right and a utilitarian or social right? Do you accept this as a legitimate distinction in the abortion dispute? Explain your position.

5. Do you think that the moderate position, as discussed at the end of this essay, is plausible? Why or why not?

NOTES

1. "Anencephalic" describes a baby born without all or a major portion of the brain. "Hydrocephalic" describes the abnormal increase in the amount of cerebrospinal fluid within the cranial cavity and expansion of the cerebral ventricles that together cause the atrophy of the brain.

2. Tay-Sachs disease results from a congenital enzyme deficiency, characterized by progressive mental and motor deterioration. It is usually fatal before age five. Spina bifida is a spinal cord defect leading to incomplete closure of the vertebrae, which can cause paralysis, bowel obstruction, and severe retardation.

3. See Joseph F. Donceel, "A Liberal Catholic's View" in Joel Feinberg, ed., *The Problem of Abortion*. Belmont, Calif.: Wadsworth, 1984, 16–17.

4. Jane English, "Abortion and the Concept of a Person," *Canadian Journal of Philosophy* 5, 2 (1975) (reprinted in this work) argues that the concept of a person is too weak to bear the weight that liberals would place on it. I think she is asking for more certainty than is necessary for moral distinctions. We have a good idea of those qualities that make adult humans over

against rocks, plants, and even lower animals valuable or morally considerable—even though we have difficulty deciding whether borderline cases like cats and dogs should count as persons. They reveal some but not all of the characteristics that are necessary for personhood.

5. Joel Feinberg, "Abortion" in *Matters of Life and Death: New Introductory Essays in Moral Philosophy*, ed. Tom Regan. New York: Random Rouse, 1980, 189f.

6. Mary Anne Warren, "On the Moral and Legal Status of Abortion," *Monist*, 57, 1, 1973, 59–60.

7. Mary Anne Warren, "Do Potential People Have Moral Rights?" *Canadian Journal of Philosophy*, 7, 2, 278.

8. Stephen Schwarz, *The Moral Question of Abortion*, Chicago: Loyola University Press, 1990, especially Chapter 7, most of which is reprinted in this work.

9. Schwarz, *Moral Question*, 94.

10. Ibid., 90.

11. Joel Feinberg, "Abortion" in *Matters of Life and Death: New Introductory Essays in Moral Philosophy*, ed. Tom Regan. New York: Random Rouse, 1980.

12. See Bruno Bettelheim, "Feral Children and Autistic Children," *The American Journal of Sociology,* 64 (March, 1959), 455–467; and *The Empty Fortress: Infantile Autism and the Birth of the Self,* New York: Free Press, 1967; see also George R. Mead, *Mind, Self and Society,* Chicago: University of Chicago Press, 1934.

14. John Noonan, "An Almost Absolute Value in History" in Noonan, ed., *The Morality of Abortion: Legal and Historical Perspectives.* Cambridge, Mass.: Harvard University Press, 1970, reprinted in this volume.

15. Robert Ginsberg, Michael Levin, Laura Purdy, and Trudy Pojman made helpful criticisms of an earlier draft of this paper.

16

Abortion and Human
Rights

NORMAN C. GILLESPIE

Norman C. Gillespie, now a lawyer in New York, for many years taught philosophy at Memphis State University. In this essay Gillespie defends a moderate position on abortion. He proceeds by examining two assumptions that give rise to the liberal-conservative dichotomy: (a) that a point somewhere between conception and adulthood defines where personhood begins and (b) that the morality of abortion depends on locating such a point. Gillespie argues against each of these assumptions and concludes that a significant moral difference exists between early and late abortions even though we cannot say where personhood begins.

Philosophical and popular thinking about abortion is influenced by the belief that the fundamental issue in settling the morality of abortion is whether a fetus is a person (is a human being, has a right to life, or has passed the point at which "life begins"). Despite widespread disagreement over "where to draw the line," many people believe (a) that there is a point somewhere between conception and adulthood that is morally significant, and (b) that the morality of a particular abortion depends on whether it occurs before or after that point. These assumptions are widely shared: Ardent anti-abortionists insist that the significant point is conception; at least one philosopher thinks that the Supreme Court, in permitting abortions during the first two trimesters of pregnancy, has "for all practical purposes...resolve[d] the difficult question of when life begins,"[1] and more than one philosopher has searched

Reprinted from *Ethics*, vol. 87, no. 3 (April 1977), © by The University of Chicago) by permission.

for criteria for determining whether or not a being is a person in order to set-tle the morality of abortion—the basic idea being that if a fetus is not a per-son, then abortion is morally permissible. All of these ideas, I shall argue, rest on mistaken assumptions, and after explicating briefly some of the principles that determine the distribution of human rights, I shall argue on the basis of those principles that (a) and (b) are false.

I

In many philosophic discussions of abortion, the problem arises: If an early abortion is morally permissible, why not a late abortion or even, as one philosopher has suggested, infanticide?[2] What is the *morally relevant difference* between them? These questions rely on some standard principles of moral reasoning; yet, as we shall see, their full implications have not been recognized by most participants in such discussions. According to the principle of univer-salizability (U), if an act is morally right for one person, then it is morally right for all relevantly similar persons, and this principle can be restated as (R). If one person has a right to *x,* then all relevantly similar persons have the same right to *x*. In analyzing these principles and the role of relevant similarities and relevant differences in moral reasoning, one finds, as Alan Gewirth puts it, that "according to the universalizability thesis, a singular moral judgment, which says that some individual subject S has some moral predicate P, is based on a reason according to which (a) S has some nonmoral property Q and (b) having Q is a sufficient justifying condition for having P, so that if one accepts the judgment and the reason then one must accept the generalization that every subject that has Q has P."[3] In short, moral properties are supervenient on nonmoral ones: Individuals are relevantly similar or relevantly different in virtue of their nonmoral properties, and whatever moral properties one has, all relevantly similar individuals share the same moral properties.

In the abortion dispute, the relevant nonmoral properties are thought to be viability, brain activity, independence, memory, and desires, and on that basis, it is argued that human beings have rights.

Some philosophers have argued that universalizability is trivial in that there can be unique nonmoral properties by virtue of which only one individual, or only one class of individuals, has certain moral properties. In responding to this criticism, Gewirth points out that "in all these cases,...the justifying [non-moral] properties in question [may] involve an important *comparative* ele-ment...The point is that even when a reason for a right or duty directly applies only to one person, where that reason logically involves a comparative ele-ment, it applies in a comparative or proportional way to other persons. The logical form of that proportionality is [L] if *x* units of some property Q justify that one have *x* units of some right of duty E, then *y* units of Q justify that one have *y* units of E. Such proportionality is a pervasive feature of traditional doctrines of distributive justice."[4]

Now, whatever nonmoral properties one selects as a basis for determining human rights, it seems likely that those properties will be comparative and thus involve (L) in any assessment of whether a being has any rights. Indeed, as is true of most people, even if someone does not know on what basis we say that adult human beings have rights, he can appreciate that children are sufficiently like adults to have some rights, that the same is true of small children, that about-to-be-born babies are comparatively like infants, and that fetuses are comparatively similar to about-to-be-born babies.

This line of reasoning is familiar. When it is used with "bald" and the number of hairs on one's head (or "poor" and the number of pennies one has), it is called "the Sorites paradox." Yet, on the basis of (L) it is not paradoxical at all; it is, instead, what reason would demand in dealing with such continuums. That "bald," "poor," and "person" are vague is widely recognized; what is not so widely appreciated is how to deal with such terms, especially in moral argument. Insisting on "drawing the line" in applying such terms is irrational; it only produces such paradoxical remarks as "it is not true that the fetus is a human being—but it is not false either," and "the indeterminateness of the fetus' humanity…means that, whatever you believe, it's not true—but neither is it false."[5]

The rational thing to do is to treat such cases on a *comparative* basis; to say that A is poorer (balder) than B, and, in the abortion dispute, that small children are not full-fledged, responsible adults, that infants are further from adulthood than small children, and fetuses further still removed from adulthood than infants. Given our awareness of the spectrum from poverty to riches, from baldness to a full head of hair, and from conception to adulthood, we can specify quite precisely where an individual falls along any of those spectrums. So precision is possible without drawing any lines, and in determining the rights of a being, we can proceed in exactly the same fashion. Thus, when an adult requests an abortion, if it is seen as a conflict of rights case, the comparative strength of the rights of the being to be aborted is determined by its stage of development. A conceptus would have a minimal right to live (supposing that an unfertilized ovum has none), whereas an almost full term fetus would have considerably more of a right, but still less than its mother. So that one morally relevant difference between an early and a late abortion is the degree of development of the fetus.

It is this reasoning, I find, that influences our moral thinking about abortion. It explains (1) why no one favors infanticide, since with infants there is no comparable *conflict* of rights, (2) why we think one should save the life of the mother if it is necessary to choose between her life and that of the unborn, (3) why we find it impossible to draw a line (say, at six months of fetal development) and insist that abortions a few minutes earlier are significantly morally different, (4) why "we are more and more reluctant [as we go back in the life of a fetus] to say that this is a human being and must be treated as such,"[6] and (5) why the use of the "morning-after pill" seems to so many people to be morally unobjectionable. On this reasoning, a fetus has a right to life, but that right is less than that of its mother. A fetus is, as the Supreme Court put it, "less than a full person," which implies that its rights are less than full—*not that it has no rights at all*. Thus, given the facts of human development, (L) explains why abortion *is* a genuine moral problem, why it is the sort of problem it is, and why it troubles us in the way it does. An abortion cannot be dismissed as simply "elective surgery," but neither is an early abortion equivalent to murder. Furthermore, (L) renders consistent the assignment of fetal rights (as some courts have done) with the Supreme Court decision that a fetus is not a person in the full legal sense of that term: One does not have to be a full-fledged person in order to have rights, or to be treated immorally.

II

The most serious distortion that affects moral discussions of abortion is the idea that abortion presents a "line-drawing problem." In introducing a series of essays on abortion, Joel Feinberg characterizes the views implicit in many of those essays when he writes, "I do not wish to suggest that 'the status of the unborn' problem is insoluble, but only that it is a problem and a difficult one, for liberal, moderate, and conservative alike, insofar as they seek principled, and not merely arbitrary solutions to line drawing problems."[7] If one thinks he must be able to "draw a line" to defend early abortions, no wonder the "status of the unborn problem" seems insoluble. Yet, Feinberg's remarks overlook entirely, as do many philosophic essays on abortion, the *principled* solution provided by (L) to that problem and the question of whether the unborn have any rights.

In his remarks, Feinberg embraces an assumption that is at the heart of the anti-abortionist position, namely, (c) if a being has a right to life, it is the same right to life that an adult human being has. In accepting (c), Feinberg considerably increases the burden that any liberal or moderate on abortion must bear. For an anti-abortionist can argue this: (d) an infant has a right to life, (e) there is no reasonable place to "draw the line" between conception and birth, therefore, (f) a conceptus has the same right to life as an infant. The inference from (d) and (e) to (f) is common; yet it depends crucially on (c). If (c) is false, (f) does not follow from (d) and (e), and the anti-abortionist must argue for (c) to defend his position. Too often, this requirement is overlooked—as Feinberg overlooks it—and liberals and moderates are left with the impression that their respective positions are unreasonable because they are unable to reasonably "draw the line." Yet, anyone who favors early abortions can emphasize the very facts about human development that are crucial for the anti-abortionist position and, in doing so, maintain that the right to life of a conceptus or zygote are minimal, whereas those of infants and about-to-be-born babies are considerable. Once one sees this possibility, the "line-drawing problem" and the intellectual burden it imposes disappear.

In other philosophical discussions of abortion, one finds such remarks as, "What properties must something have to be a person, that is, to have a serious right to life?"[8] Here, the mistake is: (g) If something is not a person, it does not have a serious right to life. And, in another discussion, the claim is made that "to stabilize his position [on abortion] the moderate would have to *invent* a new set of moral categories and principles…because our principles of justice apply solely to the relations between persons."[9] Here the fallacy is: (h) If something is not a person, our principles of justice do not apply to it. Position (g) is fallacious because being a person is a sufficient, but not a necessary condition, for having rights, and (h) is false because, as (L), which is a principle of justice, makes plain, less than full persons can have rights, and these rights can be unjustly violated.

III

More than any other position on abortion, it is the moderate position—that early abortions generally, and some late abortions, are morally justified—that has been misunderstood by failing to appreciate the role of (L) in our moral reasoning. Roger Wertheimer finds the moderate position popular, but problematic.[10] What are its problems? First, it complicates specific moral decisions: There is a great variety of possible cases, and a difference in details—especially for mid-term abortions—often requires a difference in moral judgment. Second, Wertheimer claims that a moderate, to support his position, must *invent* new categories and moral principles. Any moderate would grant the first point, perhaps even insist on it as a true account of the nature of the problem, but the second criticism is simply bizarre. After all, if the moderate position is popular, are all its adherents simply relying on their own invented moral categories and moral principles? A much more likely explanation of its popularity is that it relies on such standard moral principles as (U), (R), and (L).

Wertheimer notes that most liberals and conservatives on abortion are really only extreme moderates, since they agree that although abortion is not simply elective surgery, a fetus is not a fellow adult who must be treated as such. In short, the fetus occupies a special, intermediate place in our moral thinking. In Wertheimer's words, "it has a separate moral status, just as animals do," and he apparently infers from that claim that if the fetus has a separate status, our ordinary principles of justice do not apply to it. He argues that "our principles of justice apply solely to relations between persons," hence they do not apply to a fetus, and that argument is simply fallacious. For (L) is a principle of justice (which Wertheimer ignores), and it makes it plain that fetuses as well as animals can be treated unjustly. (Indeed, in trying to understand our moral thinking about animals, (L) would seem to be indispensable, since animals, like fetuses, are like persons in some ways, but not in others. To treat them as sticks or stones would be to ignore that fact and to violate (L).)

If one adopts a moderate position on abortion, then one requires a reason to abort a fetus, and the strength of the requisite reason is proportional to the facts of the situation and the comparative rights of the parties involved. In "A Defense of Abortion,"[11] Judith Thomson supposes, for the sake of argument, that the right to life of a fetus is the same as that of its mother, and then examines several analogous conflict of rights cases to determine whether it is always morally wrong to kill, or let die, an innocent person. Many women would reject the supposition that their rights are on a par with those of a fetus and resent anti–abortionists who make that supposition the cornerstone of their position. Since that supposition is mistaken, according to (L), their rejection of it is well founded. Yet, in Thomson's cases, the conclusion that the rights of a fetus are less than those of a normal adult only strengthens her conclusion that some abortions are morally permissible. For if it is sometimes morally permissible to let an innocent person die, or to cause his death, then the reasons required to do so with a being that is less than a full person are proportionally less. Hence the moral principles (U), (R), and (L), the supervenience analysis of the attribution of human rights, and the categories "person" and "less than a full person" provide the basis for the moderate position on abortion.

IV

Two important criticisms might be made of the position I have argued. The first is that although (L) requires a proportionality in our moral assessments based on claims of human rights, unless one knows for certain what the nonmoral or natural characteristics are for determining human rights, one cannot be certain that fetuses and infants possess such characteristics in any proportional or comparative degree. This criticism seems accurate. We do not know for certain that a fetus is less than a full person in a morally significant sense unless we know those characteristics on which we base the attribution of human rights. Yet, how would one establish what those natural characteristics are? Only, it seems, by analyzing our moral thinking about human beings and why *we think* that persons have rights. If one so proceeds, I think it is evident, or at least extremely likely, that fetuses will be found to occupy the "in-between" status I have attributed to them. That intuition, after all, is one datum that any analysis of "person" or "has rights" would have to take into account. So if not certain, the moderate position on abortion is reasonably secure.

The second criticism objects to the idea of "partial rights" or "less than full rights." A right, one might insist, is not something that grows or diminishes, or something you can have more or less of. You either have it or you do not, in the way that a statement is either true or false. But one has only to substitute "person" for "right" in that claim to argue against it. If there is a certain symmetry between being a person and having rights, then if persons can grow and develop, why should their rights not do the same? The idea that a child acquires more rights as it develops is not incoherent; it is, instead, the way most parents raise their children. And it is not simply that a child acquires more rights of different kinds as it develops; it also acquires more of the same right, such as the right to self-determination. One reply to this argument might be that, while a *child* grows and develops, a *person* does not—that is, a child becomes a person at some point and remains so from then on. So "personhood" is not elastic in the way that my position requires.

The trouble with that reply is that, if it is granted, it loses its force. Any "line-drawing" definition of "person" which insists that only those beings who satisfy the definition have any rights is simply unrealistic. For once so defined, "person" and "has rights" would be inadequate to handle the moral problems we confront in dealing with abortion. It is not the definition of "person," but the reality to which that term applies, that is crucial for moral assessments. So if someone defines "person" in such a way that a fetus, an infant, or even a small child is not a person, the continuum of human development and the moral problems it presents are still before us. It is not as if a "line-drawing" definition of "person" makes those problems disappear. So even if my use of "person" and "has rights" is revisionary, the facts of the situation require it, if those terms are to be adequate for discussing the morality of abortion. The alternative "line-drawing" approach only produces intellectual confusion and paradox.

V

Two assumptions—(a) there is a point somewhere between conception and adulthood that is morally significant, and (b) the morality of particular abortions depends on whether they occur before or after that point—underlie many discussions of the morality of abortion. In this paper, I have pointed out that if the properties in virtue of which persons have rights are comparative, then (b) is false and there is no reason to think that (a) is true. There are morally significant differences between early and late abortions, but these do not entail the conclusion that there is a point somewhere between the two at which one can draw a line and demarcate the morally right from the morally wrong abortions. Instead, mid-term and late abortions are morally complicated. Their correct resolution depends on numerous factors, some peculiar to the individual case, and not the discovery of that point at which "life begins." There are many biological reasons for doubting that there is such a point, and I have argued that it is not morally necessary that we find or create it.

STUDY QUESTIONS

1. Explain Gillespie's argument against both the liberal and the conservative. Where, according to him, do each go wrong?

2. Explain how the principles of universalizability (U and R) and comparative properties (L) lead to a conservative position. How strong is this argument?

NOTES

1. Daniel Callahan, "Remarks on the Supreme Court's Ruling on Abortion," in *The Problem of Abortion* (first ed.), ed. Joel Feinberg. Belmont, Calif., 1973, 194.

2. Michael Tooley, "In Defense of Abortion and Infanticide," in *The Problem of Abortion,* ed. Joel Feinberg.

3. Alan Gewirth, "The Non-Trivializability of Universalizability," *Australasian Journal of Philosophy* 47, 2 (1969), 123 n.2.

4. Ibid., 126.

5. Roger Wertheimer, "Understanding the Abortion Argument," *Philosophy and Public Affairs* 1, 1 (1971).

6. Phillipa Foot, "The Problem of Abortion and the Doctrine of Double Effect," *Oxford Review,* 5 (1967); reprinted in *Moral Problems,* ed. James Rachels. New York, 1971, 29.

7. Feinberg (first ed.), *The Problem of Abortion,* 4.

8. Tooley, "In Defense of Abortion and Infanticide."

9. Wertheimer, "Understanding the Abortion Argument."

10. Ibid.

11. Judith Jarvis Thomson, "A Defense of Abortion," *Philosophy and Public Affairs* 1, 1 (1971): 47–66.

17

A Defense of the
Moderate Position

L. W. SUMNER

*L. W. Sumner is Professor of Philosophy at the University of Toronto. Sumner criti-
cizes both the liberal and conservative positions on abortion and sets forth a third way
between these extremes, the moderate position The moderate position, based on the criterion of sentience, combines elements of the liberal view for early abortions with elements of the conservative view for late abortions. Sumner argues that this third way
coheres better with our overall considered moral judgments.*

When confronted with a problem as complex as that of abortion, we have
some initial reason to suspect simple solutions…We need a view of abortion responsive to all the elements whose conjunction renders the problem of
abortion so perplexing and so divisive. Such a view cannot be a simple one.

If an alternative to the established views is to be developed, three tasks
must be successfully completed. The first is to construct this third way and to
show how it is essentially different from both of the positions it supersedes
The indispensable ingredient at this stage is a criterion of moral standing that
will generate a view of the fetus and thus a view of abortion.…The second
task is to defend this view on the intuitive level by showing that it coheres
better than either of its predecessors with our considered moral judgments
both on abortion itself and on cognate issues. Then finally, the view must be
given a deep structure by grounding it in a moral theory. This chapter will

undertake the first two tasks by outlining a position on the abortion problem and justifying it by appealing to moral intuitions....

1. SPECIFICATIONS

The established views have failed in certain specific respects. Collating their points of weakness will provide us with guidelines for building a more satisfactory alternative. It will be convenient to divide these guidelines into two categories corresponding to the two ingredients that complicate the problem of abortion: the nature of the fetus and the implications of the mother-fetus relationship.

The conservative view, and also the more naive versions of the liberal view, select a precise point (conception, birth, and so on) as the threshold of moral standing, implying that the transition from no standing to full standing occurs abruptly. In doing so, these views rest more weight on these sudden events than they are capable of bearing. A view that avoids this defect will allow full moral standing to be acquired gradually. It will therefore attempt to locate not a threshold point, but a threshold period or stage.

Both of the established views attribute a uniform moral status to all fetuses, regardless of their dissimilarities. Each, for example, counts a newly conceived zygote for precisely as much (or as little) as a full-term fetus, despite the enormous differences between them. A view that avoids this defect will assign moral status differentially, so that the threshold stage occurs sometime during pregnancy.

A consequence of the uniform approach adopted by both of the established views is that neither can attach any significance to the development of the fetus during gestation.[1] Yet this development is the most obvious feature of gestation. A view that avoids this defect will base the (differential) moral standing of the fetus at least in part on its level of development. It will thus assign undeveloped fetuses a moral status akin to that of ova and spermatozoa, whereas it will assign developed fetuses a moral status akin to that of infants.

So far, then, an adequate view of the fetus must be gradual, differential, and developmental. An adequate view must also be derived from a satisfactory criterion of moral standing. The conditions of adequacy for such a criterion [are]...it must be general (applicable to beings other than fetuses), it must connect moral standing with the empirical properties of such beings, and it must be morally relevant. Its moral relevance is partly testable by appeal to intuition, for arbitrary or shallow criteria will be vulnerable to counterexamples. But the final test of moral relevance is grounding in a moral theory.

An adequate view of the fetus promises a morally significant division between early abortions (before the threshold stage) and late abortions (after the threshold stage). It also promises borderline cases (during the threshold stage). Wherever that stage is located, abortions that precede it will be private matters, since the fetus will at that stage lack moral standing. Thus the provisions of the liberal view will apply to early abortions: They will be morally innocent (as long as the usual conditions of maternal consent, and so forth, are satisfied) and ought to be legally unregulated (except for rules equally applicable to all other medical procedures). Early abortion will have the same moral status as contraception.

Abortions that follow the threshold stage will be interpersonal matters, since the fetus will at that stage possess moral standing. The provisions of Thomson's argument will apply to late abortions: They must be assessed on a case-by-case basis and they ought to be legally permitted only on appropriate grounds. Late abortions will have the same moral status as infanticide, except for the difference made by the physical connection between fetus and mother.

A third way with abortion is thus a moderate and differential view, combining elements of the liberal view for early abortions with elements of (a weakened version of) the conservative view for late abortions. The policy that a moderate view will support is a moderate policy, permissive in the early stages of pregnancy and more restrictive (though not as restrictive as conservatives think appropriate) in the later stages. So far as the personal question of the moral evaluation of particular abortions is concerned, there is no pressing need to resolve the borderline cases around the threshold stage. But a workable abortion policy cannot tolerate this vagueness and will need to establish a definite time limit beyond which the stipulated grounds will come into play. Although the precise location of the time limit will unavoidably be somewhat arbitrary, it will be defensible as long as it falls somewhere within the threshold stage. Abortion on request up to the time limit and only for cause thereafter: These are the elements of a satisfactory abortion policy.

A number of moderate views may be possible, each of them satisfying all of the foregoing constraints. A particular view will he defined by selecting (a) a criterion of moral standing, (b) the natural characteristics whose gradual acquisition during normal fetal development carries with it the acquisition of moral standing, and (c) a threshold stage. Of these three steps, the first is the crucial one because it determines both of the others.

2. A CRITERION OF MORAL STANDING

We have thus far assumed that for a creature to have moral standing is for it to have a right to life. Any such right imposes duties on moral agents; these duties can be either negative (not to deprive the creature of life) or positive (to support the creature's life). Possession of a right to life implies at least some immunity against attack by others, and possibly also some entitlement to the aid of others. As the duties can vary in strength, so can the corresponding rights. To have some moral standing is to have some right to life, whether or not it can be overridden by the rights of others. To have full moral standing is to have the strongest right to life possessed by anyone, the right to life of the paradigm person. Depending on one's moral theory, this right may or may not be inviolable and indefeasible and thus may or may not impose absolute duties on others.

Although this analysis of moral standing will later be broadened, it will still suffice for our present purposes. To which creatures should we distribute (some degree of) moral standing? On which criterion should we base this distribution? It may be easier to answer these questions if we begin with the clear case and work outward to the unclear ones. If we can determine why we ascribe full standing to the paradigm case, we may learn what to look for in other creatures when deciding whether or not to include them in the moral sphere.

The paradigm bearer of moral standing is an adult human being with normal capacities of intellect, emotion, perception, sensation, decision, action, and the like. If we think of such a person as a complex bundle of natural properties, then in principle we could employ as a criterion any of the properties common to all normal and mature members of our species. Selecting a particular property or set of properties will define a class of creatures with moral standing, namely, all (and only) those who share that property. The extension of that class will depend on how widely the property in question is distributed. Some putative criteria will be obviously frivolous and will immediately fail the tests of generality or moral relevance. But even after excluding the silly candidates, we are left with a number of serious ones. There are four that appear to be the most serious: We might attribute full moral standing to the paradigm person on the ground that he/she is (a) intrinsically valuable, (b) alive, (c) sentient, or (d) rational. An intuitive test of the adequacy of any of these candidates will involve first enumerating the class of beings to whom it will distribute moral standing and then determining whether that class either excludes creatures that on careful reflection we believe ought to be included or includes creatures that we believe ought to be excluded. In the former case the criterion draws the boundary of the moral sphere too narrowly and fails as a necessary condition of moral standing. In the latter case the criterion draws the boundary too broadly and fails as a sufficient condition. (A given criterion can, of course, be defective in both respects.)

Beings can depart from the paradigm along several different dimensions, each of which presents us with unclear cases that a criterion must resolve. These cases may be divided into seven categories: (1) inanimate objects (natural and artificial); (2) nonhuman terrestrial species of living things (animals and plants); (3) nonhuman extraterrestrial species of living things (should there be any); (4) artificial "life forms" (androids, robots, computers); (5) grossly defective human beings (the severely and permanently retarded or deranged); (6) human beings at the end of life (especially the severely and permanently senile or comatose); (7) human beings at the beginning of life (fetuses, infants, children). Since the last context is the one in which we wish to apply a criterion, it will here be set aside. This will enable us to settle on a criterion without tailoring it specially for the problem of abortion. Once a criterion has established its credentials in other domains, we will be able to trace out its implications for the case of the fetus.

The first candidate for a criterion takes a direction rather different from that of the remaining three. It is a commonplace in moral philosophy to attribute to (normal adult) human beings a special worth or value or dignity by virtue of which they possess (among other rights) a full right to life. This position implies that (some degree of) moral standing extends just as far as (some degree of) this intrinsic value, a higher degree of the latter entailing a higher degree of the former. We cannot know which things have moral standing without being told which things have intrinsic worth (and why)—without, that is, being offered a theory of intrinsic value. What is unique about this criterion, however, is that it is quite capable in principle of extending moral standing beyond the class of living beings, thus embracing such inanimate objects as rocks and lakes, entire landscapes (or indeed worlds), and artifacts. Of course, nonliving things cannot literally have a right to *life,* but it would be simple enough to generalize to a right to (continued) *existence,* where this might include both a right not to be destroyed and a right to such support as is necessary for that existence. A criterion that invokes intrinsic value is thus able to define a much more capacious moral sphere than is any of the other candidates.

Such a criterion is undeniably attractive in certain respects: How else are we to explain why it is wrong to destroy priceless icons or litter the moon even when doing so will never affect any living, sentient, or rational being? But it is clear that it cannot serve our present purpose. A criterion must connect moral standing with some property of things whose presence or absence can be confirmed by a settled, objective, and public method of investigation. The property of being intrinsically valuable is not subject to such verification. A criterion based on intrinsic value cannot be applied without a theory of intrinsic value. Such a theory will supply a criterion of intrinsic value by specifying the natural properties of things by virtue of which they possess such value. But if things have moral standing by virtue of having intrinsic value, and if they have intrinsic value by virtue of having some natural property, then it is that natural property that is serving as the real criterion of moral standing, and the middle term of intrinsic value is eliminable without loss. A theory of intrinsic value can thus entail a criterion of moral standing, but intrinsic value cannot itself serve as that criterion.

There is a further problem confronting any attempt to ground moral rights in the intrinsic worth of creatures. One must first be certain that this is not merely a verbal exercise in which attributing intrinsic value to things is just another way of attributing intrinsic moral standing to them. Assuming that the relation between value and rights is synthetic, there are then two possibilities: The value in question is moral or it is nonmoral. If it is moral, the criterion plainly fails to break out of the circle of moral properties to connect them with the nonmoral properties of things. But if it is nonmoral, it is unclear what it has to do with moral rights. If there are realms of value, some case must be made for deriving moral duties toward things from the nonmoral value of these things.

The remaining three candidates for a criterion of moral standing (life, sentience, rationality) all satisfy the verification requirement since they all rest on empirical properties of things. They can be ordered in terms of the breadth of the moral spheres they define. Since rational beings are a proper subset of sentient beings, which are a proper subset of living beings, the first candidate is the weakest and will define the broadest sphere, whereas the third is the strongest and will define the narrowest sphere. In an interesting recent discussion, Kenneth Goodpaster (1978) has urged that moral standing be accorded to all living things, simply by virtue of the fact that they are alive. Although much of his argument is negative, being directed against more restrictive criteria, he does provide a positive case for including all forms of life within the moral sphere.

Let us assume that the usual signs of life—nutrition, metabolism, spontaneous growth, reproduction—enable us to draw a tolerably sharp distinction between animate and inanimate beings, so that all plant and animal species, however primitive, are collected together in the former category. All such creatures share the property of being *teleological systems:* They have functions, ends, directions, natural tendencies, and so forth. By virtue of their teleology, such creatures have needs, in a nonmetaphorical sense—conditions that must be satisfied if they are to thrive or flourish. Creatures with needs can be benefited or harmed; they are benefited when their essential needs are satisfied and harmed when they are not. It also makes sense to say that such creatures have a good: The conditions that promote their life and health are good for them, whereas those that impair their normal functioning are bad for them. But it is common to construe morality as having essentially to do with benefits and harms or with the good of creatures. So doing will lead us to extend moral standing to all creatures capable of being benefited and harmed, that is, all creatures with a good. But this condition will include all organisms (and systems of organisms), and so life is the only reasonable criterion of moral standing.

This extension of moral standing to plants and to the simpler animals is of course highly counterintuitive, since most of us accord the lives of such creatures no weight whatever in our practical deliberations. How could we conduct our affairs if we were to grant protection of life to every plant and animal species? Some of the more extreme implications of this view are, however, forestalled by Goodpaster's distinction between a criterion of inclusion and a criterion of comparison.[2] The former determines which creatures have (some) moral standing and thus locates the boundary of the moral sphere; it is Goodpaster's contention that life is the proper inclusion criterion. The latter is operative entirely within the moral sphere and enables us to assign different grades of moral standing to different creatures by virtue of some natural property that they may possess in different degrees. Since all living beings are (it seems) equally alive, life cannot serve as a comparison criterion. Goodpaster does not provide such a criterion, though he recognizes its necessity. Thus his view enables him to affirm that all living creatures have (some) moral standing but to deny that all such creatures have equal standing. Though the lives of all animate beings deserve consideration, some deserve more than others. Thus, for instance, higher animals might count for more than lower ones, and all animals might count for more than plants.

In the absence of a criterion of comparison, it is difficult to ascertain just what reforms Goodpaster's view would require in our moral practice. How much weight must human beings accord to the lives of lichen or grass or bacteria or insects? When are such lives more important than some benefit for a higher form of life? How should we modify our eating habits, for example? There is a problem here that extends beyond the incompleteness and indeterminacy of Goodpaster's position. Suppose that we have settled on a comparison criterion; let it be sentience (assuming that sentience admits degrees in some relevant respect). Then a creature's ranking in the hierarchy of moral standing will be determined by the extent of its sentience: Nonsentient (living) beings will have minimal standing, whereas the most sentient beings (human beings, perhaps) will have maximal standing. But then we are faced with the obvious question: If sentience is to serve as the comparison criterion, why should it not also serve as the inclusion criterion? Conversely, if life is the inclusion criterion, does it not follow that nothing else can serve as the comparison criterion, in which case all living beings have equal standing? It is difficult to imagine an argument in favor of sentience as a comparison criterion that would not also be an argument in favor of it as an inclusion criterion. Since the same will hold for any other comparison criterion, Goodpaster's view can avoid its extreme implications only at the price of inconsistency.

Goodpaster's view also faces consistency problems in its claim that life is necessary for moral standing. Beings need not be organisms to be teleological systems, and therefore to have needs, a good, and the capacity to be benefited and harmed. If these conditions are satisfied by a tree (as they surely are), then they are equally satisfied by a car. To function properly most machines need periodic maintenance; such maintenance is good for them, they are benefited by it, and they are harmed by its neglect. Why then is being alive a necessary condition of moral standing? Life is but an (imperfect) indicator of teleology and the capacity to be benefited and harmed. But Goodpaster's argument then commits him to treating these deeper characteristics as the criterion of moral standing, and thus to according standing to many (perhaps most) inanimate objects.[3]

This inclusion of (at least some) nonliving things should incline us to reexamine Goodpaster's argument—if the inclusion of all living things has not already done so. The connection between morality and the capacity to be benefited and harmed appears plausible, so what has gone wrong? We may form a conjecture if we again consider our paradigm bearer of moral standing. In the case of a fully normal adult human being, it does appear that moral questions are pertinent whenever the actions of another agent promise to benefit or threaten to harm such a being. Both duties and rights are intimately connected with benefits and harms. The kinds of acts that we have a (strict) duty not to do are those that typically cause harm, whereas positive duties are duties to confer benefits. Liberty-rights protect autonomy, which is usually thought of as one of the chief goods for human beings, and the connection between welfare-rights and benefits is obvious. But if we ask what counts as a benefit or a harm for a human being, the usual answers take one or both of the following directions:

1. *The desire model.* Human beings are benefited to the extent that their desires (or perhaps their considered and informed desires) are satisfied; they are harmed to the extent that these desires are frustrated.

2. *The experience model.* Human beings benefited to the extent that they are brought to have experiences that they like or find agreeable; they are harmed to the extent that they are brought to have experiences that they dislike or find disagreeable.

We need not worry at this stage whether one of these models is more satisfactory than the other. On both models, benefits and harms for particular persons are interpreted in terms of the psychological states of those persons, in terms, that is, of their interests or welfare. Such states are possible only for beings who are conscious or sentient. Thus, if morality has to do with the promotion and protection of interests or welfare, morality can concern itself only with beings who are conscious or sentient.[4] No other beings can be beneficiaries or victims *in the morally relevant way.* Goodpaster is not mistaken in suggesting that nonsentient beings can be benefited and harmed. But he is mistaken in suggesting that morality has to do with benefits and harms as such, rather than with a particular category of them. And that can be seen the more clearly when we realize that the broadest capacity to be benefited and harmed extends not only out to but beyond the frontier of life. Leaving my lawn mower out in the rain is bad for the mower, pulling weeds is bad for the weeds, and swatting mosquitoes is bad for the mosquitoes, but there are no moral dimensions to any of these acts unless the interests or welfare of some sentient creature is at stake. Morality requires the existence of sentience in order to obtain a purchase on our actions.

The failure of Goodpaster's view has thus given us some reason to look to sentience as a criterion of moral standing. Before considering this possibility directly, it will be helpful to turn to the much narrower criterion of rationality.[5] The rational/nonrational boundary is more difficult to locate with certainty than the animate/inanimate boundary, since rationality (or intelligence) embraces a number of distinct but related capacities for thought, memory, foresight, language, self-consciousness, objectivity, planning, reasoning, judgment, deliberation, and the like.[6] It is perhaps possible for a being to possess some of these capacities and entirely lack others, but for simplicity we will assume that the higher-order cognitive processes are typically owned as a bundle. The bundle is possessed to one extent or another by normal adult human beings, by adolescents and older children, by persons suffering from the milder cognitive disorders, and by some other animal species (some primates and cetaceans for example). It is not possessed to any appreciable extent by fetuses and infants, by the severely retarded or disordered, by the irreversibly comatose, and by most other animal species. To base moral standing on rationality is thus to deny it alike to most nonhuman beings and to many human beings. Since the implications for fetuses and infants have already been examined, they will be ignored in the present discussion. Instead we will focus on why one might settle on rationality as a criterion in the first place.

That rationality is sufficient for moral standing is not controversial (though there are some interesting questions to be explored here about forms of artificial intelligence). As a necessary condition, however, rationality will exclude a good many sentient beings—just how many, and which ones, to be determined by the kind and the stringency of the standards employed. Many will find objectionable this constriction of the sphere of moral concern. Because moral standing has been defined in terms of the right to life, to lack moral standing is not necessarily to lack all rights. Thus one could hold that, although we have no duty to (nonrational) animals to respect their lives, we do have a duty to them not to cause them suffering. For the right not to suffer, one might choose a different (and broader) criterion—sentience, for example. (However, if this is the criterion appropriate for that right, why is it not also the criterion appropriate for the right to life?) But even if we focus strictly on the (painless) killing of animals, the implications of the criterion are harsh. Certainly we regularly kill nonhuman animals to satisfy our own needs or desires. But the justification usually offered for these practices is either that the satisfaction of those needs and desires outweighs the costs to the animals (livestock farming, hunting, fishing, trapping, experimentation) or that no decent life would have been available for them anyway (the killing of stray dogs and cats). Although some of these arguments doubtless are rationalizations, their common theme is that the lives of animals do have some weight (however slight) in the moral scales, which is why the practice of killing animals is one that requires moral justification (raises moral issues). If rationality is the criterion of *moral* standing, and if (most) nonhuman animals are nonrational, killing such creatures could be morally questionable only when it impinges on the interests of rational beings (as where animals are items of property). In no case could killing an animal be a wrong against it. However callous and chauvinistic the common run of our treatment of animals may be, still the view that killing a dog or a horse is morally no more serious *(ceteris paribus* than weeding a garden can be the considered judgment of only a small minority.

The standard we apply to other species we must in consistency apply to our own. The greater the number of animals who are excluded by that standard, the greater the number of human beings who will also be excluded. In the absence of a determinate criterion, it is unclear just where the moral line will be drawn on the normal/abnormal spectrum: Will a right to life be withheld from mongoloids, psychotics, the autistic, the senile, the profoundly retarded? If so, killing such persons will again be no wrong *to them*. Needless to say, most such persons (in company with many animals) are sentient and capable to some extent of enjoyable and satisfying lives. To kill them is to deprive them of lives that are of value to them. If such creatures are denied standing, this loss will be entirely discounted in our moral reasoning. Their lack of rationality may ensure that their lives are less full and rich than ours, that they consist of simpler pleasures and more basic enjoyments. But what could be the justification for treating their deaths as though they cost them nothing at all?

There is a tradition, extending back at least to Kant, that attempts just such a justification. One of its modern spokesmen is A. I. Melden (1977), who treats the capacity for moral agency as the criterion of moral standing. This capacity is manifested by participation in a moral community—a set of beings sharing allegiance to moral rules and recognition of one another's integrity. Rights can be attributed only to beings with whom we can have such moral intercourse, thus only to beings who have interests similar to ours, who show concern for the well-being of others, who are capable of uniting in cooperative endeavors, who regulate their activities by a sense of right and wrong, and who display the characteristically moral emotions of indignation, remorse, and guilt. Rationality is a necessary condition (though not a sufficient one) for possessing this bundle of capacities. Melden believes that of all living creatures known to us, only human beings are capable of moral agency.[7] Natural rights, including the right to life, are thus human rights.

We may pass over the obvious difficulty of extending moral standing to all human beings on this basis (including the immature and abnormal) and focus on the question of why the capacity for moral agency should be thought necessary for possession of a right to life. The notion of a moral community to which Melden appeals contains a crucial ambiguity. On the one hand, it can be thought of as a community of moral agents—the bearers of moral duties. Clearly to be a member of such a community, one must be capable of moral agency. On the other hand, a moral community can be thought of as embracing all beings to whom moral agents owe duties—the bearers of moral rights. It cannot simply be assumed that the class of moral agents (duty-bearers) is coextensive with the class of moral patients (right-bearers). It is quite conceivable that some beings (infants, nonhuman animals) might have rights though they lack duties (because they are incapable of moral agency). The capacity for moral agency is (trivially) a condition of having moral duties. It is not obviously also a condition of having moral rights. The claim that the criterion for rights is the same as the criterion for duties is substantive and controversial. The necessity of defending this claim is merely concealed by equivocating on the notion of a moral community.

Beings who acknowledge one another as moral agents can also acknowledge that (some) creatures who are not themselves capable of moral agency nonetheless merit (some) protection of life. The more we reflect on the function of rights, the stronger becomes the inclination to extend them to such creatures. Rights are securities for beings who are sufficiently autonomous to conduct their own lives but who are also vulnerable to the aggression of others and dependent on these others for some of the necessaries of life. Rights protect the goods of their owners and shield them from evils. We ascribe rights to one another because we all alike satisfy these minimal conditions of autonomy, vulnerability, and dependence. In order to satisfy these conditions, a creature need not itself be capable of morality; it need only possess interest that can be protected by rights. A higher standard thus seems appropriate for possession of moral duties than for possession of moral rights. Rationality appears to be the right sort of criterion for the former, but something less demanding (such as sentience) is better suited to the latter.

The moral issues raised by early abortion are precisely those raised by contraception. It is for early abortions that the liberal view is appropriate. Since the fetus at this stage has no right to life, early abortion (like contraception) cannot violate its rights. But if it violates no one's rights, early abortion (like contraception) is a private act. There are of course significant differences between contraception and early abortion, since the former is generally less hazardous, less arduous, and less expensive. A woman has, therefore, good prudential reasons for relying on contraception as her primary means of birth control. But if she elects an early abortion, then, whatever the circumstances and whatever her reasons, she does nothing immoral.

The moral issues raised by late abortion are similar to those raised by infanticide. It is for late abortions that (a weakened form of) the conservative view is appropriate. Since the fetus at this stage has a right to life, late abortion (like infanticide) might violate its rights. But if it might violate the fetus' rights, then late abortion (like infanticide) is a public act. There is, however, a morally significant difference between late abortion and infanticide. A fetus is a parasite on a unique individual in a manner in which a newborn infant is not. That parasitic relation will justify late abortion more liberally than infanticide, for they do not occur under the same circumstances.

Since we have already explored the morality of abortion for those cases in which the fetus has moral standing, the general approach to late abortions is clear enough. Unlike the simple and uniform treatment of early abortion, only a case-by-case analysis will here suffice. We should expect a serious threat to the woman's life or health (physical or mental) to justify abortion, especially if that threat becomes apparent only late in pregnancy. We should also expect a risk of serious fetal deformity to justify abortion, again especially if that risk becomes apparent (as it usually does) only late in pregnancy. On the other hand, it should not be necessary to justify abortion on the ground that pregnancy was not consented to, since a woman will have ample opportunity to seek an abortion before the threshold stage. If a woman freely elects to continue a pregnancy past that stage, she will thereafter need a serious reason to end it.

A differential view of abortion is therefore liberal concerning early abortion and conservative (in an extended sense) concerning late abortion. The status of the borderline cases in the middle weeks of the second trimester is simply indeterminate. We cannot say of them with certainty either that the fetus has a right to life or that it does not. Therefore we also cannot say either that a liberal approach to these abortions is suitable or that a conservative treatment of them is required. What we can say is that, from the moral point of view, the earlier an abortion is performed the better. There are thus good moral reasons, as well as good prudential ones, for women not to delay their abortions.

A liberal view of early abortion in effect extends a woman's deadline for deciding whether to have a child. If all abortion is immoral, her sovereignty over that decision ends at conception. Given the vicissitudes of contraception, a deadline drawn that early is an enormous practical burden. A deadline in the second trimester allows a woman enough time to discover that she is pregnant and to decide whether to continue the pregnancy. If she chooses not to continue it, her decision violates neither her duties nor any other being's rights. From the point of view of the fetus, the upshot of this treatment of early abortion is that its life is for a period merely probationary; only when it has passed the threshold will that life be accorded protection. If an abortion is elected before the threshold, it is as though from the moral point of view that individual had never existed.

Settling on sentience as a criterion of moral standing thus leads us to a view of the moral status of the fetus, and of the morality of abortion, which satisfies the constraints set out in Section 1. It is gradual, since it locates a threshold stage rather than a point and allows moral standing to be acquired incrementally. It is differential, since it locates the threshold stage during gestation and thus distinguishes the moral status of newly conceived and full-term fetuses. It is developmental, since it grounds the acquisition of moral standing in one aspect of the normal development of the fetus. And it is moderate, since it distinguishes the moral status of early and late abortions and applies each of the established views to that range of cases for which it is appropriate.

STUDY QUESTIONS

1. What are Sumner's main criticisms of the conservative view of abortion? How strong are they?

2. What are Sumner's main criticisms of the liberal view of abortion? How strong are they?

3. How does Sumner combine parts of the liberal and conservative view into a moderate position on abortion? How successful is he in his project?

4. What is the significance of "sentience" for Sumner's theory and how does it work? Consider how both liberals and conservatives would respond to Sumner's third way.

WORKS CITED

Donagan, Alan. 1977. *The Theory of Morality*. Chicago and London: University of Chicago Press.

Goodpaster, Kenneth. 1978. "On Being Morally Considerable," *Journal of Philosophy* 75, 6 (June).

Melden, A.I. 1977. *Rights and Persons*. Oxford: Basil Blackwell.

Regan, Tom. 1976. "Feinberg on What Sorts of Beings Can Have Rights," *Southern Journal of Philosophy* 14, 4 (Winter).

Tooley, Michael. 1973. "A Defense of Abortion and Infanticide," in Joel Feinberg, ed., *The Problem of Abortion*. Belmont, Calif.: Wadsworth.

Warren, Mary Anne. 1978. "On the Moral and Legal Status of Abortion," in Tom L. Beauchamp and LeRoy Walters, eds., *Contemporary Issues in Bioethics*. Encino and Belmont, Calif.: Dickenson.

NOTES

1. Both Tooley (1973) and Warren (1978) allow moral standing to be acquired gradually in the normal course of human development. But since both believe that such standing is only acquired after birth, neither attributes any importance to prenatal development—except as the groundwork of postnatal development.

2. These are my terms; Goodpaster distinguishes between a criterion of moral considerability and a criterion of moral significance (page 311). It is odd that when Goodpaster addresses the practical problems created by treating life as an inclusion criterion (page 324) he does not appeal to the inclusion/comparison distinction. Instead, he invokes the quite different distinction between its being reasonable to attribute standing to a creature and its being (psychologically and causally) possible to act on that attribution. One would have thought the question is not what we *can* bring ourselves to do but what we *ought* to bring ourselves to do, and that the inclusion/comparison distinction is precisely designed to help us answer this question.

3. Tom Regan (1976), who argues that moral standing should be distributed on the basis of possession of a good (or the capacity to be benefited and harmed), explicitly accepts the implication that inanimate things may have standing. Regan sometimes fails to distinguish between "*x* has a good (can be benefited and harmed)" and "the existence of *x* is good (has intrinsic value)." Thus his apparent endorsement of both an intrinsic value and a benefit/harm criterion.

4. Goodpaster (1978) does not shrink from attributing interests to nonsentient organisms, and Regan (1976) does not shrink from attributing interests to both nonsentient organisms and artifacts. Both authors assume that if a being has needs, a good, and a capacity to be benefited and harmed, then that being has interests.

There is much support for this assumption in the dictionary definitions of both "interest" and "welfare," though talk of protecting the interests or welfare of plants or machines seems contrived and strained. But philosophers and economists have evolved technical definitions of "interest" and "welfare" that clearly tie these notions to the psychological states of sentient beings. It is the existence of beings with interests or welfare *in this sense* that is a necessary condition of existence of moral issues.

5. Rationality is the basis of Kant's well-known distinction between persons (ends in themselves) and mere beings (means). It is also advanced as a criterion by Tooley (1973), Donagan (1977), and Warren (1978).

6. Possession of a capacity at a given time does not entail that the capacity is being manifested or displayed at that time. A person does not lose the capacity to use language, for instance, by virtue of remaining silent or being asleep. The capacity remains as long as the appropriate performance could be elicited by the appropriate stimuli. It is lost only when this performance can no longer be evoked (as when the person has become catatonic or comatose). Basing moral standing on the possession of some capacity or set of capacities does not therefore entail silly results, such as that persons lose their rights when they fall asleep. This applies of course, not only to rationality but also to other capacities, such as sentience.

7. Whether or not this is so will depend on how strong the conditions of moral agency are. Certainly many nonhuman species display altruism, if we mean by this a concern for the well-being of conspecifics and a willingness to accept personal sacrifices for their good. On page 199, Melden enumerates a number of features of our lives that are to serve as the basis of our possession of rights; virtually all mammals display all these features.

FURTHER READING

Beckwith, Francis J. *Politically Correct Death: Answering the Arguments for Abortion Rights.* Grand Rapids, Mich.: Baker Book House, 1993. Chapters 3 and 6.

Bedate, C. and R. Cefalo. "The Zygote: To Be or Not to Be a Person." *Journal of Medicine and Philosophy* 14, 6 (1989).

Brody, Baruch. *Abortion and the Sanctity of Life: A Philosophical View.* Cambridge, Mass.: MIT Press, 1975.

Devine, Philip. *The Ethics of Homicide.* Ithaca, N.Y.: Cornell University Press, 1978.

Howsepian, A. A. "Who Or What Are We?" *Review of Metaphysics* 45 (March 1992).

Irving, Dianne N. *Philosophical and Scientific Analysis of the Nature of the Early Human Embryo.* Doctoral dissertation. Washington. DC: Georgetown University, 1991.

Lee, Patrick. *Abortion and Unborn Human Life.* Washington, DC: The Catholic University of America Press, 1996.

McCormick, Richard, "Who Or What Is the Pre-Embryo?" *Kennedy Institute of Ethics Journal* 1, 1 (1991).

Noonan, John T., ed. *The Morality of Abortion: Legal and Historical Perspectives.* Cambridge, Mass.: Harvard University Press, 1970.

Schwarz, Stephen. *The Moral Question of Abortion.* Chicago: Loyola University Press, 1990.

Sumner, L. W. *Abortion and Moral Theory.* Princeton, N.J.: Princeton University Press, 1981.

Tooley, Michael. *Abortion and Infanticide.* Oxford: Oxford University Press, 1983.

Warren, Mary Anne. "On the Moral and Legal Status of Abortion." *Monist,* 57, 1 (1973).

PART VI

Beyond the Personhood Argument

INTRODUCTION

Many philosophers believe that too much weight has been put on ascertaining necessary and sufficient conditions for personhood, which grants beings a right to life. The concept of personhood, they maintain, is vague and slippery. Which conditions are necessary and how much of them? What is so valuable about rationality or self-consciousness as opposed to sentience or the potential for pleasure and pain? Isn't there something arbitrary in choosing one characteristic over another? Doesn't choosing rationality or self-consciousness simply reveal an anthropocentric chauvinism?

So a set of arguments have grown up that purport to deal with the abortion issue apart from the debate over personhood. The first kind of argument might be called the argument from autonomy or self-defense. It is morally permissible to preserve one's autonomy and defend oneself against harm even if the attacker is an innocent person (an "innocent pawn"). Jane English sets forth this argument in the first reading in this section. Rejecting Judith Jarvis Thomson's notion of an absolute right to use one's own body as one will, English argues that this right can be overridden if it affects others adversely. Nevertheless, even if the fetus is an innocent person, a woman may kill it if it poses a significant threat to her well-being, life prospects, or health. As the fetus gradually develops into a recognizable human being, the burden on the woman to justify abortion increases. English's moderate position would permit abortion "on demand" during the early stages of pregnancy, when it seems clear that the fetus lacks moral status, but seriously restrict it in the later stages, when the fetus begins to take on the characteristics of a human being.

The second type of argument involves an application of the Golden Rule. We must be consistent and reason that if it is permissible for someone to do some act (A) to someone else (X), then it would be permissible for someone to do A to you. In our second reading, Harry Gensler uses this Golden Rule argument to argue that since normally we cannot sincerely consent to the morality of our having been aborted, we cannot consistently pronounce abortion to be morally permissible.

The third kind of argument attempts to skirt the personhood issue by appealing to an analysis of the immorality of killing. What makes killing adult humans wrong? In our third reading, Don Marquis argues that the wrongness of killing derives from depriving someone of a future like ours. Fetuses also have a future like ours, so it is wrong to kill fetuses.

In our fourth and fifth readings Peter K. McInerney and Gerald H. Paske argue that Marquis's arguments are unsound and do not get beyond the personhood question. Marquis replies to their criticisms in the final essay of this section.

18

Abortion: Beyond the Personhood Argument

JANE ENGLISH

Jane English (1947–1978) taught philosophy at the University of North Carolina, Chapel Hill. English argues that the issue of whether a fetus is a person cannot be resolved and that the very concept of personhood is not clear or decisive enough to bear the weight of a solution to the abortion debate. Advancing a moderate position, similar to that of Sumner, she argues that regardless of whether a fetus is a person, the principle of self-defense permits a woman to have an abortion in some cases, especially in the early stages of pregnancy. On the other hand, even if the fetus is not a person, it is too much like a baby in the later stages of pregnancy to permit an abortion—except to avoid significant injury or death of the mother.

The abortion debate rages on. Yet the two most popular positions seem to be clearly mistaken. Conservatives maintain that a human life begins at conception and that therefore abortion must be wrong because it is murder. But not all killings of humans are murders. Most notably, self defense can justify even the killing of an innocent person.

Liberals, on the other hand, are just as mistaken in their argument that because a fetus does not become a person until birth, a woman may do whatever she pleases in and to her own body. First, you cannot do as you please with your own body if it affects other people adversely.[1] Second, if a fetus is not a person, that does not imply that you can do to it anything you wish. Animals, for example, are not persons, yet to kill or torture them for no reason at all is wrong.

Reprinted from "Abortion and the Concept of a Person," *Canadian Journal of Philosophy* vol. 5,2 (October 1975) by permission.

At the center of the storm has been the issue of just when it is between ovulation and adulthood that a person appears on the scene. Conservatives draw the line at conception, liberals at birth. In this paper, I first examine our concept of a person and conclude that no single criterion can capture the concept of a person and no sharp line can be drawn. Next I argue that if a fetus is a person, abortion is still justifiable in many cases; and if a fetus is not a person, killing it is still wrong in many cases. To a large extent, these two solutions are in agreement. I conclude that our concept of a person cannot and need not bear the weight that the abortion controversy has thrust on it.

I

The several factions in the abortion argument have drawn battle lines around various proposed criteria for determining what is and what is not a person. For example, Mary Anne Warren[2] lists five features (capacities for reasoning, self-awareness, complex communication, and so on) as her criteria for personhood and argues for the permissibility of abortion because a fetus falls outside this concept. Baruch Brody[3] uses brain waves. Michael Tooley[4] picks having-a-concept-of-self as his criterion and concludes that infanticide and abortion are justifiable), whereas the killing of adult animals is not. On the other side, Paul Ramsey[5] claims a certain gene structure is the defining characteristic. John Noonan[6] prefers conceived-of-humans and presents counterexamples to various other candidate criteria. For instance, he argues against viability as the criterion because the newborn and infirm would then be nonpersons because they cannot live without the aid of others. He rejects any criterion that calls on the sorts of sentiments a being can evoke in adults on the grounds that this would allow us to exclude other races as nonpersons if we could just view them sufficiently unsentimentally.

These approaches are typical: Foes of abortion propose sufficient conditions for personhood that fetuses satisfy, whereas friends of abortion counter with necessary conditions for personhood that fetuses lack. But these both presuppose that the concept of a person can be captured in a strait jacket of necessary or sufficient conditions.[7] Rather, "person" is a cluster of features, of which rationality, having a self concept and being conceived of humans are only part.

What is typical of persons? Within our concept of a person we include, first, certain biological factors: being descended from humans; having a certain genetic makeup; having a head, hands, arms, eyes; being capable of locomotion, breathing, eating, sleeping. There are psychological factors: sentience, perception, having a concept of self and of one's own interests and desires, the ability to use tools, the ability to use language or symbol systems, the ability to joke, to be angry, to doubt. There are rationality factors: the ability to reason and draw conclusions, the ability to generalize and to learn from past experience, the ability to sacrifice present interests for greater gains in the future. There are social factors: the ability to work in groups and respond to peer pressures, the ability to recognize and consider as valuable the interests of others, seeing oneself as one among "other minds," the ability to sympathize, encourage, love, the ability to evoke from others the responses of sympathy, encouragement, love, the ability to work with others for mutual advantage. Then there are legal factors: being subject to the law and protected by it, having the ability to sue and enter contracts, being counted in the census, having a name and citizenship, the ability to own property, inherit, and so forth.

Now the point is not that this list is incomplete, or that you can find counter-instances to each of its points. People typically exhibit rationality, for instance, but someone who was irrational would not thereby fail to qualify as a person. On the other hand, something could exhibit the majority of these features and still fail to be a person, as an advanced robot might. There is no single core of necessary and sufficient features that we can draw on with the assurance that they constitute what really makes a person: There are only features that are more or less typical.

This is not to say that no necessary or sufficient conditions can be given. Being alive is a necessary condition for being a person, and being a U.S. Senator is sufficient. But rather than falling inside a sufficient condition or outside a necessary one, a fetus lies in the penumbra region where our concept of a person is not so simple. For this reason I think a conclusive answer to the question whether a fetus is a person is unattainable.

Here we might note a family of simple fallacies that proceed by stating a necessary condition for personhood and showing that a fetus has that characteristic. This is a form of the fallacy of affirming the consequent. For example, some have mistakenly reasoned from the premise that a fetus is human (after all, it is a human fetus rather than, say, a canine fetus), to the conclusion that it is *a* human. Adding an equivocation on "being," we get the fallacious argument that since a fetus is something both living and human, it is a human being.

Nonetheless, it does seem clear that a fetus has very few of the above family of characteristics, whereas a newborn baby exhibits a much large proportion of them—and a two-year-old has even more. Note that one traditional anti-abortion argument has centered on pointing out the many ways in which a fetus resembles a baby. They emphasize its development ("it already has ten fingers...") without mentioning its dissimilarities to adults (it still has gills and a tail). They also try to evoke the sort of sympathy on our part that we only feel toward other persons ("never to laugh... or feel the sunshine?") This all seems to be a relevant way to argue, since its purpose is to persuade us that a fetus satisfies so many of the important features on the list that it ought to be treated as a person. Also note that a fetus near the time of birth satisfies many more of these factors than does a fetus in the early months of development. This could provide reason for making distinctions among the different stages of pregnancy, as the U.S. Supreme Court has done.[8]

Historically, the time at which a person has been said to come into existence has varied widely. Muslims date personhood from fourteen days after conception. Some medievals followed Aristotle in placing ensoulment at forty days after conception for a male fetus and eighty days for a female fetus.[9] In

European common law since the seventeenth century, abortion was considered the killing of a person only after quickening, the time when a pregnant woman first feels the fetus move on its own. Nor is this variety of opinions surprising. Biologically, a human being develops gradually. We shouldn't expect there to be any specific time or sharp dividing point when a person appears on the scene.

For these reasons I believe our concept of a person is not sharp or decisive enough to bear the weight of a solution to the abortion controversy. To use it to solve that problem is to clarify *obscurum per obscurius.*

II

Next let us consider what follows if a fetus is a person after all. Judith Jarvis Thomson's landmark article, "A Defense of Abortion,"[10] correctly points out that some additional argumentation is needed at this point in the conservative argument to bridge the gap between the premise that a fetus is an innocent person and the conclusion that killing it is always wrong. To arrive at this conclusion, we would need the additional premise that killing an innocent person is always wrong. But killing an innocent person is sometimes permissible, most notably in self defense. Some examples may help draw out our intuitions or ordinary judgments about self defense.

Suppose a mad scientist, for instance, hypnotized innocent people to jump out of the bushes and attack innocent passers-by with knives. If you are so attacked, we agree you have a right to kill the attacker in self defense, if killing him is the only way to protect your life or to save yourself from serious injury. It does not seem to matter here that the attacker is not malicious but himself an innocent pawn, for your killing of him is not done in a spirit of retribution but only in self defense.

How severe an injury may you inflict in self defense? In part this depends on the severity of the injury to be avoided: You may not shoot someone merely to avoid having your clothes torn. This might lead one to the mistaken conclusion that the defense may only equal the threatened injury in severity; that to avoid death you may kill, but to avoid a black eye you may only inflict a black eye or the equivalent. Rather, our laws and customs seem to say that you may create an injury somewhat, but not enormously, greater than the injury to be avoided. To fend off an attack whose outcome would be as serious as rape, a severe beating or the loss of a finger, you may shoot; to avoid having your clothes torn, you may blacken an eye.

Aside from this, the injury you may inflict should only be the minimum necessary to deter or incapacitate the attacker. Even if you know he intends to kill you, you are not justified in shooting him if you could equally well save yourself by the simple expedient of running away. Self defense is for the purpose of avoiding harms rather than equalizing harms.

Some cases of pregnancy present a parallel situation. Though the fetus is itself innocent, it may pose a threat to the pregnant woman's well-being, life prospects, or health, mental or physical. If the pregnancy presents a slight threat to her interests, it seems that self defense cannot justify abortion. But if the threat is on a par with a serious beating or the loss of a finger, she may kill the fetus that poses such a threat, even if it is an innocent person. If a lesser harm to the fetus could have the same defensive effect, killing it would not be justified. It is unfortunate that the only way to free the woman from the pregnancy entails the death of the fetus (except in very late stages of pregnancy). Thus a self-defense model supports Thomson's point that the woman has a right only to be freed from fetus, not a right to demand its death.[11]

The self-defense model is most helpful when we take the pregnant woman's point of view. In the pre-Thomson literature, abortion is often framed as a question for a third party: do you, a doctor, have a right to choose between the life of the woman and that of the fetus? Some have claimed that if you were a passer-by who witnessed a struggle between the innocent hypnotized attacker and his equally innocent victim, you would have no reason to kill either in defense of the other. These people have concluded that the self-defense model implies that a woman may attempt to abort herself, but that a doctor should not assist her. I think the position of the third party is somewhat more complex. We do feel some inclination to intervene on behalf of the victim rather than the attacker, other things being equal. But if both parties are innocent, other factors come into consideration. You would rush to the aid of your husband whether he was attacker or attackee. If a hypnotized famous violinist were attacking a skid row bum, we would try to save the individual who is of more value to society. These considerations would tend to support abortion in some cases.

But suppose you are a frail senior citizen who wishes to avoid being knifed by one of these innocent hypnotics, so you have hired a bodyguard to accompany you. If you are attacked, it is clear we believe that the bodyguard, acting as your agent, has a right to kill the attacker to save you from a serious beating. Your rights of self defense are transferred to your agent. I suggest that we should similarly view the doctor as the pregnant woman's agent in carrying out a defense she is physically incapable of accomplishing herself.

Thanks to modern technology, the cases are rare in which a pregnancy poses as clear a threat to a woman's bodily health as an attacker brandishing a switchblade. How does self defense fare when more subtle, complex, and long-range harms are involved?

To consider a somewhat fanciful example, suppose you are a highly trained surgeon when you are kidnapped by the hypnotic attacker. He says he does not intend to harm you but to take you back to the mad scientist who, it turns out, plans to hypnotize you to have a permanent mental block against all your knowledge of medicine. This would automatically destroy your career, which would in turn have a serious, adverse impact on your family, your personal relationships, and your happiness. It seems to me that if the only way you can avoid this outcome is to shoot the innocent attacker, you are justified in so doing. You are defending yourself from a drastic injury to your life prospects. I think it is no exaggeration to claim that unwanted pregnancies (most obviously among teenagers) often have such adverse life-long consequences as the surgeon's loss of livelihood.

Several parallels arise between various views on abortion and the self-defense model. Let's suppose further that these hypnotized attackers only operate at night, so that it is well known that they can be avoided completely by the considerable inconvenience of never leaving your house after dark. One view is that because you could stay home at night, if you go out and are selected by one of these hypnotized people, you have no right to defend yourself. This parallels the view that abstinence is the only acceptable way to avoid pregnancy. Others might hold that you ought to take along some defense such as Mace that will deter the hypnotized person without killing him, but that if this defense fails, you are obliged to submit to the resulting injury, no matter how severe it is. This parallels the view that contraception is all right but abortion is always wrong, even in cases of contraceptive failure.

A third view is that you may kill the hypnotized person only if he will actually kill you, but not if he will only injure you. This is like the position that abortion is permissible only if it is required to save a woman's life. Finally we have the view that it is all right to kill the attacker, even if only to avoid a very slight inconvenience to yourself and even if you knowingly walked down the very street where all these incidents have been taking place without taking along any Mace or protective escort. If we assume that a fetus is a person, this is the analogue of the view that abortion is always justifiable, "on demand."

The self-defense model allows us to see an important difference that exists between abortion and infanticide, even if a fetus is a person from conception. Many have argued that the only way to justify abortion without justifying infanticide would be to find some characteristic of personhood that is acquired at birth. Michael Tooley, for one, claims infanticide is justifiable because the really significant characteristics of person are acquired some time after birth. But all such approaches look to characteristics of the developing human and ignore the relation between the fetus and the woman. What if, after birth, the presence of an infant or the need to support it posed a grave threat to the woman's sanity or life prospects? She could escape this threat by the simple expedient of running away. So a solution that does not entail the death of the infant is available. Before birth, such solutions are not available because of the biological dependence of the fetus on the woman. Birth is the crucial point not because of any characteristics the fetus gains, but because after birth the woman can defend herself by a means less drastic than killing the infant. Hence, self defense can be used to justify abortion without necessarily thereby justifying infanticide.

On the other hand, supposing a fetus is not after all a person, would abortion always be morally permissible? Some opponents of abortion seem worried that if a fetus is not a full-fledged person, then we are justified in treating it in any way at all. However, this does not follow. Nonpersons do get some consideration in our moral code, though of course they do not have the same rights as persons have (and in general they do not have moral responsibilities), and though their interests can be overridden by the interests of persons. Still, we cannot just treat them in any way at all.

Treatment of animals is a case in point. It is wrong to torture dogs for fun or to kill wild birds for no reason at all. It is wrong Period, even though dogs and birds do not have the same rights persons do. However, few people think it is wrong to use dogs as experimental animals, causing them considerable suffering in some cases, provided that the resulting research will probably bring discoveries of great benefit to people. And most of us think it all right to kill birds for food or to protect our crops. People's rights are different from the consideration we give to animals, then, for it is wrong to experiment on people, even if others might later benefit a great deal as a result of their suffering. You might volunteer to be a subject, but this would be supererogatory; you certainly have a right to refuse to be a medical guinea pig.

But how do we decide what you may or may not do to nonpersons? This is a difficult problem, one for which I believe no adequate account exists. You do not want to say, for instance, that torturing dogs is all right whenever the sum of its effects on people is good—when it doesn't warp the sensibilities of the torturer so much that he mistreats people. If that were the case, it would be all right to torture dogs if you did it in private, or if the torturer lived on a desert island or died soon afterward, so that his actions had no effect on people. This is an inadequate account, because whatever moral consideration animals get, it has to be indefeasible, too. It will have to be a general proscription of certain actions, not merely a weighing of the impact on people on a case-by-case basis.

Rather, we need to distinguish two levels on which consequences of actions can be taken into account in moral reasoning. The traditional objections to utilitarianism focus on the fact that it operates solely on the first level, taking all the consequences into account in particular cases only. Thus utilitarianism is open to "desert island" and "lifeboat" counterexamples because these cases are rigged to make the consequences of actions severely limited.

Rawls' theory could be described as a teleological sort of theory, but with teleology operating on a higher level.[12] In choosing the principles to regulate society from the original position, his hypothetical choosers make their decision on the basis of the total consequences of various systems. Furthermore, they are constrained to choose a general set of rules that people can readily learn and apply. An ethical theory must operate by generating a set of sympathies and attitudes toward others that reinforces the functioning of that set of moral principles. Our prohibition against killing people operates by means of certain moral sentiments including sympathy, compassion, and guilt. But if these attitudes are to form a coherent set, they carry us further: We tend to perform supererogatory actions, and we tend to feel similar compassion toward person-like nonpersons.

It is crucial that psychological facts play a role here. Our psychological constitution makes it the case that for our ethical theory to work, it must prohibit certain treatment of nonpersons that are significantly person-like. If our moral rules allowed people to treat some person-like nonpersons in ways we do not want people to be treated, this would undermine the system of sympathies and attitudes that makes the ethical system work. For this reason, we would choose in the original position to make mistreatment of some sorts of animals wrong in general (not just wrong in the cases with public impact), even though animals are not themselves parties in the original position. Thus it makes sense that it is those animals whose appearance and behavior are most like those of people that get the most consideration in our moral scheme.

It is because of "coherence of attitudes," I think, that the similarity of a fetus to a baby is very significant. A fetus one week before birth is so much like a newborn baby in our psychological space that we cannot allow any cavalier treatment of the former while expecting full sympathy and nurturative support for the latter. Thus, I think that anti-abortion forces are indeed giving their strongest arguments when they point to the similarities between a fetus and a baby and when they try to evoke our emotional attachment to and sympathy for the fetus. An early horror story from New York about nurses who were expected to alternate between caring for 6-week premature infants and disposing of viable 24-week aborted fetuses is just that—a horror story. These beings are so much alike that no one can be asked to draw a distinction and treat them so very differently.

Remember however, that in the early weeks after conception, a fetus is very much unlike a person. It is hard to develop these feelings for a set of genes that doesn't yet have a head, hands, beating heart, response to touch or the ability to move by itself. Thus it seems to me that the alleged "slippery slope" between conception and birth is not so very slippery. In the early stages of pregnancy, abortion can hardly be compared to murder for psychological reasons, but in the latest stages, it is psychologically akin to murder.

Another source of similarity is the bodily continuity between fetus and adult. Bodies play a surprisingly central role in our attitudes toward persons. One has only to think of the philosophical literature on how far physical identity suffices for personal identity or Wittgenstein's remark that the best picture of the human soul is the human body. Even after death, when all agree the body is no longer a person, we still observe elaborate customs of respect for the human body; like people who torture dogs, necrophiliacs are not to be trusted with people.[13] So it is appropriate that we show respect to a fetus as the body continuous with the body of a person This is a degree of resemblance to persons that animals cannot rival.

Michael Tooley also utilizes a parallel with animals. He claims that it is always permissible to drown newborn kittens and draws conclusions about infanticide.[14] But it is only permissible to drown kittens when their survival would cause some hardship. Perhaps it would be a burden to feed and house six more cats or to find other homes for them. The alternative of letting them starve produces even more suffering than the drowning. Since the kittens get their rights second-hand, so to speak, *via* the need for coherence in our attitudes, their interests are often overridden by the interests of full-fledged persons. But if their survival would be no inconvenience to people at all, then it is wrong to drown them, *contra* Tooley.

Tooley's conclusions about abortion are wrong for the same reason. Even if a fetus is not a person, abortion is not always permissible because of the resemblance of a fetus to a person. I agree with Thomson that it would be wrong for a woman who is seven months pregnant to have an abortion just to avoid having to postpone a trip to Europe. In the early months of pregnancy when the fetus hardly resembles a baby at all, then, abortion is permissible whenever it is in the interests of the pregnant woman or her family. The reasons would only need to outweigh the pain and inconvenience of the abortion itself. In the middle months, when the fetus comes to resemble a person, abortion would be justifiable only when the continuation of the pregnancy or the birth of the child would cause harms—physical, psychological, economic, or social—to the woman. In the late months of pregnancy, even on our current assumption that a fetus is not a person, abortion seems to be wrong except to save a woman from significant injury or death.

The Supreme Court has recognized similar gradations in the alleged slippery slope stretching between conception and birth. To this point, the present paper has been a discussion of the moral status of abortion only, not its legal status. In view of the great physical, financial, and sometimes psychological costs of abortion, perhaps the legal arrangements most compatible with the proposed moral solution would be the absence of restrictions, that is, so-called abortion "on demand."

So I conclude, first, that application of our concept of a person will not suffice to settle the abortion issue. After all, the biological development of a human being is gradual. Second, whether a fetus is a person or not, abortion is justifiable early in pregnancy to avoid modest harms and seldom justifiable late in pregnancy except to avoid significant injury or death.[15]

STUDY QUESTIONS

1. Can we get beyond personhood? Has English successfully shown that we don't need to resolve the personhood issue in order to deal with the morality of abortion? Where do you agree or disagree with her?

2. English's view has been called moderate because she accepts most early stage but rejects most later stage abortions. Is her position really moderate? If so, how can this be reconciled with her proposal of abortion "on demand"?

3. Does English's argument appeal too much to our emotions and too little to reason? For example, she says "It is crucial that psychological facts play a role here. Our psychological constitution makes it the case that for our ethical theory to work, it must prohibit certain treatment of nonpersons that are significantly person-like." What does English mean? Is this an appeal to ignorance or to human irrationality?

NOTES

1. We also have paternalistic laws that keep us from harming our own bodies even when no one else is affected. Ironically, anti-abortion laws were originally designed to protect pregnant women from a dangerous but tempting procedure.

2. Mary Anne Warren, "On the Moral and Legal Status of Abortion," *Monist* 57 (1973).

3. Baruch Brody, "Fetal Humanity and the Theory of Essentialism," in Robert Baker and Frederick Elliston, eds., *Philosophy and Sex*. Buffalo, N.Y., 1975.

4. Michael Tooley, "Abortion and Infanticide," *Philosophy and Public Affairs* 2 (1971).

5. Paul Ramsey, "The Morality of Abortion," in James Rachels, ed., *Moral Problems*. New York, 1971.

6. John Noonan, "Abortion and the Catholic Church: A Summary History," *Natural Law Forum* 12 (1967), 125–131.

7. Wittgenstein has argued against the possibility of so capturing the concept of a game, *Philosophical Investigations. New York, 1958, 66–71.

8. Not because the fetus is partly a person and so has some of the rights of persons, but rather because of the rights of person-like nonpersons. This I discuss in Part III later.

9. Aristotle himself was concerned, however, with the different question of when the soul takes form. For historical data, see Jimmye Kimmey, "How the Abortion Laws Happened," *Ms.* 1 (April, 1973), 48ff, and John Noonan, "Abortion and the Catholic Church."

10. J. J. Thomson, "A Defense of Abortion," *Philosophy and Public Affairs* 1 (1971).

11. Ibid., 187.

12. John Rawls, *A Theory of Justice*. Cambridge, Mass., 1971, 3–4.

13. On the other hand, if they can be trusted with people, then our moral customs are mistaken. It all depends on the facts of psychology.

14. Rawls, *Theory of Justice,* 40, 60–61.

15. I am deeply indebted to Larry Crocker and Arthur Kuflik for their constructive comments.

19

The Golden Rule Argument Against Abortion

HARRY J. GENSLER

Harry J. Gensler is Professor of Philosophy at Loyola University in Chicago. In the article that follows, Gensler does three things. First, he analyzes the meaning of human *and the question of when human life begins. Second, he examines the major arguments in favor of abortion and concludes that none of them are successful. Third, he uses a Kantian argument based on consistency (a version of the Golden Rule) to show that normally abortion is morally wrong. In closing, he responds to six objections against his position.*

If you asked ten years ago for my view on the morality of abortion, I would have said "I don't have a view—the issue confuses me." But now I think that abortion is wrong and that certain Kantian consistency requirements more or less force us into thinking this. Part III will present my reasoning. But first, in Parts I and II, I will show why various traditional and recent arguments on abortion do not work.

I. A TRADITIONAL ANTI-ABORTION ARGUMENT

One common traditional argument goes this way:

The killing of innocent human life is wrong.

The fetus is innocent human life.

Therefore, the killing of the fetus is wrong.

From "A Kantian Argument Against Abortion," *Philosophical Studies,* No. 49 (1986), 83–98. Reprinted by permission of Kluwer Academic Publishers.

This seemingly simple argument raises some difficult questions:

It is "always wrong" or "normally wrong"? And if the latter, how do we decide the difficult cases?

Is the fetus "innocent" if it is attacking the life or health or social well-being of the woman?

Is there a clear and morally-weighty distinction between "killing" and "letting die"—or between "direct killing" and "indirect killing"?

I will not discuss these important questions; a short essay on abortion must leave many questions unanswered. But I will discuss this one:

"What does the term 'human life' in the abortion argument mean?" People sometimes presume that the meaning of the term is clear and that the major problem is the factual one of whether the fetus is "human life" (in some clear sense). But I think that the term in this context is fuzzy and could be used in different senses.

Suppose we found a Martian who could discuss philosophy; would he be "human"? We need to make distinctions: The Martian would be "human" in the sense of "animal capable of reasoning" ("rational animal") but not in the sense of "member of the species *Homo sapiens*"—so the Martian is "human" in one sense but not in another. Which of these senses should be used in the abortion argument? The fetus is not yet an "animal capable of reasoning." Is it a "member of the species *Homo sapiens*"? That depends on whether the unborn are to be counted as "members" of a species—ordinary language can use the term either way. In the biology lab we all (regardless of our views on abortion) distinguish between "human" fetuses and "mouse" fetuses—so in this sense (the "genetic sense") the fetus is human. But in counting the number of mice or humans in the city of Chicago we all (regardless of our views on abortion) count only the born—so in this sense ("the population-study sense") the fetus is not a human. So is the fetus a "human"? In two senses of this term that we have distinguished the answer would be NO, and in a third sense the answer would be YES; whether the fetus is "human" depends on what is meant by "human."

Human life has been claimed to begin at various points:

1. At conception
2. When individuality is assured (and the zygote cannot split or fuse with another)
3. When the fetus exhibits brain waves
4. When the fetus could live apart
5. At birth
6. When the being becomes self-conscious and rational

Here we do not have a factual disagreement about when there emerges, in the same clear sense of the term, a "human," rather we have six ways to use the term. Answer (1) is correct for the "genetic sense," (5) for the population-study sense," and (6) for the "rational animal sense"; answers (2) to (4) reflect other (possibly idiosyncratic) senses. And there are likely other senses of "human" besides these six. Which of these are we to use in the first premise ("The killing of innocent *human* life is wrong")? We get different principles depending on which sense of the term "human" we use.

Can we decide which sense to use by appealing to scientific data? No, we cannot. Scientific data can help us judge whether a specific individual is "human" in some specified sense (for example, sense [3] or sense [4]), but it cannot tell us which sense of "human" to use in our principle.

Can we decide by "intuition"—by following the principle that *seems* most correct? Note that moral intuitions depend greatly on upbringing and social milieu. Most Catholics were brought up to have intuitions in line with sense (1) (the "genetic sense"). Many ancient Romans and Greeks were trained to have sense (6) intuitions (allowing abortion *and* infanticide). And many Americans today are being brought up to have sense (5) intuitions (allowing abortion but not infanticide). Is there any way to resolve this clash—other than simply praising our own intuitions and insulting contrary ones? Can we carry on the argument further? I think we can and that the Kantian appeal to consistency provides a way to resolve the issue rationally.

II. SOME RECENT PRO-ABORTION ARGUMENTS

Before getting to the Kantian approach, let us consider three arguments in defense of abortion. A common utilitarian argument goes this way:

Anything having a balance of good results (considering everyone) is morally permissible.

Abortion often has a balance of good results (considering everyone).

Therefore, abortion often is morally permissible.

Here "good results" is most commonly interpreted in terms of pleasure and pain ("hedonistic act utilitarianism") or the satisfaction of desires ("preference act utilitarianism").

The second premise (on the good results of abortion) is controversial. People defending the premise say that abortion often avoids difficulties such as the financial burden of a child on poor parents or on society, the disruption of schooling or a career, and the disgrace of an unwed mother; that where these problems or probable birth defects exist, the child-to-be would have less chance for happiness; and that abortion provides a "second chance" to prevent a birth when contraceptives fail or people want to rethink an earlier choice. But opponents say that we can have equally good results without abortion, by using better social structures (more social support toward unwed mothers and poor families, better adoption practices, wiser use of contraceptives, and so on) and scientific advances (better contraceptives, artificial wombs, and so forth), and they say that abortion can harm the woman psychologically and promote callous attitudes toward human life.

I think the weaker link is the first premise—the argument's utilitarian basis. This premise would often justify killing, not just fetuses, but also infants and the sick or handicapped or elderly; many utilitarian reasons for not wanting a child around the house would also apply to not wanting grandmother around. And the premise would justify these killings, not just when they have great utilitarian benefits, but even when the utilitarian benefits are slight. Utilitarianism says that the killing of an innocent human being is justified whenever it brings even a slight increase in the sum-total of pleasure (or desire-satisfaction). This is truly bizarre.

Imagine a town where lynchings gave the people pleasure (or satisfied their desires) and the utilitarian sheriff lynches an innocent person each week because the pleasure (or desire) of the masses slightly outweighs the misery (or frustration of desire) of the person to be lynched—and so the action has a slight gain in "good results." If the utilitarian principle is correct, then the sheriff's lynchings are morally justified! But could anyone really believe that these lynchings would be morally justified?

I could pile up further examples of strange and unbelievable implications of utilitarianism. Utilitarians try to weasel out of these examples but I think not with ultimate success. So my verdict on utilitarianism is that it would justify so many bizarre actions (including so many killings) that we would not accept this principle if we were consistent and realized its logical consequences.

My second pro-abortion argument is from Michael Tooley.[1] Tooley recognizes that humans have a right to life—presumably a greater right than utilitarians would recognize, but only humans in sense (6) ("rational animals"—or, as he puts it, "persons") have such a right. The human fetus, while it might develop into a being with a right to life, presently has no more right to life than a mouse fetus. A fetus lacks a right to life because "rights" connect with "desires" conceptually—so that you can have rights only if you have desires. Tooley's argument is roughly this:

> A being has a right to X only if it desires X.
>
> No fetus desires its continued existence [because then the fetus would have to have a concept of itself as a continuing subject of experience—a concept it cannot as yet have].
>
> Therefore, no fetus has a right to its continued existence.

Tooley claims that the first premise is not correct as it stands; we must add three qualifications to make the premise harmonize with our intuitions regarding rights:

> A being has a right to X only if either it desires X or else it would desire X were it not (a) emotionally unbalanced or (b) temporarily unconscious or (c) conditioned otherwise.

He thinks the revised first premise will serve equally well (assuming obvious changes in the second premise); so he concludes that fetuses (and infants) do not have a right to life.

But we need further exceptions to make the first premise correspond to our intuitions. If we think that the dead have rights (for example, to have their wills followed), then we need to add "or (d) the being did desire X when it was alive." If we think that a child who lacks the concept "hepatitis" (and thus cannot desire not to be given this disease) does not thereby lose his right not to be given hepatitis, then we need to add "or (e) the being would desire X if it had the necessary concepts." If we think (as I do) that trees and canyons have the right not to be destroyed without good reason, then we would have to add some exception for this. And if we think that the fetus (or infant) has a right to life, then we need to add something like "or (f) if the being were to grow up to be an adult member of the rational species to which it belongs then it would desire to have had X" (presumably if the fetus were to grow up to be an adult member of *Homo sapiens* then it would desire to have had continued life—and this, with (f), allows the fetus to have a right to life).[2] The trouble with Tooley's argument is that disagreements over the main issue of the right to life of the fetus translate into disagreements over how to qualify the first premise to make it mesh with "our" intuitions; the argument cannot decide the main issue.

The third argument in defense of abortion comes from Judith Jarvis Thomson and presumes that the fetus is a "person" (in some undefined sense)[3]:

> One who has voluntarily assumed no special obligation toward another person has no obligation to do anything requiring great personal cost to preserve the life of the other.

> Often a pregnant woman has voluntarily assumed no special obligation toward the unborn child (a person), and to preserve its life by continuing to bear the unborn child would require great personal cost.

> Therefore, often a pregnant woman has no obligation to continue to bear the unborn child.

The first premise here seems acceptable. Normally you have no obligation to risk your life to save a drowning stranger; if you risk your life then you do more than duty requires. But it is different if you are a lifeguard who has assumed a special obligation—then you have to try to save the person, even at the risk of your own life. Thomson thinks that a woman getting pregnant intending to have a child is voluntarily accepting a special obligation toward the child. However, if the pregnancy is accidental (the result of a contraceptive failure or rape) then the woman has assumed no such special obligation, and, if continuing to bear the child requires great personal cost, the woman has no obligation to continue to bear it; the woman would do no wrong if she has an abortion—but if she continues to bear the child in spite of personal cost then she is doing something heroic, something beyond what duty requires.

Thomson gives an analogy. Suppose you wake up and find yourself in bed with an unconscious violinist attached to your circulatory system (his friends attached him to you because this was needed to save his life); if you disconnect him before nine months, he will die—otherwise he will live. Even though it might be praiseworthy to make the sacrifice and leave him plugged in for nine months, still you have no obligation to do so; it would be morally right for you to disconnect him, even though he will die. So also if you are pregnant under the conditions mentioned earlier, then, even though it might be praiseworthy to make the sacrifice and bear the child for nine months, still you have no obligation to do so; it would be morally right for you to have the child removed, even though it will die.

The first premise of Thomson's argument is slightly misstated. A motorist has a special obligation toward a person he has injured in an accident, even though he has not voluntarily assumed this obligation any clear way (the accident happened against his will and despite all reasonable precautions—just like an accidental pregnancy). Similarly a child has a special obligation toward his parents—even though he has not voluntarily assumed this obligation. Not all special obligations toward others are "voluntarily assumed"—so these two words should be crossed out in the premises.

My main objection to the argument can be put as a dilemma. Utilitarianism is either true or false. If it is *true*, then the first premise is false (because then the person has an obligation to do whatever has the best consequences—despite personal cost); thus, the pro-abortion utilitarian Peter Singer rejects this premise because it conflicts with utilitarianism. But if utilitarianism is *false*, then presumably Sir David Ross was right in claiming it to be morally significant that others

> stand to me in relation of promisee to promiser, of creditor to debtor, of wife to husband, *of child to parent* [my emphasis], of friend to friend, of fellow countryman to fellow countryman, and the like; and each of these relations is the foundation of a *prima facie* duty, which is more or less incumbent on me according to the circumstances of the case.[4]

If utilitarianism is *false*, then likely a person has greater obligations toward his or her offspring than toward a violinist stranger—and so the second premise, which claims that the pregnant woman has no special responsibility toward her own child, begins to look doubtful (recall that we crossed out the words "voluntarily assumed").

III. A KANTIAN ARGUMENT

My Kantian approach to abortion stresses consistency. In discussing utilitarianism I appealed to simple logical consistency (not accepting a principle without accepting its recognized logical consequences). Here I will use two further consistency requirements (based on the universalizability and prescriptivity principles) and a third consistency requirement derived from these two (a version of the golden rule). The following argument displays these three requirements and how the third follows from the first two:

> If you are consistent and think that it would be all right for someone *to do A to X*, then you will think that it would be all right for someone *to do A to you* in similar circumstances.

If you are consistent and think that it would be *all right* for someone to do *A* to you in similar circumstances, then you will *consent* to the idea of someone doing *A* to you in similar circumstances.

Therefore, if you are consistent and think that it would be *all right to do A to X,* then you will *consent* to the idea of someone *doing A to you* in similar circumstances. (GR[Golden Rule])

The first premise can be justified by the "universalizability principle," which demands that we make similar ethical judgments about the same sort of situation (regardless of the individuals involved); so if I think it would be all right to rob *Jones* but I don't think it would be all right for someone to rob *me* in an imagined exactly similar situation, then I violate universalizability and am inconsistent. The second premise can be justified by the "prescriptivity principle," which demands that we keep our ethical beliefs in harmony with the rest of our lives (our actions, intentions, desires, and so forth); so if I think an act would be all right but I don't consent to it being done, then I violate prescriptivity and am inconsistent. These and further derived requirements can be formulated and justified in a rigorous way; but I won't do that here. The conclusion GR is a form of the golden rule; if I think it would be all right to rob Jones but yet I don't consent to (or approve of) the idea of someone robbing me in similar circumstances, then I violate GR and am inconsistent.[5]

The following argument combines an instance of GR with an empirical premise about your desires:

If you are consistent and think that *stealing is normally permissible,* then you will consent to the idea of *people stealing from you* in normal circumstances. (From GR)

You do not consent to the idea of people stealing from you in normal circumstances.

Therefore, if you are consistent then you will not think that stealing is normally permissible.

Most of us do not consent to the idea of people stealing from us in normal circumstances; so we would not be consistent if we held "stealing is normally permissible" (we would then violate consistency principle GR). This argument shows that, given that a person has a certain desire (one that most people can be presumed to have), he would not be consistent if he held a given ethical view. The conclusion here concerns the consistency of holding the ethical judgment and not the judgment's truth. A person could escape this conclusion if he did not care if people robbed him; then the second premise would be false. Throughout the rest of this essay I will generally assume that the reader desires not to be robbed or blinded or killed; if you would love people to rob or blind or kill you (or you don't care whether they do this to you)—then most of my further conclusions will not apply to you.

It might seem easy to argue similarly on abortion. How would you like it if someone had aborted you? Should we say that you don't like the idea and so you can't consistently hold that abortion is permissible? Or should we say that as an ignorant fetus you would not have known enough to have been against the abortion—so that this argument won't work?

Let us slow down and try to understand GR more clearly before applying it to abortion. Properly understood, GR has to do with my *present reaction* toward a hypothetical case—not with how I *would react if I were* in the hypothetical case. A few examples may clarify things. Consider this chart:

Issue	Right Question	Wrong Question
Do I think it permissible to rob X while X is asleep?	Do I now consent to the idea of my being robbed while asleep?	If I were robbed while I was asleep would I then (while asleep) consent to this action?

(In the "Right Question" and "Wrong Question," I presume implicit "in relevantly or exactly similar circumstances" qualifiers). The point of this chart is that, by GR, to be consistent in answering YES to the ISSUE I must also answer yes to the *right question*—but I need not answer *yes* to the *wrong question*. Presumably I would answer *no* to the *right questions;* when I consider the hypothetical case of my-being-robbed-while asleep, I find that I now (while awake) do not consent to or approve of this action. But the *wrong question* has to do with what I, if I were robbed while asleep, would consent to or approve of while thus asleep (and thus ignorant of the robbery); GR, correctly understood, has nothing to do with the *wrong question*. Let me give another example:

Issue	Right Question	Wrong Question
Do I think it permissible to violate X's will after his death?	Do I now consent to the idea of my will being violated after my death?	If my will is violated after my death, would I then (while dead) consent to this action?

Again GR has to do with my *present reaction* toward a hypothetical case in which I may imagine myself as asleep or dead or even a fetus—but not with how I *would* react *while* asleep or dead or a fetus *in* the hypothetical situation.

But is it legitimate to apply the golden rule to our treatment of a fetus? Consider a case not involving abortion:

Issue	Right Question	Wrong Question
Do I think it permissible to blind X while X is a fetus?	Do *I* now consent to the idea of my having been blinded while a fetus?	If I were blinded while a fetus, would I then (while a fetus) consent to this action?

Suppose you had a sadistic mother who, while pregnant with you, contemplated injecting herself with a blindness-drug that would have no effect on her but that would cause the fetus (you) to be born blind and remain blind all its (your) life. Your mother could have done this to you. Do you think this would have been all right—and do you consent to the idea of her having done this? The answer is a clear *no*—and an equally clear *no* regardless of the time of pregnancy that we imagine the injection taking place. We could then argue as we did concerning stealing:

> If you are consistent and think that *blinding a fetus is normally permissible,* then you will consent to the idea of *your having been blinded while a fetus* in normal circumstances. (From GR)
>
> You do not consent to the idea of your having been blinded while a fetus in normal circumstances.
>
> Therefore, if you are consistent then you will not think that blinding a fetus is normally permissible.

Again, with most people the second premise will be true—most people can be presumed not to consent to (or approve of) the idea of this act having been done to them.

It is legitimate to apply the golden rule to our treatment of a fetus? Surely it is—the above reasoning makes good sense. If a pregnant woman is about to do something harmful to the fetus (like taking drugs or excessive alcohol or cigarettes), it seems appropriate for her to ask, How do I now react to the idea of my mother having done this same thing while she was pregnant with me?" Applying the golden rule to a fetus raises no special problems.

But someone might object as follows:

> Seemingly your view forces us to accept that the fetus has rights (for example, not to be blinded by the drug), even though you avoid saying it is human. But your question about "*my* having been blinded *while a fetus*" presupposes that the fetus and my present self are identical—the *same human being.* So aren't you presupposing (despite your earlier discussion on the many senses of "human") that the fetus is "human"?

Although my way of phrasing the question may presuppose this, I put my question this way only for the sake of convenience; I could rephrase my question so that it doesn't presuppose this:

Do I now consent to the idea of:

—my having been blinded while a fetus?

—the fetus that developed into my present self having been blinded?

—Helen E. Gensler having taken the blindness-drug while pregnant in 1945?

The second and third ways to phrase the question do not presuppose that the fetus and my present self are identical or the same human being; if you wish, you may rephrase my comments thusly (I will keep to the first way of speaking for the sake of brevity). I am against the idea of the drug having been given, not because I think that the fetus was in some metaphysical sense the *same human being* as I, but rather because if this drug had been given then I would be blind all my life.

The application of GR to abortion is similar—we need only switch from a blindness-drug (which blinds the fetus) to a death-drug (which kills the fetus).

Your mother could have killed you through such a death-drug (or other means of abortion). Do you think this would have been all right—and do you consent to (or approve of) the idea of her having done this? Again the answer is a clear *no*—and an equally clear *no* regardless of the time of pregnancy that we imagine the killing taking place. We can argue as we did concerning blinding:

> If you are consistent and think that *abortion is normally permissible,* then you will consent to the idea of *your having been aborted* in normal circumstances. (From GR)
>
> You do not consent to the idea of your having been aborted in normal circumstances.
>
> Therefore, if you are consistent then you will not think that abortion is normally permissible.

Again with most people the second premise will be true—most people can be presumed not to consent to (or approve of) the idea of this act having been done to them. So insofar as most people take a consistent position they will not think that abortion is normally permissible.

IV. SIX OBJECTIONS

(1) Surely a utilitarian would see your two drug cases as very different—the blindness-drug inflicts needless future suffering while the death-drug simply eliminates a life. Why wouldn't a utilitarian, moved by the greatest total happiness principle, approve of the death-drug having been given to him if this would have led to a greater total happiness? Wouldn't such a person be a consistent upholder of the view that abortion is normally permissible?

My answer is that utilitarianism leads to so many strange moral implications that, even *if* the utilitarian could be consistent on this one case, still he would likely be inconsistent in his overall position. I previously claimed that utilitarianism would justify so many bizarre actions (including so many killings) that we would not accept this principle if we were consistent and realized its logical consequences. But if there are few (if any) consistent utilitarians, then there would be few (if any) consistent utilitarian upholders of this view that abortion is normally permissible.

(2) Let us consider a *nonutilitarian* who approves of abortion but not infanticide or the blindness-drug. Why couldn't such a person consent to the idea of himself having been aborted under imagined or actual normal circumstances—and hence be consistent?

Such a person could be consistent, but only with bizarre desires about how he himself is to be treated. Let us suppose that someone combined these three judgments (as many are being brought up to do in our society today):

a. It is wrong to blind an adult or child or infant or fetus.

b. It is wrong to kill an adult or child or infant.

c. It is permissible to kill a fetus.

To be consistent the person would have to answer these questions as follows:

Do you consent to the idea of my *blinding* you now?—NO!	Do you consent to the idea of my *killing* you now?—NO!
Do you consent to the idea of my having *blinded* you yesterday?—NO!	Do you consent to the idea of my having *killed* you yesterday?—NO!
… when you were five years old?—NO!	… when you were five years old?—NO!
… when you were one day old?—NO!	… when you were one day old?—NO!
… before you were born?—NO!	… before you were born?—*YES!!!*

It is strange that the person *disapproves equally* of being *blinded* at the various times—and *disapproves equally* of being *killed* at the first four times—and yet *approves* of being *killed* at the last time. He opposes the blindings because, regardless of their timing, the effect would be the same—he would be blind. He opposes the killings at the first four times because, again the effect would be the same—he would not be alive; but killing at the fifth time has the same effect—why should he not oppose this killing also? The *yes* here seems rather strange. Of course one who thinks his life not worth living could give a *yes* to the idea of his having been killed while a fetus—but then we would expect *yes* answers to the idea of being his killed at the other times as well (which would make him inconsistent if he held that it is wrong to kill an adult or child or infant). So while a nonutilitarian who combines the three judgments *could* in principle have such desires and be consistent, still this is unlikely to happen very often—to be consistent, the person would have to have very bizarre desires.[6]

> (3) Are you saying that the desires that most people have are good whereas unusual (or "bizarre") desires are bad? How would you establish this?

I am not saying that common desires are good while unusual desires are bad—often the reverse is true; sometimes when we notice a conflict between our moral beliefs and our desires we come to change our desires and not our moral beliefs. Rather I am appealing to desires that most people have because I am trying to develop a consistency argument to show that most people who adopt the pro-abortion view are inconsistent. In effect I am challenging those who adopt such a view by saying, "Look at what you would have to desire to be consistent in your position—go and think about it and see whether you really are consistent!" I claim that most of the time, the pro-abortionist will find that he is indeed inconsistent—he is supporting certain moral principles about the treatment of others that he would not wish to have followed in their actions toward him.

(4) You question the consistency of one who holds that abortion is permissible but infanticide is wrong. But let us see whether you are consistent. If it would have been wrong for your parents to have aborted you, wouldn't it have been equally wrong for your parents not to have conceived you? The result would have been the same—there would be no YOU!

My answer here is complicated. My first reaction is to disapprove of the idea of my parents not having conceived me—to think it would have been wrong for them to have abstained or used contraceptives; but the universalizing requirement forces me to change my reactions (whereas it doesn't do this in the abortion case). If I hold "it is wrong to have an abortion in this (my) case," then I have to make the same judgment in all similar cases, but I can easily hold (consistently) that it is in general wrong to have an abortion. But if I hold "It is wrong to prevent conception (by, for example, abstinence or contraceptives) in this (my) case," then I again have to make the same judgment in all similar cases. But I cannot hold (consistently) that it is in general wrong to prevent conception—since this would commit me to desiring a policy that would bring about a greatly overpopulated world of starving people at a very low level of human life. So, to be consistent, I change my first reaction and come to judge that it would have been morally permissible for my parents not to have conceived (me) on August 5, 1944—but instead perhaps to have conceived (someone else) on September 5, 1944—and I come, though with hesitation, to consent to the possibility of their having done this. To sum up: The universalizing requirement points to an important difference between *aborting* and *not conceiving*—I can "will as a universal law" a general prohibition against *aborting,* but not one against *nonconceiving.*

(5) Suppose that reason does force us into thinking that abortion is *normally* wrong. What does "normal" here mean? And aren't the "abnormal" or "unusual" cases the more important and difficult ones to deal with? So isn't your conclusion unimportant?

My claim that abortion is *normally* wrong means that it is wrong in at least the great majority of cases but perhaps not in every conceivable case (for example, in the imagined case where Dr. Evil will destroy the world if we do not do an abortion). The question of what unusual conditions (if any) would justify abortion is indeed important and difficult. But I think that, in light of the very great number of "convenience abortions" going on today, the issue of the general moral status of abortion is at the present time far more important.

(6) Suppose that *if I am consistent* I cannot hold that abortion is normally permissible. What if I do not care about being consistent? Can you prove to me that I ought to care? Or can you prove to me that abortion is wrong without appealing to consistency?

You ask too much. Suppose I give you an argument proving that abortion is wrong (or that you ought to care about being consistent). If you do not already care about consistency, why should you not accept the premises of my argument and yet reject the conclusion? This would be inconsistent—but you don't care about this! So you presumably wouldn't care about any argument I might give—in effect you are saying that you have a closed mind. If you don't care about consistency, then I am wasting my time when I try to reason with you.

STUDY QUESTIONS

1. Is Gensler fair to the positions he criticizes, the utilitarians, Michael Tooley, and Judith Jarvis Thomson? Can you think of ways to strengthen their positions? How would Mary Anne Warren respond to the Golden Rule argument?

2. Do you see any weaknesses in the Golden Rule argument? Can you think of any counterexamples to it? Consider this one: A convicted criminal serving time in prison says to the warden, "Do you believe in the Golden Rule, Sir?" The warden replies, "Yes, I try to live my life by it." "Then," responds the prisoner, "if you were in my place, wouldn't you want me to set you free? So you should set me free."

   Or try this application of Gensler's principle. I say to myself, "Do I, rock 'n' role lover that I am, now consent to listen to rock music played at 140 decibels?" If I say "yes" does that mean I am permitted to play it that loud whether or not my roommate and neighbors can stand it?

   How would Gensler respond to these counterexamples? Do they affect Gensler's argument?

NOTES

1. Tooley's original argument was in "Abortion and Infanticide," *Philosophy and Public Affairs* 2 (1972), 37–65. He added refinements to his view in *Philosophy and Public Affairs* 2 (1973), 419–432; in a postscript to a reprint of his article in *The Rights and Wrongs of Abortion,* edited by Marshall Cohen, Thomas Nagel, and Thomas Scanlon, Princeton, 1974, 80–84; and in "In Defense of Abortion and Infanticide," in *The Problem of Abortion* (second edition), edited by Joel Feinberg, Belmont, Calif., 1984, 120–134. (The weak link in the latest version of the argument seems to be this premise: "An individual existing at one time cannot have desires at other times unless there is at least one time at which it possesses the concept of a continuing self or mental substance"; this entails the incredible "Your pet kitten cannot yesterday have had a desire to eat unless at some time it possesses the concept of a continuing self or mental substance.") Peter Singer's defense of abortion and infanticide rests partially on Tooley's earlier argument but mainly on his preference utilitarianism; see chapters 4 and 6 of his *Practical Ethics,* Cambridge, 1979.

2. Clause (f) was phrased to skirt the issue of Tooley's "superkittens" who become rational if given a certain drug; my intuitions on the superkitten (and Frankenstein) cases are not very clear. Clause (f) may require further refinement.

3. "A Defense of Abortion," in *Philosophy and Public Affairs* 1 (1971), 47–66.

4. *The Right and the Good.* Oxford, 1930, 19.

5. In arguing the abortion issue, I use some ideas from the theory of R. M. Hare, as developed in his *Freedom and Reason,* Oxford, 1963. Hare once wrote an article on "Abortion and the Golden Rule" *(Philosophy and Public Affairs* 4 [1975], 201–222), but his approach differs from mine. Hare rests his case on "We should do to others what we are glad was done to us" and on the fact that we are glad that we were conceived, not aborted, and not killed as infants; hence we too ought to conceive, not abort, and not kill infants (but contraception, abortion, and infanticide turn out to have only a weak prima facie wrongness which is easy to override by other considerations). Hare's formulation of the golden rule here is defective; if I am *glad* my parents gave me hundreds of gifts each Christmas, then perhaps to be consistent I must hold that it would be good to do this same thing in similar circumstances—but I need not hold that one *should* do this (that it is a *duty).* Also my conclusions differ from Hare's—I view abortion and infanticide (but not failing-to-conceive) as seriously wrong; I think my conclusions are what Hare's theory should lead to.

6. On the Tooley/Singer view, the cut-off point for killing is not birth but rather when the child comes to desire its continued existence as a continuing subject of experiences. (It is unclear at what age this happens.) My response to this view would be much like the previous example, except that the killing side of the chart would now have one more *yes.*

20

Why Abortion
Is Immoral

DON MARQUIS

Don Marquis is Professor of Philosophy at the University of Kansas. In this essay he argues that both anti-abortionists and prochoicers arrive at a standoff when they resort to arguments about whether the fetus is a person or a "human life." What is needed is a deeper understanding of what makes killing itself wrong. Marquis argues that what makes killing someone wrong is the fact that he or she has a future good (or "a future like ours"). He considers objections to his position, especially the objection that his arguments would entail that contraception is wrong, and argues that none of them defeats his proposal.

WHY ABORTION IS IMMORAL

The view that abortion is, with rare exceptions, seriously immoral has received little support in the recent philosophical literature. No doubt most philosophers affiliated with secular institutions of higher education believe that the anti–abortion position is either a symptom of irrational religious dogma or a conclusion generated by seriously confused philosophical argument. The purpose of this essay is to undermine this general belief. This essay sets out an argument that purports to show, as well as any argument in ethics

Reprinted from *The Journal of Philosophy.* 86 (April 1989), by permission.

can show, that abortion is, except possibly in rare cases, seriously immoral, that it is in the same moral category as killing an innocent adult human being.

The argument is based on a major assumption. Many of the most insightful and careful writers on the ethics of abortion—such as Joel Feinberg, Michael Tooley, Mary Anne Warren, H. Tristam Engelhardt, Jr., L. W. Sumner, John T. Noonan, Jr., and Philip Devine[1]—believe that whether or not abortion is morally permissible stands or falls on whether or not a fetus is the sort of being whose life it is seriously wrong to end. In this essay, I will assume, but not argue, that they are correct.

Also, this essay will neglect issues of great importance to a complete ethics of abortion. Some anti-abortionists will allow that certain abortions, such as abortion before implantation or abortion when the life of a woman is threatened by pregnancy or abortion after rape, may be morally permissible. This essay will not explore the casuistry of these hard cases. My purpose is to develop a general argument for the claim that the overwhelming majority of deliberate abortions are seriously immoral.

I

A sketch of standard anti-abortion and prochoice arguments exhibits how those arguments possess certain symmetries that explain why partisans of those positions are so convinced of the correctness of their own positions, why they are not successful in convincing their opponents, and why, to others, this issue seems to be unresolvable. An analysis of the nature of this standoff suggests a strategy for surmounting it.

Consider the way a typical anti-abortionist argues. She will argue or assert that life is present from the moment of conception or that fetuses look like babies or that fetuses possess a characteristic such as a genetic code that is both necessary and sufficient for being human. Anti-abortionists seem to believe that (1) the truth of all these claims is quite obvious, and (2) establishing any of these claims is sufficient to show that abortion is morally akin to murder.

A standard prochoice strategy exhibits similarities. The prochoicer will argue or assert that fetuses are not persons or that fetuses are not rational agents or that fetuses are not social beings. Prochoicers seem to believe that (1) the truth of any of these claims is quite obvious, and (2) establishing any of these claims is sufficient to show that an abortion is not a wrongful killing.

In fact, both the prochoice and the anti-abortion claims do seem to be true, although the "it looks like a baby" claim is more difficult to establish the earlier the pregnancy is. We seem to have a standoff. How can it be resolved?

As everyone who has taken a bit of logic knows, if any of these arguments concerning abortion is a good argument, that argument requires not only some claim characterizing fetuses, but also some general moral principle that ties a characteristic of fetuses to having or not having the right to life or to some other moral characteristic that will generate the obligation or the lack of obligation not to end the life of a fetus. Accordingly, the arguments of the anti-abortionist and the prochoicer need a bit of filling in to be regarded as adequate.

Note what each partisan will say. The anti-abortionist will claim that her position is supported by such generally accepted moral principles as "It is always prima facie seriously wrong to take a human life" or "It is always prima facie seriously wrong to end the life of a baby." Since these are generally accepted moral principles, her position is certainly not obviously wrong. The prochoicer will claim that her position is supported by such plausible moral principles as "Being a person is what gives an individual intrinsic moral worth" or "It is only seriously prima facie wrong to take the life of a member of the human community." Since these are generally accepted moral principles, the prochoice position is certainly not obviously wrong. Unfortunately, we have again arrived at a standoff.

Now, how might one deal with this standoff? The standard approach is to try to show how the moral principles of one's opponent lose their plausibility under analysis. It is easy to see how this is possible. On the one hand, the anti-abortionist will defend a moral principle concerning the wrongness of killing that tends to be broad in scope such that even fetuses at an early stage of pregnancy will fall under it. The problem with broad principles is that they often embrace too much. In this particular instance, the principle "It is always prima facie wrong to take a human life" seems to entail that it is wrong to end the existence of a living human cancer-cell culture, on the grounds that the culture is both living and human. Therefore, it seems that the anti-abortionist's favored principle is too broad.

On the other hand, the prochoicer wants to find a moral principle concerning the wrongness of killing that tends to be narrow in scope such that fetuses will *not* fall under it. The problem with narrow principles is that they often do not embrace enough. Hence, the needed principles such as "it is prima facie seriously wrong to kill only persons" or "It is prima facie wrong to kill only rational agents" do not explain why it is wrong to kill infants or young children or the severely retarded or even perhaps the severely mentally ill. Therefore, we seem again to have a standoff. The anti-abortionist charges, not unreasonably, that prochoice principles concerning killing are too narrow to be acceptable; the prochoicer charges, not unreasonably, that anti-abortionist principles concerning killing are too broad to be acceptable.

Attempts by both sides to patch up the difficulties in their positions run into further difficulties. The anti-abortionist will try to remove the problem in her position by reformulating her principle concerning killing in terms of human beings. Now we end up with "It is always prima facie seriously wrong to end the life of a human being." This principle has the advantage of avoiding the problem of the human cancer-cell culture counterexample. But this advantage is purchased at a high price. For although it is clear that a fetus is both human and alive, it is not at all clear that a fetus is a human *being*. There is at least something to be said for the view that something becomes a human being only after a process of development, and that therefore first trimester fetuses and perhaps all fetuses are not yet human beings. Hence, the anti-abortionist, by this move, has merely exchanged one problem for another.[2]

The prochoicer fares no better. She may attempt to find reasons why killing infants, young children, and the severely retarded is wrong that are independent of her major principle that is supposed to explain the wrongness of taking human life, but that will not also make abortion immoral. This is no easy task. Appeals to social utility will seem satisfactory only to those who resolve not to think of the enormous difficulties with a utilitarian account of the wrongness of killing and the significant social costs of preserving the lives of the unproductive.[3] A prochoice strategy that extends the definition of "person" to infants or even to young children seems just as arbitrary as an anti-abortion strategy that extends the definition of "human being" to fetuses. Again, we find symmetries in the two positions and we arrive at a standoff.

There are even further problems that reflect symmetries in the two positions. In addition to counterexample problems, or the arbitrary application problems that can be exchanged for them, the standard anti-abortionist principle "It is prima facie seriously wrong to kill a human being," or one of its variants, can be objected to on the grounds of ambiguity. If "human being" is taken to be a *biological* category, then the anti-abortionist is left with the problem of explaining why a merely biological category should make a moral difference. Why, it is asked, is it any more reasonable to base a moral conclusion on the number of chromosomes in one's cells than on the color of one's skin?[4] If "human being," on the other hand, is taken to be a *moral* category, then the claim that a fetus is a human being cannot be taken to be a premise in the anti-abortion argument, for it is precisely what needs to be established. Hence, either the anti-abortionist's main category is a morally irrelevant, merely biological category, or it is of no use to the anti-abortionist in establishing (non-circularly, of course) that abortion is wrong.

Although this problem with the anti-abortionist position is often noticed, it is less often noticed that the prochoice position suffers from an analogous problem. The principle "Only persons have the right to life" also suffers from an ambiguity. The term "person" is typically defined in terms of psychological characteristics, although there will certainly be disagreement concerning which characteristics are most important. Supposing that this matter can be settled, the prochoicer is left with the problem of explaining why *psychological* characteristics should make a *moral* difference. If the prochoicer should attempt to deal with this problem by claiming that an explanation is not necessary, that in fact we do treat such a cluster of psychological properties as having moral significance, the sharp-witted anti-abortionist should have a ready response. We do treat being both living and human as having moral significance. If it is legitimate for the prochoicer to demand that the anti-abortionist provide an explanation of the connection between the biological character of being a human being and the wrongness of being killed (even though people accept this connection), then it is legitimate for the anti-abortionist to demand that the prochoicer provide an explanation of the connection between psychological criteria for being a person and the wrongness of being killed (even though that connection is accepted).[5]

Feinberg has attempted to meet this objection (he calls psychological personhood "commonsense personhood"):

> The characteristics that confer commonsense personhood are not arbitrary bases for rights and duties, such as race, sex, or species membership; rather they are traits that make sense out of rights and duties and without which those moral attributes would have no point or function. It is because people are conscious; have a sense of their personal identities; have plans, goals, and projects; experience emotions; are liable to pains, anxieties, and frustrations; can reason and bargain, and so on—it is because of these attributes that people have values and interests, desires, and expectations of their own, including a stake in their own futures, and a personal well-being of a sort we cannot ascribe to unconscious or nonrational beings. Because of their developed capacities they can assume duties and responsibilities and can have and make claims on one another. Only because of their sense of self, their life plans, their value hierarchies, and their stakes in their own futures can they be ascribed fundamental rights. There is nothing arbitrary about these linkages ("Abortion," page 270).

The plausible aspects of this attempt should not be taken to obscure its implausible features. There is a great deal to be said for the view that being a psychological person under some description is a necessary condition for having duties. One cannot have a duty unless one is capable of behaving morally, and a being's capability of behaving morally will require having a certain psychology. It is far from obvious, however, that having rights entails consciousness or rationality, as Feinberg suggests. We speak of the rights of the severely retarded or the severely mentally ill, yet some of these persons are not rational. We speak of the rights of the temporarily unconscious. The New Jersey Supreme Court based their decision in the Quinlan case on Karen Ann Quinlan's right to privacy, and she was known to be permanently unconscious at that time. Hence, Feinberg's claim that having rights entails being conscious is, on its face, obviously false.

Of course, it might not make sense to attribute rights to a being that would never in its natural history have certain psychological traits. This modest connection between psychological personhood and moral personhood will create a place for Karen Ann Quinlan and the temporarily unconscious. But then it makes a place for fetuses also. Hence, it does not serve Feinberg's prochoice purposes. Accordingly, it seems that the prochoicer will have as much difficulty bridging the gap between psychological personhood and personhood in the moral sense as the anti-abortionist has bridging the gap between being a biological human being and being a human being in the moral sense.

Furthermore, the prochoicer cannot any more escape her problem by making person a purely moral category than the anti-abortionist could escape by the analogous move. For if person is a moral category, then the prochoicer is left without the resources for establishing (noncircularly, of course) the claim that a fetus is not a person, which is an essential premise in her argument. Again, we have both a symmetry and a standoff between prochoice and antiabortion views.

Passions in the abortion debate run high. There are both plausibilities and difficulties with the standard positions. Accordingly, it is hardly surprising that partisans of either side embrace with fervor the moral generalizations that support the conclusions they preanalytically favor and reject with disdain the moral generalizations of their opponents as being subject to inescapable difficulties. It is easy to believe that the counterexamples to one's own moral principles are merely temporary difficulties that will dissolve in the wake of further philosophical research and that the counterexamples to the principles of one's opponents are as straightforward as the contradiction between *A* and *O* propositions in traditional logic. This might suggest to an impartial observer (if there are any) that the abortion issue is unresolvable.

There is a way out of this apparent dialectical quandary. The moral generalizations of both sides are not quite correct. The generalizations hold for the most part, for the usual cases. This suggests that they are all *accidental* generalizations, that the moral claims made by those on both sides of the dispute do not touch on the *essence* of the matter.

This use of the distinction between essence and accident is not meant to invoke obscure metaphysical categories. Rather, it is intended to reflect the rather atheoretical nature of the abortion discussion. If the generalization a partisan in the abortion dispute adopts was derived from the reason why ending the life of a human being is wrong, then there could not be exceptions to that generalization unless some special case obtains in which there are even more powerful countervailing reasons. Such generalizations would not be merely accidental generalizations; they would point to, or be based on, the essence of the wrongness of killing—what it is that makes killing wrong. All this suggests that a necessary condition of resolving the abortion controversy is a more theoretical account of the wrongness of killing. After all, if we merely believe, but do not understand, why killing adult human beings such as ourselves is wrong, how could we conceivably show that abortion is either immoral or permissible?

II

To develop such an account, we can start from the following unproblematic assumption concerning our own case: It is wrong to kill us. Why is it wrong? Some answers can be easily eliminated. It might be said that what makes killing us wrong is that a killing brutalizes the one who kills. But the brutalization consists of being inured to the performance of an act that is hideously immoral; hence, the brutalization does not explain the immorality. It might be said that what makes killing us wrong is the great loss others would experience because of our absence. Although such hubris is understandable, such an explanation does not account for the wrongness of killing hermits, or those whose lives are relatively independent and whose friends find it easy to make new friends.

A more obvious answer is better. What primarily makes killing wrong is neither its effect on the murderer nor its effect on the victim's friends and relatives, but its effect on the victim. The loss of one's life is one of the greatest losses one can suffer. The loss of one's life deprives one of all the experiences, activities, projects, and enjoyments that would otherwise have constituted one's future. Therefore, killing someone is wrong, primarily because the killing inflicts (one of) the greatest possible losses on the victim. To describe this as the loss of life can be misleading, however. The change in my biological state does not by itself make killing me wrong. The effect of the loss of my biological life is the loss to me of all those activities, projects, experiences, and enjoyments that would otherwise have constituted my future personal life. These activities, projects, experiences, and enjoyments are either valuable for their own sakes or are means to something else that is valuable for its own sake. Some parts of my future are not valued by me now, but will come to be valued by me as I grow older and as my values and capacities change. When I am killed, I am deprived both of what I now value that would have been part of my future personal life, and what I would come to value. Therefore, when I die, I am deprived of all the value of my future. Inflicting this loss on me is ultimately what makes killing me wrong. This being the case, it would seem that what makes killing *any* adult human being prima facie seriously wrong is the loss of his or her future.[6]

How should this rudimentary theory of the wrongness of killing be evaluated? It cannot be faulted for deriving an "ought" from an "is," for it does not. The analysis assumes that killing me (or you, reader) is prima facie seriously wrong. The point of the analysis is to establish which natural property ultimately explains the wrongness of the killing, given that it is wrong. A natural property will ultimately explain the wrongness of killing only if (1) the explanation fits our intuitions about the matter and (2) there is no other natural property that provides a better explanation of the wrongness of killing. This analysis rests on the intuition that what makes killing a particular human or animal wrong is what it does to that particular human or animal. What makes killing wrong is some natural effect or other of the killing. Some would deny this. For instance, a divine-command theorist in ethics would deny it. Surely this denial is, however, one of those features of divine-command theory that renders it so implausible.

The claim that what makes killing wrong is the loss of the victim's future is directly supported by two considerations. In the first place, this theory explains why we regard killing as one of the worst of crimes. Killing is especially wrong because it deprives the victim of more than perhaps any other crime. In the second place, people with AIDS or cancer who know they are dying believe, of course, that dying is a very bad thing for them. They believe that the loss of a future to them that they would otherwise have experienced is what makes their premature death a very bad thing for them. A better theory of the wrongness of killing would require a different natural property associated with killing that better fits with the attitudes of the dying. What could it be?

The view that what makes killing wrong is the loss to the victim of the value of the victim's future gains additional support when some of its implications are examined. In the first place, it is incompatible with the view that it is wrong to kill only beings who are biologically human. It is possible that there exists a different species from another planet whose members have a future like ours. Since having a future like that is what makes killing someone wrong, this theory entails that it would be wrong to kill members of such a species. Hence, this theory is opposed to the claim that only life that is biologically human has great moral worth, a claim that many anti-abortionists have seemed to adopt. This opposition, which this theory has in common with personhood theories, seems to be a merit of the theory.

In the second place, the claim that the loss of one's future is the wrong-making feature of one's being killed entails the possibility that the futures of some actual nonhuman mammals on our own planet are sufficiently like ours that it is seriously wrong to kill them also. Whether some animals do have the same right to life as human beings depends on adding to the account of the wrongness of killing some additional account of just what it is about my future or the futures of other adult human beings that makes it wrong to kill us. No such additional account will be offered in this essay. Undoubtedly, the provision of such an account would be a very difficult matter. Undoubtedly, any such account would be quite controversial. Hence, it surely should not reflect badly on this sketch of an elementary theory of the wrongness of killing that it is indeterminate with respect to some very difficult issues regarding animal rights.

In the third place, the claim that the loss of one's future is the wrong-making feature of one's being killed does not entail, as sanctity of human life theories do, that active euthanasia is wrong. Persons who are severely and incurably ill, who face a future of pain and despair, and who wish to die will not have suffered a loss if they are killed. It is, strictly speaking, the value of a human's future that makes killing wrong in this theory. This being so, killing does not necessarily wrong some persons who are sick and dying. Of course, there may be other reasons for a prohibition of active euthanasia, but that is another matter. Sanctity-of-human-life theories seem to hold that active euthanasia is seriously wrong even in an individual case where there seems to be good reason for it independently of public policy considerations. This consequence is most implausible, and it is a plus for the claim that the loss of a future of value is what makes killing wrong that it does not share this consequence.

In the fourth place, the account of the wrongness of killing defended in this essay does straightforwardly entail that it is prima facie seriously wrong to kill children and infants, for we do presume that they have futures of value. Since we do believe that it is wrong to kill defenseless little babies, it is important that a theory of the wrongness of killing easily account for this. Personhood theories of the wrongness of killing, on the other hand, cannot straightforwardly account for the wrongness of killing infants and young children.[7] Hence, such theories must add special ad hoc accounts of the wrongness of killing the young. The plausibility of such ad hoc theories seems to be a function of how desperately one wants such theories to work. The claim that the primary wrong-making feature of a killing is the loss to the victim of the value of its future accounts for the wrongness of killing young children and infants directly; it makes the wrongness of such acts as obvious as we actually think it is. This is a further merit of this theory. Accordingly, it seems that this value of a future-like-ours theory of the wrongness of killing shares strengths of both sanctity-of-life and personhood accounts while avoiding weaknesses of both. In addition, it meshes with a central intuition concerning what makes killing wrong.

The claim that the primary wrong-making feature of a killing is the loss to the victim of the value of its future has obvious consequences for the ethics of abortion. The future of a standard fetus includes a set of experiences, projects, activities, and such that are identical with the futures of adult human beings and are identical with the futures of young children. Since the reason that is sufficient to explain why it is wrong to kill human beings after the time of birth is a reason that also applies to fetuses, it follows that abortion is prima facie seriously morally wrong.

This argument does not rely on the invalid inference that, since it is wrong to kill persons, it is wrong to kill potential persons also. The category that is morally central to this analysis is the category of having a valuable future like ours; it is not the category of personhood. The argument to the conclusion that abortion is prima facie seriously morally wrong proceeded independently of the notion of person or potential person or any equivalent. Someone may wish to start with this analysis in terms of the value of a human future, conclude that abortion is, except perhaps in rare circumstances, seriously morally wrong, infer that fetuses have the right to life, and then call fetuses "persons" as a result of their having the right to life. Clearly, in this case, the category of person is being used to state the *conclusion* of the analysis rather than to generate the *argument* of the analysis.

The structure of this anti-abortion argument can be both illuminated and defended by comparing it to what appears to be the best argument for the wrongness of the wanton infliction of pain on animals. This latter argument is based on the assumption that it is prima facie wrong to inflict pain on me (or you, reader). What is the natural property associated with the infliction of pain that makes such infliction wrong? The obvious answer seems to be that the infliction of pain causes suffering and that suffering is a misfortune. The suffering caused by the infliction of pain is what makes the wanton infliction of pain on me wrong. The wanton infliction of pain on other adult humans causes suffering. The wanton infliction of pain on animals causes suffering. Since causing suffering is what makes the wanton infliction of pain wrong and since the wanton infliction of pain on animals causes suffering, it follows that the wanton infliction of pain on animals is wrong.

This argument for the wrongness of the wanton infliction of pain on animals shares a number of structural features with the argument for the serious prima facie wrongness of abortion. Both arguments start with an obvious assumption concerning what it is wrong to do to me (or you, reader). Both then look for the characteristic or the consequence of the wrong action that makes the action wrong. Both recognize that the wrong-making feature of these immoral actions is a property of actions sometimes directed at individuals other than postnatal human beings. If the structure of the argument for the wrongness of the wanton infliction of pain on animals is sound, then the structure of the argument for the prima facie serious wrongness of abortion is also sound, for the structure of the two arguments is the same. The structure common to both is the key to the explanation of how the wrongness of abortion can be demonstrated without recourse to the category of person. In neither argument is that category crucial.

This defense of an argument for the wrongness of abortion in terms of a structurally similar argument for the wrongness of the wanton infliction of pain on animals succeeds only if the account regarding animals is the correct account. Is it? In the first place, it seems plausible. In the second place, its major competition is Kant's account. Kant believed that we do not have direct duties to animals at all because they are not persons. Hence, Kant had to explain and justify the wrongness of inflicting pain on animals on the grounds that "he who is hard in his dealings with animals becomes hard also in his dealing with men."[8] The problem with Kant's account is that there seems to be no reason for accepting this latter claim unless Kant's account is rejected. If the alternative to Kant's account is accepted, then it is easy to understand why someone who is indifferent to inflicting pain on animals is also indifferent to inflicting pain on humans, for one is indifferent to what makes inflicting pain wrong in both cases. But, if Kant's account is accepted, there is no intelligible reason why one who is hard in his dealings with animals (or crabgrass or stones) should also be hard in his dealings with men. After all, men are persons; animals are no more persons than are crabgrass or stones. Persons are Kant's crucial moral category. Why, in short, should a Kantian accept the basic claim in Kant's argument?

Hence, Kant's argument for the wrongness of inflicting pain on animals rests on a claim that, in a world of Kantian moral agents, is demonstrably false. Therefore, the alternative analysis, being more plausible anyway, should be accepted. Since this alternative analysis has the same structure as the anti-abortion argument being defended here, we have further support for the argument for the immorality of abortion being defended in this essay.

Of course, this value of a future-like-ours argument, if sound, shows only that abortion is prima facie wrong, not that it is wrong in any and all circumstances. Since the loss of the future to a standard fetus, if killed, is, however, at least as great a loss as the loss of the future to a standard adult human being who is killed, abortion, like ordinary killing, could be justified only by the most compelling reasons. The loss of one's life is almost the greatest misfortune that can happen to one. Presumably abortion could be justified in some circumstances, only if the loss consequent on failing to abort would be at least as great. Accordingly, morally permissible abortions will be rare indeed unless, perhaps, they occur so early in pregnancy that a fetus is not yet definitely an individual. Hence, this argument should be taken as showing that abortion is presumptively very seriously wrong, where the presumption is very strong—as strong as the presumption that killing another adult human being is wrong.

III

How complete an account of the wrongness of killing does the value of a future-like-ours account have to be in order that the wrongness of abortion is a consequence? This account does not have to be an account of the necessary conditions for the wrongness of killing. Some persons in nursing homes may lack valuable human futures, yet it may be wrong to kill them for other reasons. Furthermore, this account does not obviously have to be the sole reason killing is wrong where the victim did have a valuable future. This analysis claims only that, for any killing where the victim did have a valuable future like ours, having that future by itself is sufficient to create the strong presumption that the killing is seriously wrong.

One way to overturn the value of a future-like-ours argument would be to find some account of the wrongness of killing that is at least as intelligible and that has different implications for the ethics of abortion. Two rival accounts possess at least some degree of plausibility. One account is based on the obvious fact that people value the experience of living and wish for that valuable experience to continue. Therefore, it might be said, what makes killing wrong is the discontinuation of that experience for the victim. Let us call this the *discontinuation account*.[9] Another account is based on the obvious fact that people strongly desire to continue to live. This suggests that what makes killing us so wrong is that it interferes with the fulfillment of a strong and fundamental desire, the fulfillment of which is necessary for the fulfillment of any other desires we might have. Let us call this the *desire account*.[10]

Consider first the desire account as a rival account of the ethics of killing that would provide the basis for rejecting the anti-abortion position. Such an account will have to be stronger than the value of a future-like-ours account of the wrongness of abortion if it is to do the job expected of it. To entail the wrongness of abortion, the value of a future-like-ours account has only to provide a sufficient, but not a necessary, condition for the wrongness of killing. The desire account, on the other hand, must provide us also with a necessary condition for the wrongness of killing to generate a prochoice conclusion on abortion. The reason for this is that presumably the argument from the desire account moves from the claim that what makes killing wrong is interference with a very strong desire to the claim that abortion is not wrong because the fetus lacks a strong desire to live. Obviously, this inference fails if someone's having the desire to live is not a necessary condition of its being wrong to kill that individual.

One problem with the desire account is that we do regard it as seriously wrong to kill persons who have little desire to live or who have no desire to live or, indeed, have a desire not to live. We believe it is seriously wrong to kill the unconscious, the sleeping, those who are tired of life, and those who are suicidal. The value-of-a-human-future account renders standard morality intelligible in these cases; these cases appear to be incompatible with the desire account.

The desire account is subject to a deeper difficulty. We desire life, because we value the goods of this life. The goodness of life is not secondary to our desire for it. If this were not so, the pain of one's own premature death could be done away with merely by an appropriate alteration in the configuration of one's desires. This is absurd. Hence, it would seem that it is the loss of the goods of one's future, not the interference with the fulfillment of a strong desire to live, that accounts ultimately for the wrongness of killing.

It is worth noting that, if the desire account is modified so that it does not provide a necessary, but only a sufficient, condition for the wrongness of killing, the desire account is compatible with the value of a future-like-ours account. The combined accounts will yield an anti-abortion ethic. This suggests that one can retain what is intuitively plausible about the desire account without a challenge to the basic argument of this paper.

It is also worth noting that, if future desires have moral force in a modified desire account of the wrongness of killing, one can find support for an anti-abortion ethic even in the absence of a value of a future-like-ours account. If one decides that a morally relevant property, the possession of which is sufficient to make it wrong to kill some individual, is the desire at some future time to live—one might decide to justify one's refusal to kill suicidal teenagers on these grounds, for example—then, since typical fetuses will have the desire in the future to live, it is wrong to kill typical fetuses. Accordingly, it does not seem that a desire account of the wrongness of killing can provide a justification of a prochoice ethic of abortion that is nearly as adequate as the value of a human future justification of an anti-abortion ethic.

The discontinuation account looks more promising as an account of the wrongness of killing. It seems just as intelligible as the value of a future-like-ours account, but it does not justify an anti-abortion position. Obviously, if it is the continuation of one's activities, experiences, and projects, the loss of which makes killing wrong, then it is not wrong to kill fetuses for that reason, for fetuses do not have experiences, activities, and projects to be continued or discontinued. Accordingly, the discontinuation account does not have the anti-abortion consequences that the value of a future-like-ours account has. Yet, it seems as intelligible as the value of a future-like-ours account, for when we think of what would be wrong with our being killed, it does seem as if it is the discontinuation of what makes our lives worthwhile that makes killing us wrong.

Is the discontinuation account just as good an account as the value of a future-like-ours account? The discontinuation account will not be adequate at all if it does not refer to the *value* of the experience that may be discontinued. One does not want the discontinuation account to make it wrong to kill a patient who begs for death and who is in severe pain that cannot be relieved short of killing. (I leave open the question of whether it is wrong for other reasons.) Accordingly, the discontinuation account must be more than a bare discontinuation account. It must make some reference to the positive value of the patient's experiences. But, by the same token, the value of a future-like-ours account cannot be a bare future account either. Just having a future surely does not itself rule out killing this patient. This account must make some reference to the value of the patient's future experiences and projects also. Hence, both accounts involve the value of experiences, projects, and activities. So far we still have symmetry between the accounts.

The symmetry fades, however, when we focus on the time period of the value of the experiences, and so forth that has moral consequences. Although both accounts leave open the possibility that the patient in our example may be killed, this possibility is left open only by virtue of the utterly bleak future for the patient. It makes no difference whether the patient's immediate past contains intolerable pain, or consists of being in a coma (which we can imagine is a situation of indifference), or consists of a life of value. If the patient's future is a future of value, we want our account to make it wrong to kill the patient. If the patient's future is intolerable, whatever his or her immediate past, we want our account to allow killing the patient. Obviously, then, it is the value of that patient's future that is doing the work in rendering the morality of killing the patient intelligible.

This being the case, it seems clear that whether one has immediate past experiences or not does no work in the explanation of what makes killing wrong. The addition the discontinuation account makes to the value of a human future account is otiose. Its addition to the value-of-a-future account plays no role at all in rendering intelligible the wrongness of killing. Therefore, it can be discarded with the discontinuation account of which it is a part.

IV

The analysis of the previous section suggests that alternative general accounts of the wrongness of killing are either inadequate or unsuccessful in getting around the anti-abortion consequences of the value of a future-like-ours argument. A different strategy for avoiding these anti-abortion consequences involves limiting the scope of the value of a future argument. More precisely, the strategy involves arguing that fetuses lack a property that is essential for the value-of-a-future argument (or for any anti-abortion argument) to apply to them.

One move of this sort is based on the claim that a necessary condition of one's future being valuable is that one values it. Value implies a valuer. Given this, one might argue that, since fetuses cannot value their futures, their futures are not valuable to them. Hence, it does not seriously wrong them deliberately to end their lives.

This move fails, however, because of some ambiguities. Let us assume that something cannot be of value unless it is valued by someone. This does not entail that my life is of no value unless it is valued by me. I may think, in a period of despair, that my future is of no worth whatsoever, but I may be wrong because others rightly see value—even great value—in it. Furthermore, my future can be valuable to me even if I do not value it. This is the case when a young person attempts suicide but is rescued and goes on to significant human achievements. Such young people's futures are ultimately valuable to them, even though such futures do not seem to be valuable to them at the moment of attempted suicide. A fetus's future can be valuable to it in the same way. Accordingly, this attempt to limit the anti–abortion argument fails.

Another similar attempts to reject the anti–abortion position is based on Tooley's claim that an entity cannot possess the right to life unless it has the capacity to desire its continued existence. It follows that, since fetuses lack the conceptual capacity to desire to continue to live, they lack the right to life. Accordingly, Tooley concludes that abortion cannot be seriously prima facie wrong ("Abortion and Infanticide," pages 46–47).

What could be the evidence for Tooley's basic claim? Tooley once argued that individuals have a prima facie right to what they desire and that the lack of the capacity to desire something undercuts the basis of one's right to it ("Abortion and Infanticide," pages 44–45). This argument plainly will not succeed in the context of the analysis of this essay, however, since the point here is to establish the fetus's right to life on other grounds. Tooley's argument assumes that the right to life cannot be established in general on some basis other than the desire for life. This position was considered and rejected in the preceding section of this paper.

One might attempt to defend Tooley's basic claim on the grounds that, because a fetus cannot apprehend continued life as a benefit, its continued life cannot be a benefit or cannot be something it has a right to or cannot be something that is in its interest. This might be defended in terms of the general proposition that, if an individual is literally incapable of caring about or taking an interest in some X, then one does not have a right to X or X is not a benefit or X is not something that is in one's interest.[11]

Each member of this family of claims seems to be open to objections. As John C. Stevens[12] has pointed out, one may have a right to be treated with a certain medical procedure (because of a health insurance policy one has purchased), even though one cannot conceive of the nature of the procedure. And, as Tooley himself has pointed out, persons who have been indoctrinated, or drugged, or rendered temporarily unconscious may be literally incapable of caring about or taking an interest in something that is in their interest or to which they have a right, or that benefits them. Hence, the Tooley claim that would restrict the scope of the value of a future–like–ours argument is undermined by counterexamples.[13]

Finally, Paul Bassen[14] has argued that, even though the prospects of an embryo might seem to be a basis for the wrongness of abortion, an embryo cannot be a victim and therefore cannot be wronged. An embryo cannot be a victim, he says, because it lacks sentience. His central argument for this seems to be that, even though plants and the permanently unconscious are alive, they clearly cannot be victims. What is the explanation of this? Bassen claims that their lives consist of mere metabolism and mere metabolism is not enough to ground victimizability. Mentation is required.

The problem with this attempt to establish the absence of victimizability is that both plants and the permanently unconscious clearly lack what Bassen calls "prospects" or what I have called "a future life like ours." Hence, it is surely open to argument whether the real reason we believe plants and the permanently unconscious cannot be victims is that killing them cannot deprive them of a future life like ours; the real reason is not their absence of present mentation.

Bassen recognizes that his view is subject to this difficulty, and he recognizes that the case of children seems to support this difficulty, for "much of what we do for children is based on prospects." He argues, however, that, in the case of children and in other such cases, "potentiality comes into play only where victimizability has been secured on other grounds" ("Present Sakes and Future Prospects," page 333).

Bassen's defense of his view is patently question-begging, since what is adequate to secure victimizability is exactly what is at issue. His examples do not support his own view against the thesis of this essay. Of course, embryos can be victims: When their lives are deliberately terminated, they are deprived of their futures of value, their prospects. This makes them victims, for it directly wrongs them.

The seeming plausibility of Bassen's view stems from the fact that paradigmatic cases of imagining someone as a victim involve empathy, and empathy requires mentation of the victim. The victims of flood, famine, rape, or child abuse are all persons with whom we can empathize. That empathy seems to be part of seeing them as victims.[15]

In spite of the strength of these examples, the attractive intuition that a situation in which there is victimization requires the possibility of empathy is subject to counterexamples. Consider a case that Bassen himself offers: "Posthumous obliteration of an author's work constitutes a misfortune for him only if he had wished his work to endure" ("Present Sakes and Future Prospects," page 318). The conditions Bassen wishes to impose upon the possibility of being victimized here seem far too strong. Perhaps this author, due to his unrealistic standards of excellence and his low self-esteem, regarded his work as unworthy of survival, even though it possessed genuine literary merit. Destruction of such work would surely victimize its author. In such a case, empathy with the victim concerning the loss is clearly impossible.

Of course, Bassen does not make the possibility of empathy a necessary condition of victimizability; he requires only mentation. Hence, on Bassen's actual view, this author, as I have described him, can be a victim. The problem is that the basic intuition that renders Bassen's view plausible is missing in the author's case. In order to attempt to avoid counterexamples, Bassen has made his thesis too weak to be supported by the intuitions that suggested it.

Even so, the mentation requirement on victimizability is still subject to counterexamples. Suppose a severe accident renders me totally unconscious for a month, after which I recover. Surely killing me while I am unconscious victimizes me, even though I am incapable of mentation during that time. It follows that Bassen's thesis fails. Apparently, attempts to restrict the value of a future-like-ours argument so that fetuses do not fall within its scope do not succeed.

V

In this essay, I have argued that the correct ethic of the wrongness of killing can be extended to fetal life and used to show that there is a strong presumption that any abortion is morally impermissible. If the ethic of killing adopted here entails, however, that contraception is also seriously immoral, then there would appear to be a difficulty with the analysis of this essay.

But this analysis does not entail that contraception is wrong. Of course, contraception prevents the actualization of a possible future of value. Hence, it follows from the claim that futures of value should be maximized that contraception is prima facie immoral. This obligation to maximize does not exist, however; furthermore, nothing in the ethics of killing in this paper entails that it does. The ethics of killing in this essay would entail that contraception is wrong only if something were denied a human future of value by contraception. Nothing at all is denied such a future by contraception, however.

Candidates for a subject of harm by contraception fall into four categories: (1) some sperm or other, (2) some ovum or other, (3) a sperm and an ovum separately, and (4) a sperm and an ovum together. Assigning the harm to some sperm is utterly arbitrary, for no reason can be given for making a sperm the subject of harm rather than an ovum. Assigning the harm to some ovum is utterly arbitrary, for no reason can be given for making an ovum the subject of harm rather than a sperm. One might attempt to avoid these problems by insisting that contraception deprives both the sperm and the ovum separately of a valuable future like ours. On this alternative, too many futures are lost. Contraception was supposed to be wrong because it deprived us of one future of value, not two. One might attempt to avoid this problem by holding that contraception deprives the combination of sperm and ovum of a valuable future like ours. But here the definite article misleads. At the time of contraception, there are hundreds of millions of sperm, one (released) ovum and millions of possible combinations of all these. There is no actual combination at all. Is the subject of the loss to be a merely possible combination? Which one? This alternative does not yield an actual subject of harm either. Accordingly, the immorality of contraception is not entailed by the loss of a future-like-ours argument simply because there is no nonarbitrarily identifiable subject of the loss in the case of contraception.

VI

The purpose of this essay has been to set out an argument for the serious presumptive wrongness of abortion subject to the assumption that the moral permissibility of abortion stands or falls on the moral status of the fetus. Since a fetus possesses a property, the possession of which in adult human beings is sufficient to make killing an adult human being wrong, abortion is wrong. This way of dealing with the problem of abortion seems superior to other approaches to the ethics of abortion because it rests on an ethics of killing which is close to self-evident, because the crucial morally relevant property clearly applies to fetuses, and because the argument avoids the usual equivocations on "human life," "human being," or "person." The argument rests neither on religious claims nor on Papal dogma. It is not subject to the objection of "speciesism." Its soundness is compatible with the moral permissibility of euthanasia and contraception. It deals with our intuitions concerning young children.

Finally, this analysis can be viewed as resolving a standard problem—indeed, *the* standard problem—concerning the ethics of abortion. Clearly, it is wrong to kill adult human beings. Clearly, it is not wrong to end the life of some arbitrarily chosen single human cell. Fetuses seem to be like arbitrarily chosen human cells in some respects and like adult humans in other respects. The problem of the ethics of abortion is the problem of determining the fetal property that settles this moral controversy. The thesis of this essay is that the problem of the ethics of abortion, so understood, is solvable.

STUDY QUESTIONS

1. Why does Marquis think that the debate between the anti-abortionists and the prochoicers over abortion has come to a standoff? Do you agree?

2. Explain Marquis's notion of a future good. What sort of entities can have a future good? Does he exclude trees and cars from that classification? Does he exclude animals? Discuss his conditions.

3. Is Marquis against all abortions? If not, which kinds would he permit? Is he correct?

4. Why does Marquis believe that his thesis avoids condemning the use of contraceptive devices as immoral?

NOTES

1. Feinberg, "Abortion," in *Matters of Life and Death: New Introductory Essays in Moral Philosophy,* Tom Regan, ed. New York: Random House, 1986, 256–293; Tooley "Abortion and Infanticide," *Philosophy and Public Affairs,* II, 1 (1972), 37–65; Tooley, *Abortion and Infanticide,* New York: Oxford, 1984; Warren, "On the Moral and Legal Status of Abortion," *Monist,* 1.7, 1 (1973), 43–61; Engelhardt, "The Ontology of Abortion," *Ethics,* 1.34, 3 (1974), 217–234; Sumner, *Abortion and Moral Theory.* Princeton, N.J.: Princeton University Press, 1981; Noonan, "An Almost Absolute Value in History," in *The Morality of Abortion: Legal and Historical Perspectives,* Noonan, ed. Cambridge, Mass.: Harvard University Press, 1970; and Devine, *The Ethics of Homicide.* Ithaca, N.Y.: Cornell University Press, 1978.

2. For interesting discussions of this issue, see Warren Quinn, "Abortion: Identity and Loss," *Philosophy and Public Affairs,* 13, 1 (1984), 24–54; Lawrence C. Becker, "Human Being: The Boundaries of the Concept," *Philosophy and Public Affairs,* 4, 4 (1975), 334–359.

3. For example, see my "Ethics and The Elderly: Some Problems," in Stuart Spicker, Kathleen Woodward, and David Van Tassel, eds., *Aging and the Elderly: Humanistic Perspectives in Gerontology.* Atlantic Highlands, N.J.: Humanities, 1978, 341–355.

4. See Warren, "Moral and Legal Status," and Tooley, "Abortion and Infanticide."

5. This seems to be the fatal flaw in Warren's treatment of this issue.

6. I have been most influenced on this matter by Jonathan Glover, *Causing Death and Saving Lives.* New York: Penguin, 1977, Chapter 3; and Robert Young, "What Is So Wrong with Killing People?" *Philosophy* 1.4, 210 (1979), 515–528.

7. Feinberg, Tooley, Warren, and Engelhardt have all dealt with this problem.

8. "Duties to Animals and Spirits," in *Lectures on Ethics,* Louis Infeld, trans. New York: Harper, 1963, 239.

9. I am indebted to Jack Bricke for raising this objection.

10. Presumably a preference utilitarian would press such an objection. Tooley once suggested that his account has such a theoretical underpinning. See his "Abortion and Infanticide," 44–45.

11. Donald VanDeVeer seems to think this is self-evident. See his "Whither Baby Doe?" in *Matters of Life and Death: New Introductory Essays in Moral Philosophy,* Tom Regan, ed. New York: Random House, 1986, 233.

12. "Must the Bearer of a Right Have the Concepts of That to Which He Has a Right?" *Ethics,* 95, 1 (1984), 68–74.

13. See Tooley again in "Abortion and Infanticide," 47–49.

14. "Present Sakes and Future Prospects: The Status of Early Abortion," *Philosophy and Public Affairs,* 11, 4 (1982), 322–326.

15. Note carefully the reasons he gives on the bottom of page 316.

21

Does a Fetus Already
Have a Future-Like-Ours?

PETER K. McINERNEY

Peter K. McInerney is Professor of Philosophy at Oberlin College. In this essay he argues that although Don Marquis has shown that certain prochoice arguments fail, he has not established his claim that a fetus has a future-like-ours. Whereas our future is a personal one, the fetus's future is only potentially so.

DOES A FETUS ALREADY HAVE
A FUTURE-LIKE-OURS?

Some of the most interesting and underexplored issues in philosophy are those of how human beings are in time. A person's relationship to her future is very complex, particularly if time passes, as we commonsensically believe that it does. In "Why Abortion Is Immoral," Don Marquis[1] argues that what makes killing a person wrong is that it deprives the person of her future. He concludes that abortion is wrong because it deprives the fetus of a "future-like-ours." The line of argument is clear.

> The future of a standard fetus includes a set of experiences, projects, activities, and such that are identical with the futures of adult human beings and are identical with the futures of young children. Since the reason that

Reprinted from the *Journal of Philosophy* 87 (May 1990) by permission. Numbers in brackets refer to the page numbers in this book.

is sufficient to explain why it is wrong to kill human beings after the time of birth is a reason that also applies to fetuses, it follows that abortion is prima facie seriously morally wrong [347].

The unexamined premise in the argument is that a fetus *already* has a future-like-ours of which it can be deprived.[2] For the argument to be convincing, it is necessary that a fetus *at its time* "possess" or be related to a future-like-ours in a way that allows the transfer from the wrongness of killing us persons to the wrongness of killing fetuses.

Fetuses are very different from normal adult humans. The connections between a fetus at an earlier time and a person (or person stage) at a significantly later time are very different from the connections between the person stages at different times that compose one person. Philosophical investigations of personal identity through time have revealed the complexity of the biological and psychological connections between the earlier and later stages of one person. These significant differences invalidate the claim that a fetus has a personal future in the same way that a normal adult human has a personal future.

The differences between a person's relationship to her future and a fetus's relationship to its future are striking even when the passage of time is ignored. In B-series time (a time that is composed entirely of earlier and later temporal locations with their occupants), an earlier person stage has many relations with later person stages that make these later person stages be "her future." The most widely considered relations in contemporary discussions of personal identity are those of memory, continuity of character, and intention-to-action.[3] Memory relations are from later person stages to earlier person stages. The later person stages are able to remember the experiences of the earlier person stages or there is an overlapping chain of such memory connections (memory continuity). The relation of continuity of character is that in which later person stages either have a character similar to the earlier person stages or are different in ways that are explicable by the operation of normal causes.[4] The relation of intention-to-action is that between an earlier intention and a later action that carries out that intention. Normal adult humans have all sorts of plans and projects for their short- and long-term futures that take time to implement.

There are other relations that connect earlier and later person stages. Some of the "mental processing" that ordinarily goes on in normal humans, such as forming generalizations from repeated observations or "digesting" an emotionally charged experience, takes a significant amount of time and so can be considered to include relations between person stages. In addition, there are all the neurophysiological relations that underlie the ordinary continuation of mental life in persons. That a person has pretty much the same beliefs, wants, skills, and habits that she had 30 minutes (or 30 days) earlier depends on a similarity of neurophysiological conditions between the earlier and later person stages.

Most of these relations to later person stages exist even when the earlier person is asleep or temporarily unconscious. Even intentions to perform later actions might be considered to continue through periods of unconsciousness.

Since a temporarily unconscious person is still strongly related to her future, to kill her while she is unconscious is to deprive her of her future.

Young infants do not have all of the psychological complexity that adult persons have. Nevertheless, young infants are commonsensically understood to have perceptions, beliefs, desires, and emotions (whether or not the experimental data confirms this) and to learn from experience. For this reason, the neurophysiological states and processes of young infants can be understood to underlie something like the ordinary continuation of mental life in persons. A good case can be made that young infants are related in some (though not all) ways to a personal future.

The situation of a fetus at an early stage of development is very different.[5] A fetus at an early stage of development has neither a mental life of feelings, beliefs, and desires nor a developed brain and nervous system. There are none of the main relations with a personal future that exist in persons. Although there is some biological continuity between them so that there is a sense in which the later person stages "are the future" of the fetus, the fetus is so little connected to the later personal life that it cannot be deprived of that personal life. At its time the fetus does not already "possess" that future personal life in the way that a normal adult human already "possesses" his future personal life.

Our commonsense views about time and entities in time involve a past that is fixed and determinate, a future that includes alternative possibilities whose actualization may be affected by action, and a process of what is future becoming present and past. In a time of this sort, how an entity "has a future" is more complex because when some temporal part (stage) of the entity is present, there is not a fixed and fully determinate future to which that entity can now be related. With respect to persons, a present person stage is not now related to a specific determinate later person stage that will become present. A person's future includes a branching range of possibilities (including his death) from which only one life course can become present. The branching of possibilities is such that most outcomes can become present only if certain earlier possibilities have become present. The actualization of one possibility makes available those later possibilities that presuppose it. This is particularly pronounced for the acquisition of skills, abilities, and capacities, which open up ranges of possibilities that would otherwise not be available.

Many factors external to the person affect which of the person's possibilities become present. A normal adult human has only limited control over which of his possibilities become present. This control that a person exercises and attempts to exercise over his future is the most important connection that now exists with a specifically personal future. This control also depends on the person's wants, skills, abilities, and capacities. The person wants various things for his future (including wanting himself to act) and exercises his powers to affect what happens.

A fetus is separated from a personal future by many "layers" of possibility. The possibilities that are available to a person or even to a young infant are not now available to the fetus. Only if the fetus develops in the right ways (favorable possibilities become present) will it acquire the capacities that make available the infant's possibilities. A great deal of favorable development would be necessary before the fetus could control its future in the way that persons do. The fetus does not now have a personal future.

Marquis has succeeded in formulating an important feature of people's opposition to abortion: the notion that abortion "cuts off" the fetus's future. A close examination of what it is "to have a future" reveals that at its time a fetus does not have a personal future of which it can be deprived. A living human cell that might be stimulated to develop into a clone of a person does not now have a personal future. A fetus similarly has only the potentiality to develop a personal future. For this reason, killing a fetus is morally very different from killing a normal adult human.

STUDY QUESTIONS

1. What is Peter McInerney's main criticism of Marquis's argument that the fetus has a future-like-ours? How does McInerney argue for his position? How might Marquis respond to McInerney?

2. McInerney attempts to prevent his argument from allowing infanticide. How successful is this attempt?

NOTES

1. *Journal of Philosophy,* 86, 4 (April 1989), 183–202 [Reprinted in this book, pages 339–356].

2. "Since a fetus possesses a property, the possession of which in adult human beings is sufficient to make killing an adult human being wrong, abortion is wrong" [354].

3. See Derek Parfit, *Reasons and Persons.* New York: Oxford, 1984, 205–207.

4. See *Reasons and Persons,* page 207, for a brief discussion of "normal causes."

5. As the fetus develops, it becomes more similar to a young infant, and so progressively acquires more of a relationship to a personal future.

22

Abortion and the
Neo-Natal Right to Life

A Critique of Marquis's
Futurist Argument

GERALD H. PASKE

Gerald H. Paske is Professor of Philosophy at Wichita State University. The abstract he wrote for his essay follows.

ABSTRACT

In his "Why Abortion Is Immoral," Don Marquis has presented a serious challenge to the prochoice position. Marquis's argument is based on the following three claims: (1) Personhood is an inadequate foundation for the right to life. (2) The right to life is based on having a future-like-ours. (3) Normal fetuses have a future-like-ours and, hence, normal fetuses have a right to life.

I argue that (a) Marquis's own position presupposes the concept of personhood, (b) that having a future-like-ours is neither a sufficient nor a necessary condition for having a right to life, and (c) that given the concept of personhood, neonates, infants, and children have a right to life. This later point requires a discussion of a fetal right to care.

I n an influential but misleadingly entitled paper, Don Marquis has presented a serious challenge to the prochoice position.[1] Although the paper is entitled "Why Abortion Is Immoral," Marquis's argument actually allows for abortions

This essay was commissioned for this volume and appeared in print for the first time in the first edition of this book. Page numbers in brackets refer to pages in this book.

of severely mentally defective fetuses. Marquis, thus, is on the conservative end of the prochoice spectrum.

Marquis's challenge remains serious, however, because his argument, if sound, would show that from conception onward all abortions of normal fetuses are seriously immoral. Marquis's argument is based on the following three claims: (1) Personhood is an inadequate foundation for the right to life. (2) The right to life is based on having a future-like-ours. (3) Normal fetuses have a future-like-ours and, hence, normal fetuses have a right to life. Marquis also claims that the personhood concept provides an inadequate basis for the right to life of infants and children, and he takes this to constitute an additional serious challenge to the standard prochoice position.[2]

I shall argue (a) that Marquis's own position presupposes the concept of personhood, (b) that having a future-like-ours is neither a sufficient nor a necessary condition for having a right to life, and (c) that given the concept of personhood, neonates, infants, and children have a right to life.[3]

Marquis summarizes his argument as follows:

> In order to develop (my) account, we can start from the following unproblematic assumption concerning our own case: It is wrong to kill *us*....The loss of one's life is one of the greatest losses one can suffer. The loss of one's life deprives one of all the experiences, activities, projects, and enjoyments that would otherwise have constituted one's future....To describe this as the loss of life can be misleading, however. The change in my biological state does not by itself make killing me wrong. The effect of the loss of my biological life is the loss to me of all those activities, projects, experiences, and enjoyments that would otherwise have constituted my future personal life....Therefore, when I die I am deprived of all of the value of my future. Inflicting this loss on me is ultimately what makes killing me wrong. This being the case, it would seem that what makes killing *any* adult human being prima facie seriously wrong is the loss of his or her future [344–345].

Marquis applies this "deprivation argument" to the abortion issue as follows:

> The claim that the primary wrong-making feature of a killing is the loss to the victim of the value of its future has obvious consequences for the ethics of abortion. The future of a standard fetus includes a set of experiences, projects, activities, and such that are identical with the futures of adult human beings and are identical with the futures of young children. Since the reason that is sufficient to explain why it is wrong to kill human beings after the time of birth is a reason that also applies to fetuses, it follows that abortion is prima facie seriously morally wrong [347].

While granting the appeal of Marquis's argument, I shall nevertheless attack it at its foundation: the claim that having a future-like-ours is a sufficient condition for a right to life.[4] Since Marquis's positive argument is entwined with his negative claims about personhood, I shall begin with the concept of personhood.

Marquis is correct when he offers the "unproblematic assumption" that "it is wrong to kill *us*." But though the assumption is unproblematic, it requires explication. Indeed, if we are to avoid "human chauvinism" and "species bias," this unproblematic assumption must be explicated.[5] Why is it that a future-like-ours is the one that counts and not—say—the future of a pig or a cow?[6] The answer lies in the concept of personhood.

The concept of personhood is both complex and controversial. I will discuss it in some detail later, but first I shall appeal to intuitions. Given the popularity of the television show *Star Trek* and of the movie *E.T.*, most of us are comfortable with the notion of nonhuman rational beings and it is easy to ascribe a right to life to such beings. We do so because, no matter how much they differ physically, their mental lives are very similar to ours. Intuitively, then, personhood is that set of mental characteristics which hypothetical nonhuman rational beings share with humans, but which neither they nor humans share with pigs and cows. It is this personhood which makes a future-like-ours possible and it is, hence, personhood which underlies Marquis's right to life. This becomes quite clear when one examines Marquis's defense of his own position. He offers the following as points in support of his thesis:

> In the first place, (my theory) is incompatible with the view that it is wrong to kill only human beings who are biologically human....In the second place, the claim that the loss of one's future is the wrong-making feature of one's being killed entails the possibility that the futures of some actual nonhuman mammals on our own planet are sufficiently like ours that it is seriously wrong to kill them also....In the third place, the claim that the loss of one's future is the wrong-making feature of one's being killed does not entail...that active euthanasia is wrong [346].

Since Marquis offers these points in support of his thesis, one assumes that these points are more basic than the thesis itself. But, in response to his first point, if we ask what differentiates those nonhumans who have a right to life from those nonhumans who lack such a right, the answer is clear. Those nonhumans who have a right to life are persons, as are we, and those nonhumans who lack a right to life also lack personhood. With regard to Marquis's second point, the nonhuman mammals on our own planet that have something like a future-like-ours are the higher apes, and they come closest to being persons. And finally, what could justify active euthanasia except that the human *person* is either gone (comatose) or overwhelmed by excruciating pain?

Despite the fact that the Marquis thesis presupposes personhood, Marquis explicitly rejects the personhood criterion when he says that those who accept the personhood criteria are "left with the problem of explaining why *psychological* characteristics should make a *moral* difference" [342]. Insofar as this is offered as an argument it commits the *ad ignorantiam* fallacy. One is tempted, therefore, to offer the *ad hominem* response that Marquis has exactly the same problem with regard to explaining why human futures are more important than other futures. But I will not base my case on fallacies. Rather, I will provide an explanation of why certain psychological characteristics make a moral difference.

It is a basic moral principle that harming sentient life requires justification.[7] It is also an empirical fact that different kinds of harm can be done to various forms of sentient life depending on the nature of their consciousness. For example, you can cause a snake physical pain, but you cannot cause it psychological pain by insulting it. Persons can grasp and use many concepts that cannot be understood by nonpersons. Such concepts can generate attitudes and expectations that can be frustrated. Since such frustrations constitute an emotional harm, persons can be harmed in ways that nonpersons cannot. Some of these harms are the most serious that can be done to humans. Thus, what is special about human or person consciousness is that persons are capable of experiencing *conceptually based emotions.*

Conceptually based emotions are feeling states that can be experienced only if one is capable of understanding a variety of quite abstract concepts. Some examples of conceptually based emotions are the feelings of moral guilt, regret, indignation, hope, and pride. We can feel moral guilt only if we have a concept of moral wrong. We can feel indignant only if we have a concept of justice and fairness. We can feel hope only if we can foresee a variety of possible futures.

The conceptually based emotions are the basis of the demand that human beings be treated differently from other animals. For example, the desire to be an autonomous individual is a desire that can be had only by persons, and thus it is only persons whose autonomy can be violated. Also, there is nothing wrong with taking a cat's kittens away from her because, after a brief period, the cat will not and cannot miss the kittens. This is because she has no significant sense of self, nor does she have any prolonged memory of her kittens. If she were able to look forward to raising her kittens, to anticipate eventual grandkittens, and to feel a lifelong despair over the loss of her kittens, then to take her kittens from her would be immoral. But then she would be a person, a cat-person to be sure, but a person nonetheless.

Persons, and only persons, can conceptualize a distant future in which they are a participant. Only persons can anticipate and deliberately shape their own future. Only persons can desire and possess the freedom to shape their own self, their own life, their own future. Only persons can have their long-term plans frustrated by their untimely death. One aspect of the seriousness of death for a person is the loss of an anticipated, intended, longed-for future. No nonperson can be harmed in this way. It is the loss of this sort of a future that constitutes a common—but not a universal—harm arising from death. Thus, the harm constituted by the loss of *our* future presupposes that we are persons. This, in brief, is the explanation of why psychological states have moral importance.

But, for a person, what is an even more serious loss than the loss of a possible future is the loss of the actual, existent person. It is this immediate loss of personhood which constitutes the basic harm in killing. It is this loss that makes the murder of persons even on their deathbeds a serious harm. One more minute of being a living person is of great value—even if that minute is an innocuous one—and taking that minute is a great harm. The loss of a future increases the harm of a killing, but the primary harm of a killing is the loss of the life of the person. This is a serious harm even when the person has no future.

It might be replied that even if one's future amounts to no more than one more minute, it is nevertheless the loss of that minute, and not the loss of personhood, that constitutes the harm. This reply is certainly plausible, but it gets its plausibility from confusing two distinct harms that result from murder: the loss of one's personhood and the loss of one's future. If, as the reply suggests, the loss of one's future is the only harm, then the badness of the murder under discussion would arise from the harm done by the loss of the last minute of life. But surely, the difference between a life of—say—89 years and a life of 89 years and one minute, given that the minute is an innocuous one, is not sufficient to account for the serious wrongness of a deathbed murder.

Were we to derive the wrongness of a murder solely from the loss of one's future, the degree of wrongness would vary inversely with life expectancy. Murdering the elderly would be less wrong than murdering the young. While such a consequence might be appealing to some, it goes against legal practice and, I believe, it goes against moral intuition. Thus, if all murders, *qua* murder, are equally bad, it is the loss of personhood that accounts for the intrinsic wrongness of murder, and it is the failure to recognize this that constitutes the basic error involved in Marquis's deprivation thesis. However, this error is both understandable and alluring.

Having a future-like-ours and being a person are conceptually independent but empirically related properties. All persons, insofar as they retain their personhood, have a future-like-ours. Thus, whenever a person is killed, there is the simultaneous destruction of a future-like-ours.[8] This empirical entwining of personhood and having a future-like-ours makes it difficult to ascertain whether it is the loss of personhood, the loss of a future-like-ours, or the loss of both that constitutes the definitive harm done by the killing of a person.

However, consider a situation where, because of limited resources, one must choose between saving the life of a 9-year-old and saving the life of an 89-year-old. The differences in their expected futures (as well as their pasts) is surely relevant with regard to who should be saved. Surely one ought to save the child. This indicates that the value of a future-like-ours can vary in degree, one parameter being the expected length of the specific future-like-ours. It is this that makes premature death sadder than death at the end of a normal life-span.

Contrast the difference between premature and "normal" death with the difference between the murders of a 9-year-old and an 89-year-old. It is *not* the case that one murder is less wrong than the other. Both are equally wrong *qua* murder. The murders are equally wrong even though the murder of the 9-year-old causes a greater loss of a future-like-ours than does the murder of an 89-year-old. The degree of loss, the degree of harm, is not relevant to the wrongness of the murder *per se*. Rather, it is the destruction of personhood that makes all murders, *qua* murder, equally wrong.[9]

Given that we can detach the harm of the loss of personhood from the harm of the loss of a future-like-ours, we can now consider the importance of the loss of a future-like-ours when the entity undergoing the loss has not attained personhood.

Imagine that a kitten is injected with a serum that will have no significant effect on the kitten for nine months but that will, after nine months, instantaneously cause the kitten to become a person and hence, to have both a present and a future-like-ours.[10] Suppose further that an antidote to the serum is available. Would it be morally permissible to give the antidote before the kitten becomes a person? More important, would there be any moral difference between giving the antidote before the kitten becomes a person and giving the antidote after the kitten becomes a person (assuming that the antidote will then return the kitten to a normal cat state)? Giving the antidote before the acquisition of personhood changes the biological state of the kitten, but giving the antidote after the acquisition of personhood destroys an existing person. Marquis, presumably, would have to conclude that the antidote should never be given. I, on the other hand, believe that the antidote could be given before the kitten becomes a person, but not after.

Perhaps this difference merely reduces to a difference in intuitions, but I think not. It is appropriate to ask what underlies the different intuitions. Marquis and I agree that—for normal adult humans—the loss of a future-like-ours is a tragic loss. But—for normal adult humans—such a loss is simultaneous with the loss of personhood. That is, it is the simultaneous loss of personhood that underlies the tragedy of the loss of a future.

Insofar as this is correct, and insofar as killing a dying patient against their conscious will is wrong, having a future-like-ours is not a necessary condition for having a right to life. Furthermore, insofar as giving our hypothetical kitten the antidote before it becomes a person is morally permissible, having a future-like-ours is not a sufficient condition for having a right to life. What is a sufficient condition for having a right to life is *being* a person. What is wrong with killing us is not the destruction of a future but the destruction of a person.

Marquis recognizes this possibility and he discusses it under the rubric of the "discontinuation account" of the wrongness of killing. This account, he says, seems just as intelligible as the value of a future-like-ours account, but, since it does not justify an anti-abortion position, Marquis feels compelled to argue against it. His argument is as follows:

> The discontinuation account will not be adequate at all, if it does not refer to the *value of* the experience that may be discontinued. One does not want the discontinuation account to make it wrong to kill a patient who begs for death and who is in severe pain that cannot be relieved short of killing....If the patient's future is a future of value, we want our account to make it wrong to kill the patient. If the patient's future is intolerable, whatever his or her immediate past, we want our account to allow killing the patient. Obviously, then, it is the value of that patient's future that is doing the work in rendering the morality of killing the patient intelligible.
>
> This being the case, it seems clear that whether one has immediate past experiences or not does no work in the explanation of what makes killing

wrong. The addition the discontinuation account makes to the value of a human future account is otiose. Its addition to the value-of-a-future account plays no role at all in rendering intelligible the wrongness of killing [350–351].

Contrary to Marquis, what the discontinuation account is asserting is that the immediate existence of a person has great value. It is significant that in his purported refutation of this account Marquis refers to both the past and future of a person, but says absolutely nothing about the value of the instantaneous present. Thus he says: "If the patient's future is intolerable, whatever his or her immediate past, we want our account to allow killing the patient." But this is surely a mistake. Even if one is faced with a future life of intolerable pain, one ought not be killed *now*. If possible, euthanasia should be postponed until one's life *is* intolerable. Ideally, euthanasia should not be performed merely because one's life will become intolerable in the future.

In summary, Marquis's deprivation thesis acquires some initial plausibility because a full explanation of all the harms involved in a killing usually must refer to the future, for the loss of a future is *usually* part of the harm. But even if one has no (significant) future, killing one is still wrong. It is the immediate death of a person, the immediate snuffing out of personhood, that constitutes the evil of killing. The loss of a valuable future, when it accompanies the loss of personhood, is a significant *additional* loss. But it is not the loss of the future that is crucial vis-à-vis the killing. What is crucial is the loss of personhood.

The personhood account of the wrongness of killing, explicated by the concept of the conceptually based emotions, can explain the wrongness of killing, including the killing of persons who have no significant future. It is therefore superior to the future-like-ours account. However, the personhood account is still vulnerable to Marquis's claim that it cannot adequately account for the right to life of neonates. This is so, he argues, because neonates are not persons and hence would have no right to life.

Marquis's argument is unsound. His argument rests on the false assumption that a neonatal right to life must arise from the same source that generates an adult right to life. But there are many types of right. Human, or more accurately *person* rights are those rights that each person has by virtue of being a person. Social rights are those rights that are fundamental to the well functioning of a morally acceptable society. The right to life (of persons) is a human or person right. The right to—say—property is a social right. Both types of rights can be important enough to justify sacrificing one's life in their defense.

All persons have a right to life as a result of being persons. But other entities might also have a right to life, a social right to life. Indeed, I shall argue that neonates should have a social right to life. This is not a right that springs *de novo* into existence. It is rather a right that grows out of a specific fetal right, the right to care (to be cared for).

The recognition that the right to care is an increasing, dynamic right makes possible a rational defense of the widespread intuition that late abortions require more justification than early abortions. In addition, the right to care accounts for and is compatible with the equally widespread intuition that some moral significance should be attributed to conception since it is at conception that each of us as a unique biological entity first came into being.

The right to care has four sources that can be divided into two groups: those *intrinsic* to the developing entity and those that relate the entity to others, the *relational* sources. The intrinsic sources are genetic humanness and potentiality of personhood. The relational sources are both the degree to which the fetus is cared about and whether or not a decision has been made to allow it to develop.

Genetic humanness is instantaneously present at conception, and the potentiality for personhood (for normal fetuses) is generated at conception also. This is what underlies the intuition that conception is a morally significant point. Nevertheless, conception is not sufficient to generate a right to life. Conception is the beginning of a biological entity that, after extensive development, may result in the beginnings of a person, but the beginning of personhood is better thought of as occurring when sentience begins and not with mere biological existence.

The concept of brain death is relevant to this point. Brain death clearly indicates that mere genetic humanness does not generate a right to life. Indeed, biologically alive genetic human beings are humanly dead if lacking the possibility of consciousness. Brain dead individuals are biologically living human organisms, but since they permanently lack consciousness they are not living *persons.* They are biological living organisms that, because they have been persons, are now dead people.

Of course the brain dead not only lack consciousness, they also lack the potential for consciousness and, hence, are crucially different from fetuses. It is the fact that most human fetuses are potential persons that generates a minimal right to care at conception. This right is generated as follows: First, we are human and, hence, have both a right and an obligation to treat human entities in a special way even if those entities are not persons. In a sense this is species bias, but if it is thought of on the analogy of a family—the human family—it is quite plausible. If the right to care is kept within legitimate bounds, the species bias that underlies it is quite reasonable. We may legitimately treat the members of our own family in special ways so long as our doing so does not violate the rights of other entities. Family members have claims on one another that others do not. So too with the human family. Exactly what claims our family members have on us, and what responsibilities we have toward them, is a subject for another paper. Nevertheless, if human beings exist whose conceptual abilities are no more than those of a cat, we should not treat them just as we treat cats. They are one of ours, and on that basis we may and ought to treat them as one of ours. We ought to care for them.

The role of *potentiality,* though significant, is minimal. It is significant enough so that the loss of the entity is at least unfortunate, but since a potential person is not a person, its loss is not equivalent to the loss of a person. The loss of an early fetus is less sad than the loss of a more developed fetus because more of the potential becomes actualized as time passes. But at no stage is the fetus a person, and hence its loss is never the equivalent of the loss of a person. The two intrinsic properties of fetuses, therefore, generate a minimal right to care. This right can be strengthened by the relational properties of the fetus.

This first relational property is that of being cared about. Reflection dispels any doubt that merely caring about something can give it value. If we think of a family heirloom we can recognize that the objective value of the heirloom can be quite small compared with the subjective value family members attach to it. This difference in value does not mean that the family members do not know the heirloom's objective value. Its value to the family, however, grows out of the history of the object, a history that they as family members share. This subjective value transcends the mere objective value of the object.

A conceptus, like an heirloom, can acquire a great deal of relational value depending on the response to it by others, primarily its biological progenitors. If the biological progenitors want to have a child the relational value of the fetus can be enormous. Yet this relational value is contingent on the attitude of the biological progenitors. If the pregnancy is not wanted, then the conceptus gains no relational value from this source.

The second source of relational value is possible only in situations where abortions are legally permissible. In such cases, the continuation of a pregnancy is a matter of choice and the decision to continue the pregnancy increases the responsibility of the woman and thereby increases the right to care of the fetus. If a woman decides to continue her pregnancy even though she does not really want a child, that decision nevertheless increases her responsibility towards the fetus. If she decides to continue the pregnancy, the fetus will (most likely) become a person. Hence the woman's support for the continuation of the pregnancy increases the fetal right to care since the well-being of the person-to-be depends on the care given to the fetus. If you allow a process that will result in a person to continue, you acquire some responsibility toward that future person and, hence, for the fetus which will become that person. The woman's decision to continue the pregnancy gives the fetus an additional degree of the right to care. She cannot morally continue the pregnancy and neglect the fetus. If she decides to remain pregnant, she has an obligation to take care of herself for the good of the fetus, and the fetus has a right to such care.[11]

The right to care increases throughout the pregnancy because the woman's voluntary assumption of responsibility increases the longer she continues the pregnancy and the potentiality of the fetus becomes more actualized. Thus late term abortions are justifiable only to prevent the death of or serious harm to the woman. Since this final "threat" ends with birth, the neonate has a full (social) right to life.

In conclusion, personhood is the primary source of the right to life. Until a human passes through the fetal and neonatal stages and develops personhood its rights depend on the other four sources of rights. Those sources generate a range of rights beginning with a minimal and easily defeasible right to care during the early stages of the pregnancy, through an increasingly significant right to care, and culminating in a full social right to life for neonates.

STUDY QUESTIONS

1. According to Gerald Paske, why does Marquis's concept of a future-like-ours depend on the notion of personhood? Is he correct?

2. Do you agree with Paske that having conceptually based emotions is a necessary condition for Personhood? Explain your answer.

3. According to Paske, do neonates and infants have a right to life? Do they have conceptually based emotions?

4. Paske states that being wanted gives the fetus some right to life. What if an infant is not wanted? What if one parent (or grandparent) wants the fetus to live and the other doesn't? Can Paske successfully solve these problems?

NOTES

1. Marquis, Don, "Why Abortion Is Immoral," *The Journal of Philosophy,* 86, 4 (April 1989), 183–202. This article is reprinted in the following: (1) *Midwest Medical Ethics,* 5, Summer 1989. (2) *Social Ethics,* Mappes and Zembaty, eds., 4th ed., 1992. (3) *Taking Sides: Clashing Views on Controversial Moral Issues,* Stephen Satris, ed., 3rd ed., 1992. (4) *Today's Moral Issues,* Daniel Bonevac, ed., 1st ed., 1992. (5) *Social and Personal Ethics,* William H. Shaw, ed., 1st ed., 1992. (6) *Personal Values: Moral Problems in Daily Life,* Eric H. Gampel, ed., 1992. (7) *Gender Basics,* Anne Minas, ed., 1993. (8) *Moral Controversies: Race, Gender and Class,* Steven Gold, ed., 1993. (9) *Arguing About Abortion,* Lewis M. Schwartz, ed., 1st ed., 1993.

2. There are several concepts of personhood but the relevant notion vis-à-vis the abortion debate is that persons are capable of highly abstract thought. It is generally agreed that some higher mammals may be capable of such thought but mammals such as cows and pigs are not. It is also generally assumed that human fetuses and neonates lack this capacity.

3. In the rest of the paper I shall use "fetus" to mean "normal fetus." The question of whether seriously defective fetuses and neonates have a right to life complicates matters but cannot he discussed here.

4. For other points of attack see McInerney, Peter K., "Does a Fetus Already Have a Future-Like-Ours" and Norcross, Alastair, "Killing, Abortion, and Contraception: A Reply to Marquis," both in the *Journal of Philosophy,* 87, 5 (May 1990). I believe that Marquis has met these attacks in his unpublished paper "Abortion and the Deprivation of a Future: A Reply."

5. See, for example, Routley, R. and Routley, V., "Against the Inevitability of Human Chauvinism," *Ethics and Problems of the 21st Century,* K. E. Goodpaster, and K. M. Sayre, eds., Notre Dame, Ind.: University of Notre Dame Press, 1979. For a discussion of species bias see Regan, Tom, *The Case for Animal Rights,* Berkeley: University of California Press, 1983.

6. For the purposes of this paper I assume that cows and pigs have no right to life. I make no such assumption with regard to the higher apes. For a discussion of animal rights, see Paske, Gerald H., "Why Animals Have No Right to Life," *Australasian Journal of Philosophy,* 66, 4 (December 1988).

7. For an argument that sentience is a necessary condition for a right to life, see Paske, Gerald H., "The Life Principle: A (metaethical) Rejection," *Journal of Applied Philosophy,* 6, 2 (1989).

8. At first glance it may appear that the reverse is not true, that the loss of future-like-ours by a person does not entail the loss of that person. However, this is a mistake. Consider a person who is struck in the head and, although not killed, is so brain damaged that he or she no longer has a future-like-ours. In such cases personhood has been destroyed even though biological life continues The extreme forms of this are cases of brain death where the loss of personhood, despite the continuation of biological life, is explicitly recognized as constituting human (or person) death. Unfortunately there are intermediate cases with which the law has not yet adequately dealt. A discussion of such cases, of which higher brain death is one, is beyond the scope of this paper.

9. Some may feel, contrary to my intuition, that there is a difference in the degree of wrongness of the murders. Even so, the difference in degree of harm between the murder of a 9-year-old and an 89-year-old, such that there is much less harm done to the 89-year-old, does not correspond to any plausible difference in the wrongness of the two murders. To claim otherwise would be to trivialize murdering the elderly.

10. This distinction has already been drawn by Michael Tooley with his well-known cat example. See his "Abortion and Infanticide," *Philosophy and Public Affairs,* 2, 1, (Fall 1972), 60–62. However, because the animal rights movement has become influential since Tooley's article first appeared, I have modified the example so that the kitten need not be killed.

11. I have restricted my discussion to the decision of the woman. Men also can participate in the decision to continue a pregnancy, and by doing so they can affect the relational value of the fetus. However, the role, of men in this regard is secondary to my thesis and is too complex to be integrated into this article.

23

A Future Like Ours and the Concept of Person

A Reply to McInerney and Paske

DON MARQUIS

Don Marquis is Professor of Philosophy at the University of Kansas. In this essay Marquis distinguishes his position, "the future-like-ours account" (FLO) from other related but different positions and argues that neither McInerney nor Paske defeats his argument. Moreover, the personhood strategy has severe difficulties of its own which make it less satisfactory than the future-like-ours account.

According to the future-like-ours account of the ethics of abortion (hereafter, the FLO account) depriving an individual of a future like ours is what makes killing that individual wrong. Surely the misfortune of premature death underlies the wrongness of killing. People who have cancer or AIDS do regard the loss of their futures as constituting the misfortune of their premature deaths. Ending the life of a fetus involves depriving it of a future like ours. If the misfortune of premature death is what underlies the wrongness of killing, and if the deprivation of a future like ours is what underlies the misfortune of premature death, and if ending the life of a fetus involves depriving it of a future like ours, then ending the life of a fetus is presumptively wrong. Accordingly abortion is presumptively wrong. Since the presumption that killing a human being is wrong is a very strong presumption, the presumption that abortion is wrong is a very strong presumption.[1]

This essay was commissioned for the first edition of this volume. Page numbers in brackets refer to pages in this book.

The main, although certainly not the only, competitor to this FLO account of the ethics of abortion is the personhood strategy. On standard versions of this strategy; some account is given of the concept of person. Then it is argued that because fetuses are not persons, they do not have the right to life and because fetuses do not have the right to life, abortion is morally permissible.[2]

I believe that personhood strategies are inferior to the FLO account for at least two reasons. In the first place, personhood strategies do not provide an adequate account of the connection between the wrongness of taking a human life and the concept of a person. In the second place, such strategies are subject to the problem of infanticide: They rule out an adequate account of the wrongness of killing individuals who are not persons, such as infants. More generally, they rule out an adequate account of why wrongful behavior toward individuals who are not persons is wrong.[3] The FLO account is not subject to these difficulties because the concept of person plays no role whatsoever in the account.

Gerald Paske and Peter McInerney have both criticized the FLO account of the wrongness of abortion. Their objections revolve around the claim that the concept of person plays an essential role in the correct account of the wrongness of killing. Their views are interesting because examination of the views of each suggests many different ways in which the concept of a person might enter into an account of the wrongness of killing. I shall argue, however, that neither Paske nor McInerney is successful in showing that the concept of person enters *in any essential way* into an adequate account of the wrongness of killing. I shall also argue that neither of them have dealt successfully with the other Achilles heel of personhood strategies: the problem of infanticide.

I

Paske claims that the concept of person is tacitly presupposed by the FLO account of the wrongness of killing. According to Paske if we ask, "Why is it that a future-like-ours is the one that counts and not—say—the future of a pig or a cow?," the answer "lies in the concept of personhood" [363]. By personhood, Paske means "that set of mental characteristics that hypothetical nonhuman rational beings share with humans, but that neither they nor humans share with pigs and cows" [363]. Let me explain why Paske's claim is incorrect.

One account of the wrongness of abortion, an account that is more difficult to defend than the FLO account, might be called "the future as a person (FAP) account." According to this account, what makes our futures worth having is that we will or would exist as beings capable of relatively abstract thought, that is, as beings who meet Paske's definition of "person" [364]. What makes our premature deaths a misfortune for us is that we are deprived of the future we would have had as persons. Since being deprived of a FAP is what makes causing the premature death of an individual wrong, it is presumptively wrong to cause the death of a fetus.

In contrast, the FLO account is deliberately neutral concerning the nature of the future that an individual must have for it to be wrong to kill that individual. One could adopt the FLO view and also adopt the view that what makes a future valuable is the enjoyments it will contain. One might wish to argue that, as a consequence, it is wrong to kill cows and pigs because they will be deprived of a future that contains enjoyments such as chewing their cuds, wallowing in the mud, and feeling the warm sun on their backs. Let us call such a view the future of enjoyment or FOE view. There is room under the FLO umbrella for both the FAP and the FOE view. The FAP account and the FOE account each entail the FLO account, but the FLO account entails neither. On either the FAP account or the FOE account, the abortion of human beings will be wrong. Accordingly, if one is interested in constructing the most plausible account one can of the wrongness of abortion, there is no need to commit oneself in an overly specific way on the issue of just what it is about our futures that makes them valuable. Therefore, I did not.

The FLO view takes for granted the consensus among civilized human beings that it is presumptively very wrong to kill adult human beings and children. According to the FLO view, what accounts for this consensus view is that adult human beings and children have FLOs. It follows that a characterization of a FLO must be sufficiently broad so that it accounts for this consensus. I regard my own future as valuable because it (presumably) involves doing philosophy, but the future as philosopher view is too narrow to account for the consensus, so it is inadequate as an account of the wrongness of killing human beings. Any version of the FLO view that accounts for the consensus will lead (given a few apparently obvious assumptions) to the view that abortion is immoral. This is because the futures of standard human fetuses will contain the futures of children and adults. Accordingly, whatever it is in the futures of children and adults that makes it wrong to kill them will also be found in the futures of human fetuses. Thus Paske's view that the FLO account excludes extension to ordinary animals is incorrect. Paske supposes that some notion of personhood is required to justify active euthanasia, but this is clearly incorrect [363–364]. People often have an animal euthanized because they believe that the animal will not have a future that is valuable from the animal's point of view.

II

In the previous section I considered Paske's suggestion that the FLO account presupposes the concept of person. Paske's suggestion is compatible with the use of the FLO account to defend the wrongness of abortion. In this section I want to consider Peter McInerney's claim that the FLO account presupposes the concept of person. If McInerney's claim is correct, then the FLO account cannot be used to justify the immorality of abortion.

McInerney draws our attention to the ways in which persons are connected to their futures. At least some of our present life will be remembered by us in the future (if we do not die in the meantime). Our present and future are connected by continuity of character. We project our plans and projects onto our futures. Our futures are those in which our plans and projects are realized, or frustrated. Learning through experience connects our present and our future. There are neurophysiological connections between present and future person-stages. Our future is *ours* as opposed to being someone else's by virtue of all these ways in which persons are connected to their futures. All of these relations between present and future connect different stages of a person [358].

What are we supposed to conclude from all of this? McInerney wants us to conclude that persons are related to their futures in ways that fetuses are not. This conclusion is plainly true. How do we get from it to the thesis that there is something wrong with the FLO argument for the wrongness of abortion? McInerney thinks that we should further conclude that (1) "the fetus is so little connected to the later personal life that it cannot be deprived of that personal life" [359]; (2) at its time the fetus does not already "possess" that future personal life or have a personal future [359]; (3) "a fetus is separated from a personal future by many 'layers' of possibility" [359]; and (4) "a fetus similarly has only the potentiality to develop a personal future" [360]. Thus, McInerney believes that if a fetus does not have or possess a personal future or if it is too much separated from a personal future, then it cannot be deprived of that future. If it cannot be deprived of a future, then the FLO argument fails to show that abortion is immoral. Persons stand in the appropriate relations to their future such that they can be deprived of them, whereas fetuses do not. In this way, the concept of person is necessary to the FLO argument for the wrongness of killing. Seeing how that concept is relevant shows why the FLO argument for the immorality of abortion fails.

McInerney's view seems to be subject to the following difficulty. On the one hand, McInerney seems to be claiming that a fetus cannot be deprived of its future as a person in any sense whatsoever. If this is his claim, then his claim is both a *non sequitur* and known to be false. It is a *non sequitur* because the claim that a fetus is not related to its future in all of the ways persons, *qua* persons, are related to their futures does not entail that fetuses are not related to their futures at all. It is known to be false because a fetus is simply a human being at a very early stage of its life. It is not wrong to say it has been deprived of its future if it is killed and is, for that reason, unable to complete its natural life span.

On the other hand, McInerney claims that "for the [FLO] argument to be convincing, it is necessary that a fetus *at its time* 'possess' or be related to a future-like-ours in a way that allows the transfer from the wrongness of killing us persons to the wrongness of killing fetuses" [358]. This suggests that, instead of concluding that a fetus does not possess a future at all, McInerney should have concluded that there is no *morally relevant* sense in which a fetus possesses and, therefore, could be deprived of its future. If this is his conclusion, then his conclusion is not obviously false. The trouble is that McInerney provides no argument whatsoever for *this* conclusion.[4] There are, however, considerations found in Paske's essay that could provide a basis for such an argument.

III

Paske also claims that "the harm constituted by the loss of *our* future presupposes that we are persons." (5) He supplies considerations that appear to support this claim:

> Persons, and only persons, can conceptualize a distant future in which they are a participant. Only persons can anticipate and deliberately shape their own future. Only persons can desire and possess the freedom to shape their own self, their own life, their own future. Only persons can have their long-term plans frustrated by their untimely death. One aspect of the seriousness of death for a person is the loss of an anticipated, intended, longed-for future. [364]

These considerations can serve two important functions. In the first place, in view of the fact that I have criticized personhood strategies for lack of moral relevance, they can provide a basis for a response to that criticism. In the second place, presumably considerations such as these could be used to support McInerney's suggestion that the wrongness of depriving a person of his or her FLO cannot be transferred to fetuses or other nonpersons. If the wrongness of the deprivation of a FLO presupposes reference to the previous considerations and the previous considerations are considerations involving only persons (which they plainly are), then we are not justified in concluding that it is wrong to deprive fetuses of their futures.

Paske's claim that persons can be harmed by their deaths in ways that non-persons cannot is undoubtedly correct. Furthermore, it is undoubtedly true that these harms are very serious and important. Nevertheless, there are, it seems to me, two problems with using these considerations to suggest that the FLO account of the wrongness of killing applies only to persons. In the first place, Paske's undoubtedly true claims do not entail that the harms of death are not very great for a nonperson, especially when that death deprives that nonperson of the experience of a rich personal life. We place a very high value on such a life. If we did not, we would not care whether we will die prematurely. But we do care. Thus, we know how great a loss death is for someone who dies, whether or not they anticipate that loss. There seems to be no reason why *this* misfortune cannot be transferred from persons to nonpersons. Since this misfortune underlies the wrongness of killing, the wrongness can be transferred also.

The problem for what I am now supposing to be Paske's view can be seen in another way. Suppose that we knew that someone's future would not be the future that he intends, anticipates and longs for, but would be a different future that human beings typically value highly. It would be no less wrong to deprive such a person of that future.

In the second place, if Paske were challenged to defend the view that the considerations he offers show that only persons can be wrongly deprived of their futures, one of the following two lines of argument might seem attractive. Paske might argue that the wrongness of depriving an individual of her future presupposes either that such an individual *does* have a pro attitude toward her future life or *can* have a pro attitude toward her future life. Since only persons have the conceptual apparatus to have such attitudes, then it follows that the deprivation of a future argument yields only the result that it is wrong to kill persons.

These two arguments are subject to problems. Suppose, on the one hand, that Paske would wish to claim that the wrongness of killing someone presupposes that one *does* have the pro attitude toward one's future that only persons can possess. This view has great intuitive plausibility. It is presumptively wrong to interfere with the self-regarding wishes of another. Basing the serious wrongness of the interference with what that person cares deeply about falls out of this general moral truth rather nicely. The trouble with the "does care" view is that it does not account for why it is wrong to kill those who are suicidal, those who are just tired or bored with life, and those who are depressed. Accordingly, the general wrongness of killing people cannot be dependent on the fact that the individual who is killed *does* have a pro attitude toward her future.

This suggests that Paske should hold, on the other hand, that the class of those who are wronged by being killed should be limited to those who *can* care in a conceptually sophisticated way about their futures. The great advantage of this "can care" view is that it avoids the counterexamples to the "does care" view. However, this advantage is obtained at a price. The price is that the intuitive plausibility of the "does care" view is given up. The fact that a person possesses the conceptual apparatus to care about some state of affairs does not, by itself, give one a reason for action. The fact that a person *can* have a pro attitude toward her future is sometimes quite compatible with having a presumptive reason for ending her life. If her future will be one laden with pain and despair and she knows that it will be laden with pain and despair, we do have a presumptive (although plainly not conclusive) reason for killing her. Furthermore, it is presumptively wrong to kill temporarily unconscious persons who are incapable of any mentation at all and who are therefore incapable of conceptually based emotions.

Thus, I suspect that only if we confuse the "can care" and the "does care" versions of the arguments that apparently underlie Paske's considerations would we be tempted to construe those remarks as showing that the deprivation of a future arguments cannot be applied to fetuses. Thus, the fact that only persons and not fetuses, have *intentional* relations to their actual or anticipated futures seems not to be capable of underwriting the view that the FLO argument shows that the presumption that killing is wrong applies only to persons.

IV

If I have understood him correctly, Paske believes that the FLO argument is unsound because it should, if correctly formulated, refer to the value of the FLO of a *present person*. If I have understood him correctly, Paske *also* believes that the FLO argument should, if correctly formulated, refer to a personal future (that is, a *future as a person)* of a present individual. *In addition,* Paske defends the claim that one's right to life is not based on the value of one's future to oneself at all. He claims that "what is a sufficient condition for having a right to life is *being a* person. What is wrong with killing us is not the destruction of a future but the destruction of a person" [366]. He says that this is because "the immediate existence of a person has great value" [367]. To speak only of the value of a future leaves out something of highest importance: "the value of the instantaneous present" [367]. Thus, in addition to his previous arguments, Paske wants to cash out the importance of the concept of person in an account of what is wrong with killing in terms of the value of the instantaneous present of a person [367].

Why should we believe that the instantaneous present has great value? One of Paske's arguments is based on the analysis of a case in which one might attempt to justify active euthanasia on the grounds that a patient faces a future of intolerable pain and suffering and, therefore, faces a future full of disvalue. Paske says that such a patient "ought not be killed *now*. If possible, euthanasia should be postponed until one's life *is* intolerable." [367] Paske is wrong about this. Ideally, euthanasia should be performed at that precise moment that divides a patient's past bearable life from the patient's future intolerable life.[5] This is entirely compatible with holding that the morality of killing a person turns on the value of that person's future.

Paske also bases his view on an analysis of the case of a kitten that is injected with a serum that will turn it into a person [366]. However, Paske admits that different people will have different intuitions about this case. Accordingly, the case does not seem to show that his instantaneous present account is superior to the FLO account.

I suspect (and this entirely speculation) that someone who would take Paske's line about the immediate present would have something like the following argument in mind: I can be wronged only by what happens to me in the immediate present. The future is not yet. It will not affect me until the future becomes the present. Thus, the harm of killing must be understood primarily in terms of the loss of my immediate present, not my future.

However, this argument leads directly to Epicurean puzzles. If death does not affect the living because they are not yet dead, death does not affect the dead because they do not exist. Thus, death is not a deprivation at all.[6] No doubt, Paske would not welcome this conclusion.[7]

I think that there are two reasons (that are not entirely independent) for thinking that an individual's instantaneous present is of little value. (1) The instantaneous present is so short that it is hard to believe that anyone would hold that it did matter most in an ethics of the wrongness of killing. The future we will experience if we continue to live is *so* much longer. Indeed, it is infinitely longer. Therefore, it is of infinitely greater value. (2) Suppose that you have early colon cancer. Your surgeon says that without *immediate* surgery you will die within a year. Surgery requires anesthesia. Therefore, surgery requires giving up what is valuable about your immediate present (but isn't it really your immediate future?). However, after surgery you can have a future of roughly the same value that you would have had in the absence of the colon cancer. Surgery is plainly the rational choice. Furthermore, I suspect that one's choice of surgery would be even more decisive if the surgery actually could be done in the immediate present rather than in the immediate future. This shows that a rational individual values his future far more than he values his immediate present. This, in turn, seems sufficient for claiming that it is the value of our future rather than the value of our immediate present that accounts for the great misfortune of premature death.

V

Paske's most important argument for the importance of the concept of person in the correct account of the wrongness of killing is based on the claim that all murders are equally wrong. On the FLO account, he argues, it is far worse to kill a 9-year-old than to kill an eighty-nine-year old because the future of which the 9-year-old would be deprived is typically so much longer than the future of the 89-year-old. But both murders are equally wrong. Since the 9-year-old and the 89-year-old are equally persons, the concept of person can be used in the account of the equality of the wrongness of murder. Therefore, the wrongness of murder should be based on the concept of person [365].

Is the doctrine of that all murders are equally wrong true? Paske defends it by appealing to moral intuition and to legal practice [365]. However, plainly the doctrine of the legal equality of the wrongness of murder might be based on considerations other than the doctrine of the moral equality of the wrongness of murder. There are reasons for equalizing the punishment for murder. The differences in the values of the lost futures caused by actual murders are so difficult to estimate that it might be better for juries to take for granted that all murders are equally wrong. Mere appeal to moral intuition is not an adequate defense of any doctrine.

Since murder deprives the 9-year-old of so much more than it does the 89-year-old, there is something to be said for the view that not all murders are equally morally wrong. Such a view seems less counterintuitive when one realizes that it does not imply the trivialization of the murder of the elderly (compare Paske, note 9). Someone who adopts the FLO account might believe that the murder of an 89-year-old deserves at least the death penalty or life imprisonment and that the murder of a 9-year-old deserves 10 death penalties or 10 lives in prison because it deprives the victim of so much more. Such an individual might be willing to settle for equality of punishment, and, therefore, the legal equality of murder, on the grounds that executing a person ten times or imprisoning him for ten lifetimes is impossible.

There may be ways of arriving at the doctrine of the moral and legal equality of murder that are compatible with the argument that the wrongness of murder is based on the loss of one's future of value. A friend of mine, who recently retired, claims that the subjective value of each of his remaining Tuesdays is greater than the subjective value of each of the future Tuesdays of younger people because there will be fewer Tuesdays for him. People who are approaching death often remark on how much more they treasure life because they realize how little of it there is left. This suggests that the value of each day of a person's future from her own point of view varies directly with age. If this is so, then the values of our futures as a whole tend toward equality.

Furthermore, we regard murder as one of the worst of crimes because it deprives the victim of more than almost any other crime. This provides some with a reason for punishing murderers as much as possible within the limit of the Eighth Amendment prohibition of cruel and unusual punishment. Given this not implausible rationale, equality of punishment makes sense even if we believe that the amount of loss when life is lost varies inversely with the age of the victim. In addition, if the real point of punishing murderers is deterrence, then it does not make a difference whether the punishments for different murders vary with the losses experienced by the victims.

Finally, it seems that the old utilitarian problem concerning interpersonal comparisons of utility emerges when we try to compare the values of the futures of different people. Since comparing units of value among persons seems impossible, comparing the value of the futures of different people seems impossible. These difficulties seem so insuperable that the doctrine of the legal equality of murder may be the only satisfactory public policy. But if this is so, then a FLO account of the wrongness of killing is compatible with the doctrine of the legal equality of murder. Thus, for many reasons, Paske's equality objection to the FLO account of the wrongness of killing fails.

VI

Let us summarize and put in perspective the preceding analysis. On the one hand, personhood strategies for justifying abortion rights involve arguing for (or sometimes just assuming) that the concept of person is the central concept in an account of the wrongness of killing. Personhood strategists conclude that because no fetuses are persons, all abortions are morally permissible. On the other hand, according to the FLO account having a FLO is the natural property that is the basis for the wrongness of killing. Because almost all fetuses have FLOs, it is wrong intentionally to end their lives. On the FLO account, the personhood of the victim is irrelevant. Both Paske and McInerney argue, in many different ways, that the FLO analysis fails because it does not include the concept of person. I have argued that they are mistaken.

There is another important difference between personhood strategies and the FLO account. On the FLO account, infanticide is typically wrong for the quite straightforward reason that infants typically have FLOs. Personhood strategists argue that abortion is morally permissible because fetuses aren't persons. Because no infants are persons, they have trouble explaining why infanticide is morally wrong. Some individuals make the mistake of throwing out the baby with the bath water. Personhood strategists make the error of throwing out the baby with the fetus.

The nature of the problem concerning infanticide deserves discussion. According to Paske, my "argument rests on the false assumption that a neonatal right to life must arise from the same source that generates an adult right to life" [367]. Paske's claim is untrue. No such assumption is required. All one needs to do to discover that personhood strategists have a problem accounting for the wrongness of infanticide is to examine their arguments for the wrongness of infanticide. These arguments are, without exception, very weak. This difficulty for personhood strategists is no accident. It is an outgrowth of the structure of the personhood strategy itself.

Personhood strategists wish to account for the wrongness of killing persons in terms, somehow, of their personhood to defend abortion rights. It is not open to the personhood strategist to argue that killing babies is immoral because infants are persons, because infants are not persons. It is not open to the personhood strategist to argue that killing infants is immoral because babies are potential persons or because babies have FLOs or because killing a baby is intentionally ending an innocent human life because, if such arguments were sound, they would show that abortion is immoral. Thus, the problem for the personhood strategist is to find an argument that *actually shows* that infanticide is wrong in a dialectical context in which all the standard candidates for such arguments are not available. I doubt that any such argument exists. This cannot be shown *a priori*. One must examine the accounts of the wrongness of infanticide that personhood strategists actually propose.

Michael Tooley, Mary Anne Warren, Stanley Benn, Tris Engelhardt, and Joel Feinberg all have adopted personhood strategies.[8] On the one hand, Michael Tooley has dealt with the infanticide issue by arguing that there is nothing at all wrong with killing unwanted little babies. On the other hand, Feinberg, Benn, Warren, and Engelhardt have all offered special accounts of the wrongness of infanticide. Since Feinberg is surely no less able than the other members of this group, let us consider Feinberg's defense of the claim that killing normal infants is wrong. Here is his entire argument:

> Nature has apparently implanted in us an instinctive tenderness toward infants that has proven extremely useful to the species, not only because it leads us to protect our young from death, and thus keep our population up, but also because infants usually grow into adults, and in Benn's words, "if as infants *they* are not treated with some minimal degree of tenderness and consideration, they will suffer for it later, as persons." One might add that when they are adults, others will suffer for it too, at their hands. Spontaneous warmth and sympathy toward babies then clearly has a great deal of social utility, and insofar as infanticide would tend to weaken that socially valuable response, it is, on utilitarian grounds, morally wrong.[9]

Unless we wish to quibble, we can grant that everything Feinberg says is true. Notice that Feinberg does not claim that permitting infanticide would *actually* weaken the socially valuable response he describes. However, the argument succeeds only if that response would actually be weakened. Furthermore, the argument succeeds only if the response would be weakened so much that the considerable utilitarian benefits of killing some babies were overridden. Do either of these conditions on the success of Feinberg's argument obtain?

If the puppies and kittens who will become our pets are not treated with tenderness and consideration, then they may suffer for it later as mature dogs and cats. Furthermore, we may suffer later because we treated the puppies and kittens badly. Yet we euthanize *other* dogs and cats.

If fetuses who are wanted are not treated well, then the adults they become will suffer for it later as persons. Furthermore, we will suffer later because those fetuses had been treated badly.[10] Yet we kill *other* fetuses. Plainly there are analogues to Feinberg's argument that infanticide does not promote social utility. The analogues are plainly weak arguments. The fact that we are willing to end the existence of some members of a class because they are not wanted does not at all entail nor does it seem to be necessarily psychologically connected to the claim that the other members of the same class who *are* wanted will not be treasured. (Think of furniture, plants, and houses.)

Feinberg also neglects to discuss the considerable utilitarian benefits that could be obtained by killing infants. (I'm assuming, for the sake of argument, Feinberg's view of their moral personhood.) We do not permit young adolescents to vote or to drive. That is because we have good reason to believe that many of them would vote and would drive in a socially irresponsible fashion. We have good evidence that a substantial percentage of children parented by young adolescents do not turn out well. Since, according to the personhood strategy, infants do not have the right to life, the utilitarian advantages of killing the infants of other children who are often not sufficiently responsible to be either parents voters, or drivers seem evident (I assume we could not find good homes for all these babies elsewhere). Thus, I am inclined to think that if the personhood strategists are correct, infanticide is not only morally permissible, but, in some cases, obviously good social policy.

VII

The argument of the last section should be enough to establish the presumption that accounting for the wrongness of infanticide is a major difficulty for personhood strategists. Plainly, however, the fact that Feinberg fails to show that infanticide is wrong does not entail that neither Paske nor McInerney can show that infanticide is wrong. Have they succeeded where Feinberg has not?

Consider first McInerney. McInerney claims that only persons have a personal future, or are significantly related to a personal future, or are related in morally important ways to their futures. Since infants are not persons, infanticide should be a problem for him. Here (in full) is how McInerney deals with this problem:

> Young infants do not have all of the psychological complexity that adult persons have. Nevertheless, young infants are commonsensically understood to have perceptions, beliefs, desires, and emotions (whether or not the experimental data confirms this) and to learn from experience. For this reason, the neurophysiological states and processes of young infants

can be understood to underlie something like the ordinary continuation of mental life in persons. A good case can be made that young infants are related in some (though not all) ways to a personal future [367].

McInerney's claim that young infants have perceptions, desires and emotions seems reasonable. Whether they have beliefs and learn from experience is surely more controversial. The trouble for McInerney is that what is controversially true about his claim obviously does not entail that there is any continuity in an infant's mental life at all. Yet, the presence of that continuity in persons and its absence in fetuses is the entire basis of McInerney's argument that the FLO account of the wrongness of killing does not apply to fetuses.

Let us make the counterfactual supposition that McInerney has established that there is some continuity in an infant's mental life. It seems, therefore, legitimate to allow him the inference that infants are related in some ways to a personal future. Such relations would be far less sophisticated than an adult human being's relations to a personal future. Why then should we conclude that the primitive relations between stages of an infant's mental life are sufficient to make it wrong to kill infants? McInerney supplies us with nothing whatsoever to fill this inferential account of the wrongness of infanticide.

McInerney might reply that what is significant is that infants have some relation to a personal future whereas "at its time a fetus does not have a personal future of which it can be deprived." [360]. The trouble with this reply is that his claim about fetuses is, as we have already seen, plainly false. Thus, McInerney faces a dilemma. Either fetuses have no relation to a personal future or fetuses have some relation to a personal future. On the one hand, if he claims that a fetus has no relation to his personal future, then he can distinguish in a relevant way between the absence of a fetus's relation to his future and (given our counterfactual supposition) the presence of an infant's relation to his future. This provides him with a basis for justifying the wrongness of killing infants without also justifying the wrongness of killing fetuses. The trouble with this horn of the dilemma, however, is that the claim that fetuses have no relation to their personal futures is plainly false. On the other hand, if he admits that fetuses have some relation to their personal futures, then he can exchange a true claim about fetuses for a false one. However, the price he pays is that he loses a basis for distinguishing between the permissibility of abortion and the wrongness of infanticide. Thus, McInerney, like other personhood strategists, is unable to account for the immorality of infanticide.

VIII

Has Paske succeeded where Feinberg and McInerney have not? Paske claims that, in general, a neonate's right to life grows out of the right of a fetus who will not be aborted to be cared for [367]. More specifically, according to Paske, an infant's right to life has four sources: (1) the obligations a woman has when pregnant toward the person the infant will become (for example, the obligation to refrain from more than minimal alcohol consumption) [369], (2) the fact that some pregnant women care for their fetuses and newborns before they become persons [369], (3) the biological humanity of the newborn [367] and (4) the potential personhood of the newborn [368]. If we assume that Paske's version of the personhood strategy is successful, do any or all of these considerations provide an adequate foundation for a neonatal right to life?

Paske bases a fetal right to care on the obligations a woman has toward the person her fetus will become. The obligations of the woman are, in turn, based on that person's right not to be harmed. By killing her infant or her fetus, a woman can guarantee that there will be no person to be the basis of the fetal right to care. Accordingly, both infanticide and abortion are entirely compatible with the obligations Paske justifies. Thus, Paske's first consideration provides no basis for a neonatal right to life.

That some women care for their unborn (or recently born) children confers value only on children actually cared for, not on all newborns. It confers no value on other children. In addition, something can be valued without acquiring a right to exist (consider a child's favorite blanket). Thus, Paske's fact about caring does not come close to generating a neonatal right to life for infants who are *not* cared for.

Paske does not give arguments for his view that a fetus's or infant's potential personhood helps to generate a minimal right to care [368]. This aspect of his view consists merely of assertions.

According to Paske, fetuses and infants acquire a right to care because they are biologically human. Why should this be so? Human cancer cells are biologically human. Human cancer cells can be preserved in a laboratory. They do not, as a consequence, acquire a *right* to care (although they may be useful to us). Paske claims that fetuses and newborns acquire a minimal right to care because we are all members of the human family [368]. However, "family" in this usage is nothing more than a metaphorical term for "group." Plainly, it is not the case that members of all the groups to which we belong have a right to care. After all, we are members of the animal kingdom and members of the class of things that consist in part of hydrogen atoms. Thus, there seems to be no reason at all to believe that something acquires the right to care merely because it is biologically human.

Norwood Russell Hanson used to tell a story about a preacher who was finally persuaded that none of the arguments for the existence of God is valid. The preacher cheerfully concluded that the conjunction of those arguments must be valid because there are so many of them. Short of adopting the stance of Hanson's preacher, I see no basis for holding that although *each* of Paske's considerations constitutes no basis whatsoever for a neonatal right to life, their *conjunction* is a sufficient basis for a right to life. And plainly the fact that the fetus grows during pregnancy does not entail that either the right to life or the right to care (whatever that is) grows also. Thus, Paske has failed to show that his version of the personhood strategy avoids the infanticide problem.

Paske, and Mcinerney, and Feinberg have all espoused versions of the personhood strategy. They all realize that their use of the personhood strategy entails that they deal with the problem of infanticide. They all have offered special accounts of the immorality of infanticide. Each account is inadequate.

Are my standards for adequacy too high? Three considerations suggest that they are not. In the first place, on the FLO account, which is the competing account, the wrongness of infanticide is a perfectly straightforward matter, because infants have FLOs. In the second place, when we do moral philosophy of any sort, we want to be able to criticize accounts of morality on the grounds that they are too narrow, that they do not account for some of our obligations when our obligations are plain. If we allow obligations to be based on weak arguments, then philosophers who propose theories that are too narrow will always be able to meet criticism by appealing to weak *ad hoc* arguments. Thus, accepting arguments such as Paske's sets back our ability to do a significant bit of moral philosophy. In the third place, prochoice philosophers have (rightly in my view) criticized the weakness of prolife arguments that appeal to the humanity of the fetus. Such prolife arguments seem to be no weaker, however, than Paske's, McInerney's and Feinberg's arguments for the wrongness of infanticide. Prochoicers cannot have it both ways. I prefer their more stringent standards of argument.

IX

In my original essay, I argued that the concept of a future like ours plays an essential role in the correct analysis of the wrongness of killing and that the concept of person is not involved in the correct account. I also argued there that the essential role of a FLO and the inessential role of the concept of person in the correct account of the wrongness of killing provides a basis for showing that abortion is immoral. Both Gerald Paske and Peter McInerney have argued, on the contrary, that the FLO account of the immorality of abortion is incorrect because it does not acknowledge the essential role the concept of person plays in the correct account of the wrongness of killing. I have argued that they have failed to show that the concept of person is central to such an analysis. I have also argued that their accounts, like other personhood strategies, fail to account for the immorality of infanticide. Thus, unless some other challenge to the FLO analysis is successful, we have good reasons for believing that abortion is, except in unusual circumstances, immoral.

STUDY QUESTIONS

1. What does Marquis mean by "the future-like-ours account" of the ethics of abortion? Is it a clear thesis? Is he correct in his claims about it?

2. What are Marquis's arguments against the personhood strategy? Assess their merits.

3. How does Marquis respond to Paske's and McInerney's criticisms? Is he successful in rebutting these criticisms? Explain your answer.

NOTES

1. This view is elaborated and defended in more detail in my paper, "Why Abortion Is Immoral," *The Journal of Philosophy*, 86 (April 1989), 183–202.

2. The two classic versions of personhood strategies are those of Michael Tooley, "Abortion and Infanticide," *Philosophy* and *Public Affairs*, 2, 1 (1972), 37–65 and Mary Anne Warren, "On the Moral and Legal Status of Abortion," *Monist*, 58, 1 (1973), 43–61. Revised versions of the views of each can be found in Michael Tooley *Abortion and Infanticide,* New York: Oxford University Press, 1984, and Mary Anne Warren, "The Abortion Issue," in *Health Care Ethics,* Donald VanDeVeer and Tom Regan, eds., Philadelphia: Temple University Press, 1987, 184–214. Other important versions of the personhood strategy can be found in Joel Feinberg, "Abortion," *Matters of Life and Death: New Introductory Essays in Moral Philosophy,* Tom Regan, ed., New York: Random House, 1986, 256–293; H. Tristam Engelhardt, Jr., *The Foundations of Bioethics,* New York: Oxford University Press, 1986; and Stanley I. Benn, "Abortion, Infanticide, and Respect for Persons," in *The Problem of Abortion,* J. Feinberg, ed., Belmont, Calif.: Wadsworth, 1973.

3. Kant's account of our obligations toward animals has been often and rightly criticized. The reason that Kant has difficulty dealing with animals is that they are not persons and the concept of person is a central concept in Kant's ethical theory. Accordingly, the problem with his account and the infanticide problem are first cousins. See Immanuel Kant, *Lectures on Ethics,* Louis Infield, tr. New York: Harper Torchbooks, 1963, 239–241.

4. It is, of course, possible to speculate on the arguments McInerney might offer in defense of this claim, but an analysis based on such speculations would unduly lengthen this essay.

5. I am, for purposes of this argument, assuming the absence of important public policy considerations. In fact, of course, public policy considerations are of the greatest importance in the discussion of the morality of euthanasia.

6. This line of argument can be found in Epicurus, "Letter to Menoeceus." tr. C. Bailey, in *The Stoic and Epicurean Philosophers,* Whitney J. Oates ed. New York: Modern Library, 1940.

7. Fred Feldman has, I believe, laid this Epicurean problem to rest. See his excellent discussion in his *Confrontations with the Reaper: A Philosophical Study of the Nature and Valise of Death* (New York: Oxford University Press, 1992, Chapter 8.

8. See footnote 2.

9. Feinberg. "Abortion," 271.

10. There is reason to think that the long-run social costs of crack addiction and alcoholism during pregnancy are, and will be, substantial.

FOR FURTHER READING

Beckwith, Francis J. *Politically Correct Death: Answering the Arguments for Abortion Rights.* Grand Rapids, Mich.: Baker Books, 1993.

Brody, Baruch. *Abortion and the Sanctity of Human Life: A Philosophical View.* Cambridge, Mass.: MIT Press, 1975.

Callahan, Daniel. *Abortion Law, Choice and Morality.* New York: Macmillan, 1970.

Kamm, F.M. *Creation and Abortion: A Study in Moral and Legal Philosophy.* New York: Oxford University Press, 1992.

Norcross, Alastair. "Killing, Abortion, and Contraception: A Reply to Marquis." *Journal of Philosophy* 87 (May 1990).

Schwarz, Stephen D. *The Moral Question of Abortion.* Chicago: Loyola University Press, 1990.

PART VII

Feminist Arguments on Abortion

INTRODUCTION

Many varieties of feminism exist: liberal feminism, which emphasizes evolutionary reform rather than revolution; socialist feminism, which aims at restructuring the economic and social structures of society; and radical feminism, which aims at thoroughly transforming our way of looking at the world—to name the most prominent current varieties. Feminists, with notable exceptions, advocate a prochoice position on abortion, supporting its legalization. Although women such as Judith Jarvis Thomson, Jane English, Laura Purdy, and Mary Anne Warren were among the early supporters of a prochoice position of abortion, their arguments were based on traditional philosophical theories and concepts (for example, the right to use one's own body as one wishes, the nature of personhood). There was nothing especially distinctive about their arguments.

Recently, however, a growing number of feminists have argued for a distinctive feminist understanding of abortion. Appealing to insights from the work of Carole Gilligan, Sarah Ruddick, Nel Nodding, Annette Baier, and others, they juxtapose a feminine ethic of caring, nondualist egalitarianism, nonviolence, and openness to nature against the more male-oriented ethic of rationality, impartiality, dualism, hierarchical dominance, and power.

Other feminists seek to make us aware of the oppression of women in a male dominated "sexist" society and at the same time aware of a woman's perspective as the child-bearer who must face poverty, illegitimacy, rape, and neglect. Catherine MacKinnon in her article *"Roe v. Wade:* A Study in Male Ideology" (reprinted in Part III) argues that because in a male-dominated society women do not control their sexual behavior and so do not freely choose to engage in sexual intercourse, basing the right to an abortion on the right to privacy, as *Roe v. Wade* does, fails to come to grips with the problem of sexism in society.

Sally Markowitz, in our first selection "Abortion and Feminism," argues that although abortion is a bad thing, even if fetuses are persons, it is permissible for women in a sexist society to have abortions. Women are oppressed and so cannot be called on to make the tremendous sacrifice required by prohibiting abortions. This principle does not apply to fetuses, however, because fetuses are only disadvantaged, not oppressed. If men are really concerned about the rights of fetuses, they must work for an egalitarian society in which abortion would not be necessary.

Writer Naomi Wolf, in this section's second essay, argues for a prochoice feminism that is sensitive to the moral quandary undergirding the abortion decision for women. For this reason, Wolf suggests that the prochoice movement rethink its political rhetoric. Although she does not want to recriminalize abortion, she does want to inject moral judgment of abortion into the prochoice movement because, in her judgment, there is nothing inconsistent in defending the right to abortion while saying that abortion is in some cases not right. This, according to Wolf, will push the "mushy middle" in the abortion debate to the prochoice side.

In our third reading, Celia Wolf-Devine argues that a contradiction exists in the radical feminist movement. On the one hand, feminists advocate a rejection of "male" norms of rights-based ethics, power, dominance, impersonal judgment, and violence and, instead, profess to hold to a nurturing, relational, nonviolent, egalitarian ethic of love. On the other hand, they, all too often, advocate a male mode when it comes to abortion.

In our final essay Caroline Whitbeck argues that not only are women oppressed but they have not been taken seriously as persons. Few understand the hardship of being pregnant in our society: the vulnerability, risk of poverty, risk of fetal defects, stigma of illegitimacy, and threat of abuse by men. Women do not want abortions. They are grim options, but they must remain legal as the lesser of evils. A presumption exists that the pregnant woman is the best one to make a decision about whether to have an abortion.

24

⬛

A Feminist Defense of
Abortion

SALLY MARKOWITZ

Sally Markowitz teaches philosophy at Willamette University in Salem, Oregon. In this essay she argues that philosophical analysis of the abortion issue has neglected women and feminism. One must examine this issue in the context of a sexist society that oppresses women. Because of this oppression arguments for the personhood or non-personhood of fetuses or the autonomy of women are inadequate to deal with the morality of the issue. Markowitz appeals to two principles: the Feminist Proviso (that is, that women are oppressed) and the Impermissible Sacrifice Principle (that is, it is wrong to require oppressed groups to make sacrifices that will exacerbate this oppression) to argue for the moral right to abortion.

In the past few decades, the issue of abortion, long of concern to women, has gained a prominent place in the platforms of politicians and a respectable, if marginal, one in the writings of moral philosophers. It is natural to speculate that the rise of and reactions to the women's liberation movement explain the feverish pitch of the recent debate, and no doubt there is much to this speculation. And yet, philosophical analyses of abortion have had surprisingly little to say directly about either women or feminism. Instead, their primary concern has been to decide whether or not the fetus is a person, with a right to life like yours or mine. That this question deserves philosophical attention becomes especially clear when we consider the frightening (if fanciful) ways it is asked and answered by those in power. Nevertheless, as many feminists and

Reprinted from *Social Theory and Practice*, vol. 16.1 (Spring 1990) by permission.

some philosophers have recognized, the way we respond to the problem of personhood will not necessarily settle the dispute over abortion once and for all. On some views, a full account must deal with the rights of pregnant women as well.

In fact, one popular defense of abortion is based on the woman's right to autonomy and avoids the personhood issue altogether. The central claim of the autonomy defense is that anti–abortion policies simply interfere in an impermissible way with the pregnant woman's autonomy. In what has become the classic philosophical statement of this view, Judith Jarvis Thomson ingeniously argues that even if the fetus has a right to life, it need not also have the right to use its mother's body to stay alive. The woman's body is her own property, to dispose of as she wishes.[1] But autonomy theorists need not rest their case on the vaguely disturbing notion of the pregnant woman's property rights to her own body. For example, Jane English, in another version of the view, argues that a woman is justified in aborting if pregnancy and childbearing will prevent her from pursuing the life she wants to live, the expression of her own autonomy.[2]

Philosophers have come to call this strategy the "feminist" or "woman's liberation" approach, and indeed some version of it seems to be favored by many feminists.[3] This is no surprise since such a view may seem to be quite an improvement over accounts that regard personhood as the only essential issue. At least it recognizes women as bearers of rights as well as of babies. In what follows, however, I shall suggest that this defense may fall short of the feminist mark. Then I shall offer another defense, one derived not from the right to autonomy, but from an awareness of women's oppression and a commitment to a more egalitarian society.

I will assume throughout that the fetus has a serious right to life. I do so not because I believe this to be true, but rather because a feminist defense of abortion rights should be independent of the status of the fetus. For if, as many feminists believe, the move towards a sexually egalitarian society requires women's control of their reproductive lives, and if the permissibility of this control depends ultimately on the status of the fetus, then the future of feminism rests on how we resolve the personhood issue. This is not acceptable to most feminists. No doubt many feminists are comforted by arguments against the fetus's personhood. But regardless of the fetus's status, more must be said.

1

What, then, from a feminist point of view, is wrong with an autonomy defense? Feminists should be wary on three counts. First, most feminists believe not only that women in our society are oppressed, but also that our failure to face the scope and depth of this oppression does much to maintain it. This makes feminists suspicious of perspectives, often called humanist or liberal ones, that focus only on the individual and deemphasize the issue of gender by either refusing to acknowledge that women have less power than men or denying that this inequity is worth much attention. While liberals and humanists may try to discuss social issues, including abortion, with as little mention as possible of gender, feminists tend to search for the hidden, unexpected, and perhaps unwelcome ways in which gender is relevant. From this perspective, defenses of abortion that focus only on the personhood of the fetus are not essentially or even especially feminist defenses since they completely avoid any mention of gender. Autonomy arguments, though, are not much of an improvement. They may take into account the well-being of individual women, but they manage to skirt the issue of women's status, as a group, in a sexist society.

Second, the autonomy defense incorporates a (supposedly) gender-neutral right, one that belongs to every citizen; there's nothing special about being a woman—except, of course, for the inescapable fact that only women find themselves pregnant against their wills. Some feminists have become disillusioned with this gender-neutral approach. They reject it both on principle, because it shifts attention away from gender inequality, and for practical reasons, because it often works against women in the courts.[4] Instead, feminists have come to realize that sometimes gender should be relevant in claiming rights. Some of these rights, like adequate gynecological care, may be based on women's special physiology; others may stem from the special needs experienced by female casualties of a sexist society: the impoverished, divorced, or unwed mother, the rape victim, the anorexic teen, the coed who has been convinced that she lacks (or had better lack) mathematical aptitude. A thoroughly feminist analysis, then will not hesitate, when appropriate, to claim a right on the basis of gender, rather than in spite of it.[5] And to do otherwise in the case of abortion may be not only to deny the obvious, but also to obscure the relation of reproductive practices to women's oppression.

The third problem feminists might have with an autonomy defense involves the content of the human ideal on which the right to autonomy rests. Some feminists, influenced by Marxist and socialist traditions, may reject an ideal that seems to be so intimately connected with the individualistic ideology of capitalism. Others may suspect that this ideology is not just capitalist but male-biased. And if feminists hesitate to justify abortion by appeal to a gender-neutral right derived from a gender-neutral ideal, they are even more suspicious of an ideal that seems to be gender-neutral when really it's not. Increasingly, feminists reject the ideals of older feminists, like Simone de Beauvoir, who, in promoting for women what appeared to be an androgynous human ideal, unwittingly adopted one that was androcentric, or male-centered. Instead, feminists seek to free themselves from the misogynist perspective that sees women as incomplete men and ignores, devalues, or denies the existence of particularly female psychologies, values, and experiences. On this view, to fashion a feminist human ideal we must look to women's values and experiences—or, at least, we must not look only to men's.[6]

This reevaluation has important implications for the abortion issue because many feminists consider an overriding right to autonomy to be a characteristically male ideal, while nurturance and responsibility for others (the paradigmatic case of which, of course, is motherhood) to be characteristically female ones. Indeed, in the name of such women's values, some women who call themselves feminists have actually joined the anti-abortionist camp.[7] Most feminists, of course, don't go this far. But, paradoxically, many seem to find the ideal of autonomy less acceptable than the right to abortion it is supposed to justify. Clearly, something is awry. (I shall have more to say in section 4 about how autonomy is important to feminists.)

Feminists, therefore, need another argument. Instead of resting on an ideal many feminists reject, a feminist defense of abortion should somehow reflect an awareness of women's oppression and a commitment to ending it.

2

Of all the philosophers, feminist and otherwise, who have discussed abortion, Alison Jaggar seems to be the only one to address the problem from this perspective. Jaggar argues that in societies where mothers bear the responsibility for pregnancy, birth, and child-rearing, women should control abortion decisions. Women who live in other, more cooperative social communities (wherever they are), where members of both sexes share such responsibilities, cannot claim a right of the same force. The strength of a woman's say about whether or not to abort, then should be relative to the amount of support (financial, emotional, physical, medical and otherwise) she can expect from those around her.[8]

It is disheartening that the philosophical community has not paid Jaggar's paper the attention it merits in the decade and a half since its publication, but this lapse is hardly surprising. The notion of the individual's right to autonomy is so firmly entrenched that we have difficulty even entertaining other approaches. We find ourselves invoking such rights perhaps without realizing it even when we neither want nor need to. And, indeed, Jaggar is no exception; despite the promising intuition with which she starts, Jaggar finally offers us another, albeit more sophisticated, version of the autonomy argument. Quite simply, her argument implies that if abortion ought to be permissible in some societies but not in others, this is only because pregnancy and motherhood create obstacles to personal autonomy in some societies but not in others.

Jaggar bases her argument for abortion rights in our society on two principles. The first, or Right to Life principle, holds that

> the right to life, when it is claimed for a human being, means the right to a full human life and to whatever means are necessary to achieve this...To be born, then, is only one of the necessary conditions for a full human life. The others presumably include nutritious food, breathable air, warm human companionship, and so on. If anyone has a right to life, she or he must be entitled to all of these.[9]

According to the second, or Personal Control Principle, "Decisions should be made by those, and only by those, who are importantly affected by them."[10] In our society, then, the state cannot legitimately set itself up as the protector of the fetus's right to life (as Jaggar has characterized it) because the mother and not the state will be expected to provide for this right, both during pregnancy and afterwards. But since, by the Personal Control Principle, only those whose lives will be importantly affected have the right to make a decision, in our society the pregnant woman should determine whether to continue her pregnancy.

Jaggar's argument incorporates both liberal and feminist perspectives, and there is a tension between them. Her argument is feminist rather than merely liberal because it does not rest exclusively on a universal right to autonomy. Instead, it takes seriously the contingent and socially variable features of reproduction and parenting, their relationship to women's position in a society, and the effect of anti-abortion policy on this position. But her argument is also a liberal one. Consider, for example, the Personal Control Principle. While Jaggar doesn't explicitly spell out its motivation, she does state that the principle "provides the fundamental justification for democracy and is accepted by most shades of political opinion."[11] Surely this wide acceptance has something to do with the belief, equally widely held, that citizens should be able to decide for themselves what courses their lives should take, especially when some courses involve sacrifices or burdens. This becomes clear when Jaggar explains that an individual or organization has no moral claim as a protector of the right to life "that would justify its insistence on just one of the many conditions necessary to a full human life, in circumstances where this would place the burden of fulfilling all the other conditions squarely on the shoulders of some other individual or organization."[12] Once again we have an appeal to a universal right to personal autonomy, indeed a right based on an ideal that not only might be unacceptable to many feminists, but may cast the net too widely even for some liberals. For example, one might claim that taxation policies designed to finance social programs interfere with personal choices about how to spend earnings, a matter that will have important consequences for one's life. Such a view also permits a range of private actions that some liberals may believe are immoral: for example, an adult grandchild may decide to stop caring for a burdensome and senile grandparent if such care places a heavy burden on the grandchild.

I shall not attempt to pass judgment here on the desirability of either redistributing income through taxation or passing laws requiring us to be Good Samaritans in our private lives. Nor do I want to beg the question, which I shall discuss later, of whether reproductive autonomy is, in all circumstances, overridingly important in a way other sorts of autonomy may not be. I can leave these matters open because a feminist defense of abortion need not depend on how we settle them. For there is a significant difference between the sacrifices required by restrictive abortion policies and those required by enforcing other sorts of Good Samaritanism: taxes and laws against letting the aged or handicapped starve to death apply to everyone; those prohibiting abortion apply only to women. Although anyone might end up with a helpless, cantankerous grandparent and most of us end up paying taxes, only women end up pregnant. So anti-abortion laws require sacrifice not of everyone, but only of women.

3

This brings us to what I regard as the crucial question: When, if ever, can people be required to sacrifice for the sake of others? And how can feminists answer this question in a way that rests not on the individual right to personal autonomy, but on a view of social reality that takes seriously power relations between genders? I suggest the following principle, which I shall call the Impermissible Sacrifice Principle: *When one social group in a society is systematically oppressed by another, it is impermissible to require the oppressed group to make sacrifices that will exacerbate or perpetuate this oppression.* (Note that this principle does not exempt the members of oppressed groups from *all* sorts of sacrifices just because they are oppressed; they may be as morally responsible as anyone for rendering aid in some circumstances. Only sacrifices that will clearly perpetuate their oppression are ruled out.)

The Impermissible Sacrifice Principle focuses on power relationships between groups rather than on the rights of individuals. This approach will suit not only feminists but all who recognize and deplore other sorts of systematic social oppression as well. Indeed, if we take our opposition to oppression seriously, this approach may be necessary. Otherwise, when policy decisions are made, competing goals and commitments may distract us from the conditions we claim to deplore and encourage decisions that allow such conditions to remain. Even worse, these other goals and commitments can be used as excuses for perpetuating oppression. Testing policies against the Impermissible Sacrifice Principle keeps this from happening

Feminists should welcome the applicability of the Impermissible Sacrifice Principle to groups other than women. Radical feminists are sometimes accused of being blind to any sort of oppression but their own. The Impermissible Sacrifice Principle, however, enables feminists to demonstrate solidarity with other oppressed groups by resting the case for abortion on the same principle that might, for example, block a policy requiring the poor rather than the rich to bear the tax burden, or workers rather than management to take a pay cut. On the other hand, feminists may worry that the Impermissible Sacrifice Principle, taken by itself, may not yield the verdict on abortion feminists seek. For if some radical feminists err by recognizing only women's oppression, some men err by not recognizing it at all. So the Impermissible Sacrifice Principle must be supplemented by what I shall call the Feminist Proviso: *Women are, as a group, sexually oppressed by men, and this oppression can neither be completely understood in terms of, nor otherwise reduced to, oppressions of other sorts.*

Feminists often understand this oppression to involve men's treating women as breeding machines, sexual or aesthetic objects, nurturers who need no nurturance. Women become alienated from their bodies, their sexuality, their work, their intellect, their emotions, their moral agency. Of course, feminists disagree about exactly how to formulate this analysis, especially since women experience oppression differently depending on their class, race, and ethnicity. But however we decide to understand women's oppression, we can be sure an anti-abortion policy will make it worse.

Adding the Feminist Proviso, then, keeps (or makes) sexism visible, ensuring that women are one of the oppressed groups to which the Principle applies. This should hardly need saying. Yet by focusing on other sorts of oppression the Principle might cover, men often trivialize or ignore feminists' demands and women's pain. For example, someone (perhaps a white male) who is more sympathetic to the claims of racial minorities or workers than to those of women might try to trivialize or deny the sexual oppression of a white, affluent woman (perhaps his wife) by reminding her that she's richer than an unemployed black male and so should not complain. The Feminist Proviso also prevents an affluent white woman who rejects the unwelcome sexual advances of a minority or working class male from being dismissed (or dismissing herself) as a racist or classist. She may well be both. But she also lives in a world where, all things being equal, she is fair sexual game, in one way or another, for any male.[13] Finally, the Impermissible Sacrifice Principle in conjunction with the Feminist Proviso might be used to block the view that a black or Third World woman's first obligation is to bear children to swell the ranks of the revolution, regardless of the consequences of maternity within her culture. Having children for this reason may be a legitimate choice, but she also may have independent grounds to refuse.

I have added the Feminist Proviso so that the Impermissible Sacrifice Principle cannot be used to frustrate a feminist analysis. But I must also emphasize that the point is not to pit one oppressed group against another, but to make sure that the men in otherwise progressive social movements do not ignore women's oppression or, worse, find "politically correct" justifications for it. Women refuse to wait until "after the revolution" not just because they are impatient, but also because they have learned that not all revolutions are feminist ones.

The Impermissible Sacrifice Principle and the Feminist Proviso together, then, justify abortion on demand for women *because they live in a sexist society.* This approach not only gives a more explicitly feminist justification of abortion than the autonomy defense, it also gives a stronger one. For autonomy defenses are open to objections and qualifications that a feminist one avoids. Consider the ways the feminist approach handles these four challenges to the autonomy defense.

First, some philosophers have dismissed autonomy defenses by suggesting blithely that we simply compensate the pregnant woman.[14] Of what, though, will such compensation consist? Maternity leave? Tax breaks? Prenatal health care? Twenty points added to her civil-service exam score? Such benefits lighten one's load, no doubt. But what women suffer by being forced to continue unwanted pregnancies is not merely a matter of finances or missed opportunities; in a sexist society, there is reason to expect that an anti-abortion policy will reinforce a specifically *sexual* oppression, whatever sorts of compensation are offered. Indeed, even talk of compensation may be misguided because it implies a prior state when things were as they should be; compensation seeks to restore the balance after a temporary upset. But in a sexist society, there is no original balance; women's oppression is the status quo. Even if individual women are compensated by money, services, or opportunities, sexual oppression may remain.

Second, an autonomy defense may seem appropriate only in cases where a woman engages in "responsible" sex: It is one thing to be a victim of rape or even contraceptive failure, one might argue; it is quite another voluntarily to have unprotected intercourse. A feminist defense suggests another approach. First, we might question the double standard that requires that women pay for "irresponsible" sex while men don't have to, even though women are oppressed by men. More important, if we focus on the *way* women are oppressed, we may understand many unwanted pregnancies to result from fear and paralysis rather than irresponsibility. For in a sexist society, many women simply do not believe they can control the conditions under which they have sex. And, sad to say, often they may be right.[15]

Third, what about poor women's access to abortion? The sort of right the autonomy theorists invoke, after all, seems to be a right to noninterference by the state. But this negative right seems to be in tension with a demand for state-funded abortions, especially since not everyone supports abortion. At any rate, we will need another argument to justify the funding of abortion for poor women. The defense I suggest, however, is clearly committed to providing all women with access to abortion because to allow abortions only for those who can afford them forces poor women, who are doubly oppressed, to make special sacrifices. An egalitarian society must liberate all women, not just rich ones.

Finally, autonomy defenses allow, indeed invite, the charge that the choice to abort is selfish. Even Thomson finds abortion, while not unjust, often to be "selfish" or "indecent." Although she has deprived nothing of its rights, the woman who aborts has chosen self-interested autonomy over altruism in the same way one might choose to watch while a child starves. Of course, one is tempted to point out the (largely male) world of commerce and politics thrives on such "morally indecent" but legal actions. But then feminists are reduced to claiming a right to be as selfish as men are. Moreover, once the specter of selfishness is raised, this defense does not allow feminists to make enough of male anti-abortionists' motives. On an autonomy defense, these motives are simply not relevant, let alone damning, and feminists who dwell on them seem to be resorting to *ad hominems*. From a feminist perspective, however, abortion is a political issue, one that essentially concerns the interests of and power relations between men and women. Thus, what women and men can expect to gain or lose from an abortion policy becomes the point rather than the subject of *ad hominem* arguments.[16]

The approach I propose does well on each of these important counts. But its real test comes when we weight the demands of the Impermissible Sacrifice Principle against fetal rights; for we have required that a feminist analysis be independent of the status of the fetus. Indeed, we may even be tempted to regard fetuses as constituting just the sort of oppressed group to whom the principle applies, and surely a fetus about to be aborted is in worse shape than the woman who carries it.

However, it may not make sense to count fetuses as an oppressed group. A disadvantaged one, perhaps. But the Impermissible Sacrifice Principle does not prescribe that more disadvantaged groups have a right to aid from less disadvantaged ones; it focuses only on the particular disadvantage of social oppression. That the fetus has a serious right to life does not imply that it's the sort of being that can be oppressed, if it cannot yet enter into the sorts of social relationships that constitute oppression. I cannot argue for this here; in any case, I suspect my best argument will not convince everyone. But feminists have another, more pointed response.

Whether or not we can weigh the disadvantage of fetuses against the oppression of women, we must realize what insisting on such a comparison does to the debate. It narrows our focus, turning it back to the conflict between the rights of fetuses and of women (even if now this conflict is between the rights of groups rather than of individuals). This is certainly not to deny that fetal rights should be relevant to an abortion policy. But feminists must insist that the oppression of women should be relevant too. And it is also relevant that unless our society changes in deep and global ways, anti-abortion policies, intentionally or not, will perpetuate women's oppression by men. This, then, is where feminists must stand firm.

Does this mean that instead of overriding the fetus's right to life by women's rights to autonomy, I am proposing that feminists override the fetus's right by the right of women to live in a sexually egalitarian society? This is a difficult position for feminists but not an impossible one, especially for feminists with utilitarian leanings. Many feminists, for example, see sexism as responsible for a culture of death: war, violence, child abuse, ecological disaster. Eradicate sexism, it might be argued, and we will save more lives than we will lose. Some feminists might even claim that an oppressed woman's fate can be worse than that of an aborted fetus. Although I will not argue for such claims, they may be less implausible than they seem. But feminists need not rest their case on them. Instead, they may simply insist that society must change so that women are no longer oppressed. Such changes, of course, may require of men sacrifices unwelcome beyond their wildest dreams. But that, according to a feminist analysis, is the point.

So we should not see the choice as between liberating women and saving fetuses, but between two ways of respecting the fetus's right to life. The first requires women to sacrifice while men benefit. The second requires deep social changes that will ensure that men no longer gain and women lose through our practices of sexuality, reproduction, and parenthood. To point out how men gain from women's compulsory pregnancy is to steal the misplaced moral thunder from those male authorities—fathers, husbands, judges, congressmen, priests, philosopher—who, exhorting women to do their duty, present themselves as the benevolent, disinterested protectors of fetuses against women's selfishness. Let feminists insist that the condition for refraining from having abortions is a sexually egalitarian society. If men do not respond, and quickly, they will have indicated that fetal life isn't so important to them after all, or at least not important enough to give up the privileges of being male in a sexist society. If this makes feminists look bad, it makes men look worse still.

STUDY QUESTIONS

1. Why does Sally Markowitz think that the personhood arguments and autonomy arguments are inadequate to deal with the abortion issue? Is she correct?

2. Reflect on her two principles: the Feminist Proviso and the Impermissible Sacrifice Principle. Do you agree that they are valid principles? Do you think that they are adequate to justify abortion in the way Markowitz argues?

3. Do you agree with the author that the Impermissible Sacrifice Principle cannot be used to protect fetuses because fetuses are not oppressed, only disadvantaged? What is the relevant difference? Could one argue that fetuses are really more oppressed than women because women are not being killed simply because they are not wanted?

4. What are the implications of the Impermissible Sacrifice Principle? Suppose I belong to a group that is being oppressed by a majority. May I commit acts of kidnapping or murder of other innocent people if it will lessen my own oppression?

NOTES

1. Judith Jarvis Thomson, "A Defense of Abortion," *Philosophy and Public Affairs* 1 (1971): 47–66.

2. Jane English, "Abortion and the Concept of a Person," in *Today's Moral Problems,* ed. by Richard A. Wasserstrom. New York: Macmillan, 1985, 448–457.

3. Peter Singer, *Practical Ethics.* Cambridge: Cambridge University Press, 1979, 113.

4. Catherine A. MacKinnon, *Feminism Unmodified: Discourses on Life and Law.* Cambridge: Harvard University Press, 1987, 35–36.

5. See, for example, Alison Jaggar, *Feminism Politics and Human Nature.* Totowa, New Jersey: Rowman and Allanheld, 1983, especially Parts One and Two; and Catharine A. MacKinnon, *Feminism Unmodified: Discourses on Life and Law.*

6. See Sara Ruddick, "Maternal Thinking," *Feminist Studies* 6 (1980): 345–346; Nancy Chodorow, *The Reproduction of Mothering: Psychoanalysis and the Sociology of Gender,* Berkeley and Los Angeles: University of California Press, 1978; Carol Gilligan, *In a Different Voice: Psychological Theory and Women's Development,* Cambridge: Harvard University Press, 1982.

7. Sidney Callahan, "A Pro-Life Feminist Makes Her Case," *Commonweal* (April 25, 1986), quoted in the *Utne Reader* 20 (1987): 104–108.

8. Alison Jaggar, "Abortion and a Woman's Right to Decide," in *Philosophy and Sex,* ed. Robert Baker and Frank Elliston. Buffalo: Prometheus Press, 1975, 324–337.

9. Ibid., 328.

10. Ibid., 328.

11. Ibid., 329.

12. For classic discussions of sexism in the civil rights movement, see Susan Brownmiller, *Against Our Will: Men, Women, and Rape,* New York: Simon and Schuster, 1975, especially 210–255; and Michelle Wallace, *Black Macho and the Myth of the Superwoman,* New York: Dial Press, 1978.

13. [This reference, apparently to Jaggar, is missing in the original—Eds.]

14. Michael Tooley, "Abortion and Infanticide," in Joel Feinberg, ed., *The Problem of Abortion.* Belmont, Calif.: Wadsworth, 1983.

15. MacKinnon, *Feminism Unmodified,* 95.

16. This approach also allows us to understand the deep divisions between women on this issue. For many women in traditional roles fear the immediate effects on their lives of women's liberation generally and a permissive abortion policy in particular. On this, see Kristen Luker, *Abortion and the Politics of Motherhood,* Berkeley: University of California Press, 1984, especially 158–215.

25

Our Bodies, Our Souls

NAOMI WOLF

Naomi Wolf is a social commentator and bestselling author who has published widely on a variety of topics relating to feminism and American culture. According to Wolf, prochoice feminists should shift their political rhetoric to a moral framework that would truly capture the sentiments of a majority of Americans: Abortion is a moral tragedy, though it should be legally permitted at least in the first trimester of pregnancy. Wolf maintains that many prochoice feminists have dehumanized the fetus to draw attention to the legitimate plight of pregnant women in a patriarchal society. Unfortunately, writes Wolf, this strategy treats the fetus as a valueless blob, which it is not. In addition, it reduces the abortion decision to something less than a moral quandary because killing what is valueless cannot be morally problematic. Yet, explains Wolf, this is not the experience of a vast majority of women who have been pregnant, given birth, or have had abortions. This is why Wolf suggests that prochoice feminists obey what she calls "the first commandment of real feminism: When in doubt, listen to women."

I had an abortion when I was a single mother and my daughter was two years old. I would do it again. But you know how in the Greek myths when you kill a relative you are pursued by furies? For months, it was as if baby furies were pursuing me.

These are not the words of a benighted, superstition-ridden teenager lost in America's cultural backwaters. They are the words of a Cornell-educated, urban-dwelling, Democratic-voting 40-year-old cardiologist—I'll call her

Published by permission from *The New Republic* (16 October 1995).

Clare. Clare is exactly the kind of person for whom being prochoice is an un-shakable conviction. If there were a core constituent of the movement to se-cure abortion rights, Clare would be it. And yet: Her words are exactly the words to which the prochoice movement is not listing.

At its best, feminism defends its moral high ground by being simply faithful to the truth: to women's real-life experiences. But, to its own ethical and politi-cal detriment, the prochoice movement has relinquished the moral frame around the issue of abortion. It has ceded the language of right and wrong to abortion foes. The movement's abandonment of what Americans have always, and rightly, demanded of their movements—an ethical core—and its reliance instead on a political rhetoric in which the fetus means nothing are proving fatal.

The effects of this abandonment can be measured in two ways. First, such a position causes us to lose political ground. By refusing to look at abortion within a moral framework, we lose the millions of Americans who want to support abortion as a legal right but still need to condemn it as a moral iniq-uity. Their ethical allegiances are then addressed by the prolife movement, which is willing to speak about good and evil.

But we are also in danger of losing something more important than votes; we stand in jeopardy of losing what can only be called our souls. Clinging to a rhetoric about abortion in which there is no life and no death, we entangle our beliefs in a series of self-delusions, fibs, and evasions. And we risk becom-ing precisely what our critics charge us with being: callous, selfish and casually destructive men and women who share a cheapened view of human life.

In the following pages, I will argue for a radical shift in the prochoice movement's rhetoric and consciousness about abortion: I will maintain that we need to contextualize the fight to defend abortion rights within a moral framework that admits that the death of a fetus is a real death; that there are degrees of culpability, judgment, and responsibility involved in the decision to abort a pregnancy; that the best understanding of feminism involves holding women as well as men to the responsibilities that are inseparable from their rights; and that we need to be strong enough to acknowledge that this coun-try's high rate of abortion—which ends more than a quarter of all pregnan-cies—can only be rightly understood as what Dr. Henry Foster was brave enough to call it: "a failure."

Any doubt that our current prochoice rhetoric leads to disaster should be dispelled by the famous recent defection of the woman who had been Jane Roe. What happened to Norma McCorvey? To judge by her characterization in the elite media and by some prominent prochoice feminists, nothing very impor-tant. Her change of heart about abortion was relentlessly "explained away" as having everything to do with the girlish motivations of insecurity, fickleness, and the need for attention, and little to do with any actual moral agency.

This dismissive (and, not incidentally, sexist and classist) interpretation was so highly colored by subjective impressions offered by the very institutions that define objectivity that it bore all the hallmarks of an exculpatory cultural myth: Poor Norma—she just needed stroking. She was never very stable, the old dear—first she was a chess-piece for the prochoice movement ("just some anonymous person who suddenly emerges," in the words of one NOW member) and then a codependent of the Bible-thumpers. Low self-esteem, a history of substance abuse, ignorance—these and other personal weaknesses explained her turnaround.

To me, the first commandment of real feminism is when in doubt, listen to women. What if we were to truly, respectfully listen to this woman who began her political life as, in her words, just "some little old Texas girl who got in trouble"? We would have to hear this: Perhaps Norma McCorvey actually had a revelation that she could no longer live as the symbol of a belief system she increasingly repudiated.

Norma McCorvey should be seen as an object lesson for the prochoice movement—a call to us to search our souls and take another, humbler look at how we go about what we are doing. For McCorvey is in fact an American Everywoman: She is the lost middle of the abortion debate, the woman whose allegiance we forfeit by our refusal to use a darker and sterner and more honest moral rhetoric. McCorvey is more astute than her critics; she seems to understand better than the prochoice activists she worked with just what the woman-in-the-middle believes: "I believe in the woman's right to choose. I'm like a lot of people. I'm in the mushy middle," she said. McCorvey still supports abortion rights through the first trimester—but is horrified by the brutality of abortion as it manifests more obviously further into a pregnancy. She does not respect the black-and-white ideology on either side and insists on referring instead, as I understand her explanation, to her conscience. What McCorvey and other Americans want and deserve is an abortion-rights movement willing publicly to mourn the evil—necessary evil though it may be—that is abortion. We must have a movement that acts with moral accountability and without euphemism.

With the prochoice rhetoric we use now, we incur three destructive consequences—two ethical, one strategic: hardness of heart, lying, and political failure.

Because of the implication of a Constitution that defines rights according to the legal ideal of "a person," the abortion debate has tended to focus on the question of "personhood" of the fetus. Many prochoice advocates developed a language to assert that the fetus isn't a person, and this, over the years, has developed into a lexicon of dehumanization. Laura Kaplan's *The Story of Jane,* an important forthcoming account of a pre-*Roe* underground abortion service, inadvertently sheds light on the origins of some of this rhetoric: Service staffers referred to the fetus—well into the fourth month—as "material" (as in "the amount of material that had to be removed..."). The activists felt exhilaration at learning to perform abortions themselves instead of relying on male doctors: "When [a staffer] removed the speculum and said, 'There, all done,' the room exploded in excitement." In an era when women were dying of illegal abortion, this was the understandable exhilaration of an underground resistance movement.

Unfortunately, though, this cool and congratulatory rhetoric lingers into a very different present. In one woman's account of her chemical abortion, in the January/February 1994 issue of *Mother Jones,* for example, the doctor says,

"By Sunday you won't see on the monitor *what we call the heartbeat*" (my italics). The author of the article, D. Redman, explains that one of the drugs the doctor administered would "end the growth of the fetal tissue." And we all remember Dr. Joycelyn Elders's remark, hailed by some as refreshingly frank and pro-woman, but which I found remarkably brutal: "We really need to get over this love affair with the fetus...."

How did we arrive at this point? In the early 1970s, Second Wave feminism adopted this rhetoric in response to the reigning ideology in which motherhood was invoked as an excuse to deny women legal and social equality. In a climate in which women risked being defined as mere vessels while their fetuses were given "personhood" at their expense, it made sense that women's advocates would fight back by depersonalizing the fetus. The feminism complaint about the prolife movement's dehumanization of the pregnant woman in relation to the humanized fetus is familiar and often quite valid: *The Silent Scream* portrayed the woman as "a vessel"; Ellen Frankfort's *Vaginal Politics,* the influential feminist text, complained that the fetus is treated like an astronaut in a spaceship.

But, say what you will, pregnancy confounds Western philosophy's idea of the autonomous self: The pregnant woman is in fact both a person in her body and a vessel. Rather than seeing both beings as alive and interdependent—seeing life within life—and acknowledging that sometimes, nonetheless, the woman must choose her life over the fetus's, Second Wave feminists reacted to the dehumanization of women by dehumanizing the creatures within them. In the death-struggle to wrest what Simone de Beauvoir called transcendence out of biological immanence, some feminists developed a rhetoric that defined the unwanted fetus as at best valueless; at worst an adversary, a "mass of dependent protoplasm."

Yet that has left us with a bitter legacy. For when we defend abortion rights by emptying the act of moral gravity we find ourselves cultivating a hardness of heart.

Having become pregnant through her partner's and her own failure to use a condom, Redman remarks that her friend Judith, who has been trying to find a child to adopt, begs her to carry the pregnancy to term. Judith offers Redman almost every condition a birth-mother could want: "'Let me have the baby,'" she quotes her friend pleading. "'You could visit her anytime, and if you ever wanted her back, I promise I would let her go.'" Redman does not mention considering this possibility. Thinking, rather about the difficulty of keeping the child—"My time consumed by the tedious, daily activities that I've always done my best to avoid. Three meals a day. Unwashed laundry..."—she schedules her chemical abortion.

The procedure is experimental, and the author feels "almost heroic," thinking of how she is blazing a trail for other women. After the abortion process is underway, the story reaches its perverse epiphany: Redman is on a Women's Day march when the blood from the abortion first appears. She exults at this: "'Our bodies, our lives, our right to decide.'...My life feels luxuriant with possibility. For one precious moment, I believe that we have the power to dismantle this system. I finish the march, borne along by the women...." As for the pleading Judith, with everything she was ready to offer a child, and the phantom baby? They are both off-stage, silent in this chilling drama of "feminist" triumphalism.

And why should we expect otherwise? In this essay, the fetus (as the author writes, "the now-inert material from my womb" is little more than a form of speech: a vehicle to assert the author's identity and autonomy.

The prolife warning about the potential of widespread abortion to degrade reverence for life does have a nugget of truth: A free-market rhetoric about abortion can, indeed, contribute to the eerie situation we are now facing, wherein the culture seems increasingly to see babies not as creatures to whom parents devote their lives but as accouterments to enhance parental quality of life. Day by day, babies seem to have less value in themselves, in a matrix of the sacred, than they do as products with a value dictated by a market economy.

Stories surface regularly about "worthless" babies left naked on gratings or casually dropped out of windows, while "valuable," genetically correct babies are created at vast expense and with intricate medical assistance for infertile couples. If we fail to treat abortion with grief and reverence, we risk forgetting that, when it comes to the children we choose to bear, we are here to serve them—whomever they are; they are not here to serve us.

Too often our rhetoric leads us to tell untruths. What Norma McCorvey wants, it seems, is for abortion-rights advocates to face, really face, what we are doing: "Have you ever seen a second-trimester abortion?" she asks. "It's a baby. It's got a face and a body, and they put him in a freezer and a little container."

Well, so it does; and so they do.

The prochoice movement often treats with contempt the prolifers' practice of holding up to our faces their disturbing graphics. We revile their placards showing an enlarged scene of the aftermath of a D & C abortion; we are disgusted by their lapel pins with the little feet, crafted in gold, of a 10-week-old fetus; we mock the sensationalism of *The Silent Scream*. We look with pity and horror at someone who would brandish a fetus in formaldehyde—and we are quick to say that they are lying: "Those are stillbirths, anyway," we tell ourselves.

To many prochoice advocates, the imagery is revolting propaganda. There is a sense among us, let us be frank, that the gruesomeness of the imagery *belongs* to the prolifers; that it emerges from the dark, frightening minds of fanatics; that is represents the violence of imaginations that would, given half a chance, turn our world into a scary, repressive place. "People like us" see such material as the pornography of the prolife movement.

But feminism at its best is based on what is simply true. While prolifers have not been beyond dishonesty, distortion, and the doctoring of images (preferring, for example, to highlight the results of very late, very rare abortions), many of those photographs are in fact the footprints of a 10-week-old fetus; the prolife slogan, "Abortion stops a beating heart," is incontrovertibly true. While images of violent fetal death work magnificently for prolifers as political polemic, the pictures are not polemical in themselves: They are bio-logical facts. We know this.

Since abortion became legal nearly a quarter-century ago, the fields of embryology and perinatology have been revolutionized—but the prochoice view of the contested fetus has remained static. This has led to a bizarre bifur-cation in the way we who are prochoice tend to think about wanted as op-posed to unwanted fetuses; the unwanted ones are still seen in schematic black-and-white drawings while the wanted ones have metamorphosed into vivid and moving color. Even while Elders spoke of our need to "get over" our love affair with the unwelcome fetus, an entire growth industry—Mozart for your belly; framed sonogram photos; home fetal-heartbeat stethoscopes—is devoted to sparking fetal love affairs in other circumstances and aimed espe-cially at the hearts of overscheduled yuppies. If we avidly cultivate love for the ones we bring to term, and "get over" our love for the ones we don't, do we not risk developing a hydroponic view of babies—and turn them into a prod-uct we can cull for our convenience?

Any happy couple with a wanted pregnancy and a copy of *What to Expect When You're Expecting* can see the cute, detailed drawing of the fetus whom the book's owner presumably is not going to abort and can read the excited descriptions of what that fetus can do and feel, month by month. Anyone who has had a sonogram during pregnancy knows perfectly well that the four-month-old fetus responds to outside stimulus—"Let's get him to look this way," the technician will say, poking gently at the belly of a delighted mother-to-be. *The Well Baby Book,* the kind of whole-grain, holistic guide to preg-nancy and childbirth that would find its audience among the very demographic that is most solidly prochoice reminds us that "Increasing knowl-edge is increasing the awe and respect we have for the unborn baby and is causing us to regard the unborn baby as a real person long before birth...."

So, what will it be: Wanted fetuses are charming, complex, REM-dreaming little beings whose profile on the sonogram looks just like Daddy, but unwanted ones are mere "uterine material"? How can we charge that it is vile and repul-sive for prolifers to brandish vile and repulsive images if the images are real? To insist that the truth is in poor taste is the very height of hypocrisy. Besides, if these images *are* often the facts of the matter, and if we then claim that it is of-fensive for prochoice women to be confronted by them, then we are making the judgment that women are too inherently weak to face a truth about which they have to make a grave decision. This view of women is unworthy of femi-nism. Free women must be strong women, too; and strong women, presum-ably, do not seek to cloak their most important decisions in euphemism.

Other lies are not lies to others, but to ourselves. An abortion–clinic doc-tor, Elizabeth Karlin, who wrote a recent "Hers" column in *The New York Times,* declared that "There is only one reason I've ever heard for having an abortion: the desire to be a good mother."

While that may well be true for many poor and working-class women—and indeed research shows that poor women are three time more likely to have abortions than are better-off women—the elite, who are the most vociferous in their morally unambiguous prochoice language, should know perfectly well how untrue that statement often is in their own lives. All abortions occupy a spectrum, from full lack of alternatives to full moral accountability. Karlin and many other prochoice activists try to situate all women equally at the extreme endpoint of that spectrum, and it just isn't so. Many women, including middle-class women, do have abortions because, as one such woman put it, "They have a notion of what a good mother is and don't feel they can be that kind of mother at this phase of their lives." In many cases, that is still a morally defensible place on the spectrum, but it is not the place of absolute absolution that Dr. Karlin claims it to be. It is, rather, a place of moral struggle, of self-interest mixed with selflessness, of wished-for-good intermingled with necessary evil.

Other abortions occupy places on the spectrum that are far more culpable. Of the abortions I know of, these were some of the reasons: to find out if the woman could get pregnant; to force a boy or man to take a relationship more seriously; and, again and again, to enact a rite of passage for affluent teenage girls. In my high school, the abortion drama was used to test a boyfriend's character. Seeing if he would accompany the girl to the operation or, better yet, come up with the money for the abortion could almost have been the 1970s Bay Area equivalent of the '50s fraternity pin.

The affluent teenage couples who conceive because they can and then erase the consequences—and the affluent men and women who choose abortion because they were careless or in a hurry or didn't like the feel of latex— are not the moral equivalent of the impoverished mother who responsibly, even selflessly, acknowledges she already has too many mouths to feed. Feminist rights include feminist responsibilities; the right to obtain an abortion brings with it the responsibility to contracept. Fifty-seven percent of unintended pregnancies come about because the parents used no contraception at all. Those millions certainly include women and men too poor to buy contraception, girls and boys too young and ill-informed to know where to get it, and countless instances of marital rape, coerced sex, incest, and couplings in which the man refused to let the woman use protection.

But they also include millions of college students, professional men and women, and middle- and upper-middle-class people (11 percent of abortions are obtained by people in households with incomes of higher than $50,000)— who have no excuse whatsoever for their carelessness. "There is only one reason I've ever heard for having an abortion: the desire to be a good mother"—this is a falsehood that condescends to women struggling to be true agents of their own souls, even as it dishonors through hypocrisy the terminations that are the writer's subject.

Not to judge other men and women without judging myself, I know this assertion to be false from my own experience. Once, I made the choice to take a morning-after pill. The heavily pregnant doctor looked at me, as she dispensed it, as if I were the scum of the earth.

If what was going on in my mind had been mostly about the well-being of the possible baby, that pill would never have been swallowed. For that potential baby, brought to term, would have had two sets of loving middle-income grandparents, an adult mother with an education and even, as I discovered later, the beginning of diaper money for its first two years of life (the graduate fellowship I was on forbade marriage but, frozen in time before women were its beneficiaries, said nothing about unwed motherhood). Because of the baby's skin color, even if I chose not to rear the child, a roster of eager adoptive parents awaited him or her. If I had been thinking only or even primarily about the baby's life, I would have had to decide to bring the pregnancy, had there been one, to term.

No: there were two columns in my mind—"Me" and "Baby"—and the first won out. And what was in it looked something like this: unwelcome intensity in the relationship with the father; desire to continue to "develop as a person" before "real" parenthood; wish to encounter my eventual life partner without the off-putting encumbrance of a child; resistance to curtailing the nature of the time remaining to me in Europe. Essentially, this column came down to this: I am not done being responsive only to myself yet.

At even the possibility that the cosmos was calling my name, I cowered and stepped aside. I was not so unlike those young louts who father children and run from the specter of responsibility. Except that my refusal to be involved with this potential creature was as definitive as a refusal can be.

Stepping aside in this way is analogous to draft evasion; there are good and altruistic reasons to evade the draft, and then there are self-preserving reasons. In that moment, feminism came to one of its logical if less-than-inspiring moments of fruition: I chose to sidestep biology; I acted—and was free to act—as if I were in control of my destiny, the way men more often than women have let themselves act. I chose myself on my own terms over a possible someone else, for self-absorbed reasons. But "to be a better mother"? "*Dulce et decorum est...*"? Nonsense.

Now, freedom means that women must be free to choose self or to choose selfishly. Certainly for a woman with fewer economic and social choices than I had—for instance, a woman struggling to finish her higher education, without which she would have little hope of a life worthy of her talents—there can indeed be an *obligation* to choose self. And the defense of some level of abortion rights as fundamental to women's integrity and equality has been made fully by others, including, quite effectively, Ruth Bader Ginsberg. There is no easy way to deny the powerful argument that a woman's equality in society must give her some irreducible rights unique to her biology, including the right to take the life within her life.

But we don't have to lie to ourselves about what we are doing at such a moment. Let us at least look with clarity at what that means and not whitewash self-interest with the language of self-sacrifice. The landscape of many such decisions looks more like Marin County than Verdun. Let us certainly not be fools enough to present such spiritually limited moments to the world with a flourish of pride, pretending that we are somehow pioneers and heroines and even martyrs to have snatched the self, with its aims and pleasures, for the pressure of biology.

That decision was not my finest moment. The least I can do, in honor of the being that might have been, is simply to know that.

Using amoral rhetoric, we weaken ourselves politically because we lose the center. To draw an inexact parallel, many people support the choice to limit the medical prolongation of life. But, if a movement arose that spoke of our "getting over our love affair" with the terminally ill, those same people would recoil into a vociferous interventionist position as a way to assert their moral values. We would be impoverished by a rhetoric about the end of life that speaks of the ill and dying as if they were meaningless and of doing away with them as if it were a bracing demonstration of our personal independence.

Similarly, many people support necessary acts of warfare (Catholics for a Free Choice makes the analogy between abortion rights and such warfare). There are legal mechanisms that allow us to bring into the world the evil of war. But imagine how quickly public opinion would turn against a president who waged war while asserting that our sons and daughters were nothing but cannon fodder. Grief and respect are the proper tones for all discussions about choosing to endanger or destroy a manifestation of life.

War is legal; it is sometime even necessary. Letting the dying die in peace is often legal and sometimes even necessary. Abortion should be legal; it is sometimes even necessary. Sometimes the mother must be able to decide that the fetus, in its full humanity, must die. But it is never right or necessary to minimize the value of the lives involved or the sacrifice incurred in letting them go. Only if we uphold abortion rights within a matrix of individual conscience, atonement, and responsibility can we both correct the logical and ethical absurdity in our position—and consolidate the support of the center.

Many others, of course, have wrestled with this issue: Camille Paglia, who has criticized the "convoluted casuistry" of some prochoice language; Roger Rosenblatt, who has urged us to permit but discourage abortion; Laurence Tribe, who has noted that we place the fetus in shadow in order to advance the prochoice argument. But we have yet to make room for this conversation at the table of mainstream feminism.

And we can't wait much longer. Historical changes—from the imminent availability of cheap chemical abortifacients to the ascendancy of the religious right to Norma McCorvey's defection—make the need for a new abortion-rights language all the more pressing.

In a time of retrenchment, how can I be so sure that a more honest and moral rhetoric about abortion will consolidate rather than scuttle abortion rights? Look at what Americans themselves say. When a recent *Newsweek* poll asked about support for abortion using the rare phrasing, "It's a matter between a woman, her doctor, her family, her conscience and her God," a remarkable 72 percent of the respondents called that formulation "about right." This represents a gain of thirty points over the abortion-rights support registered in the latest Gallup poll, which asked about abortion without using the words "God" or "conscience." When participants in the Gallup poll were asked if they supported abortion "under any circumstances" only 32 percent agreed; only 9 percent more supported it under "most" circumstances. Clearly abortion rights are safest when we are willing to submit them to a morality beyond just our bodies and our selves.

But how, one might ask, can I square a recognition of the humanity of the fetus, and the moral gravity of destroying it, with a prochoice position? The answer can only be found in the context of a paradigm abandoned by the left and misused by the right: the paradigm of sin and redemption.

It was when I was four months pregnant, sick as a dog, and in the middle of an argument, that I realized I could no longer tolerate the fetus-is-nothing paradigm of the prochoice movement. I was being interrogated by a conservative, and the subject of abortion rights came up. "You're four months pregnant," he said. "Are you going to tell me that's not a baby you're carrying?"

The accepted prochoice response at such a moment in the conversation is to evade: to move as swiftly as possible to a discussion of "privacy" and "difficult personal decisions" and "choice." Had I not been so nauseated and so cranky and so weighed down with the physical gravity of what was going on inside me, I might not have told what is the truth for me. "Of course it's a baby," I snapped. And went rashly on: "And if I found myself in circumstances in which I had to make the terrible decision to end this life, then that would be between myself and God."

Startlingly to me, two things happened: The conservative was quiet; I had said something that actually made sense to him. And I felt the great relief that is the grace of long-delayed honesty.

Now, the G-word is certainly a problematic element to introduce into the debate. And yet "God" or "soul"—or, if you are secular and prefer it, "conscience"—is precisely what is missing from prochoice discourse. There is a crucial difference between "myself and my God" or "my conscience"—terms that imply moral accountability—and "myself and my doctor" the phrasing that Justice Harry Blackmun's working in *Roe* ("inherently, and primarily, a medical decision") has tended to promote in the prochoice movement. And that's not even to mention "between myself and myself" (Elders: "It's not anybody's business if I went for an abortion"), which implies just the relativistic relationship to abortion that our critics accuse us of sustaining.

The language we use to make our case limits the way we let ourselves think about abortion. As a result of the precedents in *Roe* (including *Griswold v. Connecticut* and *Eisenstadt v. Baird*), which based a woman's right to an abortion on the Ninth and Fourteenth Amendments' implied right to personal privacy, other unhelpful terms are also current in our discourse. Prochoice advocates tend to cast an abortion as "an intensely personal decision." To which we can say, No: one's choice of *carpeting* is an intensely personal decision. One's struggles with a life-and-death issue must be understood as a matter of personal conscience. There is a world of difference between the two, and it's the difference a moral frame makes.

Stephen L. Carter has pointed out that spiritual discussion has been robbed of a place in American public life. As a consequence we tend—often disastrously—to use legislation to work out right and wrong. That puts many in the position of having to advocate against abortion rights in order to proclaim their conviction that our high rate of avoidable abortion (one of the highest in developed countries, five times that of the Netherlands, for example) is a social evil, and, conversely, many must pretend that abortion is not a transgression of any kind if we wish to champion abortion rights. We have no ground on which to say that abortion is a necessary evil that should be faced and opposed in the realm of conscience and action and even soul; yet remain legal.

But American society is struggling to find its way forward to a discourse of right and wrong that binds together a common ethic for the secular and the religious. When we do that, we create a moral discourse that can exist in its own right independent of legislation, and we can find ground to stand on.

Norma McCorvey explained what happened to her in terms of good and evil: She woke in the middle of the night and felt a presence pushing violently down on her. "I denounce you, Satan," she announced. This way of talking about evil is one of the chief class divisions in America: Working-class people talk about Satan, and those whom Paul Fussell calls "the X group"—those who run the country—talk instead about neurotic guilt. While the elite scoff at research that shows that most Americans maintain a belief in the embodiment of evil—"the devil"—they miss something profound about the human need to make moral order out of chaos. After all, the only real difference between the experience described by Clare, the Cornell-educated prochoicer, and McCorvey, the uneducated ex-alcoholic, is a classical allusion.

There is a hunger for a moral framework that we prochoicers must reckon with. In the Karlin "Hers" column, the author announced proudly that pregnant women are asked by the counselor in the office, "So, how long have you been prochoice?" Dr. Karlin writes that "laughter and the answer, 'About ten minutes,' is the healthiest response. 'I still don't believe in abortion,' some women say, unaware that refusal to take responsibility for the decision means that I won't do the procedure."

How is this "feminist" ideological coercion any different from the worst of prolife shaming and coercion? The women who come to a clinic that is truly feminist—that respects women—are entitled not only to their abortions but also to their sense of sin.

To use the term "sin" in this context does not necessarily mean, as Dr. Karlin believes, that a woman thinks she must go to hell because she is having an abortion. It may mean that she has fallen short of who she should be, and that she needs to ask forgiveness for that, and atone for it. As I understand such a woman's response, she *is* trying to take responsibility for the decision.

We on the left tend to twitch with discomfort at that word "sin." Too often we have become religiously illiterate, and so we deeply misunderstand the word. But in all of the great religious traditions, our recognition of sin, and then our atonement for it, brings on God's compassion and our redemption. In many faiths, justice is linked, as it is in medieval Judaism and in Buddhism, to compassion. From Yom Kippur and the Ash Wednesday-to-Easter cycle to the Hindu idea of karma, the individual's confrontation with her or his own culpability is the first step toward ways to create and receive more light.

How could one live with a conscious view that abortion is an evil and still be prochoice? Through acts of redemption, or what the Jewish mystical tradition calls *tikkun;* or "mending." Laurence Tribe, in *Abortion: The Clash of Absolutes,* notes that "Memorial services for the souls of aborted fetuses are fairly common in contemporary Japan," where abortions are both legal and readily available. Shinto doctrine holds that women should make offerings to the fetus to help it rest in peace; Buddhists once erected statues of the spirit guardian of children to honor aborted fetuses (called "water children" or "unseeing children"). If one believes that abortion is killing and yet is still prochoice, one could try to use contraception for every single sex act; if one had to undergo an abortion, one could then work to provide contraception, or jobs, or other choices to young girls; one could give money to programs that provide prenatal care to poor women; if one is a mother or father, one can remember the aborted child every time one is tempted to be less than loving—and give renewed love to the living child. And so on: *tikkun.*

But when you insist, as the "Hers" column writer did, on stripping people of their sense of sin, they react with a wholesale backing-away into a rigid morality that reimposes order: hence, the ascendancy of the religious right.

Just look at the ill-fated nomination of Dr. Henry Foster for Surgeon General. The Republicans said "abortion," and the discussion was over. The Democrats, had they worked out a moral framework for progressivism, could have responded, "Yes: Our abortion rate is a terrible social evil. Here is a man who can help put a moral framework around the chaos of a million and a half abortions a year. He can bring that rate of evil down. And whichever senator among you has ever prevented an unplanned pregnancy—and Dr. Foster has—let him ask the first question."

Who gets blamed for our abortion rate? The ancient Hebrews had a ritual of sending a "scapegoat" into the desert with the community's sins projected on it. Abortion doctors are our contemporary scapegoats. The prolifers obviously scapegoat them in one way: If prolifers did to women what they do to abortion doctors—harassed and targeted them in their homes and workplaces—public opinion would rapidly turn against them; for the movement would soon find itself harassing the teachers and waitresses, housewives and younger sisters of their own communities. The prolife movement would have to address the often all-too-pressing good reasons that lead good people to abort. That would be intolerable, a tactical defeat for the prolife movement, and as sure to lose it "the mushy middle" as the prochoice movement's tendency toward rhetorical coldness loses it the same constituency.

But prochoicers, too, scapegoat the doctors and clinic workers. By resisting a moral framework in which to view abortion, we who are pro-abortion-rights leave the doctors in the front lines, with blood on their hands: the blood of repeat abortions—at least 43 percent of the total; the suburban summer country-club rite-of-passage abortions; the "I don't know what came over me, it was such good Chardonnay" abortions; as well as the blood of the desperate and the unpreventable and accidental and the medically necessary and the violently conceived abortions. This is blood that the doctors and clinic workers often see clearly, and that they heroically rinse and cause to flow and rinse again. And they take all our sins, the prochoice as well as the prolife among us, on themselves.

And we who are prochoice compound their isolation by declaring that that blood is not there.

As the world changes and women, however incrementally, become more free and more powerful, the language in which we phrase the goals of feminism must change as well. As a result of the bad old days before the Second Wave of feminism, we tend to understand abortion as a desperately needed exit from near-total male control of our reproductive lives. This scenario posits an unambiguous chain of power and powerlessness in which men control women and women, in order to survive, must have unquestioned control over fetuses. It is this worldview, all too real in its initial conceptualization, that has led to the dread among many prochoice women of departing from a model of woman-equals-human-life, fetus-equals-not-much.

This model of reality may have been necessary in an unrelenting patriarchy. But today, in what should be, as women continue to consolidate political power, a patriarchy crumbling in spite of itself, it can become obsolete.

Now: Try to imagine real gender equality. Actually, try to imagine an American that is female-dominated, since a true working democracy in this country would reflect our 54–46 voting advantage.

Now imagine such a democracy, in which women would be valued so very highly, as a world that is accepting and responsible about human sexuality; in which there is no coerced sex without serious jailtime; in which there are affordable, safe contraceptives available for the taking in every public health building; in which there is economic parity for women—and basic economic subsistence for every baby born, and in which every young American woman knows about and understands her natural desire as a treasure to cherish, and responsibly, when the time is right, on her own terms, to share.

In such a world, in which the idea of gender as a barrier has become a dusty artifact, we would probably use a very different language about what would be—then—the rare and doubtless traumatic event of abortion. That language would probably call on respect and responsibility, grief and mourning. In that world we might well describe the unborn and the never-to-be-born with the honest words of life.

And in that world, passionate feminists might well hold candlelight vigils at abortion clinics, standing shoulder to shoulder with the doctors who work there, commemorating and saying good-bye to the dead.

STUDY QUESTIONS

1. What is the main point that Naomi Wolf is trying to make in her essay and how does she defend it? Do you think she succeeds? Why or why not? Explain your answer.

2. Wolf seems to be according the fetus higher moral status than many pro-choice feminists are willing to accord it. In your judgment, how high a status is Wolf willing to grant the fetus? How does she argue for this position? And how does she reconcile what some may see as an apparent conflict between her prochoice position and the moral wrongness of killing what is both valuable and human (a fetus)?

3. Many people have been critical of Wolf's position, arguing that she has betrayed her prochoice sisters. Do you agree with this assessment? Why or why not? Could you speculate why anyone would think that about Wolf? Explain your answer.

4. Wolf maintains that there was a strategic reason why the previous generation of feminists (in her words, "Second Wave Feminists") sought to dehumanize the fetus. According to Wolf, what was that reason? Do you think that strategy was wise? Why or why not?

26

Abortion and the "Feminine Voice"

CELIA WOLF-DEVINE

Celia Wolf-Devine is Professor of Philosophy at Stonehill College in Massachusetts. In this essay she first describes the growing movement within feminism to see women as nurturing, nonviolent, egalitarian, and relational as opposed to males and the male character traits of dominance, rationality, violence, hierarchy, and power. Next Wolf-Devine shows the discrepancy between this holistic and nonviolent "feminine voice" and the practice of abortion, which actually fits the male, not female, model. Finally, she responds to objections to her position.

A growing number of feminists now seek to articulate the "feminine voice," to draw attention to women's special strengths, and to correct the systematic devaluation of these by our male-dominated society. Carol Gilligan's book, *In a Different Voice,* was especially important to the emergence of this strain of feminist thought. It was her intention to help women identify more positively with their own distinctive style of reasoning about ethics, instead of feeling that there is something wrong with them because they do not think like men (as Kohlberg's and Freud's theories would imply). Inspired by her work, feminists such as Nel Noddings, Annette Baier, and the contributors to *Women and Moral Theory,*[1] have tried to articulate further the feminine voice in moral reasoning. Others such as Carol McMillan, Adrienne Rich, Sara Ruddick, and Nancy Harstock argue that women have distinct virtues and argue that these need not be self-victimizing.[2] When

Reprinted from *Public Affairs Quarterly* vol. 3, no. 3 (July 1989), by permission.

properly transformed by a feminist consciousness, women's different characteristics can, they suggest, be productive of new social visions.

Similar work is also being done by feminists who try to correct for masculine bias in other areas such as our conception of human nature, the way we
view the relationship between people and nature, and the kinds of paradigms
we employ in thinking about society.[3]

Some of those engaged in this enterprise hold that women *by nature* possess certain valuable traits that men do not, but, more frequently, they espouse
the weaker position that, on the whole, the traits they label "feminine" are
more common among women (for reasons that are at least partly cultural), but
that they also can be found in men, and that they should be encouraged as
good traits for a human being to have, regardless of sex.[4]

Virtually all those feminists who are trying to reassert the value of the
feminine voice also express the sort of unqualified support for free access to
abortion that has come to be regarded as a central tenet of feminist "ortho-
doxy." What I wish to argue in this paper is that (1) abortion is, by their own
accounts, clearly a masculine response to the problems posed by an unwanted
pregnancy, and is thus highly problematic for those who seek to articulate
and defend the "feminine voice" as the proper mode of moral response; and
that (2) on the contrary, the "feminine voice" as it has been articulated generates a strong presumption against abortion as a way of responding to an unwanted pregnancy.[5]

These conclusions, I believe, can be argued without relying on a precise
determination of the moral status of the fetus. A case at least can be made that
the fetus is a person because it is biologically a member of the human species
and will, in time, develop normal human abilities. Whether the burden of
proof rests on those who defend the personhood of the fetus, or on those who
deny it, is a matter of moral methodology and, for that reason, will depend in
part on whether one adopts a masculine or feminine approach to moral issues.

I. MASCULINE VOICE/FEMININE VOICE

A. Moral Reasoning

According to Gilligan, girls, being brought up by mothers, identify with them,
whereas males must define themselves through separation from their mothers.
As a result, girls have "a basis for empathy built into their primary definition
of self in a way that boys do not."[6] Thus, while masculinity is defined by separation and threatened by intimacy, femininity is defined through attachment
and threatened by separation; girls come to understand themselves as imbedded within a network of personal relationships.

A second difference concerns attitudes toward general rules and principles.
Boys tend to play in larger groups than girls and become "increasingly fasci-
nated with the legal elaboration of rules and the development of fair procedures for adjudicating conflicts."[7] We thus find men conceiving of morality

largely in terms of adjudicating fairly between the conflicting rights of self-assertive individuals.

Girls play in smaller groups and accord a greater importance to relationships than to following rules. They are especially sensitive to the needs of the particular other, instead of emphasizing impartiality, which is more characteristic of the masculine perspective. They think of morality more in terms of having responsibilities for taking care of others and place a high priority on preserving the network of relationships that makes this possible. While the masculine justice perspective requires detachment, the feminine care perspective sees detachment and separation as themselves the moral problem.[8]

Inspired by Gilligan, many feminist philosophers have discovered a masculine bias in traditional ethical theories. Nel Noddings has written a book called *Caring: A Feminine Approach to Ethics.* Annette Baier has praised Hume for his emphasis on the role of the affections in ethics[9] and proposed that trust be taken as the central notion for ethical theory.[10] Christina Hoff Sommers has argued for giving a central role to special relationships in ethics.[11] And Virginia Held has suggested that the mother-child relationship be seen as paradigmatic of human relationships, instead of the economic relationship of buyer/seller (which she sees to be the ruling paradigm now).[12]

The feminine voice in ethics attends to the particular other, thinks in terms of responsibilities to care for others, is sensitive to our interconnectedness, and strives to preserve relationships. It contrasts with the masculine voice, which speaks in terms of justice and rights, stresses consistency and principles, and emphasizes the autonomy of the individual and impartiality in one's dealings with others.

B. Human Nature: Mind and Body

Feminist writers have also discovered a masculine bias in the way we think of mind and body and the relationship between them. A large number of feminists, for example, regard radical mind/body dualism as a masculine way of understanding human nature. Alison Jaggar, for example, criticizes what she calls "normative dualism" for being "male biased"[13] and defines "normative dualism" as "the belief that what is especially valuable about human beings is a particular 'mental' capacity, the capacity for rationality."[14]

Another critic of dualism is Rosemary Radford Reuther, a theologian. Her book *New Woman, New Earth* is an extended attack on what she calls transcendent hierarchical dualism, which she regards as a "male ideology."[15] By "transcendent dualism," she means the view that consciousness is "transcendent to visible nature"[16] and that there is a sharp split between spirit and nature. In the attempt to deny our own mortality, our essential humanity is then identified with a "transcendent divine sphere beyond the matrix of coming to be and passing way."[17] In using the term "hierarchical," she means that the mental or spiritual component is taken to be superior to the physical. Thus "the relation of spirit and body is one of repression, subjugation, and mastery."[18]

Dodson Gray, whose views resemble Reuther's, poetically contrasts the feminine attitude with the masculine one as follows:

I see that life is not a line but a circle. Why do men imagine for themselves the illusory freedom of a soaring mind, so that the body of nature becomes a cage? 'Tis not true. To be human is to be circled in the cycles of nature, rooted in the processes that nurture us in life, breathing in and breathing out human life just as plants breathe in and out their photosynthesis.[19]

Feminists critical of traditional masculine ways of thinking about human nature also examine critically the conception of "reason" that has become ingrained in our Western cultural heritage from the Greeks on. Genevieve Lloyd, for example, in *The Man of Reason: Male and Female in Western Philosophy*,[20] suggests that the very notion of reason itself has been defined in part by the exclusion of the feminine. And if the thing that makes us distinctively human—namely our reason—is thought of as male, women and the things usually associated with them such as the body, emotion, and nature, will be placed in an inferior position.

C. Our Relationship with Nature

Many feminists hold that mind-body dualism that sees mind as transcendent to and superior to the body, leads to the devaluation of both women and nature. For the transcendent mind is conceived as masculine, and women, the body, and nature are assigned an inferior and subservient status.[21] As Rosemary Radford Reuther puts it:

> The woman, the body, and the world are the lower half of a dualism that must be declared posterior to, created by, subject to, and ultimately alien to the nature of (male) consciousness in whose image man made his God.[22]

Women are to be subject to men, and nature may be used by man in any way he chooses. Thus the male ideology of transcendent dualism sanctions unlimited technological manipulation of nature; nature is an alien object to be conquered.

Carolyn Merchant, in her book *The Death of Nature: Women, Ecology and the Scientific Revolution*,[23] focuses on the Cartesian version of dualism as particularly disastrous to our relationship with nature and finds the roots of our present ecological crisis to lie in the seventeenth century scientific revolution—itself based on Cartesian dualism and the mechanization of nature. According to Merchant, both feminism and the ecology movement are egalitarian movements that have a vision of our interconnectedness with each other and with nature.

Feminists who stress the deep affinities between feminism and the ecology movement are often called "ecofeminists." Stephanie Leland, radical feminist and co-editor of a recent collection of ecofeminist writings, has explained that

> Ecology is universally defined as the study of the balance and interrelationship of all life on earth. The motivating force behind feminism is the expression of the feminine principle. As the essential impulse of the feminine principle is the striving towards balance and interrelationship, it follows that feminism and ecology are inextricably connected.[24]

The masculine urge is, she says, to "separate, discriminate, and control," while the feminine impulse is "toward belonging, relationship, and letting be."[25] The urge to discriminate leads, she thinks, to the need to dominate "in order to feel secure in the choice of a particular set of differences."[26] The feminine attitude springs from a more holistic view of the human person and sees us as imbedded in nature rather than standing over and above it. It entails a more egalitarian attitude, regarding the needs of other creatures as important and deserving of consideration. It seeks to "let be" rather than to control and maintains a pervasive awareness of the interconnectedness of all things and the need to preserve this if all are to flourish.

Interconnectedness, which we found to be an important theme in feminist ethics, thus reappears in the writings of the ecofeminists as one of the central aspects of the feminine attitude toward nature.

D. Paradigms of Social Life

Feminists' descriptions of characteristically masculine and feminine paradigms of social life center around two different focuses. Those influenced by Gilligan tend to stress the contrast between individualism (which they take to be characteristic of the masculine "justice tradition") and the view of society as "a web of relationships sustained by a process of communication"[27] (which they take to characterize the feminine "care perspective"). According to them, the masculine paradigm sees society as a collection of self-assertive individuals seeking rules that will allow them to pursue their own goals without interfering with each other. The whole contractarian tradition from Locke and Hobbes through Rawls is thus seen as a masculine paradigm of social life; we are only connected to others and responsible to them through our own choice to relinquish part of our autonomy in favor of the state. The feminine care perspective guides us to think about societal problems in a different way. We are already imbedded in a network of relationships and must never exploit or hurt the other. We must strive to preserve those relationships as much as possible without sacrificing the integrity of the self.

The ecofeminists, pacifist feminists, and those whose starting point is a rejection of dualism, tend to focus more on the contrast between viewing social relationships in terms of hierarchy, power, and domination (the masculine paradigm) and viewing them in a more egalitarian and nonviolent manner (the feminine one). Feminists taking this position range from the moderate ones who believe that masculine social thought tends to be more hierarchical than feminine thought, to the extreme radicals who believe males are irredeemably aggressive and dominating, and prone to violence in order to preserve their domination.

The more moderate characterization of masculine social thought would claim that men tend to prefer a clear structure of authority; they want to know who is in control and have a clear set of procedures or rules for resolving difficult cases. The more extreme view, common among ecofeminists and a large number of radical feminists, is that males seek to establish and maintain patriarchy (systematic domination by males) and use violence to maintain their control. These feminists thus see an affinity between feminism (which combats male violence against women) and the pacifist movement (which does so on a more global scale). Mary Daly, for example, holds that "the rulers of patriarchy—males with power—wage an unceasing war against life itself...female energy is essentially biophilic."[28] Another radical feminist, Sally Miller Gearhart, says that men possess the qualities of objectification, violence, and competitiveness, whereas women possess empathy, nurturance, and cooperation.[29] Thus the feminine virtues must prevail if we are to survive at all, and the entire hierarchical power structure must be replaced by "horizontal patterns of relationship."[30]

Women are thus viewed by the pacifist feminists as attuned in some special way to the values and attitudes underlying a pacifist commitment. Sara Ruddick, for example, believes that maternal practice, because it involves "preservative love" and nurtures growth, involves the kinds of virtues that, when put to work in the public domain, lead us in the direction of pacifism.[31]

II. ABORTION

A person who had characteristically masculine traits, attitudes, and values as defined earlier would very naturally choose abortion and justify it ethically in the same way in which most feminists do. Conversely, a person manifesting feminine traits, attitudes and values would not make such a choice, or justify it in that way.

According to the ecofeminists, the masculine principle is insensitive to the interconnectedness of all life; it strives to discriminate, separate, and control. It does not respect the natural cycles of nature, but objectifies it, and imposes its will on it through unrestrained technological manipulation. Such a way of thinking would naturally lead to abortion. If the woman does not *want* to be pregnant, she has recourse to an operation involving highly sophisticated technology to defend her control of her body. This fits the characterization of the masculine principle perfectly.

Abortion is a separation—a severing of a life-preserving connection between the woman and the fetus. It thus fails to respect the interconnectedness of all life. Nor does it respect the natural cycles of nature. The mother and the developing child together form a delicately balanced ecosystem with the woman's entire hormonal system geared towards sustaining the pregnancy.[32] The abortionist forces the cervical muscles (which have become thick and hard in order to hold in the developing fetus) open and disrupts her hormonal system by removing it.

Abortion has something further in common with the behavior ecofeminists and pacifist feminists take to be characteristically masculine; it shows a willingness to use violence to maintain control. The fetus is destroyed by being pulled apart by suction, cut in pieces, or poisoned. It is not merely killed inadvertently as fish might be by toxic wastes, but it is deliberately targeted for destruction. Clearly this is not the expression of a "biophilic" attitude. This point was recently brought home to me by a Quaker woman who had reached the conclusion that the abortion she had had was contrary to her pacifist principles. She said, "we must seek peaceableness both within and without."

In terms of social thought, again, it is the masculine models that are most frequently employed in thinking about abortion. If masculine thought is naturally hierarchical and oriented toward power and control, then the interests of the fetus (who has no power) would naturally be suppressed in favor of the interests of the mother. But to the extent that feminist social thought is egalitarian, the question must be raised of why the mother's interests should prevail over the child's.

Feminist thought about abortion has, in addition, been deeply pervaded by the individualism that they so ardently criticize. The woman is supposed to have the sole authority to decide the outcome of the pregnancy. But what of her interconnectedness with the child and with others? Both she and the unborn child already exist within a network of relationships ranging from the closest ones—the father, grandparents, siblings, uncles and aunts, and so on—to ones with the broader society—including the mother's friends, employer, employees, potential adoptive parents, taxpayers who may be asked to fund the abortion or subsidize the child, and all the numerous other people affected by her choice. To dismiss this already existing network of relationships as irrelevant to the mother's decision is to manifest the sort of social atomism that feminist thinkers condemn as characteristically masculine.

Those feminists who are seeking to articulate the feminine voice in ethics also face a prima facie inconsistency between an ethics of care and abortion. Quite simply, abortion is a failure to care for one living being who exists in a particularly intimate relationship to oneself. If empathy, nurturance, and taking responsibility for caring for others are characteristic of the feminine voice, then abortion does not appear to be a feminine response to an unwanted pregnancy. If, as Gilligan says, "an ethic of care rests on the premise of nonviolence—that no one should be hurt,"[33] then surely the feminine response to an unwanted pregnancy would be to try to find a solution that does not involve injury to anyone, including the unborn.

"Rights" have been invoked in the abortion controversy in a bewildering variety of ways, ranging from the "right to life" to the "right to control one's body." But clearly those who defend unrestricted access to abortion in terms of such things as the woman's right to privacy or her right to control her body are speaking the language of an ethics of justice rather than an ethics of care. For example, Judith Jarvis Thomson's widely read article "A Defense of Abortion"[34] treats the moral issue involved in abortion as a conflict between the rights of the fetus and the mother's rights over her own body. Mary Anne Warren also sees the issue in terms of a conflict of rights, but since the fetus does not meet her criteria for being a person, she weighs the woman's rights to "freedom, happiness and self-determination" against the rights of other people in the society who would like to see the fetus preserved for whatever reason.[35] And, insofar as she appeals to consciousness, reasoning, self-motivated activity, the capacity to communicate, and the presence of self-concepts and self-awareness as criteria of personhood, she relies on the kind of opposition between mind and nature criticized by many feminists as masculine. In particular, she is committed to what Jaggar calls "normative dualism"—the view that what is especially valuable about humans is their mental capacity for rational thought.

It is rather striking that feminists defending abortion lapse so quickly into speaking in the masculine voice. Is it because they feel they must do so to be heard in our male dominated society, or is it because no persuasive defense of abortion can be constructed from within the ethics of care tradition? We now consider several possible "feminine voice" defenses of abortion.

III. POSSIBLE RESPONSES AND REPLIES

Among the feminists seeking to articulate and defend the value of the feminine voice, very few have made any serious attempt to grapple with abortion. The writings of the ecofeminists and the pacifist feminists abound with impassioned defenses of such values as nonviolence, a democratic attitude towards the needs of all living things, letting others be and nurturing them, and so on, existing side by side with impassioned defenses of "reproductive rights." They see denying women access to abortion as just another aspect of male domination and violence against women.

This will not do for several reasons. First, it is not true that males are the chief opponents of abortion. Many women are strongly opposed to it. The prolife movement at every level is largely composed of women. For example, as of May 1988, 38 of the state delegates to the National Right to Life Board of Directors were women, and only 13 were men. Indeed as Jean Bethke Elshtain has observed,[36] the prolife movement has mobilized into political action an enormous number of women who were never politically active before. And a Gallup poll in 1981 found that 51 percent of women surveyed believed a person is present at conception, compared with only 33 percent of the men. The prolife movement, thus, cannot be dismissed as representing male concerns and desires only. Granted, a prochoice feminist could argue that women involved in the prolife movement suffer from "colonized minds," but this sort of argument clearly can be made to cut both directions. After all, many of the strongest supporters of "reproductive rights" have been men—ranging from the Supreme Court in *Roe v. Wade* to the Playboy Philosopher.

Second, terms like violence and domination are used far too loosely by those who condemn anti-abortion laws. If there are laws against wife abuse, does this mean that abusive husbands are being subjected to domination and violence? One does not exercise violence against someone merely by crossing his or her will, or even by crossing his or her will and backing this up by threats of legal retribution.

Finally, those who see violence and domination in laws against abortion, but not in abortion itself, generally fail to look at the nature of the act itself, and thus fail to judge that act in light of their professed values and principles.

This is not surprising; abortion is a bloody and distressing thing to contemplate. But one cannot talk about it intelligently without being willing to look concretely at the act itself.

One line of thought is suggested by Gilligan, who holds that at the highest level of moral development, we must balance our responsibility to care for others against our need to care for ourselves. Perhaps we could, then, see the woman who has an abortion as still being caring and nurturing in that she is acting out of a legitimate care for herself. This is an implausible view of the actual feelings of women who undergo abortions. They may believe they are "doing something for themselves" in the sense of doing what they must do to safeguard their legitimate interests. But the operation is more naturally regarded as a violation of oneself than as a nurturing of oneself. This has been noted, even by feminists who support permissive abortion laws. For example, Caroline Whitbeck speaks of "the unappealing prospect of having someone scraping away at one's core,"[37] and Adrienne Rich says that "Abortion is violence: a deep, desperate violence inflicted by a woman on, first of all, herself."[38]

We here come up against the problem that a directive to care, to nurture, to take responsibility for others, and so on, provides a moral orientation, but leaves unanswered many important questions and hence provides little guidance in problem situations. What do we do when caring for one person involves being uncaring toward another? How widely we must extend our circle of care? Are some kinds of not caring worse than others? Is it caring to give someone what they want even though it may be bad for them?

Thinking in terms of preserving relationships suggests another possible "feminine" defense of abortion—namely that the woman is striving to preserve her interconnectedness with her family, husband, or boyfriend. Or perhaps she is concerned to strengthen her relationship with her other children by having enough time and resources to devote to their care To simply tell a woman to preserve *all* her existing relationships is not the answer. Besides the fact that it may not be possible (women *do* sometimes have to sever relationships), it is not clear that it would be desirable even if it were possible. Attempting to preserve our existing relationships has conservative tendencies in several unfortunate ways. It fails to invite us to reflect critically on whether those relationships are good, healthy, or worthy of preservation.[39] It also puts the unborn at a particular disadvantage, since the mother's relationship with him or her is just beginning, while her relationships with others have had time to develop. And not only the unborn, but any needy stranger who shows up at our door can be excluded on the grounds that caring for them would disrupt our existing pattern of relationships. Thus the care perspective could degenerate into a rationalization for a purely tribal morality: I take care of myself and my friends.

But how are decisions about severing relationships to be made? One possibility is suggested by Gilligan in a recent article. She looks at the network of connections within which the woman who is considering abortion finds herself entangled and says "to ask what actions constitute care or are more caring directs attention to the parameters of connection and the *costs of detachment...* (emphasis added)"[40] Thus, the woman considering abortion should reflect on the comparative costs of severing various relationships. This method of decision, however, makes her vulnerable to emotional and psychological pressure from others, by encouraging her to sever whichever connection is easiest to break (the squeaky wheel principle).[41]

But perhaps we can lay out some guidelines (or, at least, rules of thumb) for making these difficult decisions. One way we might reason, from the point of view of the feminine voice, is that since preserving interconnectedness is good, we should prefer a short term estrangement to an irremediable severing of relationship. And we should choose an action that *may* cause an irremediable break in relationship over one which is certain to cause such a break. By either of these criteria, abortion is clearly to be avoided.[42]

Another consideration suggested by Gilligan's work is that since avoiding hurt to others (or nonviolence) is integral to an ethics of care, severing a relationship where the other person will be only slightly hurt would be preferable to severing one where deep or lasting injury will be inflicted by our action. But on this criterion, again, it would seem she should avoid abortion, since loss of life is clearly a graver harm than emotional distress.

Two other possible criteria that would also tell against abortion are (1) that it is permissible to cut ties with someone who behaves unjustly and oppressively toward one, but not with someone who is innocent of any wrong against one, or (2) we have special obligations to our own offspring, and thus should not sever relationship with them.

Criteria can, perhaps, be found that would dictate severing relationship with the fetus rather than others, but it is hard to specify one that clearly reflects the feminine voice. Certainly the right to control one's body will not do. The claim that the unborn is not a person and therefore does not deserve moral consideration can be faulted on several grounds. First, if the feminine voice is one that accepts the interconnectedness of all life and strives to avoid harm to nature and to other species, then the non-personhood of the fetus (supposing it could be proved) would not imply that its needs can be discounted. And second, the entire debate over personhood has standardly been carried on very much in the masculine voice.[43] One feminist, Janice Raymond,[44] has suggested that the question of when life begins is a masculine one, and if this is a masculine question, it would seem that personhood, with its juridical connotations, would be also. It is not clear that the care perspective has the resources to resolve this issue. If it cannot, then, one cannot rely on the non-personhood of the fetus in constructing a "feminine voice" defense of abortion. A care perspective would at least seem to place the burden of proof on those who would restrict the scope of care, in this case to those that have been born.

It seems that the only way open to the person who seeks to defend abortion from the point of view of the feminine voice is to deny that a relationship (or at least any morally significant relationship) exists between the embryo/fetus and the mother. The question of how to tell when a relationship (or a morally significant relationship) exists is a deep and important one, which has, as yet, received insufficient attention from those who are trying to

articulate the feminine voice in moral reasoning. The whole ecofeminist position relies on the assumption that our relationship with nature and with other
species is a real and morally significant one. They, thus, have no basis at all for
excluding the unborn from moral consideration.

There are those, however, who wish to define morally significant relationships more narrowly—thus effectively limiting our obligation to extend care.
While many philosophers within the "justice tradition" (for example, Kant)
have seen moral significance only where there is some impact on rational beings, Nel Noddings, coming from the "care perspective" tries to limit our
obligation to extend care in terms of the possibility of "completion" or "reciprocity" in a caring relationship.[45] Since she takes the mother-child relationship to be paradigmatic of caring, it comes as something of a surprise that she
regards abortion as a permissible response to an unwanted pregnancy.[46]

There are, on Noddings' view, two different ways in which we can be
bound, as caring persons, to extend our care to one for whom we do not already have the sort of feelings of love and affection that would lead us to do the
caring action naturally. One is by virtue of being connected with our "inner
circle" of caring (which is formed by natural relations of love and friendship)
through "chains" of "personal or formal relations."[47] As an example of a person
appropriately linked to the inner circle, she cites her daughter's fiancé. It would
certainly *seem* that the embryo in one's womb would belong to one's "inner
circle" (via natural caring), or at least be connected to it by a "formal relation"
(that is, that of parenthood). But Noddings does not concede this. Who is part
of my inner circle, and who is connected to it in such a way that I am obligated
to extend care to him or her seems to be, for Noddings, largely a matter of my
feelings toward the person and/or my choice to include him or her. Thus the
mother *may* "confer sacredness" on the "information speck"[48] in her womb,
but need not if, for example, her relationship with the father is not a stable and
loving one. During pregnancy "many women recognize the relation as established when the fetus begins to move about. it Is not a question of when life
begins, but of when relation begins."

But making the existence of a relation between the unborn and the mother
a matter of her choice or feelings, seems to run contrary to one of the most
central insights of the feminine perspective in moral reasoning—namely that
we already *are* interconnected with others and, thus, have responsibilities to
them. The view that we are connected with others only when we choose to
be or when we *feel* we are presupposes the kind of individualism and social
atomism that Noddings and other feminists criticize as masculine

Noddings also claims that we sometimes are obligated to care for "the
proximate stranger." She says:

> We cannot refuse obligation in human affairs by merely refusing to enter
> relation; we are, by virtue of our mutual humanity, already and perpetu-
> ally in potential relation.[49]

Why, then, are we not obligated to extend care to the unborn? She gives
two criteria for when we have an obligation to extend care: there must be

"the existence of or potential for present relation" and the "dynamic potential for growth in relation, including the potential for increased reciprocity…" Animals are, she believes, excluded by this second criterion since their response is nearly static (unlike a human infant).

She regards the embryo/fetus as not having the potential for present relationships of caring and reciprocity, and thus as having no claim on our care. As the fetus matures, he or she develops increasing potential for caring relationships, and thus our obligation in creases also. There are problems with her position, however.

First, the only relationships that can be relevant to *my* obligation to extend care, for Noddings, must be relationships with *me*. Whatever the criteria for having a relationship are, it must be that at a given time, an entity either has a relationship with me or it does not. If it does not, it may either have no potential for a morally significant relationship with me (for example, my word processor), or it may have such potential in several ways: (1) The relationship may become actual at the will of one or both parties (for example, the stranger sitting next to me on the bus). (2) The relationship may become actual only after a change in relative spatial locations which will take time, and thus can occur only in the future (for example, walking several blocks to meet a new neighbor, or traveling to Tibet to meet a specific Tibetan). Or, (3) the relationship may become actual only after some internal change occurs within the other (for example by waiting for a sleeping drug to wear off, for a deep but reversible coma to pass, or for the embryo to mature more fully) and thus can also happen only in the future.

In all three of these cases, there is present now in the other the potential for relations of a caring and reciprocal sort. In cases (1) and (2) this is uncontroversial, but (3) requires some defense in the case of the unborn. The human embryo differs now from a rabbit embryo in that it possesses potential for these kinds of relationships although neither of them is presently able to enter into relationships of any sort.[50] That potential becomes actualized only over time, but it can become actualized only because it is there to be actualized (as it is not in the rabbit embryo).[51] Noddings fails to give any reason why the necessity for some internal change to occur in the other before relation can become actual has such moral importance that we are entitled to kill the other in case (3), but not in the others, especially since my refraining from killing it is a sufficient condition for the actualization of the embryo's potential for caring relationships. Her criterion as it stands would also seem to imply that we may kill persons in deep but predictably reversible comas.

Whichever strand of Noddings' thought we choose, then, it is hard to see how the unborn can be excluded from being ones for whom we ought to care. If we focus on the narrow, tribal morality of "inner circles" and chains," then an objective connection exists tying the unborn to the mother and other relatives. If we are to be open to the needy stranger because of the real potential for relationship and reciprocity then we should be open to the unborn because he or she also has the real and present potential for a relationship of reciprocity and mutuality that comes with species membership.

Many feminists will object to my argument so far on the grounds that they do not, after all, consider abortion to be a *good* thing. They aren't pro-abortion in the sense that they encourage women to have abortions. They merely regard it as something that must be available as a kind of "grim option"— something a woman would choose only when the other alternatives are all immeasurably worse.[52]

First, the grim options view sounds very much like the "masculine voice"—we must grit our teeth, and do the distasteful but necessary deed (the more so where the deed involves killing).[53] Furthermore, it is in danger of collapsing into total subjectivism unless one is willing to specify some criteria for when an option is a genuinely grim one, beyond the agent's feeling that it is. What if she chooses to abort in order not to have to postpone her trip to Europe, or because she prefers sons to daughters? Surely these are not grim options no matter what she may say. Granted, the complicated circumstances surrounding her decision are best known to the woman herself. But this does not imply that no one is *ever* in a position to make judgments about whether her option is sufficiently grim to justify abortion. We do not generally concede that only the agent is in a position to judge the morality of his or her action.

Feminists standardly hold that absolutely no restrictions may be placed on a woman's right to choose abortion.[54] This position cannot be supported by the grim options argument. One who believes something is a grim option will be inclined to try to avoid or prevent it, and thus be willing, at least in principle, to place some restrictions on what counts as a grim option. Granted, practical problems exist about how such decisions are to be made and by whom. But someone who refuses in principle to allow any restrictions on women's right to abort, cannot in good faith claim that they regard abortion only as a grim option.

Some feminists will say, yes, feminine virtues are a good thing for any person to have, and yes, abortion is a characteristically masculine way of dealing with an unwanted pregnancy, but in the current state of things we live in a male dominated society, and we must be willing to use now weapons that, ideally, in a good, matriarchal society, we would not use.[55] But there are no indications that an ideal utopian society is just around the corner; thus we are condemned to a constant violation of our own deepest commitments. If the traits, values, and attitudes characteristic of the "feminine voice" are asserted to be good ones, we ought to act according to them. And such values and attitudes simply do not lend support to either the choice of abortion as a way of dealing with an unwanted pregnancy in individual cases, or to the political demand for unrestricted[56] access to abortion that has become so entrenched in the feminist movement. Quite the contrary.[57]

STUDY QUESTIONS

1. Has Celia Wolf-Devine made a strong case that abortion is radically opposed to the "feminine voice" of caring and relationships?

2. How might feminists like Markowitz and Whitbeck respond to Wolf-Devine's arguments? And how would she treat their responses? Where does the truth lie?

3. Is there a feminine way of looking at morality that is different from the masculine way, as some feminists aver? If so, is this more due to nature or nurture (biological causes or environmental conditioning)?

NOTES

1. See Nel Noddings, *Caring: A Feminine Approach to Ethics,* Berkeley: University of California Press, 1984; Annette Baier, "What Do Women Want in a Moral Theory?," *Nous,* 19 (March, 1985), and "Hume, the Women's Moral Theorist?," in *Women and Moral Theory,* (eds.) Kittay and Meyers, Minneapolis: University of Minnesota Press, 1987.

2. Carol McMillan, *Woman, Reason and Nature,* Princeton: Princeton University Press, 1982; Adrienne Rich, *Of Woman Born,* N.Y.: Norton, 1976; Sara Ruddick, "Remarks on the Sexual Politics of Reason" in *Woman and Moral Theory,* (eds.) Kittay and Meyers, Minneapolis: University of Minnesota Press, 1987, and "Maternal Thinking" and "Preservative Love and Military Destruction: Some Reflections on Mothering and Peace" in Joyce Treblicot (ed.) *Mothering: Essays in Feminist Theory,* Totowa, N.J.: Rowman & Allanheld, 1983; and Nancy Harstock "The Feminist Standpoint" in *Discovering Reality,* Harding (ed.), Boston: D. Reidel, 1983.

3. Among them are such writers as Rosemary Radford Reuther, Susan Griffin, Elizabeth Dodson Gray, Brian Easla, Sally Miller Gearhart, Carolyn Merchant, Genevieve Lloyd, the pacifist feminists, and a number of feminists involved in the ecology movement.

4. In this paper I shall use the terms "masculine" and "feminine" only in this weaker sense, which is agnostic about the existence of biologically based differences.

5. A strong presumption against abortion is not, of course, the same thing as an absolute ban on all abortions. I do not attempt here to resolve the really hard cases; it is not clear that the feminine voice (at least as it has been articulated so far) is sufficiently fine-grained to tell us exactly where to draw the line in such cases.

6. See Carol Gilligan, *In a Different Voice,* Cambridge, Mass.: Harvard University Press, 1982, 8.

7. Ibid., 10.

8. See Gilligan, "Moral Orientation and Moral Development" in *Women and Moral Theory,* (eds.) Kittay and Meyers, Minneapolis: University of Minnesota Press, 1987, 31.

9. Annette Baier, "Hume, the Woman's Moral Theorist?," 37–35.

10. "What do Women Want in a Moral Theory," *Nous,* 19 (March, 1985), 53.

11. Christina Hoff Sommers, "Filial Morality," in *Women and Moral Theory,* (eds.) Kittay and Meyers, Minneapolis: University of Minnesota Press, 1987, 69–84.

12. Virginia Held, "Feminism and Moral Theory," in *Women and Moral Theory,* (eds.) Kittay and Meyers. Minneapolis: University of Minnesota Press, 1987, 111–128.

13. Alison Jaggar, *Feminist Politics and Human Nature.* Totowa, N.J.: Rowman & Allanheld, 1983, 46.

14. Ibid., 28.

15. Rosemary Radford Reuther, *New Woman, New Earth.* New York: Seabury Press, 1975, 195.

16. Ibid., 188.

17. Ibid., 195.

18. Ibid., 189.

19. Elizabeth Dodson Gray, *Why the Green Nigger.* Wellesley, Mass.: Roundtable Press, 1979, 54.

20. Genevieve Lloyd, *The Man of Reason: Male and Female in Western Philosophy.* Minneapolis: University of Minnesota Press, 1984.

21. See, for example, Rosemary Radford Reuther, *New Woman, New Earth*; Elizabeth Dodson Gray, *Why the Green Nigger;* and Brian Easla, *Science and Sexual Oppression,* London: Weidenfeld & Nicolson, 1981.

22. Reuther, *New Woman, New Earth,* 195.

23. Carolyn Merchant, *The Death of Nature: Women, Ecology and the Scientific Revolution.* San Francisco: Harper & Row, 1980.

24. Stephanie Leland and Leonie Caldecott, (eds.) *Reclaim the Earth: Women Speak out for Life on Earth.* London: Women's Press, 1983, 72. For an overview of ecofeminist thought that focuses on the role of mind/body dualism, see Val Plumwood, "Ecofeminism: An Overview," *Australasian Journal of Philosophy,* Supplement to Vol. 64 (June, 1986), 120–138.

25. Leland and Caldecott, *Reclaim the Earth,* 71.

26. Ibid., 69.

27. Introduction to *Women and Moral Theory,* by Kittay and Meyers. Minneapolis: University of Minnesota Press, 1987, 7.

28. Cited by Barbara Zanotti, "Patriarchy: A State of War," in *Reweaving the Web of Life,* Pam McAllister, (ed.). Philadelphia: New Society Publishers, 1982, 17.

29. See, for example, Sally Miller Gearhart, "The Future—if there is one— is Female," in *Reweaving the Web of Life,* Pam McAllister, (ed.). Philadelphia: New Society Publishers, 1982, 266.

30. Ibid., 272.

31. See Sara Ruddick, "Remarks on the Sexual Politics of Reason."

32. I owe the idea of regarding mother and child as an ecosystem to a conversation with Leonie Caldecott, co-editor of *Reclaim the Earth.*

33. Gilligan, *In a Different Voice,* 174.

34. Judith Jarvis Thomson, "A Defense of Abortion," *Philosophy and Public Affairs,* 1, (1971), 47–66.

35. Mary Anne Warren, "On the Moral and Legal Status of Abortion," *Monist,* 57 (January 1973), reprinted in Wasserstrom, *Today's Moral Problems.* New York: Macmillan, 1985, 448.

36. Jean Bethke Elshtain, *Public Man, Private Woman.* Princeton, N.J.: Princeton University Press, 1981, 312.

37. Carolyn Whitbeck, "Women as People: Pregnancy and Personhood," in *Abortion and the Status of the Fetus,* W.B. Bondeson, et al. (ed.). Boston: D. Reidel, 1983, 252.

38. Rich, *Of Woman Born,* 269.

39. Joan Tronto makes this point in "Beyond Gender Differences to a Theory of Care," *Signs,* 22 (Summer, 1987), 666.

40. Carol Gilligan, "Moral Orientation and Moral Development," 24.

41. This was evident in the reasoning of the women in Gilligan's case studies, many of whom had abortions to please or placate other significant persons in their lives.

42. Some post-abortion counselors find the sense of irremediable break in relationship to be one of the most painful aspects of the post-abortion experience and try to urge the woman to imaginatively re-create a relationship with the baby to be better able to complete the necessary grieving

process. Conversation with Teresa Patterson, post-abortion counselor at Crisis Pregnancy Center in Walnut Creek, California.

43. For an excellent "masculine voice" discussion of the personhood issues, see, for example, Philip E. Devine, *The Ethics of Homicide,* Ithaca, N.Y.: Cornell University Press, 1978.

44. Janice Raymond, *The Transsexual Empire.* Boston: Beacon Press, 1979, 114.

45. It would seem that in using the term "obligation," Noddings is blurring the distinction between the masculine and feminine voice because obligations imply rights. When she speaks of obligations to extend care, however, these are not absolute, but relative to the individual's choice of being a caring person as an ethical ideal. They are binding on us only as a result of our own prior choice, and our care is not something the other can claim as a matter of justice.

46. Noddings' discussion of abortion occurs on pages 87–90 of *Caring: A Feminine Approach to Ethics,* and all quotes are from these pages unless otherwise noted.

47. Ibid., 47.

48. It is inaccurate to call even the newly implanted zygote an "information speck." Unlike a blueprint or pattern of information, it is alive and growing.

49. I realize that Noddings would not be happy with the extent to which I lean on her use of the term "criteria," since she prefers to argue by autobiographical example. However, because moral intuitions about abortion vary so widely, this sort of argument is not effective here.

50. I omit here consideration of such difficult cases as severe genetic retardation.

51. The notion of potentiality I am relying on here is roughly an Aristotelian one.

52. Caroline Whitbeck articulates a view of this sort in "Women as People: Pregnancy and Personhood."

53. Granted, this sort of judgment is, at least in part, an impressionistic one. It is supported, however, by Gilligan's findings about the difference between boys and girls in their response to the "Heinz dilemma" (where the man is faced with a

choice between allowing his wife to die or stealing an expensive drug from the druggist to save her). Although the females she studies do not all respond to the dilemma in the same way (for example, Betty at first sounds more like Hobbes than like what has been characterized as the feminine voice—pages 75–76), some recurring patterns that she singles out as representative of the feminine voice are resisting being forced to accept either horn of the dilemma, seeing all those involved as in relationship with each other, viewing the dilemma in terms of conflicting responsibilities rather than rights, and seeking to avoid or minimize harm to anyone (see, for example, Sarah, page 95). Because the abortion decision involves killing and not merely letting die, it would seem that the impetus to find a way through the horns of the dilemma would be, if anything, greater than in the Heinz dilemma.

54. For example, one feminist, Roberta Steinbach, argues that we must not restrict a woman's right to abort for reasons of sex selection *against females* because it might endanger our hard won "reproductive rights"! (See "Sex Selection: From Here to Fraternity" in Carol Gould (ed.) *Beyond Domination,* Totowa, N.J.: Rowman & Allanheld, 1984, 280.)

55. For example, Annette Baier regards trust as the central concept in a feminine ethics, but speaks of "the principled betrayal of the exploiter's trust" (Baier, "What Do Women Want in a Moral Theory?," 62.)

56. Restrictions can take many forms, including laws against abortion, mandatory counseling that includes information about the facts of fetal development and encourages the woman to choose other options, obligatory waiting periods, legal requirements to notify (or obtain the consent of) the father, or in the case of a minor the girl's parents, and so on. To defend the appropriateness of any particular sort of restrictions goes beyond the scope of this paper.

57. I wish to thank the following for reading and commenting on an earlier draft of this paper: Edith Black, Tony Celano, Phil Devine, James Nelson, Alan Soble, and Michael Wreen.

27

Taking Women Seriously as People

The Moral Implications for Abortion

CAROLINE WHITBECK

Caroline Whitbeck is Research Fellow at the Center for Policy Alternatives, Massachusetts Institute of Technology. She seeks to redirect our attention from the status of the fetus to the situation of the pregnant woman faced with the inadequate financial resources, the prospect of fetal defects, the stigma of illegitimacy, and the increased dependency on unkind men. Given this oppressive context, abortion should be seen not as a good, but as a lesser evil. Virtually no woman would choose to have an abortion, but given these exigencies, not to mention ignorance about or lack of adequate contraceptive devices, abortion should be kept legal as an option.

One of the striking things about the philosophical debate on the ethics of abortion is how few women enter it. I believe that the relatively small number of women who enter the discussion is a result as well as a cause of the way in which the subject is demarcated and the way in which it is conceptualized. Given the way in which the issue is presently framed, it is difficult for many women to find any position for which they wish to argue. I shall argue, first, that abortion is actually a fragment of several other moral issues surrounding pregnancy and childbirth so that the moral situation can be adequately understood only if this larger context is considered, and, second, that the choice of the terms in which the analysis is generally carried out is mistaken. In particular, I shall argue that neglect of matters that cannot be adequately expressed in terms of "rights" and the employment of an atomistic model of people (a model that represents moral relationships as incidental to being a person) confuses many moral issues but especially those concerning pregnancy, childbirth, and infant care. It is my purpose in this paper to argue for a re-framing of the issues regarding pregnancy and childbirth. Such a reframing will yield different questions from those that have typically been raised in debates about abortion.

An important factor contributing to the inadequate formulation of the issues that I shall discuss is the neglect of interpretations of the human condition from women's perspective. (The problem is not confined to philosophy, but the neglect of women's perspective in philosophy is symptomatic of the neglect of women's experience in the culture generally.) It is not my purpose to give an extensive critique of the existing literature but to at least to identify many of the neglected issues and to show how attention to the perspective of women will generate new approaches to these issues.

1. ON THE DENIAL THAT WOMEN ARE PEOPLE

It is striking that the culture has managed to ignore the implications of the fact that women are people. Of course, our own culture is strongly influenced by a number of scientific and religious traditions that explicitly deny that women have in full measure those characteristics that are taken to distinguish man from the animals. Thus, St. Paul in his first letter to the Corinthians interprets the second of the two accounts of creation in Genesis as denying that woman is created in the image of God, as man is. Woman, Paul says, stands in relation to man as man does to Christ. Woman was created for man. Paul concedes that man cannot do without woman, however, since man is born of woman. In short, Paul represents women as failing to have the property of being made in God's image, although they are a necessary means to the existence of such beings.[1]

Aristotle in his work, *On the Generation of Animals,* tells us that the most common kind of deformity is to be born a woman and that the rational part of the soul, that which distinguishes man from the lower animals, is inoperative in woman. Because women do not have enough soul heat, women cannot cook their menstrual blood into semen, says Aristotle, and therefore, to put the matter in modern terms, women do not contribute any gametes to the formation of the embryo. According to Aristotle, not only are women not people in the sense of failing to be rational animals (recall that Aristotle regarded "rational animal" as definition of "man"), women are, in a sense, not even full parents of people on Aristotle's account, but only necessary as the custodians and nurturers of men's "seed." I have termed this, "the flowerpot theory of generation." Ideas found in Paul and Aristotle are to be found in the work of many other thinkers, although these quotations from Paul and Aristotle are among the most influential on subsequent views of women [38].

These days, it is less common to assert outright that women lack some or all of the characteristics taken to distinguish people from lower animals. Many implications of the view that women are people are routinely ignored, however, and women's experience continues to be disregarded as though it were not relevant to understanding the human condition. (I venture that by this stage in the present volume, we will have had a remarkable amount of discussion of fetuses with little or no mention of pregnancy.)

The problem is not one of sloth on the part of individual scholars, but of general neglect within the culture. The neglect of discussion of the experience of pregnancy and childbirth within our culture and the neglect of women's perspective on the subject of human sexuality are subjects that I have discussed in detail elsewhere [37]. The problem can be illustrated by considering some of your own experience. How many of you have seen films or read novels about men's experience in war? How many have seen or read at least four such works? How many of you have seen films and read novels that deal with women's experience in pregnancy and childbirth? (I do not count Lamaze and other childbirth training films any more than I count combat training films.) My contention is that of those people who have not borne children, more have identified imaginatively with Lassie than with a pregnant woman.

Women and men alike are given cultural representations of what is stereotypically men's experience, whether in war or playing football, and few if any representations of women's experience, not only for activities and roles that are regarded as subsidiary activities but even for activities and roles such as those of mothering that are regarded as essential. The implication is that although women may figure importantly *in* people's experience, as do horses and automobiles, there is nothing in *women's experience* that merits attention. Furthermore, the subjects of women's needs and women's moral integrity and bodily integrity are omitted regularly, as is the issue of matching women's responsibilities with the authority to carry them out. Often, indeed, an ethical double standard has been implicit, so that people in general are regarded as constrained morally by the requirement not to violate anyone else's rights, but the moral expectation on women is that they be nurturant, that is, that they ought to go beyond respecting rights and meet the needs of others, perhaps any and all others. Some even push the double standard further and maintain that women do not have rights equal to those of men.

2. THE LIMITS OF THE APPLICABILITY OF THE CONCEPT OF A MORAL RIGHT

Like recent discussions of other ethical issues, much of the literature on abortion discusses its subject exclusively in terms of rights. The emphasis on rights often stems from the implicit assumption of what I shall call, a "rights view of ethics." According to a rights view of ethics, the concept of a moral right is the fundamental moral notion, or at least the one that is of preeminent significance, so that a moral issue is settled by consideration of rights. According to this view, a person is assumed to be nothing more than a being having certain rights, human rights. (Indeed it has now become common for philosophers to define explicitly the concept of a person as a being possessing certain rights, particularly the right to life.[2]) Persons are viewed as social and moral atoms, actually or potentially in competition with one another. If any attention is given to human relationships, it is assumed that they exist on a contractual (or quasi-contractual) basis and that the moral requirements arising from them are limited to rights and obligations.

In contrast with obligations that generally specify what acts or conduct are morally required, permitted, or forbidden, responsibilities (in the prospective sense of "responsibility for") specify the ends to be achieved rather than the conduct required.[3] Thus, responsibilities require an exercise of discretion on the part of their bearers. People without medical knowledge cannot bear a moral responsibility to give someone good medical care, and newborns cannot have any moral responsibilities at all.

In contrast with the rights view of ethics, what I shall call "the responsibilities view" of ethics takes moral responsibility arising out of relationships as the fundamental moral notion, and regards people as beings who can (among other things) act for moral reasons and who come to this status through relationships with other people.[4] Such relationships are not assumed to be contractual. The relationship of a child to his or her parents is a good example of a relationship that is not contractual. In general, relationships between people place moral responsibilities on both parties. Each party is responsible for ensuring some aspect of the other's welfare or, at least, for achieving some ends that contribute to the other's welfare or achievement. This holds even in asymmetrical relationships (whether personal or professional), such as the relationship between parent and child or between client and lawyer.

Rights and obligations do have a place within the responsibilities view. Human rights are claims on society and on other people that are necessary if a person is to be able to meet the responsibilities of her or his relationships. Although only moral agents can have moral responsibilities and thus can have moral rights, according to this view, moral agents can, and probably do, have some moral obligations toward, or responsibility for the welfare of other beings who are not moral agents, that is, beings who do not themselves have the moral status of people. For example, people may have a moral obligation to treat corpses with respect, or not be cruel to animals.

I maintain that a rights view of ethics yields an inadequate view of the moral status of people or "persons" and disregards the importance of the special responsibilities that go with personal and professional relationships. In some cases, notably in situations involving adults who are strangers, the situation can be described adequately in terms of rights and obligations alone. For issues relating to pregnancy, childbirth and infant care, however, where the relationships between the parties are those that are central and indeed necessary for one of the parties ever to become a moral agent, adequate representation of the situation requires that attention be given to responsibilities.

3. THE SCOPE AND LIMITS OF RIGHTS AS THEY BEAR UPON PREGNANCY AND ITS TERMINATION

Although the question of when it is moral to terminate a pregnancy is not answered adequately if we attend only to rights, some rights are relevant.

Let us pose a question: Supposing you were able to do so, how many of you would like to have an abortion?

Of course, women do not want abortions any more than they want to have mastectomies, even if the risks from each are minimal. (One of the most striking examples of misogyny in our society is the way in which women who resort to abortion are portrayed as Medea figures, that is as people who wish to destroy the fetuses they carry. Medea herself is a product of the masculine imagination and is represented as having ripped her children's bodies limb from limb and strewing the parts on the ocean out of rage toward their father, Jason.) Philosophers have long struggled to formulate the distinction between what people straightforwardly want (such as equal pay for equal work) and those options that are selected only because of a still greater aversion to the only available alternatives. I shall call the latter sorts of options "grim options."[5]

One example of a grim option that philosophers employ is the option of being hung with a noose made with silk rope as opposed to being hung with a noose made of hemp rope. The prisoner making the choice does not want to be hung with a silk rope in the straightforward sense of want, but only chooses that over being hung with a hemp rope. Such cases are not easily subsumed under the heading of what is wanted only as a means. Although the selected options could be represented as a means for avoiding the alternatives, grim options cases differ from usual cases in which something is wanted only as a means, in that the causal relation between the means and end is at best remote, and the end is the *avoidance* of some outcome rather than the *attainment* of one.

It would be a mistake to regard abortion as a means to the end of being childless, since most women who have abortions do bear children at some other time in their lives. A woman seeks an abortion most often not to avoid having children *per se,* but to avoid such alternatives as the risk of becoming an invalid as a result of the pregnancy; the inability to keep a major commitment to someone; the prospect of being reduced to poverty by loss of her livelihood; dependency on someone who would batter or mistreat her or her children; or the stigma of "illegitimacy" on herself, her child, and her family.[6] (Often in human history giving birth to an illegitimate child has meant the death of the mother, either by execution or through probable starvation, as well as social ostracism and probable death of the child.) In this country laws discriminating against bastards were not declared unconstitutional until the landmark Supreme Court decision in the case of *Levy v. Louisiana* [19] in 1968, and informal discrimination and ostracism continues. Many of the facts that impel a woman to resort to abortion would be changed with a change in social conditions. In particular, safe, effective means of contraception and sterilization and the elimination of rape would guarantee a woman's control of her fertility without resort to abortion.

Abortion is in many ways a prototype of a grim option, but this point seems to have been neglected in both the philosophical and popular literature on abortion. In addition to the two commonly discussed issues, the risks of an abortion and the killing of the fetus in abortion (the moral significance of which we are assessing), there is the unappealing prospect of having someone scraping away at one's inner core.

Thus, women do not want abortions, although under duress they may resort to them. Nonetheless, people can, and many do, want safe abortions available, just as people want safe mastectomies to be available. It is estimated that approximately 84,000 women die every year as a result of abortion ([6],page 1), although a legal first trimester abortion in the United States has a mortality risk no greater than that of a penicillin shot. The distinction between what one wants and what one *wants to be available* is crucial for understanding the resort to a grim option. Further, since the development of therapeutic medicine is a prime example of society's preparation for an undesired turn of events, the distinction between what one wants and what one wants to be available is a particularly important one in the philosophy of medicine.[7] The right that would correspond to this desire would be the right of entitlement to a *safe* abortion. It would correspond precisely to a putative right to other forms of surgical care such as mastectomies, appendectomies, and the like. The desire for the availability of good care of this sort cannot be equated with actually wanting such operations. Indeed, there has been a good deal of lay criticism of surgeons for encouraging patients to have operations, especially appendectomies and hysterectomies, for trivial reasons. Therefore, rights to medical care are importantly unlike such other rights of entitlement as the right to a basic education, in that people prefer *not* to be in the position of actually needing to exercise these rights.

The second example of something that people might want and claim as a right is the general right of control of one's body. This is a prototype of the privacy rights that must be honored if one is to function as a person. (I generally agree with J. H. Reiman [25] and S. I. Benn [2] that rights of privacy are not derivative rights. On the contrary, they are fundamental to being (or becoming) a person. Although the rules and conventions regarding privacy vary from one society to another, in *every* society privacy exists as the social practice by which the individual moral right to control the matters relating to one's own person is recognized. I disagree with Reiman's use of the term "moral ownership" in this context, since it suggests that the right connected with one's body or one's person is a species of property right. Sara Ann Ketchum [14] argues convincingly that it is not.)

The claim that abortion should be available "on demand" may be intended as any one of several different claims. It may, and most often does, mean that it should always be legal for a woman to have an abortion without obtaining the approval of anyone else. What is in question is a negative right, a right to be free of interference when seeking an abortion. In contrast, the claim that abortion should be available on demand is often interpreted as closely linked to the claim that women are entitled to this surgical intervention regardless of ability to pay, which is a right of entitlement. Some, usually those who are in opposition to abortion on demand on one of the preceding interpretations, treat the view that abortion should be available on demand as a claim that abortion is *morally justified* under all circumstances. They then argue that one should deny availability of abortion on the grounds that it would sometimes be morally wrong to have an abortion. The view that women have a moral and legal right to obtain an abortion without the approval of others does not imply that it is always, on balance, morally justified for a given woman to exercise that right. It does at least suggest that the woman is prima facie the best person to decide when abortion is morally justified.

Although the rights that I have just discussed are relevant to the moral issues involved, the moral aspects of the condition or relation of pregnancy is of even greater importance, and it is that subject to which I now turn.

4. THE MORAL ASPECTS OF PREGNANCY AND THE STATUS OF THE FETUS

I have already given some examples of the blindness of our culture to the experience of pregnancy. As a consequence of this blindness, the relationship between the pregnant woman and the fetus is inadequately conceptualized, as is the ontological and moral status of the fetus. What we find in the abortion literature is a conceptualization based on the categories that are familiar to men's experience, so that being pregnant is represented on the one hand as similar to having a tumor, or on the other as being hooked up to an adult stranger who is dependent on that hookup for survival, or more remote yet, as occupying a house with another person whose presence constitutes more or less of a threat to one's life. Although philosophers have offered some ingenious arguments, the unsatisfying nature of these treatments should warn us that the conceptualizations on which these arguments are based are mistaken.

Judith J. Thomson's [32] analogy about being hooked up to the ailing violinist is helpful in that it reveals some of the special nature of one's rights to one's own body and the problem with the view that one person could have rights to another's body.[8] Beyond shedding some light on the issue of one's rights to one's body, Thomson's paper comes close to constituting a *reductio ad absurdum* of the view that the relation of a woman to the fetus she carries is to be understood on the model of her relation to an adult stranger who wants or needs the use of her body to survive and, hence, of the view that the fetus should be understood on the model of an adult stranger (so that rights are all that matter in this case). A claim more worthy of examination is the claim that human fetuses are relevantly like newborn human beings and have the same moral status as newborns or one that is very similar, and that likewise their moral relationships are importantly similar to those of newborns.

I shall return to this claim in a moment but first wish to clarify my use of terms. By "fetus," I mean "fetus" in the strict biological sense, not a blastomere, an embryo, and so forth. Because the papers by Professors Biggers [3] and Soupart [30] discuss embryonic development, I will only make a few points about the stages in this process. After the ovum is fertilized, some authorities in medicine continue to refer to it as "an ovum" until about four weeks after the last menstrual period or two weeks after fertilization. This way of speaking reflects the continuity of biological development before and after the addition of the sperm ([11], page 125), and is in sharp contrast to the masculist neo-Aristotelian assumption that the male contribution of the sperm makes the crucial ontological and moral difference. (The neo-Aristotelian view is the basis of what became the claim of the biological father that his offspring were his property.) The demarcation between embryos and fetuses is not sharp. It occurs at roughly ten weeks after the last menstrual period or eight weeks after fertilization. Nonetheless, there are established criteria for distinguishing between embryos and fetuses. These are reflected in the definition that Van Nostrand's *Scientific Encyclopedia* gives for the term "embryo":

> The developing individual between the union of the germ cells and the completion of the organs which characterize its body when it becomes a separate organism. The term is difficult to limit because some development occurs after birth or hatching and in some species considered growth intervenes between the completion of the essential structures of the individual and its assumption of separate life. In the latter stage, the organism is called a fetus if it is a mammal ([34], page 943).

A fetus then is a mammal with the "essential structures," that is, the major organ systems characteristic of its species, but prior to its assumption of a "separate life." Differentiation of the tissues continues during fetal life and some differentiation takes place after birth as well. For example, sexual differentiation is not complete until puberty.

The reason that the biological category, fetus, looks as though it might have ethical import, is that fetuses are sentient, that is, possessing major human organ systems gives fetuses the ability to experience as opposed to merely react to their environment. Sentience provides one basis for the analogy between fetuses and newborns. Furthermore, whereas, as Professor Biggers has shown, a fertilized ovum has less than a 40 percent chance of developing into a newborn, fetuses have a very good chance, statistically speaking. (I do not intend to suggest that the killing of even an embryo has no moral significance. I am inclined to regard the killing of at least higher animal forms as something requiring at least *some* moral justification, and thus not something that it is morally acceptable to do on whim.)

Membership in the species *Homo sapiens* is often mentioned as though it were morally significant, but it is hard to see how species identity could be significant in the absence of other similarities. Mere species identity (the fact that the cells of some being have the human chromosomal pattern) is hardly a morally relevant trait, since this is something that human people share with some human tissue cultures.[9] If life forms on other planets should turn out to act as moral agents and have other morally relevant characteristics of people, then mere species difference ought not to prejudice our treatment of them, or justify a failure to regard them as people. Similarly two nonpersons who are similar in morally significant respects ought to be treated similarly, regardless of their species. Although the termination of a pregnancy even at the embryonic stage is a grim option, killing of a sentient human raises additional moral questions. Obviously there are differences between fetuses at ten weeks after the last menstrual period and those at term, not the least of which is viability, the subject discussed in Professor Engelhardt's [10] essay. I leave it open as to what, if any, moral significance these differences have.

The term "person" has been used in many disparate technical senses, only some of which are morally significant. Because of the variety of technical uses to which the term "person" has been put, I try to avoid using it and its plural "persons," and make do with the term "people" and use "person" only when it is necessary to use a singular noun.

As I argued, an individual acquires the moral status of a person in and through relationships with other people. Furthermore, people's behavior is understandable only by reference to their participation in human communities. Even in the unusual circumstance in which a person is living in isolation from other people, that person's behavior is strongly influenced by social understandings and practices that are acquired in relationships with other people. For example, Robinson Crusoe lived as a Britisher even when he lived alone.

I take it that being a human being and having language are jointly sufficient to indicate that one is a person. (Such people may be immature people, neurotic people, mad people, or for some other reasons, of limited competence, but that is another matter.) I choose the indicators of being human and having language because of what I know, or think I know, about the process of language learning in humans, its prerequisites and its consequences. I trust that it is clear that I am not suggesting that the properties of being human and possessing language are indicators that must necessarily be present for one to be counted as a person, much less that these indicators provide a definition of the concept. Rather, I propose to use the term "people" in a way that retains all the richness and fuzziness of that concept, so that we will be less likely to overlook features of people that are germane to their special moral status.

People are (among other things) moral agents, that is, beings who can act for moral reasons and whose acts can be reasonably evaluated in moral terms. The claim that fetuses are people is absurd if it is taken to imply that fetuses are, or are very much like, moral agents, that they have moral integrity, have moral responsibilities and are capable of making choices. The same is true, however, of newborns. Concern over responsibilities for the welfare of the fetus is better expressed by asking whether the fetus is similar to a newborn (in ways that are morally relevant) than by asking whether the fetus is a person.[10]

One motive for insisting that a fetus is a person has been to give grounds for saying that feticide is homicide. Replacing the question of whether the fetus is a person by the question of the extent of the similarity in moral status of fetuses and newborns, does not prejudge the question of whether feticide should count as homicide, since infanticide is generally regarded as homicide. Furthermore, it should be clear that saying that we need to examine the claim that human fetuses are like newborn human beings is not asserting that the moral status of fetuses is the same as that of newborns. To examine the claim, however, we would need an understanding of the ontological and moral status of newborns and, interestingly enough, we lack even this.

The absence of a developed philosophical account of the moral status of newborns is further evidence of the blindness of the culture to women's experience. The care of newborns has been left almost entirely to women, and therefore the store of knowledge that we have regarding newborns and the conceptual understanding that has been developed in the course of this practice has been largely ignored. It is well to remember that when Freud put forward his theory of childhood sexuality, he recognized that what he was saying was already known by those who tended the nursery. Nonetheless, his ideas were counted as startling new discoveries.

If the day-to-day realities concerning toddlers and children have been omitted from the background knowledge on which philosophers and other scholars and scientists rely, this is even more true of our knowledge concerning newborns.[11] Indeed, because the organization of modern life gives little opportunity for the transmission of the knowledge and practices of the subculture that is or was women's culture (for example, we no longer see our neighbors through labor and delivery), the disregard of newborns in the philosophical literature is now matched by an ignorance of them even on the part of a large number of women. For example, it is common for people expecting their first child and attending childbirth classes never to have seen a newborn, and thus they must be warned not to expect that their newborn will look like the chubby, social, emerging people depicted on diaper boxes and baby food jars. (I recall one father-to-be who regarded Elizabeth Janeway's description of infants as "voracious" as a shocking and perhaps even hostile statement, whereas in fact, "voracious" aptly describes newborns whose only coordinated movements are those of sucking and who do that with total involvement.)

Although we need an adequate account of the moral aspects of the relation of parents and their newborns to one another and to others in society, in order to assess the scope and limits of the analogy between the parent-newborn relation and the relation of the pregnant woman to the fetus she carries, I will at least point out points of negative and positive analogy between fetuses and newborns. For example, both fetuses and newborns are extremely vulnerable to permanent detriments later in life as a result of short-term deprivation or exposure to noxious influences. On the negative side, it is impossible for the pregnant woman to do something analogous to putting the newborn up for adoption.

A difference in the practice with regard to the disposal of the bodies of fetuses and newborns indicates a *perceived* difference between fetuses and newborns. Statistics on premature birth in the United States are compiled using the figure of 500 grams as the cutoff between miscarriage and premature birth. In many other countries the figure used is 1000 grams. The weight of 500 grams represents a weight that has been the lower limit for survival, that is, survival *supported and assisted by high technology.* (Therefore it is not an estimate of the lower limit for viability in Engelhardt's sense.) According to the law in many states, fetuses *ex utero* over 500 grams are considered premature newborns, and therefore birth certificates must be issued for them and they must be buried. Fetuses under 500 grams are treated as other tissue, and hospitals dispose of them accordingly. The procedures are no different at any Roman Catholic hospital with which I am familiar, that is, *no* hospital buries the bodies of fetuses less than 500 grams. As far as I have been able to ascertain, when a spontaneous abortion occurs outside of the hospital, people do not bury the body of fetuses and this is true even of those who profess to regard not only fetuses, but all products of conception, as people.

Whatever the extent of the analogy between fetuses and newborns, it must be the same for wanted and unwanted fetuses. If feticide that results from induced abortion is homicide, so is feticide that is a consequence of an accidental action on the part of the pregnant woman. If such an accident involved negligence by the pregnant woman, she would then be guilty of negligent homicide. It may be clear that deciding the scope and the limits of the analogy between the relation of parents to newborns and pregnant women to fetuses is not a simple matter and will have consequences reaching far beyond its impact on induced abortions.

5. THE TRADITION WHICH REGARDS WOMEN AND WOMEN'S BODIES AS A RESOURCE TO BE USED BY MEN

I have argued that our culture has neglected women's experience and the status of women as moral individuals with a need to maintain moral as well as bodily integrity, particularly in connection with pregnancy and childbirth. How then has the culture represented women? There is a long tradition that regards women and women's bodies as property to be bartered, bestowed, or used by men. Usually women have lacked the power to refuse to accept sexual partners, have had little or no option as to whether to prevent or seek pregnancy, or whether to carry to term or abort. That the prohibition of abortion has often coexisted with the practice of infanticide, infanticide controlled either by the father of the infant or by the state, shows that the prohibition of abortion often evidences the view that women or women's bodies are a resource to be controlled by men, rather than a concern about feticide. The prohibition of abortion within Nazi Germany evidences the same view. We find the legacy of this tradition still very much with us when opposition to abortion is supported with the reason that women should not be allowed to have abortions because this allows them to escape the consequences of what is seen as their probable sexual "misconduct."

The book of *Deuteronomy* (22:13–21) stipulates that if any new husband accuses his bride of not having been a virgin at her marriage and her male relative cannot produce the "tokens of her virginity" as evidence that she was, she is to be stoned to death. *Deuteronomy* (22:22) also lists the death penalty as punishment for extramarital relations on the part of a married woman with no sanctions at all on similar activity on the part of a married man. Until the late 1960s, the legal definition of adultery in the state of Connecticut was extramarital activity involving a married woman. Extramarital sexual activity on the part of a married man was not covered by the statute. The Bible not only exempts men from similar jeopardy for extramarital sexual activity, but as the example of Abraham *(Genesis,* 12:11–16) and Isaac *(Genesis,* 26:7–10) show, men were excused for giving their wives for the sexual use of other men, and Lot *(Genesis,* 19:1–8) and the Ephremite of Judges 19 (19:22–24) are approved for offering their virgin daughters to be raped to ensure that that fate does not befall their male guests. Not only is it a common assumption in our heritage that women's bodies are at the disposal first of their fathers and then of their husbands, but until recently, the prevailing view was that if women wandered out of the care of such "protectors" they were "asking for" trouble, and "fair game" for rape. The threat of rape still severely restricts the mobility of women in society, notwithstanding the fact that rape frequently occurs within the victim's home.[12]

B. Nathanson and R. N. Ostling in their book, *Aborting America* [21] profess that their regard for the fetus leads them to oppose all abortion although they do have some concern about one kind of problem pregnancy. This is not the pregnancy that results from rape or that which involves the pregnant 12-year-old. It is the pregnancy that results from adultery. Nathanson expresses sympathy with the view he attributes to George Williams of Harvard Divinity School, that in the case of pregnancy from adultery, the husband has the right to demand an abortion. This sentiment continues to evidence the view that women's bodies ought to be under the control of their husbands.

We find that the interest of the state or of those in power in controlling women's bodies, and through that controlling fertility, is equally represented in the tradition. In the *Republic* (Bk. 5, 460), Plato casually recommends infanticide for unpromising infants, and the recent history of fluctuations in the policies of Eastern European countries with regard to contraception and abortion show that the availability of both are manipulated to suit economic interests of those in power. The sentiment favoring such manipulation is also illustrated in an article by Alan L. Otten that appeared on the front page of the *Wall Street Journal,*[13] in which Otten speaks of a "people shortage," which turns out to be a shortage, not of people in general, but of "native populations" of the countries of Northwestern Europe [23]. In this article, Otten raises the specter of shrinking markets and mentions such remedies as anti-abortion laws, but does not mention caring for children. If pronatalist policies were desired, then a rational and humane implementation would involve addressing the concern of women that they cannot adequately care for additional children and would make provision to care for both existing and future children. This does not seem to have occurred to Otten who does not discuss either adjusting work life to accommodate the existence of children, or providing good inexpensive day care for children. Otten seems oblivious to the fact that even in industrialized countries, and in the United States in particular, *most* women seek paid employment out of economic necessity. Perhaps Otten is not interested in most women, but only wants to get the more affluent "native population" women back to breeding.

A frequent complaint of feminists is that little priority has been given to the development of contraceptives that are both safe and effective. As it now stands, the methods of contraception that are reputed to be most effective have proved to have a greater mortality risk than does a legal first trimester abortion in the United States.[14]

In the seventeenth century, John Locke put forward a view that husbands do not have the power of life and death over their wives, but do have ultimate authority in decisions affecting the family's common interest, including the power to decide the control of their joint property. Since, according to seventeenth century English law, the husband was given total control not only of his wife's property, but also of her person, and he had the right to imprison her and beat her so long as he stopped short of killing her, Mary Ann Warren argues that Locke's views were advanced for his time and should be termed "protofeminist" [35]. Indeed, Locke's view that all men are naturally free and equal was taken up and interpreted to apply to women by early feminist writers such as Mary Wollstonecraft.

In Rousseau's *Émile* [27], we find further evidence of the way in which the tradition of regarding women and women's bodies as a resource for men continues, even in the work of those writers usually taken to have placed the greatest emphasis on individual dignity and autonomy. In this work, Rousseau sets out a plan for the education of a child from infancy to manhood. The emphasis is on an upbringing that will place little or no restraint on the child Émile. This absence of restraint extends from the elimination of swaddling clothes to having as much playtime as the child likes. Rather than giving Émile commands, the tutor will arrange circumstances so that Émile learns the desired lessons from experience. Émile is to be taught to believe nothing except what is evident to his own reason. It is an education supposedly geared toward autonomy, but given the absence of responsibility for the welfare of others, one might ask whether the self-governance implied in autonomy would indeed be present. The suggestion that it would not finds support in the plan of education laid down for Sophie, Émile's future bride, who must, Rousseau tells us, like all girls "be trained to bear the yoke from the first so that they may not feel it, to master their own caprices and to submit themselves to the will of others" ([27], page 332). Indeed Rousseau maintains that she should even be deliberately subjected to injustice since she is "formed to obey a creature so imperfect as man, a creature so often vicious and always faulty, she should learn early to submit to injustice and to suffer the wrong inflicted on her by her husband without complaint" ([27], page 333). Unlike Émile, Sophie is to be taught to believe on the basis of authority, rather than to believe on the basis of reason.

In this sort of social scheme, it is easy to recognize the fantasies of an infant or toddler centering on having control of the mother who will forever act as a willing buffer between him and harsh reality. It is the realization of this fantasy for men at least that explains the implicit double standard that I mentioned earlier, according to which men are at liberty so long as they do not unduly violate the rights of other men, but which holds that women are morally required to meet the needs of others and perhaps are denied equal rights in addition. The rights of women, and the responsibilities of others to meet the needs of women if women are to be able to meet their responsibilities, are rarely mentioned.

This asymmetry between the way in which the ethical situations of men and women are construed is found again in a recent article on abortion by Rosaline Weiss, in "The Perils of Personhood" [36]. In her article, Weiss points out some of the weaknesses of the argument that the fetus is a person and therefore has a right to life. She suggests that the abortion issue be reexamined from the perspective of duties rather than of rights. The duties and responsibilities that she mentions, however, are exclusively duties and responsibilities that might exist on the part of the woman to promote the welfare of the fetus. It does not occur to her to ask what might be the duties and responsibilities of others toward pregnant women and new mothers. It is as though women are regarded as Earth Mothers, having access to all resources and being able to meet all the needs simultaneously, if they were only willing to do so. The literature on abortion shows that many people are readily able to image themselves in the place of fetus but not in the place of the pregnant woman,[15] but *if one is able to look at the matter from the perspective of the pregnant woman, it becomes clear how much violence is done to the woman by abortion, and therefore that the woman's self interest would lead her to avoid (unwanted pregnancy and) abortion if she had other options genuinely available.*

6. SOME MORAL DILEMMAS OF
PREGNANT WOMEN

Some of the moral issues that are commonly involved in decisions to seek or attempt an abortion are specific instances of dilemmas that face pregnant women generally. Over the centuries, pregnant women have taken pains to avoid those influences thought to be teratogenic, and an extensive lore purporting to identify these influences developed. The existence of this lore attests to the longstanding nature of women's concern to promote the healthy development of the fetus.

One dilemma commonly faced by a pregnant woman with existing children is that she must weigh some benefits to those children against some risk to the fetus, usually in the nature of increased risk of abortion and of premature delivery and of the damage that commonly results from premature birth. For example, the medical center at which I worked is the only referral in the state. Patients who cannot afford private care may need to travel 700 miles or more to obtain treatment. A woman in the late stages of pregnancy with a child who needs treatment may have to choose between the increased risk of abortion, or premature delivery that attends a long automobile trip and having her child's ailments go untreated.

The typical woman in Asia and the Middle East who seeks an abortion (or attempts to abort herself) is an older married woman who has given birth to many children. In circumstances of poverty where the welfare, and indeed the survival of existing children, are likely to be put in question by another birth, that fact must figure in the woman's response to her pregnancy (unless she has been so conditioned to "bear the yoke" or is so debilitated by malnutrition and disease that she has little or no response to what happens to her).

Even in this country, half of the women who have abortions are already mothers for whom the welfare of existing children is likely to be an important consideration. As Justice Brennan pointed out in his dissent on the Gilbert decision (the decision that struck down the EEOC guidelines calling on employers to provide maternity disability benefits), the United States is the only industrialized country in the world with no universal legal and social provisions for maternity. The woman whose children depend on her income may regard the welfare of those children (or of aged parents or others who depend on her) as incompatible with continuing a pregnancy, even if she could bear the thought of giving up a newborn for adoption. Considering how many women are supporting children on salaries at or below the poverty line in this country, such fears are likely to be common. Although children in this country do not starve to death in significant numbers, many children live in conditions of poverty where their physical safety is always in question. Recent figures on poverty in the United States show that families consisting of women and their children are the most rapidly growing segment of the poor. A survey in the State of Illinois in 1980, for example, found that one child in six is being raised in poverty. The moral dilemmas facing a pregnant woman because of the competing responsibility for the welfare of her fetus and the welfare of existing children (or aged parents, and so on) are real and deserve systematic attention.

The woman who is pregnant by rape and is struggling to come to terms with and recover from the experience of rape, faces a special dilemma that exists in some form for all pregnant women, that of coming to terms with the experience of pregnancy. One author of a well-known pregnancy manual describes the early describes the early fetus in the following terms: "It is already alive, a human being, although its movements are still too feeble to be felt. And it has immense power. It can make a person take care of it, and adjust her whole organism to serve it" ([13], [40]). Small wonder that a woman pregnant by rape frequently experiences her pregnancy as a nine-month continuation of that rape. Not only does she, like many raped women, wake up at night screaming, but when she does, she finds that her body is still possessed by another. It is a significant omission that the philosophical literature on abortion has considered the rape issue only in connection with the question of whether the woman bears some responsibility for having become pregnant by having consented to sexual relations!

Being taken over by another being is an idea that has evoked both wonder and horror through the ages. It evokes wonder where it represents a desired union with God or some divine force (for example, being filled with the Holy Spirit, or being inspired by a Muse). It evokes horror where it represents being taken over unwillingly by some human or demonic force (for example, being possessed by a troubled spirit or the ghost of a person who has died, or by a demon, witch, or sorcerer). Possession and inspiration provide the closest analogy to the ultimately unique experience of pregnancy. The experience of a wanted pregnancy is as different from that of an unwanted pregnancy as the two experiences of inspiration and possession. (Perhaps all or most experiences of inspiration have some element of possession in them and vice versa, and similarly with wanted and unwanted pregnancies.)

It should be noted that, like inspiration and possession, pregnancy whether wanted or unwanted is a psychologically hazardous path. The rate of significant mental illness after delivery is high and is considerably higher than that following abortion. According to Freedman and Kaplan's *Comprehensive Textbook of Psychiatry* [22], postpartum psychoses, while uncommon, stand at the significantly high rate of one to two per thousand deliveries. (Notice that this rate is for *all* pregnancies carried to term, both wanted and unwanted.) This high rate of significant postpartum reaction is not surprising when one considers that bringing another person into full social being requires continual renegotiation of the self-other boundaries. Of course to say that some experience is risky is not to say that the risks are not worth taking, but it does suggest that those bearing the risk should decide whether to undertake it.

In parts of Africa and Latin America, the typical woman seeking an abortion is young and unmarried ([6], page 106), and this is the profile of about half of the women seeking abortions in the United States. The young unmarried woman may face the same threat of poverty that confronts an older married woman and, like the oldest, the youngest pregnant women often face greatly increased risks to their own health from pregnancy. The unmarried woman, however, faces the additional stigma of "illegitimacy." The stigmatization of women who dare or are forced to bring forth children without being married, serves to control not merely a woman's sexual behavior but, perhaps more importantly, her option of creating families with or without men.

The postulation of a "Principle of Legitimacy" as a "universal sociological law" and as "the most important moral and legal rule" concerning kinship was made in the 1930s by Bronislaw Malinowski. According to Laslett, it has continued to dominate discussions of birth out of wedlock ever since. The version of the "Principle of Legitimacy" that he quotes from Malinowski is.

> The most important moral and legal rule concerning the physiological state of kinship is that no child should be brought into this world without a man—and one man at that—assuming the role of sociological father, that is guardian and protector, the male link between the child and the rest of the community. I think that this generalization amounts to a universal sociological law, and as such I have called it…The Principle of Legitimacy ([18], page 5).

The only alternative to bringing a child into the world once pregnancy has begun is to abort it.

Today in the United States there are three million teenage girls having sexual intercourse who are not protected by any form of contraception. They are at high risk for pregnancy and cannot be assumed to have made a considered decision to undertake the responsibilities of parenthood.[16] If women's knowledge and control of their bodies were fostered generally (I have in mind here promulgation of the sort of knowledge found in the women's health movement), then decisions about contraception could be approached forthrightly. Although I do not believe that engaging in heterosexual intercourse without contraceptive protection when pregnancy is undesired is *necessarily* an unreflective or uninformed choice, the evidence is that teenagers frequently do so because of lack of information or because of social pressure.

We still live with the legacy of the view expressed by Rousseau that women should not be educated to make responsible decisions but to learn "to bear the yoke." While factions quarrel over *which yoke* the young teenage girl should bear, the present situation will continue. On the one hand, those who would forbid the young teenager heterosexual intercourse have often convinced her that premeditated contraceptive preparation shows that she is cheap, that is, too available. (The opposite of being "cheap" is being "expensive," which means that one still is a commodity but the price is higher. The way out of the commodity mentality is not to avoid "being cheap" but to reclaim one's body, to reclaim it in the way expressed by the phrase "Our Bodies Ourselves.") On the other hand, societal arrangements that make the girl dependent on pleasing men pressure her into sexual intercourse at an early age. As long as we are content to leave girls subject to pressures, and simply try to see that "the right" yoke is placed on them, rather than support the development of their capacity to make decisions they can live with concerning their lives in general and sexual activity in particular, the only alternatives to increased maternity (and resulting morbidity and mortality) among teenagers, will be the grim options of legal abortion or illegal abortion.

If we take seriously women's role as decision makers and moral agents then we must give greater attention to the issue of providing accurate information to the woman facing a decision about abortion. Such information must of course include information about the embryo or fetus that will die as a result of the abortion procedure. It is unfortunate that there has not been more attention to this point on the part of feminists. Perhaps this is because the phrase "informed consent" has been misapplied to inaccurate information designed to frighten and punish the woman seeking an abortion. Probably the most famous attempt to force misinformation on women was the Akron ordinance that required that, among other things, a woman seeking an abortion be told that abortion was "major surgery" (contrary to the view of the American College of Obstetrics and Gynecology) [1]. Dr. Willard Cates, Jr., Director of the Abortion Surveillance Branch of the National Center for Disease Control, Atlanta, Georgia, has recently discussed the harmful consequences of the Akron ordinance and other measures designed to restrict abortion services [4].

Perhaps some of the people interested in ensuring a woman's right to a safe, early abortion have failed to provide a pregnant woman full and accurate information about the embryo or fetus because they wish to spare the woman—but then the behavior is paternalistic. It fails to respect the woman's need to maintain her moral integrity, that is, to face her situation and make a decision that she can live with. (I also regard the effort as misguided in that there is considerable evidence that this sort of deception actually increases psychological damage in the long run.)

Dr. Raymond S. Duff has written extensively on the process of facing grim choices and of supporting parents in facing the grim choices that arise when a baby is born with severe deformities.[17] He emphasizes the harm done when hospital staff think they are sparing the parents by failing to give them all the information or failing to cooperate with the uncoerced choice of parents to see or hold their deformed or dead babies. In a recent letter to the *New England Journal of Medicine* [9], Duff explicitly extends this to fetuses, recommending that the staff be prepared to accede to women's requests to be shown their aborted fetuses. I concur with Duff and argue that just as women who have *spontaneously* aborted have been left puzzled and angry by the paternalism of physicians who dismiss their loss as "a matter of little consequence,"[18] so women who resort to induced abortion have been inadequately prepared by those counselors who avoid discussing the embryo or fetus that will die as a result of the procedure.

7. CONCLUSION

I have argued that the moral issues involving decisions to resort to abortion need to be reformulated. Recent philosophical discussion of the subject, and most of the popular discussion, has systematically ignored certain important features of the moral situation, most commonly features that are more prominent in women's experience than in men's. A major point that has been neglected is that abortion is not something that anyone would straightforwardly want, but rather is a surgical intervention that, like most surgical interventions, is resorted to only if the alternatives are even worse. It is therefore misleading to speak of a right to abortion because this makes it sound as if abortion were something, like equal pay, that people might want. The right to control one's body is of course something that people can and do straightforwardly want. Indeed that right is a fundamental right of privacy, that is, exercising control over one's body is requisite for functioning as a person. An adequate representation of the moral situation involving abortion would need to come to terms with the fact that it is in the interests of women not to have to resort to abortion in order to control their bodies, just as it is in the interests of women to prevent breast cancer rather than treat it with mastectomies or "lumpectomies" even if these operations constituted one hundred percent safe and effective treatments for breast cancer.

Of course being pregnant is importantly different from having a tumor, and often unwanted pregnancy would be wanted if there were a change in other conditions, for example if there were more social support for child rearing or no stigma attached to giving birth to children out of wedlock. Pregnancy has remained one of the least discussed subjects in philosophy in spite of much recent discussion of fetuses and abortion. There has been no attention given to the moral dilemmas commonly faced by pregnant women other than decisions about whether to induce abortion, even though decisions about how to choose between risks to the fetus and risks to existing children or between a risk of deformity and an increased risk of (spontaneous) abortion raise many of the same philosophical questions. These questions concern the moral status of the fetus; the nature of the relationships of pregnant women to their fetuses and of each to others in society; and the relative importance of future deformity, present or future pain, and continuance of life in assessing the well-being of the fetus. These philosophical questions might well be brought together by examining the scope and limits of the analogy between fetuses and newborns. To do this would require a developed philosophical account of newborns, and modern philosophy has none to offer. Intimate relationships with newborn babies and with the practices that transform them into people in the full social sense that is so commonly a part of women's experience as mothers,[19] nurses, aunts, and so forth, has been omitted from the background knowledge on which philosophers rely in choosing their problems and framing their arguments. If we are to understand the philosophical issues concerning fetuses, pregnant women, and the nature of the relationship created in pregnancy, we will need to give close attention to women's experience and to the practices involved that have traditionally been regarded as women's work, especially infant and child care and nursing (in all the senses of that term). It is only then that we will be able to frame ethical issues in an adequate manner, that is, in a way that takes account of all the morally relevant features of the situation.[20]

STUDY QUESTIONS

1. Describe Whitbeck's views on the morality of abortion. What is her main idea with regard to seeing abortion from the vantage point of the pregnant woman?

2. Compare Whitbeck's feminist thesis with Markowitz's (Chapter 24). How are they similar and different? Evaluate them.

3. Do you agree with Whitbeck that abortion, even though not a good thing, should be mainly left to the pregnant woman to decide on? If the fetus is a person, does the suffering of the woman justify killing the fetus? Explain your reasoning.

4. What does Whitbeck mean by shifting from a *rights* view to a *responsibility* view of morality? How does this apply to the problem of abortion?

NOTES

★ I owe many intellectual debts to feminist writing and writings and, more important, to specific examples of feminist practice. I am no longer able to keep track of them all. Certainly extended discussions with Carol P. Christ, particularly in 1971 and 1972 were of inestimable value to me in developing my own thought on women's issues. I note how congenial to the views presented here is Christ's reading of Atwood's *Surfacing* as showing that abortion "is not a matter of little consequence" ([5], page 52). One of the many catalysts to my thinking on the present issue was Adrienne Rich's discussion of abortion in *Of Woman Born* from which the following passage is taken:

"No free woman, with 100 perfect effective, non-harmful birth control readily available, would 'choose' abortion. At present, it is certainly likely that a woman can—through many causes—become so demoralized as to use abortion as a form of violence against herself—a penance, an expiation. But this needs to be viewed against the ecology of guilt and victimization in which so many women grow up. In a society where women entered sexual intercourse willingly, where adequate contraception was a genuine social priority, there would be no "abortion issue." And in such a society there would be a vast diminishment of female self-hatred—a psychic source of many unwanted pregnancies.

"Abortion is violence: a deep desperate violence inflicted by a woman upon, first of all, herself. It is the offspring, and will continue to be the accuser, of a more pervasive and prevalent violence, the violence of rapism" ([26], 273–274).

I wish to thank James B. Speer, Jr. and Eleanor Kuykendall for their detailed criticism of this paper.

1. Paul suggests a very different view of the spiritual significance of gender in *Galatians,* 3: 28 but repeats the views he expressed in *Corinthians,* in *1st. Timothy* (2:12–15) and *Ephesians* (5:22–23).

2. For example, Michael Tooley in "A Defense of Abortion and Infanticide" stipulates "In my usage the sentence "X is a person" will be synonymous with the sentence "X has a (serious) moral right to life" ([33], page 40); and Edward A. Langerak, in his article "Abortion: Listening to the Middle," stipulates that he uses the term "person" to refer to "those human beings that will have as strong a claim to life as a normal adult" ([17], page 25).

3. Since the line between description of acts or actions and the ends achieved by those acts or actions is not sharp, obligations shade into responsibilities.

4. Readers may notice the similarity between ideas I express here and ideas put forward by John Ladd in his article "Legalism and Medical Ethics" [15]. However, in the abbreviated version of this article, which appeared in the March 1979, *Journal of Medicine and Philosophy* [16], Ladd omits what, to my mind, were crucial parts of the view of an ethics of responsibility. That is, he does not bring out the importance of respect for rights in safeguarding people's moral integrity and because his work does not go into the view of the person implicit in different views of ethics, I hesitate to say how close my views are to Ladd's, although I owe much to having read his work.

5. Some philosophers have argued that a person cannot choose freely when faced with grim options. I have discussed problems with some of these arguments in "Towards an Understanding of Motivational Disturbance and Freedom of Action" [40].

6. For a social history of illegitimacy or bastardy, see [18].

7. In "A Theory of Health" [39], I have developed some related distinctions and shown these implications for the concepts of health and disease, and therefore for understanding the medical enterprise.

8. Ketchum's [14] argument that one's right to one's body is not a property right.

9. Those who argue that killing a fertilized ovum is just as bad, morally speaking, as killing a viable fetus do not seem to realize that the view commits them to a position that killing a viable fetus is *no worse* than killing a fertilized ovum.

10. Birth constitutes a major change in status according to many *religious* traditions. In the New Testament, for example, birth is the principal metaphor for beginning, and generates such expressions as "reborn in Christ," rather than, say "reconceived in Christ." Of course, those who are willing to question the ethical validity of such religious sources can still consider the possibility that the moral status of the fetus may be close to that of a newborn.

11. The way in which philosophers employ background knowledge is aptly illustrated in Solomon's paper [29] where he refers to the experience of being a stranger in a strange city; however, it is reasonable to assume that people attending a conference like the one generating this volume will have had this experience many times in their lives. Background knowledge about newborn care is not something that philosophers, other than a few feminist philosophers, use in their arguments. For an interesting example of philosophical attention to infants and child care, see [28].

12. This point has been thoroughly argued by Susan Peterson in "Rape and Coercion: The State as a Male Protection Racket" [24].

13. 1 am indebted to Barbara Tilley for bringing this article to my attention.

14. An extensive bibliography on the hazards of various forms of birth control, together with a multifaceted discussion of the subject, is contained in [12]. See also [43].

15. As Mary Daly observes, the analogy between the fetus in the womb and the space traveler in a capsule is a recurrent theme, and she maintains that the popularity of the identification of fetus with space travelers explains some of the popular fascination with, and generous findings of space exploration [8].

16. The many different reasons that women have for not using contraception are discussed in [20].

17. By "severe deformities" one generally means deformities that produce severe retardation, or pain throughout life and not "merely" crippling or disfigurement.

18. Victoria Spelman informs me that there is a book forthcoming on the subject of a woman's experience of spontaneous abortion, which takes as its ironic title, *A Matter of Little Consequence.*

19. Notice that Carol Christ uses the same form of words and denies that abortion is a "matter of little consequence" for the woman involved. See ★ Note. For 1974, the percentage of women in the United States bearing children some time in their lives stood at 91 percent as compared with 73 percent in 1910 [31].

20. After the paper was written I became familiar with Carol Gilligan's psychological studies that lend empirical support to the thesis that the responsibilities view is more adequate for expressing women's moral concerns. See *In a Different Voice,* Cambridge: Harvard University Press, 1982.

WORKS CITED

(When "in this volume" follows a citation, it refers to the book in which Whitbeck's piece originally appeared—Eds.)

1. *Akron Center for Reproductive Heath, Inc. v. City of Akron,* 651 F. 2d 1198 (C.A. 6 Ohio, June 12, 1981; re hearings denied, July 10, 1981, and July 22, 1981).

2. Benn, S. I., "Privacy, Freedom and Respect for Persons," in *Today's Moral Problems,* ed. R. Wasserstrom. New York: Macmillan, 1975, 1–20.

3. Biggers, J. D., "Generation of the Human Life Cycle," in this volume, 1983, 31–53.

4. Cates, W., Jr. "Restricting Abortion Services: Harm and Misfortune," *Medical News* 26 (1980): 3.

5. Christ, C. P., *Diving Deep and Surfacing.* Cambridge, Mass.: Beacon, 1980.

6. "Complications of Abortion in Developing Countries," *Population Reports,* Series F, No. 7, Population Information Program, The Johns Hopkins University, Baltimore, July 1980.

7. Connery, J. R., "Abortion: Roman Catholic Perspectives," in *Encyclopedia of Bioethics,* vol. 1, ed. W. Reich. New York: Macmillan and Free Press, 1978, 9–13.

8. Daly, M., *Gyn/Ecology: Metaethics of Radical Feminism.* Cambridge, Mass.: Beacon, 1978.

9. Duff, R. S., "Care in Childbirth and Beyond," *New England Journal of Medicine* (1980), 302, 685–686.

10. Engelhardt, H. T., Jr., "Viability and the Use of the Fetus," in this volume, 1982, 183–208.

11. Hellman, L. M. and J. Pritchard (eds.), *Williams Obstetrics.* New York: Appleton Century Crofts, 1971.

12. Holmes, H. et al. (eds.), *Birth Control and Controlling Birth.* Clifton, N.J.: Humana, 1981.

13. Ingelman-Fundberg, A., *A Guide for the Mother To Be.* Clifton, N.J.: Humana, 1975.

14. Ketchum, S. A., "The Moral Status of the Bodies of Persons," unpublished manuscript, 1980

15. Ladd, J., "Legalism and Medical Ethics," in *Contemporary Issues in Biomedical Ethics,* ed. J. W. Davis, B. Hoffmaster, and S. Shorten. Clifton, N.J.: Humana, 1978, 1–33.

16. Ladd, J., "Legalism and Medical Ethics," *Journal of Medicine and Philosophy* 4 (1979): 70–80.

17. Langerak, E. A., "Abortion: Listening to the Middle," *Hastings Center Report* 9 (1979): 24–48.

18. Laslett, K., K. Oatween, and R. M. Smith (eds.), *Bastardy and Its Comparative History.* Cambridge, Mass.: Harvard University Press, 1980.

19. *Levy v. Louisiana,* 391 U.S. 68 (1968).

20. Luker, K., *Taking Chances.* Berkeley: University of California Press, 1978.

21. Nathanson, B. N. and R. N. Ostling, *Aborting America.* New York: Doubleday, 1979.

22. Normand, W. C ., "Postpartum Disorders," in *Comprehensive Textbook of Psychiatry,* ed. A. M. Freedman and H. I. Kaplan. Baltimore: Williams and Wilkins, 1967, 1161–1163.

23. Otten, A. L., 1979, "People Shortage: A Growing Problem," *Wall Street Journal* 64 (38): 1.

24. Peterson, S. "Rape and Coercion: The State as a Male Protection Racket," in *Feminism and Philosophy,* (ed.) M. Vetterlin-Braggin, et al. Totowa, N.J.: Littlefield Adams, 1977, 54–61.

25. Reiman, J. H., "Privacy, Intimacy and Personhood," *Philosophy and Public Affairs* 6 (1976), 26–44.

26. Rich, A., *Of Woman Born; Motherhood as Experience and Institution.* New York: Norton, 1976.

27. Rousseau, J. J., *Émile,* trans. by B. Foxley and J. M. Denton. London: Heineman, 1963.

28. Ruddick, S. "Maternal Thinking," *Feminist Studies* 6 (1980): 87–96.

29. Solomon, R., "Reflections on the Meaning of (Fetal) Life," in this volume, 1981, 209–226.

30. Soupart, P., "Present and Possible Future Research in the Use of Human Embryos," in this volume, 1981, 67–104.

31. Stellman, J. M., *Women's Work, Women's Health: Myths and Realties.* New York: Pantheon, 1978.

32. Thomson, J. J., "Rights and Death," *Philosophy and Public Affairs* 2 (1973): 146–159.

33. Tooley, M., "A Defense of Abortion and Infanticide," *Philosophy and Public Affairs,* 2 (1972): 37–65.

34. Van Nostrand, R., *Scientific Encyclopedia.* New York: Free Press, 1976.

35. Warren, M. A. *The Nature of Woman, An Encyclopedia and Guide to the Literature.* Inverness, Calif.: Edgepress, 1980

36. Weiss, R., "The Perils of Personhood," *Ethics* 89 (1978): 66–75.

37. Whitbeck, C., "The Maternal Instinct," *The Philosophical Forum* 6 (1975): 265–273.

38. Whitbeck, C., "Theories of Sex Difference," in *Women and Philosophy: Towards a Philosophy of Liberation,* (eds.) C. C. Gould and M. W. Wartofsky. New York: Putnam's, 1976, 54–80

39. Whitbeck, C., "A Theory of Health," in *Concepts of Health and Disease,* eds. A. Caplan, H. T. Engelhardt, and J. McCartney. Reading, Mass.: Addison-Wesley, 1981, 611–626.

40. Whitbeck, C., "Towards an Understanding of Motivational Disturbance and Freedom of Action," in *Mental Health: Philosophical Perspectives,* eds. H. T. Engelhardt Jr. and S. F. Spicker. Dordrecht, Holland: D. Reidel, 1977, 221–231.

41. Whitbeck, C., "What Are We Teaching When We Teach Human Sexuality?," *Connecticut Medicine* 42 (1978): 657–661.

42. Wirsen, B., C. Wirsen, and A. McMillan (eds.), *Obstetrician.* New York: Dell, 1966, 80.

43. "Women and Health," *Public Health Reports,* Superintendent of Documents, Washington, DC: U.S. Government Printing Office, (September-October, 1980): 27.

FOR FURTHER READING

Annas, George J. "Pregnant Women as Fetal Containers." *Hastings Center Report* 16 (December 1986).

Gatens-Robinson, Eugenia. "A Defense of Woman's Choice: Abortion and the Ethics of Care." *Journal of Social Philosophy* 30.3 (Fall 1992).

Gordon, Doris. "Abortion and Rights: Applying Libertarian Principles Correctly," *Studies in Prolife Feminism* 1.2 (Spring 1995).

Harrison, Beverly Wildung. *Our Right to Choose: Toward a New Ethic of Abortion.* Boston: Beacon, 1983.

MacKinnon, Catharine. *Feminism Unmodified: Discourses on Life and Law.* Cambridge, Mass.: Harvard University Press, 1987.

Mavrodes, George. "Abortion and Imagination: Reflections on Mollenkott's 'Reproductive Choice.'" *Christian Scholar's Review* 18 (December 1988).

Mollenkott, Virginia Ramey. "Reproductive Choices Basic to Justice for Women." *Christian Scholar's Review* 17 (March 1988).

PART VIII

Abortion, Faith, and State Neutrality

Concerning freedom of religion, the United States Constitution reads, "Congress shall make no law respecting the establishment of religion, or prohibiting the free exercise thereof..." Some have interpreted this to mean that the state should remain neutral on questions that deal with people's fundamental beliefs about reality, such as one's view of the good, the meaning of life, or even when human life begins. This seems to be the reasoning behind the U.S. Supreme Court's upholding of abortion rights in *Planned Parenthood v. Casey* (1992):

> Our law affords constitutional protection to personal decisions relating to marriage, procreation, family relationships, child rearing, and education... These matters, involving the most intimate and personal choices a person may make in a lifetime, choices central to personal dignity and autonomy, are central to the liberty protected by the Fourteenth Amendment. At the heart of liberty is the right to define one's own concept of existence, of meaning, of the universe, and of the mystery of human life. Beliefs about these matters could not define the attributes of personhood were they formed under compulsion by the State.[1]

In his dissenting opinion in *Webster v. Reproductive Health Services* (1989), Supreme Court Justice John Paul Stephens writes, "The Missouri Legislature [which said that human life begins at conception] may not inject its endorsement of a particular religious tradition in this debate, for 'the Establishment Clause does not allow public bodies to foment such disagreement.'"[2]

Consequently, when the prolife advocate proposes that women should be prohibited from undergoing abortions, on the basis that human personhood begins at conception or at least sometime before birth, she not only is calling for violating women's right to privacy but also their free exercise of religion. As prochoice supporter Virginia Ramey Mollenkott argues,

> Women who believe that abortion is murder may *never* justly be required to have an abortion. Anti-abortion laws would not affect such women for obvious reasons. But for women whose religious beliefs do permit them to consider abortion (and under certain circumstances require them to do so), anti-abortion legislation would forbid their following these religious convictions.[3]

In this section, Professors Francis J. Beckwith and Ronald Dworkin wrestle with the question of whether anti-abortion legislation violates state neutrality. Beckwith argues that *both* prolife and prochoice legislation violate state neutrality because they both make certain claims about the nature of fetuses and what sorts of living beings the state ought to protect. Therefore, Beckwith concludes, there is no principled way for the state to be neutral on the issue of abortion rights. Dworkin disagrees. He maintains that prolife legislation violates the principle of state neutrality because its proponents are using state coercion to force agreement by those who disagree with the prolife movement's controversial beliefs about ultimate things. Although the state may discourage abortion, writes Dworkin, it would be wrong for the state to prohibit it entirely.

NOTES

1. *Planned Parenthood v. Casey*, 112 Sup. Ct. 2791, 2807 (1992).

2. *Webster v. Reproductive Services* (1989), as found in *The United States Law Week* 57.50 (27 July 1989): 5044–5045.

3. Virginia Ramey Mollenkott, "Reproductive Choice: Basic to Justice for Women," *Christian Scholar's Review* 17 (March 1988): 291.

28

Pluralism, Tolerance, and Abortion Rights

FRANCIS J. BECKWITH

Francis J. Beckwith is Associate Professor of Philosophy, Culture, and Law and W. Howard Hoffman scholar, at Trinity Graduate School and Trinity Law School, Trinity International University (Deerfield, IL), California campus. In this essay, Beckwith maintains that attempts to defend the right to abortion by appealing to tolerance, pluralism, or state neutrality do not succeed. According to Beckwith, to say that women have the "right to choose" abortion is tantamount to denying the prolife position that fetuses are worthy of protection. And to affirm that fetuses are fully human with a "right to life" is tantamount to denying the prochoice perspective that women have a fundamental right to abortion. In any event, it seems that neutrality concerning abortion is an intellectual impossibility. In this essay, Beckwith critiques four prochoice arguments that are often employed to defend state neutrality.

Many people in the abortion-rights movement argue that their position is more tolerant than the prolife position. After all, they reason, the abortion-rights movement is not forcing pro-life women to have abortion, but the pro-life movement *is* trying to deny all women the option to make a choice. Abortion-rights advocates use at least four arguments to articulate this position.

Used by permission from Francis J. Beckwith, "Pluralism, Tolerance, and Abortion Rights," in *Life and Learning: Proceedings of the Third University Faculty for Life Conference*, ed. Joseph Koterski (Washington, DC: University Faculty for Life, 1993). This essay is an abridged version of a portion of Chapter 5 of Francis J. Beckwith, *Politically Correct Death: Answering the Arguments for Abortion Rights* (Grand Rapids, Mich.: Baker Book House, 1993).

ARGUMENT FROM RELIGIOUS PLURALISM

It is sometimes argued that the question of when protectable human life begins is a religious question that one must answer for oneself. Justice Blackmun writes in *Roe v. Wade,* "We need not resolve the difficult question of when life begins. When those trained in the respective disciplines of medicine, philosophy, and theology are unable to arrive at any consensus, the judiciary at this point in the development of man's knowledge, is not in a position to speculate." Hence, the state should not take one theory of life and force those who do not agree with that theory to subscribe to it. Blackmun writes in *Roe,* "In view of all this, we do not agree that, by adopting one theory of life, Texas may override the rights of the pregnant woman that are at stake." In his dissenting opinion in *Webster,* Justice Stevens goes even further than Blackmun: "The Missouri Legislature [which said that life begins at conception] may not inject its endorsement of a particular religious tradition in this debate, for 'the Establishment Clause does not allow public bodies to foment such disagreement.'" Thus for the prolife advocate to propose that women should be forbidden from having abortions, on the basis that personhood begins at conception or at least sometime before birth, not only violates their right to privacy but also violates the separation of church and state. Such a separation is supposedly necessary to sustain tolerance in a pluralistic society...

There are several problems with this argument. First, it is self-refuting and question-begging. To claim, as Justices Blackmun and Stevens do, that the decision should be left up to each pregnant woman as to when protectable human life begins, is to propose a theory of life that hardly has a clear consensus in this country. Once one claims that certain individuals (pregnant women) have the right to bestow personhood on unborn humans, one implies that the bestowers are fully human. This is a theory of life held by a number of religious denominations and groups, whose amicus briefs Stevens oddly enough cites in a footnote in his *Webster* dissent. Moreover, what if a religious group arose that believed that personhood did not begin until the age of two and before that time parents could sacrifice their children to the devil? By forbidding child-killing after birth, the Court would be infringing on the religious beliefs of this group, would it not? And in doing so, the Court would obviously be proposing one theory of life over another. Hence, in attempting not to propose one theory of life, Blackmun and Stevens in fact assume a particular theory of life, and by doing so clearly beg the question and show that their opinions cannot abide by their own standard of not proposing one theory of life.

Second, the fact that a particular theory of life is consistent with a religious view does not mean that it is exclusively religious or that it is in violation of the Establishment Clause of the Constitution. For example, many prolife advocates argue for their position by emphasizing that there is nontheological support for their position, whereas many abortion-rights advocates, such as Virginia Ramey Mollenkott, argue that their position is theologically grounded in the Bible. Hence, the prolife advocate could argue that the fact that a philosophically and scientifically plausible position is also found in religious literature, such as the Bible, does not make such a view exclusively religious. If it did, our society would have to dispense with laws forbidding such crimes as murder and robbery simply because such actions are prohibited in the Hebrew-Christian Scriptures. Furthermore, some public policies, such as civil-rights legislation and elimination of nuclear testing—policies supported by many clergymen who find these policies in agreement with and supported by their doctrinal beliefs—would have to be abolished simply because they are believed by some to be supported by a particular religious theory of life. It is well-known that those who sought to abolish slavery in nineteenth-century America were unashamed to admit that their moral convictions were based almost exclusively on their Christian beliefs...

Third, this argument asks the prolife movement to act as if its fundamental view of human life is incorrect and to accept the abortion-rights view of what constitutes both a just society and a correct view of human life. This asks too much of the prolife movement, as philosopher George Mavrodes shows:

> Let us imagine a person who believes that Jews are human persons, and that the extermination of Jews is murder. Many of us will find that exercise fairly easy, because we are people of that sort ourselves. So we may as well take ourselves to be the people in question. And let us now go on to imagine that we live in a society in which the "termination" of Jews is an everyday routine procedure, a society in which public facilities are provided in every community for this operation, and one in which any citizen is free to identity and denounce Jews and to arrange for their arrest and termination. In that imaginary society, many of us will know people who have themselves participated in these procedures, many of us will drive past the termination centers daily on our way to work, we can often see the smoke rising gently in the late afternoon sky, and so on. And now imagine that someone tells us that if we happen to believe that Jews are human beings then that's O.K., we needn't fear any coercion, nobody requires us to participate in the termination procedures ourselves. We need not work in the gas chamber, we don't have to denounce a Jew, and so on. We can simply mind our own business, walk quietly past the well-trimmed lawns, and (of course) pay our taxes.
>
> Can we get some feel for what it would be like to live in that context?...And maybe we can then have some understanding of why they [the right-to-lifers] are unlikely to be satisfied by being told that they don't have to get an abortion themselves.

Since the abortion-rights advocate asks the pro-life advocate to act as if his fundamental view of human life is false, the pro-life advocate may legitimately view his adversary's position as a subtle and patronizing form of intolerance. When the "prochoicer" rails at the prolifer, "Don't like abortion, don't have one," the prolifer hears, "Don't like murder, don't commit one" or "Don't like slavery, don't own a slave."

ARGUMENT FROM IMPOSING MORALITY

Some abortion-rights advocates argue that it is wrong for anyone to force his or her own view of what is morally right on someone else. They argue that prolifers, by attempting to forbid women from having abortions, are trying to force their morality on others. Aside from the fact that this argument make the controversial assumption that all morality is subjective and relative, there are at least three other problems with it.

First, it does not seem obvious that it is always wrong to demand that people behave in accordance with certain moral precepts. For instance, laws against drunk driving, murder, smoking crack, robbery, and child molestation all are intended to impose a particular moral perspective on the free moral agency of others. Such laws are instituted because the acts they are intended to limit often obstruct the free agency of other persons. For example, a person killed by a drunk driver is prevented from exercising his free agency. These laws seek to maintain a just and orderly society by limiting some free moral agency so that free moral agency is increased for a greater number. Therefore, a law forbidding abortion would unjustly impose a moral perspective on another only if the act of abortion does not limit the free agency of another. That is to say, if the unborn entity is fully human, forbidding abortions would be just, since nearly every abortion limits the free agency of another (that is, the unborn human).

Although it does not seriously damage their entire position, it is interesting to note that some abortion-rights advocates do not hesitate to impose their moral perspective on others when they call for the use of other people's tax dollars (many of whom do not approve of this use of funds) to help pay for the abortions of poor women.

Second, although he presents his position in the rhetoric of freedom, the abortion-rights advocate nevertheless imposes his perspective on others. All rights imply obligations on the part of others, and all obligations impose a moral perspective on others, to make them act in a certain way. Thus, the abortion-rights advocate, by saying that the prolifer is obligated not to interfere with the free choice of pregnant women to kill their unborn offspring, is imposing his moral perspective on the prolifer who believes it is her duty to rescue the unborn because these beings are fully human and hence deserve, like all human beings, our society's protection. Therefore, every right, whether it is the right to life or the right to abortion, imposes some moral perspective on others to either act or not act in a certain way.

Third, it follows that the abortion-rights advocate begs the question. If the unborn are not fully human, the abortion-rights advocate is correct in saying that the prolifers are trying to force their morality onto women who want abortions. But if the unborn are fully human, a woman receiving an abortion is imposing her morality on another. Therefore, unless the abortion-rights advocate assumes that the unborn are not fully human, his argument is not successful. Hence, the question of whose morality is being forced on whom hinges on the status of the unborn.

ARGUMENT AGAINST A PUBLIC POLICY
FORBIDDING ABORTION

There is another variation on the first argument from pluralism. Some people argue that it is not wise to make a public-policy decision in one direction when there is wide diversity of opinion within society. This argument can be outlined in the following way:

1. There can never be a just law requiring uniformity of behavior on any issue on which there is widespread disagreement.

2. There is widespread disagreement on the issue of forbidding abortion on demand.

3. Therefore, any law that forbids abortion on demand is unjust.

One way to show that this argument wrong is to show that premise 1 is false. There are several reasons to believe that it is. First, if premise 1 is true, then the abortion-rights advocate must admit that the United States Supreme Court decision, *Roe v. Wade,* is an unjust decision because the Court ruled that the states, whose statutes before the ruling disagreed on the abortion issue, must behave uniformly in accordance with the Court's decision. If, however, the abortion-rights advocate denies that *Roe* was an unjust decision, then he is conceding that it is false that "there can never be a just law requiring uniformity of behavior on any issue on which there is widespread disagreement." Second, if premise 1 is true, then the abolition of slavery was unjust because there was widespread disagreement of opinion among Americans in the nineteenth century. Yet nobody would say that slavery should have remained as an institution. Third, if premise 1 is true, then much of civil-rights legislation, about which there was much disagreement, would be unjust. Fourth, if premise 1 is true, then a favorite abortion-rights public policy proposal is also unjust. Some abortion-rights advocates believe that the federal or state government should use the tax dollars of the American people to fund the abortions of poor women. Large numbers of Americans, however, some of whom support abortion rights, do not want their tax dollars used in this way. And fifth, if premise 1 is true, then laws forbidding prolife advocates from preventing their unborn neighbors from being aborted would be unjust. One cannot say that there is not widespread disagreement concerning this issue. But these are the very laws that the abortion-rights advocate supports. Hence, this argument is self-refuting because by legislating the "prochoice" perspective, the government is "requiring uniformity of behavior on an issue on which there is widespread disagreement." That is to say, the abortion-rights advocate is forcing the prolifer to act as if she were a prochoicer. By making "no law," the government is implicitly affirming the view that the unborn are not fully human, which is hardly a neutral position,

Another way to show that this argument is not successful is to challenge the second premise and show that there is not widespread disagreement on the question of whether abortion on demand should be forbidden. Recent polls have shown that a great majority of Americans, although supporting a woman's right to an abortion in the rare "hard cases" (such as rape, incest, and severe fetal deformity), do not support abortion on demand, the abortion-rights position that asserts that abortion should remain legal during the entire nine months of pregnancy for any reason the woman deems fit. According to one poll, taken by *The Boston Globe* and WBZ Broadcasting, the vast majority of Americans would ban abortions in the following circumstances: "a woman is a minor" (50%), "wrong time in life to have a child" (82%), "fetus not of the desired sex" (93%), "woman cannot afford a child" (75%), "as a means of birth control" (89%), "pregnancy would cause too much emotional strain" (64%), "father unwilling to help raise the child" (83%), "father absent" (81%), "mother wants abortion/father wants baby" (72%), "father wants abortion/mother wants baby" (75%). This is why the journalist who reported this poll concluded that "most Americans would ban the vast majority of abortions performed in this country…While 78 percent of the nation would keep abortion legal in limited circumstances, according to the poll, *those circumstances account for a tiny percentage of the reasons*" (emphasis added). Therefore, the second premise in this argument is wrong. There is not "widespread disagreement on the issue of forbidding abortion on demand."

ARGUMENT FROM "COMPULSORY" PREGNANCY

Some abortion-rights advocates, wanting to get a rhetorical edge in public debate, refer to pro-life legislation as "tantamount to advocating compulsory pregnancy." This is not really an argument in a technical sense, because it has only a conclusion and contains no premises to support the conclusion. It is merely an assertion that begs the question because it assumes the non-personhood of the unborn—the point under question. To cite an example, a man who murdered his wife and children would be begging the question as to the personhood of his victims if he referred to the laws that forbid murder as tantamount to advocating *compulsory marriage* and *compulsory fatherhood.* Can you imagine a father or a mother arguing that he or she is not obligated to obey child-support laws because they are "tantamount to advocating *compulsory parenthood"*? A rapist could argue on the same grounds and conclude that laws against rape are "tantamount to advocating *compulsory chastity."* And the slave owner, the prochoicers of the mid-nineteenth-century political scene, could easily conclude that Lincoln's Emancipation Proclamation because it robbed him of slave ownership, was "tantamount to advocating compulsory government-mandated relinquishing of private property."

In sum, a law that forbids the brutal victimizing of another person is inherently a just law, whether the victim is an unborn child, an adult woman, a youngster, or an African-American. Hence, the real question is whether the unborn are fully human, not whether prolife legislation advocates "compulsory pregnancy."

STUDY QUESTIONS

1. Briefly summarize the first two arguments for abortion rights that Beckwith evaluates. What are his criticisms of each argument? Do you find any flaws in his evaluations? If so, present and explain those flaws.

2. Briefly summarize the second two arguments for abortion rights that Beckwith evaluates. What are his criticisms of each argument? Do you find any flaws in his evaluations? If so, present and explain those flaws.

3. Beckwith maintains throughout his essay that "the real question is whether the unborn is fully human." Do you think he is correct about that? If not, explain why. If he is correct, are there still ways for a pro-choice advocate to defend abortion rights? Present and explain your answer.

4. Beckwith does not seem to address two questions many prochoice advocates might raise in response to his essay: "Assuming you are correct that the issue is whether the unborn is fully human, how would you legally and socially address abortion given that many intelligent people of good will continue to disagree on the question of what constitutes full personhood? Isn't a 'neutral' solution the only way to solve it, at least until our society arrives at a consensus on the issue?" How do you think Beckwith would reply to these questions?

29

Abortion, the Court, and State Neutrality

RONALD DWORKIN

Ronald Dworkin is Professor of Law at New York University and university professor of jurisprudence at Oxford University in England. In this essay, Professor Dworkin argues that although state regulation and coercion is legitimate in certain areas, it is not legitimate when it comes to the question of whether women should have a right to control their own bodies. He maintains that because the nature of the abortion decision involves a woman's belief-system as well as her ultimate commitments, the state should remain neutral on the matter, neither forcing women to have abortions nor forcing them not to have abortions. This does not mean that the state may not require its citizens to think seriously about the abortion decision (for example, require that information about fetal development be provided to women seeking abortions); it just means that the state may not use its coercive power to force its citizens to think one way on the matter.

[have] said that the difficult constitutional question in *Roe v. Wade* was not whether states are permitted under the Constitution to treat a fetus as a constitutional person. They plainly are not. I set out two other, much more difficult questions that our reformulation of the moral argument about abortion helps us to identify as the central issues in the constitutional debate. First, do women have a constitutional right of procreative autonomy—a right to control their own role in procreation unless the state has a compelling reason for denying them that control? Second, do states have this compelling reason not

Used by permission from Ronald Dworkin, *Life's Dominion: An Argument About Abortion, Euthanasia, and Freedom* (New York: Alfred A. Knopf, 1993).

because a fetus is a person but because of a detached responsibility to protect the sanctity of human life considered as an intrinsic value?

Most of the lawyers who think *Roe v. Wade* was wrong have directed their arguments to the first of these questions. They say that women do not have a constitutionally protected right to procreative autonomy because no such right is mentioned in the text and because none of the "framers" of the Constitution intended women to have such a right. I have tried to show that these objections are misplaced because the constitutional provisions that command liberty and equality are abstract. The key legal question is whether the best interpretation of these abstract provisions, respecting the requirements of integrity I described, supports this right of procreative autonomy. If it does, then in the pertinent sense the Constitution *does* "mention" such a right, and those who created the Constitution *did* "intend" it.

The second question, too, is a matter of interpretation. On the best interpretation of the abstract provisions of the Bill of Rights, does government have the detached power to protect intrinsic values as well as the derivative power to protect particular people? Some people believe that government should not have this detached power at all, that government can properly act only to protect the rights or interests of particular people or creatures, not intrinsic values, which it must leave to individual conscience. (That was apparently the position of John Stuart Mill.) But this restricted view of the powers the United States Constitution allows government is ruled out by the constraints of integrity because too much of American political practice assumes the contrary.

Neither cultural achievements nor animal species nor future human beings are creatures with rights or interests. But no one doubts that government may treat art and culture as having intrinsic value, or that government may act to protect the environment, endangered animal species, and the quality of life of future generations. Government may properly levy taxes that will be used to support museums, for example; it can forbid people to destroy their own buildings if it deems these to be of historical architectural value; it can prohibit manufacturing practices that threaten endangered species or injure future generations. Why should government not have the power to enforce a much more passionate conviction—that abortion is a desecration of the inherent value that attaches to every human life?

It is not true that an individual woman's decision to have an abortion affects only herself (or only herself and the fetus's father), for individual decisions inevitably affect shared collective values. Part of the sense of the sacred is a sense of taboo, and it is surely harder to maintain a taboo against abortion, and to raise one's children to respect it, in a community where others not only reject it but violate it openly, especially if they receive official financial or moral support.

So if, on the best understanding of the Constitution's abstract provisions, American states lack the power to forbid abortion, then this must be because of something specific about abortion or reproduction; it is not because states may not legislate to protect intrinsic values at all. I distinguished two issues—

whether a woman has a right to procreative autonomy and whether states have a compelling interest in protecting the intrinsic value of human life. Our discussion has now brought them together as two sides of the same issue. Is there something special about procreation and abortion so that, though government may regulate people's behavior in other ways to protect intrinsic values, pregnant women have a right that government not forbid them to terminate their pregnancies?

The question so described lies at the intersection of two sometimes competing traditions, both of which are part of America's political heritage The first is the tradition of personal freedom The second assigns government responsibility for guarding the public moral space in which all citizens live. A good part of constitutional law consists in reconciling these two ideas. What is the appropriate balance in the case of abortion?

Both the majority and dissenting opinions in *Roe v. Wade* said that a state has an interest in "protecting human life." We have now assigned a particular sense to that ambiguous claim; it means that any political community has a legitimate concern in protecting the *sanctity* or *inviolability* of human life by requiring its members to acknowledge the intrinsic value of human life in their individual decisions. But this is still ambiguous. It might describe either of two goals, and the distinction between them is extremely important.

One is the goal of responsibility A state might aim that its citizens treat decisions about abortion as matters of moral importance; that they recognize that fundamental intrinsic values are at stake in such decisions and decide reflectively, not out of immediate convenience but out of examined conviction. The second is the goal of conformity. A state might aim that its citizens obey rules and practices that the majority believes best express and protect the sanctity of life, that women abort, if ever, only in circumstances in which a majority thinks abortion appropriate or, at least, permissible.

These goals of responsibility and conformity are not only different but antagonistic. If we aim at responsibility, we must leave citizens free, in the end, to decide as they think right, because that is what moral responsibility entails. But if we aim at conformity, we demand instead that citizens act in a way that might be contrary to their own moral convictions; this discourages rather than encourages them to develop their own sense of when and why life is sacred.

The traditional way of understanding the abortion controversy, which we have now rejected, submerges the distinction between these two goals. If a fetus is a person, then of course the state's dominant goal must be to protect it, just as it protects all other people. And the state must therefore subordinate any interest it has in developing its citizens' sense of moral responsibility to its interest that they act on a specific moral conclusion: that killing people is wrong.

But when we shift the state's interest, as we have, to protecting an intrinsic value, then the opposition between the two goals moves into the foreground. The sanctity of life is a highly controversial, *contestable* value. It is controversial, for example, whether abortion or childbirth best serves the intrinsic value of life when a fetus is deformed, or when having a child would seriously depress a woman's chance to make something valuable of her own life. Does a state protect a contestable value best by encouraging people to accept it *as* contestable, understanding that they are responsible for deciding for themselves what it means? Or does the state protect a contestable value best by itself deciding, through the political process, which interpretation is the right one, and then forcing everyone to conform? The goal of responsibility justifies the first choice, the goal of conformity justifies the second. A state cannot pursue both goals at the same time.

RESPONSIBILITY

I can think of no reason why government should not aim that its citizens treat decisions about human life and death as matters of serious moral importance. So in my view, the United States Constitution does allow state governments to pursue the goal of responsibility—but only in ways that respect the crucial difference between advancing that goal and wholly or partly coercing a final decision. May a state require a woman contemplating abortion to wait twenty-four hours before having the procedure? May it require that she be given information explaining the gravity of a decision to abort? May it require a pregnant teenage woman to consult with her parents, or with some other adult? Or a married woman to inform her husband, if she can? Must the government help to pay for abortion services for those too poor to pay themselves if it helps pay for childbirth?

Since many constitutional lawyers think that the only issue in *Roe v. Wade* was whether states may treat a fetus as a person, they do not distinguish between the goals of coercion and responsibility; they have therefore assumed that if *Roe v. Wade* is right, and states may not coerce women by forbidding abortion altogether, it directly follows that states must include abortion in their medical aid programs and that they may not require that women delay abortion or consult with others or be given information. That explains why many lawyers thought that the Supreme Court's decisions in the years following *Roe,* which did allow states to discriminate in financial support and to regulate abortion in these various ways, amounted to a partial overruling or undermining of *Roe...*

But when we understand *Roe* as I have suggested—as about inherent value and not about personhood—then we see that *Casey* [*Planned Parenthood of Southeastern Pennsylvania v. Casey* (1992)] dealt primarily with issues not resolved by *Roe.* It is perfectly consistent to insist that states have no power to impose on their citizens a particular view of how and why life is sacred, and yet also to insist that states do have the power to encourage their citizens to treat the question of abortion seriously. The joint opinion of Justices O'Connor, Kennedy, and Souter in *Casey* made that distinction clear: The three justices affirmed *Roe's* rule that states may not prohibit abortion but nevertheless affirmed a state's legitimate interest in encouraging responsibility. "What is at stake is the woman's right to make the ultimate decision, not a right to be insulated from all others in doing so," they said, and therefore "states are free to enact laws to provide a reasonable framework for a woman to make a decision that has such profound and lasting meaning." A state may reasonably think, they added, that a woman considering abortion should at least be aware of arguments against it that others in the community believe important, so that "even in the earliest stages of pregnancy, the State may enact rules and regulations designed to encourage her to know that there are philosophic and social arguments of great weight that can be brought to bear in favor of continuing the pregnancy...."

COERCION

...Do the states of the United States have the power to decide for everyone that abortion insults the intrinsic value of human life and to prohibit it on that ground? In *Casey,* four justices said that they still aim to reverse *Roe* and declare that states do have that power. Are they right, as a matter of American constitutional law? Should any state or nation have that power, as a matter of justice and decent government?

As I said, government sometimes acts properly when it coerces people to protect certain intrinsic values: when it collects taxes to finance national museums or when it imposes conservation measures to protect endangered animal species, for example. Why is abortion different? Why can a state not forbid abortion on the same ground: that the majority of its citizens thinks that aborting a fetus, except, perhaps, when the mother's own life is at stake, is an intolerable insult to the inherent value of human life? There are two central and connected reasons why prohibiting abortion is a very different matter.

First, in the case of abortion, the effect of coercion on particular people—pregnant women—is far greater. Making abortion criminal may destroy a woman's life. Protecting art or historic buildings or endangered animal species of future generations is rarely as damaging to particular people and might well be unconstitutional if it were. Second, our convictions about how and why human life has intrinsic importance, from which we draw our views about abortion, are much more fundamental to our overall moral personalities than our convictions about culture or about endangered species, even though these too concern intrinsic values. Our beliefs about human life are decisive in forming our opinions about *all* life-and-death matters—abortion, suicide, euthanasia, the death penalty, and conscientious objection to war. Indeed, their power is even greater than this, because our opinions about how and why our *own* lives have intrinsic value influence every major decision we make about how we live. Very few people's opinions about conserving the artifacts of a culture or saving endangered species are as foundational to their moral personality, as interwoven with the structural choices of their lives.

These interconnections are most evident in the lives of people who are religious in traditional ways. The connection between their faith and their opinions about abortion is not contingent but constitutive—the latter are shadows of religious beliefs about why human life itself is important, and these beliefs are at work in every aspect of their lives. Most people who are not religious also have general, instinctive convictions about whether, why, and how any human life has intrinsic value. No one can lead even a mildly reflective life without revealing such convictions, and they surface, for almost everyone, at the same critical moments in life—in opinions and decisions about children, death, and war, for example. An atheist can have convictions about the point or meaning of human life that are just as pervasive, just as foundational to his moral personality, as those of a devout Catholic, Jew, Muslim, Hindu, or Buddhist. An atheist's system of beliefs can have, in the words of a famous Supreme Court opinion, "a place in the life of its possessor parallel to that filled by the orthodox belief in God." We may describe most people's beliefs about the inherent value of human life—beliefs deployed in their opinions about abortion—as *essentially* religious beliefs...

The Supreme Court, in denying the state the specific power to make contraception criminal, presupposed the more general principle of procreative autonomy I am defending. That is important, as I have said, because almost no one believes that the Court's contraception decisions should now be overruled. The law's integrity demands that the principles necessary to support an authoritative set of judicial decisions must be accepted in other contexts as well. It might seem an appealing political compromise to apply the principle of procreative autonomy to contraception, which almost no one now thinks states can forbid, but not to abortion, which powerful constituencies violently oppose. But the point of integrity—the point of law itself—is exactly to rule out political compromises of that kind. We must be one nation of principle: Our Constitution must represent conviction, not the tactical strategies of justices eager to satisfy as many political constituencies as possible.

Integrity does not, of course, require that judges respect principles embedded in past decisions that they and others regard as *mistakes*. It permits the Supreme Court to declare, as it has several times in the past, that a given decision or string of decisions was in error because the principles underlying it are inconsistent with more fundamental principles embedded in the Constitution's structure and history. The Court cannot declare everything in the past a mistake; that would destroy integrity under the pretext of serving it. It must exercise its power to disregard past decisions modestly, and it must exercise it in good faith. It cannot ignore principles underlying past decisions it purports to approve, decisions it would ratify if asked to do so, decisions almost no one, not even among the sternest critics of the Court's past performance, now disapproves of or regards as mistakes. The contraception cases fall into that category, and it would be both dangerous and offensive for the Court cynically to ignore the principles these cases presupposed in any decision it reaches about abortion.

So integrity demands general recognition of the principle of procreative autonomy, and therefore of the right of women to decide for themselves not only whether to conceive but whether to bear a child. If you remain in doubt—if you are not yet convinced that *Roe* was right on the most basic issues—then consider the possibility that in some states a majority of voters might come to think that it shows *disrespect* for the sanctity of life to continue a pregnancy in some circumstances—in cases of fetal deformity, for example. If a majority has the power to impose its own views about the sanctity of life on everyone, then the state could *require* someone to abort, even if that were against her own religious or ethical convictions, at least if abortion had become physically as safe as, for example, the vaccinations and inoculations we now expect our governments to require...

The *Casey* decision was important because it made plainer than ever before how central the abortion issue is to the very idea of freedom. Not just for America, but for any nation dedicated to liberty, the question of how far government may legitimately impose collective judgments about spiritual matters on individual citizens is absolutely crucial. It is hardly surprising that American law leaves women freer to follow their own conscience than do the laws of many other nations, for the Bill of Rights places more emphasis on individual liberty, especially in matters touching conscience and the sacred, than does any other constitution. *Roe v. Wade* is not yet wholly safe: If a single new justice is appointed who believes it should be overruled, it will fall. That would be a bleak day in American constitutional history, for it would mean that American citizens were no longer secure in their freedom to follow their own reflective convictions in the most personal, conscience-driven, and religious decisions many of them will ever make.

STUDY QUESTIONS

1. Summarize and explain Dworkin's defense of abortion rights. What does he mean by the state's goal of responsibility and the state's goal of conformity, and why does he believe that the state cannot pursue both simultaneously?

2. Since prolifers believe that *all* fetuses deserve state protection, not just those carried in the wombs of prolife women, how do you think Dworkin would reply to the prolifer who would argue in the following way: "Because I believe that all fetuses are human persons, your perspective is violating my humanitarian autonomy to defend all human persons to the best of my ability. Consequently, is not your perspective doing to me what you accuse my perspective of doing to others, namely, making me 'no longer secure in [my] freedom to follow [my] own reflective convictions in the most personal, conscience-driven, and religious [decision I] will ever make?'"

3. How does Dworkin define a "religious belief" and how does this definition apply to his defense of abortion rights?

4. What does Dworkin mean by judicial integrity, and how does he apply that notion of integrity to the question of abortion rights?

FOR FURTHER READING

Beckwith, Francis J. "Philosophical Commitments, Public Policy, and Family Law." *Focus on Law Studies* (American Bar Association) 12 (Fall 1996).

Beckwith, Francis J. *Politically Correct Death: Answering the Arguments for Abortion Rights.* Grand Rapids, Mich.: Baker Book House, 1993, Chapter 5.

Canavan, Francis. *The Pluralist Game: Pluralism, Liberalism, and the Moral Conscience.* Lanham, Md.: Rowan & Littlefield, 1995.

Dworkin, Ronald. *Life's Dominion: An Argument About Abortion, Euthanasia, and Freedom.* New York: Knopf, 1993.

Dworkin, Ronald. "Neutrality, Equality, and Liberalism." In *Liberalism Reconsidered*, eds. Douglas MacLean and Claudia Mills. Totowa, N.J.: Rowan and Allanheld, 1983.

George, Robert P. *Making Men Moral: Civil Liberties and Public Morality.* Oxford: Clarendon, 1993.

Macedo, Stephen. *Liberal Virtues.* Oxford: Oxford University Press, 1990.

Mavrodes, George. "Abortion and Imagination: Reflections on Mollenkott's 'Reproductive Choice.'" *Christian Scholar's Review* 18 (December 1988).

Mollenkott, Virginia Ramey. "Reproductive Choice: Basic to Justice for Women." *Christian Scholar's Review* 17 (March 1988).

Pavlischek, Keith. *John Courtney Murray and the Dilemma of Religious Toleration.* Kirksville, Mo.: Thomas Jefferson University Press, 1994.

Rawls, John. *Political Liberalism.* New York: Columbia University Press, 1993.

Raz, Joseph. *The Morality of Freedom.* Oxford: Oxford University Press, 1986.

Sher, George. *Beyond Neutrality: Perfectionism and Politics.* New York: Cambridge University Press, 1997.